T0178523

Lecture Notes in Computer Science   14254

Founding Editors

Gerhard Goos
Juris Hartmanis

The series Lecture Notes in Computer Science (LNCS), including its subseries Lecture Notes in Artificial Intelligence (LNAI) and Lecture Notes in Bioinformatics (LNBI), has established itself as a medium for the publication of new developments in computer science and information technology research, teaching, and education.

LNCS enjoys close cooperation with the computer science R & D community, the series counts many renowned academics among its volume editors and paper authors, and collaborates with prestigious societies. Its mission is to serve this international community by providing an invaluable service, mainly focused on the publication of conference and workshop proceedings and postproceedings. LNCS commenced publication in 1973.

Lazaros Iliadis · Antonios Papaleonidas ·
Plamen Angelov · Chrisina Jayne
Editors

Artificial Neural Networks and Machine Learning – ICANN 2023

32nd International Conference on Artificial Neural Networks
Heraklion, Crete, Greece, September 26–29, 2023
Proceedings, Part I

Springer

Editors
Lazaros Iliadis ⓘ
Democritus University of Thrace
Xanthi, Greece

Antonios Papaleonidas ⓘ
Democritus University of Thrace
Xanthi, Greece

Plamen Angelov ⓘ
Lancaster University
Lancaster, UK

Chrisina Jayne ⓘ
Teesside University
Middlesbrough, UK

ISSN 0302-9743   ISSN 1611-3349 (electronic)
Lecture Notes in Computer Science
ISBN 978-3-031-44206-3   ISBN 978-3-031-44207-0 (eBook)
https://doi.org/10.1007/978-3-031-44207-0

This Springer imprint is published by the registered company Springer Nature Switzerland AG
The registered company address is: Gewerbestrasse 11, 6330 Cham, Switzerland

Paper in this product is recyclable.

Preface

The European Neural Network Society (ENNS) is an association of scientists, engineers and students, conducting research on the modelling of behavioral and brain processes, and on the development of neural algorithms. The core of these efforts is the application of neural modelling to several diverse domains. According to its mission statement ENNS is the European non-profit federation of professionals that aims at achieving a worldwide professional and socially responsible development and application of artificial neural technologies.

The flagship event of ENNS is ICANN (the International Conference on Artificial Neural Networks) at which contributed research papers are presented after passing through a rigorous review process. ICANN is a dual-track conference, featuring tracks in brain-inspired computing on the one hand, and machine learning on the other, with strong crossdisciplinary interactions and applications.

The response of the international scientific community to the ICANN 2023 call for papers was more than satisfactory. In total, 947 research papers on the aforementioned research areas were submitted and 426 (45%) of them were finally accepted as full papers after a peer review process. Additionally, 19 extended abstracts were submitted and 9 of them were selected to be included in the front matter of ICANN 2023 proceedings. Due to their high academic and scientific importance, 22 short papers were also accepted.

All papers were peer reviewed by at least two independent academic referees. Where needed, a third or a fourth referee was consulted to resolve any potential conflicts. Three workshops focusing on specific research areas, namely Advances in Spiking Neural Networks (ASNN), Neurorobotics (NRR), and the challenge of Errors, Stability, Robustness, and Accuracy in Deep Neural Networks (ESRA in DNN), were organized.

The 10-volume set of LNCS 14254, 14255, 14256, 14257, 14258, 14259, 14260, 14261, 14262 and 14263 constitutes the proceedings of the 32nd International Conference on Artificial Neural Networks, ICANN 2023, held in Heraklion city, Crete, Greece, on September 26–29, 2023.

The accepted papers are related to the following topics:

Machine Learning: Deep Learning; Neural Network Theory; Neural Network Models; Graphical Models; Bayesian Networks; Kernel Methods; Generative Models; Information Theoretic Learning; Reinforcement Learning; Relational Learning; Dynamical Models; Recurrent Networks; and Ethics of AI.

Brain-Inspired Computing: Cognitive Models; Computational Neuroscience; Self-Organization; Neural Control and Planning; Hybrid Neural-Symbolic Architectures; Neural Dynamics; Cognitive Neuroscience; Brain Informatics; Perception and Action; and Spiking Neural Networks.

Neural applications in Bioinformatics; Biomedicine; Intelligent Robotics; Neuro-robotics; Language Processing; Speech Processing; Image Processing; Sensor Fusion; Pattern Recognition; Data Mining; Neural Agents; Brain-Computer Interaction; Neuromorphic Computing and Edge AI; and Evolutionary Neural Networks.

September 2023

Lazaros Iliadis
Antonios Papaleonidas
Plamen Angelov
Chrisina Jayne

Organization

General Chairs

Iliadis Lazaros   Democritus University of Thrace, Greece
Plamen Angelov   Lancaster University, UK

Program Chairs

Antonios Papaleonidas   Democritus University of Thrace, Greece
Elias Pimenidis   UWE Bristol, UK
Chrisina Jayne   Teesside University, UK

Honorary Chairs

Stefan Wermter   University of Hamburg, Germany
Vera Kurkova   Czech Academy of Sciences, Czech Republic
Nikola Kasabov   Auckland University of Technology, New Zealand

Organizing Chairs

Antonios Papaleonidas   Democritus University of Thrace, Greece
Anastasios Panagiotis Psathas   Democritus University of Thrace, Greece
George Magoulas   University of London, Birkbeck College, UK
Haralambos Mouratidis   University of Essex, UK

Award Chairs

Stefan Wermter   University of Hamburg, Germany
Chukiong Loo   University of Malaysia, Malaysia

Communication Chairs

Sebastian Otte	University of Tübingen, Germany
Anastasios Panagiotis Psathas	Democritus University of Thrace, Greece

Steering Committee

Stefan Wermter	University of Hamburg, Germany
Angelo Cangelosi	University of Manchester, UK
Igor Farkaš	Comenius University in Bratislava, Slovakia
Chrisina Jayne	Teesside University, UK
Matthias Kerzel	University of Hamburg, Germany
Alessandra Lintas	University of Lausanne, Switzerland
Kristína Malinovská (Rebrová)	Comenius University in Bratislava, Slovakia
Alessio Micheli	University of Pisa, Italy
Jaakko Peltonen	Tampere University, Finland
Brigitte Quenet	ESPCI Paris, France
Ausra Saudargiene	Lithuanian University of Health Sciences, Lithuania
Roseli Wedemann	Rio de Janeiro State University, Brazil

Local Organizing/Hybrid Facilitation Committee

Aggeliki Tsouka	Democritus University of Thrace, Greece
Anastasios Panagiotis Psathas	Democritus University of Thrace, Greece
Anna Karagianni	Democritus University of Thrace, Greece
Christina Gkizioti	Democritus University of Thrace, Greece
Ioanna-Maria Erentzi	Democritus University of Thrace, Greece
Ioannis Skopelitis	Democritus University of Thrace, Greece
Lambros Kazelis	Democritus University of Thrace, Greece
Leandros Tsatsaronis	Democritus University of Thrace, Greece
Nikiforos Mpotzoris	Democritus University of Thrace, Greece
Nikos Zervis	Democritus University of Thrace, Greece
Panagiotis Restos	Democritus University of Thrace, Greece
Tassos Giannakopoulos	Democritus University of Thrace, Greece

Program Committee

Abraham Yosipof	CLB, Israel
Adane Tarekegn	NTNU, Norway
Aditya Gilra	Centrum Wiskunde & Informatica, Netherlands
Adrien Durand-Petiteville	Federal University of Pernambuco, Brazil
Adrien Fois	LORIA, France
Alaa Marouf	Hosei University, Japan
Alessandra Sciutti	Istituto Italiano di Tecnologia, Italy
Alessandro Sperduti	University of Padua, Italy
Alessio Micheli	University of Pisa, Italy
Alex Shenfield	Sheffield Hallam University, UK
Alexander Kovalenko	Czech Technical University in Prague, Czech Republic
Alexander Krawczyk	Fulda University of Applied Sciences, Germany
Ali Minai	University of Cincinnati, USA
Aluizio Araujo	Universidade Federal de Pernambuco, Brazil
Amarda Shehu	George Mason University, USA
Amit Kumar Kundu	University of Maryland, USA
Anand Rangarajan	University of Florida, USA
Anastasios Panagiotis Psathas	Democritus University of Thrace, Greece
Andre de Carvalho	Universidade de São Paulo, Brazil
Andrej Lucny	Comenius University, Slovakia
Angel Villar-Corrales	University of Bonn, Germany
Angelo Cangelosi	University of Manchester, UK
Anna Jenul	Norwegian University of Life Sciences, Norway
Antonios Papaleonidas	Democritus University of Thrace, Greece
Arnaud Lewandowski	LISIC, ULCO, France
Arul Selvam Periyasamy	Universität Bonn, Germany
Asma Mekki	University of Sfax, Tunisia
Banafsheh Rekabdar	Portland State University, USA
Barbara Hammer	Universität Bielefeld, Germany
Baris Serhan	University of Manchester, UK
Benedikt Bagus	University of Applied Sciences Fulda, Germany
Benjamin Paaßen	Bielefeld University, Germany
Bernhard Pfahringer	University of Waikato, New Zealand
Bharath Sudharsan	NUI Galway, Ireland
Binyi Wu	Dresden University of Technology, Germany
Binyu Zhao	Harbin Institute of Technology, China
Björn Plüster	University of Hamburg, Germany
Bo Mei	Texas Christian University, USA

Brian Moser	Deutsches Forschungszentrum für künstliche Intelligenz, Germany
Carlo Mazzola	Istituto Italiano di Tecnologia, Italy
Carlos Moreno-Garcia	Robert Gordon University, UK
Chandresh Pravin	Reading University, UK
Chao Ma	Wuhan University, China
Chathura Wanigasekara	German Aerospace Centre, Germany
Cheng Shang	Shanghai Jiaotong University, China
Chengqiang Huang	Huawei Technologies, China
Chenhan Zhang	University of Technology, Sydney, Australia
Chenyang Lyu	Dublin City University, Ireland
Chihuang Liu	Meta, USA
Chrisina Jayne	Teesside University, UK
Christian Balkenius	Lund University, Sweden
Chrysoula Kosma	Ecole Polytechnique, Greece
Claudio Bellei	Elliptic, UK
Claudio Gallicchio	University of Pisa, Italy
Claudio Giorgio Giancaterino	Intesa SanPaolo Vita, Italy
Constantine Dovrolis	Cyprus Institute, USA
Coşku Horuz	University of Tübingen, Germany
Cunjian Chen	Monash, Australia
Cunyi Yin	Fuzhou University, Singapore
Damien Lolive	Université Rennes, CNRS, IRISA, France
Daniel Stamate	Goldsmiths, University of London, UK
Daniel Vašata	Czech Technical University in Prague, Czech Republic
Dario Pasquali	Istituto Italiano di Tecnologia, Italy
David Dembinsky	German Research Center for Artificial Intelligence, Germany
David Rotermund	University of Bremen, Germany
Davide Liberato Manna	University of Strathclyde, UK
Dehao Yuan	University of Maryland, USA
Denise Gorse	University College London, UK
Dennis Wong	Macao Polytechnic University, China
Des Higham	University of Edinburgh, UK
Devesh Jawla	TU Dublin, Ireland
Dimitrios Michail	Harokopio University of Athens, Greece
Dino Ienco	INRAE, France
Diptangshu Pandit	Teesside University, UK
Diyuan Lu	Helmholtz Center Munich, Germany
Domenico Tortorella	University of Pisa, Italy
Dominik Geissler	American Family Insurance, USA

DongNyeong Heo	Handong Global University, South Korea
Dongyang Zhang	University of Electronic Science and Technology of China, China
Doreen Jirak	Istituto Italiano di Tecnologia, Italy
Douglas McLelland	BrainChip, France
Douglas Nyabuga	Mount Kenya University, Rwanda
Dulani Meedeniya	University of Moratuwa, Sri Lanka
Dumitru-Clementin Cercel	University Politehnica of Bucharest, Romania
Dylan Muir	SynSense, Switzerland
Efe Bozkir	Uni Tübingen, Germany
Eleftherios Kouloumpris	Aristotle University of Thessaloniki, Greece
Elias Pimenidis	University of the West of England, UK
Eliska Kloberdanz	Iowa State University, USA
Emre Neftci	Foschungszentrum Juelich, Germany
Enzo Tartaglione	Telecom Paris, France
Erwin Lopez	University of Manchester, UK
Evgeny Mirkes	University of Leicester, UK
F. Boray Tek	Istanbul Technical University, Turkey
Federico Corradi	Eindhoven University of Technology, Netherlands
Federico Errica	NEC Labs Europe, Germany
Federico Manzi	Università Cattolica del Sacro Cuore, Italy
Federico Vozzi	CNR, Italy
Fedor Scholz	University of Tuebingen, Germany
Feifei Dai	Chinese Academy of Sciences, China
Feifei Xu	Shanghai University of Electric Power, China
Feixiang Zhou	University of Leicester, UK
Felipe Moreno	FGV, Peru
Feng Wei	York University, Canada
Fengying Li	Guilin University of Electronic Technology, China
Flora Ferreira	University of Minho, Portugal
Florian Mirus	Intel Labs, Germany
Francesco Semeraro	University of Manchester, UK
Franco Scarselli	University of Siena, Italy
François Blayo	IPSEITE, Switzerland
Frank Röder	Hamburg University of Technology, Germany
Frederic Alexandre	Inria, France
Fuchang Han	Central South University, China
Fuli Wang	University of Essex, UK
Gabriela Sejnova	Czech Technical University in Prague, Czech Republic
Gaetano Di Caterina	University of Strathclyde, UK
George Bebis	University of Nevada, USA

Gerrit Ecke	Mercedes-Benz, Germany
Giannis Nikolentzos	Ecole Polytechnique, France
Gilles Marcou	University of Strasbourg, France
Giorgio Gnecco	IMT School for Advanced Studies, Italy
Glauco Amigo	Baylor University, USA
Greg Lee	Acadia University, Canada
Grégory Bourguin	LISIC/ULCO, France
Guillermo Martín-Sánchez	Champalimaud Foundation, Portugal
Gulustan Dogan	UNCW, USA
Habib Khan	Islamia College University Peshawar, Pakistan
Haizhou Du	Shanghai University of Electric Power, China
Hanli Wang	Tongji University, China
Hanno Gottschalk	TU Berlin, Germany
Hao Tong	University of Birmingham, UK
Haobo Jiang	NJUST, China
Haopeng Chen	Shanghai Jiao Tong University, China
Hazrat Ali	Hamad Bin Khalifa University, Qatar
Hina Afridi	NTNU, Gjøvik, Norway
Hiroaki Aizawa	Hiroshima University, Japan
Hiromichi Suetani	Oita University, Japan
Hiroshi Kawaguchi	Kobe University, Japan
Hiroyasu Ando	Tohoku University, Japan
Hiroyoshi Ito	University of Tsukuba, Japan
Honggang Zhang	University of Massachusetts, Boston, USA
Hongqing Yu	Open University, UK
Hongye Cao	Northwestern Polytechnical University, China
Hugo Carneiro	University of Hamburg, Germany
Hugo Eduardo Camacho Cruz	Universidad Autónoma de Tamaulipas, Mexico
Huifang Ma	Northwest Normal University, China
Hyeyoung Park	Kyungpook National University, South Korea
Ian Nabney	University of Bristol, UK
Igor Farkas	Comenius University Bratislava, Slovakia
Ikuko Nishikawa	Ritsumeikan University, Japan
Ioannis Pierros	Aristotle University of Thessaloniki, Greece
Iraklis Varlamis	Harokopio University of Athens, Greece
Ivan Tyukin	King's College London, UK
Iveta Bečková	Comenius University in Bratislava, Slovakia
Jae Hee Lee	University of Hamburg, Germany
James Yu	Southern University of Science and Technology, China
Jan Faigl	Czech Technical University in Prague, Czech Republic

Jan Feber	Czech Technical University in Prague, Czech Republic
Jan-Gerrit Habekost	University of Hamburg, Germany
Jannik Thuemmel	University of Tübingen, Germany
Jeremie Cabessa	University Paris 2, France
Jérémie Sublime	ISEP, France
Jia Cai	Guangdong University of Finance & Economics, China
Jiaan Wang	Soochow University, China
Jialiang Tang	Nanjing University of Science and Technology, China
Jian Hu	YiduCloud, Cyprus
Jianhua Xu	Nanjing Normal University, China
Jianyong Chen	Shenzhen University, China
Jichao Bi	Zhejiang Institute of Industry and Information Technology, China
Jie Shao	University of Electronic Science and Technology of China, China
Jim Smith	University of the West of England, UK
Jing Yang	Hefei University of Technology, China
Jingyi Yuan	Arizona State University, USA
Jingyun Jia	Baidu, USA
Jinling Wang	Ulster University, UK
Jiri Sima	Czech Academy of Sciences, Czech Republic
Jitesh Dundas	Independent Researcher, USA
Joost Vennekens	KU Leuven, Belgium
Jordi Cosp	Universitat Politècnica de Catalunya, Spain
Josua Spisak	University of Hamburg, Germany
Jozef Kubík	Comenius University, Slovakia
Junpei Zhong	Hong Kong Polytechnic University, China
Jurgita Kapočiūtė-Dzikienė	Vytautas Magnus University, Lithuania
K. L. Eddie Law	Macao Polytechnic University, China
Kai Tang	Independent Researcher, China
Kamil Dedecius	Czech Academy of Sciences, Czech Republic
Kang Zhang	Kyushu University, Japan
Kantaro Fujiwara	University of Tokyo, Japan
Karlis Freivalds	Institute of Electronics and Computer Science, Latvia
Khoa Phung	University of the West of England, UK
Kiran Lekkala	University of Southern California, USA
Kleanthis Malialis	University of Cyprus, Cyprus
Kohulan Rajan	Friedrich Schiller University, Germany

Koichiro Yamauchi	Chubu University, Japan
Koloud Alkhamaiseh	Western Michigan University, USA
Konstantinos Demertzis	Democritus University of Thrace, Greece
Kostadin Cvejoski	Fraunhofer IAIS, Germany
Kristína Malinovská	Comenius University in Bratislava, Slovakia
Kun Zhang	Inria and École Polytechnique, France
Laurent Mertens	KU Leuven, Belgium
Laurent Perrinet	AMU CNRS, France
Lazaros Iliadis	Democritus University of Thrace, Greece
Leandro dos Santos Coelho	Pontifical Catholic University of Parana, Brazil
Leiping Jie	Hong Kong Baptist University, China
Lenka Tĕtková	Technical University of Denmark, Denmark
Lia Morra	Politecnico di Torino, Italy
Liang Ge	Chongqing University, China
Liang Zhao	Dalian University of Technology, China
Limengzi Yuan	Shihezi University, China
Ling Guo	Northwest University, China
Linlin Shen	Shenzhen University, China
Lixin Zou	Wuhan University, China
Lorenzo Vorabbi	University of Bologna, Italy
Lu Wang	Macao Polytechnic University, China
Luca Pasa	University of Padova, Italy
Ľudovít Malinovský	Independent Researcher, Slovakia
Luis Alexandre	Universidade da Beira Interior, Portugal
Luis Lago	Universidad Autonoma de Madrid, Spain
Lukáš Gajdošech Gajdošech	Comenius University Bratislava, Slovakia
Lyra Puspa	Vanaya NeuroLab, Indonesia
Madalina Erascu	West University of Timisoara, Romania
Magda Friedjungová	Czech Technical University in Prague, Czech Republic
Manuel Traub	University of Tübingen, Germany
Marcello Trovati	Edge Hill University, UK
Marcin Pietron	AGH-UST, Poland
Marco Bertolini	Pfizer, Germany
Marco Podda	University of Pisa, Italy
Markus Bayer	Technical University of Darmstadt, Germany
Markus Eisenbach	Ilmenau University of Technology, Germany
Martin Ferianc	University College London, Slovakia
Martin Holena	Czech Technical University, Czech Republic
Masanari Kimura	ZOZO Research, Japan
Masato Uchida	Waseda University, Japan
Masoud Daneshtalab	Mälardalen University, Sweden

Mats Leon Richter	University of Montreal, Germany
Matthew Evanusa	University of Maryland, USA
Matthias Karlbauer	University of Tübingen, Germany
Matthias Kerzel	University of Hamburg, Germany
Matthias Möller	Örebro University, Sweden
Matthias Müller-Brockhausen	Leiden University, Netherlands
Matus Tomko	Comenius University in Bratislava, Slovakia
Mayukh Maitra	Walmart, India
Md. Delwar Hossain	Nara Institute of Science and Technology, Japan
Mehmet Aydin	University of the West of England, UK
Michail Chatzianastasis	École Polytechnique, Greece
Michail-Antisthenis Tsompanas	University of the West of England, UK
Michel Salomon	Université de Franche-Comté, France
Miguel Matey-Sanz	Universitat Jaume I, Spain
Mikołaj Morzy	Poznan University of Technology, Poland
Minal Suresh Patil	Umea universitet, Sweden
Minh Tri Lê	Inria, France
Mircea Nicolescu	University of Nevada, Reno, USA
Mohamed Elleuch	ENSI, Tunisia
Mohammed Elmahdi Khennour	Kasdi Merbah University Ouargla, Algeria
Mohib Ullah	NTNU, Norway
Monika Schak	Fulda University of Applied Sciences, Germany
Moritz Wolter	University of Bonn, Germany
Mostafa Kotb	Hamburg University, Germany
Muhammad Burhan Hafez	University of Hamburg, Germany
Nabeel Khalid	German Research Centre for Artificial Intelligence, Germany
Nabil El Malki	IRIT, France
Narendhar Gugulothu	TCS Research, India
Naresh Balaji Ravichandran	KTH Stockholm, Sweden
Natalie Kiesler	DIPF Leibniz Institute for Research and Information in Education, Germany
Nathan Duran	UWE, UK
Nermeen Abou Baker	Ruhr West University of Applied Sciences, Germany
Nick Jhones	Dundee University, UK
Nicolangelo Iannella	University of Oslo, Norway
Nicolas Couellan	ENAC, France
Nicolas Rougier	University of Bordeaux, France
Nikolaos Ioannis Bountos	National Observatory of Athens, Greece
Nikolaos Polatidis	University of Brighton, UK
Norimichi Ukita	TTI-J, Japan

Oleg Bakhteev	EPFL, Switzerland
Olga Grebenkova	Moscow Institute of Physics and Technology, Russia
Oliver Sutton	King's College London, UK
Olivier Teste	Université de Toulouse, France
Or Elroy	CLB, Israel
Oscar Fontenla-Romero	University of A Coruña, Spain
Ozan Özdenizci	Graz University of Technology, Austria
Pablo Lanillos	Spanish National Research Council, Spain
Pascal Rost	Universität Hamburg, Germany
Paul Kainen	Georgetown, USA
Paulo Cortez	University of Minho, Portugal
Pavel Petrovic	Comenius University, Slovakia
Peipei Liu	School of Cyber Security, University of Chinese Academy of Sciences, China
Peng Qiao	NUDT, China
Peter Andras	Edinburgh Napier University, UK
Peter Steiner	Technische Universität Dresden, Germany
Peter Sutor	University of Maryland, USA
Petia Georgieva	University of Aveiro/IEETA, Portugal
Petia Koprinkova-Hristova	Bulgarian Academy of Sciences, Bulgaria
Petra Vidnerová	Czech Academy of Sciences, Czech Republic
Philipp Allgeuer	University of Hamburg, Germany
Pragathi Priyadharsini Balasubramani	Indian Institute of Technology Kanpur, India
Qian Wang	Durham University, UK
Qinghua Zhou	King's College London, UK
Qingquan Zhang	Southern University of Science and Technology, China
Quentin Jodelet	Tokyo Institute of Technology, Japan
Radoslav Škoviera	Czech Technical University in Prague, Czech Republic
Raoul Heese	Fraunhofer ITWM, Germany
Ricardo Marcacini	University of São Paulo, Brazil
Riccardo Renzulli	University of Turin, Italy
Richard Duro	Universidade da Coruña, Spain
Robert Legenstein	Graz University of Technology, Austria
Rodrigo Clemente Thom de Souza	Federal University of Parana, Brazil
Rohit Dwivedula	Independent Researcher, India
Romain Ferrand	IGI TU Graz, Austria
Roman Mouček	University of West Bohemia, Czech Republic
Roseli Wedemann	Universidade do Estado do Rio de Janeiro, Brazil

Rufin VanRullen	CNRS, France
Ruijun Feng	China Telecom Beijing Research Institute, China
Ruxandra Stoean	University of Craiova, Romania
Sanchit Hira	JHU, USA
Sander Bohte	CWI, Netherlands
Sandrine Mouysset	University of Toulouse/IRIT, France
Sanka Rasnayaka	National University of Singapore, Singapore
Sašo Karakatič	University of Maribor, Slovenia
Sebastian Nowak	University Bonn, Germany
Seiya Satoh	Tokyo Denki University, Japan
Senwei Liang	LBNL, USA
Shaolin Zhu	Tianjin University, China
Shayan Gharib	University of Helsinki, Finland
Sherif Eissa	Eindhoven University of Technology, Afghanistan
Shiyong Lan	Independent Researcher, China
Shoumeng Qiu	Fudan, China
Shu Eguchi	Aomori University, Japan
Shubai Chen	Southwest University, China
Shweta Singh	International Institute of Information Technology, Hyderabad, India
Simon Hakenes	Ruhr University Bochum, Germany
Simona Doboli	Hofstra University, USA
Song Guo	Xi'an University of Architecture and Technology, China
Stanislav Frolov	Deutsches Forschungszentrum für künstliche Intelligenz (DFKI), Germany
Štefan Pócoš	Comenius University in Bratislava, Slovakia
Steven (Zvi) Lapp	Bar Ilan University, Israel
Sujala Shetty	BITS Pilani Dubai Campus, United Arab Emirates
Sumio Watanabe	Tokyo Institute of Technology, Japan
Surabhi Sinha	Adobe, USA
Takafumi Amaba	Fukuoka University, Japan
Takaharu Yaguchi	Kobe University, Japan
Takeshi Abe	Yamaguchi University, Japan
Takuya Kitamura	National Institute of Technology, Toyama College, Japan
Tatiana Tyukina	University of Leicester, UK
Teng-Sheng Moh	San Jose State University, USA
Tetsuya Hoya	Independent Researcher, Japan
Thierry Viéville	Domicile, France
Thomas Nowotny	University of Sussex, UK
Tianlin Zhang	University of Manchester, UK

Tianyi Wang	University of Hong Kong, China
Tieke He	Nanjing University, China
Tiyu Fang	Shandong University, China
Tobias Uelwer	Technical University Dortmund, Germany
Tomasz Kapuscinski	Rzeszow University of Technology, Poland
Tomasz Szandala	Wroclaw University of Technology, Poland
Toshiharu Sugawara	Waseda University, Japan
Trond Arild Tjostheim	Lund University, Sweden
Umer Mushtaq	Université Paris-Panthéon-Assas, France
Uwe Handmann	Ruhr West University, Germany
V. Ramasubramanian	International Institute of Information Technology, Bangalore, India
Valeri Mladenov	Technical University of Sofia, Bulgaria
Valerie Vaquet	Bielefeld University, Germany
Vandana Ladwani	International Institute of Information Technology, Bangalore, India
Vangelis Metsis	Texas State University, USA
Vera Kurkova	Czech Academy of Sciences, Czech Republic
Verner Ferreira	Universidade do Estado da Bahia, Brazil
Viktor Kocur	Comenius University, Slovakia
Ville Tanskanen	University of Helsinki, Finland
Viviana Cocco Mariani	PUCPR, Brazil
Vladimír Boža	Comenius University, Slovakia
Vojtech Mrazek	Brno University of Technology, Czech Republic
Weifeng Liu	China University of Petroleum (East China), China
Wenxin Yu	Southwest University of Science and Technology, China
Wenxuan Liu	Wuhan University of Technology, China
Wu Ancheng	Pingan, China
Wuliang Huang	ICT, China
Xi Cheng	NUPT, Hong Kong, China
Xia Feng	Civil Aviation University of China, China
Xian Zhong	Wuhan University of Technology, China
Xiang Zhang	National University of Defense Technology, China
Xiaochen Yuan	Macao Polytechnic University, China
Xiaodong Gu	Fudan University, China
Xiaoqing Liu	Kyushu University, Japan
Xiaowei Zhou	Macquarie University, Australia
Xiaozhuang Song	Chinese University of Hong Kong, Shenzhen, China

Xingpeng Zhang	Southwest Petroleum University, China
Xuemei Jia	Wuhan University, China
Xuewen Wang	China University of Geosciences, China
Yahong Lian	Nankai University, China
Yan Zheng	China University of Political Science and Law, China
Yang Liu	Fudan University, China
Yang Shao	Hitachi, Japan
Yangguang Cui	East China Normal University, China
Yansong Chua	China Nanhu Academy of Electronics and Information Technology, Singapore
Yapeng Gao	Taiyuan University of Technology, China
Yasufumi Sakai	Fujitsu, Japan
Ye Wang	National University of Defense Technology, China
Yeh-Ching Chung	Chinese University of Hong Kong, Shenzhen, China
Yihao Luo	Yichang Testing Technique R&D Institute, China
Yikemaiti Sataer	Southeast University, China
Yipeng Yu	Tencent, China
Yongchao Ye	Southern University of Science and Technology, China
Yoshihiko Horio	Tohoku University, Japan
Youcef Djenouri	NORCE, Norway
Yuan Li	Military Academy of Sciences, China
Yuan Panli	Shihezi University, China
Yuan Yao	Tsinghua University, China
Yuanlun Xie	University of Electronic Science and Technology of China, China
Yuanshao Zhu	Southern University of Science and Technology, China
Yucan Zhou	Institute of Information Engineering, Chinese Academy of Sciences, China
Yuchen Zheng	Shihezi University, China
Yuchun Fang	Shanghai University, China
Yue Zhao	Minzu University of China, China
Yuesong Nan	National University of Singapore, Singapore
Zaneta Swiderska-Chadaj	Warsaw University of Technology, Poland
Zdenek Straka	Czech Technical University in Prague, Czech Republic
Zhao Yang	Leiden University, Netherlands
Zhaoyun Ding	NUDT, China
Zhengwei Yang	Wuhan University, China

Zhenjie Yao	Chinese Academy of Sciences, Singapore
Zhichao Lian	Nanjing University of Science and Technology, China
Zhiqiang Zhang	Hosei University, Japan
Zhixin Li	Guangxi Normal University, China
Zhongnan Zhang	Xiamen University, China
Zhongzhan Huang	Sun Yat-sen University, China
Zi Long	Shenzhen Technology University, China
Zilong Lin	Indiana University Bloomington, USA
Zuobin Xiong	Georgia State University, USA
Zuzana Cernekova	FMFI Comenius University, Slovakia

Invited Talks

Developmental Robotics for Language Learning, Trust and Theory of Mind

Angelo Cangelosi

University of Manchester and Alan Turing Institute, UK

Growing theoretical and experimental research on action and language processing and on number learning and gestures clearly demonstrates the role of embodiment in cognition and language processing. In psychology and neuroscience, this evidence constitutes the basis of embodied cognition, also known as grounded cognition (Pezzulo et al. 2012). In robotics and AI, these studies have important implications for the design of linguistic capabilities in cognitive agents and robots for human-robot collaboration, and have led to the new interdisciplinary approach of Developmental Robotics, as part of the wider Cognitive Robotics field (Cangelosi and Schlesinger 2015; Cangelosi and Asada 2022). During the talk we presented examples of developmental robotics models and experimental results from iCub experiments on the embodiment biases in early word acquisition and grammar learning (Morse et al. 2015; Morse and Cangelosi 2017) and experiments on pointing gestures and finger counting for number learning (De La Cruz et al. 2014). We then presented a novel developmental robotics model, and experiments, on Theory of Mind and its use for autonomous trust behavior in robots (Vinanzi et al. 2019, 2021). The implications for the use of such embodied approaches for embodied cognition in AI and cognitive sciences, and for robot companion applications, was also discussed.

Challenges of Incremental Learning

Barbara Hammer

CITEC Centre of Excellence, Bielefeld University, Germany

Smart products and AI components are increasingly available in industrial applications and everyday life. This offers great opportunities for cognitive automation and intelligent human-machine cooperation; yet it also poses significant challenges since a fundamental assumption of classical machine learning, an underlying stationary data distribution, might be easily violated. Unexpected events or outliers, sensor drift, or individual user behavior might cause changes of an underlying data distribution, typically referred to as concept drift or covariate shift. Concept drift requires a continuous adaptation of the underlying model and efficient incremental learning strategies. Within the presentation, I looked at recent developments in the context of incremental learning schemes for streaming data, putting a particular focus on the challenge of learning with drift and detecting and disentangling drift in possibly unsupervised setups and for unknown type and strength of drift. More precisely, I dealt with the following aspects: learning schemes for incremental model adaptation from streaming data in the presence of concept drift; various mathematical formalizations of concept drift and detection/quantification of drift based thereon; and decomposition and explanation of drift. I presented a couple of experimental results using benchmarks from the literature, and I offered a glimpse into mathematical guarantees which can be provided for some of the algorithms.

Reliable AI: From Mathematical Foundations to Quantum Computing

Gitta Kutyniok[1,2]

[1]Bavarian AI Chair for Mathematical Foundations of Artificial Intelligence, LMU Munich, Germany
[2]Adjunct Professor for Machine Learning, University of Tromsø, Norway

Artificial intelligence is currently leading to one breakthrough after the other, both in public life with, for instance, autonomous driving and speech recognition, and in the sciences in areas such as medical diagnostics or molecular dynamics. However, one current major drawback is the lack of reliability of such methodologies.

In this lecture we took a mathematical viewpoint towards this problem, showing the power of such approaches to reliability. We first provided an introduction into this vibrant research area, focussing specifically on deep neural networks. We then surveyed recent advances, in particular concerning generalization guarantees and explainability methods. Finally, we discussed fundamental limitations of deep neural networks and related approaches in terms of computability, which seriously affects their reliability, and we revealed a connection with quantum computing.

Intelligent Pervasive Applications for Holistic Health Management

Ilias Maglogiannis

University of Piraeus, Greece

The advancements in telemonitoring platforms, biosensors, and medical devices have paved the way for pervasive health management, allowing patients to be monitored remotely in real-time. The visual domain has become increasingly important for patient monitoring, with activity recognition and fall detection being key components. Computer vision techniques, such as deep learning, have been used to develop robust activity recognition and fall detection algorithms. These algorithms can analyze video streams from cameras, detecting and classifying various activities, and detecting falls in real time. Furthermore, wearable devices, such as smartwatches and fitness trackers, can also monitor a patient's daily activities, providing insights into their overall health and wellness, allowing for a comprehensive analysis of a patient's health. In this talk we discussed the state of the art in pervasive health management and biomedical data analytics and we presented the work done in the Computational Biomedicine Laboratory of the University of Piraeus in this domain. The talk also included Future Trends and Challenges.

Contents – Part I

A Classification Performance Evaluation Measure Considering Data Separability

Lingyan Xue, Xinyu Zhang$^{(\boxtimes)}$, Weidong Jiang, Kai Huo, and Qinmu Shen

National University of Defense Technology, Changsha, China
zhangxinyu90111@163.com

Abstract. Machine learning and deep learning classification models are data-driven, and the model and the data jointly determine their classification performance. It is biased to evaluate the model's performance only based on the classifier accuracy while ignoring the data separability. Sometimes, the model exhibits excellent accuracy, which might be attributed to its testing on highly separable data. Most of the current studies on data separability measures are defined based on the distance between sample points, but this has been demonstrated to fail in several circumstances. In this paper, we propose a new separability measure–the rate of separability (RS), which is based on the data coding rate. We validate its effectiveness as a supplement to the separability measure by comparing it to four other distance-based measures on synthetic dataset. Then, we discover the positive correlation between the proposed measure and recognition accuracy in a multi-task scenario constructed from a real dataset. Finally, we discuss the methods for evaluating the classification performance of machine learning and deep learning models considering data separability.

Keywords: Machine learning · Classification accuracy · Data separability · Classification difficulty · Performance evaluation

1 Introduction

As an important branch in data mining, classification aims to construct a classification model to learn a mapping regularity from existing data to class labels. The research of model is essential, yet data also determines the performance [2]. A specific example is the impact of spectral separability on classification accuracy [17]. Numerous classification models have been proposed, including KNN, SVM, logistic regression, neural networks, etc., but studies on data separability are substantially fewer. A recent study in hyperspectral image classification has argued that insufficient data may limit the assessment capability of existing accuracy indexes [9]. That leads to the problem of whether a model performs best on a classification case is unclear or inconclusive [15]. It is acknowledged that a good classification model provides greater generalization potential, which means finding rules consistent with available data that apply widely to predict

L. Iliadis et al. (Eds.): ICANN 2023, LNCS 14254, pp. 1–13, 2023.
https://doi.org/10.1007/978-3-031-44207-0_1

the class of unknown data [20]. Yet the criteria for assessing the model's generalization ability remain debated. To simplify the performance evaluation process, researchers generally tend to adopt measures based on the confusion matrix [7], like accuracy, precision, kappa statistic, and F-score. Each measure is represented with a single score number, making it straightforward to compare and analyze classification models quantitatively. Although the result is intuitive, its comparability is invalid when confronted with a multi-task classification situation more representative of the real-world environment.

A contradictory example is that a classifier reaches the highest accuracy in one task but the lowest in another. What causes the problem is that such classifier-oriented measures treat the different instances of a dataset as statistical objects and ignore the classification difficulty of each instance. For the above issue, Yu et al. [18] proposed an instance-oriented measure but only apply to data with few samples due to the computational complexity of classification difficulty for each instance. Therefore, we require a measure to statistically characterize the classification difficulty of datasets. Fortunately, previous research has established that separability is an intrinsic characteristic of a dataset [4] to describe how instances belonging to different classes mix. Measuring the data quality is critical for estimating the problem's difficulty in advance since a classification model's accuracy strongly depends on the data quality [1]. Obviously, the more separable the dataset, the simpler the classification. Eventually, we consider data separability as a metric of classification difficulty.

There are several measures of data separability that can quantify classification difficulty. The Fisher discriminant ratio [8] has been used in many studies, which measures the data separability using the mean and standard deviation of each class, but it fails in some cases like a two-class circle data. A more effective issue is data complexity which measures the distance of intra classes as well as the inter class. Ho and Basu [6] conducted a groundbreaking review of data complexity measures. Recently, Lorena et al. [11] summarized existing methods for the measurement of classification complexity, showing that some of those may have large time cost.

As an alternative to the distance-based criterion, we consider explaining data separability from the perspective of probability theory. Inspired by Cover and Thomas [3], the process of minimizing the data rate distortion is equivalent to the process of solving the optimal solution of the likelihood function, i.e., the data coding rate has strong consistency with the parameter estimation performance [13]. That means if the data can be fitted with better distribution model after segmentation, then the data should be effectively encoded in relation to such model. Ma et al. [12] argued that the coding rate (subject to a distortion) provides a natural measure of the goodness of segmentation for real-valued mixed data.

Since there is no research verifying the feasibility of using coding rate as a measure of data separability, this is the first study to construct a separability measure based on rate-distortion theory called the rate of separability (RS). The main contributions of this paper are summarized as follows.

1) We propose a data separability measure based on rate-distortion theory, and verify its effectiveness in theory and experiments.

2) We find a positive correlation between classification accuracy and data separability in a multi-task noisy environment.

3) In a multi-task noisy environment, we design a task-oriented classifier performance evaluation method considering data separability as the task difficulty. Unlike the classification accuracy changing with different tasks, this method obtains classifier ability as the classifier's inherent property under certain assumptions.

4) We build a modular classifier performance evaluation model to explain the function of deep learning convolutional blocks using data separability.

The rest of this paper is structured as follows. Section 2 introduces the method of constructing coding-rate-based measure. Section 3 provides experimental methods for validating measure validity and evaluates the classification model performance; results and analysis are also given in this section. Finally, we conclude in Sect. 4.

2   Data Separability Measure

In this section, we apply rate-distortion theory in constructing a new data separability measure.

2.1   Coding-Rate Based Data Separability Measure

Given a data $\mathbf{X} = [\mathbf{x}_1, ..., \mathbf{x}_m] \in \mathbb{R}^{d \times m}$ with m samples of d dimension and a encoding precision $\varepsilon > 0$, let $\mathbf{\Pi} = \{\mathbf{\Pi}^j \in \mathbb{R}^{m \times m}\}_{j=1}^k$ be the label matrix of the $\mathbf{X}$ in the k classes, and $\mathbf{\Pi}^j(i, i)$ is the label of $\mathbf{x}_i$ belonging to class j, our proposed data separability measure based on rate-distortion is:

$$\mathrm{R_S}(\mathbf{X}) = \frac{\mathrm{R_C}(\mathbf{X}, \varepsilon | \mathbf{\Pi})}{\mathrm{R}(\mathbf{X}, \varepsilon)}. \tag{1}$$

In Eq. (1), the $\mathrm{R_C}(\mathbf{X}, \varepsilon | \mathbf{\Pi})$ and $\mathrm{R}(\mathbf{X}, \varepsilon)$ denote the local and global coding rate of the data, respectively. Unlike Yu et al. [19], who utilized $\Delta \mathrm{R}(\mathbf{X}) = \mathrm{R}(\mathbf{X}, \varepsilon) - \mathrm{R_C}(\mathbf{X}, \varepsilon | \mathbf{\Pi})$ as the optimization problem's objective function subjecting to $\left\| \mathbf{X}^j \right\|_F^2 = \mathrm{tr}(\mathbf{\Pi}^j)$, here we discard the constraint and adopt a ratio form between $\mathrm{R}(\mathbf{X}, \varepsilon | \mathbf{\Pi})$ and $\mathrm{R}(\mathbf{X}, \varepsilon)$, resulting in a data separability measure $\mathrm{R_S}(\mathbf{X})$ in the range of [0,1] with low values indicating high separability. It means that the smaller the $\mathrm{R_C}(\mathbf{X}, \varepsilon | \mathbf{\Pi})$, the more clustered the samples within the class, and the larger the $\mathrm{R}(\mathbf{X}, \varepsilon)$, the more dispersed the samples between classes. Next we introduce the definition of the coding rate and explain how the measure we proposed reflects the data intrinsic separability.

2.2   Definition and Computation of the Coding Rate

According to Cover and Thomas' [3] definition of rate-distortion: the rate-distortion $R(\mathbf{X}, \varepsilon)$ is the minimal number of binary bits needed to encode $\mathbf{X}$ and the expected decoding error is less than ε. The actual estimation coding rate of $\mathbf{X}$ with zero mean is as follows:

$$R(\mathbf{X}, \varepsilon) = \frac{m}{2} \log \det(\mathbf{I} + \frac{d}{m\varepsilon^2} \mathbf{X}\mathbf{X}^T). \tag{2}$$

Furthermore, suppose $\mathbf{X}$ has k-class samples, then $\mathbf{X} = \mathbf{X}^1 \cup \mathbf{X}^2 \cup ... \cup \mathbf{X}^k$. the data $\mathbf{X}^j$ in each class j also occupy a certain volume in its low dimensional subspace. For each subset, the above coding rate (2) is applied, then $R_C(\mathbf{X}, \varepsilon|\mathbf{\Pi})$ is given by

$$R_C(\mathbf{X}, \varepsilon|\mathbf{\Pi}) = \sum_{j=1}^{k} \frac{tr(\mathbf{\Pi}^j)}{2} \log \det \left(\mathbf{I} + \frac{d}{tr(\mathbf{\Pi}^j)\varepsilon^2} \mathbf{X}\mathbf{\Pi}^j \mathbf{X}^T \right) \tag{3}$$

The equation for the coding rate in Eq. (2) is for the scenario where the mean value of the given data is zero mean. More generally, when $\mathbf{X} = [\mathbf{x}_1, ..., \mathbf{x}_m] \in \mathbb{R}^{d \times m}$ is not zero mean, we have the mean $\boldsymbol{\mu} = \frac{1}{m} \sum_{i=1}^{m} \mathbf{x}_i \in \mathbb{R}^d$ and the zero mean part of the data $\bar{\mathbf{X}}$, thus the total coding rate of $\mathbf{X}$ with non-zero mean is:

$$R(\mathbf{X}) = \frac{m}{2} \log \det(\mathbf{I} + \frac{d}{m\varepsilon^2} \bar{\mathbf{X}}\bar{\mathbf{X}}^T) + \frac{d}{2}\log_2 \left(1 + \frac{\boldsymbol{\mu}^T \boldsymbol{\mu}}{\varepsilon^2} \right). \tag{4}$$

2.3   Correlation Between RS and Data Separability

This section discusses the connection between RS and data separability. Under the condition that the data follows a Gaussian distribution, we prove Theorem 1. Theorem 1 gives the lower bound of the data coding rate and the necessary and sufficient conditions for it to reach the lower bound. This condition illustrates that if and only if every class $\mathbf{X}$ has the same distribution, the total coding rate of $\mathbf{X}$ is identical to the sum of $\mathbf{X}^j$'s coding rate.

Theorem 1. *For any* $\left\{ \mathbf{X}^j \in \mathbb{R}^{d \times m_j} \right\}_{j=1}^{k}$ *and any* $\varepsilon > 0$, *let* $\mathbf{X} = [\mathbf{x}_1, ..., \mathbf{x}_m] = [\mathbf{X}^1, \cdots \mathbf{X}^k] \in \mathbb{R}^{d \times m}$ *with* $m = \sum_{j=1}^{k} m_j$ *and* $\boldsymbol{\mu} = \frac{1}{m} \sum_{i=1}^{m} \mathbf{x}_i \in \mathbb{R}^d$, *then we define the zero mean part* $\bar{\mathbf{X}} = \mathbf{X} - \boldsymbol{\mu} \cdot \mathbf{1}_{1 \times m}$. *Let* $\mathbf{X}^j = [\mathbf{x}_1^j, ..., \mathbf{x}_{m_j}^j] \in \mathbb{R}^{d \times m_j}$ *with* $\boldsymbol{\mu}^j = \frac{1}{m_j} \sum_{i=1}^{m_j} \mathbf{x}_i^j \in \mathbb{R}^d$ *and* $\bar{\mathbf{X}}^j = \mathbf{X}^j - \boldsymbol{\mu}^j \cdot \mathbf{1}_{1 \times m_j}$. *We have* $R(\mathbf{X}, \varepsilon) \geq R_C(\mathbf{X}, \varepsilon|\mathbf{\Pi})$,

$$\frac{m}{2} \log \det(\mathbf{I} + \frac{d}{m\varepsilon^2} \bar{\mathbf{X}}\bar{\mathbf{X}}^T) + \frac{d}{2}\log_2 \left(1 + \frac{\boldsymbol{\mu}^T \boldsymbol{\mu}}{\varepsilon^2} \right) \geq$$
$$\sum_{j=1}^{k} \frac{m_j}{2} \log \det(\mathbf{I} + \frac{d}{m_j\varepsilon^2} \bar{\mathbf{X}}^j (\bar{\mathbf{X}}^j)^T) + \frac{d}{2k}\log_2 \left(1 + \frac{(\boldsymbol{\mu}^j)^T \boldsymbol{\mu}^j}{\varepsilon^2} \right). \tag{5}$$

where the equality holds if and only if

$$\frac{\bar{\mathbf{X}}^1(\bar{\mathbf{X}}^1)^T}{m_1} = \frac{\bar{\mathbf{X}}^2(\bar{\mathbf{X}}^2)^T}{m_2} = \cdots = \frac{\bar{\mathbf{X}}^k(\bar{\mathbf{X}}^k)^T}{m_k} = \frac{\bar{\mathbf{X}}(\bar{\mathbf{X}})^T}{m}$$

$$\boldsymbol{\mu}^1 = \boldsymbol{\mu}^2 = \cdots = \boldsymbol{\mu}^k = \boldsymbol{\mu}. \tag{6}$$

The Proof of Theorem 1 is based on the concave property of the $\log\det(\cdot)$ and $\log(\cdot)$ functions, and they satisfy Jensen's inequality.

Proof. Since $\log\det(\cdot)$ and $\log(\cdot)$ is strictly concave, The Jensen's inequality is satisfied. We have

$$f(\sum_{j=1}^k \beta_j \mathbf{S}^j) \geq \sum_{j=1}^k \beta_j f(\mathbf{S}^j). \tag{7}$$

for all $\{\beta_j > 0\}_{j=1}^k$, $\sum\limits_{j=1}^k \beta_j = 1$ and $\{\mathbf{S}^j \in \mathbb{S}_{++}^n\}_{j=1}^k$, where equality holds if and only if $\mathbf{S}^1 = \mathbf{S}^2 = \cdots = \mathbf{S}^k$.

For function $\log\det(\cdot)$, take $\beta^j = \frac{m_j}{m}$ and $\mathbf{S}^j = \mathbf{I} + \frac{d}{m_j\varepsilon^2}\bar{\mathbf{X}}^j(\bar{\mathbf{X}}^j)^T$, we get

$$\log\det(\mathbf{I} + \frac{d}{m\varepsilon^2}\bar{\mathbf{X}}\bar{\mathbf{X}}^T) \geq \sum_{j=1}^k \frac{m_j}{m} \log\det(\mathbf{I} + \frac{d}{m_j\varepsilon^2}\bar{\mathbf{X}}^j(\bar{\mathbf{X}}^j)^T). \tag{8}$$

with equality holds if and only if $\frac{\bar{\mathbf{X}}^1(\bar{\mathbf{X}}^1)^T}{m_1} = \frac{\bar{\mathbf{X}}^2(\bar{\mathbf{X}}^2)^T}{m_2} = \cdots = \frac{\bar{\mathbf{X}}^k(\bar{\mathbf{X}}^k)^T}{m_k} = \frac{\bar{\mathbf{X}}(\bar{\mathbf{X}})^T}{m}$.

For function $\log(\cdot)$, take $\beta^j = \frac{1}{k}$ and $\mathbf{S}^j = 1 + \frac{d}{\varepsilon^2}(\boldsymbol{\mu}^j)^T\boldsymbol{\mu}^j$, we get

$$\log(1 + \frac{\boldsymbol{\mu}^T\boldsymbol{\mu}}{\varepsilon^2}) \geq \sum_{j=1}^k \frac{1}{k} \log(1 + \frac{(\boldsymbol{\mu}^j)^T\boldsymbol{\mu}^j}{\varepsilon^2}). \tag{9}$$

with equality holds if and only if $\boldsymbol{\mu}^1 = \boldsymbol{\mu}^2 = \cdots = \boldsymbol{\mu}^k = \boldsymbol{\mu}$, and the last equality is from $\sum\limits_{j=1}^k m_j\boldsymbol{\mu}^j = m\boldsymbol{\mu}$. From formula (8) and (9), Theorem 1 can be proved.

From Theorem 1, we can conclude that the sum of the various classes of data coding rate is a lower bound on the overall data coding rate. When the overall data coding rate reaches the lower bound, its necessary and sufficient condition indicate: for the Gaussian distributed data, each category of data has the same distribution, which also means that the feature vectors of each class have a high degree of coincidence, corresponding to the most inseparable situation.

3   Experiments

3.1   Validation on Two-Class Synthetic Datasets

We first verify the proposed measure RS's effectiveness using a two-class synthetic dataset[1] with adjustable separability, and contrast its separability evalua-

---

[1] The datasets are created by the Samples Generator in sklearn.datasets https://scikit-learn.org/stable/modules/classes.html#samples-generator.

tion results with distance-based measures [5] (e.g., DSI, N2, LSC, Density). We experiment on the data following a Gaussian distribution, the region of feature overlap can be adjusted by changing the feature standard deviation (SD). We set the SD parameter from 1 to 9. Four instances are depicted in Fig. 1, the results are presented in Fig. 2.

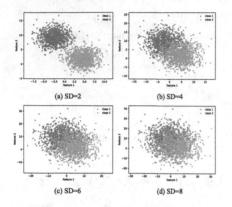

(a) SD=2   (b) SD=4

(c) SD=6   (d) SD=8

Fig. 1. The data with different cluster standard deviations (SD). A high SD value denotes a significant overlap area

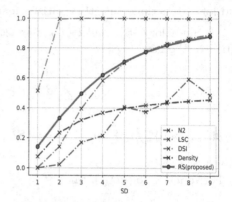

Fig. 2. Comparison of data separability evaluation results with varying degrees of feature overlap. For measures, a high value on the y-axis indicates low separability

In this condition, both N2 and LSC fail to assess the data separability. Among them, LSC can only distinguish the case of features with or without overlap and is not sensitive to the change of feature overlap area. At the same time, N2 fluctuates with the deterioration of data separability, suggesting a lower evaluation precision. Besides, RS, DSI, and Density can correctly reflect the trend of data separability, i.e., a high SD value corresponds to a high measure value. Furthermore, both DSI and RS have an extensive dynamic change range.

3.2 Correlation Between Classification Accuracy and Data Separability

After verifying the validity of RS as a measure of data separability, we characterize the data separability using RS values. This section discusses the experimental procedures used to investigate the correlation between classification accuracy and data separability. The experiment framework is shown in Fig. 3.

Step I is to add Gaussian white noise with a specific variance to the original data to create a test set with a signal-to-noise ratio (SNR) of 5–20 dB.

In Step II, we deploy four standard machine learning classifiers. Nonlinear classifiers such as K-Nearest Neighbor (KNN) and Support Vector Machine with

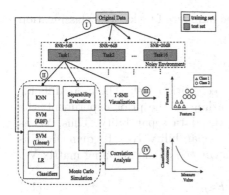

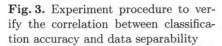

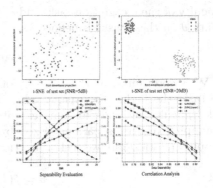

Fig. 3. Experiment procedure to verify the correlation between classification accuracy and data separability

Fig. 4. Analysis results to verify the correlation between classification accuracy and data separability

Radial Basis Function (SVM with RBF) can generate nonlinear decision boundaries. Linear classifiers include linear SVM and logistic regression (LR). The Iris data from UCI repository [10] are utilized in the experiment.

In step III, the T-SNE tool is used to visualize the influence of noise on data separability. And in step IV, we compute noisy data's RS value and analyze the classification accuracy correlation. Here we apply the Monte Carlo simulation to average the randomness of the results due to noise.

The analysis results on the Iris data are shown in Fig. 4. When the SNR is lower than 5 dB, the test data separability becomes extremely poor relative to the training data. And when the SNR is high as 20dB, its separability is equivalent to the training data. Referring to the separability evaluation and correlation analysis, as SNR grows, the separability of test data gradually improves, and the classification accuracy increases along with it. Thus we can conclude a positive correlation between data separability and recognition accuracy.

3.3 Classifier's Ability Evaluated by Classification Accuracy Under Data Separability

In this section, we evaluate the classifier's generalization ability in the group of tasks constricted in Sect. 3.2. Specifically, as shown in Fig. 4, for the dataset Iris, the classification accuracy of SVM (RBF) is consistently higher than other classifiers at $SNR = 20\,dB$, but the lowest at $SNR = 5\,dB$. Since the 5 dB task is more difficult than the 20 dB one, we can't conclude whether the classifier performance is good or not. At this point, how could the classifier's performance be measured?

The simple idea is to assign a certain weight $\mathbf{W} \in \mathbb{R}^n$ to the recognition accuracy $\mathbf{P}_{acc} \in \mathbb{R}^n$ of the classifier on that group of tasks according to the difficulty of the recognition task, and n is the number of tasks. The classification ability θ on these tasks is defined as

$$\theta = \mathbf{W}^T \mathbf{P}_{acc}. \tag{10}$$

$\mathbf{W}$ is determined by the difficulty of the recognition task. The more difficult the task, the higher the weight value. According to the prior experiment, the task difficulty depends to some extent on the data separability. Thus, $\mathbf{W}$ as a mapping matrix is parameterized by the separability $\mathbf{R}_S$. To quantify this mapping relationship, we seek a functional form $f(\cdot)$ of the mapping matrix $\mathbf{W}$.

$$\theta = f(P_{acc}; R_S) \tag{11}$$

$f(\cdot)$ needs to be obtained by fitting a given P_{acc} and θ. P_{acc} can be derived directly from the classification results, whereas θ is uncertain. Therefore, it is first necessary to construct the known θ based on the following assumptions.

1) For different difficulty tasks, homogeneous classifiers with fixed parameters exhibit different recognition accuracies.

2) For the same dataset, homogeneous classifiers with fixed parameters exhibit consistent recognition ability values.

3) For homogeneous classifiers with different parameter settings, their relative ability value can be inferred from the recognition accuracy.

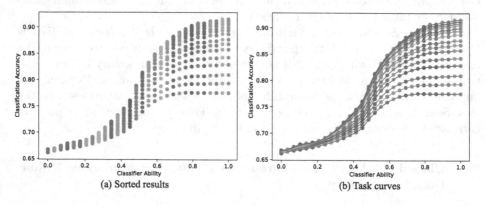

(a) Sorted results   (b) Task curves

Fig. 5. The map of $\mathbf{P}_{acc}$ and θ. Here, $k = 30$, $n = 15$. Each column of $\mathbf{P}_{acc}$ records the classification accuracy of an SVM model on 16 tasks associated with the same color point column in Figure (a). Each row of $\mathbf{P}_{acc}$ records the classification accuracy of 30 SVM models on a single task. The row values are sequentially concatenated to obtain the task curve shown in Figure (b)

Based on the assumptions stated above, we choose the SVM (Linear) model on the Iris dataset to perform the anti-noise experiment depicted in Fig. 3. k SVMs with relative ability values θ were obtained by adjusting the regular parameter C. $\theta \in \mathbb{R}^k$ take k values evenly from 0 to 1. Each SVM tests on n noisy tasks, and get $\mathbf{P}_{acc}^{j} \in \mathbb{R}^{n}(j = 1, 2, ..., k)$. k-group $\mathbf{P}_{acc}^{j}$ is sorted from small to large according to its largest element, and we have $\mathbf{P}_{acc} = [\mathbf{P}_{acc}^{1}, \mathbf{P}_{acc}^{2}, ..., \mathbf{P}_{acc}^{k}] \in \mathbb{R}^{n \times k}$. Figure 5 shows the mapping of $\mathbf{P}_{acc}$ and θ.

Observe that the shape of the curve in Fig. 5(b) is more consistent with that of the Sigmoid function, but the upper and lower bounds of the task curve are variable; thus, Eq. (12) is adopted as the fitting function.

$$P_{acc} = \frac{u - l}{1 + \exp(-a * (\theta - b))} + u \tag{12}$$

Plotting the curve of Eq. (12) in Fig. 6, we explore the properties of this function.

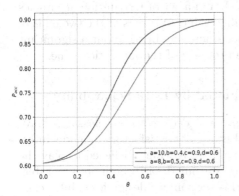

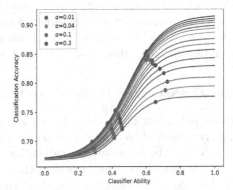

Fig. 6. Fitting function plot

Fig. 7. The fitting task curves and the mapping points

The parameters u, l, a, and b reflect the function properties as follows.

1) u and l can represent the classifier's upper and lower bounds of recognition accuracy on a set of recognition tasks, respectively.

2) $(u - l) * a$ reflects the slope of the function. The flatter the function, the harder the task and the lower the recognition accuracy.

3) b affects the right shift rate of the function. The larger the right shift magnitude, the more difficult the task is, and the less accurate the classifier is.

Then we employ the polynomial fitting approach, with a and b represented by R_S

$$f_a(R_S) = h_0 + h_1 R_S + h_2 R_S^2$$
$$f_b(R_S) = p_0 + p_1 R_S + p_2 R_S^2. \tag{13}$$

The mapping function $f^{-1}(\cdot)$ from classification accuracy to classifier ability with separability R_S as a parameter is now obtained.

$$P_{acc} = f^{-1}(\theta; R_S) = \frac{u - l}{1 + \exp(-f_a(R_S) * (\theta - f_b(R_S)))} + u \qquad (14)$$

To examine the validity of this mapping function, we need to substitute the recognition accuracy of another classifier into the Eq. (14) to ensure the uniqueness of its recognition ability value, demonstrating that the recognition ability value exists as an inherent property of the classifier.

Figure 7 shows the results of fitting the task curve with the SVM model as a reference and an evaluation of the LR (with adjusted parameter α) models' recognition ability on this curve.

This evaluation method has a high assessment accuracy in the middle of the task curve. The evaluation of the LR model ability values for $\alpha = 0.01$ and $\alpha = 0.1$ are distributed over a small interval, and a set of recognition accuracies essentially map to a unique recognition ability value. Whereas at the two ends of the curve, a slight change in recognition accuracy may bring about a significant deviation in recognition ability due to the presence of the saturation zone.

3.4 CNN Layers' Performance Evaluated by Data Separability

As an extension of machine learning classifiers, deep learning classifiers have greatly improved recognition performance but are not satisfactory in model interpretability. The convolution module, for example, is widely believed to play the role of feature extraction, enabling the final output data to be more separable, but how do we measure this function? In this section, we design a modular classifier recognition performance evaluation method to evaluate the performance of each convolutional component of the CNN.

Effective separability indices are invaluable for the performance evaluation of radar signal classification algorithms [14]. Since radar image is more difficult to identify the classes to which they belong after their semantic features are extracted by the convolutional layer, we use the typical radar image MSTAR[2] as the experimental data. The evaluation method proposed is to insert a feature separability analysis module after each convolutional block to monitor its performance, and the separability measure used is RS.

On the MSTAR dataset, we evaluate the performance of some convolutional blocks of CNN provided by Chen et al. [16]. And to reduce the computational effort of RS, we apply a 2 * 2 average pooling to the feature map. The network structure and the feature separability analysis module are shown in Fig. 8.

After 100 epochs of training, the convergence of recognition accuracy on the test set and the variation of feature separability extracted by each convolutional block are set out in Fig. 9.

The most striking result from Fig. 9 is that the separability of features extracted by each convolutional block keeps step with the final classification accuracy. When classification accuracy improves dramatically, the RS value falls

---

[2] The URL for downloading the dataset: https://www.sdms.afrl.af.mil/datasets/mstar/.

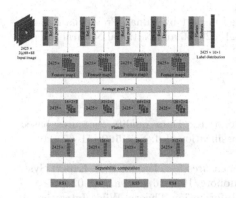

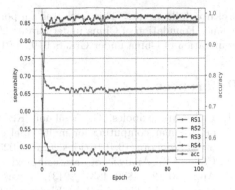

Fig. 8. Network architecture and feature separability analysis module

Fig. 9. Classification accuracy and feature separability analysis results

precipitously. And when the classification accuracy converges, the RS value becomes steady. Furthermore, we also find that the convolutional block in a deeper network has a more significant function in extracting a more separable feature with a lower RS value (RS1 > RS2 > RS3 > RS4). And the deeper feature map exhibits a wider dynamic range of RS value (ΔRS1 < ΔRS2 < ΔRS3 < ΔRS4).

4   Conclusion

Data separability quantification provides some basis for analyzing, understanding, and enhancing model performance. In this paper, we validate the effectiveness of the proposed measure on a typical synthetic two-class dataset and confirm its positive correlation with the classification accuracy in a series of noisy tasks constructed from real datasets. Then we designed machine learning and deep learning classifier model evaluation methods based on the above two basic argumentation experiments. We build a functional mapping model for machine learning classifiers from classification accuracy to classifier ability. In the model, the task difficulty is characterized by the measure, and the classification accuracy assesses the classifiers' capability value as its inherent properties with a separability measure as a parameter. For deep learning classifiers, we use a modular evaluation approach. Each convolutional block's ability to extract separable features is assessed using the proposed measure. Finally, we explain why neural networks work effectively from the perspective of feature separability.

In fact, the separability measure can also be applied to evaluate clustering results, understand the demerit of each feature, provide a theory for building multi-classifier decisions, or reduce data complexity as a loss function. In general, explaining and improving classification performance by exploiting data separability still deserves further study.

Acknowledgments. This work was supported in part by Hunan Provincial Natural Science Foundation of China under Grants 2021JJ20056 and National Natural Science Foundation of China under Grants 61921001.

References

1. Bello, M., Nápoles, G., Vanhoof, K., Bello, R.: Data quality measures based on granular computing for multi-label classification. Inf. Sci. **560**, 51–67 (2021). https://doi.org/10.1016/j.ins.2021.01.027
2. Cano, J.R.: Analysis of data complexity measures for classification. Expert Syst. Appl. **40**(12), 4820–4831 (2013). https://doi.org/10.1016/j.eswa.2013.02.025
3. Cover, T.M., Thomas, J.A.: Elements of Information Theory. Wiley Interscience, New York (2006)
4. Fernández, A., García, S., Galar, M., Prati, R.C., Krawczyk, B., Herrera, F.: Data intrinsic characteristics. In: Learning from Imbalanced Data Sets, pp. 253–277. Springer, Cham (2018). https://doi.org/10.1007/978-3-319-98074-4_10
5. Guan, S., Loew, M.: A novel intrinsic measure of data separability (2022). https://doi.org/10.1007/s10489-022-03395-6
6. Ho, T.K., Basu, M.: Complexity measures of supervised classification problems. IEEE Trans. Pattern Anal. Mach. Intell. **24**(3), 289–300 (2002). https://doi.org/10.1109/34.990132
7. Hossin, M., Sulaiman, M.N.: A review on evaluation metrics for data classification evaluations. Int. J. Data Min. Knowl. Manage. Process **5**(2), 1–11 (2015). https://doi.org/10.5121/ijdkp.2015.5201
8. Li, C., Wang, B.: Fisher linear discriminant analysis. CCIS Northeastern University (2014)
9. Li, S., Hao, Q., Gao, G., Kang, X.: The effect of ground truth on performance evaluation of hyperspectral image classification. IEEE Trans. Geosci. Remote Sens. **56**(12), 7195–7206 (2018). https://doi.org/10.1109/TGRS.2018.2849225
10. Lichman, M.E.A.: UCI machine learning repository (2013). https://archive.ics.uci.edu/ml/datasets.php
11. Lorena, A.C., Garcia, L.P.F., Lehmann, J., Souto, M.C.P., Ho, T.K.: How complex is your classification problem?: A survey on measuring classification complexity. ACM Comput. Surv. **52**(5), 1–34 (2019). https://doi.org/10.1145/3347711
12. Ma, Y., Derksen, H., Hong, W.: Segmentation of multivariate mixed data via lossy data coding and compression. IEEE Trans. Pattern Anal. Mach. Intell. **29**(9), 1546–1562 (2007). https://doi.org/10.1109/TPAMI.2007.1085
13. Madiman, M., Harrison, M., Kontoyiannis, I.: Minimum description length versus maximum likelihood in lossy data compression. In: International Symposium on Information Theory. IEEE, Chicago (2004). https://doi.org/10.1109/ISIT.2004.1365499
14. Mishra, A.K.: Separability indices and their use in radar signal based target recognition. IEICE Electron. Express **6**(14), 1000–1005 (2009). https://doi.org/10.1587/elex.6.1000
15. Oprea, M.: A general framework and guidelines for benchmarking computational intelligence algorithms applied to forecasting problems derived from an application domain-oriented survey. Appl. Soft Comput. **89**, 106103 (2020). https://doi.org/10.1016/j.asoc.2020.106103

16. Sizhe, C., Haipeng, W., Feng, X., Yaqiu, J.: Target classification using the deep convolutional networks for SAR images. IEEE Trans. Geosci. Remote Sens. **54**(8), 4806–4817 (2016). https://doi.org/10.1109/TGRS.2016.2551720
17. Wicaksonoa, P., Aryagunab, P.A.: Analyses of inter-class spectral separability and classification accuracy of benthic habitat mapping using multispectral image. Remote Sens. Appl. Soc. Environ. **19**, 100335 (2020). https://doi.org/10.1016/j.rsase.2020.100335
18. Yu, S., Li, X., Feng, Y., Zhang, X., Chen, S.: An instance-oriented performance measure for classification. Inf. Sci. **580**, 598–619 (2021). https://doi.org/10.1016/j.ins.2021.08.094
19. Yu, Y., Chan, K.H.R., You, C., Song, C., Ma, Y.: Learning diverse and discriminative representations via the principle of maximal coding rate reduction (2020). https://doi.org/10.48550/arXiv.2006.08558
20. Zhang, C., Samy, B., Moritz, H., Benjamin, R., Oriol, V.: Understanding deep learning (still) requires rethinking generalization. Commun. ACM **64**(3), 107–115 (2021). https://doi.org/10.1145/3446776

A Cross-Modal View to Utilize Label Semantics for Enhancing Student Network in Multi-label Classification

Yuzhuo Qin, Hengwei Liu, and Xiaodong Gu$^{(\boxtimes)}$ ®

Department of Electronic Engineering, Fudan University, Shanghai 200438, China
xdgu@fudan.edu.cn

Abstract. Knowledge transfer has become a promising approach for improving the performance and efficiency of relatively lightweight networks. Previous research has focused on identifying suitable knowledge and enhancing network structures to obtain more valuable knowledge. However, the introduction of extra information such as semantics remains an unexplored area. In this study, we introduce a multi-label classifier with label embeddings to replace the traditional GAP layer and incorporate semantics. Our approach adopts a cross-modal view for classification and employs the correlation matrix of visual and label modalities as knowledge to enhance the performance of the student. Furthermore, due to the same classification head, we initiate the student's head with trained teacher's and enable the label embeddings more representative. Experimental results show that our proposed method outperforms existing typical methods. Additionally, further analysis confirms the effectiveness of our approach.

Keywords: Label semantics · Knowledge transfer · Cross-Modal

1 Introduction

Knowledge-Transfer is widely used in deep learning as a means of transferring knowledge from a large, complex model to a smaller, simpler one. While these methods have shown promise in improving the performance and efficiency of neural networks, they also have several drawbacks that need to be considered.

One of the main drawbacks of existing Knowledge-Transfer methods is that they rely heavily on the design of a novel training strategy. This means that researchers must spend a significant amount of time and resources developing new algorithms and techniques to optimize the transfer of knowledge between models. While this approach can lead to improvements in performance and efficiency, it can also be time-consuming and expensive. Another drawback of existing Knowledge-Transfer methods is that they often focus on the selection of what knowledge to transfer. This means that the teacher model is designed to provide a specific subset of information that the student model is expected to learn. While this approach can be effective in certain cases, it can also lead to a loss

L. Iliadis et al. (Eds.): ICANN 2023, LNCS 14254, pp. 14–25, 2023.
https://doi.org/10.1007/978-3-031-44207-0_2

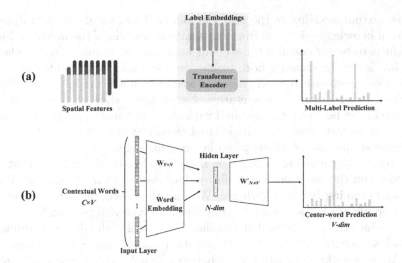

Fig. 1. The illustration of the process for obtain (a). label embedding and (b). word embedding

of generalization and adaptability in the student model. However, the amount of knowledge that a naive model can carry is limited, which also determines the maximum gain that can be achieved through knowledge transfer.

Multi-label classification is a popular technique used to classify instances into multiple labels or categories simultaneously. In recent years, there has been a significant amount of research devoted to improving the accuracy of multi-label classification models. However, one area that has been largely overlooked is the use of Knowledge-Transfer techniques for improving multi-label classification performance. Recently, some works such as [10,15] introduced label embeddings to represent each unique category and fed them together with the spatial features extracted from backbone network into a transformer encoder block, then pools the features rich in label semantics and predicts the logits for corresponding categories. The process for the obtain of label embeddings is similar to word embeddings, which trains a neural network on a large corpus of text to represent words as numerical vectors in a high-dimensional space, as shown in Fig. 1 respectively. And this provides a cross-modal (text-image) view to treat the multi-label classification task as the fusion of visual and label features to gain a better classification performance.

As illustrated above, in the literature of Transfer-Knowledge for multi-label classification, there is a significant gap in this field. Current methods focus on what knowledge should be selected or how to design better architectures to fully exploit the potential of teacher networks.

Therefore, in this paper, we propose to replace the traditional gap-based classification head with label-embedding one, to fully extract semantic information from images. Inspired by paper [13], which used the tags of visual regions as a intermediate to transfer contextual knowledge (i.e., the label correlation matrix) from the textual modality to the visual modality. Thus, we also make full use of the refined knowledge obtained from the similarity matrix of the image and label embeddings to better enhance the student network. Furthermore, as the classification heads are the same for both teacher and student, we initial the student's classification head with trained teacher's weight to make the label embeddings in student network more representative. Experiments show that our proposed method achieves best results compared with classical Knowledge-Transfer methods that are transplanted from single-label classification.

In general, our contributions could be summarized as:

(a) We analyze existing Knowledge-Transferred methods and find that they either focus on the selection of transferred knowledge or the promotion of algorithm for obtaining better knowledge. We find that decoupling the model and adopt a proper classification head is important in Knowledge-Transfer.

(b) We introduce a multi-label classification model with label embeddings to introduce semantics and treat the classification from a cross-modal review.

(c) We utilize the similarity matrix between visual features and label embeddings as knowledge and initial the student's classification head with teacher's trained weights, experimental results show that our method gains great performance among existing classical Knowledge-Transfer methods.

2   Related Works

Knowledge-Transfer is a concept that involves the transfer of knowledge from one domain or task to another. It is a promising area of research that aims to improve the performance and efficiency of deep learning models by leveraging pre-existing knowledge or models. Knowledge transfer can take different forms, including transfer learning, domain adaptation, and multi-task learning. Transfer learning is the most common form of knowledge transfer in deep learning, where a pre-trained model is used as a starting point for a new task, which is deemed as teacher network in this work.

The transfer of knowledge can assist in training a model by learning the data distribution from another model, thereby improving the performance of both models. Due to its effectiveness in aligning different domains, knowledge transfer is commonly used in knowledge distillation. Knowledge distillation was first proposed by [5] to adopt teacher's soft target as hint to guide the training of student. Besides logit-based form, intermediate representations in network could also be treated as a powerful form of knowledge, [16] selected intermediate blocks of a teacher and forced the student to mimic the way how teacher outputs. Besides, [21] refined the attention information of feature maps from the final block of network into a single map. As a combined form of both logit-based and feature-based, [19] proposed to force the student's logits continuous with teacher's instead of only using feature matching loss.

Multi-label Classification aims at assigning multiple labels to a given input image. This type of classification problem is often encountered in many real-world applications, where an instance may belong to multiple categories or

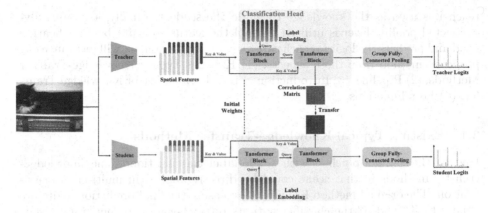

Fig. 2. Illustration of the classification network and knowledge-transfer, dashed lines denote the process for knowledge transfer. "Teacher" and "Student" represent the backbone networks

classes simultaneously. A straightforward way to impose multi-label classification is to transform it into several independent binary classification tasks, which switches the *Softmax* activation in single-label classification network to the *Sigmoid* activation. There are several popular topics in multi-label classification, such as loss functions improvement [8,14], label correlation modeling [1,2,20] and classification head design [10,15]. Specifically, to address the negative-positive imbalance in multi-label classification, [14] proposed asymmetric loss to introduce a restricted factor to reduce the dominance of negative samples in loss function based on [8]. [1,2] both constructed a graph based on the statistical label co-occurrence and class-aware maps respectively. And [20] updated static graph to dynamic graph by using a dynamic graph convolutional network (GCN) module for robust representations. Furthermore, [10] utilized transformer decoders to extract features with multi-head attentions focusing on different parts or views of an object category and learning label embeddings. And [15] modified Query2Label by utilizing group-wise queries and removing the self-attention module for better computational friendliness.

3   Method

To enable transferred knowledge rich in label semantics, we replace the GAP layer in a typical classification network with a query2label [10] head which consists of label embeddings. The main pipeline of our knowledge-transferred method is illustrated in Fig. 2. Firstly, an identical raw image is firstly fed into teacher and student networks respectively, which are usually large as well as complex and small as well as simple backbone networks. Then the spatial features are sent into the classification head to be fused with label embeddings, where the module consists of two transformer decoders. The correlation matrix from teacher is used as the knowledge to guide the student. Finally, a group fully-connected pooling layer is utilized to pool the features output by classification head and predicts the logit for each category. In this section, we will introduce our proposed method from those aspects: (1) Existing Typical Knowledge-Transfer Methods, (2) Pipeline, (3) Introduction of Label Semantics for Knowledge Transfer, (4) Loss Functions.

3.1   Existing Typical Knowledge-Transfer Methods

Due to the similar pipeline with single-label classification, some knowledge-transfer methods in that scene could be directly applied in multi-label classification. The original method KD [5] is to measure the final prediction logits, we denote by T_i^o and S_i^o the classifier outputs of teacher and student respectively, thus the logit-based knowledge transfer loss could be presented as

$$\mathcal{L} = \tau^2 \sum_{i=1}^{K} KL(T_i \| S_i) \tag{1}$$

where τ is the temperature, K is the category number and $KL(\cdot)$ represents the Kullback-Leibler divergence. Different from single-label classification, multi-label classification consists of multiple independent binary classifiers, thus the *activation* in multi-label knowledge transfer is switched to *Sigmoid* activation function.

Besides, intermediate representations could also be treated as knowledge. Fit-Nets [16] selected blocks inside network and guided the student to learn the way how those networks output. Attention Transfer [21] operated quadratic computation along the channel-wise dimension of feature maps and activated the spatial areas which the network focuses most for taking its output decision. Mathematically, we denote by Fea_t, Fea_s the feature knowledge of teacher and student respectively, the loss for feature-based knowledge transfer could be presented as

$$\mathcal{L} = \sum_{i \in K} L_2(Fea_t^i, Fea_s^i), \tag{2}$$

3.2   Pipeline

The whole pipeline, as shown in Fig. 2 can be divided into two parts: multi-label classification and knowledge transfer. In multi-label classification task we adopt the pipeline of Query2Label [10]. Given an input image, among a set of categories of interest, multi-label classification is to predict whether each category is present. Assume that there are K categories, the corresponding label for the given image X is denoted as $y = \{y_k | k = 1, \cdots, K, y_k \in \{0, 1\}\}$. Generally, the given image, which is denoted by $X \in \mathbf{R}^{H \times W \times 3}$, is first input into a backbone network and obtains the spatial feature maps $F \in \mathbf{R}^{H_o \times W_o \times d}$. $H \times W, H_o \times W_o$ are the size (height and width) of the original input image and the feature maps respectively. d represents the channel size of spatial feature maps. Spatial features maps are then sent into a transformer-based classification head, which contains several stacked Transformer blocks for query updating and adaptive feature pooling, and a linear projection layer for computing prediction logits. For each Transformer block, label embedding $Q_0 \in R^{K \times d}$ is used as Queries and spatial feature map is used as Key and Value. Specifically, for the $i - th$ block, an iteration of Query can be formulated as:

$$Q_i^{(1)} = MultiHead(\widetilde{Q}i - 1, \widetilde{Q}i - 1, Q_{i-1}),$$
$$Q_i^{(2)} = MultiHead(\widetilde{Q}_i^{(2)}, \widetilde{F}, F), \tag{3}$$
$$Q_i = FFN(Q_i^{(2)}),$$

Both the $MultiHead(\texttt{Query},\texttt{Key},\texttt{Value})$ and $FFN(\cdot)$ functions are the same as defined in the standard Transformer decoder [18]. Assuming that there are L blocks, the queried feature Q_L is used the final representation for predicting the probability of each category. We treat each label prediction as a binary classification task and project the feature of each class to a logit value using a linear projection layer followed with a sigmoid function:

$$p_k = Sigmoid(W_k^T Q_{L,k} + b_k) \tag{4}$$

where $W_k \in R^d$, $W = [W_1, \cdots, W_K]_T \in R^{K \times d}$, and $b = [b_1, \cdots, b_K]_T \in R^K$ are parameters in the linear layer, and $p = [p_1, \cdots, p_K] \in R^K$ is the predicted probabilities for corresponding categories.

3.3   Introduction of Label Semantics for Knowledge Transfer

Classification head utilizes MultiHeadAttention to fuse the spatial feature maps and the label embeddings. The process of cross-attention operation enables it convenient to obtain the similarity between each spatial feature and each category, which can also considered the correlation knowledge between location and semantic. And due to the larger capacity of network, teacher is more sophisticated to capture greater spatial feature maps to achieve better fusion with label semantics. Thus, we directly adopt the similarity matrix extracted from the second decoder module as the transferred knowledge to guide student learn a better correlation between the visual modality and the labeling modality, which can be considered a cross-modal view. Specifically, we denote by $M_t \in R^{H_o W_o \times K}$ and $M_s \in R^{H_o W_o \times K}$ as the similarity matrices from teacher and student respectively, thus the loss function to measure the similarity of them can be presented as

$$\mathcal{L}_{cor} = \sum_{i \in K} p_i L_2(M_t^i, M_s^i), \tag{5}$$

where p_i represents the teacher's probability for the $i\text{-}th$ category and the similarity matrix is pre-normalized. $L_2(\cdot)$ represents the L_2 loss function.

3.4 Loss Functions

Knowledge Transfer usually obeys a paradigm that the final object function consists of two elements, *i.e.* the original task one and the one for measuring the knowledge similarity. In this work, the original task is to predict multiple labels for a given instance, where the logits output from group fully-connected pooling is used to be closer to the ground-truths. We denote by p_i the probability for the *i-th* category and y_i the corresponding label. To address the negative-positive problem in multi-label classification, we leverage the asymmetric focal loss for calculation, which is presented as

$$\mathcal{L}_{cls} = \frac{1}{K} \sum_{i \in K} \begin{cases} (1 - p_i)^{\lambda^+} log(p_i), y_i = 1, \\ (p_i)^{\lambda^-} log(1 - p_i), y_i = 0, \end{cases}$$

Thus the final object function of our proposed correlation knowledge transfer could be presented as

$$\mathcal{L} = \mathcal{L}_{cls} + \alpha \mathcal{L}_{cor}, \tag{6}$$

where α is the weight to balance two losses.

4 Experiments

4.1 Datasets and Evaluation Metrics

Datasets. We conduct our experiments on MS-COCO [9], which is a public datasets constructed for object detection and segmentation tasks, and can also be used for multi-label classification. It contains 123,287 images totally with 80 categories covered. It is split into 82,783 and 40,504 as training and validation sets respectively.

Evaluation Metrics. Due to the overall precision (OP) and the overall recall (OR) are determined by the threshold for the probabilities. Following previous works, we adopt the mean average precision (mAP) over all categories for evaluation.

4.2 Implementation Details

In this section we will introduce more detailed experimental settings for our proposed model. The input image is resized into 448×448 and adopt random augmentation for better performance. We select ResNet101 [4] and SwinLarge [11] as teacher networks, ResNet18 [4] and MobileNetv3 [6] as student networks. For all knowledge transfer settings, backbone networks are pre-trained on ImageNet [3], spatial feature maps extracted from backbones are projected into the dimension size of 2048. We train models using the Adam optimizer [7], with True-Weight-Decay [12] set to 1×10^{-2}, and a cycle learning rate schedule [17] with a maximum learning rate of 1×10^{-4}. The batch-size is set to 256. Additionally, we employ the exponential moving average trick [14] to improve performance.

Table 1. mAP(%) results of knowledge transfer with different combinations of backbones on MS-COCO. Best results are in bold font.

	CNN-CNN		Transformer-CNN	
Teacher	ResNet101 [4]	ResNet101 [4]	SwinLarge [11]	SwinLarge [11]
Student	ResNet18 [4]	MobileNetV3 [6]	ResNet18 [4]	MobileNetV3 [6]
Teacher	84.88	84.88	91.44	91.44
Student	78.47	79.03	78.47	79.03
KD [5]	79.37	79.86	79.18	79.55
FitNets [16]	78.70	79.29	78.48	79.24
AT [21]	78.78	79.27	78.54	79.05
Ours	**80.83**	**81.14**	**80.75**	**81.44**

4.3 Experiment Results

We conduct experiments on MS-COCO [9] dataset and report different combinations of networks in Table 1, including CNN-CNN and Transformer-CNN as teacher and student networks respectively. As comparisons, results of classical methods such as KD [5], FitNets [16] and AT [21] are also reported. It is noteworthy that for FitNets, only representations from the last block are utilized, because they are directly fed into the classification head and responsible to the performance of the prediction. From the table, it could be seen that our proposed method outperforms existing methods by a large margin. Among three classical methods, KD works the best, which validates that using the teacher's logits to guide the student also works in the multi-label classification with label-embedding classification head. Process for the final logits in both training and validation stages are independent among different categories and it may cause the helplessness of logits for student. However, the similarity matrix inside transformer block is computed by *Softmax* operation and it may help incorporate information among categories, leading to the effectiveness of KD. For FitNets, the information stored in feature maps is too redundant and brings little gains for student. And we can also observe that the performances of AT on Transformer-CNN are inferior than that on CNN-CNN, which may due to the non-locality inside transformer structure and makes it less able to capture the local attention areas in an image.

In general, our method improves the performance by 2.36% and 2.11% in CNN-CNN settings, 2.28% and 2.41% in Transformer-CNN settings respectively. Interestingly, as a stronger teacher comparison with ResNet101, SwinLarge couldn't enlighten a better student. We argue that the structure of ResNet101 is much more similar to that of ResNet18, thus enabling student easier to capture the correlation and improves itself. Still, compared with classical methods, results could also validate that with initializing the student's classification head, and utilizing the correlation matrix between spatial features and label embeddings could promote student networks effectively in multi-label classification.

4.4   Ablation Studies

Table 2. Ablation studies for our proposed method. "ClsInit" represents initializing the student's classification head with teacher's weight

Teacher	ResNet101 [4]	ResNet101 [4]
Student	ResNet18 [4]	MobileNetV3 [6]
Teacher	84.88	84.88
Student	78.47	79.03
KD [5]	79.37	79.86
FitNets [16]	78.70	79.29
AT [21]	78.78	79.01
Ours w/o ClsInit	80.73	80.89
Ours	**80.83**	**81.14**

To further validate the effectiveness of our proposed two approaches, *i.e.* knowledge transfer with correlation matrix and initialization student's classification with teacher's weight, we conduct ablation studies and also compare the result of each method with classical knowledge transfer methods. As shown in Table 2, we fist directly utilize the correlation matrix as knowledge to guide student, it could be seen that the incorporation of label semantics works well and shows the validity of treating this process with a cross-modal view.

Furthermore, after initializing the student's classification head with teacher's weight, namely "ClsInit", the performances of students are further improved. It proves that teacher network with a larger capacity could learn better label embeddings, and endow them richer semantics, thus provides a better starting point for the training of student networks.

4.5   Further Analyses

Improvement of Student After Knowledge Transfer. In our proposed method, we utilize the similarity matrix between spatial feature maps and label embeddings as transferred knowledge. Thus the similarity matrix is able to exhibit the local activation for each category, which could be utilized to visualize and for better comprehension. In order to qualitatively analyse how correlation knowledge works during knowledge transfer, we illustrate the activation maps for corresponding categories in Fig. 3. The two rows represent student without and with knowledge transfer respectively.

From the first row of Fig. 3, it could be seen that lightweight student network is less able to activate accurate locations for specific categories, such as the "bird" and "elephant". However, with correlation knowledge learned from teacher network, the location of those instances are improved obviously. The

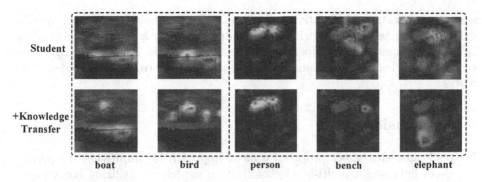

Fig. 3. Illustration of the visualization of category activation for student without and with knowledge transfer respectively. The label below each picture represents its corresponding category.

visualization results demonstrate that with the help of correlation knowledge transferred from teacher, student is much easier to be enlightened to acquire the relationship between spatial and semantic domains.

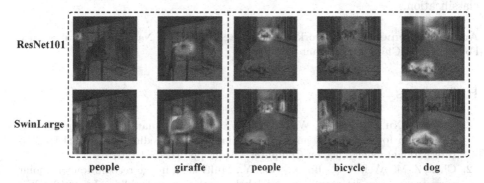

Fig. 4. Illustration of the visualization of category activation extracted from similarity matrix in transformer decoder. The label below each picture represents its corresponding category

Comparison of Correlation Between Different Teachers. From Table 1, we could observe that with MobileNet chosen as student, a greater teacher could bring a better student. We conjecture that due to the larger capacity of Transformer backbones, they could obtain better spatial features and enable label embeddings richer semantics, which leads to a better correlation between spatial and semantic domains. Besides, the gain of student in Transformer-CNN is not such drastic as CNN-CNN combination, this may because that less capacity couldn't make students thoroughly learn how to output the identical spatial features as transformer teachers. Still, as shown in Fig. 4, we could observe that with a stronger backbone, the activation for each category could be better. Specifically, a better teacher network is able to appropriately activate corresponding instances in space, such as people, giraffe, and bicycle. Thus knowledge from teacher could convey more comprehensive semantic information to student networks.

5   Conclusion

In conclusion, this paper proposed a novel approach for improving the performance of lightweight multi-label classification models by utilizing Knowledge-Transfer techniques. We identified the limitations of existing Knowledge-Transfer methods and proposed a solution that replaces the traditional gap-based classification head with a label-embedding one, which fully extracts semantic information from images. Our approach utilizes the refined knowledge obtained from the similarity matrix of image and label embeddings to enhance the student network. We also initialized the student's classification head with the trained teacher's weight to make the label embeddings in the student network more representative. Experimental results demonstrate that our proposed method outperforms classical Knowledge-Transfer methods that are transplanted from single-label classification.

Acknowledgements. This work was supported in part by National Natural Science Foundation of China under grant 62176062.

References

1. Chen, T., Xu, M., Hui, Z., Wu, H., Lin, L.: Learning semantic-specific graph representation for multi-label image recognition. In: Proceedings of the IEEE/CVF International Conference on Computer Vision, pp. 522–531 (2019)
2. Chen, Z.-M., Wei, X.-S., Jin, X., Guo, Y.: Multi-label image recognition with joint class-aware map disentangling and label correlation embedding. In: 2019 IEEE International Conference on Multimedia and Expo (ICME), pp. 622–627. IEEE (2019)
3. Deng, J., Dong, W., Socher, R., Li, L.-J., Li, K., Fei-Fei, L.: ImagenNet: a large-scale hierarchical image database. In: 2009 IEEE Conference on Computer Vision and Pattern Recognition, pp. 248–255. IEEE (2009)
4. He, K., Zhang, X., Ren, S., Sun, J.: Deep residual learning for image recognition. In: Proceedings of the IEEE Conference on Computer Vision and Pattern Recognition, pp. 770–778 (2016)
5. Hinton, G., Vinyals, O., Dean, J.: Distilling the knowledge in a neural network. arXiv preprint arXiv:1503.02531 (2015)
6. Howard, A.G., et al.: MobileNets: efficient convolutional neural networks for mobile vision applications. arXiv preprint arXiv:1704.04861 (2017)
7. Kingma, D.P., Ba, J.: Adam: a method for stochastic optimization. arXiv preprint arXiv:1412.6980 (2014)

8. Lin, T.-Y., Goyal, P., Girshick, R., He, K., Dollár, P.: Focal loss for dense object detection. In: Proceedings of the IEEE International Conference on Computer Vision, pp. 2980–2988 (2017)
9. Lin, T.-Y., et al.: Microsoft COCO: common objects in context. In: Fleet, D., Pajdla, T., Schiele, B., Tuytelaars, T. (eds.) ECCV 2014. LNCS, vol. 8693, pp. 740–755. Springer, Cham (2014). https://doi.org/10.1007/978-3-319-10602-1_48
10. Liu, S., Zhang, L., Yang, X., Su, H., Zhu, J.: Query2Label: a simple transformer way to multi-label classification. arXiv preprint arXiv:2107.10834 (2021)
11. Liu, Z., et al.: Swin transformer: hierarchical vision transformer using shifted windows. In: Proceedings of the IEEE/CVF International Conference on Computer Vision (ICCV) (2021)
12. Loshchilov, I., Hutter, F.: Decoupled weight decay regularization. arXiv preprint arXiv:1711.05101 (2017)
13. Qin, Y., Xiaodong, G., Tan, Z.: Visual context learning based on textual knowledge for image-text retrieval. Neural Networks **152**, 434–449 (2022)
14. Ridnik, T., et al.: Asymmetric loss for multi-label classification. In: Proceedings of the IEEE/CVF International Conference on Computer Vision, pp. 82–91 (2021)
15. Ridnik, T., Sharir, G., Ben-Cohen, A., Ben-Baruch, E., Noy, A.: ML-Decoder: scalable and versatile classification head. In: Proceedings of the IEEE/CVF Winter Conference on Applications of Computer Vision, pp. 32–41 (2023)
16. Romero, A., Ballas, N., Kahou, S.E., Chassang, A., Gatta, C., Bengio, Y.: FitNets: hints for thin deep nets. arXiv preprint arXiv:1412.6550 (2014)
17. Smith, L.N., Topin, N.: Super-convergence: very fast training of neural networks using large learning rates. In: Artificial Intelligence and Machine Learning for Multi-domain Operations Applications, vol. 11006, pp. 369–386. SPIE (2019)
18. Vaswani, A., et al.: Attention is all you need. In: Guyon, I., et al. (eds.) Advances in Neural Information Processing Systems: Annual Conference on Neural Information Processing Systems, 4–9 December 2017, Long Beach, CA, USA, vol. 30, pp. 5998–6008 (2017)
19. Yang, J., Martinez, B., Bulat, A., Tzimiropoulos, G., et al.: Knowledge distillation via softmax regression representation learning. In: International Conference on Learning Representations (ICLR) (2021)
20. Ye, J., He, J., Peng, X., Wu, W., Qiao, Yu.: Attention-driven dynamic graph convolutional network for multi-label image recognition. In: Vedaldi, A., Bischof, H., Brox, T., Frahm, J.-M. (eds.) ECCV 2020, Part XXI. LNCS, vol. 12366, pp. 649–665. Springer, Cham (2020). https://doi.org/10.1007/978-3-030-58589-1_39
21. Zagoruyko, S., Komodakis, N.: Paying more attention to attention: improving the performance of convolutional neural networks via attention transfer. arXiv preprint arXiv:1612.03928 (2016)

A Hybrid Model Based on Samples Difficulty for Imbalanced Data Classification

Ao Shan[✉][iD] and Yeh-Ching Chung[iD]

The Chinese University of Hong Kong (Shenzhen), Shenzhen 518172, China
18840824080@163.com

Abstract. Imbalanced data classification is a challenging problem with wide applications in machine learning and data mining. Most researchers attempt to solve this problem from the data level or algorithm level. Nevertheless, these methods have their limitations. In addition, most of them focus on dealing with the imbalance in the number of data samples while ignoring the imbalance caused by sample difficulty. Thus, we design a hybrid model to handle this problem. Our model integrates data space improvement, sample selection, sampling strategy, and loss function. To evaluate the performance of our hybrid model, we conduct experiments on several real-world imbalanced datasets. The experimental results prove that our hybrid model is effective.

Keywords: Class imbalance · Machine learning · Imbalanced data

1 Introduction

Imbalanced data classification is challenging [10,13], and it has wide applications in the machine learning field [3,11,19]. The main characteristic of the imbalanced data is its skewed data distribution, which means that most samples belong to one class (the majority class) and the rest belong to the other (the minority class). The skewed data distribution usually leads to conventional machine learning classifiers having poor classification performance.

To address imbalanced data classification, researchers have proposed plenty of methods. Existing methods mainly contain two categories: data-level techniques and algorithm-level techniques. Data-level techniques solve the imbalanced data by changing the data distribution. Algorithm-level techniques increase the importance of the minority class in adjusting the learning or decision process.

However, we notice the weakness of the above existing methods. On the one hand, traditional data-level methods usually do not consider the impact of different types of samples in the imbalanced dataset to train the model. The study [16] indicates that some of the samples are useless and even negatively impact model training. On the other hand, traditional algorithm-level methods [6,8] usually focus on giving a higher loss to the minority class but ignore the impact of sample difficulty.

L. Iliadis et al. (Eds.): ICANN 2023, LNCS 14254, pp. 26–37, 2023.
https://doi.org/10.1007/978-3-031-44207-0_3

This paper aims to remedy the above weaknesses from two aspects. Firstly, this paper introduces the concept of "sample classification importance" to select suitable samples for sampling. Intuitively, classification importance represents the importance of a sample for classifier training. For a dataset, we divide all samples into three kinds, i.e., important informative samples, negative informative samples, and general informative samples. Such sample classification importance can guide the selection of suitable samples for sampling to obtain satisfactory results. Secondly, we propose a loss function that is based on sample difficulty. This loss function can give different costs to different samples according to their sample difficulty.

Then, we further propose a hybrid model to solve imbalanced data classification. Our model integrates data space improvement, sample selection, and loss function based on sample difficulty. Specifically, it contains three blocks: (1) Data space block, which transforms the data space to make samples close to their nearest neighbors belonging to the same class and separates samples from other classes by a large margin. This block can make samples easier to be separated. (2) Sample selection block finds suitable samples for sampling to obtain a balanced dataset. This block aims to find valuable samples. (3) Sample Difficulty block applies a novel loss function that adds larger loss to samples with greater difficulty for training the classifier.

In summary, our contributions lie in the following aspects. (1) Firstly, we propose a new sample selection approach that can use fewer samples but get better classification results. (2) Secondly, we design a novel loss function based on sample difficulty for imbalanced data training. (3) Thirdly, we design a hybrid model that integrates space improvement, sample selection, sampling, and loss function to handle this problem. (4) Finally, experimental results on real-world imbalanced datasets have shown that our hybrid model performs better than competing methods, and each block of our model is valid.

2   Related Work

2.1   Data-Level Methods

Data-level approaches [7] aim to solve imbalanced data by changing the data distribution. They can be further divided into undersampling methods and oversampling methods. Under-sampling methods reduce the number of majority instances from the original dataset to balance the dataset. The simplest undersampling form is random undersampling [10]. This method removes the majority of instances randomly. Unlike undersampling methods, oversampling methods generate minority instances to obtain a balanced dataset. Random oversampling is the most straightforward way that randomly generates minority instances from the original data. In addition, plenty of advanced sampling methods have been designed. SMOTE [5] is the commonly used sampling method that selects close instances, drawing a line between instances and generating a new instance at a point along that line. ADASYN [9], MWMOTE [1], and ADMO [18] are representative sampling methods that generate the minority synthetic instances.

However, the weaknesses of data-level methods are apparent: The technique of selecting suitable instances for sampling is still being determined [4].

2.2 Algorithm-Level Methods

Algorithm-level approaches solve imbalanced data by increasing the importance of the minority class in adjusting the learning or decision process. These methods mainly contain cost-sensitive learning and novel loss functions. Cost-sensitive learning approaches modify the cost matrix to reduce bias towards the majority class. However, determining a matrix is difficult for cost-sensitive learning-based methods. Researchers have recently designed several new loss functions [6,8] for training deep neural networks for solving imbalanced data classification. The most widely used loss for imbalanced data is the focal loss [15] that assigns a weight to each instance according to its prediction accuracy in model training.

3 Proposed Method

3.1 Overview

As shown in Fig.1, our model consists of three blocks: (1) Data space block (DSB), which transforms the data space to make samples close to their nearest neighbors with the same class. This block can make samples easier to be separated. (2) Sample selection block (SSB) finds valuable samples and builds up a set based on valuable samples. This block aims to find valuable samples for sampling. (3) Sample Difficulty block (SDB) applies a novel loss function that adds larger loss to samples with higher sample difficulty for the training classifier.

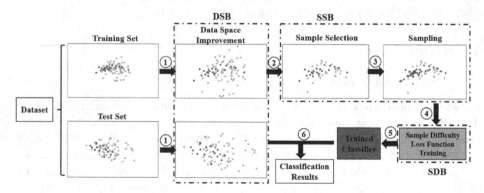

Fig. 1. The architecture of our hybrid model

3.2 Data Space Block

Our model integrates the data space improvement technique to make the imbalanced data easier to be separated. In this work, we use the LMNN [17] technique that builds up an algorithm to pull samples with the same class label close to the target sample and push samples that belong to different class labels away from the target sample, as shown in Fig. 2. The algorithm of the LMNN technique is as follows: $\varphi(H) = (1-\mu)\varphi_{\text{pull}}(H) + \mu\varphi_{\text{push}}(H)$, where H is the linear transformation of the input space and μ is a positive real number utilized as the weight. The first part of this loss penalizes large distances between the sample and its k nearest neighbors belonging to the same class, which is defined as $\varphi_{\text{pull}}(H) = \sum_{p,q \in M(p)} \|L(x_p - x_q)\|^2$, where $M(p)$ is the k nearest neighbor of sample p with the same class label as p.

The second part penalizes small distances between the sample and others with different classes, which is defined as:

$$\varphi_{\text{push}}(H) = \sum_{p,q,l} (1 - \delta_{pl}) \max\left\{1 + \|H(s_p - s_q)\|^2 - \|H(s_p - s_l)\|^2, 0\right\},$$

where δ_{il} is utilized to decide whether samples s_l and s_p belong to different classes or not. If samples belong to different classes, $\delta_{pl} = 0$; otherwise, $\delta_{pl} = 1$.

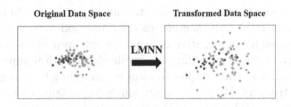

Fig. 2. Using the LMNN algorithm, the comparison between original data space and transformed data space

3.3   Sample Selection Block

Traditional data-level methods usually select all samples for sampling to obtain a balanced dataset. However, study [16] has indicated that not all samples are useful for model training. Thus, it is necessary to distinguish the types of samples and select suitable samples for sampling. In this part, we first introduce the definition of sample classification importance and propose a method to finish sample selection based on this definition.

Definition: Sample classification importance represents the importance of a sample for the classifier training.

Intuitively, we divide samples into three kinds, i.e., important informative samples, negative informative samples, and general informative samples, as shown in Fig. 3 .

Important informative samples: They are the most informative samples during the classifier training. For instance, as we can see in Fig.3, important informative instances are usually located close to the classification boundary of the classifier. Improving the importance of these instances is helpful in improving the performance of the classification [16].

Negative informative samples: By contrast, negative informative samples harm the model training. For example, negative informative samples are in Fig. 3 are usually caused by indistinguishable noise, which could lead the model to serious overfitting. Thus, we need to reduce the impact of these samples.

General informative samples: Most of the samples are general informative samples that the model can correctly classify, as shown in Fig.3. Each general informative sample only contributes minor importance. However, the overall contribution is enormous because of its large number. For this type of sample, we only need a small part of them to remain their " skeleton " to prevent overfitting, then remove most of them.

We evaluate sample classification importance based on the kNN method [2]. If all neighbors of a sample belong to a different class, then it is a negative informative sample. On the contrary, if all neighbors of a sample and itself belong to the same class, then it is a general informative sample. In other cases, the sample can be seen as an important informative sample, which means that it will have a large value when a sample locates on the borderline between different classes. Then, we introduce the sample selection method. Given a dataset, it can be divided into three parts: negative informative set, important informative set, and general informative set according to sample classification importance. We do not use negative informative samples to sample since they have negative impacts on the classifier training. We focus on sampling important informative samples because they are essential in finding the classification boundary. In addition, we only use small parts of general informative samples to sample because we only need a small part of them to retain their "skeleton". Based on the above analysis, our sample selection method is shown in Algorithm 1 in detail.

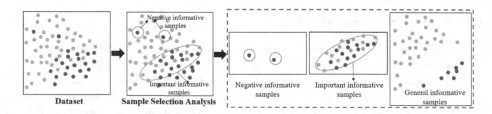

Fig. 3. Illustration of types of samples

3.4 Sample Difficulty Block

This block applies a new loss function based on sample difficulty to train the classifier with the imbalanced data. We first introduce the sample difficulty and then propose our loss function. Based on the analysis in the sample selection part, finding suitable samples that can learn the classification boundary as precisely as possible is important. In addition, we also notice that different suitable samples

---

Algorithm 1. Sample Selection

Input: Dataset D, the quantity of samples N, the parameter of kNN method k, the percent of general informative samples m.

1: **for** $i \leftarrow 1$ to N **do**
2:    Use the kNN method to calculate the number of its neighbors that have different labels with itself: $kNN(x_{i,j}, D - D_j)$;
3:    **if** $kNN(x_{i,j}, D - D_j) = k$ **then**
4:        $x_{i,j}$ is a negative informative sample;
5:    **else if** $kNN(x_{i,j}, D - D_j) = 0$ **then**
6:        $x_{i,j}$ is a general informative sample;
        Add $x_{i,j}$ to the set of general informative samples $D_{general}$;
7:    **else**
8:        $x_{i,j}$ is an important informative sample;
        Add $x_{i,j}$ to the set of important informative samples $D_{important}$;
9:    **end if**
10: **end for**
11: Based on $D_{general}$, use random undersampling to obtain m percent of general informative samples $D_{sampledgeneral}$.
    $D_{selection} = D_{important} \cup D_{sampledgeneral}$
    Output: The dataset after Sample Selection $D_{selection}$

---

may also have different difficulties in model training. Thus, we propose a method to calculate the level of sample difficulty.

Intuitively, a sample with more nearest neighbors with different class labels will have a high sample difficulty level. Based on this, we provide formula (1) to evaluate the sample difficulty (SD), where k is the number of nearest neighbors. $kNN(x_{i,j}, D - D_j)$ is the number of k nearest neighbors of sample $x_{i,j}$ that do not belong to class j.

$$SD(x_{i,j}) = \frac{kNN(x_{i,j}, D - D_j)}{k} \tag{1}$$

Then, We introduce our novel loss starting from the cross-entropy (CE) loss for classification. For a classification of p categories, the CE loss is defined as:

$$L_{CE} = -\frac{1}{n} \sum_{i=1}^{n} \sum_{j=1}^{p} y_{i,j} \log \hat{y}_{i,j} \tag{2}$$

where n is the sample size. $y_{i,j} \in \{1, 0\}$ specifies the ground truth sample, and $\hat{y}_{i,j} \in [0, 1]$ is the model's estimated probability for the sample with ground truth i, j.

Based on the CE loss, we add a factor that can consider the different types of samples in a dataset, as mentioned in the sample selection block. The parameter $w_{i,j}$ is related to the sample difficulty. We use formulas (1) and (3) to calculate the value of $w_{i,j}$. Then we define our sample difficulty loss function as formula

(4). We notice the property of our proposed loss function. The parameter $w_{i,j}$ gives samples that are more difficult to train a large loss.

$$w_{i,j} = \log(1 + SD(x_{i,j})) \tag{3}$$

$$L_{SD} = -\frac{1}{n}\sum_{i=1}^{n}\sum_{j=1}^{p} w_{i,j}y_{i,j}\log\hat{y}_{i,j} \tag{4}$$

4   Experiments

4.1   Data Description and Compared Methods

We employ several real-world imbalanced datasets by imblearn toolbox [14] (These datasets are from UCI, LIBSVM, and KDD repository.) to test the performance of our hybrid model. These datasets have different characteristics in terms of the number of samples, IR (Imbalance Ratio), and features. The detailed information on datasets is shown in Table 1. Besides, we randomly split datasets into training sets (60%), valid sets (20%), and test sets (20%).

Table 1. Summary of imbalanced datasets

Datasets	Samples	Features	IR
optical-digits	5620	64	9.1
satimage	6435	36	9.3
pen-digits	10992	16	9.4
abalone	4177	10	9.7
sick-euthyroid	3163	42	9.8
spectrometer	531	93	11
isolet	7797	617	12
us-crime	1994	100	12
yeast-ml8	2417	103	13
scene	2407	294	13
thyroid-sick	3772	52	15
coil-2000	9822	85	16
arrhythmia	452	278	17
oil	937	49	22
car-eval-4	1728	21	26
wine-quality	4898	11	26
abalone-19	4177	10	130

We compare our hybrid model with the following methods, including data-level methods: Random oversampling (ROS), MWMOTE [1], ADASYN [9], SMOTE [5], and AMDO [18]; algorithm-level methods: Focal loss [15], Class-balanced loss [6], and DWE loss [8].

4.2   Evaluation Metrics

We employ commonly used metrics, G-mean and AUC [12], to evaluate the performance of imbalanced data classification. Let FN, FP, TP, and TN be false negative, false positive, true positive, and true negative. TNR and TPR measure the number of correctly classified positive instances and negative instances, respectively. G-mean combines TNR and TPR . AUC is the area under the receiver operating characteristic curve that reflects the relationship between the false positive and true positive ratios. This area describes the trade-off between incorrectly classified positive and correctly classified negative instances.

$$TNR = \frac{TN}{TN + FP} \tag{5}$$

$$TPR = \frac{TP}{TP + FN} \tag{6}$$

$$G - \text{Mean} = \sqrt{TPR \times TNR} \tag{7}$$

4.3   Implementation Details

We select Multilayer perception (MLP) as the classifier and a batch size of 32 to train it for 100 epochs based on the TensorFlow framework. The classifier utilizes Adam as the optimizer, with a learning rate is 0.001. We ran all experiments ten times and took the average of ten times as the final result to obtain a reliable result. Our model finds suitable samples and evaluates the sample difficulty level based on the kNN method (k = 7).

4.4   Experimental Results

Tables 2 and 3 reports AUC and G-mean values on imbalanced datasets. From the experimental results, we find that no single method can achieve the best performance on all datasets. In contrast, our hybrid model achieves decent performance in most cases. The reasons that our model can perform well lie in the following aspects.

First, we use a data space block to make samples easier to be classified. Second, unlike traditional imbalance resolution methods, we select suitable samples based on sample selection for model training. This method retains the critical classification information. Third, our sample difficulty loss function gives each sample a loss corresponding to its sample difficulty. This loss function fully considers the impact of sample difficulty and offers a higher loss to the samples with higher sample difficulty and more challenging to distinguish. Combining the findings above, our model is effective for imbalanced data classification.

Table 2. Valus of AUC on 17 real-world imbalanced datasets

Dataset	MWMOTE	ADASYN	SMOTE	AMDO	ROS	Focal	DWE	BCE	Our model
optical-digits	0.9792	0.9772	0.9810	0.9747	0.9861	0.5000	0.5000	0.9826	**0.9940**
satimage	0.7931	0.7946	0.7985	0.5302	0.8060	0.5000	0.5000	0.7964	**0.8437**
pen-digits	0.9951	0.9963	0.9977	0.9956	0.9985	0.5000	0.5000	0.9952	**0.9985**
abalone	0.7206	**0.7389**	0.7122	0.4990	0.7362	0.5048	0.5416	0.6504	0.6700
sick-euthyroid	0.9224	**0.9404**	0.8988	0.9006	0.9201	0.5000	0.5000	0.9283	0.9092
spectrometer	**0.9948**	0.9928	0.9726	0.9231	0.9574	0.5000	0.5000	0.9716	0.9776
isolet	0.9637	0.9581	0.9480	0.9621	0.9734	0.6846	0.5000	0.9617	**0.9937**
us-crime	0.6874	0.6685	0.6527	0.6870	0.6905	0.6555	0.6858	0.6947	**0.8011**
yeast-ml8	0.5193	0.5126	0.5196	0.4964	0.5126	0.5136	0.5102	0.5195	**0.5916**
scene	0.5924	0.6036	0.5850	0.5658	0.5841	0.5767	0.5000	0.5809	**0.7827**
thyroid-sick	0.9098	0.8941	0.8831	0.8536	0.8968	0.5000	0.5000	0.9098	**0.9102**
coil-2000	0.5572	0.5492	0.5641	0.5252	0.5581	0.5290	0.5331	0.5787	**0.5923**
arrhythmia	0.6101	0.6112	0.6100	0.6066	0.6089	0.5000	0.5000	0.6712	**0.9965**
oil	0.6799	0.8132	0.6443	0.6367	0.6028	0.5000	0.5000	0.7282	**0.8475**
car-eval-4	0.9072	0.9267	0.9170	0.9725	0.9470	0.9079	0.9023	0.8970	**0.9880**
wine-quality	0.6512	0.6522	**0.6819**	0.5438	0.6781	0.5000	0.5000	0.6532	0.6542
abalone-19	0.4892	0.5018	0.4896	0.4996	0.4898	0.4995	0.5000	0.5018	**0.5818**

Table 3. Valus of G-mean on 17 real-world imbalanced datasets

Dataset	MWMOTE	ADASYN	SMOTE	AMDO	ROS	Focal	DWE	BCE	Our model
optical-digits	0.9788	0.9769	0.9807	0.9743	0.9860	0.0000	0.0000	0.9825	**0.9940**
satimage	0.7893	0.7892	0.7968	0.2582	0.8032	0.0000	0.0000	0.7936	**0.8425**
pen-digits	0.9951	0.9963	0.9977	0.9956	0.9985	0.0000	0.0000	0.9952	**0.9985**
abalone	0.7080	**0.7347**	0.7029	0.0000	0.7292	0.0605	0.2951	0.6129	0.6338
sick-euthyroid	0.9221	**0.9403**	0.8953	0.8980	0.9185	0.0000	0.0000	0.9281	0.8952
spectrometer	**0.9948**	0.9928	0.9721	0.9120	0.9558	0.0000	0.9372	0.9710	0.9445
isolet	0.9632	0.9574	0.9451	0.9615	0.9732	0.3844	0.0000	0.9612	**0.9937**
us-crime	0.6247	0.5936	0.5639	0.6118	0.6284	0.5646	0.6176	0.6375	**0.7849**
yeast-ml8	0.2287	0.2254	0.2412	0.0755	0.2302	0.1884	0.1939	0.2830	**0.4853**
scene	0.4736	0.4964	0.4527	0.3955	0.4483	0.4323	0.0000	0.4511	**0.7652**
thyroid-sick	0.9098	0.8904	0.8786	0.8436	0.8930	0.0000	0.0000	0.9072	**0.9089**
coil-2000	0.3921	0.3770	0.4210	0.2545	0.4098	0.2623	0.2994	0.4637	**0.5298**
arrhythmia	0.4924	0.4930	0.4924	0.4907	0.4918	0.0000	0.0000	0.6055	**0.9965**
oil	0.5201	0.8091	0.4144	0.3503	0.3683	0.0000	0.0000	0.7282	**0.8383**
car-eval-4	0.9031	0.9439	0.9212	0.9087	0.9236	0.9026	0.8954	0.8917	**0.9880**
wine-quality	0.6070	0.6059	**0.6454**	0.3003	0.6390	0.0000	0.0000	0.5883	0.6365
abalone-19	0.0000	0.0696	0.0000	0.0000	0.0000	0.0000	0.0000	0.1380	**0.4926**

5 Discussion

5.1 The Impact of Important Informative Samples

In our model, we select suitable samples to train the classifier because samples are essential for finding the classification boundary. Thus, we run experiments on both original and datasets that only contain important informative samples to further illustrate the impact of important informative samples. From Table 4, we observe that training the classifier with datasets containing only important informative samples can obtain better results than training the classifier with original datasets, which verifies the effectiveness of important informative samples. In addition, we also noticed that by selecting suitable samples for training, we improved the classification results while reducing the number of samples used for model training. In summary, selecting suitable samples to deal with imbalanced data classification is a new perspective, which can both reduce the number of samples used for the classifier training and improve the performance of the classifier.

5.2 The Impact of Parameters

To analyze the impact of parameter k in our model, we conduct experiments with varying k from 1 to 13 on three real-world imbalanced datasets. From the experimental results in Fig. 4, we find that the performance of our model is stable with the change of k and when $k = 7$ achieves the best performance.

Table 4. The Impact of Important Informative Samples

Dataset	Original Samples		Suitable Samples	
	AUC	G-mean	AUC	G-mean
pen-digits	0.9976	0.9976	0.9985	0.9985
abalone	0.6561	0.6207	0.6700	0.6338
yeast-ml8	0.5330	0.2956	0.5916	0.4853

5.3 Ablation Study

Our model consists of three blocks: Data Space Block (DSB), Sample Selection Block (SSB), and Sample Difficulty Block (SDB). To analyze the effectiveness of each block, we build some variants of our hybrid model: (1) DSB, which is our model without DSB; (2) SSB, which is our model without SSB; (3) SDB, which is our model without SDB. Fig. 5 shows experimental results on abalone-19 and us-crime datasets. We find that all of these variants perform worse than our model on both datasets, which illustrates that our model effectively integrates three blocks to take advantage of each. Moreover, we find that SSB performs the worst, which demonstrates that SSB has a more critical impact among all blocks.

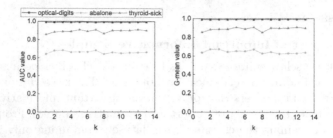

Fig. 4. Impact of parameter k in our model

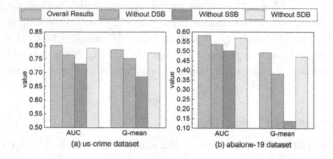

Fig. 5. Ablation Study

6 Conclusion

We aim to overcome the weakness of existing imbalanced learning methods from perspectives of sample selection and sample difficulty. First, we divide samples into different types in an imbalanced dataset according to their impacts on imbalanced data classification. Based on this, we can select suitable samples for sampling. Then, we propose a loss function based on sample difficulty. After that, we design a hybrid model to solve imbalanced data classification. To the best of our knowledge, this is the first model that integrates data space improvement, sample selection, and loss function into imbalanced data classification. Experiments on real-world imbalanced datasets have shown that our hybrid model performs better than competing methods. The ablation study verifies that each model block is valid.

References

1. Barua, S., Islam, M.M., Yao, X., Murase, K.: Mwmote-majority weighted minority oversampling technique for imbalanced data set learning. IEEE Trans. Knowl. Data Eng. **26**(2), 405–425 (2012)
2. Borsos, Z., Lemnaru, C., Potolea, R.: Dealing with overlap and imbalance: a new metric and approach. Pattern Anal. Appl. **21**(2), 381–395 (2018)

3. Bugnon, L.A., Yones, C., Milone, D.H., Stegmayer, G.: Deep neural architectures for highly imbalanced data in bioinformatics. IEEE Trans. Neural Netw. Learn. Syst. **31**(8), 2857–2867 (2019)
4. Cao, P., Zhao, D., Zaïane, O.R.: A PSO-based cost-sensitive neural network for imbalanced data classification. In: Li, J., et al. (eds.) PAKDD 2013. LNCS (LNAI), vol. 7867, pp. 452–463. Springer, Heidelberg (2013). https://doi.org/10.1007/978-3-642-40319-4_39
5. Chawla, N.V., Bowyer, K.W., Hall, L.O., Kegelmeyer, W.P.: Smote: synthetic minority over-sampling technique. J. Artifi. Intell. Res. **16**, 321–357 (2002)
6. Cui, Y., Jia, M., Lin, T.Y., Song, Y., Belongie, S.: Class-balanced loss based on effective number of samples. In: Proceedings of the IEEE/CVF Conference on Computer Vision and Pattern Recognition, pp. 9268–9277 (2019)
7. Das, B., Krishnan, N.C., Cook, D.J.: Racog and wracog: two probabilistic over-sampling techniques. IEEE Trans. Knowl. Data Eng. **27**(1), 222–234 (2014)
8. Fernando, K.R.M., Tsokos, C.P.: Dynamically weighted balanced loss: class imbalanced learning and confidence calibration of deep neural networks. IEEE Trans. Neural Netw. Learn. Syst. (2021)
9. He, H., Bai, Y., Garcia, E.A., Li, S.: Adasyn: adaptive synthetic sampling approach for imbalanced learning. In: 2008 IEEE International Joint Conference on Neural Networks (IEEE World Congress on Computational Intelligence), pp. 1322–1328. IEEE (2008)
10. He, H., Garcia, E.A.: Learning from imbalanced data. IEEE Trans. Knowl. Data Eng. **21**(9), 1263–1284 (2009)
11. Hu, Y., Zhang, Y., Gong, D., Sun, X.: Multi-participant federated feature selection algorithm with particle swarm optimizaiton for imbalanced data under privacy protection. IEEE Trans. Artifi. Intell. (2022)
12. Johnson, J.M., Khoshgoftaar, T.M.: Survey on deep learning with class imbalance. J. Big Data **6**(1), 1–54 (2019)
13. Krawczyk, B.: Learning from imbalanced data: open challenges and future directions. Progress Artifi. Intell. **5**(4), 221–232 (2016)
14. Lemaître, G., Nogueira, F., Aridas, C.K.: Imbalanced-learn: a python toolbox to tackle the curse of imbalanced datasets in machine learning. J. Mach. Learn. Res. **18**(1), 559–563 (2017)
15. Lin, T.Y., Goyal, P., Girshick, R., He, K., Dollár, P.: Focal loss for dense object detection. In: Proceedings of the IEEE International Conference on Computer Vision, pp. 2980–2988 (2017)
16. Liu, Z., et al.: Self-paced ensemble for highly imbalanced massive data classification. In: 2020 IEEE 36th International Conference on Data Engineering (ICDE), pp. 841–852. IEEE (2020)
17. Weinberger, K.Q., Saul, L.K.: Distance metric learning for large margin nearest neighbor classification. J. Mach. Learn. Res. **10**(2) (2009)
18. Yang, X., Kuang, Q., Zhang, W., Zhang, G.: Amdo: an over-sampling technique for multi-class imbalanced problems. IEEE Trans. Knowl. Data Eng. **30**(9), 1672–1685 (2017)
19. Zhao, H., Wang, R., Lei, Y., Liao, W.H., Cao, H., Cao, J.: Severity level diagnosis of parkinson's disease by ensemble k-nearest neighbor under imbalanced data. Expert Syst. Appli. **189**, 116113 (2022)

A New Dataset for Hair Follicle Recognition and Classification in Robot-Aided Hair Transplantation

Xinyu Gu[1], Xiaoxu Zhang[1,2](✉), Hongbin Fang[1,2], Wenyu Wu[1,3,4], Jinran Lin[3], and Kai Yang[4]

[1] Academy for Engineering and Technology, Fudan University, Shanghai 200433, China
zhangxiaoxu@fudan.edu.cn
[2] MOE Engineering Research Center of AI and Robotics, Shanghai 200433, China
[3] Department of Dermatology, Shanghai Institute of Dermatology, Huashan Hospital, Fudan University, Shanghai 200040, China
[4] Department of Dermatology, Jing'an District Central Hospital, Shanghai 200040, China

Abstract. We have created a publicly available scalp hair follicle dataset containing 1652 images and 20697 annotated vectors for 4 object classes, which can be used for hair follicle classification and target detection in hair transplantation. The dataset is derived from clinical data from Huashan Hospital of Fudan University and contains 158MB of image data. To demonstrate the accuracy and superiority of our dataset, we calculated the mean and variance of the image dataset and statistically analyzed the information such as the distribution of each category and the size of the labeled targets. In addition, we conducted experiments on Faster R-CNN and SSD to validate the usability of the dataset, and both were trained successfully. By comparing the average precision (AP) and average recall (AR) of the two experimental results, we demonstrate that the dataset can converge on the target detection network and find that SSD works better.

Keywords: Follicle Database · Computer Vision · Deep Learning · Hair Transplantation Robot

1 Introduction

Hair loss is a global problem. It is not only an index of people's health but also increases the psychological and mental burden of young people. According to statistics, the average hair loss rate of adult men in Asia is between 20% and 30%. Asia has a population of 402 million people with hair loss, of which China has more than 250 million patients with hair loss. By referring to the latest epidemiological survey in China, the prevalence of androgenetic alopecia in Chinese men is 21.3% and in women 6.0% [1, 2]. Furthermore, the latest survey found that the post-90s account for 39% of the hair loss population and the post-80s account for about 38%, showing a younger trend. These results indicate that the problem of hair loss is becoming more and more serious.

© The Author(s), under exclusive license to Springer Nature Switzerland AG 2023
L. Iliadis et al. (Eds.): ICANN 2023, LNCS 14254, pp. 38–49, 2023.
https://doi.org/10.1007/978-3-031-44207-0_4

Although some medications are available to treat certain types of hair loss problems, e.g., male pattern baldness, they are often accompanied by certain side effects. In contrast, surgical treatment is more reliable. A commonly adopted operation is follicular unit extraction (FUE) which has a quick recovery and leaves no visible scars, and is currently the mainstream option for manual surgery. However, this process is slow and requires the cooperation of several healthcare professionals, indicating that the efficiency is limited. The FUE-based hair transplant robot is a good solution to this problem. This robot is divided into two modules: the hair follicle visual recognition system and the mechanical actuator. The hair follicle visual recognition system determines the category and position information of hair follicles, and its accuracy is related to the execution of the whole hair transplantation procedure.

Most of the work on hair follicle detection still relies on image processing algorithms, such as image filtering, enhancement, feature extraction, segmentation, etc. For example, Shih et al. [3] solved the problem of overlapping hair by using a hair bundling algorithm and proposed a hair counting algorithm for curved hair; Zhang et al. [4] designed an automatic hair counting system using the Otsu algorithm and Hough transform; Kim et al. [5] first preprocessed the images using contrast stretching and morphological operations, and then measured the hair density by converting skeletonized images and applying a line endpoint search algorithm.

However, the accuracy of image processing algorithms for identifying overlapping areas is still limited, and they cannot distinguish between the root and tip of the hair. Moreover, they are easily affected by environmental factors. The rapid development of deep learning in the field of medical imaging provides us with new directions. For example, Chang et al. [6] developed an intelligent scalp detection and diagnostic system called ScalpEye based on deep learning, which can detect four types of conditions, including dandruff, folliculitis, hair loss, and oily hair. ERDOĞAN et al. [7] used multiple depth cameras to build a 3D model of the patient's head and combined it with deep learning methods to detect and segment hair follicles, creating an FUE hair transplant analysis system. Kim et al. [8] used deep learning techniques for hair density measurement and compared the performance of multiple object detection algorithms, with experimental results showing that YOLOv4 [9] performed the best.

Whereas the model accuracy and generalization ability largely depends on the size and quality of the training dataset, no publicly available hair follicle dataset can be used as a standard for hair follicle detection. To this end, we cooperate with the top dermatology team in China, who are also co-authors of this paper, to establish a professional-grade hair follicle dataset for hair follicle classification and detection. We also conduct a comprehensive statistical analysis of the dataset itself, the categories, and the labeled target attributes to verify the superiority and reliability of our dataset. Finally, we successfully trained two mature target detection networks, Faster R-CNN and SSD, using FDU_HairFollicleDataset and proved the usability of the dataset. It can be used within the field of hair transplantation. FDU_HairFollicleDataset is available at GoogleDrive [1], and if used, please cite this paper.

---

[1] https://drive.google.com/file/d/1rMw8OzgxuTOSqKD8EBPN_BYXW18q9d3H/view?usp=sharing.

The rest of this paper is organized as follows. Section 2 describes the work related to dataset annotation. Section 3 provides the specific methods for dataset preparation and statistical analysis. Section 4 presents the experiments for validating the usability of the dataset. Finally, Sect. 5 summarizes the paper.

2   Related Work

This section will briefly describe the existing work on datasets and their evaluation metrics.

As deep learning techniques evolve rapidly, there is an increasing demand for high-quality datasets to support the training and validation of deep learning algorithms. For example, the Pascal Visual Object Classes (VOC) challenge committee has released multiple versions of computer vision datasets since 2005, which have been widely applied in object detection and image segmentation. Taking Pascal VOC2012 [10] as an example, it contains 20 categories, 17,125 original images, of which 5,717 are labeled training images, 5,823 are labeled validation images, and 5,799 are labeled testing images. In addition, the Pascal VOC2012 dataset provides evaluation tools for different metrics, such as mean average precision (mAP), precision, and recall, to evaluate the performance of object detection algorithms. The ImageNet dataset [11], which has been collected since 2007, has surpassed 14 million images and more than 20,000 class labels. Its openness has greatly promoted the development of computer vision. The Microsoft Common Objects in Context (MS COCO) dataset [12] has also been widely used for object detection, segmentation, and image captioning. As of its last update in 2017, it includes 328,000 images, 80 object categories, and 5,000,000 annotations, and has been compared with other datasets in terms of the number of categories, the number of annotation instances per category, and the average size of objects. The Open Image dataset [13] released by Google has reached version 4 as of 2019, with over 9 million images, over 300 million annotated bounding boxes, and approximately 2 million annotated key points. It also provides statistics on label histograms, image-level label percentages, positive and negative sample counts, and annotation box sizes to evaluate dataset quality.

In recent years, some work has been done on hair follicle datasets with varying sizes, resolutions, and annotation qualities. Zhou et al. [14] collected 340 raw 3D hair models, divided hair into 12 categories based on different criteria, and created a hair dataset with over 40k samples using mirroring and mixed-filling techniques. Chang et al. [6] obtained scalp hair symptom microscope images from a hairdressing company, annotated them using four common scalp hair symptom categories, and created a dataset that includes 615 seborrheic dermatitis symptom images, 312 folliculitis symptom images, 859 alopecia symptom images, and 412 oily hair symptom images. AI Hub [15] also created a scalp image dataset about patients with hair loss, containing 4492 enlarged images and corresponding annotation data, which were classified based on the number of hairs in the follicles. Kim et al. [16] collected 600 images from 10 male participants and had them annotated by a physician, resulting in a hair follicle dataset with a total of 24012 labels.

Although existing scalp hair follicle datasets and labeling tools have greatly facilitated research in this field, they still have certain limitations. Firstly, the image data quality is poor and often obscured by noise. Secondly, most aggregated images are directly sourced from the internet, which is inconsistent with clinical application scenarios. Thirdly, although some are hair epidermal datasets, they are not suitable for hair transplantation. Fourthly, there is a lack of guidance from professional doctors, resulting in inaccurate judgments for different categories of hair. Fifthly, the annotated bounding boxes are mostly in the vicinity of the hair follicles, which is not in line with the real application scenarios and makes it difficult to calculate the three-dimensional pose of the hair follicles. Sixthly, there is a lack of statistical information about the datasets themselves. Therefore, the development of the hair transplantation field still requires the creation of large-scale, high-quality scalp hair follicle datasets.

3   Dataset Preparation

In this section, we will introduce the sources of the images, the criteria for labeling categories, and how we annotated the dataset. We also conducted data statistics on the dataset. The specific dataset preparation was carried out according to Fig. 1.

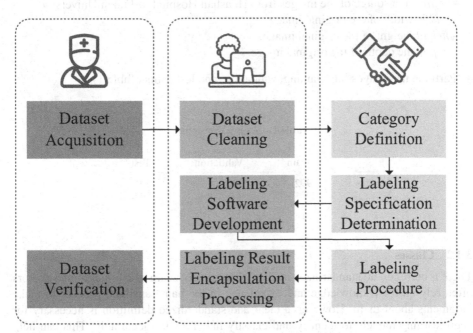

Fig. 1. Flowchart of dataset preparation. Shades of color indicate the work done by the dermatologists, our work, and the work done together.

3.1   Dataset Acquisition and Annotation

3.1.1   Dataset Acquisition

The availability of reliable and authentic images is a fundamental requirement for creating a high-quality dataset. Unlike others facing challenges in developing hair follicle datasets, we collaborated with the Department of Dermatology at Huashan Hospital of Fudan University, a top medical institution in China. We obtained the most comprehensive clinical photographs of hair follicles, along with professional guidance from expert physicians. We have received permission from these physicians to disclose the dataset to interested parties. The dataset is organized according to the format of PASCAL VOC2012.

In summary, the FDU_HairFollicleDataset comprises approximately 1600 images, collected through a rigorous process:

1. 1652 original images with an image resolution of 1280x1024 and a field of view size of about 3x3 mm were provided successively by Huashan Hospital of Fudan University.
2. Remove duplicate images.
3. Relevant metadata of all images were extracted to assign the appropriate attributes.

- *folder*: address of the dataset.
- *filename*: the file name of each image.
- *source*: the source of the images from Huashan Hospital of Fudan University.
- *width*: width of the original image.
- *height*: height of the original image.
- *depth*: the depth of the original image.

4. Partition the images into training, validation, and test splits (Table 1).

Table 1. Dataset divisions.

	Train	Validation	Test
Images	992	330	330

3.1.2 Classes

There is currently no standardized medical definition of scalp hair follicles, and doctors often rely on their knowledge and experience in the hair transplant process to make judgments about them. However, a clear and standardized definition is necessary for deep learning models to identify and classify hair follicles accurately. This can help improve the accuracy and efficiency of the model by mapping image features to specific classes.

To accurately describe the different characteristics of hair follicles on the scalp, we have identified four categories: Premium, Single, Undersize, and Abnormal. Premium follicles are large and healthy, typically containing multiple thick, full heels of hair. Single follicles grow only one hair, while Undersize follicles tend to produce fine, fragile hair. Finally, Abnormal follicles exhibit atypical features, such as twisted shapes, abnormal growth patterns, or hair fragments and flakes that do not meet the definition of a hair follicle. Typical category characteristics are shown in Fig. 2.

By classifying hair follicles in this way, we can provide a more detailed and precise analysis of scalp health and hair growth. It is worth noting that the criteria for hair follicles may differ between doctors, so a standardized definition is especially important in the context of deep learning and large-scale data analysis.

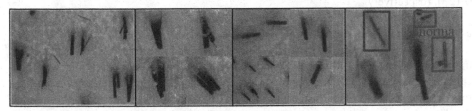

Fig. 2. Schematic diagram of various categories of hair follicles. (a) The actual scenario of hair follicles. (b) Illustration of hair follicles in the Premium category. (c) Illustration of hair follicles in a Single category. (d) Special types of hair follicles (Undersize & Abnormal).

3.2 Labeling Specifications and Processes

Annotation specifications and processes for the dataset are crucial to ensure the quality and efficiency of the data labeling. In the hair transplant procedure, to facilitate the surgery, the surgeon usually requests the subject to shave their hair to 1–2 mm, allowing for better observation of the hair follicles. The number of hairs present in each follicle is an essential criterion for classification, and as such, we require a directed line segment as the marking method, with the hair follicles pointing towards the hair tips. The starting point of the line segment indicates the location of the hair follicles.

We utilized the LabelBoundingBox [17] labeling tool, which enables us to import the original image and sort it into categories. This tool accurately labels the boundaries of each target by drawing rectangular boxes and generates information about the image's category and coordinate position. To better meet our specific requirements, we have made improvements to the tool:

1. To accurately label the linear characteristics of hair, we have adopted a vector labeling format instead of using rectangular boxes.
2. To distinguish between hair roots and tips, we have added a solid yellow circle to indicate the location of the hair follicle.
3. Unlike typical target detection tasks, our scene contains multiple targets in a single image. To increase annotation efficiency, we have introduced a new feature where clicking on different annotations changes the corresponding target annotation vector's shade in the main interface, making it easier to distinguish between different targets.

Our dataset has benefited from the guidance of dermatologists from Huashan Hospital. The annotation process involved the following steps: first, two doctors jointly labeled 100 images to establish accurate classification criteria. Next, two other doctors independently labeled 200 images according to the established criteria, serving as our reference. Finally, the remaining images were annotated by our annotators and then reviewed and verified by the doctors.

3.3 Statistical Analysis of Dataset Quality

Our dataset consists of 1,652 scalp images, all derived from real clinical scenes, and split into the train, validation, and test sets as shown in Table 1. We also calculated the mean and variance of the dataset, which were [0.525, 0.521, 0.540] and [0.102, 0.105, 0.128], respectively.

To better understand the distribution of information within our dataset, we conducted a statistical analysis of the categories and annotation vectors.

Specifically, the FDU_HairFollicleDataset is divided into four categories based on the quality of the hair follicles: Premium, Single, Undersize, and Abnormal. We then calculated the total and average number of each category within the training set, validation set, and test set to gain insight into the distribution of these categories throughout the dataset.

Table 2. Distribution of each category on the dataset.

	Train		Validation		Test	
	Sum	Average	Sum	Average	Sum	Average
Premium	8096	8.16	2891	8.76	2741	8.31
Single	2825	2.85	949	2.88	944	2.86
Undersize	929	0.94	249	0.75	315	0.95
Abnormal	429	0.43	160	0.48	169	0.51

Table 2 shows that the proportion of each category in the training, validation, and test sets is nearly identical, with a ratio of about 18:6:2:1. This indicates that our dataset is stable and well-balanced.

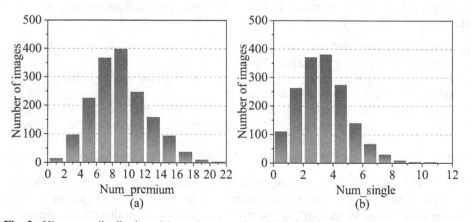

Fig. 3. Histogram distribution of the main categories of hair follicles in the dataset, (a) Premium, (b) Single.

Considering the proportion of categories in Table 2, the Premium category accounted for approximately 66.3% of the total hair follicles, and the Single category for approximately 22.8%. We focused on the histogram of these two categories of hair follicles and observed that the Premium and Single categories showed distributions that approximated Gaussian distributions with maxima of 9 and 3, respectively in Fig. 3.

Annotation vectors are a crucial component of our dataset, and their quality is a significant indicator of the dataset's reliability. We conducted a comprehensive analysis of the annotation vectors, including their number, size, and distribution, to accurately assess the quality of our dataset.

Table 3. Annotated vector distribution and average number.

	Train	Validation	Test
Images	992	330	330
Vector	12279	4269	4169
per image	*12.4*	*12.9*	*12.6*

In our study, we counted the total number and average size of annotation vectors in the training, validation, and test sets. We found that the average number of vectors was 12.4, 12.9, and 12.6, respectively, which were very similar in Table 3. This result demonstrates the consistency and stability of our dataset across the three sets.

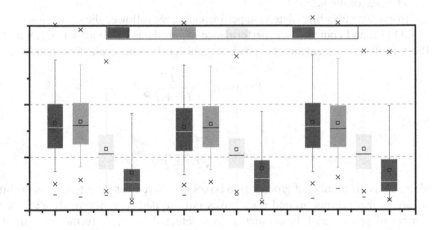

Fig. 4. Box plots for each class of annotated vectors on each set.

Moreover, in Fig. 4, we analyzed the size distribution of annotation vectors for different categories. We found that the hair follicles of the Premium and Single types had similar sizes, which were the largest among all categories. This finding is consistent with our selection criteria of prioritizing high-quality hair follicles. In contrast, the Abnormal type had smaller hair follicles, some of which were less than half the size of those in the Premium and Single categories. These results highlight the usefulness and reliability of our dataset in supporting research and innovation in hair follicle transplantation.

4 Dataset Availability Validation

In this section, we aim to demonstrate the utility of our dataset. To achieve this, we carried out experiments on Faster R-CNN [18] and Single Shot MultiBox Detector (SSD) [19], respectively. We compare and analyze the results obtained from the experiments.

4.1 Experimental Environment and Evaluation Metrics

To validate the usability of our dataset, for the Faster R-CNN, we trained with vgg16 [20] as the backbone network using 992 images from the training set. To speed up the training, our training strategy involved using a pre-training approach, where we froze the prior features to extract the network weights, trained the RPN and the final prediction network for 20 cycles, and then trained the entire network weights for 81 cycles to complete the usability validation experiments. The SGD optimizer with a learning rate of 0.005, a momentum of 0.9, a weight decay of 0.0005, and a batch size of 4 was used during the training process. We conducted the experiments on an Ubuntu operating system using a GeForce RTX 3090 GPU with 24GB memory for accelerated computation. And for SSD, we used the same hyperparameters and trained 101 epochs to get the experimental results. The evaluation metrics used in this study were accuracy, recall, and loss values at each stage of the network.

To evaluate the object detection performance, we followed the evaluation metrics of COCO [12] and compared the performance of our dataset on Faster R-CNN and SSD. The formulae for calculating the precision and recall in the evaluation metrics are:

$$Precision = \frac{TP}{TP + FP} \tag{1}$$

and

$$Recall = \frac{TP}{TP + FN} \tag{2}$$

where TP is the number of ground truth boxes that have been detected, FP is the number of targets that are not ground truth boxes but are detected incorrectly and FN is the number of ground truth boxes that are not detected. Then by further plotting the PR curves, we can obtain the COCO metrics at different scales.

In addition, we observed the classification loss and regression loss values of Faster R-CNN in both global and RPN stages, where the classification loss is a binary cross-entropy loss and the regression loss is calculated by the smooth L1 function.

4.2 Comparison and Analysis of Experimental Results

Based on the equipment and environment described above, we trained Faster R-CNN and SSD on our dataset. In Fig. 5 (a), we can find that the training loss of each Faster R-CNN is less than 0.2, and convergence is achieved. The COCO metrics of the training results of the two types of target detection networks are counted to obtain the AP performance of our dataset in both networks in Table 4 and the AR performance in Table 5, respectively. It can be found that SSD performs better than Faster R-CNN across the board except for the AP metric for Intersection over Union (IOU) of 0.5. The change curves of AP (IOU = 0.5) and AR (area = large) for the two types of data with the largest statistical values are plotted in Fig. 5(b), (c), where the difference between the AP values of SSD and Faster R-CNN is not much, while the AR value is ahead by about 15.6%, and the convergence speed is also better than that of Faster R-CNN, which verifies that SSD does work better.

Table 4. Each AP value on Faster R-CNN and SSD.

	AP	AP (0.5)	AP (0.75)	AP (small)	AP (medium)	AP (large)
Faster R-CNN	0.2237	**0.4680**	0.1896	0.0101	0.2093	0.2916
SSD	**0.2432**	0.4565	**0.2268**	**0.0136**	**0.2120**	**0.3247**

Table 5. Each AR value on Faster R-CNN and SSD.

	AR (1)	AP (10)	AR (100)	AR (small)	AR (medium)	AR (large)
Faster R-CNN	0.1239	0.3116	0.3301	0.0505	0.3251	0.3882
SSD	**0.1268**	**0.3453**	**0.3620**	**0.0690**	**0.3374**	**0.4489**

The curves in Fig. 5 show that our dataset achieves convergence during training, which is a good proof of its usability. And SSD also performs basically better than Faster R-CNN in training with Faster R-CNN across the board.

However, there is still room for improvement in our dataset. On the one hand, we need to expand it further, especially regarding the total number and the number of undersized and anomalous categories. On the other hand, the two types of target detection networks detecting target frames may not fully satisfy the hair follicle recognition application scenario because some target frames have unbalanced aspect ratios, which will filter out some samples and affect the accuracy. Therefore, a detection network using linear target recognition may perform better in this scenario.

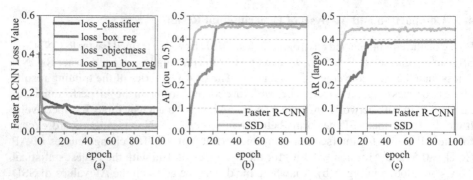

Fig. 5. The performance of our dataset on target detection network results. (a) Epoch versus loss values for our dataset in Faster R-CNN. (b) Epoch versus AP for IOU of 0.5 in Faster R-CNN and SSD. (c) Epoch versus AR for the area of large in Faster R-CNN and SSD.

5 Conclusion

This paper introduces the FDU_HairFollicleDataset, a dataset comprising 1652 clinical scalp images and 20697 hair follicle targets annotated using a unified standard for hair follicle classification and detection in hair transplant surgery. The process of data acquisition and annotation is meticulously described, and an extensive statistical analysis of the dataset is provided. We also showcase the application of the dataset in Faster R-CNN and SSD, and present a comparative analysis of their performance. Our results indicate that SSD performs better than Faster R-CNN. In future work, we aim to scale up the FDU_HairFollicleDataset to enhance the dataset quality, add more data in the Undersize and Abnormal categories, and include additional attributes such as truncation and overlap. The diversity of the dataset will promote research and innovation in hair follicle transplantation.

Acknowledgements. This work was supported by the National Natural Science Foundation of China (Grant No. 11902077), Medical and Industrial Integration Project (Grant No. yg2021-002), Shanghai Engineering Research Center of Hair Medicine (Grant No. 19DZ2250500), Leading Talent Project of Shanghai Health Commission (Grant No. 2022LJ017), Clinical Research Plan of SHDC (Grant No. SHDC22022302, SHDC2020CR2033B).

References

1. Wang, T.L., et al.: Prevalence of androgenetic alopecia in China: a community-based study in six cities. Br. J. Dermatol. **162**(4), 843–847 (2010)
2. Xu, F., et al.: Prevalence and types of androgenetic alopecia in Shanghai, China: a community-based study. Br. J. Dermatol. **160**(3), 629–632 (2009)
3. Shih, H.C.: An unsupervised hair segmentation and counting system in microscopy images. IEEE Sens. J. **15**(6), 3565–3572 (2014)
4. Zhang, Q., Sung-Jong, E.: Design and implementation of an automatic hair counting system. J. Dig. Art Eng. Multimedia **1**(2), 75 (2014)

5. Kim, W., et al.: A hair density measuring scheme using smartphone. In: Proceedings of the Korea Information Processing Society Conference, pp. 1416–1419. Korea Information Processing Society (2015)
6. Chang, W.J., et al.: ScalpEye: a deep learning-based scalp hair inspection and diagnosis system for scalp health. IEEE Access **8**, 134826–134837 (2020)
7. Erdogan, K., et al.: KEBOT: an artificial intelligence based comprehensive analysis system for FUE based hair transplantation. IEEE Access **8**, 200461–200476 (2020)
8. Kim, M., Kang, S., Lee, B.D.: Evaluation of automated measurement of hair density using deep neural networks. Sensors **22**(2), 650 (2022)
9. Bochkovskiy, A., Wang, C.Y., Liao, H.Y.M.: Yolov4: optimal speed and accuracy of object detection. arXiv preprint arXiv:2004.10934 (2020)
10. Everingham, M., et al.: The pascal visual object classes challenge: a retrospective. Int. J. Comput. Vision **111**, 98–136 (2015)
11. Deng, J., et al.: Imagenet: a large-scale hierarchical image database. In: 2009 IEEE Conference on Computer Vision and Pattern Recognition, pp. 248–255. IEEE (2009)
12. Lin, T.Y. et al.: Microsoft COCO: common objects in context. In: Fleet, D., Pajdla, T., Schiele, B., Tuytelaars, T. (eds.) Computer Vision – ECCV 2014. ECCV 2014. Lecture Notes in Computer Science, vol. 8693. Springer, Cham (2014). https://doi.org/10.1007/978-3-319-10602-1_48
13. Kuznetsova, A., et al.: The open images dataset v4: unified image classification, object detection, and visual relationship detection at scale. Int. J. Comput. Vision **128**(7), 1956–1981 (2020)
14. Zhou, Y., et al.: Hairnet: single-view hair reconstruction using convolutional neural networks. In: Proceedings of the European Conference on Computer Vision (ECCV), pp. 235–251 (2018)
15. AI Hub. https://aihub.or.kr. Accessed 23 Nov 2021
16. Kim, J.H., et al.: Hair follicle classification and hair loss severity estimation using mask R-CNN. J. Imaging **8**(10), 283 (2022)
17. LabelBoundingBox. https://github.com/hjptriplebee/LabelBoundingBox. Accessed 14 Feb 2022
18. Ren, S., He, K., Girshick, R.B., Sun, J.: Faster R-CNN: towards real-time object detection with region proposal networks. In: Advances in Neural Information Processing Systems, vol. 28 (2015)
19. Liu, W., et al.: SSD: single shot multibox detector. In: Leibe, B., Matas, J., Sebe, N., Welling, M. (eds.) Computer Vision – ECCV 2016. ECCV 2016. Lecture Notes in Computer Science, vol. 9905. Springer, Cham (2016). https://doi.org/10.1007/978-3-319-46448-0_2
20. Simonyan, K., Zisserman, A.: Very deep convolutional networks for large-scale image recognition. arXiv preprint arXiv:1409.1556 (2014)

A Policy for Early Sequence Classification

Alexander Cao[1(✉)], Jean Utke[2], and Diego Klabjan[1]

[1] Department of Industrial Engineering and Management Sciences,
Northwestern University, Evanston, IL, USA
`a-cao@u.northwestern.edu`, `d-klabjan@northwestern.edu`
[2] Data, Discovery and Decision Science, Allstate Insurance Company,
Northbrook, IL, USA
`jutke@allstate.com`

Abstract. Sequences are often not received in their entirety at once, but instead, received incrementally over time, element by element. Early predictions yielding a higher benefit, one aims to classify a sequence as accurately as possible, as soon as possible, without having to wait for the last element. For this early sequence classification, we introduce our novel classifier-induced stopping. While previous methods depend on exploration during training to learn when to stop and classify, ours is a more direct, supervised approach. Our classifier-induced stopping achieves an average Pareto frontier AUC increase of 11.8% over multiple experiments.

Keywords: Early classification · Sequence classification

1 Introduction

Practical use cases for early sequence classification exist in many domains. Holding your smartphone's microphone up to a speaker, in seconds a music recognition app can tell which song is being played. There are two competing objectives with respect to the app making a real-time classification from audio. On one hand, a longer sequence from the song may yield a more accurate classification. On the other hand, the user may not have the patience to wait very long.

Generally, we are interested in scenarios in which a classifier receives elements of a sequence over time. This kind of ongoing flow of data immediately suggests a need for a real-time ability to stop waiting for new elements and classify given the received elements at this point in time at sufficient accuracy. We call this early classifying to differentiate from classification after a 'complete' sequence or a pre-set number of sequence elements is received. Optimally deciding when one has received enough data, and then making an accurate classification from that data, is the crux of the problem we are investigating.

To this end, we introduce our novel classifier-induced stopping (CIS) in this paper. Previous methods depend on exploration during training (when there is access to the entire sequence) to learn (i) a policy to decide when to stop

© The Author(s), under exclusive license to Springer Nature Switzerland AG 2023
L. Iliadis et al. (Eds.): ICANN 2023, LNCS 14254, pp. 50–61, 2023.
https://doi.org/10.1007/978-3-031-44207-0_5

waiting for new elements and classify and (ii) the classifier itself. Exploration, in an early sequence classification context, means the policy affects how much of the sequence is ingested or used to learn. In contrast, CIS learns both policy and classifier in a more direct, supervised approach inspired by imitation learning [1]. CIS learns to classify as accurately as possible at every time step, after receiving a new element. Concurrently, it learns to stop and classify at the optimal time (based off a reward) induced from its own classifications at each time step. CIS removes notions of exploration and learns to follow the ideal decision-making based off its own classification predictions; hence, we call it classifier-induced. The main contributions of our work are as follows. We introduce a novel, supervised framework to learn a stopping time for early classifiers that avoids exploration. Instead, it learns when to stop from its own classifications. We demonstrate that CIS outperforms benchmarks in terms of a Pareto frontier AUC measure across diverse experiments.

Our paper is structured as follows. In Sect. 2, we establish notation and review related work, specifically the two benchmark methods used in experiments. Following in Sect. 3, we discuss CIS in detail. Section 4 presents results from three sets of experiments on a variety of problems and data. Section 5 gives a summary.

2   Related Work

2.1   Problem Setup Notation

The framework of early classification we consider here is as follows. The set of training data $\mathcal{X}$ comprises sequences $x^{(i)}$ paired with one-hot encoded labels $y^{(i)} \in \{0,1\}^C$ for C classes, where $x^{(i)} = \left(x_1^{(i)}, x_2^{(i)}, ..., x_{T_{\text{end}}}^{(i)}\right)$ is a sequence of tensors. At time $t \leq T_{\text{end}}$, its state is given by $s_t^{(i)} = \left(x_1^{(i)}, x_2^{(i)}, ..., x_t^{(i)}\right)$.

A *classifier* neural network $f_\alpha(s_t) = \widehat{y}_\alpha(\cdot|s_t)$ parameterized by α takes s_t as input[1] and outputs predicted class distribution vector $\widehat{y}_\alpha(\cdot|s_t)$ at time t. A *policy* neural network $g_\beta(s_t) = \pi_\beta(\cdot|s_t)$ parameterized by β takes s_t as input and outputs policy distribution vector $\pi_\beta(\cdot|s_t)$ over two actions ('wait' and 'stop and classify') at time t.

At each time step t, we take an action a_t according to policy $\pi_\beta(\cdot|s_t)$. This is done stochastically via sampling or deterministically via taking the most likely action. We keep waiting another time step and receive new element x_{t+1} until we decide to stop. Once we decide to stop and classify, we make a classification according to $\widehat{y}_\alpha(\cdot|s_t)$. To encourage a model to early classify as accurately as possible, as quickly as possible, we use the following reward function at each time step t

$$R_t^\alpha(s_t, a_t)$$
$$= \begin{cases} -\mu & \text{if } a_t = \text{'wait'} \\ -\mu - \text{CE}\left(y, \widehat{y}_\alpha(\cdot|s_t)\right) & \text{if } a_t = \text{'stop and classify' or } t = T_{\text{end}} \end{cases} \quad (1)$$

---

[1] We omit the $^{(i)}$ indices unless needed.

where μ is a time penalty parameter and CE is cross-entropy. At each time step, a constant penalty of $-\mu$ is incurred. Early classification is completed once the model decides to stop and classify at a time T. The problem is to solve

$$\max_{\alpha,\beta} \mathbb{E}_{\mathcal{X}} \sum_t R_t^\alpha \left(s_t, a_t\left(\beta\right)\right). \tag{2}$$

Maximizing the cumulative reward is equivalent to classifying as accurately as possible (so that the cross entropy is low), as quickly as possible (so that the sum of time penalties is low). The time penalty parameter μ controls how much waiting another time step is penalized. If μ is large, we may sacrifice more accuracy for an earlier classification, and vice-versa.

The problem has two challenges. When a policy decides to stop, it never directly learns what would happen if it waited longer. In essence, the ability to look forward and learn from information after the stopping time is important. Second, and more subtly, the policy and classifier need to be cohesively learned together as the time penalty relates the two.

2.2   Early Classification via Reinforcement Learning

Several papers treat early classification as a standard reinforcement learning problem. [5] ingests text sentence-by-sentence and answers given questions (via classification) when the model decides enough information has been read. [2] applies a very similar methodology to obtain early diagnoses from healthcare vital signs like EEGs. It is important to note that [2,5] still train their models with the REINFORCE algorithm [10], a standard policy gradient method. They compare against full-sequence-length classifiers or utilize a fixed threshold on each time step's classification as a stopping rule. We choose the Proximal Policy Optimization (PPO) algorithm [7] as our standard reinforcement learning benchmark to compare against CIS; details are in Sect. 2.3.

2.3   PPO

Policy gradient methods work by first creating episodes

$$(s_1, a_1, R_1^\alpha), (s_2, a_2, R_2^\alpha), ..., (s_T, a_T, R_T^\alpha)$$

with actions determined by the current policy. The policy is then updated in gradient ascent direction so that actions leading to greater future rewards become more probable. PPO, following [7], maximizes the clipped surrogate objective

$$\mathcal{L}_{\text{PPO}}$$
$$= \mathbb{E}_{\mathcal{X},t} \left[\min \left\{ \frac{\pi_\beta\left(a_t|s_t\right)}{\pi_{\beta_{\text{old}}}\left(a_t|s_t\right)} \widehat{A}_t^\alpha, \text{clip}\left(\frac{\pi_\beta\left(a_t|s_t\right)}{\pi_{\beta_{\text{old}}}\left(a_t|s_t\right)}, 1-\epsilon, 1+\epsilon \right) \widehat{A}_t^\alpha \right\} \right]. \tag{3}$$

The estimated advantage $\widehat{A}_t^\alpha$ is given by $\widehat{A}_t^\alpha = \sum_{t'=t}^T \gamma^{t'-t} R_{t'}^\alpha - V\left(s_t\right)$ where γ is a discount factor and $V\left(s_t\right)$ is a learned state-value function. PPO's exploration hindrance is evident as any information after time T is not used in learning. Keeping in line with previous work relying on exploration, we opt to keep the policy stochastic during inference [2,4,7].

Policy gradient reinforcement learning methods are, by nature, trial and error-based. They cannot take advantage of the fact that stopping and classifying later for a given sample would have been better. Put differently, they do not utilize the entire sequence during training.

2.4   LARM

Length Adaptive Recurrent Model (LARM) [4] and CIS remedy this inability to look forward in the sequence. LARM takes a more probabilistic interpretation to early classification. Let $A_T = (a_1 = $ 'wait', $a_2 = $ 'wait', $..., a_{T-1} = $ 'wait', $a_T = $ 'stop and classify') be a decision sequence where the policy decided to wait the first $T - 1$ time steps and stopped to classify at time T. Given A_T and $\pi_\beta (\cdot | s_t)$, we can explicitly factor the probability of sequence A_T as

$$\mathbb{P}(A_T | s_T) = \prod_{t=1}^{T} \pi_\beta (a_t | s_t). \tag{4}$$

With respect to this stopping time probability, LARM seeks to maximize the expected cumulative reward in (2) with the objective

$$\max_{\alpha,\beta} \mathbb{E}_{\mathcal{X}} \left[-\text{CE} \left(y, \sum_{T=1}^{T_{\text{end}}} (\widehat{y}_\alpha | s_T) \mathbb{P}(A_T | s_T) \right) - \mu \sum_{T=1}^{T_{\text{end}}} T \cdot \mathbb{P}(A_T | s_T) \right].$$

The first term is a micro-averaged cross-entropy loss and the second term is the expected stopping time.

Because $\mathbb{P}(A_T | s_T)$ is a product whose value may exponentially decrease, LARM takes special care to prevent this. During training, the factors $\pi_\beta (a_t = $ 'wait'$| s_t)$ are set to 1 with probability ρ. This forces the model to wait for more elements in the sequence and not get stuck stopping too soon. In terms of early classification, waiting is tantamount to ingesting more information and so ρ is a parameter controlling this aspect. Even so, there is an exploration drawback here in that learning accurate classifications at low probability stopping times is difficult. For inference, LARM opts for stochastic policy rollout with deterministic classification.

3   Classifier-Induced Stopping

As previously stated, early classification can be framed as maximizing the cumulative reward given in (2). We can recast this quantity as a function r depending on label y, classification prediction $\widehat{y}_\alpha (\cdot | s_T)$, and classification time T given by $r(y, \widehat{y}, T) = -\text{CE}(y, \widehat{y}) - \mu T$. Note, for a fixed $\widehat{y}$ and y this is a univariate function of time T. With this in mind, we aim to learn (i) when to stop and classify and (ii) what classification to make in a more direct, supervised manner. First, CIS seeks to make the most accurate classification prediction at every single time step. Second and simultaneously, CIS learns the corresponding policy which yields the resulting optimal classification time. In this way, our policy learns the ideal policy based off of its own classifications. Hence, we name it classifier-induced. The loss function is given by $\min_{\alpha,\beta} \mathcal{L}_{\text{CIS}} = \min_{\alpha,\beta} \mathbb{E}_{\mathcal{X}} \left[\mathcal{L}_{\hat{y}} + \lambda \cdot \mathcal{L}_{\pi} \right]$ where

$$\mathcal{L}_{\hat{y}} = \frac{1}{T_{\text{end}}} \sum_{t=1}^{T_{\text{end}}} \text{CE}\left(y, \hat{y}_\alpha\left(\cdot|s_t\right)\right), \quad \mathcal{L}_{\pi} = \frac{1}{T_{\text{end}}} \sum_{t=1}^{T_{\text{end}}} \text{CE}\left(\tilde{\pi}_\alpha\left(\cdot|x,t\right), \pi_\beta\left(\cdot|s_t\right)\right)$$

(5)

$$\tilde{\pi}_\alpha\left(\cdot|x,t\right) = \begin{cases} (1,0) & \text{if } t < \tilde{T}_\alpha\left(x,y\right) \\ (0,1) & \text{if } t \geq \tilde{T}_\alpha\left(x,y\right), \end{cases} \quad \tilde{T}_\alpha\left(x,y\right) = \arg\max_t r\left(y, \hat{y}_\alpha\left(\cdot|s_t\right), t\right).$$

(6)

We write $(1,0)$ to mean 'wait' with probability 1 and $(0,1)$ as 'stop and classify' with probability 1. There is hyperparameter λ. Figure 1 below offers an intuitive visual walkthrough of CIS.

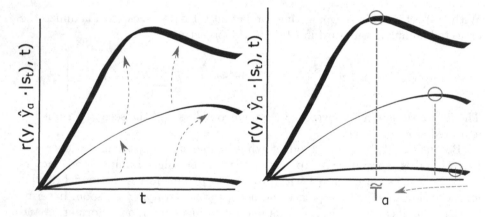

Fig. 1. (Left) $\mathcal{L}_{\hat{y}}$ is increasing cumulative reward r at each time step. (Right) Concurrently, for the rendered reward curve, there exists an optimal time to stop and classify $\tilde{T}_\alpha$ that maximizes r and therefore an optimal policy $\tilde{\pi}_\alpha\left(\cdot|x,t\right)$. $\mathcal{L}_{\pi}$ aims to learn this policy.

Unlike PPO and LARM, our novel CIS does not rely on any notion of exploration. The entire sequence is wholly used in training and we are able to directly learn the optimal classification time in a supervised manner. During training $\tilde{\pi}_\alpha\left(\cdot|x,t\right)$ and $\tilde{T}_\alpha$ are treated as fixed labels in minibatch updates. Since there is no exploration in CIS, the policy does not have an exploratory nature; hence, in inference we simply take the argmax action.

4 Experimental Results

4.1 Datasets and Pareto Metric

Our first experiment is with the IMDB movie reviews sentiment analysis dataset [6]. We do not need to ingest the entire review to classify its sentiment. Instead, we read word by word and classify the review after ingesting a minima number of words. The dataset comprises 50,000 movie reviews; half the reviews are positive and the other half negative. We reserve a random 15% of samples to be the hold-out validation set, separate from the training set. We set $T_{end} = 236$, which is the mean training review length, and pad up or truncate down all reviews to this length.

The second experiment uses Electrocardiography (ECG) waveforms of multiple cardiovascular diagnoses from PTB-XL [9]. ECGs record electrical signals from the heart and help to assess cardiac clinical status of patients. Instead of a diagnostic tool alone, early classification aids in continuous monitoring for heart conditions. The sooner an early classifier can detect a heart attack, the sooner medical attention can be given. Here we early classify ECG signals by ingesting small segments sequentially. After following [8] and filtering out some ECGs (those with uncertain diagnoses, for instance), we are left with 17,221 samples in the dataset. There are five classes which are reasonably balanced. We reserve a random 10% of samples to be the validation set, again separate from the training set. Each ECG length is 10 s, sampled at 100 Hz. Consistent with the procedure in [11], the network input is the log spectrogram of each ECG (using a Tukey window of length 32 with 50% overlap). In essence, spectrograms are consecutive fragments of a signal in Fourier space to represent frequencies varying over time. Therefore our early classifier, in effect, receives each ECG in consecutive 0.16 s fragments in Fourier space.

Our third and final experiment is motivated by European call options. They give the holder the right to buy a stock at a specified strike price only on a given expiration date (betting the stock will go up). However, after buying the option, if the option holder could predict that the stock price will not be above the strike price on the option expiration date, then the holder could attempt to sell the option in the secondary market to recoup the original cost of the option. To be clear, in this problem context we are concerned only with the prediction aspect and not the option sale.

From [3], it is reasonable to assume a strike price equal to the stock price on the option origination purchase date. With this in mind, we simulate 1-month European call options in the following way. Samples are generated from 65 current S&P 500 technology stocks based on daily data ranging from 1962 to 2017. For the training set, we divide each technology stock into disjoint 30-day stock price samples, through 2016. We consider a binary classification of whether the stock closing price on day 30 is greater than or less than the stock closing price on day 1 (proxying strike price). Thus, stopping to classify is akin to committing on day T to exercise the option or not upon expiration. This process yields 9,313 training samples with 59% of these options as profitable to exercise. For validation, we wish to roll out the early classifier more organically and continuously. Accordingly, we take the remaining year 2017 after the training set from each stock for validation. The assumption is that we will have year-long stock price sequence to continually roll out early classifiers and 'purchase' new options the day after stopping and deciding what to do with the current one. Table 1 summarizes daily technical indicators used along with the standard open, high, low, and close prices plus volume to form the daily features.

Table 1. Stock price sequence technical indicators, using standard parameters

Feature	Description
Exponential moving average	Measures trend direction,
(open, high, low, close, volume)	heavier weighting on more recent days
Bollinger Bands	Relative highs and lows of price movement
On-balance volume	Measures buying and selling of stock
Accumulation/distribution	Gauges supply and demand
Average directional	Measures trend strength
Aroon oscillator	Indicates uptrend or downtrend
Moving average	Measures momentum
convergence/divergence	
Relative strength	Measures speed of price changes
Stochastic oscillator	Measures momentum

In all experiments, we holistically compare early classifiers from PPO, LARM, and CIS by their Pareto frontiers. This allows us to examine the entire performance spectrum of their accuracy-timeliness tradeoffs. Our procedure for constructing a Pareto frontier is as follows. For a given μ value, we roll out the early classifier over the validation set and compute the mean classification time and accuracy after each training epoch. This is repeated for varying μ to get the entire collection of such accuracy-timeliness tradeoff points. Finally, all dominated points are removed which yields the Pareto frontier. The Pareto frontier (piecewise-constant) AUC is a holistic measure of accuracy-timeliness tradeoff efficacy. We treat μ as a hyperparameter, controlling the dichotomous balance between accuracy and timeliness, and sweep multiple values to trace the Pareto frontier. In a real-world use case, extrinsic factors from the problem itself should guide which Pareto point is optimal.

4.2   Implementation

Before describing network design and hyperparameters, we modify PPO's objective. Learning a state-value baseline function leads to more unstable training and ultimately poorer results. So in our case we remove it, and the advantage reduces to the sum of future rewards $\widehat{A}_t^\alpha = \sum_{t'=t}^{T} \gamma^{t'-t} R_{t'}^\alpha$. In addition to PPO's main objective, we add a classification term to help directly teach the classifier. The combined objective is then

$$\min_{\alpha,\beta} \left(\mathbb{E}_{\mathcal{X},t} \left[\text{CE} \left(y, \widehat{y}_\alpha \left(\cdot | s_t \right) \right) \right] - \mathcal{L}_{\text{PPO}} \right) \quad .$$

While the policy and classifier can be disjoint networks, in practice it is common to have them as two heads of the same body network [4]. We choose this for our implementations of PPO, LARM, and CIS, with the body network being an LSTM. Elements of sequential data (or embeddings) are inputs to the LSTM. The recurrent hidden states are in turn inputs to separate, feed-forward networks: one for the policy and one for the classifier. Each of these feed-forward heads is composed of a single hidden-layer with ReLU activation and softmax output. Next, we explicate all of the hyperparameters used in our experiments.

For all three experiments, we sweep $\mu \in \{0.001, 0.003, 0.005, 0.007, 0.01, 0.03, 0.05, 0.07, 0.1\}$. We keep the standard PPO clip value of $\epsilon = 0.2$ and a discount factor $\gamma = 1$ yields the best results (and does not scale the cumulative reward). To further aid PPO waiting longer and ingesting more information initially, yielding better results, we initialize the policy head's final layer's bias to $(10, 0)$. For CIS, we set the scaling constant $\lambda = 1$. The training set is optimized by using Adam with batch size 128 until validation accuracies and mean classification times plateau.

For the IMDB experiment specifically, the word embedding dimension is 32. For the network size, the LSTM hidden state is of dimension 64 and the two FFN hidden layers are of dimension 32. Learning rates for PPO and LARM are 10^{-4} and 10^{-3} for CIS. Following [4], we keep LARM's waiting parameter $\rho = 0.9$.

For the ECG experiment specifically, the hidden vector of the LSTM is of dimension 128 and the two FFN hidden layers are of dimension 64. All three learning rates are set to 10^{-4}. Again, we keep LARM's $\rho = 0.9$.

Finally, for the stock option experiment specifically, we implement a chronological rolling normalization so that all features are scaled in range $[0, 1]$. The network dimensions are 32, 16, and 16. All three learning rates are set to 10^{-4}. In this experiment, LARM performs poorly with $\rho = 0.9$ and lowering it to $\rho = 0.6$ lead to significantly better performance.[2]

4.3 IMDB Experiment

Figure 2 displays the Pareto frontiers for the IMDB experiment. CIS's AUC is 17.7% greater than PPO's AUC and 2.4% greater than LARM's AUC. CIS outperforms PPO and LARM, and we stress this is due to the forward-looking, supervised nature of the algorithm.

While CIS and LARM performs well globally, they are also coherent on an individual review level. Let us consider each early classifier at a mean T of about 40 words (red circles in Fig. 2). In Fig. 3 we present their respective outputs for a very stark negative movie review. For this review, CIS and LARM are able to

---

[2] Code is available at this repository: https://github.com/alexcao828/cis..

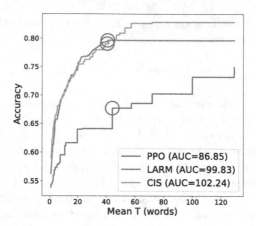

Fig. 2. Pareto frontiers for the IMDB experiment.

quickly and correctly stop soon after 'a really awful movie' while PPO continues to wait. Additionally, in Fig. 3 we also show CIS and LARM's abilities to early classify a long-winded, positive movie review. The first 20 words in this review are not actually about the movie itself. It is not until 'i loved it then and i love it now' that the models sense the review's sentiment and act and classify accordingly. Again PPO seems to need more information. These two didactic examples indicate the discerning patience and linguistic understanding of CIS and LARM over PPO, contributing to the gap in accuracies.

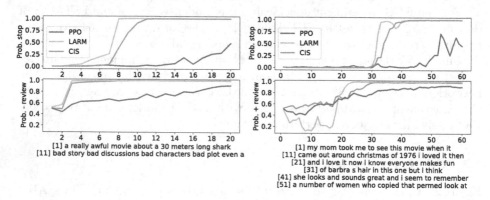

Fig. 3. Early classifer performances on an example (left) stark negative and (right) long-winded positive IMDB movie review.

4.4 ECG Experiment

Figure 4 (left) displays the Pareto frontiers for the ECG experiment. CIS holistically outperforms PPO and LARM. CIS's AUC is 35.3% greater than PPO's

AUC and 2.9% greater than LARM's AUC. Although it is worthwhile to note that CIS performs worst for mean T below 0.3 s. This is due to those Pareto points coming from early, un-converged epochs.

To be sure, there is significant nuance in differentiating ECGs. To again highlight CIS's discerning patience, we investigate the distribution of stopping times for each diagnosis compared to LARM. Figure 4 (right) shows just this using CIS and LARM at 68% accuracy (red circles in Fig. 4 (left)). We can see that CIS (i) on average stops sooner for NORM and MI diagnoses and (ii) has smaller interquartile ranges for all diagnoses.

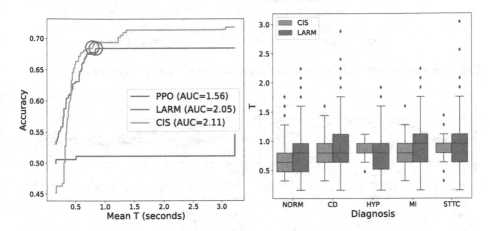

Fig. 4. (Left) Pareto frontiers for the ECG experiment. (Right) Box plots showing distribution of CIS and LARM classification times T for each ground truth ECG diagnosis. For HYP, CIS's first quartile coincides with the median because of repeating values. Similarly for STTC, CIS's third quartile coincides with the median.

4.5 Stock Option Experiment

For our stock option experiment, we construct two Pareto frontier comparisons, shown in Fig. 5. On the left, are the standard accuracy-time Pareto frontiers. However, in the financial scenario inspiring this experiment, dollars and profit is a more apt axis. So on the right, we also present profit-classification time Pareto frontiers. Here, we take a perfect hindsight definition of profit to include potential money gained and lost by not exercising the option. Since in this experiment we roll out the early classifiers continuously, the stochastic policies of PPO and LARM affect the future options (or samples). Accordingly, each Pareto frontier point is the average of 100 trials. One hundred trials is sufficient as the maximum ratio of standard error to mean is 2.7% across all points' mean accuracies, profits, and classification times.

Again, our CIS holistically outperforms the benchmarks. In the accuracy sense, CIS's AUC is 6.5% greater than PPO's AUC and 5.4% greater than LARM's AUC. Turning to profit, CIS's AUC is 10.3% greater than PPO's AUC and 18.4% greater than LARM's AUC.

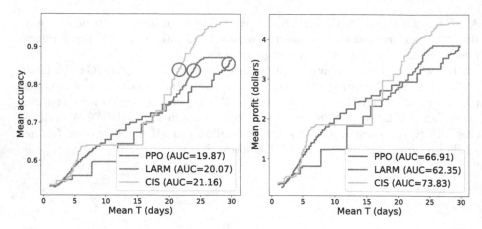

Fig. 5. Accuracy (left) and profit (right) Pareto frontiers for the options experiment.

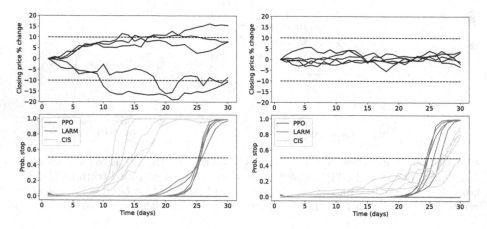

Fig. 6. (Left plots) Five options with their daily percent change in closing price compared to day 1 exceeding ±10%, marked with black dashed lines in the upper panel. We also mark 0.5 in the lower panel. (Right plots) Similar to left, except note the percent changes within ±10% for these options.

While stock price movements are complex random walks, CIS is able to discern recognizable patterns better than LARM and PPO. If a stock displays strong and consistent growth or loss in the early days (drift in a random walk), one is more likely able to extrapolate a trend sooner. Similarly, if a stock continuously fluctuates around the first day's price, waiting longer becomes necessary to observe a trend, if any exist. Figure 6 demonstrates this hypothesis on an individual sample level using each early classifier at around 84% mean accuracy (red circles in Fig. 5 (left)). CIS stops much sooner for stock price movements with strong positive or negative drift. LARM consistently classifies around 25 days and PPO waits until the end (very low time penalty).

5   Conclusion

From our experiments, we stress CIS performs holistically better than state-of-the-art PPO and LARM in terms of a Pareto frontier AUC measure. On average, CIS is 3.6% more accurate than LARM, and 19.8% more accurate than PPO, given the same stopping time. Directly learning when to stop from its own classifications provides a better framework than exploration.

References

1. Attia, A., Dayan, S.: Global overview of imitation learning. arXiv preprint arXiv:1801.06503 (2018)
2. Hartvigsen, T., Sen, C., Kong, X., Rundensteiner, E.: Adaptive-halting policy network for early classification. In: Proceedings of the 25th ACM SIGKDD International Conference on Knowledge Discovery & Data Mining, pp. 101–110 (2019)
3. Huang, J.Z., Wu, L.: Specification analysis of option pricing models based on time-changed lévy processes. J. Finance **59**(3), 1405–1439 (2004)
4. Huang, Z., Ye, Z., Li, S., Pan, R.: Length adaptive recurrent model for text classification. In: Proceedings of the 2017 ACM on Conference on Information and Knowledge Management, pp. 1019–1027 (2017)
5. Liu, X., Mou, L., Cui, H., Lu, Z., Song, S.: Finding decision jumps in text classification. Neurocomputing **371**, 177–187 (2020)
6. Maas, A.L., Daly, R.E., Pham, P.T., Huang, D., Ng, A.Y., Potts, C.: Learning word vectors for sentiment analysis. In: Proceedings of the 49th Annual Meeting of the Association for Computational Linguistics: Human Language Technologies, pp. 142–150. Association for Computational Linguistics, Portland, Oregon, USA (June 2011), http://www.aclweb.org/anthology/P11-1015
7. Schulman, J., Wolski, F., Dhariwal, P., Radford, A., Klimov, O.: Proximal policy optimization algorithms. arXiv preprint arXiv:1707.06347 (2017)
8. Śmigiel, S., Pałczyński, K., Ledziński, D.: ECG signal classification using deep learning techniques based on the ptb-xl dataset. Entropy **23**(9), 1121 (2021)
9. Wagner, P., et al.: Ptb-xl, a large publicly available electrocardiography dataset. Scientific Data **7**(1), 154 (2020)
10. Williams, R.J.: Simple statistical gradient-following algorithms for connectionist reinforcement learning. Mach. Learn. **8**(3), 229–256 (1992)
11. Zihlmann, M., Perekrestenko, D., Tschannen, M.: Convolutional recurrent neural networks for electrocardiogram classification. In: 2017 Computing in Cardiology (CinC), pp. 1–4. IEEE (2017)

A Study of Data-Driven Methods for Adaptive Forecasting of COVID-19 Cases

Charithea Stylianides[ID], Kleanthis Malialis[✉][ID], and Panayiotis Kolios[ID]

KIOS Research and Innovation Center of Excellence,
University of Cyprus, Nicosia, Cyprus
{stylianides.charithea,malialis.kleanthis,kolios.panayiotis}@ucy.com.cy

Abstract. Severe acute respiratory disease SARS-CoV-2 has had a profound impact on public health systems and healthcare emergency response especially with respect to making decisions on the most effective measures to be taken at any given time. As demonstrated throughout the last three years with COVID-19, the prediction of the number of positive cases can be an effective way to facilitate decision-making. However, the limited availability of data and the highly dynamic and uncertain nature of the virus transmissibility makes this task very challenging. Aiming at investigating these challenges and in order to address this problem, this work studies data-driven (learning, statistical) methods for incrementally training models to adapt to these nonstationary conditions. An extensive empirical study is conducted to examine various characteristics, such as, performance analysis on a per virus wave basis, feature extraction, "lookback" window size, memory size, all for next-, 7-, and 14-day forecasting tasks. We demonstrate that the incremental learning framework can successfully address the aforementioned challenges and perform well during outbreaks, providing accurate predictions.

Keywords: incremental learning · data streams · neural networks · time-series forecasting

1 Introduction

The COVID-19 pandemic has caused a massive disruption to society since its emergence in December 2019. An unprecedented number of people were infected, hospitalized and had COVID-19 being their leading cause of death. Moreover, the consequences of the pandemic are still impacting our social and economic ecosystems. Evidently, many countries still impose restrictions and measures

This work was supported by the European Union's Horizon 2020 research and innovation programme under grant agreement No 739551 (KIOS CoE - TEAMING) and from the Republic of Cyprus through the Deputy Ministry of Research, Innovation and Digital Policy. It was also supported by the CIPHIS (Cyprus Innovative Public Health ICT System) project of the NextGenerationEU programme under the Republic of Cyprus Recovery and Resilience Plan under grant agreement C1.1l2.

L. Iliadis et al. (Eds.): ICANN 2023, LNCS 14254, pp. 62–74, 2023.
https://doi.org/10.1007/978-3-031-44207-0_6

based on the evolution of the infected population. Hence, effective modelling and prediction of the evolution of the viral load in the society can be of detri-mental factor in decision making. By taking proactive measures for closures and lockdowns, restricting public events, health guidelines and vaccine policies, gov-ernments can increase their effectiveness and limit transmissibility. A way to capture the spread of the virus is by tracking and predicting the number of positive cases. This constitutes a challenging task because of:

Data non-stationarity. The data exhibit a highly dynamic behaviour, i.e., the data distribution evolves over time [6]. In the COVID-19 case, for instance, there have been many variants of the virus (e.g., Delta and Omicron), as well as many measures which have been imposed (e.g., vaccination and school closure).

Limited data. This refers to the problem of having limited availability of historical data. Evidently most countries reported positive cases on a daily basis which accumulates to a mere 365 data points over the course of a year.

As a result, it is necessary to have an online learning model which is able to adapt to non-stationary environments, and to be incrementally trained from limited data. The contributions of this work are the following.

- The primary focus of this study is on COVID-19 cases forecasting for Cyprus, a European country with a population of around one million.
- We conduct an extensive empirical analysis where we examine the roles of (i) traditional/offline vs online incremental learning; (ii) "look-back" window size; (iii) feature extraction; (iv) memory size; (v) learning (neural network) vs statistical (ARIMA) models. Furthermore, all these are considered in three tasks (next-, 7-, and 14-day forecasting) and we provide a per-wave analysis.

The remainder of the paper is structured as follows. Section 2 discusses work related to ours. Section 3 describes the problem formulation and the incremental learning framework for adaptive forecasting. The experimental setup and results are provided in Sect. 4 and 5 respectively. We conclude in Sect. 6.

2   Related Work

2.1   Compartmental Models

These models, like the well-known Susceptible Exposed Infectious Recovered (SEIR) [11] and any variations of it, split the population into mutually exclu-sive states that describe a path of infection dynamics through mathematical modelling [15]. For maximum accuracy, studies [4,10] have deduced parame-ters describing the transition between states that are time-varying capturing the social changes, medical advancements and non-pharmaceutical interventions during a pandemic [10]. For example, the "DELPHI" model [15] consists of 11 compartments and forecasts detected cases and deaths for about 2 weeks, accounting for government measures and limited population testing. The vast majority of existing work on COVID-19 cases forecasting lie within this domain.

2.2 Data-Driven Methods

The focus of our work is on data-driven methods. Forecasting using data-driven methods can also be successfully achieved through statistical and machine learning methods. Isaac B. et al. [3] compared the performance of a model that combines Convolutional and Long Short Term Memory (LSTM) layers to that of a standard neural network, using a 14-day window of positive cases to predict those of the next seven days both at the regional and national level. Several studies have compared the performance of LSTM to that of other models including Recurrent Neural Networks (RNNs) [2], Gradient Boosting Trees [18] and the statistical model ARIMA [12]. Research includes time series of just confirmed cases for generalizability [3], added features like number of cured patients and deaths [12] and aggregated features [12,18] for improved accuracy. The superiority of the LSTM is concluded in all the last comparisons. Another comparative study in [25] used LSTM, RNN, Bidirectional LSTM, Gated Recurrent Units (GRUs) and Variational AutoEncoder (VAE) to predict new and recovered cases for the next 17-days where VAE showed the best performance. Encoders of self-attention and recurrent layers, that consider among other factors travelling from each country to predict the spread were also proposed in [13].

The aforementioned methods consider offline learning. Continual or online learning is starting to be used to capture the concept of drift in the spread of COVID-19 and adapt models in real time. The study in [24] evaluates the best number of training samples needed at each time step to minimize the prediction error and, thus, capture drift. Ridge regression is used for predictions of hospitalizations from new cases, severe cases from hospitalizations and deaths from severe cases for the next 7 d using 14-day windows [24]. In [23] an ensemble of regression models predicts 30-day mortality allowing for adaptation of the models at every instance by i) fitting them again on the whole data, ii) fitting them again on just the new instance, or iii) fitting a completely new ensemble on the new data. A linear model with LASSO (least absolute shrinkage and selection operator) penalty [16] and a feed-forward network with autoregressive input (predictions at each time step used for training for the next forecast) [22], were also able to incrementally train and produce 2-day cases predictions [16] and 30-day predictions of hospitalizations and deaths [22], respectively.

2.3 Hybrid

A study [5] has used data from a compartmental model (exposed, infected, recovered and dead population) to evaluate the best lags of each out of time series windows in an ARIMA model, for predicting each of the variables and susceptible population. Based on this, new data is then continuously bootstrapped out of a data stream, predicting and updating incrementally an ensemble of algorithms each time [5]. In [7,8] incremental learning of a neural network provides 5 parameters (rate of infection during lockdown, time lockdown begins, rate of death, rate of recovery) needed for a Susceptible Infected Recovered Vaccinated Deceased (SIRVD) model. The SIRVD model forecasts monthly trajectories of deaths under different senarios [7] and monthly total number of cases, active infections and deaths [8].

Algorithm 1 Data-driven framework for adaptive forecasting

   Input:
   D: number of days to forecast
   W: "Lookback" window size
   M: Memory / queue size
1: Wait W days, observe instance $x^W = \{n^1, ..., n^W\}$
2: Create model $f^W.init()$
3: Predict $\hat{y}^{W+1} = f^W.predict(x^W)$
4: **for** each time step $t \in [W+1, W+D-1]$ **do**
5:     Get ground truth $y^t = n^t$
6:     Observe instance $x^t = \{n^t, n^{t-1}, .., n^{t-W+1}\}$
7:     Predict $\hat{y}^{t+1} = f^W.predict(x^t)$
8: Initialise memory $q^t = \{\}$
9: **for** each time step $t \in [W+D, \infty)$ **do**
10:    Get ground truth $y^t = n^t$
11:    Observe $y^t = \{n^t, n^{t-1}, .., n^{t-D+1}\}$
12:    Append example to memory $q^t = q^{t-1}.append((x^{t-D}, y^t))$
13:    Incremental training $f^t = f^{t-1}.train(q^t)$
14:    Observe instance $x^t = \{n^t, n^{t-1}, .., n^{t-W+1}\}$
15:    Predict $\hat{y}^{t+1} = f^t.predict(x^t)$

---

3 Incremental Learning Framework for Adaptive Forecasting

We consider a data generating process $S = \{n^t\}_{t=1}^T$ that provides at each day t a number $n^t \in \mathbb{R}$ of positive cases, from an unknown and evolving probability distribution $p^t(n)$, where $T \in [1, \infty)$. The instances constitute a univariate time series, and n^t corresponds to the number of COVID-19 cases on day t.

To address the temporal aspects of the data, we consider a sliding window of size $W \in \mathbb{Z}^+$, such that, $x^t = \{n^t, n^{t-1}, ..., n^{t-W+1}\} \in \mathbb{R}^W$ is a W-dimensional vector belonging to input space $X \subset \mathbb{R}^W$. The task is to forecast $D \in \mathbb{Z}^+$ days of the COVID-19 cases, that is, at any day $t > W$ to predict $\hat{y}^{t+D} = \{\hat{n}^{t+D}, ..., \hat{n}^{t+2}, \hat{n}^{t+1}\} \in \mathbb{R}^D$, a D-dimensional vector belonging to $Y \subset \mathbb{R}^D$.

A regression model f^t receives a new example $x^t \in \mathbb{R}^W$ at time step t and makes a prediction $\hat{y}^{t+D} \in \mathbb{R}^D$, based on a concept $f : X \rightarrow Y$ such that $\hat{y}^{t+D} = f^t(x^t)$. In this study, we will be using neural networks as our regression models, which they have been demonstrated to be effective incremental learners [17,20,21]. The loss function used between a prediction $\hat{y}^t \in \mathbb{R}^D$ and ground truth $y^t \in \mathbb{R}^D$ at time t is the Mean Squared Error (MSE) defined as:

$$J^t = MSE(\hat{y}^t, y^t) = \frac{1}{D}\sum_{d=1}^{D}(\hat{y}_d^t - y_d^t)^2, \tag{1}$$

The model is continually updated using incremental learning, which is defined as the gradual adaptation of a model without complete re-training, that is, $f^t = f^{t-1}.train((x^{t-D}, y^t))$. Learning is performed using incremental Stochastic

Gradient Descent where each neural network weight w is updated according to the formula $w^t \leftarrow w^{t-1} - \alpha \frac{\partial J^t}{w}$, where $\frac{\partial J^t}{w}$ is the partial derivative with respect to w, and α is the learning rate.

Furthermore, we introduce a memory component implemented as a queue q of size M, which stores historical examples. For instance, at time t, it will append to memory the example (x^{t-D}, y^t), i.e., $m^t = m^{t-1}.append((x^{t-D}, y^t))$. As a result, incremental learning is now performed using $f^t = f^{t-1}.train(q^t)$, and the loss function is defined as the average MSE of all memory examples.

The framework's pseudocode is shown in Alg. 1. Initially, we wait for W days (Line 1). Subsequently and until day $t < W + D$, we only perform prediction (i.e., forecasting) without any incremental training (Lines 2 - 7). From day $t \geq W + D$ we perform both prediction and incremental learning (Lines 8 - 15).

4   Experimental Setup

4.1   Dataset

Our data consist of reported daily SARS-CoV-2 cases in Cyprus from 15/10/20 to 08/10/22 as they appear in the TESSy platform of the European Center of Disease Prevention and Control (ECDC) in the RESPISURV dataset. Data preprocessing included creating sliding windows of 7, 14, 30 d and removal of daily cases of under 100 for reduced noise and easier learning of the models. Any missing values were imputed with the mean of their row or the previous row and data were normalized by dividing by maximum number of cases. Six periods of interest, referred to as "waves", are considered in this study and are shown in Fig. 1. The time periods of each wave are as follows: Wave 1: 13/12/20-11/01/21; Wave 2: 04/04/21-03/05/21; Wave 3: 02/07/21-31/07/21; Wave 4: 19/12/21-07/01/22; Wave 5: 17/06/22-26/07/22. Also, we will be referring to the remaining (i.e., non-waves) time period as "normal".

4.2   Compared Methods

The compared methods follow the same framework shown in Algorithm 1.

MLP. It refers to the standard feed-forward, fully-connected Multilayer Perceptron (MLP) model. In all experiments, its hyper-parameters are: He Normal [9] weight initialisation, the Adam [14] optimisation algorithm, LeakyReLU [19] and ReLU for the hidden and output activation function respectively, the MSE loss function, and mini-batch size of one. The rest of them (architecture, learning rate, regularisation, and number of epochs) slightly vary for each experiment.

ARIMA. The Autoregressive Integrated Moving Average (ARIMA) model is a classical forecasting method. Despite the fact that ARIMA is often considered as a baseline method, it is emphasised that due to the limited availability of historical data, it is actually demonstrated to be very effective particularly during normal and small outbreaks. In all experiments, its hyper-parameters are number of lagged observations for auto-regression: 1, number of times the raw observations are differenced: 0 and moving average window size: 0.

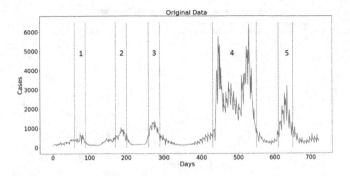

Fig. 1. COVID-19 cases in Cyprus (15/10/20-18/10/22)

4.3   Evaluation Method and Metrics

To evaluate and compare the aforementioned methods, we have been using the following widely adopted metrics for regression forecasts.

MAE. This refers to the Mean Absolute Error (MAE).

MAPE. This refers to the Mean Absolute Percentage Error (MAPE) between actual $y^t \in \mathbb{R}^D$ and predicted $\hat{y}^t \in \mathbb{R}^D$ values as defined below:

$$MAPE(\hat{y}, y) = \frac{100\%}{N} \sum_{d=1}^{D} \frac{|y_d - \hat{y}_d|}{|y_d|}, \tag{2}$$

For all experiments involving neural networks, we run each one over 10 repetitions and provide the average and standard deviation for both metrics, for an overall time period, as well as during wave and normal periods.

5   Experimental Results

5.1   Role of Incremental Learning

This section compares the performance of MLP using offline learning to that of online incremental learning. For offline learning, the MLP was pre-trained on one month of data and with no further training. For the next-day prediction task, Fig. 2 shows the results of the two paradigms on a daily basis, while Table 1 provides the relevant aggregated metrics. The standard deviation of the error is shown in brackets. The corresponding results for the 7- and 14-day forecasting tasks are shown in Table 2 and Table 3. It is observed that online learning significantly outperforms offline learning in all tasks and all time periods.

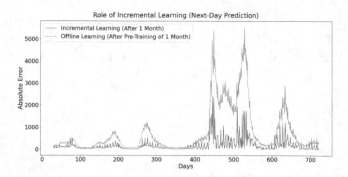

Fig. 2. Online vs offline learning for next-day predictions

Table 1. MLP with online vs offline learning for next-day predictions

	Overall		Waves		Normal	
	MAE	MAPE	MAE	MAPE	MAE	MAPE
Online	**186.1 (47.4)**	**26.3 (14.3)**	**378.4 (62.5)**	**25.5 (9.1)**	**148.2 (50.4)**	**26.7 (17.9)**
Offline	767.9 (405.3)	83.9 (43.8)	1714.1 (934.0)	96.7 (57.1)	588.2 (302.7)	79.9 (40.5)

Table 2. MLP with online vs offline learning for 7-day predictions

	Overall		Waves		Normal	
	MAE	MAPE	MAE	MAPE	MAE	MAPE
Online	**342.3 (48.0)**	**43.7 (5.3)**	**714.1 (105.8)**	**46.0 (5.0)**	**267.9 (36.5)**	**43.5 (5.5)**
Offline	598.7 (59.4)	65.4 (6.3)	1319.8 (140.0)	75.1 (7.3)	461.2 (45.0)	62.7 (6.5)

Table 3. MLP with online vs offline learning for 14-day predictions

	Overall		Waves		Normal	
	MAE	MAPE	MAE	MAPE	MAE	MAPE
Online	**524.2 (42.1)**	**75.9 (4.1)**	**1011.1 (97.9)**	**67.9 (4.9)**	**413.6 (31.6)**	**74.5 (4.3)**
Offline	686.7 (47.2)	83.6 (7.8)	1416.5 (101.4)	88.3 (10.4)	546.3 (35.5)	82.0 (6.9)

5.2   Role of the Sliding Window Size

This section examines the impact of the sliding window size on the performance of MLP using incremental learning. Results are provided in Table 4 and Table 5 for next- and seven-day prediction tasks, respectively.

Using MLP, the 7-day window performs better compared to the 14-day and 30-day ones for all prediction tasks. Regarding average performance across waves, the 30-day window performs best for next-day and 7-day prediction and the 7-day window performs best for 14-day prediction task (not shown here). Normal periods benefit the most from a 7-day window for all prediction tasks. While not shown due to space restrictions, for ARIMA, a 30-day window performs the best on the overall data, wave and normal periods for all tasks.

Table 4. MLP with 7-, 14- and 30-day sliding window (next-day prediction)

	Overall		Waves		Normal	
Window	MAE	MAPE	MAE	MAPE	MAE	MAPE
7	**186.1 (47.4)**	**26.3 (14.3)**	378.4 (62.5)	25.5 (9.1)	**148.2 (50.4)**	**26.7 (17.9)**
14	343.9 (258.0)	48.2 (28.8)	698.6 (569.1)	42.5 (30.9)	270.0 (201.5)	47.4 (29.9)
30	187.8 (20.8)	28.3 (7.1)	**368.5 (23.0)**	**25.2 (5.2)**	154.1 (23.6)	28.6 (8.7)

Table 5. MLP with 7-, 14- and 30-day sliding window (7-day prediction)

	Overall		Waves		Normal	
Window	MAE	MAPE	MAE	MAPE	MAE	MAPE
7	**342.3 (48.0)**	**43.7 (5.3)**	714.1 (105.8)	46.0 (5.0)	**267.9 (36.5)**	**43.5 (5.5)**
14	378.0 (43.5)	46.5 (4.7)	795.5 (95.5)	48.8 (4.9)	292.6 (32.9)	45.2 (4.6)
30	350.6 (38.9)	46.4 (5.0)	**709.2 (81.1)**	**44.9 (4.7)**	281.6 (32.1)	45.9 (5.5)

The better performance of a 7-day window can be attributed to the fewer window days suggesting more recent data, which can increase performance. On the other hand, it is speculated that a 30-day window works best because of the more data and fluctuations considered.

5.3 Role of Feature Extraction

This section describes the role of 20 features in our model, aggregated across a 14-day window. The features are: school closing strictness (mean), public events cancellation strictness (mean), positive cases (min, max), unvaccinated cases (min, median), second dose vaccinated population (min, range), second dose vaccinated cases (mean, median), first dose vaccinated cases (median, mean), weekly deaths (mean), workplace closing strictness (mean), weekly ICU cases (mean), weighted stringency index (median), recovered (s.d.), 70+ aged cases (mean), first dose vaccinated population (median) and 18–24 aged cases (mean).

The results for next- and seven-day prediction tasks are shown in Table 6 and Table 7, respectively. Using the features, MAPE is reduced by 8.3%, 7.2% and 0.2% for overall, wave and normal periods, respectively, for the 7-day prediction. The features seem to be more informative when making later predictions.

5.4 Role of the Memory Size

In this section, the role of the memory size using i) raw data and ii) features is assessed. For these experiments, raw data was used in 7-day windows for 14-day predictions and features were extracted from 14-day windows for 7-day predictions. Window size here is chosen based on best windows for raw data and features, respectively, as stated in Sects. 5.2 and 5.3. The results for the memory use with raw data are shown in Table 8 and with features in Table 9.

70   C. Stylianides et al.

In the first case, it is deduced that increasing memory size improves overall, wave and normal periods performance by up to 17%, 12.7% and 16.1%, respectively. Interestingly, in the second case, using memory decreases performance.

Table 6. MLP with raw data vs features (next-day prediction)

	Overall		Waves		Normal	
Data	MAE	MAPE	MAE	MAPE	MAE	MAPE
Raw	**186.1 (47.4)**	**26.3 (14.3)**	**378.4 (62.5)**	25.5 (9.1)	**148.2 (50.4)**	**26.7 (17.9)**
Features	211.5 (42.1)	30.5 (11.8)	423.2 (57.1)	29.4 (9.1)	172.0 (43.8)	31.8 (14.1)

Table 7. MLP with raw data vs features (7-day prediction)

	Overall		Waves		Normal	
Data	MAE	MAPE	MAE	MAPE	MAE	MAPE
Raw	342.3 (48.0)	43.7 (5.3)	714.1 (105.8)	46.0 (5.0)	267.9 (36.5)	43.5 (5.5)
Features	**284.7 (11.1)**	**35.4 (2.9)**	**603.1 (15.4)**	**38.8 (2.0)**	**238.7 (13.5)**	**43.3 (5.5)**

Table 8. MLP performance with raw data per memory size (7-day window, 14-day prediction)

	Overall		Waves		Normal	
Memory	MAE	MAPE	MAE	MAPE	MAE	MAPE
1	524.2 (42.1)	75.9 (4.1)	1011.1 (97.9)	67.9 (4.9)	413.6 (31.6)	74.5 (4.3)
30	570.0 (35.7)	98.7 (3.8)	981.1 (93.9)	67.9 (4.1)	464.3 (27.5)	98.2 (4.4)
90	505.9 (50.7)	78.9 (5.8)	917.8 (106.9)	63.4 (5.0)	421.8 (38.9)	82.9 (6.2)
180	428.7 (35.2)	65.5 (3.4)	798.2 (77.2)	57.8 (3.9)	350.3 (25.5)	67.0 (3.2)
240	445.1 (40.4)	65.6 (3.7)	846.8 (90.6)	59.0 (4.3)	349.8 (32.1)	63.9 (4.0)
360	**418.7 (46.1)**	**58.9 (4.3)**	**820.7 (97.7)**	**55.2 (5.2)**	**329.3 (36.6)**	**58.4 (4.7)**

Table 9. MLP performance with features per memory size (14-day window, 7-day prediction)

	Overall		Waves		Normal	
Memory	MAE	MAPE	MAE	MAPE	MAE	MAPE
1	**284.7 (11.1)**	**35.4 (2.9)**	**603.1 (15.4)**	**38.8 (2.0)**	**238.7 (13.5)**	**43.3 (5.5)**
30	513.8 (13.4)	84.9 (0.9)	880.1 (37.3)	56.1 (2.0)	440.2 (11.3)	94.4 (4.4)
90	622.8 (3.7)	132.2 (0.9)	912.2 (5.6)	51.9 (1.4)	581.1 (13.6)	158.2 (7.1)
180	702.7 (2.0)	142.5 (0.6)	1071.6 (2.2)	57.2 (0.6)	580.3 (7.9)	147.6 (4.5)
240	696.7 (3.5)	134.2 (0.9)	1115.2 (5.5)	57.3 (1.4)	537.8 (13.8)	130.1 (6.9)
360	651.0 (2.2)	110.4 (0.6)	1181.4 (2.5)	57.0 (0.6)	496.7 (8.1)	107.7 (4.6)

5.5 Comparative Study

This section aims to compare the best MLP experiments in this study to the traditional forecasting ARIMA method. Results refer to overall, wave and normal periods, as well as each wave. For next-day predictions, they are reported in Table 10 and Table 11, and for 14-day predictions in Table 12 and Table 13. Next-day prediction learning curves for the two models are shown in Fig. 3.

It is observed that for next-day predictions, the neural network outperforms ARIMA at Waves 4 and Wave 5 (Table 11), with MAE of 529.1 (against 557.1) at Wave 4 and MAE of 371.5 (against 385.4) at Wave 5. For 14-day predictions, MLP captures the data distribution shift at Wave 4 (Table 13) better than ARIMA with MAE of 1209 (against 1433.5).

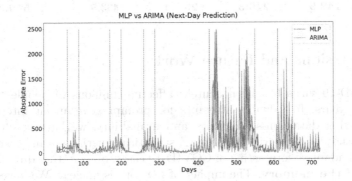

Fig. 3. MLP vs ARIMA (next-day prediction)

Table 10. MLP vs ARIMA (next-day prediction)

	Overall		Waves		Normal	
Model	MAE	MAPE	MAE	MAPE	MAE	MAPE
MLP	186.1 (47.4)	26.3 (14.3)	378.4 (62.5)	25.5 (9.1)	148.2 (50.4)	26.7 (17.9)
ARIMA	176.2	20.3	371.7	20.5	137.6	19.6

Table 11. MLP vs ARIMA per wave (next-day prediction)

	Wave 1	Wave 2	Wave 3	Wave 4	Wave 5
Model	MAE	MAE	MAE	MAE	MAE
MLP	167.3 (131.5)	168.2 (174.4)	206.4 (264.4)	**529.1 (13.8)**	**371.5 (18.2)**
ARIMA	103.5	123.5	128.4	557.1	385.4

Table 12. MLP vs ARIMA (14-day prediction)

	Overall		Waves		Normal	
Model	MAE	MAPE	MAE	MAPE	MAE	MAPE
MLP	418.7 (46.1)	58.9 (4.3)	**820.7 (97.7)**	55.2 (5.2)	329.3 (36.6)	58.4 (4.7)
ARIMA	412.7	42.8	861.6	48.3	322.6	40.9

Table 13. MLP vs ARIMA per wave (14-day prediction)

	Wave 1	Wave 2	Wave 3	Wave 4	Wave 5
Model	MAE	MAE	MAE	MAE	MAE
MLP	247.6 (29.2)	339.8 (50.5)	392.5 (58.8)	**1209.0 (153.5)**	767.4 (65.4)
ARIMA	142.9	246.3	297.9	1433.5	**569.3**

6 Conclusions and Future Work

The COVID-19 virus has been acutely affecting millions of people for more than three years. In valuable attempts for prompt government interventions and addressing data non-stationarity and availability, we have conducted an empirical study of data-driven (learning, statistical) methods using incremental training for adaptive forecasting of COVID-19 cases. Some future directions are:

Role of the memory. The impact of memory is unclear. We have demonstrated its effectiveness on the performance of MLP with raw data, however, performance declined for MLP with features. Future work will investigate this.

Statistical models with features. In this study we examine the impact of features in MLP. We plan to use ARIMAX [1] to incorporate features to ARIMA.

Advanced neural architectures. Future work will investigate more complex neural architectures, such as, autoregressive networks and LSTMs.

References

1. Aji, B.S., Rohmawati, A.A., et al.: Forecasting number of Covid-19 cases in Indonesia with arima and arimax models. In: 2021 9th International Conference on Information and Communication Technology (ICoICT), pp. 71–75. IEEE (2021)
2. Alassafi, M.O., Jarrah, M., Alotaibi, R.: Time series predicting of Covid-19 based on deep learning. Neurocomputing **468**, 335–344 (2022)
3. Boyd, I., Hedges, D., Carter, B.T., Whitaker, B.M.: Using neural networks to model the spread of COVID-19. In: 2022 Intermountain Engineering, Technology and Computing (IETC), IEEE (2022)
4. Calafiore, G.C., Novara, C., Possieri, C.: A time-varying SIRD model for the Covid-19 contagion in Italy. Annu. Rev. Control. **50**, 361–372 (2020)
5. Camargo, E., Aguilar, J., Quintero, Y., Rivas, F., Ardila, D.: An incremental learning approach to prediction models of SEIRD variables in the context of the COVID-19 pandemic. Health Technol. (Berl.) **12**(4), 867–877 (2022)

6. Ditzler, G., Roveri, M., Alippi, C., Polikar, R.: Learning in nonstationary environments: a survey. IEEE Comput. Intell. Mag. **10**(4), 12–25 (2015)
7. Farooq, J., Bazaz, M.A.: A novel adaptive deep learning model of Covid-19 with focus on mortality reduction strategies. Chaos Solitons Fractals **138**(110148), 110148 (2020)
8. Farooq, J., Bazaz, M.A.: A deep learning algorithm for modeling and forecasting of COVID-19 in five worst affected states of India. Alex. Eng. J. **60**(1), 587–596 (2021)
9. He, K., Zhang, X., Ren, S., Sun, J.: Delving deep into rectifiers: Surpassing human-level performance on ImageNet classification. In: Proceedings of the IEEE International Conference on Computer Vision, pp. 1026–1034 (2015)
10. IHME COVID-19 Forecasting Team: Modeling COVID-19 scenarios for the united states. Nat. Med. **27**(1), 94–105 (2021)
11. Kermack, W.O., McKendrick, A.G., Walker, G.T.: A contribution to the mathematical theory of epidemics. Proc. Royal Society of London. Series A, Containing Papers of a Math. Phys. Character **115**(772), 700–721 (1927)
12. Ketu, S., Mishra, P.K.: India perspective: CNN-LSTM hybrid deep learning model-based COVID-19 prediction and current status of medical resource availability. Soft. Comput. **26**(2), 645–664 (2022)
13. Kim, M., et al.: Hi-covidnet: Deep learning approach to predict inbound covid-19 patients and case study in south korea. In: Proceedings of the 26th ACM SIGKDD International Conference on Knowledge Discovery & Data Mining, pp. 3466–3473. KDD '20, Association for Computing Machinery, New York, NY, USA (2020)
14. Kingma, D.P., Ba, J.: Adam: A method for stochastic optimization. In: Proceedings of the 3rd International Conference on Learning Representations (ICLR) (2015)
15. Li, M.L., Bouardi, H.T., Lami, O.S., Trikalinos, T.A., Trichakis, N., Bertsimas, D.: Forecasting COVID-19 and analyzing the effect of government interventions. Oper. Res. **71**(4) (2022)
16. Liu, D., et al.: Real-time forecasting of the COVID-19 outbreak in chinese provinces: Machine learning approach using novel digital data and estimates from mechanistic models. J. Med. Internet Res. **22**(8), e20285 (2020)
17. Losing, V., Hammer, B., Wersing, H.: Incremental on-line learning: a review and comparison of state of the art algorithms. Neurocomputing **275**, 1261–1274 (2018)
18. Luo, J., Zhang, Z., Fu, Y., Rao, F.: Time series prediction of COVID-19 transmission in america using LSTM and XGBoost algorithms. Results Phys. **27**(104462), 104462 (Aug2021)
19. Maas, A.L., Hannun, A.Y., Ng, A.Y.: Rectifier nonlinearities improve neural network acoustic models. In: Proceedings of the 30th International Conference on Machine Learning (2013)
20. Malialis, K., Panayiotou, C.G., Polycarpou, M.M.: Online learning with adaptive rebalancing in nonstationary environments. IEEE Trans. Neural Netw. Learn. Syst. **32**(10), 4445–4459 (2021)
21. Malialis, K., Panayiotou, C.G., Polycarpou, M.M.: Nonstationary data stream classification with online active learning and Siamese neural networks. Neurocomputing **512**, 235–252 (2022)
22. Rodríguez, A.: Deepcovid: an operational deep learning-driven framework for explainable real-time Covid-19 forecasting. Proc. AAAI Conf. Artif. Intell. **35**(17), 15393–15400 (2022)
23. Tetteroo, J., Baratchi, M., Hoos, H.H.: Automated machine learning for Covid-19 forecasting. IEEE Access **10**, 94718–94737 (2022)

24. Uchida, T., Yoshida, K.: Concept drift in Japanese Covid-19 infection data. Proc. Comput. Sci. **207**, 380–387 (2022) knowledge-Based and Intelligent Information & Engineering Systems: Proceedings of the 26th International Conference KES2022
25. Zeroual, A., Harrou, F., Dairi, A., Sun, Y.: Deep learning methods for forecasting covid-19 time-series data: a comparative study. Chaos, Solitons & Fractals **140**, 110121 (2020)

An Ensemble Scheme Based on the Optimization of TOPSIS and AdaBoost for In-Class Teaching Quality Evaluation

Junqi Guo[1,2], Aohua Song[1,2(✉)] [iD], Ludi Bai[1], Ziyun Zhao[1,2], and Siyu Zheng[1]

[1] Beijing Normal University, Beijing, China
[2] Engineering Research Center of Intelligent Technology and Educational
Application, Ministry of Education, Beijing, China
`aohuasong@mail.bnu.edu.cn`

Abstract. As artificial intelligence has grown, intelligent technology has steadily been used in the classroom. Intelligent in-class evaluation has gained popularity in recent years. In this study, we apply two models: AE-SIS (Analytic Hierarchy Process-Entropy Weight-TOPSIS) and AW-AB (Adjusted Weight in Adaptive Boosting) to evaluate in-class teaching quality. We provide an ensemble scheme for intelligent in-class evaluation that combines the benefits of the two models. We test the current in-class evaluation criteria using classroom datasets for comparison. The outcomes show how great and successful the suggested plan is.

Keywords: in-class teaching · intelligent evaluation · statistical modeling · machine learning

1 Introduction

Education informatization is a breakthrough that stimulates improvements in the outdated educational system while also supporting students in fully developing themselves. It does this by leveraging several information approaches [15,17], including big data and AI methodology. For instance, Malaysia encourages cloud resources while developing innovative curricula, instructional methods, and learning resources [12]. Japan employs a platform for collaborative home-schooling to raise awareness of electronic textbooks and other learning materials [20]. China has started to gradually digitize education with support from the strong policy. Governments must raise the degree of information infrastructure building and set up a top-notch education support system, according to "The 14th Five-Year-Plan of National Informatization Plan" [1] in 2021. Governments should adopt strategic efforts to hasten the digital education transformation and intelligent updates as well as integrate information technology and educational innovations, according to the "Work Highlights of the Ministry of Education" from 2022 [2].

L. Iliadis et al. (Eds.): ICANN 2023, LNCS 14254, pp. 75–86, 2023.
https://doi.org/10.1007/978-3-031-44207-0_7

In related research, intelligent education quality evaluation is a crucial component of education informatization. It may evaluate learning outcomes, evaluate teaching quality, and help intelligent systems manage instruction. The observation-based scale method and the questionnaire-based research method, both of which are manual processes, are the two types of in-class teaching quality evaluation techniques that are traditionally used [9]. As a result of the assessor's subjective elements, it is impossible to draw a more unbiased and trustworthy conclusion. Also, it would take more time and effort to manually create questionnaires and observe teaching. Therefore, how to make education quality evaluation more intelligent has become a research hotpot [19].

The Distance Education Center at Beijing Normal University, for instance, has developed a methodology for measuring student involvement in distant learning based on LMS data that considers four factors [10], including online participation and interaction. To gauge student learning, the New Future firm created the Wisroom smart classroom system [18]. The Gradescope platform was developed by the University of California's Department of Computer Science to assist teachers in classifying and revising more than 250 million student assignments [11]. However, most current intelligent systems are analytic techniques such as behavior recognition, and in-class teaching quality models are scarce and have yet to be evaluated. To address the above problem, we propose an ensemble scheme for intelligent in-class evaluation.

2 Background

2.1 Statistical Learning

The Analytic Hierarchy Process and the Entropy Weight Method. By reducing complex problems down into smaller, more manageable components, the Analytic Hierarchy Process (AHP) [13] assists people and organisations in prioritising and making decisions. It entails building a hierarchy of choice criteria and options, then performing pairwise comparisons to ascertain their relative weight. The Entropy Weight Method (EWM) [3,21], a multi-criteria decision analysis technique, uses information theory and entropy to evaluate the relative weight of selection criteria. It works by assessing the degree of diversity or uncertainty among the selection criteria and assigning weights based on the importance of each criterion.

TOPSIS. In the Technique for Order Preference by Similarity to an Ideal Solution (TOPSIS), the solutions are ranked according to how closely they resemble the ideal answer.

Denote n as the number of samples, m as the number of features, and x_{ij} as the j_{th} feature of the i_{th} sample. The steps for using the TOPSIS method to perform the calculations are listed as follows:

(1) Regularization. Features need to be classified into four categories: extremely large features (larger is better), extremely small features (smaller is

better), intermediate features (closer to a certain value is better) and interval features (within a certain range is better). All features that are not extremely large must be transformed into the type where larger features are considered preferable.

(2) Normalization. Normalize all the feature series to eliminate the influence of the magnitude.

(3) Calculation of the distance between each sample and the positive ideal solution and negative ideal solution. Denote $X^+ = \{X_1^+, \ldots, X_m^+\}$ as the positive ideal solution, where X_j^+, $j \in \{1, \ldots, m\}$ is the maximum value of j_{th} feature. Denote $X^- = \{X_1^-, \ldots, X_m^-\}$ as the negative ideal solution, where X_j^-, $j \in \{1, \ldots, m\}$ is the minimum value of j_{th} feature. Denote D_i^+ as the distance between i_{th} sample and X^+, D_i^- as the distance between i_{th} sample and X^-. They are calculated as:

$$D_i^+ = \sqrt{\sum_{j=1}^{m} \left(X_j^+ - x_{ij}\right)^2} \qquad (1)$$

$$D_i^- = \sqrt{\sum_{j=1}^{m} \left(X_j^- - x_{ij}\right)^2} \qquad (2)$$

(4) Calculation of the final score. The final score for each sample is calculated as:

$$S_i = \frac{D_i^-}{D_i^+ + D_i^-} \qquad (3)$$

2.2   Ensemble Learning

Ensemble Learning (EL) is a supervised learning algorithm that has gradually become popular [6]. Freund and Schapire [7] proposed the Adaptive Boosting algorithm (AB), which automatically adjusts the weight of each base learner according to the error rate. All base learners are assigned weights according to error rates to obtain an ensemble learner.

3   Method

3.1   The Analytic Hierarchy Process-Entropy Weight-TOPSIS (AE-SIS) Model

Although the TOPSIS technique reveals sample differences clearly and correctly, it tends to equally weight each aspect or relies on subjective experience, which makes it inadequate for assessing the effectiveness of in-class instruction. As a result, appropriate weights must be provided for each model feature. Using the AHP-EW model with the TOPSIS technique results in more appropriate weights for assessing the quality of classroom instruction because the AHP-EW model incorporates subjective and objective data [16]. The structure of the AE-SIS model is shown in Fig. 1. For different indicators, the specific process of the AE-SIS model is described in Fig. 2.

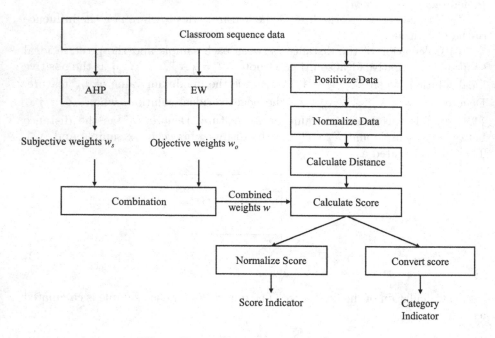

Fig. 1. Framework of the AE-SIS model.

The steps for using the AE-SIS model to evaluate in-class teaching quality are presented as follows:

(1) By the in-class teaching quality evaluation system [8], choose and standardize the features that correspond to the indicators.

(2) Calculate the comprehensive weights of the features. The subjective and objective weights of the features were determined and ranked using the AHP and EWM, respectively. Then, based on the data intensity and order of the objective and subjective weights, the comprehensive weights are decided.

(3) Calculate the scores of the samples. The samples are first evaluated and scored based on TOPSIS. The combined weights derived in the previous step are then introduced in the calculation of the distances to the positive and negative ideal solutions. The updated equation is as follows:

$$D_i^+ = \sqrt{\sum_{j=1}^{m} w_j \left(X_j^+ - x_{ij}\right)^2} \tag{4}$$

$$D_i^- = \sqrt{\sum_{j=1}^{m} w_j \left(X_j^- - x_{ij}\right)^2} \tag{5}$$

where w_j is the comprehensive weight of the j_{th} feature.

(4) Output of the corresponding results. For category indicators, we will compare and analyze the scores of each sample, identify the classification threshold and convert the scores into category results. For the score indicators, the scores need to be normalized so that they meet the requirements.

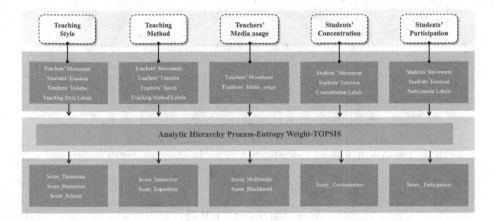

Fig. 2. The AE-SIS-based statistical model for in-class teaching evaluation.

3.2   The Adjusted Weight in Adaptive Boosting (AW-AB) Model

Even while Adaptive Boosting excels at solving classification and regression issues, it is highly sensitive to unusual data. The algorithm will give aberrant samples more weight throughout the iterative training phase, which will change the weight of regular samples and thus result in low accuracy. To increase accuracy, we implement a penalty mechanism to lessen the weight of samples with multiple errors. For different indicators, the specific process of the AE-SIS model is described in Fig. 3.

The steps for using the AW-AB model to evaluate in-class teaching quality are described as follows:

Dataset $A = \{(x_1, y_1), \ldots, (x_n, y_n)\}$, where n is the number of the samples, x_i and y_i are the data and label of the i_{th} sample, respectively. h is the base learner, and c is the number of iterations.

(1) Determination of the base learner and dataset. The corresponding features and dataset are determined according to the indicator system.

(2) Initialization of the sample weights as $\frac{1}{n}$.

(3) The base learner h_c is trained using the current weight W_c, and the error e_c is calculated at each iteration. h_c is calculated as:

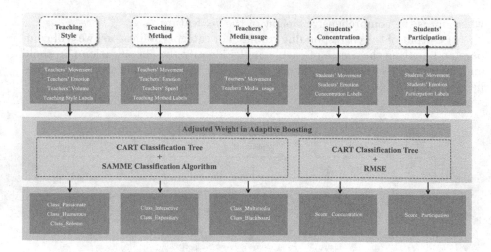

Fig. 3. The AW-AB-based ensemble model for in-class teaching evaluation.

$$h_c = AdaBoost\,(A, W_c) \tag{6}$$

$$e_c = \sum_{i=1}^{N} w_{ci} I\,[h_c(x) \neq y] \tag{7}$$

(4) The weighting factor α_c and normalization factor Z_c are calculated based on e_c. It is calculated as:

$$\alpha_c = \frac{1}{2} \ln \left(\frac{1 - e_c}{e_c} \right) \tag{8}$$

$$Z_c = \sum_{i=1}^{n} W_{ci} e^{-\alpha_c y_i h_c(x_i)} \tag{9}$$

(5) A penalty mechanism is introduced to update the sample weights W_{c+1}. We introduce the weighting threshold th. After a certain iteration, if a sample is assigned weights above this threshold due to a consistently high e_c, the sample will be judged as an anomaly. We then add penalties to reduce the weight of the sample, thus reducing the impact of the sample on the overall model e_c. β is the weight adjustment parameter after the threshold is exceeded. The process is calculated as follows:

(6) Synthetic ensemble learner $H(x)$. The combination of C weak learners into AW-AB ensemble learners is calculated as:

$$H(x) = \text{sign} \left(\sum_{c=1}^{c} \alpha_c h_c(x) \right) \tag{10}$$

Table 1. Formulas for updating weights based on the AW-AB model

Conditions		Weighting update formula
If $h_c(x_i) = y_i$		$W_{c+1} = \dfrac{W_c(i)e^{-\alpha_c}}{Z_c}$
If $h_c(x_i) \neq y_i$	If $W_c(x_i) \leq th$	$W_{c+1} = \dfrac{W_c(i)e^{\alpha_c}}{Z_c}$
	If $W_c(x_i) > th$	$W_{c+1} = \dfrac{W_c(i)e^{\frac{1-\beta}{2}}}{Z_c}$

4   Experiment

4.1   Dataset

We selected 200 sessions of audio and video data of smart informatization class-rooms in primary and secondary schools at Beijing Normal University. After processing by artificial intelligence algorithms such as object detection, speech recognition, and action recognition [4,5,14], we obtained a total of 200 sets of teacher samples and a total of 300 sets of student samples.

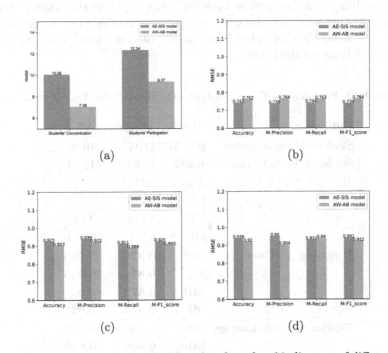

Fig. 4. Performance comparison of students' and teachers' indicators of different models. (a) Performance of students' indicators (b) Performance of teaching style (c) Performance of teaching method (d) Performance of teachers' media_usage.

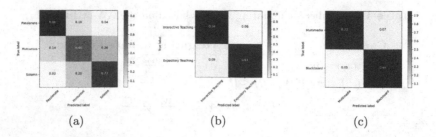

(a)   (b)   (c)

Fig. 5. Confusion matrix for teachers' indicators evaluated by the AE-SIS model. (a) Performance of teaching style (b) Performance of teaching method (c) Performance of teachers' media_usage.

The teacher samples are divided into six categories-movement, emotion, volume, speed, speech text and labels. The student samples are divided into three categories-movement, emotion, and labels. Both teacher data and student emotion data include two categories: laughing or not laughing. Teacher movement data include 9 categories: raising hands, gesturing with both hands, moving around, teaching without gestures, bending over to operate the desktop, holding textbooks, writing on the blackboard, turning over and fingering the multimedia. Student movement data included 5 categories: raising hands, reading, writing, head up, and lying on the table.

Table 2. Performance Comparison of TOPSIS and the AE-SIS model

Indicator	Metric	TOPSIS	AE-SIS
Students' Concentration	RMSE	11.17	10.06
Students' Participation	RMSE	13.99	12.34
Teaching Style	Acc	0.712	0.742
	MP	0.715	0.738
	MR	0.712	0.744
	MF	0.712	0.739
Teaching Method	**Acc**	**0.876**	**0.925**
	MP	**0.878**	**0.925**
	MR	**0.876**	**0.925**
	MF	**0.876**	**0.925**
Teachers' Media_usage	**Acc**	**0.909**	**0.939**
	MP	**0.909**	**0.939**
	MR	**0.909**	**0.939**
	MF	**0.909**	**0.939**

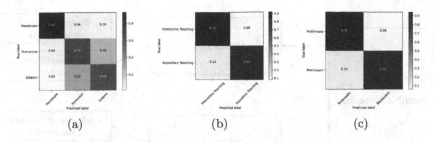

(a)   (b)   (c)

Fig. 6. Confusion matrix for teachers' indicators evaluated by the AE-AB model. (a) Performance of teaching style (b) Performance of teaching method (c) Performance of teachers' media_usage.

Table 3. Performance Comparison of the AB and AW-AB models.

Indicator	Metric	AB	AW-AB
Students' Concentration	**RMSE**	**9.22**	**7.06**
Students' Participation	**RMSE**	**10.66**	**9.37**
Teaching Style	**Acc**	**0.718**	**0.762**
	MP	**0.729**	**0.764**
	MR	**0.718**	**0.763**
	MF	**0.713**	**0.764**
Teaching Method	Acc	0.896	0.903
	MP	0.896	0.904
	MR	0.896	0.904
	MF	0.896	0.903
Teachers' Media_usage	Acc	0.891	0.920
	MP	0.891	0.920
	MR	0.891	0.920
	MF	0.891	0.920

4.2 Results

We drew on the existing evaluation systems as the in-class teaching quality evaluation system for this trial [8]. In this section, we compare the performance of the AE-SIS model, AW-AB model and proposed ensemble model.

Comparison of the AE-SIS and AW-AB Models. Fig. 4(a) shows a comparison of students' indicator evaluations. Figure 4(b)(c)(d) shows a comparison of teachers' indicator evaluations. From the results, we know that two-category classification tasks are simple, that the AE-SIS model fits well, and that the AW-AB model is more suitable for complex tasks such as teaching style classification.

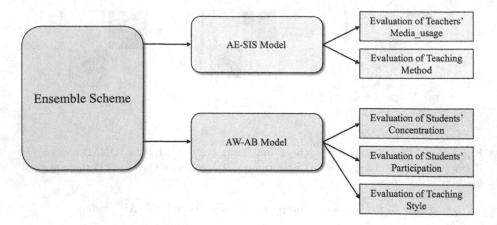

Fig. 7. Framework of the ensemble scheme.

Table 4. Performance Comparison of the Traditional model and Combination model.

Classification	Indicator	Metric	TOPSIS	AdaBoost	Ensemble Scheme
Students' Score Indicators	Students' Concentration	RMSE	11.17	9.22	7.06
	Students' Participation	RMSE	13.99	10.66	9.37
Teachers' Category Indicators	Teaching Style	Acc	0.712	0.718	0.762
		MP	0.715	0.729	0.764
		MR	0.712	0.718	0.763
		MF	0.712	0.713	0.764
	Teaching Method	Acc	0.876	0.896	0.925
		MP	0.878	0.896	0.925
		MR	0.876	0.896	0.925
		MF	0.876	0.896	0.925
	Teachers' Media_usage	Acc	0.909	0.891	0.939
		MP	0.909	0.891	0.939
		MR	0.909	0.891	0.939
		MF	0.909	0.891	0.939

The Results of the AE-SIS Model. The RMSE between the predicted value and the label value of students' concentration is 10.06, and the RMSE of students' participation is 12.34. Figure 5 shows the confusion matrix of the teachers' indicators. Table 2 shows a comparison of the AE-SIS model and TOPSIS method of in-class teaching evaluation. The results show that the proposed AE-SIS model is overall better than the TOPSIS method, which performs well in the classification of teaching methods and teachers' media_usage. The results demonstrate the effectiveness of statistical models in in-class intelligence teaching quality evaluation.

The Results of the AW-AB Model. The RMSE between the predicted value and the label value of students' concentration is 7.058, and the RMSE of students' participation is 9.370. Figure 6 shows a confusion matrix of the teachers' indicators. Table 3 shows a comparison of the AW-AB model and AB model. The proposed AW-AB model has significant improvements in the classification of teaching style and regression task of students' indicators, is better than the AB model. The results demonstrate the advantages of the proposed model in in-class intelligence teaching quality evaluation.

Comparison of the Ensemble Scheme and Traditional Method. Thus, for different indicators, we choose different suitable models to obtain the combination model, as shown in Fig. 7.

Table 4 shows a comparison of our proposed ensemble scheme and the traditional method:TOPSIS and AdaBoost. The ensemble scheme performs better on the in-class student regression tasks and teacher classification tasks.

5 Conclusion

In this study, we propose an ensemble technique for intelligent in-class evaluation, and we experimentally show how better and more efficient it is. The AE-SIS model outperforms the TOPSIS technique via entropy weighting and analytic hierarchy process feature weighting. The AW-AB model outperforms the AdaBoost method by tweaking basic learners' weight updates to lessen the influence of aberrant samples. In addition to providing a more thorough and varied framework than a single model, the ensemble scheme efficiently addresses the issues with traditional in-class teaching evaluation.

References

1. The 14th five-year-plan of national informatization plan was released. Modern Educ. Technol. **32**(1), 15 (2022)
2. Highlights of the ministry of education 2022. www.moe.gov.cn/jyb_sjzl/moe_164/202202/t20220208_597666.html (2022)
3. Bao, Q., Yuxin, Z., Yuxiao, W., Feng, Y.: Can entropy weight method correctly reflect the distinction of water quality indices? Water Resour. Manage **34**(11), 3667–3674 (2020)
4. Bochkovskiy, A., Wang, C.Y., Liao, H.Y.M.: Yolov4: Optimal speed and accuracy of object detection. arXiv preprint arXiv:2004.10934 (2020)
5. Cao, Z., Simon, T., Wei, S.E., Sheikh, Y.: Realtime multi-person 2d pose estimation using part affinity fields. In: Proceedings of the IEEE Conference on Computer Vision and Pattern Recognition, pp. 7291–7299 (2017)
6. Dong, X., Yu, Z., Cao, W., Shi, Y., Ma', Q.: A survey on ensemble learning. Front. Comp. Sci. **14**(2), 241–258 (2020)
7. Freund, Y., Schapire, R.E.: A decision-theoretic generalization of on-line learning and an application to boosting. J. Comput. Syst. Sci. **55**(1), 119–139 (1997)
8. Guo, J., Bai, L., Yu, Z., Zhao, Z., Wan, B.: An AI-application-oriented in-class teaching evaluation model by using statistical modeling and ensemble learning. Sensors **21**(1), 241 (2021)

9. Liu, H., Zhu, Y.: Research on the construction of teaching quality evaluation system. In: J. Phys.: Conf. Series. **1673**, 012055 IOP Publishing (2020)
10. Luan, L., Hong, J.C., Cao, M., Dong, Y., Hou, X.: Exploring the role of online EFL learners' perceived social support in their learning engagement: a structural equation model. Interact. Learn. Environ. 28(9), 1–12 (2020)
11. Singh, A., Karayev, S., Gutowski, K., Abbeel, P.: Gradescope: a fast, flexible, and fair system for scalable assessment of handwritten work. In: Proceedings of the Fourth (2017) ACM Conference on Learning@ Scale, pp. 81–88 (2017)
12. Thang, S.M., Hall, C., Murugaiah, P., Azman, H.: Creating and maintaining online communities of practice in Malaysian smart schools: challenging realities. Educ. Action Res. **19**(1), 87–105 (2011)
13. Vaidya, O.S., Kumar, S.: Analytic hierarchy process: an overview of applications. Eur. J. Oper. Res. **169**(1), 1–29 (2006)
14. Van Lancker, D., Kreiman, J., Wickens, T.D.: Familiar voice recognition: patterns and parameters part II: recognition of rate-altered voices. J. Phon. **13**(1), 39–52 (1985)
15. Wang, B., Xing, H.: The application of cloud computing in education informatization. In: 2011 International Conference on Computer Science and Service System (CSSS), pp. 2673–2676. IEEE (2011)
16. Xing, Y., Zhang, Z., Wu, J., Zhao, H., Tu, C., Xue, C.: Evaluation system of distribution network admission to roof distributed photovoltaic based on ahp-ew-topsis. In: 2021 IEEE 5th Conference on Energy Internet and Energy System Integration (EI2), pp. 1349–1352. IEEE (2021)
17. Yan, S., Yang, Y.: Education informatization 2.0 in China: Motivation, framework, and vision. ECNU Rev. Educ. **4**(2), 410–428 (2021)
18. Yu, T.: A case study on the development strategy of TAL education group. J. Innov. Social Sci. Res. ISSN **2591**, 6890 (2020)
19. Zhu, Z.T.: New development of smart education: From flipped classroom to smart classroom and smart learning space. vol. 22, p. 18 (2016)
20. Zhang, W., Li, Z., Okubayashi, T., Jia, R.: Analysis of the educational informatization policies in Japan and significances for China. Modern Educ. Technol. **27**(3), 5–12 (2017)
21. Zhu, Y., Tian, D., Yan, F.: Effectiveness of entropy weight method in decision-making. Math. Problems Eng. **2020**, 0–5 (2020)

Architecturing Binarized Neural Networks for Traffic Sign Recognition

Andreea Postovan and Mădălina Eraşcu[✉]

Faculty of Mathematics and Informatics, West University of Timisoara, 4 blvd. V.,
Parvan 300223, Romania
{andreea.postovan99,madalina.erascu}@e-uvt.ro

Abstract. Traffic signs support road safety and managing the flow of traffic, hence are an integral part of any vision system for autonomous driving. While the use of deep learning is well-known in traffic signs classification due to the high accuracy results obtained using convolutional neural networks (CNNs) (state of the art is 99.46%), little is known about binarized neural networks (BNNs). Compared to CNNs, BNNs reduce the model size and simplify convolution operations and have shown promising results in computationally limited and energy-constrained devices which appear in the context of autonomous driving.

This work presents a bottom-up approach for architecturing BNNs by studying characteristics of the constituent layers. These constituent layers (binarized convolutional layers, max pooling, batch normalization, fully connected layers) are studied in various combinations and with different values of kernel size, number of filters and of neurons by using the German Traffic Sign Recognition Benchmark (GTSRB) for training. As a result, we propose BNNs architectures which achieve an accuracy of more than 90% for GTSRB (the maximum is 96.45%) and an average greater than 80% (the maximum is 88.99%) considering also the Belgian and Chinese datasets for testing. The number of parameters of these architectures varies from 100k to less than 2M. The accompanying material of this paper is publicly available at https://github.com/apostovan21/BinarizedNeuralNetwork.

Keywords: binarized neural networks · XNOR architectures · traffic sign classification · GTSRB

1 Introduction

Traffic signs are important both in city and highway driving for supporting road safety and managing the flow of traffic. Therefore, *traffic sign classification (recognition)* is an integral part of any vision system for autonomous driving. It consists of: *a)* isolating the traffic sign in a bounding box, and *b)* classifying the sign into a specific traffic class. This work focuses on the second task.

This work was supported by a grant of the Romanian National Authority for Scientific Research and Innovation, CNCS/CCCDI - UEFISCDI, project number PN-III-P1-1.1-TE-2021-0676, within PNCDI III.

L. Iliadis et al. (Eds.): ICANN 2023, LNCS 14254, pp. 87–98, 2023.
https://doi.org/10.1007/978-3-031-44207-0_8

Building a traffic sign classifier is challenging as it needs to cope with complex real-world traffic scenes. A well-know problem of the classifiers is the lack of *robustness* to *adversarial examples* [29] and to occlusions [30]. *Adversarial examples* are traffic signs taken as input which produce erroneous outputs and, together with *occlusions*, they naturally occur because the traffic scenes are unique in terms of weather conditions, lighting, aging.

One way to alleviate the lack of robustness is to formally verify that the trained classifier is robust to adversarial and occluded examples. For constructing the trained model, binary neural networks (BNNs) have shown promising results [14] even in computationally limited and energy-constrained devices which appear in the context of autonomous driving. BNNs are neural networks (NNs) with weights and/or activations binarized and constrained to ±1. Compared to NNs, they reduce the model size and simplify convolution operations utilized in image recognition task.

Our long term goal, which also motivated this work, is to give formal guarantees of properties (e.g. robustness) which are true for a trained classifier. The formal *verification problem* is formulated as follows: given a trained model and a property to be verified for the model, does the property hold for that model? To do so, the model and the property are translated into a constrained satisfaction problem and use, in principle, existing tools to solve the problem [22]. However, the problem is NP-complete [17], so experimentally beyond the reach of general-purpose tool.

This work makes an attempt to arrive at BNN architectures specifically for traffic signs recognition by making an extensive study of variation in accuracy, model size and number of parameters of the produced architectures. In particular, we are interested in BNNs architectures with high accuracy and small model size in order to be suitable in computationally limited and energy-constrained devices but, at the same time, reduced number of parameters in order to make the verification task easier. A bottom-up approach is adopted to design the architectures by studying characteristics of the constituent layers of internal blocks. These constituent layers are studied in various combinations and with different values of kernel size, number of filters and of neurons by using the German Traffic Sign Recognition Benchmark (GTSRB) for training. For testing, similar images from GTSRB, as well as from Belgian and Chinese datasets were used.

As a result of this study, we propose the network architectures (see Sect. 6) which achieve an accuracy of more than 90% for GTSRB [13] and an average greater than 80% considering also the Belgian [1] and Chinese [3] datasets, and for which the number of parameters varies from 100k to 2M.

2   Related Work

Traffic Sign Recognition Using CNNs. Traffic sign recognition (TSR) consists in predicting a label for the input based on a series of features learned by the trained classifier. CNNs were used in traffic sign classification since long time ago [8,27]. These works used GTSRB [13] which is maintained and used on a large scale also nowadays. Paper [8] obtained an accuracy of 99.46% on the test images which is better than the human performance of 98.84%, while [27] with 98.31% was very close. These accuracies were obtained either modifying traditional models for image recognition (e.g. ResNet [27]) or coming up with new ones (e.g. multi-column deep neural network [8]). The architecture from [8] (see Fig. 1) contains a number of parameters much higher than those of the models trained by us and it is not amenable for verification although the convolutional layers would be quantized. The work of [8] is still state of the art for TSR using CNNs.

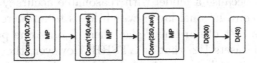

Fig. 1. Architecture for recognizing traffic signs [8]. Image sz: 48×48 (px $\times$ px)

Binarized Neural Networks Architectures. Quantized neural networks (QNNs) are neural networks that represent their weights and activations using low-bit integer variables. There are two main strategies for training QNNs: *post-training quantization* and *quantization-aware training* [18] (QAT). The drawback of the post-training quantization is that it typically results in a drop in the accuracy of the network with a magnitude that depends on the specific dataset and network architecture. In our work, we use the second approach which is implemented in Larq library [11]. In QAT, the imprecision of the low-bit fixed-point arithmetic is modeled already during the training process, i.e., the network can adapt to a quantized computation during training. The challenge for QNNs is that they can not be trained directly with stochastic gradient descent (SGD) like classical NNs. This was solved by using the straight-through gradient estimator (STE) approach [15] which, in the forward pass of a training step, applies rounding operations to computations involved in the QNN (i.e. weights, biases, and arithmetic operations) and in the backward pass, the rounding operations are removed such that the error can backpropagate through the network.

BinaryConnect [9] is one of the first works which uses 1-bit quantization of weights during forward and backward propagation, but not during parameter update to maintain accurate gradient calculation during SGD. As an observation, the models used in conjuction with BinaryConnect use only linear layers which is sufficient for MNIST [20] dataset, but convolutional layers for CIFAR-10 [19] and SVHN [24]. Paper [14] binarizes the activations as well. Similarly, for MNIST dataset they use linear layers, while for CIFAR-10, SVHN and ImageNet [10] they use variants of ConvNet, inspired by VGG [28], with the binarization of the activations.

In XNOR-Net [25], both the weights and the inputs to the convolutional and fully connected layers are approximated with binary values which allows an efficient way of implementing convolutional operations. The paper uses ImageNet

dataset in experiments. We use XNOR-Net architectures in our work but for a
new dataset, namely traffic signs.

Research on BNNs for traffic sign detection and recognition is scarce.
Paper [7] uses the binarization of RetinaNet [21] and ITA [6] for traffic sign
detection, in the first phase, and then recognition. Differently, we focus only on
recognition, hence the architectures used have different underlying principles.

Verification of Neural Networks. Properties of neural networks are subject to
verification. In the latest verification competition there are various benchmarks
subject to verification [2], however, there is none involving traffic signs. We
believe that this is because a model with reasonable accuracy for classification
task must contain convolutional layers which leads to an increase of number of
parameters. To the best of our knowledge there is only one paper which deals
with traffic signs datasets [12] that is GTSRB. However, they considered only
subsets of the dataset and their trained models consist of only fully connected
layers with ReLU activation functions ranging from 70 to 1300. They do not
mention the accuracy of their trained models. BNNs [5,23] are also subject to
verification but we did not find works involving traffic signs datasets.

3   Binarized Neural Networks

A BNN [14] is a feedforward network where weights and activations are mainly
binary. [23] describes BNNs as sequential composition of blocks, each block consisting of linear and non-linear transformations. One could distinguish between
internal and *output blocks.*

There are typically several *internal blocks.* The layers of the blocks are chosen
in such a way that the resulting architecture fulfills the requirements of accuracy,
model size, number of parameters, for example. Typical layers in an internal
block are: *1)* linear transformation (LIN), *2)* binarization (BIN), *3)* max pooling
(MP), *4)* batch normalization (BN). A linear transformation of the input vector
can be based on a fully connected layer or a convolutional layer. In our case
is a convolution layer since our experiments have shown that a fully connected
layer can not synthesize well the features of traffic signs, therefore, the accuracy
is low. The linear transformation is followed either by a binarization or a max
pooling operation. Max pooling helps in reducing the number of parameters. One
can swap binarization with max pooling, the result would be the same. We use
this sequence as Larq [11], the library we used in our experiments, implements
convolution and binarization in the same function. Finally, scaling is performed
with a batch normalization operation [16].

There is *one output block* which produces the predictions for a given image.
It consists of a dense layer that maps its input to a vector of integers, one for
each output label class. It is followed by function which outputs the index of the
largest entry in this vector as the predicted label.

We make the observation that, if the MP and BN layers are omitted, then
the input and output of the internal blocks are binary, in which case, also the

input to the output block. The input of the first block is never binarized as it drops down drastically the accuracy.

4 Datasets and Experimental Setting

We use GTSRB [4] for training and testing purposes of various architectures of BNNs. These architectures were also tested with the Belgian data set [1] and the Chinese [3].

GTSRB is a multi-class, single-image dataset. The dataset consists of images of German road signs in 43 classes, ranging in size from 25×25 to 243×225, and not all of them are square. Each class comprises 210 to 2250 images including prohibitory signs, danger signs, and mandatory signs. The training folder contains 39209 images; the remaining 12630 images are selected as the testing set. For training and validation the ratio 80:20 was applied to the images in the train dataset. GTSRB is a challenging dataset even for humans, due to perspective change, shade, color degradation, lighting conditions, just to name a few.

The *Belgium Traffic Signs* dataset is divided into two folders, training and testing, comprising in total 7095 images of 62 classes out of which only 23 match the ones from GTSRB. Testing folder contains few images for each remaining classes, hence, we have used only the images from the training folder which are 4533 in total. The *Chinese Traffic Signs* dataset contains 5998 traffic sign images for testing of 58 classes out of which only 15 match the ones from GTSRB. For our experiments, we performed the following pre-processing steps on the Belgium and Chinese datasets, otherwise the accuracy of the trained model would be very low: *1)* we relabeled the classes from the Belgium, respectively Chinese, datasets such that their common classes with GTSRB have the same label, and *2)* we eliminated the classes not appearing in GTSRB.

In the end, for testing, we have used 1818 images from the Belgium dataset and 1590 from the Chinese dataset.

For this study, the following points are taken into consideration.

1. Training of network is done on Intel Iris Plus Graphics 650 GPU using Keras v2.10.0, Tensorflow v2.10.0 and Larq v0.12.2.
2. From the open-source Python library Larq [11], we used the function QuantConv2D in order to binarize the convolutional layers except the first. Subsequently, we denote it by QConv. The bias is set to False as we observed that does not influence negatively the accuracy but it reduces the number of parameters.
3. Input shape is fixed either to 30×30, 48×48, or 64×64 (px $\times$ px). Due to lack of space, most of the experimental results included are for 30×30, however all the results are available at https://github.com/apostovan21/BinarizedNeuralNetwork.
4. Unless otherwise stated, the number of epochs used in training is 30.
5. Throughout the paper, for max pooling, the kernel is fixed to non-overlapping 2×2 dimension.

6. Accuracy is measured with variation in the number of layers, kernel size, the number of filters and of neurons of the internal dense layer. Various combination of the following values considered are: *(a)* Number of blocks: 2, 3, 4; *(b)* Kernel size: 2, 3, 5; *(c)* Number of filters: 16, 32, 64, 128, 256; *(d)* Number of neurons of the internal dense layer: 0, 64, 128, 256, 512, 1024.
7. ADAM is chosen as the default optimizer for this study. For initial training of deep learning networks, ADAM is the best overall choice [26].

Following section discusses the systematic progress of the study.

5 Proposed Methodology

We recall that the goal of our work is to obtain a set of architectures for BNNs with high accuracy but at the same time with small number of parameters for the scalability of the formal verification. At this aim, we proceed in two steps. First, we propose two simple two internal blocks XNOR architectures[1] (Sect. 5.1). We train them on a set of images from GTSRB dataset and test them on similar images from the same dataset. We learned that MP reduces drastically the accuracy while the composition of a convolutional and binary layers (QConv) learns well the features of traffic signs images. In Sect. 5.2.1, we restore the accuracy lost by adding a BN layer after the MP one. At the same time, we try to increase the accuracy of the architecture composed by blocks of the QConv layer only by adding a BN layer after it.

Second, based on the learnings from Sects. 5.1 and 5.2.1, as well as on the fact that a higher number of internal layers typically increases the accuracy, we propose several architectures (Sect. 5.2.2). Notable are those with accuracy greater than 90% for GTSRB and an average greater than 80% considering also the Belgian and Chinese datasets, and for which the number of parameters varies from 100k to 2M.

5.1 XNOR Architectures

We consider the two XNOR architectures from Fig. 2. Each is composed of two internal blocks and an output dense (fully connected) layer. Note that, these architectures have only binary parameters. For the GTSRB, the results are in Table 1. One could observe that a simple XNOR architecture gives accuracy of at least 70% as long as MP layers are not present but the number of parameters and the model size are high. We can conclude that QConv synthesizes the features well. However, MP layers reduce the accuracy tremendously.

5.2 Binarized Neural Architectures

5.2.1 Two Internal Blocks

As of Table 1, the number of parameters for an architecture with MP layers is at least 15 times less than in a one without, while the size of the binarized models

---

[1] An XNOR architecture [25] is a deep neural network where both the weights and the inputs to the convolutional and fully connected layers are approximated with binary values.

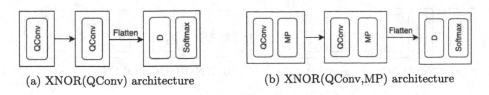

(a) XNOR(QConv) architecture   (b) XNOR(QConv,MP) architecture

Fig. 2. XNOR architectures

Table 1. XNOR(QCONV) and XNOR(QCONV, MP) architectures. Image size: 30px × 30px. Dataset for train and test: GTSRB.

Model description	Acc	#Binary Params	Model Size (in KiB)	
			Binary	Float-32
QConv(32, 3×3), QConv(64, 2×2), D(43)	77.91	2015264	246.5	7874.56
QConv(32, 3×3), MP(2×2), QConv(64, 2×2), MP(2×2), D(43)	5.46	108128	13.2	422.38
QConv(64, 3×3), QConv(128, 2×2), D(43)	70.05	4046912	495.01	15810.56
QConv(64, 3×3), MP(2×2), QConv(128, 2×2), MP(2×2) D(43)	10.98	232640	28.4	908.75
QConv(16, 3×3), QConv(32, 2×2), D(43)	81.54	1005584	122.75	3932.16
QConv(16, 3×3), MP(2×2), QConv(32, 2×2), MP(2×2), D(43)	1.42	52016	6.35	203.19

is approx. 30 times less than the 32 bits equivalent. Hence, to benefit from these two sweet spots, we propose a new architecture (see Fig. 3b) which adds a BN layer in the second block of the XNOR architecture from Fig. 2b. The increase in accuracy is considerable (see Table 2)[2]. However, a BN layer following a binarized convolution (see Fig. 3a) typically leads to a decrease in accuracy (see Table 3). The BN layer introduces few real parameters in the model as well as a slight increase in the model size. This is because only one BN layer was added. Note that the architectures from Fig. 3 are not XNOR architectures.

5.2.2 Several Internal Blocks

Based on the results obtained in Sects. 5.1 and 5.2.1, firstly, we trained an architecture where each internal block contains a BN layer only after the MP (see Fig. 4a). This is based on the results from Tables 2 (the BN layer is crucial after MP for accuracy) and 3 (BN layer after QConv degrades the accuracy). There is an additional internal dense layer for which the number of neurons varies in the set {64, 128, 256, 512, 1028}. The results are in Table 4. One could observe that the conclusions drawn from the 2 blocks architecture do not persist. Hence, motivated also by [14] we propose the architecture from Fig. 4b.

---

[2] A BN layer following MP is also obtained by composing two blocks of XNOR-Net proposed by [25].

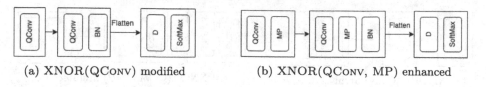

(a) XNOR(QCONV) modified   (b) XNOR(QCONV, MP) enhanced

Fig. 3. BNNs architectures which are not XNOR

Table 2. XNOR(QCONV, MP) enhanced. Image size: 30px ×30px. Dataset for train and test: GTSRB.

Model description	Acc	#Params			Model Size (in KiB)	
		Binary	Real	Total	Binary	Float-32
QConv(32, 3×3), MP(2×2), QConv(64, 2×2), MP(2×2), BN, D(43)	50.87	108128	128	108256	13.7	422.88
QConv(64, 3×3), MP(2×2), QConv(128, 2×2), MP(2×2), BN, D(43)	36.96	232640	256	232896	29.4	909.75
QConv(16, 3×3), MP(2×2), QConv(32, 2×2), MP(2×2), BN, D(43)	39.55	52016	64	52080	6.6	203.44

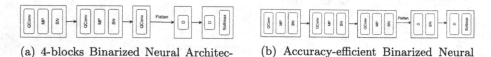

(a) 4-blocks Binarized Neural Architecture   (b) Accuracy-efficient Binarized Neural Architectures

Fig. 4. Binarized Neural Architectures

6   Experimental Results and Discussion

The best accuracy for GTSRB and Belgium datasets is 96, 45 and 88, 17, respectively, and was obtained for the architecture from Fig. 5, with input size 64 × 64 (see Table 5). The number of parameters is almost 2M and the model size 225, 67 KiB (for the binary model) and 6932, 48 KiB (for the Float-32 equivalent). There is no surprise the same architecture gave the best results for GTSRB and Belgium since they belong to the European area. The best accuracy for Chinese dataset (83, 9%) is obtained by another architecture, namely from Fig. 6, with input size 48 × 48 (see Table 6). This architecture is more efficient from the point of view of computationally limited devices and formal verification having 900k parameters and 113, 64 KiB (for the binary model) and 3532, 8 KiB (for the Float-32 equivalent). Also, the second architecture gave the best average accuracy and the decrease in accuracy for GTSRB and Belgium is small, namely 1, 17% and 0, 39%, respectively.

If we investigate both architectures based on confusion matrix results, for GTSRB we observe that the model failed to predict, for example, the *End of speed limit 80* and *Bicycle Crossing*. The first was confused the most with *Speed limit (80 km/h)*, the second with *Children crossing*. One reason for the first confu-

Table 3. XNOR(QCONV) modified. Image size: 30px × 30px. Dataset for train and test: GTSRB.

Model description	Acc	#Params			Model Size (in KiB)	
		Binary	Real	Total	Binary	Float-32
QConv(32, 3×3), QConv(64, 2×2), BN, D(43)	82.01	2015264	128	2015392	246.5	7874.56
QConv(64, 3×3), QConv(128, 2×2), BN, D(43)	69.12	4046912	256	4047168	495.01	15810.56
QConv(16, 3×3), QConv(32, 2×2), BN, D(43)	73.11	1005584	64	1005648	123	3932.16

Table 4. Results for the architecture from the column Model Description. Image size: 30px ×30px. Dataset for train and test: GTSRB.

Model Description	#Neur	#Ep	Acc	#Params			Model size (in KiB)	
				Binary	Real	Total	Binary	Float-32
QConv(32, 5x5), MP(2x2), BN, QConv(64, 5x5), MP(2x2), BN, QConv(64, 3x3), D(#Neur), D(43)	0	30	41.17	101472	192	101664	13.14	397.12
		100	52.17					
	64	30	4.98	109600	192	109792	14.13	428.88
		100	5.7					
	128	30	7.03	128736	192	128928	16.46	503.62
		100	5.70					
	256	30	12.43	167008	192	167200	21.14	653.12
		100	8.48					
	512	30	19.82	243552	192	243744	30.48	952.12
		100	32.13					
	1024	30	46.05	396640	192	396832	49.17	1546.24
		100	50.91					

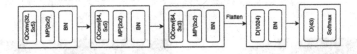

Fig. 5. Accuracy Efficient Architecture for GTSRB and Belgium dataset

sion could be that *End of speed limit (80 km/h)* might be considered the occluded version of *Speed limit (80 km/h)*.

For Belgium test set, the worst results were obtained, for example, for *Bicycle crossing* and *Wild animals crossing* because the images differ a lot from the images on GTSRB training set (see Fig. 7a). Another bad prediction is for *Double Curve* which was equally confused with *Slippery road* and *Children crossing*.

In the Chinese test set, the *Traffic signals* failed to be predicted at all by the model proposed by us and was assimilated with the *General Caution* class from the GTSRB, however *General Caution* is not a class in the Chinese test set (see Fig. 7b, top). Another bad prediction is for *Speed limit (80 km/h)* which was equally confused with *Speed limit (30 km/h), Speed limit (50 km/h)* and *Speed limit (60 km/h)* but not with *Speed limit (70 km/h)*. One reason could be the quality of the training images compared to the test ones (see Fig. 7b, bottom).

Table 5. Results for the architecture from Fig. 5. Dataset for train: GTSRB.

Input size	#Neur	Accuracy			#Params			Model Size (in KiB)	
		German	China	Belgium	Binary	Real	Total	Binary	Float-32
64px × 64px	0	93.83	77.86	79.75	159264	320	159584	20.69	623.38
	64	94.43	75.09	82.39	195616	448	196064	25.63	765.88
	128	95.42	74.71	83.44	300768	576	301344	38.96	1177.60
	256	94.75	80.37	81.40	511072	832	511904	65.64	1996.80
	512	95.65	78.49	85.64	931680	1344	933024	118.98	3645.44
	1024	**96.45**	**81.50**	**88.17**	1772896	2368	1775264	225.67	6932.48

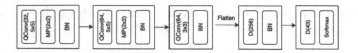

Fig. 6. Accuracy Efficient Architecture for Chinese dataset

Table 6. Results for the architecture from Fig. 6. Dataset for train: GTSRB.

Input size	#Neur	Accuracy			#Params			Model Size (in KiB)	
		German	China	Belgium	Binary	Real	Total	Binary	Float-32
48px × 48px	0	94.67	82.13	83.16	225312	320	225632	28.75	881.38
	64	94.56	82.38	85.75	293920	448	294368	37.63	1146.88
	128	95.02	81.50	87.45	497376	576	497952	62.96	1945.60
	256	**95.28**	**83.90**	**87.78**	904288	832	905120	113.64	3532.80
	512	95.90	76.22	87.34	1718112	1344	1719456	214.98	6717.44
	1024	95.37	81.76	86.74	3345760	2368	3348128	417.67	13076.48

(a) Difference between Belgium (left) and GRSRB (right) dataset

(b) Difference between Chinese (left) and GRSRB (right) dataset

Fig. 7. Differences between traffic sign in the datasets

In conclusion, there are few cases when the prediction failures can be explained, however the need for formal verification guarantees of the results is urgent which we will be performed as future work.

References

1. Belgian Traffic Sign Database. www.kaggle.com/datasets/shazaelmorsh/trafficsigns. Accessed March 25 2023
2. Benchmarks of the 3rd International Verification of Neural Networks Competition (VNN-COMP'22). www.github.com/ChristopherBrix/vnncomp2022_benchmarks. Accessed Feb 22 2023
3. Chinese Traffic Sign Database. www.kaggle.com/datasets/dmitryyemelyanov/chinese-traffic-signs. Accessed March 25 2023
4. German Traffic Sign Recognition Benchmark. www.kaggle.com/datasets/meowmeowmeowmeowmeow/gtsrb-german-traffic-sign?datasetId=82373&language=Python. Accessed March 25 2023
5. Amir, G., Wu, H., Barrett, C., Katz, G.: An SMT-based approach for verifying binarized neural networks. In: TACAS 2021. LNCS, vol. 12652, pp. 203–222. Springer, Cham (2021). https://doi.org/10.1007/978-3-030-72013-1_11
6. Chen, E.H., Röthig, P., Zeisler, J., Burschka, D.: Investigating low level features in CNN for traffic sign detection and recognition. In: 2019 IEEE Intelligent Transportation Systems Conference (ITSC), pp. 325–332. IEEE (2019)
7. Chen, E.H., et al.: Investigating Binary Neural Networks for Traffic Sign Detection and Recognition. In: 2021 IEEE Intelligent Vehicles Symposium (IV), pp. 1400–1405. IEEE (2021)
8. Ciregan, D., Meier, U., Schmidhuber, J.: Multi-column deep neural networks for image classification. In: 2012 IEEE Conference on Computer Vision and Pattern Recognition, pp. 3642–3649. IEEE (2012)
9. Courbariaux, M., Bengio, Y., David, J.P.: BinaryConnect: Training deep neural networks with binary weights during propagations. Adv. Neural Inform. Process. Syst. **28** (2015)
10. Deng, J., Dong, W., Socher, R., Li, L.J., Li, K., Fei-Fei, L.: ImageNet: a large-scale hierarchical image database. In: 2009 IEEE Conference on Computer Vision and Pattern Recognition, pp. 248–255. Ieee (2009)
11. Geiger, L., Team, P.: Larq: an open-source library for training binarized neural networks. J. Open Source Softw. **5**(45), 1746 (2020)
12. Guo, X., Zhou, Z., Zhang, Y., Katz, G., Zhang, M.: OccRob: Efficient SMT-Based Occlusion Robustness Verification of Deep Neural Networks. arXiv preprint arXiv:2301.11912 (2023)
13. Houben, S., Stallkamp, J., Salmen, J., Schlipsing, M., Igel, C.: Detection of traffic signs in real-world images: the German traffic sign detection benchmark. In: The 2013 International Joint Conference on Neural Networks (IJCNN), pp. 1–8. IEEE (2013)
14. Hubara, I., Courbariaux, M., Soudry, D., El-Yaniv, R., Bengio, Y.: Binarized neural networks. Adv. Neural Inform. Process. Syst. **29** (2016)
15. Hubara, I., Courbariaux, M., Soudry, D., El-Yaniv, R., Bengio, Y.: Quantized neural networks: training neural networks with low precision weights and activations. J. Mach. Learn. Res. **18**(1), 6869–6898 (2017)

16. Ioffe, S., Szegedy, C.: Batch Normalization: accelerating deep network training by reducing internal covariate shift. In: International Conference on Machine Learning, pp. 448–456. PMLR (2015)
17. Katz, G., Barrett, C., Dill, D.L., Julian, K., Kochenderfer, M.J.: Reluplex: an efficient SMT solver for verifying deep neural networks. In: Majumdar, R., Kunčak, V. (eds.) CAV 2017. LNCS, vol. 10426, pp. 97–117. Springer, Cham (2017). https://doi.org/10.1007/978-3-319-63387-9_5
18. Krishnamoorthi, R.: Quantizing Deep Convolutional Networks for Efficient Inference: A whitepaper. arXiv preprint arXiv:1806.08342 (2018)
19. Krizhevsky, A., Hinton, G., et al.: Learning Multiple Layers of Features from Tiny Images (2009)
20. LeCun, Y.: The MNIST Database of Handwritten Digits. www.yann.lecun.com/exdb/mnist/ (1998)
21. Lin, T.Y., Goyal, P., Girshick, R., He, K., Dollár, P.: Focal Loss for Dense Object Detection. In: Proceedings of the IEEE International Conference on Computer Vision, pp. 2980–2988 (2017)
22. de Moura, L., Bjørner, N.: Z3: an efficient SMT solver. In: Ramakrishnan, C.R., Rehof, J. (eds.) TACAS 2008. LNCS, vol. 4963, pp. 337–340. Springer, Heidelberg (2008). https://doi.org/10.1007/978-3-540-78800-3_24
23. Narodytska, N.: Formal analysis of deep binarized neural networks. In: IJCAI, pp. 5692–5696 (2018)
24. Netzer, Y., Wang, T., Coates, A., Bissacco, A., Wu, B., Ng, A.Y.: Reading Digits in Natural Images with Unsupervised Feature Learning (2011)
25. Rastegari, M., Ordonez, V., Redmon, J., Farhadi, A.: XNOR-Net: ImageNet classification using binary convolutional neural networks. In: Leibe, B., Matas, J., Sebe, N., Welling, M. (eds.) ECCV 2016. LNCS, vol. 9908, pp. 525–542. Springer, Cham (2016). https://doi.org/10.1007/978-3-319-46493-0_32
26. Ruder, S.: An Overview of Gradient Descent Optimization Algorithms. arXiv preprint arXiv:1609.04747 (2016)
27. Sermanet, P., LeCun, Y.: Traffic sign recognition with multi-scale convolutional networks. In: The 2011 International Joint Conference on Neural Networks, pp. 2809–2813. IEEE (2011)
28. Simonyan, K., Zisserman, A.: Very Deep Convolutional Networks for Large-Scale Image Recognition. arXiv preprint arXiv:1409.1556 (2014)
29. Szegedy, C., et al.: Intriguing Properties of Neural Networks. arXiv preprint arXiv:1312.6199 (2013)
30. Zhang, J., Wang, W., Lu, C., Wang, J., Sangaiah, A.K.: Lightweight deep network for traffic sign classification. Ann. Telecommun. **75**, 369–379 (2020)

Boosting Few-Shot Classification with Lie Group Contrastive Learning

Feihong He and Fanzhang Li[✉] [iD]

School of Computer Science and Technology, Soochow University, 215006 Suzhou,
China
fhheloafei@stu.suda.edu.cn, lfzh@suda.edu.cn

Abstract. Few-shot learning can alleviate the issue of sample scarcity,
however, there remains a certain degree of overfitting. There have been
solutions for this problem by combining contrastive learning with few-
shot learning. In previous works, sample pairs are usually constructed
with traditional augmentation. The fitting of traditional data augmentation methods to real sample distributions poses difficulties. In this
paper, our method employs Lie group transformations for data augmentation, resulting in the model learning more discriminative feature representations. Otherwise, we consider the congruence between contrastive
learning and few-shot learning with respect to classification objectives.
We also incorporate an attention mechanism into the model. Utilizing
the attention module obtained through contrastive learning, the performance of few-shot learning can be improved. Inspired by the loss function
of contrastive learning, we incorporate a penalty term into the loss function for few-shot classification. This penalty term serves to regulate the
similarity between classes and non-classes. We conduct experiments with
two different feature extraction networks on the standard few-shot image
classification benchmark datasets, namely miniImageNet and tieredImageNet. The experimental results show that the proposed method effectively improves the performance of the few-shot classification.

Keywords: Few-shot learning · Contrastive learning · Lie group

1 Introduction

In recent years, deep neural networks perform satisfactorily with the support of
large amounts of data. However, acquiring large amounts of labeled data requires
too many human and financial resources. And, in many sample-sparse domains,
obtaining enough samples for deep neural network training is impossible. Under
such circumstances, deep learning often fails to demonstrate its full efficacy. As
a result of these challenges, there has been significant interest in the field of
few-shot learning [5, 7, 12, 22, 24, 25].

Few-shot learning allows the model to adapt to a task with a very small number of labeled samples. Meta-learning [5, 7, 22, 24, 25] is a popular class of methods

L. Iliadis et al. (Eds.): ICANN 2023, LNCS 14254, pp. 99–111, 2023.
https://doi.org/10.1007/978-3-031-44207-0_9

used in few-shot learning. We usually divide meta-learning into two general directions: optimization-based [7] and metric-based [22]. Specifically, metric learning is used to classify samples by learning transferable feature extraction capabilities on the training set. It learns the feature representation capabilities specific to that task from a small number of samples during the testing phase and constructs a feature space to classify the samples by the metric. In meta-learning, feature extraction networks also suffer from overfitting problems due to sample sparsity. Unsupervised learning is proposed to address the problem of labeled sample scarcity. Contrastive learning is a class of methods for unsupervised learning. Networks trained by contrastive learning exhibit strong generalizations and are commonly used in diverse downstream tasks.

Inspired by the generalization capability of contrastive learning across diverse tasks, we propose a method that combines contrastive learning and meta-learning, aiming to endow meta-learning with enhanced generalization ability. Specifically, we divided the model training into two phases, the contrastive training phase and the meta-training phase. In the contrastive learning phase, we improve the data augmentation method for constructing sample pairs. Typically, traditional image augmentation, such as cropping, flipping, and color distortion, is commonly employed in contrastive learning. Recent works combining contrastive learning and few-shot learning have shown exceptional performance but have relied on traditional image augmentation methods. More powerful image augmentation can facilitate the creation of more diverse sample pairs. More diverse sample pairs enable the model to learn more discriminative expressions. We introduce Lie group transformations in the comparative learning stage to construct more diverse sample pairs. Specifically, we utilize the SO3 group, which conforms to the structure of Lie groups, to implement an image augmentation module. We refer to this module as the Lie transformation. Meanwhile, we incorporated an attention module in the contrastive learning phase. In meta-training phase, we will transfer the attention module trained in the contrastive learning phase. This transfer will enable the sample features to exhibit diverse expressive abilities in the channel dimension. Moreover, we formulate a penalty term based on contrastive learning in the meta-training phase. This penalty term implements inter-class constraints on samples by constructing positive and negative sample pairs based on the support set. The contributions of this paper are as follows:

- · Using the Lie group transformation method, we improve the image augmentation module in contrastive learning. By integrating it with meta-learning, we enhance the sample representation capability of meta-learning.
- · We introduce an attention module and add a penalty term to the meta-learning loss function to correct the deviation of prototype points in the sample space.
- · The result of our experiments on two popular few-shot classification benchmark datasets – miniImagenet and tieredImagenet, demonstrate that our algorithm outperforms state-of-the-art methods significantly on both 1-shot and 5-shot tasks.

2 Related Work

2.1 Few-Shot Learning

We can divide few-shot learning into two categories: initialization-based method and metric-based method. The main idea of initialization-based few-shot learning methods is to find an optimal set of initialization parameters for the model through training on different tasks. These initialization parameters can be trained with a small amount of data and quickly adapt to new tasks to achieve good results. Chelsea Finn et al. proposed a classic model [7] in 2017, pioneering the field of initialization-based few-shot learning methods. The main idea of metric-based few-shot learning methods is to acquire prior knowledge through training the model with a large number of tasks, map the samples to a reasonable space using the prior knowledge, and classify the samples using a predetermined metric method. Prototypical Networks [22], Matching Network [25], and Siamese Network [5] are classic models in metric learning. Many subsequent works are based on the idea of these models and have made improvements. The current metric-based few-shot learning shows excellent performance.

2.2 Contrativate Learning

The two mainstream methods of unsupervised learning currently are contrastive learning and masked image modeling [10,13]. Contrastive learning is an unsupervised learning method that learns representations by contrasting positive and negative data pairs. The goal of contrastive learning is to make the representations of positive pairs similar while making the representations of negative pairs dissimilar. Contrastive learning recently gains a lot of attention in deep learning due to its impressive performance in various computer vision tasks, such as image recognition and object detection. Inst Disc [27] pushes the class discrimination task to the extreme and proposes for the first time an instance discrimination method that achieves remarkable performance in the unsupervised domain. In the unsupervised domain, a large number of contrastive learning works [2,9] emerge and make rapid progress. In our work, we exploit the powerful generalization of contrastive learning to improve the performance of few-shot learning.

2.3 Lie Group Machine Learning

Recent years, Lie groups plays an important role in driving the development of machine learning research. In [28], Lie algebra is used to perform unsupervised augmentation of unlabeled samples and improve the performance of the model using an expanded dataset. In [29], the intrinsic mean of Lie groups is introduced to describe remote sensing images, which better reflects the commonalities of objects and the relationship between feature expressions, thereby achieving better results. In order to preserve shallow features and enhance local features, Lie groups are introduced in [30] to achieve satisfactory results. In our work, we also apply Lie groups to contrastive learning to improve the performance of few-shot learning.

3   Method

In this section, we introduce two parts in detail. In the first part, we introduce the improvement of contrastive learning through Lie group transformations in the contrastive learning phase. And the second part, we present the combination of meta-learning and contrastive learning, which is integrated with attention mechanisms and loss penalty terms.

Fig. 1. Original Image means the image that has not been augmented. Traditional is the image augmented with traditional cropping, flipping, and color transformation. Lie Mean is the image augmented with Lie transformation module and blank filled with image mean. Lie Original is the image augmented with Lie transformation module and blank filled with the original image.

We adopt a traditional few-shot learning setup to evaluate our method. In meta-learning, we usually divide samples into a training set $D_t = \{(x_i, y_i) ; i = 1 \cdots N_t\}$ and a validation set $D_v = \{(x_i, y_i) ; i = 1 \cdots N_v\}$ $(D_t \cap D_v = \emptyset)$. Following the N-way K-shot few-shot learning task setting, we draw N categories from the dataset, with $K + Q$ samples per category. Of these, $N \times K$ samples are used as the support set $D_s = \{(x_{i,j}, y_i); i = 1 \cdots N, j = 1 \cdots K\}$, with their category labels are visible to the model. Where $N \times Q$ samples are used as the query set $D_q = \{(x_{i,j}, y_i); i = 1 \cdots N, j = 1 \cdots Q\}$ and their category labels are not visible to the model.

3.1   Lie Contrative Learning

A Lie group is a mathematical object that simultaneously possesses a group structure and a smooth manifold structure. Firstly, we provide a formal definition for the structure of a Lie group. $(G, \bullet)$ is a group if it satisfies the following conditions:

1. $a \bullet b \in G, \forall a, b \in G$
2. $(a \bullet b) \bullet c = a \bullet (b \bullet c), \forall a, b, c \in G$

3. $\exists e \in G, \forall a \in G, e \bullet a = a \bullet e = a$
4. $\forall a \in G, \exists a^{-1}, a^{-1} \bullet a = a \bullet a^{-1} = e$

When a group structure satisfies the above conditions and it is also a differentiable manifold with the property that the group operations are compatible with the smooth structure, we call it a Lie group. It is commonly understood that matrix multiplication groups consisting of non-singular matrices can form Lie groups.

We define a new image augmentation operator as $r : R^3 \to R^3$. We demand that the operator satisfies the following conditions:

1. $\|r(v)\| = \sqrt{\langle r(v), r(v) \rangle} = \sqrt{\langle v, v \rangle} = \|v\|, \forall v \in R^3$
2. $\langle r(v), r(w) \rangle = \langle v, w \rangle = \|v\|\|w\| \cos \alpha, \forall v, w \in R^3$
3. $u \times v = w \longleftrightarrow r(u) \times r(v) = r(w)$

Based on the above properties, we can define:

$$SO(3) : \{r : R^3 \to R^3 \forall v, w \in R^3, \|r(v)\| = \|v\|, r(v) \times r(w) = r(v \times w)\}$$

Thus, we have obtained a transformation method, denoted by r, for an image in Euclidean space. Specifically, we can obtain a decomposed representation of the operator r by performing a decomposition on it:

$$r = R_x(\alpha) \bullet R_y(\beta) \bullet R_z(\gamma)$$

By decomposing its expression, we can construct a specific operator r based on three parameters α, β and γ:

$$R_x(\alpha) = \begin{bmatrix} 1 & 0 & 0 \\ 0 & \cos \alpha & -\sin \alpha \\ 0 & \sin \alpha & \cos \alpha \end{bmatrix} R_y(\beta) = \begin{bmatrix} \cos \beta & 0 & \sin \beta \\ 0 & 1 & 0 \\ -\sin \beta & 0 & \cos \beta \end{bmatrix} R_z(\gamma) = \begin{bmatrix} \cos \gamma & -\sin \gamma & 0 \\ \sin \gamma & \cos \gamma & 0 \\ 0 & 0 & 1 \end{bmatrix}$$

All possible operators that exist in r form a group structure known as SO3. For the sake of brevity in our exposition, we shall denote this process as $r(x)$. In Fig. 1, we compare the commonly used augmentation methods in contrastive learning and our two augmentation methods.

In contrastive learning phase, we put the samples in the training set through two traditional data augmentations and the random operator r to obtain the augmented samples $\{(r_l(x_i), r_r(x_i)); x_i \in D_t, i = 1 \cdots N_t\}$ after two different data augmentation methods. We treat two augmentations from the same sample as positive pairs, and one of the augmentations with two augmentations from the other sample as negative pairs. We expect more similarity between positive sample pairs and more variability between negative pairs, and have following loss function:

$$L = -\log \frac{\exp(r_l(x_i) \cdot r_r(x_i)/T)}{\sum_{i \neq j} \exp(r(x_i) \cdot r(x_j)/T)}$$

3.2   Attention and Penalty Items

It can be readily comprehended that the loss has a similar geometric meaning as the prototype network loss. In Fig. 2, it is evident that in contrastive learning, the positive sample pairs exhibit a closer distance in the corresponding metric space, whereas the negative sample pairs are farther apart. In prototypical networks, instances of the same class exhibit clustering, while instances of different classes demonstrate dispersion. Due to similar optimization objectives for the loss function, we can enhance the expressive ability of feature channels in meta-learning by training an attention module during the contrastive learning phase. This attention module assigns distinct weights to the embeddings of sample features in different channels. In the meta-learning phase, we transfer this attention module to the meta-learning model to improve the channel-wise representation capability of features in meta-learning.

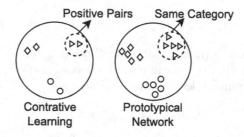

Fig. 2. The figure shows the spatial distribution of samples obtained from comparative learning and the spatial distribution characteristics of samples in the prototypical network (few-shot learning).

In the meta-training phase, we construct a penalty term by defining positive and negative pairs in the support set. Specifically, we consider samples within the support set belonging to the same class as positive pairs, and construct negative pairs from different classes. Therefore, our penalty term can be formulated as:

$$L_c = \frac{\sum_{i=1}^{N} d\left(x_{ip}, x_{iq}\right)}{\sum_{j,k=1}^{N} \sum_{m,n=1}^{K} d\left(x_{jm}, x_{kn}\right)}$$

The d function here represents the measurement method. After adding a penalty term, the meta-training loss can be uniformly expressed as: $L = L_{CE} + tL_c$. The t serves as a hyperparameter that balances the penalty term and cross-entropy loss function.

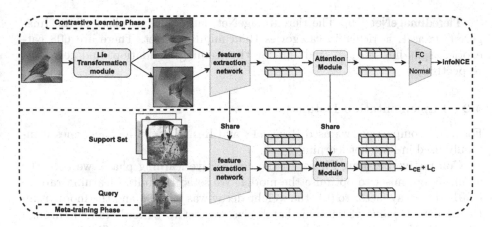

Fig. 3. The overall process framework of our method.

In Fig. 3, we present the overall workflow of the proposed method. Our method divides the training process into two stages: contrastive learning phase and meta-training phase. In the contrastive learning phase, we subject the input samples to two augmentations using a Lie transformation module, and obtain a pair of augmented samples. These augmented samples are first input into a feature extraction network. Then, the output is fed into an attention module, before being processed through two fully connected layers to obtain the sample feature representation. Following the conventional setup of instance discrimination tasks, InfoNCE is computed using sample feature representations to optimize the network. We incorporated attention modules following the feature extraction network in the meta-training phase. We shared the parameters of both the feature extraction network and attention modules trained in the contrastive learning phase, and then optimize the model by incorporating a meta-training loss function with a penalty term.

4   Experiments

In this section, we verify the method's performance through extensive experiments.

4.1   Datasets

We test our method on two public few-shot learning datasets with the 5way-5shot and 5way-1shot tasks, respectively.

MiniImageNet [25]: The miniImageNet dataset is selected from the sizeable visual dataset ImageNet. It contains 100 categories, 600 samples per category, and a total of 60,000 color images. Each image's resolution is set to 84×84. It is partitioned into a training set of 64 categories, a validation set of 16 categories, and a test set of 20 categories.

TieredImageNet [19]: The tieredImageNet dataset, as a subset of the ImageNet dataset, is richer in categories than miniImageNet. There are 608 categories, split into 351, 97 and 160 for the training, validation, and test sets, respectively.

4.2   Implementation Details

For a fair comparison, we used ResNet18 and ResNet12 as the backbones commonly used in few-shot learning.

Contrastive Learning Phase: In the contrastive learning phase, we used the adam [6] optimiser to optimise the model. We seted the initial learning rate to 0.001, the decay factor to 0.1 ,the weight decay was 0.00006 and the momentum to the default value of 0.9. Our batch size was set to 64 and trained through 200 epochs. In the image augmentation phase, we used cropping, flipping, colour transformation and Lie transformation to generate sample pairs. We seted the three randomly generated variables α, β, and γ in the Lie transformation to range between -0.5 and 0.5. We seted the temperature parameter to 0.5 in the loss function of the contrastive learning phase.

Meta-Training Phase: In the meta-training phase, we used the adam [6] optimiser to optimise the model. The optimiser parameters were the same as those used in the comparative learning phase. In the loss function, we seted the temperature parameter t of the penalty term to 0.5. In the 5way-5shot task, we randomly selected 5 categories in the training set. Each category had 5 samples to form the support set and 16 to form the query set. Each task consisted of 105 samples. In the 5way-1shot task, we randomly selected 5 categories in the training set, with 1 sample from each category formed the support set and 16 samples formed the query set. Each task consisted of 85 samples. In 1-shot tasks, the limited number of samples precludes the calculation of penalty terms. We employed Lie transformations to generate auxiliary samples for penalty term computation to address this issue. Each batch contained one task in both the 5shot and 1shot tasks, and there were 100 batches in each epoch, and 400 epochs were used for training.

Evaluation Metric: For the sake of fairness, we followed the assessment scheme unchanged. We evaluate our method with 1000 tasks and report the average accuracy with 95% confidence intervals.

4.3   Results

Following the standard setting, we conducted experiments using ResNet18 as the backbone, employing the original image and mean padding methods to fill the image's blank spaces. We conducted experiments on both miniImagenet and tieredImageNet, and the results are shown in Table 1. The state-of-the-art comparative methods were categorized into Baselines, Optimization-based and Metric-based. As our approach is metric-based, we selected more metric-based models for comparative analysis. We use the Prototypical Network [22] as the baseline, which we re-implemented using ResNet18 as the backbone, and test it

Table 1. FEW-SHOT LEARNING CLASSIFICATION OF RESNET-18 ACCURA-CIES ON MINI-IMAGENET AND TIERED-IMAGENET UNDER THE SETTING OF 5-WAY 1-SHOT AND 5-WAY 5-SHOT WITH 95% CONFIDENCE INTERVAL. ('-' NOT REPORTED)

Model	Backbone	mini-ImageNet		tiered-ImageNet	
		1-shot	*5-shot*	*1-shot*	*5-shot*
Optimization-based					
MAML [7]	Resnet-18	49.68 ± 0.84	65.73 ± 0.83	-	-
LEO [20]	WRN-28-10	61.76 ± 0.08	77.59 ± 0.12	66.33 ± 0.05	81.44 ± 0.09
Metrics-based					
Matching network [25]	Resnet-18	52.92 ± 0.81	68.93 ± 0.65	-	-
Relation network [24]	Resnet-18	52.19 ± 0.83	70.20 ± 0.66	54.48 ± 0.93	71.32 ± 0.78
SimpleShot [26]	Resnet-18	62.92 ± 0.83	79.07 ± 0.70	69.09 ± 0.22	84.58 ± 0.16
Neg-Cosine [15]	Resnet-18	62.31 ± 0.81	80.97 ± 0.55	-	-
TEAM [17]	Resnet-18	60.10 ± 0.24	75.94 ± 0.23	-	-
CTM [14]	Resnet-18	64.12 ± 0.28	80.51 ± 0.86	68.41 ± 0.39	84.28 ± 1.73
TADAM [16]	Resnet-18	58.50 ± 0.60	76.70 ± 0.45	-	-
PFA [18]	Resnet-18	59.60 ± 0.49	73.74 ± 0.36	-	-
CC+rot [8]	WRN-28-10	62.93 ± 0.45	79.87 ± 0.33	62.93 ± 0.45	79.87 ± 0.33
PSST [4]	WRN-28-10	64.16 ± 0.44	80.64 ± 0.32	-	-
Baseline	Resnet-18	61.18 ± 0.74	79.58 ± 0.64	66.82 ± 0.12	80.82 ± 0.53
Ours:LieOrigin	Resnet-18	62.68 ± 0.49	80.41 ± 0.54	67.22 ± 0.42	82.16 ± 0.61
Ours:LieMean	Resnet-18	**64.92** ± 0.52	**82.63** ± 0.62	**69.23** ± 0.34	**84.92** ± 0.63

using the same settings. By observation, our method shows excellent advantages compared to the baseline. Our method also shows better performance compared to optimization-based methods. Compared with the metric-based methods of the same category, [22,24,25] only focus on existing samples and do not solve the problem of sample scarcity, whereas our method expands the sample set and solves the problem to some extent. Our approach exploits the similarity between contrastive learning and metric learning by acquiring a channel attention module during training, enabling it to develop a more discriminative feature. Our method shows better performance in similar methods that exploit the attention mechanism [14,16]. In methods [4,8], which are similar to ours, we use the lie group approach to expand the image set and introduce channel attention to obtain more discriminative features to achieve a more competitive result.

We compare using ResNet-12 as the backbone in the same experimental setup, as shown in Table 2. By observation, our method shows equally competitive experimental results under ResNet-12.

4.4 Ablation Study

This section verifies the effectiveness of the proposed Lie group image augmentation method and attention module through ablation experiments. We used only

Table 2. FEW-SHOT LEARNING CLASSIFICATION OF RESNET-12 ACCURA-CIES ON MINI-IMAGENET AND TIERED-IMAGENET UNDER THE SETTING OF 5-WAY 1-SHOT AND 5-WAY 5-SHOT WITH 95% CONFIDENCE INTERVAL.

Model	Backbone	mini-ImageNet		tiered-ImageNet	
		1-shot	5-shot	1-shot	5-shot
MAML [7]	ConvNet-4	47.78 ± 1.75	64.31 ± 1.1	52.07 ± 0.91	71.10 ± 1.67
Prototypical Network [22]	Resnet-12	60.76 ± 0.39	78.44 ± 0.21	66.25 ± 0.34	80.11 ± 0.91
Cosine Classifier [1]	Resnet-12	55.43 ± 0.81	77.18 ± 0.61	61.49 ± 0.91	82.37 ± 0.67
MTL [23]	Resnet-12	61.20 ± 1.80	75.50 ± 0.80	65.62 ± 1.80	80.61 ± 0.90
TapNet [31]	Resnet-12	61.65 ± 0.15	76.36 ± 0.10	63.08 ± 0.15	80.26 ± 0.12
Meta-Baseline [3]	Resnet-12	63.17 ± 0.23	79.26 ± 0.17	68.62 ± 0.27	83.29 ± 0.18
DSN-MR [21]	Resnet-12	64.60 ± 0.72	79.51 ± 0.50	67.39 ± 0.82	82.85 ± 0.56
MetaOptNet [11]	Resnet-12	62.64 ± 0.61	78.63 ± 0.46	65.99 ± 0.72	81.56 ± 0.63
Ours:LieMean	**Resnet-12**	**64.94 ± 0.62**	**80.22 ± 0.68**	**68.78 ± 0.64**	**83.48 ± 0.58**

ResNet-18 as the feature extractor and the same experimental settings as in the comparison experiments section.

We conducted separate ablation experiments on the mean padding and original image padding Lie group augmentation methods and the attention module employed in the approach. Table 3 shows that the mean padding effect significantly outperforms the original image padding. This may be due to the fact that the positive pairs filled with the original image have a large number of identical features, and the network model found a classification shortcut. This method further improves the model effect and enhances the sample feature representation ability by adding an attention module. Figure 4 shows the Grad-CAM visualization results obtained by our method and prototypical network on the miniImageNet. In the Grad-CAM visualization, our proposed approach demonstrates a stronger capability to focus on the object of interest that requires classification in the image.

Table 3. ABLATION EXPERIMENTS ON MODULE. ('✓' WITH; '-' WITHOUT)

	Lie Group			mini-ImageNet	
	Mean	Origin	AT	1-shot	5-shot
(I)	-	-	-	61.18	79.58
(II)	✓	-	-	63.28	82.52
(III)	-	✓	-	62.32	80.21
(VII)	-	✓	✓	62.68	80.41
(IV)	✓	-	✓	64.92	82.63

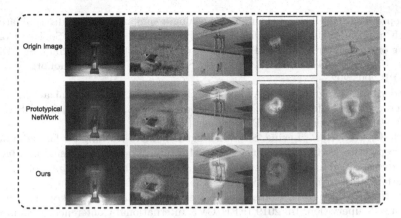

Fig. 4. Grad-CAM visualization of prototypical network and our method sampled randomly from mini-ImageNet.

5 Conclusion

In this paper, we propose a method of few-shot learning based on Lie group contrastive method. Specifically, we are inspired by contrastive learning's strong generalization and use Lie group to improve it. We apply it to few-shot learning to enhance its generalization capabilities. In addition, we use an attention mechanism and a loss penalty term in our approach. They optimize the model regarding sample channels and sample space distribution, respectively. Experimental results show that our method performs significantly on popular few-shot classification benchmark datasets.

Acknowledgments. This work is Supported by the National Key Research and Development Program of China (No. 2018YFA0701700; No. 2018YFA0701701) and National Natural Science Foundation of China (62002253, 62176172, 61672364).

References

1. Chen, W., Liu, Y., Kira, Z., et al.: A closer look at few-shot classification. In: 7th International Conference on Learning Representations, New Orleans, LA, USA, May 6–9, 2019 (2019)
2. Chen, X., Fan, H., Girshick, R., He, K.: Improved baselines with momentum contrastive learning. arXiv preprint arXiv:2003.04297 (2020)
3. Chen, Y., Wang, X., Liu, Z., Xu, H., Darrell, T., et al.: A new meta-baseline for few-shot learning. arXiv preprint arXiv:2003.04390 2(3), 5 (2020)
4. Chen, Z., Ge, J., Zhan, H., et al.: Pareto self-supervised training for few-shot learning. In: IEEE Conference on Computer Vision and Pattern Recognition, virtual, June 19–25, 2021, pp. 13663–13672. Comput. Vision Found. / IEEE (2021). https://doi.org/10.1109/CVPR46437.2021.01345

5. Chopra, S., Hadsell, R., LeCun, Y.: Learning a similarity metric discriminatively, with application to face verification. In: 2005 IEEE Computer Society Conference on Computer Vision and Pattern Recognition, 20–26 June 2005, San Diego, CA, USA, pp. 539–546. IEEE Computer Society (2005). https://doi.org/10.1109/CVPR.2005.202

6. Diederik, P., Kingma, E.A.: Adam: a method for stochastic optimization. In: 3rd International Conference on Learning Representations, San Diego, CA, USA, May 7–9, 2015, Conference Track Proceedings (2015)

7. Finn, C., Abbeel, P., Levine, S.: Model-agnostic meta-learning for fast adaptation of deep networks. In: Proceedings of the 34th International Conference on Machine Learning, Sydney, NSW, Australia, 6–11 August 2017. Proceedings of Machine Learning Research, vol. 70, pp. 1126–1135. PMLR (2017)

8. Gidaris, S., Bursuc, A., Komadakis, N., et al.: Boosting few-shot visual learning with self-supervision. In: 2019 IEEE/CVF International Conference on Computer Vision, Seoul, Korea (South), October 27 - November 2, 2019, pp. 8058–8067. IEEE (2019). https://doi.org/10.1109/ICCV.2019.00815

9. Grill, J., et al.: Bootstrap your own latent - a new approach to self-supervised learning. In: Advances in Neural Information Processing Systems 33: Annual Conference on Neural Information Processing Systems 2020, December 6–12, 2020, virtual (2020)

10. He, K., Chen, X., Xie, S., Li, Y., Dollár, P., Girshick, R.: Masked autoencoders are scalable vision learners. In: Proceedings of the IEEE/CVF Conference on Computer Vision and Pattern Recognition, pp. 16000–16009 (2022)

11. Lee, K., Maji, S., Ravichandran, A., Soatto, S.: Meta-learning with differentiable convex optimization. In: IEEE Conference on Computer Vision and Pattern Recognition, Long Beach, CA, USA, June 16–20, 2019, pp. 10657–10665. Computer Vision Foundation / IEEE (2019). https://doi.org/10.1109/CVPR.2019.01091

12. Li, G., Zheng, C., Su, B.: Transductive distribution calibration for few-shot learning. Neurocomputing **500**, 604–615 (2022)

13. Li, G., Zheng, H., Liu, D., Wang, C., Su, B., Zheng, C.: Semmae: Semantic-guided masking for learning masked autoencoders. arXiv preprint arXiv:2206.10207 (2022)

14. Li, H., Eigen, D., Dodge, S., Zeiler, M., Wang, X.: Finding task-relevant features for few-shot learning by category traversal. In: IEEE Conference on Computer Vision and Pattern Recognition, Long Beach, CA, USA, June 16–20, 2019, pp. 1–10. Computer Vision Foundation / IEEE (2019). https://doi.org/10.1109/CVPR.2019.00009

15. Liu, B., et al.: Negative margin matters: Understanding margin in few-shot classification. In: Computer Vision - ECCV 2020–16th European Conference, Glasgow, UK, August 23–28, 2020, Proceedings, Part IV. Lecture Notes in Computer Science, vol. 12349, pp. 438–455. Springer (2020). https://doi.org/10.1007/978-3-030-58548-8_26

16. Oreshkin, B.N., López, P.R., Lacoste, A.: TADAM: task dependent adaptive metric for improved few-shot learning. In: Advances in Neural Information Processing Systems 31: December 3–8, 2018, Montréal, Canada, pp. 719–729 (2018)

17. Qiao, L., Shi, Y., Li, J., Wang, Y., Huang, T., Tian, Y.: Transductive episodic-wise adaptive metric for few-shot learning. In: 2019 IEEE/CVF International Conference on Computer Vision, Seoul, Korea (South), October 27 - November 2, 2019, pp. 3602–3611. IEEE (2019). https://doi.org/10.1109/ICCV.2019.00370

18. Qiao, S., Liu, C., et al.: Few-shot image recognition by predicting parameters from activations. In: 2018 IEEE Conference on Computer Vision and Pattern Recognition, Salt Lake City, UT, USA, June 18–22, 2018, pp. 7229–7238. Computer Vision Foundation / IEEE Computer Society (2018). https://doi.org/10.1109/CVPR.2018.00755
19. Ren, M., et al.: Meta-learning for semi-supervised few-shot classification. In: 6th International Conference on Learning Representations, Vancouver, BC, Canada, April 30 - May 3, 2018, Conference Track Proceedings. OpenReview.net (2018)
20. Rusu, A.A., et al.: Meta-learning with latent embedding optimization. In: 7th International Conference on Learning Representations, New Orleans, LA, USA, May 6–9, 2019. OpenReview.net (2019)
21. Simon, C., Koniusz, P., Nock, R., Harandi, M.: Adaptive subspaces for few-shot learning. In: 2020 IEEE/CVF Conference on Computer Vision and Pattern Recognition, Seattle, WA, USA, June 13–19, 2020, pp. 4135–4144. Computer Vision Foundation / IEEE (2020). https://doi.org/10.1109/CVPR42600.2020.00419
22. Snell, J., Swersky, K., Zemel, R.: Prototypical networks for few-shot learning. In: Advances in Neural Information Processing Systems 30: December 4–9, 2017, CA, USA, pp. 4077–4087 (2017)
23. Sun, Q., et al.: Meta-transfer learning for few-shot learning. In: IEEE Conference on Computer Vision and Pattern Recognition, USA, June 16–20, 2019, pp. 403–412. Computer Vision Foundation / IEEE (2019). https://doi.org/10.1109/CVPR.2019.00049
24. Sung, F., Yang, Y., Zhang, L., Xiang, T., Torr, P.H., Hospedales, T.M.: Learning to compare: Relation network for few-shot learning. In: 2018 IEEE Conference on Computer Vision and Pattern Recognition, Salt Lake City, UT, USA, June 18–22, 2018, pp. 1199–1208. Computer Vision Foundation / IEEE Computer Society (2018). https://doi.org/10.1109/CVPR.2018.00131
25. Vinyals, O., Blundell, C., Lillicrap, T., Wierstra, D.: Matching networks for one shot learning. In: Advances in Neural Information Processing Systems 29: Annual Conference on Neural Information Processing Systems 2016, December 5–10, 2016, Barcelona, Spain, pp. 3630–3638 (2016)
26. Wang, Y., Chao, W.L., Weinberger, K.Q., van der Maaten, L.: Simpleshot: Revisiting nearest-neighbor classification for few-shot learning. arXiv preprint arXiv:1911.04623 (2019)
27. Wu, Z., Xiong, Y., Yu, S.X., Lin, D.: Unsupervised feature learning via non-parametric instance discrimination. In: Proceedings of the IEEE Conference On Computer Vision and Pattern Recognition, pp. 3733–3742 (2018)
28. Xu, C., Zhu, G.: Semi-supervised learning algorithm based on linear lie group for imbalanced multi-class classification. Neural Process. Lett. 52(1), 869–889 (2020). https://doi.org/10.1007/s11063-020-10287-8
29. Xu, C., Zhu, G., Shu, J.: Robust joint representation of intrinsic mean and kernel function of lie group for remote sensing scene classification. IEEE Geosci. Remote Sens. Lett. 18(5), 796–800 (2021). https://doi.org/10.1109/LGRS.2020.2986779
30. Xu, C., Zhu, G., Shu, J.: A combination of lie group machine learning and deep learning for remote sensing scene classification using multi-layer heterogeneous feature extraction and fusion. Remote. Sens. 14(6), 1445 (2022)
31. Yoon, S.W., Seo, J., Moon, J.: Tapnet: Neural network augmented with task-adaptive projection for few-shot learning. In: Proceedings of the 36th International Conference on Machine Learning, 9–15 June 2019, Long Beach, California, USA. Proceedings of Machine Learning Research, vol. 97, pp. 7115–7123. PMLR (2019)

Context Enhancement Methodology for Action Recognition in Still Images

Jiarong He, Wei Wu$^{(\boxtimes)}$, and Yuxing Li

Inner Mongolia University, Hohhot 010021, Inner Mongolia, China
cswuwei@imu.edu.cn

Abstract. Action recognition in still images is a popular research topic in the field of computer vision, but it is to remain challenging due to the lack of motion information. Contextual information is a significant factor in the task of recognizing image action, which is inseparable from a predefined action class. And the existing research strategy does not ensure adequate use of contextual information. To address this issue, we propose a Contextual Enhancement Module (CEM) that combines the self-attention mechanism and the contextual attention mechanism. Specifically, the context enhancement module uses self-attention to learn pixel-level contextual information, after which separates the image into parts and uses contextual attention to learn region-level contextual information. In this way, the model can emphasize the significance of various pixels and regions in the image and significantly improve feature representation. We performed a lot of experiments on the PASCAL VOC 2012 Action dataset and the Stanford 40 Actions dataset. The results demonstrate that our method performs effectively, with the state-of-the-arts outcomes being obtained on both datasets.

Keywords: Action recognition · Attention mechanism · Contextual information

1 Introduction

Action recognition is a difficult study area in the world of computer vision and is widely applied in domains like as surveillance, robotics, human-computer interaction, and other areas [1]. The two categories of action recognition are image-based action recognition and video-based action recognition. However, recognizing actions in images is more challenging due to the lack of motion information, complex background, and high intra-class variance and low inter-class variance in some categories [2].

Images contain more information, such as human beings, interactive objects and scenes, which are composed of pixels. Humans can accurately distinguish these pieces of information, which indicates that there are certain connections between pixels of different information, we call these connections as the context information of images. Context information is one of the important clues in images, which is used in many image action recognition methods, however, most of the methods [7–10] consider from the perspective of multiple features fusion, and do not focus on the extraction of context

L. Iliadis et al. (Eds.): ICANN 2023, LNCS 14254, pp. 112–122, 2023.
https://doi.org/10.1007/978-3-031-44207-0_10

information. Only a few researchers have proposed the recognition method [11] using context information, but the experimental results are not satisfactory.

After achieving success in the field of natural language processing, attention mechanism [3] found widespread application in computer vision. Self-attention mechanism [4] is a special attention mechanism, which pays more attention to the key information contained in the input data itself. The self-attention mechanism assigns weights to each pixel in an image and then aggregates local features based on weighted summation. Therefore, we use the self-attentive mechanism to capture the correlation between pixels of an image to better describe global contextual information.

Regions can capture the object-parts relationships better, but they cannot be represented richly with only pixel-level contextual information. To truly describe an image, we must consider not only the spatial arrangement of the parts, but also their appearance and importance in distinguishing subtle differences. The context attention [5] can learn to emphasize potential representations of multiple regions, as well as encode spatial arrangements of various regions. It enables our model to selectively focus on more relevant integral regions to generate holistic context information.

Motivated by the observations above, in this paper, we propose a context enhancement module that uses a novel way to add two kinds of attention to the network, which can efficiently encode the spatial layout and visual appearance of parts. The contributions of this paper are summarized as follows:

- We propose a Context Enhancement Module (CEM). This module has a two-layer attention structure that combines a self-attention module and a contextual attention module to make the contextual information wealthy.
- We conduct experiments on the Stanford 40 Actions and PASCAL VOC 2012 Action datasets to demonstrate the effectiveness of CEM and the experiment parameters and network structure are introduced in detail. The results show that our methodology achieves the state-of- the-art performance.

2 Related Work

In 2006, Wang et al. [6] published the first paper on still image action recognition algorithms, and since then, with the rapid development of computer technology, especially the appearance of neural networks, more and more scholars have turned their attention to this aspect of deep learning.

In the field of deep learning, Gkioxari et al. proposed R*CNN [7], which incorporates contextual information as features in the recognition model. Zhao et al. [8] proposed a proposed method to arrange the features of different semantic parts in spatial order, arranging these features in a top-down order. Zhao et al. [9] proposed a method to improve human action recognition using semantic partial actions by merging local actions with contextual information.

With the occurrence of the attention mechanism, many authors began to try to bring it into their own models. Yan et al. [10] proposed a multi-branch attention network which has three branches, the scene attention branch, the target sub-region classification branch and the local region attention branch, thus capturing both global and local information. Zheng et al. [12] proposes a multi-stage deep learning method called Spatial Attention based Action Mask Networks (SAAM-Nets). The model adds a spatial attention layer to the convolutional neural network to create a specific action mask for each image that has only an action label.

Additionally, some researchers are attempting to recognize actions in static images by using a variety of features. Ma et al. [13] proposed a new approach to action recognition by considering the relation between human and object as an important cue to enhance the features of action classification by computing the information of pair-wise relation between human and object. Wang et al. [14] proposed the pose enhanced relation module, which can extract the implicit relation between pose and human body output the pose enhanced relation feature with powerful representation capability. Surrounding objects information is also applied to strengthen the solution.

Most of the above methods only use convolutional neural networks to extract context information, and do not extract the context of images in depth. Some approaches conduct extensive research on context information, but the experimental results are not good. Compared with these methods, our proposed method can extract more detailed context information, which is conducive to improving the performance of recognizing actions in images.

3   Method

In this section, we introduce the model in detail. First, we'll go over the network's overall structure. Then, the two components of the Context Enhancement Module (CEM) are introduced in detail: the self-attention submodule and the context attention submodule.

3.1   Overview

Figure 1 shows the model's overall structure. First, ResNet-50 [15] is used for feature extraction, and the convolutional feature map of the last residual block in the network is retained. Then, the feature map is input into the Context Enhancement Module (CEM), where self-attention is employed to aggregates the contextual information of the overall image based on weighted summation, and contextual attention is used to enhance the feature representation of various regions and encode their spatial arrangement. Thus, the context enhancement module can emphasize the significance of individual pixels and regions in the image and obtain more detailed contextual information. Eventually, the dimension of the feature vectors is reduced by two fully connected layers to get the final recognition results. The next part gives a detailed presentation of the context enhancement module's structure.

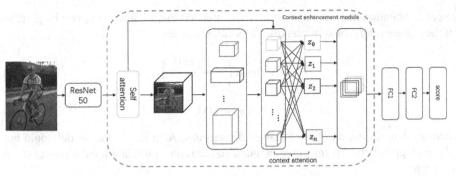

Fig. 1. Overview of our proposed methodology for action recognition in still images.

3.2 Context Enhancement Module (CEM)

The context enhancement module (CEM) structure is shown in Fig. 2. The module consists of two parts, namely self-attention submodule and contextual attention submodule. First, the image features are entered into the self-attention submodule, which learns pixel-level context information and generates a new feature map with self-attention weight. The context attention submodule takes this feature map as input and divides it into n integral regions, then extracts context information at the region level to produce n feature vectors. Finally, the module stacks these feature vectors to produce the final output feature map for the context enhancement module. As a result, the model could emphasize pixels and different-sized regions in the image as well learning contextual information in a hierarchical way.

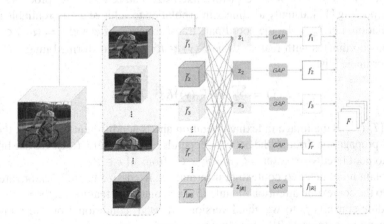

Fig. 2. The structure of the Context Attention Module (CEM)

Self-attention Submodule. In order to learn the relations among all pixels, we add a self-attentive module [16] to the model. $f(x), g(x), h(x)$ are 1×1 convolutions, and the output of $f(x)$ is transposed and multiplied with the output of $g(x)$. Through softmax, we get an attention map θ_p, and multiply the attention map θ_p and $h(x)$ pixel by pixel to get the feature map o of self-attention. It is calculated as:

$$\theta_p = Softmax\left(\frac{g(x)f(x)^T}{\sqrt{d_k}}\right) \tag{1}$$

$$o = \theta_p * h(x) \tag{2}$$

where d_k denotes the number of feature dimensions. As a result, the model could not only learn global context information, but also focus on significant local information in the image.

Contextual Attention Submodule. For further extracting contextual information, we capture many regions with different roughness levels from the feature map, and the level of roughness is determined by the size of the region. The minimum region is $r(i, j, \Delta x, \Delta y)$, where Δx denotes the width and Δy denotes the height, located (top-left corner) in the ith column and j^{th} row of the feature map o. We derive a set of regions by varying their widths and heights. The set of regions can be expressed as follows:

$$R = \{r(i, j, m\Delta x, n\Delta y)\} \tag{3}$$

Where $m, n = 1, 2, 3, \ldots$ and $i < i + m\Delta x \leq w$, $j < j + \Delta y \leq$ H. W and H denote the width and height of the feature map o, respectively. This method can obtain regions with different roughness in the feature map, so that the model can learn the subtle changes of different hierarchical structures in the image and obtain richer context information.

Since the size of region $r \in R$ is different, the goal is to represent these variable size regions $(X \times Y \times C) \rightarrow (w \times h \times C)$ with a fixed size feature vector, we process it using a bilinear pooling [17], usually a bilinear interpolation to achieve a differentiable image transformation. Let $T_\varphi(y)$ be the coordinate transformation of φ and $y = (i, j) \in R^2$ be the region coordinates with feature value $F(y) \in R^C$. The transformed image $\tilde{F}$ at the target coordinate $\tilde{y}$ is:

$$\tilde{F}(\tilde{y}) = \sum_y F(T_\varphi(y)) K(\tilde{y}, T_\varphi(y)) \tag{4}$$

where $F(T_\varphi(y))$ is the image indexing operation and is nondifferentiable; thus, the way gradients propagation through the network depends on the kernel $K(., .)$. We use bilinear pooling to pool fixed size features $f_r(w \times h \times C)$ from all $r \in R$.

To obtain more detailed contextual information, fixed-size feature vectors are used as input to the contextual attention module [5] and contextual feature vector z_r as output. This module converts f_r to weighted versions of itself, conditional on the remaining feature mapping $f_{r'}(r, r' \in R)$. This allows our model to selectively focus on the more relevant integration regions to generate overall contextual information. It is calculated as:

$$g_{r,r'} = \tanh\left(W_g(f_r) + W_{g'}(f_{r'}) + b_g\right) \tag{5}$$

$$\alpha_{r,r'} = softmax\left(W_\alpha g_{r,r'} + b_\alpha\right) \tag{6}$$

$$z_r = \sum\nolimits_{r'=1}^{R} \alpha_{r,r'} f_{r'} \tag{7}$$

where W_g, $W_{g'}$ are the weight matrices of f_r and $f_{r'}$, W_α is the weight matrix of their nonlinear combination, and b_α and b_g are the bias matrices. The attention element $\alpha_{r,r'}$ captures the similarity between the feature maps f and $f_{r'}$ of regions r and r'. The attention focused context vector z_r determines the strength of f_r in focus conditioned on itself and its neighborhood context. This applies to all integral regions r.

In order to improve the extensibility of the model and reduce the computational complexity of the model, we use global average pooling to integrate the spatial information of the feature vector $z_r(r = 1, 2, 3, \cdots) \in \mathbb{R}^{w \times h \times C}$ and obtain the context feature $f_r \in \mathbb{R}^{1 \times C}$. To create the context attention sub-module's final output vector $F \in \mathbb{R}^{|\mathcal{R}| \times C}$, all of feature vectors f_r are finally stacked.

4 Experiments

In this section, we first provide a description of the experimental datasets and parameter settings, then compare our experimental results with the state-of-the-art models, and finally perform ablation experiments to prove the effectiveness of our proposed model.

4.1 Datasets and Evaluation Metric

We use the PASCAL VOC 2012 Action [18] dataset and the Stanford 40 Actions [19] dataset to train and evaluate the image action recognition task.

The PASCAL VOC 2012 Action dataset, which contains 9157 images covering 10 categories of actions. For training and validation, 400–500 images from each category in the dataset are used, and the remaining images are used for testing. The Stanford 40 Actions dataset consists of 9532 images total, separated into 40 classes of actions, with 100 pictures every class used for training and the rest images used for testing. The two datasets are split similarly to other methods that are currently in use in the field, allowing for a performance comparison with those.

For action recognition in images, we measure the performance by Average Precision (AP) and mean Average Precision (mAP). Average Precision (AP) is used to measure the performance of the model on each category, and mean Average Precision (mAP) is used to measure the overall performance of the model.

4.2 Experimental Setup

In our experiments, we set the input image size to 224 × 224 and the training epoch to 100 on all datasets. we utilize stochastic gradient descent (SGD) [20] with a momentum of 0.9 and a learning rate of 0.0001 to optimize the model during the training period. The entire model is constructed using the Tensorflow framework and trained on single NVIDIA Tesla P40 GPU.

4.3 Comparisons with the State-of-the-Art Models

In this section, we show the result of other state-of-the-art methods to provide a comprehensive perspective on the performance of our proposed model.

We firstly evaluate our model on the Pascal VOC 2012 Action dataset. The results and comparison with state-of-the-art approaches on the validation and test set are respectively shown in Tables 1 and 2. On the validation and test sets, the mAP of our method achieves 93.1% and 94.2%, which is the State-of-the-art result among all methods. Especially on the test set, our approach significantly improved the AP values for the categories of 'playing instrument', 'using computer' and 'walking' etc.

Table 1. Performance comparison on the PASCAL VOC 2012 Action validation set

Method	Jumping	Phoning	Playing instrument	Reading	Riding bike	Riding horse	Running	Taking photo	Using computer	Walking	Mean AP
R*CNN [7]	87.7	80.1	94.8	81.1	**95.5**	97.2	87.0	84.7	94.6	70.1	87.3
Yan et al. [10]	87.8	78.4	93.7	81.1	95.0	97.1	86.0	85.5	93.1	73.4	87.1
Ma et al. [13]	89.2	**89.8**	96.5	87.6	98.2	99.1	**92.3**	**91.6**	95.2	79.2	91.9
Zhao et al. [9]	89.6	86.9	94.4	88.5	94.9	97.9	91.3	87.5	92.4	76.4	90.0
Ours	**92.4**	84.5	**98.8**	**92.7**	**95.5**	**99.8**	91.6	91.2	**98.4**	**85.5**	**93.1**

Table 2. Performance comparison on the PASCAL VOC 2012 Action test set

Method	Jumping	Phoning	Playing instrument	Reading	Riding bike	Riding horse	Running	Taking photo	Using computer	Walking	Mean AP
R*CNN [7]	91.5	84.4	93.6	83.2	96.9	98.4	93.8	85.9	92.6	81.8	90.2
Yan et al. [10]	92.7	86.0	93.2	83.7	96.6	98.8	93.5	85.3	91.8	80.1	90.2
Ma et al. [13]	91.1	89.8	95.4	87.7	98.6	98.8	**95.4**	**91.4**	95.8	84.3	92.8
Zhao et al. [9]	95.0	**92.4**	97.0	88.3	**98.9**	99.0	94.5	91.3	95.1	87.0	93.9
Ours	**96.6**	89.5	**99.1**	**91.9**	97.8	**99.2**	91.4	87.7	**98.6**	**90.6**	**94.2**

We further evaluate the proposed model on the Stanford 40 Actions dataset. As shown in Table 3, The mAP of our proposed method is 95.0%, achieving the state-of-the-art performance. In particularly, The approach [13, 14, 21] focuses more on recognizing the features of the interaction relationship between people and objects, but our approach evaluates from the aspect of context information, increasing the mAP value by 1.8–5.5%. The method [7, 10, 23] approaches the problem from a similar perspective as ours, but these methods perform worse than ours, with a performance difference of 1.2–4.3%.

Table 3. Performance comparison on the Stanford 40 Actions validation set

Method	Networks	Mean AP(%)
Mi et al. [21]	ResNet-101	89.5
Yan et al. [10]	VGG-16	90.7
R*CNN [7]	VGG-16	90.9
Zhao et al. [9]	ResNet-50	91.2
Ma et al. [13]	ResNet-50	93.1
Wang et al. [14]	ResNet-50	93.2
Wu et al. [22]	ResNet-50	93.7
Li et al. [23]	ResNet-50	93.8
Ours	ResNet-50	**95.0**

4.4 Ablation Study and Analysis

In this section, we conducted detailed ablation experiments on two datasets to demonstrate the effectiveness of our proposed method.

Table 4. Ablation study on the two datasets

Method	ResNet-50	Context Enhancement Module		Mean AP(%)	
		Self-Attention Submodule	Context Attention Submodule	PASCAL VOC 2012	Stanford 40
1	✓			70.3	78.8
2	✓	✓		73.7	80.5
3	✓		✓	93.9	94.6
4	✓		✓	**94.2**	**95.0**

Firstly, we explored the impact of the model's three components on the experimental results, and the data are shown in Table 4. As shown in the table, the contextual attention submodule plays a much significant role than the self-attention submodule. The experimental results of adding the Context Enhancement Module into the model is the greatest, with mAP of 94.2% and 95.0%, respectively, confirming that the proposed hierarchical learning approach of pixel-level and region-level context information is beneficial for recognizing action in still image.

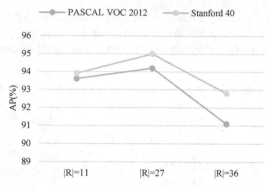

Fig. 3. Experimental results of different number $|R|$ of integral regions

Figure 3 illustrates the effect of the number $|R|$ of Integral Regions on model performance. There are 10, 26, and 35 integral regions that can be obtained by altering the values of m and n in Formula (3) of Sect. 3, including the input image, the total number of regions is 11, 27, and 36. When the number of regions was increased to 27, the PASCAL VOC 2012 and Stanford 40 Actions datasets had the highest mAP values, proving that the region provides the most contextual information in this setting. When the number of regions is 36, the mAP values of the PASCAL VOC 2012 and Stanford 40 actions datasets are the lowest, which means that the different regions overlapped more at this time and the information contained in the feature maps was in an oversaturated state, causing the performance of the model to decrease. This experiment shows that when there are 27 regions, the model performs best on both datasets.

5   Conclusions

This paper presents a novel action recognition model based on contextual information. Context information is an important clue of image activity recognition, but the existing methods do not make full use of it, resulting in poor recognition effect of static images. We created a multiple-attention fusion strategy to solve this problem, which build the context-enhanced modules by applying attention mechanisms in order to gather more valuable contextual information for enhancing feature representation. Experimental results demonstrates that our method performs better than the state-of-the-art models on PASCAL VOC 2012 and Stanford 40 Actions datasets.

Acknowledgement. This work is supported by the Inner Mongolia Science and Technology Project (No. 2021GG0166).

References

1. Zhu, Y., et al.: A comprehensive study of deep video action recognition. arXiv preprint arXiv: 2012.06567 (2020)
2. Girish, D., Singh, V., Ralescu, A.: Understanding action recognition in still images. In: Proceedings of the IEEE/CVF Conference on Computer Vision and Pattern Recognition Workshops, pp. 370–371 (2020)
3. Dosovitskiy, A., et al.: An image is worth 16 x 16 words: transformers for image recognition at scale. arXiv preprint arXiv:2010.11929 (2020)
4. Vaswani, A., et al.: Attention is all you need. Adv. Neural Inf. Process. Syst. **30** (2017)
5. Behera, A., Wharton, Z., Hewage, P.R., Bera, A.: Context-aware attentional pooling (cap) for fine-grained visual classification. Proc.AAAI Conf. Artif. Intell. **35**(2), 929–937 (2021)
6. Wang, Y, et al.: Unsupervised discovery of action classes. In: 2006 IEEE Computer Society Conference on Computer Vision and Pattern Recognition (CVPR 2006), vol. 2. IEEE (2006)
7. Gkioxari, G., Girshick, R., Malik, J.: Contextual action recognition with r* CNN. In: Proceedings of the IEEE International Conference on Computer Vision, pp. 1080–1088 (2015)
8. Zhao, Z., Ma, H., Chen, X.: Semantic parts based top-down pyramid for action recognition. Patt. Recogn. Lett. **84**, 134–141 (2016)
9. Zhao, Z., Ma, H., You, S.: Single image action recognition using semantic body part actions. In: Proceedings of the IEEE International Conference on Computer Vision, pp. 3391–3399 (2017)
10. Yan, S., Smith, J.S., Lu, W., Zhang, B.: Multibranch attention networks for action recognition in still images. IEEE Trans. Cognitive Dev. Syst. **10**(4), 1116–1125 (2017)
11. Zhu, H., Hu, J.F., Zheng, W.S.: Learning hierarchical context for action recognition in still images. In: Advances in Multimedia Information Processing–PCM 2018: 19th Pacific-Rim Conference on Multimedia, Hefei, China, 21–22 September, 2018, Proceedings, Part III 19, pp. 67–77 (2018)
12. Zheng, Y., Zheng, X., Lu, X., Wu, S.: Spatial attention based visual semantic learning for action recognition in still images. Neurocomputing **413**, 383–396 (2020)
13. Ma, W., Liang, S.: Human-object relation network for action recognition in still images. In: 2020 IEEE International Conference on Multimedia and Expo (ICME), pp. 1–6 (2020)
14. Wang, J., Liang, S.: Pose-enhanced relation feature for action recognition in still images. In: Þór Jónsson, B., et al. MultiMedia Modeling. MMM 2022. Lecture Notes in Computer Science, vol. 13141. Springer, Cham (2022). https://doi.org/10.1007/978-3-030-98358-1_13
15. He, K., Zhang, X., Ren, S., Sun, J.: Deep residual learning for image recognition. In: Proceedings of the IEEE Conference on Computer Vision and Pattern Recognition, pp. 770–778 (2016)
16. Zhang, H., Goodfellow, I., Metaxas, D., Odena, A.: Self-attention generative adversarial networks. In: International Conference on Machine Learning, pp. 7354–7363 (2019)
17. Yu, C., Zhao, X., Zheng, Q., Zhang, P., You, X.: Hierarchical bilinear pooling for fine-grained visual recognition. In: Proceedings of the European Conference on Computer Vision (ECCV), pp. 574–589 (2018)
18. Everingham, M., Van Gool, L., Williams, C.K., Winn, J., Zisserman, A.: The pascal Visual Object Classes (voc) challenge. Int. J. Comput. Vision **88**, 303–338 (2010)
19. Yao, B., Jiang, X., Khosla, A., Lin, A.L., Guibas, L., Fei-Fei, L.: Human action recognition by learning bases of action attributes and parts. In: 2011 International Conference on Computer Vision, pp. 1331–1338 (2011)
20. Ruder, S.: An overview of gradient descent optimization algorithms. arXiv preprint arXiv: 1609.04747(2016)

21. Mi, S., Zhang, Y.: Pose-guided action recognition in static images using lie-group. Appl. Intell. 1–9(2022)
22. Wu, W., Yu, J.: An improved deep relation network for action recognition in still images. In: ICASSP 2021–2021 IEEE International Conference on Acoustics, Speech and Signal Processing (ICASSP), pp. 2450–2454 (2021)
23. Li, Y., Li, K., Wang, X.: Recognizing actions in images by fusing multiple body structure cues. Patt. Recogn. **104**, 107341 (2020)

Discrete Denoising Diffusion Approach to Integer Factorization

Kārlis Freivalds[1][(✉)], Emīls Ozoliņš[2], and Guntis Bārzdiņš[2]

[1] Institute of Electronics and Computer Science, Riga, Latvia
karlis.freivalds@edi.lv
[2] Institute of Mathematics and Computer Science, Riga, Latvia

Abstract. Integer factorization is a famous computational problem unknown whether being solvable in the polynomial time. With the rise of deep neural networks, it is interesting whether they can facilitate faster factorization. We present an approach to factorization utilizing deep neural networks and discrete denoising diffusion that works by iteratively correcting errors in a partially-correct solution. To this end, we develop a new seq2seq neural network architecture, employ relaxed categorical distribution and adapt the reverse diffusion process to cope better with inaccuracies in the denoising step. The approach is able to find factors for integers of up to 56 bits long. Our analysis indicates that investment in training leads to an exponential decrease of sampling steps required at inference to achieve a given success rate, thus counteracting an exponential run-time increase depending on the bit-length.

1 Introduction

Deep Neural Networks have shown excellent results not only for real-world tasks but also for intellectually demanding algorithmic tasks such as sorting and multiplication [5], NP-hard problems including Boolean Satisfiability (SAT) [17], Travelling Salesman Problem (TSP) [7] and game playing [21]. But there are algorithmic tasks that are too complex for a neural network to predict the solution directly. One of such tasks is integer factorization (the inverse of multiplication) where the goal is to find the prime factors of an integer number. Integer factorization [15] is a famous computational problem believed not to be solvable in polynomial time but also suspected that it is not NP-complete. There exists a fast quantum algorithm [20] for factorization but it is questionable whether a sufficiently capable quantum computer can be built. Therefore it is tempting to

Supported by Latvian Council of Science, project "Smart Materials, Photonics, Technologies and Engineering Ecosystem", project No. VPP-EM-FOTONIKA-2022/1-0001; Latvian Quantum Initiative under European Union Recovery and Resilience Facility project no. 2.3.1.1.i.0/1/22/I/CFLA/001; the Latvian Council of Science project lzp-2021/1-0479; Google Research Grants; NVIDIA Academic Grant "Deep Learning of Algorithms".

© The Author(s), under exclusive license to Springer Nature Switzerland AG 2023
L. Iliadis et al. (Eds.): ICANN 2023, LNCS 14254, pp. 123–134, 2023.
https://doi.org/10.1007/978-3-031-44207-0_11

find out whether neural networks can facilitate finding the factors quickly and this is the subject of our research.

The best algorithm is General Number Field Sieve which, for factoring a b bit number, is of complexity $\exp((64/9)^{1/3} + o(1))b^{1/3}\log(b)^{2/3})$ [3]. Simple algorithms can factor small integers quickly, for example, Pollard's rho algorithm [18] factorizes a 56-bit number in about 0.03 s but struggles on large numbers. The largest factored cryptographic-hard number is 829 bits long.

Some attempts have been made to predict integer factors using neural networks. In [16] experiments were done with tiny neural networks and encoding the input and output as a single real number. In [12] binary encoding was used reaching 37% success at factoring 20-bit numbers using a neural network only and 90% when followed by brute-force post-processing to correct up to 4 bits in the solution.

In this paper, we propose an indirect way of approaching integer factorization that requires the neural network to learn a simpler task i.e. to correct errors in a given partially-correct solution. Then, at inference time such error correction is applied iteratively in a randomized fashion to search for a fully-correct solution. Our approach is derived from Denoising Diffusion [22] which gives a strong theoretical basis for such a randomized search strategy. Diffusion models naturally allow sampling from the entire solution distribution, rather than only giving the most probable solution – a feature needed for our task since there can be many ways to factor a given number. Also, diffusion models can be conditioned on subsidiary data – the number to be factored, in our case.

We adapt the diffusion algorithm so that it works well for factorization. First, we modify the sampling algorithm to retain the full probability information from step to step and sample only when presenting data to the denoising neural network. Second, we relax the discrete distribution using Gumbel-Softmax [11] technique to make the denoising task easier to learn. We show that these modifications improve the factorization performance. For the denoising task, we evaluate several existing neural architectures and develop a new one that outperforms the existing ones.

We evaluate our approach on integers up to 56 bits long. The success of factoring a given number depends on the number of sampling steps that we perform at the inference and in this paper we give detailed analysis with respect to different number of sampling steps and bit lengths. For example, we get 98% correctly factored 32-bit numbers in 8192 sampling steps and 31% correctly factored 40-bit numbers given 16384 sampling steps. We also evaluate the scaling behavior which reveals two trends: (a) longer numbers require exponentially more sampling steps and (b) longer training results in an exponential decrease of required sampling steps.

2   Background: Diffusion Models

Diffusion models have achieved state-of-the-art results for image generation [9, 19,25]. Diffusion has been applied to discrete binary [22] and categorical [10] data, text generation [1]. But not for such hard combinatorial problems like integer factorization.

Given data x_0, a diffusion model [22] consists of predefined variational distributions $q(x_t|x_{t-1})$ that gradually introduces noise over time steps $t \in \{1, ..., T\}$. The diffusion trajectory is defined such that $q(x_t|x_{t-1})$ adds a small amount of noise around x_t. This way, information is gradually destroyed and at the final time step, x_T carries almost no information about x_0. A nice property of the diffusion process is that it can be reversed if the gradient of the distribution can be estimated which is often expressed as a function that denoises the data. Usually, Normal distribution is employed which is simple to work with and produces excellent results for images [9] and sound [14].

To deal with discrete values, here we employ diffusion for categorical data, namely the Multinomial Diffusion [10]. Having K categories, x_t is encoded as one-hot vector $x_t \in \{0,1\}^K$. The multinomial diffusion process is defined using a categorical distribution that has a small probability β_t of resampling a category uniformly and a large $(1 - \beta_t)$ probability of sampling the previous value x_{t-1}:

$$q(x_t|x_{t-1}) = \mathcal{C}(x_t|(1 - \beta_t)x_{t-1} + \beta_t/K), \tag{1}$$

where $\mathcal{C}$ denotes a categorical distribution with probability parameters after |. For such diffusion process the probability of any x_t given x_0 is expressed as:

$$q(x_t|x_0) = \mathcal{C}(x_t|\bar{\alpha}_t x_0 + (1 - \bar{\alpha}_t)/K), \tag{2}$$

where $\alpha_t = 1 - \beta_t$ and $\bar{\alpha}_t = \prod_{\tau=1}^{t} \alpha_\tau$. For reverse distribution step, we follow the common practice to parametrize it using x_0. According to [10], the distribution for the previous time step $t - 1$ can be computed from the value x_t at the next step and the initial value x_0 as:

$$q(x_{t-1}|x_t, x_0) = \mathcal{C}(x_{t-1}|\theta_{post}(x_t, x_0)), \tag{3}$$

$$\theta_{post}(x_t, x_0) = \tilde{\theta} / \sum_{k=1}^{K} \tilde{\theta}_k, \tag{4}$$

$$\tilde{\theta} = [\alpha_t x_t + (1 - \alpha_t)/K] \odot [\bar{\alpha}_{t-1} x_0 + (1 - \bar{\alpha}_{t-1})/K] \tag{5}$$

During the reverse process, an approximation $\hat{x}_0$ is used instead of x_0 which is produced by a neural network μ: $\hat{x}_0 = \mu(x_t, \bar{\alpha}_t)$. The neural network is trained by feeding it with the cumulative noise[1] at time t and noisy sample x_t which is produced by the forward diffusion and asking the network to produce a clean sample $\hat{x}_0$. We use a linear schedule of $\bar{\alpha}$ both during training and inference. The loss function for training is the KL divergence between the true distribution and the predicted one:

$$KL(\mathcal{C}(\theta_{post}(x_t, x_0))|\mathcal{C}(\theta_{post}(x_t, \hat{x}_0))) \tag{6}$$

---

[1] [10] parametrize the neural network with t, instead. This is equivalent once we fix the noise schedule.

3   Diffusion for Factorization

We wish to apply the diffusion process to produce two integer numbers a,b given their product ab. Such function cannot be directly approximated by a neural network for two reasons. First, this function is generally accepted to be extremely hard for which no efficient algorithm is known [15] and also our experiments confirm the inability of direct learning (see Fig. 1 portion with the large noise level, for evidence). Second, the factors are not unique prohibiting a straightforward supervised learning approach. Therefore we took the denoising approach where the neural network is asked to correct errors in a partially correct solution instead of outputting a fully correct solution from scratch. Such function we found to be learnable and also it allows obtaining samples from the whole distribution of factors, not only one particular.

To make the diffusion process work well for factorization, several modifications to the standard diffusion schema are introduced. At first, all functions need to be conditioned on the given number ab to be factored. We augment the neural network with an additional input in which ab is represented in binary one-hot encoding. Similarly, each x_t consists of one-hot encoded a and b: $\hat{a}, \hat{b} = \hat{x}_0 = \mu(x_t, \bar{\alpha}_t, ab)$.

To train the model, we generate training examples consisting of two odd random numbers of $n/2$ bits each (by selecting each bit randomly, hence some leading bits may be zeros), calculate their product ab and form x_0 by concatenating one-hot encodings of a and b. Then, we sample uniformly $\bar{\alpha}_t$ and obtain x_t by sampling $q(x_t|x_0)$ as given in Eq. 2. All three inputs to the neural network are concatenated along the feature axis forming a sequence of length n (the inputs ab and x_t are n bits long and $\bar{\alpha}_t$ is replicated in each sequence position). The neural network $\mu(x_t, \bar{\alpha}_t, ab)$ is trained using KL divergence given by Eq. 6 to estimate x_0. We use a dataset of 10M examples generated this way, smaller datasets in our setup lead to overfitting.

When the model is trained, we can use it for sampling to find the factors of a given number ab. For testing, we use composite numbers having exactly two prime factors each of length roughly $n/2$. We form a test set of 1K examples and explicitly make sure that none of these factors are used as multiplicands in the training set.

Diffusion models are meant for producing samples of some distribution. Here, the distribution, conditioned on the number ab to be factorized, consists of all the factorizations of ab. During training, we use randomly generated a and b which may be composite numbers themselves, so the neural network learns to factorize any composite number. But we test only on the most interesting (and possibly the hardest) case when both a and b are primes. So the distribution to sample from at test time consists of two discrete points (a, b) and (b, a).

The sampling algorithm is inspired by the reverse diffusion but it has two differences: (a) it uses additive update instead of multiplicative and (b) it retains the full probability distribution from step to step and performs sampling from it only to present data to the neural network. Given the total number of steps T, the algorithm (see Algorithm 1) works backward from step T toward step 1.

The initial distribution x_T is created with equal probabilities of 0 and 1 for each bit and then at each step a sample x_{sample} from it is drawn which is presented to the neural network μ. The neural network returns an approximation of the correct bits $\hat{x}_0$. The probabilities of the previous timestep x_{t-1} are calculated by taking the weighted average of x_t and $q(x_{t-1}|\hat{x}_0)$ with a coefficient γ. We use $\gamma = 0.9$. The algorithm returns the bit probabilities at the final step (or at an intermediate step if the solution is found) which should be close to binary if the neural network produces a good approximation, but in practice, we take the argmax over its category dimension as the bit values. This algorithm assumes that the neural network μ returns probabilities that sum to 1 for each bit; that is achieved by placing softmax as the last layer in μ.

The motivation behind deviating from the standard sampling algorithm is that the neural network produces a very inexact approximation $\hat{x}_0$ which by Eq. 5 is often converging to a pair of numbers a, b whose product is not the required ab. Also, the multiplicative nature of Eq. 5 prohibits recovering from confident errors i.e. if, at some step the network gives a wrong 0 in some position, it is almost impossible to get it to 1 by using multiplication in the subsequent steps. The proposed modifications remedy these pitfalls. Use of the additive update allows easy recovery from confident mistakes and keeping the full probabilities instead of one sample retains more information and places less weight on each individual (and possibly wrong) update. A drawback of these modifications is that we lose the diversity of samples. That means that we may get only one factorization solution of ab instead of all of them. But we are happy with that since there is essentially only one way to factor examples in the test set. We have confirmed experimentally that the proposed sampling algorithm works better.

Algorithm 1. Sampling

1: $x_T = 0.5^{n \times 2}$
2: **for** $t = T...1$ **do**
3:     $\bar{\alpha}_{t-1} = 1 - (t-1)/T$
4:     $x_{sample} \sim \mathcal{C}(x_t)$
5:     $\hat{x}_0 = \mu(x_{sample}, \bar{\alpha}_{t-1}, ab)$
6:     **if** a and b encoded in $\hat{x}_0$ multiply to ab **then return** $\hat{x}_0$
7:     $x_{t-1} = \gamma x_t + (1 - \gamma)[\bar{\alpha}_{t-1}\hat{x}_0 + (1 - \bar{\alpha}_{t-1})/K]$
8: **return** x_0

Another modification is that we use relaxed categorical distribution (with a temperature equal to 1) instead of categorical. Their difference is how samples are produced. Categorical distribution introduces discrete noise characterized as bit flips. Relaxed distribution has more fine-grained noise which facilitates training and obtains a better success rate at inference. To work with the relaxed distribution we employ all the formulas given above except for sample generation where we apply the Gumbel Softmax technique [11]. We have confirmed experimentally that using the relaxed distribution is beneficial.

4   Choice of the Neural Model

The architecture of the neural network used to perform denoising has a significant impact on the overall performance. As the integer numbers are encoded as binary sequences, the task is of sequence-to-sequence nature. We evaluated three suitable architectures: Transformer [26], Neural GPU [13] and Residual Shuffle-Exchange Networks (RSE) [4,6] but were not satisfied with their performance on our task. Therefore we tried to implement a new architecture, which turned out to be about 10% better than Transformer and RSE.

The new architecture is a sequence-to-sequence recurrent convolutional neural network based on the combination of Neural GPU and Shuffle-Exchange networks. It operates on hidden state $s \in \mathbb{R}^{n \times m}$ where n is the sequence length and m is the number of feature maps. It applies the following transformation, named Convolutional Shuffle Unit (CSU), to the sequence transforming the state s_r at the recurrent-step r to the state at the next step s_{r+1}:

$$s_{drop} = dropout(s_r)$$
$$s_F = \text{ForwardShuffle}(s_{drop})$$
$$s_R = \text{ReverseShuffle}(s_{drop})$$
$$g = \text{GELU}(\text{InstanceNorm}(W \circledast [s_{drop}|s_F|s_R] + B))$$
$$c = W'g + B'$$
$$s_{r+1} = \sigma(S) \odot s_r + Z \odot c$$

In the above equations, W is a convolution weight matrix of size $3m \times h \times 3$, where h is the hidden size; W' is a linear transformation weight matrix of size $h \times m$; S and Z are vectors of size m; B and B' are biases − all of those are learnable parameters; $\odot$ denotes element-wise vector multiplication and σ is the sigmoid function, $\circledast$ denotes convolution, — denotes concatenation along the feature axis. We choose the hidden size $h = 4m$.

The CSU starts by regularizing its input with dropout [23] (we use dropout rate 0.1), then the input is concatenated with its forward- and reverse-shuffled versions [6] (ForwardShuffle and ReverseShuffle, accordingly). The forward shuffle divides the sequence into halves and interleaves the halves. The reverse shuffle does the opposite – places even elements consecutively in the first half of the sequence and the odd elements in the second half. Convolution of kernel size 3 is then applied to the concatenated sequence followed by Instance Normalization [24] and GELU [8]. It is shown in [6] that repeated application of forward or reverse shuffle together with combining adjacent sequence elements allows rapid (in $O(\log n)$ steps) flow of information between any, possibly distant, sequence positions. In the new model, we use both shuffles together to even more facilitate long-range information flow and combine them with convolution to deal with short-range interactions.

The last step of the CSU is a scaled residual connection. The candidate c is scaled by a zero-initialized parameter Z and added to the scaled input state s_r. The input scale parameter S is chosen such that $\sigma(S) \approx 0.95$. Scaling both values in this way was shown to allow stable training of very deep residual networks [2] and lead to excellent performance in recurrent networks [27].

The whole neural architecture consists of the input projection part, the recurrent part, and the output projection part. In the input part, two linear layers with GELU in-between are applied to data in each input sequence position independently to obtain the initial hidden state s_0. Then, CSU is applied $\max(n/2, 4\lceil\log_2(n)\rceil)$ times in a recurrent fashion sharing the same parameters. Such recurrent depth was chosen as a reasonable compromise between the high expressive power of a deep network and the faster training of a shallow one. Each position of the last state is projected by a linear mapping to two values followed by softmax to obtain the bit probabilities of a and b.

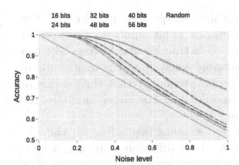

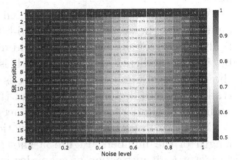

Fig. 1. Bit prediction accuracy of the trained model depending on the noise level. The diagonal is a trivial baseline achieved by rounding.

Fig. 2. Prediction accuracy of each bit depending on the noise level for 16-bit factors of 32-bit numbers. We can see that for small noise all bits are predicted precisely, for large noise only the lowest and the highest bit can be predicted.

5   Results

We have implemented the proposed method in Tensorflow, the code is available at https://github.com/KarlisFre/diffusion-factorization. To present our main results, we trained the model to factor 16–56-bit numbers. The length 56 was chosen roughly to be the maximum for which we can get a non-zero success rate. The model itself is independent of the sequence length, so we create batches of inputs in length increments of 8 in the given range and one training step consists of minimizing the loss for all these batches simultaneously like in [5]. The training was performed for 1M steps using AdaBelief optimizer [28] taking 2 weeks on two NVIDIA RTX A6000 GPUs. We chose the number of feature maps $m = 384$ yielding a model with 5.8M trainable parameters. This choice was obtained experimentally in a few trials to get good results within the given training budget.

All the results presented below are the averages over a batch of 256 examples. We repeated each experiment 5 times with different batches and depict the standard deviation as a shaded area in the line charts.

At first, let us explore how well the neural model is able to learn denoising. Fig. 1 shows bit accuracy depending on the amount of introduced noise which is equal to $1 - \bar{\alpha}_t$. For small amounts of noise, we get good prediction accuracy. For large noise, the model performs only slightly better than the trivial baseline that rounds each bit of the input x_t. Poor prediction in case of large noise is expected to some extent because there can be two possible results a, b or b, a, and with purely random x_t it is impossible to determine which order is the right one.

We can inspect more closely which bits are well-predicted in Fig. 2. The figure shows the accuracy for each 16-bit factor of 32-bit numbers. The first bit is always correct since we use only odd numbers in training and testing. The last bit is also predicted accurately which is possible solely from the magnitude of the composite number ab. And there is a general tendency that the leading or trailing bits are better predicted than the middle ones. For larger numbers, the findings are similar, only the overall accuracy is lower.

Next, we investigate the factorization performance depending on the bit-length of the numbers. Figure 3a shows how many diffusion steps are needed to factor a given fraction of examples in the batch. Since diffusion is a random process that may skip off an already found solution, we mark the example as factored if it happened at least in one of the diffusion steps. We see that small examples can be factored in a few steps but, for longer examples, the increase is exponential. Note that the model has indeed learned how to factor unseen numbers since we explicitly made sure that none of the prime factors used for testing were shown to the model during training.

Often the goal is to factor one given number. We can replicate this number to fill the whole batch, process the batch in parallel, and expect that some of the replicas will be factorized faster due to randomness in sampling. Figure 3b shows such a scenario. We see that the general shape of the lines is similar to those in Fig. 3a only the variance is higher. The same mean in both these charts is expected since the data is the same, only replicated in the latter case. The variance is higher because some numbers appear to be easier to be factorized. We see that the line regarding 1/256 is significantly below the two other lines even taking the variance into account, indicating that some instances (of the same number) in the batch get solved faster than the others, hence it is indeed useful to use such replicated batches. Also, at least one of the replicated numbers up to 48 bits got solved within the step limit showing that there are no hard numbers that the method is unable to factorize at all.

It is interesting to analyze how much resources it is advisable to invest in training. If we invest more time in training, fewer diffusion steps (and computation time, respectively) are necessary to factor the given numbers. Notably, the one-time investment for training pays off for each number we wish to factor in afterward. Fig. 4 shows a heat map depicting the success rate (fraction of solved examples in the batch) depending on the training and diffusion steps for 32 and 40-bit numbers. We can see that the success rate increases both with training time and diffusion steps where the increase with training time is roughly linear. It can be observed that borders of equal success rate (one of such is marked in blue color) form almost straight lines. Since training steps are presented linearly but diffusion steps logarithmically, it means that a linear increase in training time leads to an exponential reduction of diffusion steps. This is very good news showing that investing in training pays off. The bad news is that the success rate decreases exponentially with sequence length.

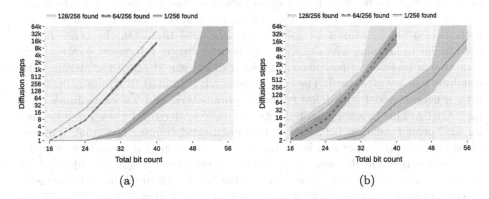

Fig. 3. Diffusion steps taken to reach a given fraction of fully solved instances on batches containing different numbers (a) and on batches of equal numbers (b). Note that diffusion steps are presented log-scale.

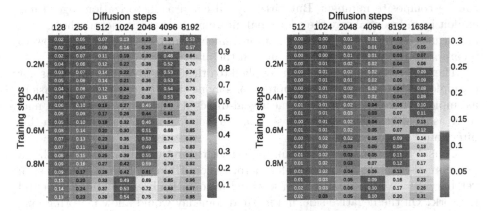

Fig. 4. Success rate depending on training steps and diffusion steps on 32 bit (left) and 40 bit (right) integers. Note that diffusion steps are depicted in log-scale.

6 Conclusion and Outlook

We have presented an approach that solves the integer factorization problem using neural networks and discrete denoising diffusion. We found that neural networks can learn error correction in integer factors and, although being too imprecise to be used directly, it can gradually arrive at the correct solution when applied iteratively, like in denoising diffusion. As a subsidiary result, we have presented a novel neural architecture that performs well on the denoising task. This new architecture, when properly validated, may find applications in other sequence-to-sequence tasks.

We have analyzed how the method scales with respect to training and sampling steps and the bit-length of the numbers. Increasing the bit-length requires an exponential increase of the sampling steps at the inference or exponential investment in training to reach the same success rate suggesting that the factorization problem cannot be solved in polynomial time. On the other hand, investment in training gives exponential benefit during inference. So we might hint that a huge one-time investment in training would allow factorizing long numbers quickly afterward. The current research is limited to numbers up to 56 bits, a neural model with 5.8M trainable parameters, and 2 week training time on 2 GPUs. This is a very limited setup to fully understand the scaling behavior and proper relation between the two mentioned trends. The small integers considered in this paper can be factorized in a fraction of a second using standard methods while the neural approach can take several minutes (depending on the number of diffusion steps). So, further work with much more investment in computing resources is definitely needed to see whether the neural methods can present an asymptotic speedup.

Although tested only on primes, the algorithm itself deals with a more general problem – factoring the given integer into two multiplicands which themselves can be composite numbers. But virtually all classical factorization algorithms exploit in an essential way the additional information that the factors themselves are primes. A further direction for improvement could be investigating how to incorporate the properties of primality in the algorithm.

The same denoising idea may be applied to other discrete search problems, for example, SAT. Currently, the main tool for solving them is tree-search. Diffusion, as employed here, is essentially a linear goal-directed randomized search that may serve as an alternative to the tree-search. We look forward to new results in this direction.

Considering a broader scope, an important theoretical question is whether a polynomial-time algorithm exists for factorization. Humans have not found such yet but, if it exists, could it be discovered automatically via learning a neural network? On the negative side, if a method someday would allow factoring long integers quickly, it will yield many cryptosystems insecure and secrets, currently protected by them, revealed.

References

1. Austin, J., Johnson, D.D., Ho, J., Tarlow, D., Van Den Berg, R.: Structured denoising diffusion models in discrete state-spaces. Adv. Neural Inform. Process. Syst. **34**, 17891–17993 (2021)
2. Bachlechner, T., Majumder, B.P., Mao, H., Cottrell, G., McAuley, J.: Rezero is All You Need: Fast Convergence At Large Depth. arXiv preprint arXiv:2003.04887 (2020)
3. Buhler, J.P., Lenstra, H.W., Pomerance, C.: Factoring integers with the number field sieve. In: Lenstra, A.K., Lenstra, H.W. (eds.) The development of the number field sieve. LNM, vol. 1554, pp. 50–94. Springer, Heidelberg (1993). https://doi.org/10.1007/BFb0091539
4. Draguns, A., Ozoliņš, E., Šostaks, A., Apinis, M., Freivalds, K.: Residual shuffle-exchange networks for fast processing of long sequences. Proceedings of the AAAI Conference on Artificial Intelligence, vol. 35, pp. 7245–7253 (2021)
5. Freivalds, K., Liepins, R.: Improving the neural GPU architecture for algorithm learning. The ICML workshop Neural Abstract Machines and Program Induction v2 (NAMPI 2018) (2018)
6. Freivalds, K., Ozoliņš, E., Šostaks, A.: Neural shuffle-exchange networks - sequence processing in $O(n \log n)$ time. Adv. Neural Inform. Process. Syst. **32**, 6626–6637 Curran Associates Inc (2019)
7. Gaile, E., Draguns, A., Ozoliņš, E., Freivalds, K.: Unsupervised training for neural tsp solver. In: Learning and Intelligent Optimization: 16th International Conference, LION 16, Milos Island, Greece, June 5–10, 2022, Revised Selected Papers, pp. 334–346. Springer (2023). https://doi.org/10.1007/978-3-031-24866-5_25
8. Hendrycks, D., Gimpel, K.: Gaussian Error Linear Units (GELUs). arXiv preprint arXiv:1606.08415 (2016)
9. Ho, J., Saharia, C., Chan, W., Fleet, D.J., Norouzi, M., Salimans, T.: Cascaded diffusion models for high fidelity image generation. J. Mach. Learn. Res. **23**(47), 1–33 (2022)
10. Hoogeboom, E., Nielsen, D., Jaini, P., Forré, P., Welling, M.: Argmax flows and multinomial diffusion: Learning categorical distributions. Adv. Neural Inform. Process. Syst. **34**, 12454–12465 (2021)
11. Jang, E., Gu, S., Poole, B.: Categorical reparameterization with gumbel-softmax. arXiv preprint arXiv:1611.01144 (2016)
12. Jansen, B., Nakayama, K.: Neural networks following a binary approach applied to the integer prime-factorization problem. In: Proceedings. 2005 IEEE International Joint Conference on Neural Networks, 2005, vol. 4, pp. 2577–2582. IEEE (2005)
13. Kaiser, Ł., Sutskever, I.: Neural GPUs learn algorithms. arXiv preprint arXiv:1511.08228 (2015)
14. Kong, Z., Ping, W., Huang, J., Zhao, K., Catanzaro, B.: DiffWave: a versatile diffusion model for audio synthesis. In: 9th International Conference on Learning Representations, ICLR 2021, Virtual Event, Austria, May 3–7, 2021. OpenReview.net (2021)
15. Lenstra, A.K.: Integer factoring. Towards a quarter-century of public key cryptography: A Special Issue of DESIGNS, CODES AND CRYPTOGRAPHY An International Journal. **19**(2/3), 31–58 (2000)
16. Meletiou, G., Tasoulis, D.K., Vrahatis, M.N.: A first study of the neural network approach to the RSA cryptosystem. In: IASTED 2002 Conference on Artificial Intelligence, pp. 483–488 (2002)

17. Ozolins, E., Freivalds, K., Draguns, A., Gaile, E., Zakovskis, R., Kozlovics, S.: Goal-aware neural sat solver. In: 2022 International Joint Conference on Neural Networks (IJCNN), pp. 1–8. IEEE (2022)
18. Pollard, J.M.: Monte Carlo methods for index computation. Math. Comput. **32**(143), 918–924 (1978)
19. Rombach, R., Blattmann, A., Lorenz, D., Esser, P., Ommer, B.: High-Resolution Image Synthesis with Latent Diffusion Models. arXiv preprint arXiv:2112.10752 (2021)
20. Shor, P.W.: Algorithms for quantum computation: discrete logarithms and factoring. In: Proceedings 35th Annual Symposium on Foundations of Computer Science, pp. 124–134 (1994)
21. Silver, D., et al.: A general reinforcement learning algorithm that masters chess, shogi, and go through self-play. Science **362**(6419), 1140–1144 (2018)
22. Sohl-Dickstein, J., Weiss, E., Maheswaranathan, N.: Deep unsupervised learning using nonequilibrium thermodynamics. In: International Conference on Machine Learning, pp. 2256–2265. PMLR (2015)
23. Srivastava, N., Hinton, G., Krizhevsky, A., Sutskever, I., Salakhutdinov, R.: Dropout: a simple way to prevent neural networks from overfitting. J. Mach. Learn. Res. **15**(1), 1929–1958 (2014)
24. Ulyanov, D., Vedaldi, A., Lempitsky, V.: Instance normalization: The missing ingredient for fast stylization. arXiv preprint arXiv:1607.08022 (2016)
25. Vahdat, A., Kreis, K., Kautz, J.: Score-based generative modeling in latent space. Adv. Neural Inform. Process. Syst. **34**, 11287–11302 (2021)
26. Vaswani, A., et al.: Attention is All you Need. In: Guyon, I., Luxburg, U.V., et al., editors. Adv. Neural Inform. Process. Syst. **30**, 5998–6008. Curran Associates Inc (2017)
27. Zakovskis, R., Draguns, A., Gaile, E., Ozolins, E., Freivalds, K.: Gates are not what you need in RNNs. arXiv preprint arXiv:2108.00527 (2021)
28. Zhuang, J., et al.: Adabelief optimizer: adapting stepsizes by the belief in observed gradients. Adv. Neural Inform. Process. Syst. **33**, 18795–18806 (2020)

Distinguishing the Correctness of Knowledge Makes Knowledge Transfer Better

Chao Cheng[1], Bin Fang[2], and Jing Yang[1(✉)]

[1] College of Computer Science and Technology, East China Normal University,
Shanghai 200333, Putuo, China
chaocheng@stu.ecnu.edu.cn, jyang@cs.ecnu.edu.cn
[2] Viterbi School of Engineering, University of Southern California, Los Angeles,
California 90007, USA
binfang@usc.edu

Abstract. Using the Large Language Model(LLM) for in-context learning to solve Natural Language Processing(NLP) tasks has become one of the most popular and effective methods. There has been a sea of works to elicit knowledge from LLM to perform commonsense reasoning, but those methods consume a lot of time and space. Our work considers how to transfer the generated knowledge from LLM to a small model for knowledge generation. We find that the incorporation of wrong knowledge is important in knowledge transfer, which has been neglected by previous work. We propose different filter methods to different generated knowledge to distinguish the correctness of knowledge, and use both correct and wrong knowledge in Contrastive-Learning for knowledge transfer to improve the ability of small models to generate knowledge. In this paper, we first figure out what kind of prompts in in-context learning can better motivate LLM to generate knowledge that has higher generalization and is more helpful in answering questions. Then, we compare various filtering methods for knowledge correctness determination. At last, we use Contrastive-Learning based knowledge generation for transferring knowledge from LLM to the small model. In this way, the knowledge generated by the small model are not only richer but also more correct, which boost reasoning tasks with performance improved up to 1.7% on the *CommonsenseQA* and 3.2% on the *OpnebookQA* comparing the knowledge generated by simply fine-tuned on all knowledge.

Keywords: Commonsense Reasoning · Large Language Model · Neural Network

1 Introduction

LLM has shown its strong capability on in-context learning, and has achieved impressive results on various baseline tasks in the NLP tasks. GPT3 [2] propose to solve NLP tasks using in-context learning, allowing the model to directly

© The Author(s), under exclusive license to Springer Nature Switzerland AG 2023
L. Iliadis et al. (Eds.): ICANN 2023, LNCS 14254, pp. 135–146, 2023.
https://doi.org/10.1007/978-3-031-44207-0_12

predict results when facing with new sample inputs simply by giving task instructions and examples as the context of the model input, it can be seen as Direct Prompt, Fig. 1(a) are results of using Direct prompt to perform Question Answering(QA), it can directly predict the answers to simple questions. But this method lacks in explainability, and when it encounters a more complicated problem, the prediction failed. GKP [8] further proposes to steer LLM for generating relevant knowledge based on questions to perform commonsense reasoning, which achieves a considerable improvement compared to Direct Prompt, but sometimes the generated knowledge is incomplete and irrelevant to the question. As shown in Fig. 1(b), "Wood is a common building material" is a piece of factual knowledge, but it does not help to derive the Ground Truth(GT) answer.

How to use LLM to generate more relevant knowledge for answering questions has become the focus of recent research. People establish the relationship between concepts in the question through the chain of thought and use such chain to derive the correct answer, CoT [17] uses LLM to simulate this chain of thought to solve Numerical Reasoning and Commonsense Reasoning tasks and has achieved better performance. Furthermore, [9,18] proposed Rationalization, which gives the correct answer as an additional hint in the prompt and guide the LLM to explain such answer. The generated knowledge have more information, which help not only infer the correct answer but also distinguish the wrong answer. The knowledge generated by Rationalization of Quesiton2 in Fig. 1(c) can not only infer the correct answer "(c)desk drawer", but also explain why not choose the incorrect answer "(a)backpack".

However, the knowledge generated by LLM is not always correct. CoT and Rationalization do not always perform well when a quesiton require more complex reasoning. For the question "To locate a choker not located in a jewelry box or boutique where would you go? (a)jewelry store, (b)neck, (c) jewelry box, (d)jewelry, or (e)boutique?", the corresponding generated knowledge is "We can find chokers in jewelry stores or boutiques, but if not in jewelry stores, then we will find them in boutiques." This is a wrong knowledge to help answer the correct answer "(a)jewelry store". [18] and [19] also found that the knowledge generated by language models is unreliable and sometimes produces nonfactual knowledge, which is unacceptable for downstream tasks. The correctness of knowledge can be determined by using metrics that approximate the factuality of knowledge. Although LLM have strong knowledge generation capabilities, judging the correctness of generated knowledge is still the focus of research. Meanwhile, due to the large cost of LLM in storage and inference, [6] proposed to use the knowledge of LLM to improve the reasoning ability of small models, but it didn't distinguish the correctness of knowledge generated by Rationalization and utilized wrong knowledge when transferring, we demonstrate that the knowledge generated by this method is sup-optimal through plenty of experiments. Our work follows this setting, but we focus on how to use small model to generate knowledge.

In this paper, we focus on how to distinguish the correctness of knowledge generated by LLM and transfer it to a small model. First, We use Rationalization and CoT to leverage knowledge generation on LLM respectively. Then, the knowledge generated by Rationalization is filtered by an additional inference model and False Rejection is used to filter the knowledge generated by CoT. At last, we propose a Contrastive-Learning based method to utilize both correct and wrong knowledge to perform knowledge transfer in a small model. We use the generated knowledge by the small model to perform Commonsense Reasoning for validation. Numerous experiments have shown that compared with simply fine-tuned on all knowledge generated by LLM, the participation of wrong knowledge in the transfer stage can prevent the model from overfitting and retard generating wrong knowledge. It has increased by up to 1.7% On the *CommonsenseQA*, and 3.2% on the *OpenbookQA*, which proves that our proposed method can effectively improve the knowledge generation ability of small models.

The following are the main contributions of this paper:

(1) We propose a pipeline method to extract, filter knowledge from LLM, and transfer it to a small models.

(2) We use two filter methods to distinguish the correctness of knowledge and propose a Contrastive-Learning based method to transfer these knowledges to a small model for knowledge generation.

(3)We use knowledge generated by the small model to perform commonsense reasoning, achieving up to 1.7% and 3.2% improvements in *CommonsenseQA* and *OpenbookQA* respectively.

Method	Prompt	Question1	Question2	Question3
(a) Easy prompt	Generate the answer from candidates of the input. Examples: Input: Google Maps and other highway and street GPS services have replaced what? (a) united states, (b) mexico, (c)countryside, (d)atlas, (e)oceans Answer: atlas ... Input: {question} Answer:	Generation: clothing store Prediction: (b) clothing store ☑	Generation: backpack Prediction: (a) backpack ✗	Generation: lumberyard Prediction: (b) lumberyard ✗
(b) GKP	Generate some knowledge about the concepts in the input. Examples: Input: Google Maps and other highway and street GPS services have replaced what? (a) united states, (b) mexico, (c)countryside, (d)atlas, (e)oceans Knowledge: Electronic maps are the modern version of paper atlas. ... Input: {question} Knowledge:	Generation: Clothing stores sell clothing. Prediction: (b) clothing store ☑	Generation: The desk is the most common place to keep a pen. Prediction: (c) desk drawer ☑	Generation: Wood is a common building material. Prediction: (b) lumberyard✗
(c) Rationalization	Generate explanations for the answer to questions. Examples: Input: The christian Sunday school teacher gave out a punishment, this happened when the students did what to her orders? Candidates: (a) stumble, (b)rebel, (c)disobey, (d)go astray, (e)commit sin Answer: (c)disobey Explanation: The teacher will give orders to the students in the school, but if the students do not obey, the teacher will punish the students. ... Input: {question} Answer: {answer} Explanation:	Generation: People can find body coverings in clothing stores, and they can also find them in clothing stores. Prediction: (b) clothing store☑	Generation: We can usually find ballpoint pens in desk drawers, but if not in desk drawers, then we will find them in backpack. Prediction: (c) desk drawer ☑	Generation: Carpets can be placed on top of wood. Prediction: (d) Carpets ☑

Fig. 1. Three samples in CSQA: Quesiton1 is "Where can a human find body coverings? (a)phone booth, (b)clothing store, (c)workplace, (d)swimming pool or (e)closets?", it's GT is (b)clothing store. Quesiton2 is "Where in your home would you keep a ballpoint pen when not in use? (a)backpack, (b)bank, (c)desk drawer, (d)eat cake or (e)office desk?", it's GT is (c)desk drawer. Quesiton3 is "What could go on top of wood? (a)lumberyard, (b)synagogue, (c)floor, (d)carpet or (e)hardware store?", it's GT is (d)carpet. Use blue, green, and red to denote generation, correct predictions, and incorrect predictions respectively.

2   The Proposed Method

We divide our proposed method into three stages. First, we select examples
for constructing Prompt and use LLM's in-context Learning ability to generate
knowledge candidates for each sample on the training set. Then, using Knowledge
Filter to distinguish the correctness of the generated knowledge. Finally, we
perform knowledge transfer by simply fine-tuned and Contrastive-Learning based
method to guide the small model to generate knowledge. The overview of our
proposed method is shown in Fig. 2:

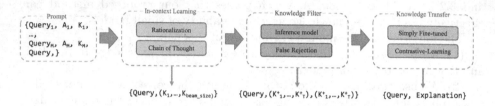

Fig. 2. A overview of our proposed method

In the validation stage, the transferred small model is used to generate knowledge to questions for validation. We concatenate the question with the generated
knowledge, and using inference models to select the highest-scoring option from
candidates as the prediction, we compare the prediction and GT, so the generated knowledge can be verified by whether it helps to answer questions correctly.

2.1   Task Formulation

We focus on the impact of knowledge generated by our method on commonsense
reasoning tasks:

Given a natural language question $Query$ and c options $(candidate_1,$
$..., candidate_c)$, select GT $Answer$ from c options, and denotes the dataset
D with N training examples as: $D=\{Query_i, candidate_1, ..., candidate_c,$
$Answer_i\}_N$, $i \in N$. We follow settings of previous works, select M samples
$(M \ll N)$ from the N training examples, manually write prompt P and create $Demonstration = \{P_1,...,P_M\}$. Use LLM to generate a knowledge set
$K = \{knowledge_1,...,knowledge_b\}$ for each sample in the training set. Exe-
cuting different filter methods to distinguish the correctness of $knowledge_i$,
$i \in \{1,...,b\}$. Mark the correct knowledge as $Knowledge^+$ and the wrong knowledge as $Knowledge^-$. Both $Knowledge^+$ and $Knowledge^-$ will guide the small
model g to generate Knowledge according to the input $(Query, candidate_1, ...,$
$candidate_c)$ in training stage. In validation stage, we connect the input and the
generation $Knowledge'$ as $(Query, candidate_1,..., candidate_c, Knowledge')$ to
make prediction, denoted as $Answer'$. The effectiveness of $Knowledge'$ is measured by the exact matching of $Answer'$ and $Answer$. We conduct validation
experiments on different inference models.

2.2   Select Examples to Construct Demonstration for Knowledge Generation

The aspects of the question include mathematical reasoning, negative reasoning, relational reasoning, and other types of reasoning in the commonsense reasoning task. We hope that the selected M samples are the most representative ones in this task so that it can generate multi-aspect knowledge for new samples. Inspired by [7], we use the K-means method to cluster the input representation to obtain M cluster centers and select the M samples with the closest distance to the cluster centers to construct demonstrations. This process can be expressed as the follow:

$$K - means(D) = \{Query_1, ..., Query_M\}$$

We use various strategies to generate knowledge that helps answer commonsense reasoning questions. The specific way is to control the form of the prompt to realize different strategies by focusing on problems from different angles. For each sample, we have:

$$\{Query, candidate_1, \ldots, candidate_c, Answer\}$$

The prompt designed by [17] derives the correct answer by simulating the chain of thought of human beings. As an intermediate step in reasoning, it can also be regarded as a piece of knowledge that helps answer questions. It defines prompt as:

$$P = \{Query_1^P, Knowledge_1^P, Answer_1^P, ...,$$
$$Query_M^P, Knowledge_M^P, Answer_M^P, Query_i\}$$

The prompt of Rationalization is similar to the data in the Cos-E [14]. Based on the question and GT, an explanation corresponding to GT is put forward. We assume that such explanation can also be used as knowledge to help answer the question. It defines prompt as:

$$P = \{Query_1^P, Answer_1^P, Knowledge_1^P, ...,$$
$$Query_M^P, Answer_M^P, Knowledge_M^P, Query_i, Answer_i\}$$

Different from the previous two prompt methods, Rationalization sees GT during the learning process, since GT is obviously invisible in the validation stage, this can only be used for knowledge generation and cannot be used to generate answers directly on the validation set.

For LLM G, we use beam-search to generate and search knowledge. We express the generated knowledge as:

$$K_{set} = \{Knowledge_1, ..., Knowledge_b\} = G(Knowledge_i|P)$$

where b=beam size.

Nevertheless, due to the randomness in the process of knowledge generation, it may lead to generate wrong knowledge, so it is necessary to distinguish the correctness of knowledge.

2.3   Knowledge Filter

For CoT, the answer finally generated by the chain can be directly used to filter knowledge by *False Rejections*. If the answer in the generated result is the GT, it proves that the knowledge corresponding to this chain of thought can deduce the GT, which can be regarded as correct knowledge. Otherwise, it is wrong knowledge. According to prompt, the generation is $\{Knowledge_i, Answer_i\}$, if $Answer_i = Answer$, then we mark $Knowledge_i$ as correct knowledge $Knowledge_i^+$, otherwise mark it as $Knowledge_i^-$.

For Rationalization, we regard the explanation about GT as a piece of knowledge. Since there is no answer in its generation, it cannot be filtered by *False Rejections*. We consider a reverse process, if GT can be easily answered after adding these explanations, we can consider these explanations to be correct knowledge. There are models fine-tuned on many reasoning and QA datasets, which have strong knowledge perception ability, so these models can be used to perform this reverse process. We use the inference model to compute the loss for generating candidate answers, and select the candidate with the lowest loss as the final prediction. If the prediction is the same as the GT, we consider this piece of knowledge to be correct knowledge, otherwise it is considered to be wrong knowledge. The process can be expressed as the following:

$$Answer' = I_{argmax}(candidates_i | Query, candidates_1, \ldots, candidates_c, Knowledge_i)$$

We mark $Knowledge_i$ as correct knowledge $Knowledge_i^+$ if $Answer' == Answer$, otherwise mark it as $Knowledge_i^-$.

We use different filter methods to distinguish each piece of knowledge, and finally generate a training data set D' consist of questions and associated correct knowledge and wrong knowledge.

$$D' = \{Query_i, Knowledge_1^+, .., Knowledge_T^+, Knowledge_1^-, .., Knowledge_F^-\}_N$$

Where T is the number of correct knowledge, F is the number of wrong knowledge, and we have $T+F=b$, and NF is the size of the entire training dataset.

2.4   Contrastive-Learning Based Knowledge Transfer

The previous work [6] proposed that transferring the knowledge generated by LLM to the small model can improve its reasoning ability, but he did not distinguish the correctness of knowledge and ignored the influence of wrong knowledge in transfer learning. The goal of Contrastive-Learning is to learn a better representation of the positive and negative samples and lead the distance between the positive samples closer, make its farther away from the negative samples at the same time. Using transfer learning in our task allows the model to learn what kind of knowledge is correct and what kind of knowledge is wrong. The framework of the Contrastive-Learning we use in transfer learning is shown in Fig. 3:

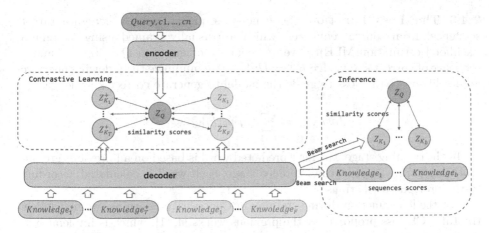

Fig. 3. The training stage and the generation stage of Contrastive-Learning

2.4.1 Sample Construction for Contrastive-Learning. The negative samples used in previous work are sampled from batch[3], but for this task, each sample in the batch has different questions, so simply using different knowledge of different problems for Contrastive-Learning has little effect. Since we have distinguished the correctness of different knowledge for each question in 2.3, we can use $Knowledge^+$ as a positive sample and $Knowledge^-$ as a negative sample for generation target for a question in a sample.

2.4.2 Learning Object and Inference of Contrastive-Learning. The generated different knowledge can be regarded as different perspectives of the same question, we can make the representation of the problem close to the representation of correct knowledge and away from the representation of wrong knowledge. We use sequence-to-sequence model [15] for knowledge generation and take the output Z_Q and Z_K of the encoder and decoder as the feature representation of question and knowledge respectively, then perform affine transformation and cosine similarity to calculate the *similarity_scores* of Z_Q and Z_K, we maximize *similarity_scores* of Z_Q and representation of correct knowledge Z_K^+ and minimize *similarity_scores* of Z_Q and representation of wrong knowledge Z_K^-. In the inference stage, we first use the beam-search algorithm to generate b(beam-size) knowledge and get the normalized *sequences_scores* of each generated knowledge. Then the learned affine transformation is used to calculate the *similarity_scores* of the question's representation and generated knowledge's representation. At last, we sum up *sequences_scores* and *similarity_scores* to get the final score for each piece of knowledge, and select the knowledge with the highest score as the final generated knowledge. The process of selecting the final generated knowledge is expressed as follows:

$$Knowledge' = argmax\{sequences\_scores_i + similarity\_scores_i\}_b, i \in \{1, ..., b\}$$

2.4.3 The Loss Function. Sequence-to-sequence models generate target sequences from source sequences, which are usually trained using maximum likelihood estimation(MLE). Given a sequence of question $Q = \{q_i\}_{i=1}^{M}$ and a sequence of correct knowledge $K^+ = \{k_i\}_{i=1}^{N}$, we minimize the following negative log-likelihood (NLL) loss to guide the model to generate correct knowledge:

$$loss_{NLL} = \sum_{t=1}^{N} log\ p_\theta(k_t|Q, k_{<t}) \tag{1}$$

In the training stage, the next predicted word is based on all previous ground truth inputs $k_{<t}$, and in the inference stage, each word is calculated according to the previous predictions.

For the loss function during training in Contrastive-Learning, we first follow the InfoNCE loss proposed by the previous works [4,11], which is implemented in this method as:

$$loss_{NCE} = -log \sum_{i=1}^{T} \frac{exp(cos(Z_Q, Z_K^+))}{mean(\sum_{j=1}^{F} exp(Z_Q, cos(Z_K^-)))} \tag{2}$$

where Z_Q, Z_K^+, and Z_K^- is the representation of input question, correct knowledge and wrong knowledge respectively. The goal of InfoNCE is to learn a similarity function, make Z_Q get closer to Z_K^+ and farther away from Z_K^-.

Inspired by [1], we compare the representation of each correct knowledge Z_K^+ with each wrong knowledge Z_K^- pairwise to obtain better Contrastive-Learning performance. We construct each correct knowledge K^+ and wrong knowledge K^- into a sample pair (K^+, K^-), we denote the set of multiple sample pairs as P, and calculate the loss using margin_loss:

$$loss_{PAIR} == \sum_{(K^+,K^-)} max(0, cos(Z_Q, Z_K^-) - cos(Z_Q, Z_K^+)) \tag{3}$$

The learning object of Pair loss is similar to InfoNCE loss, but each correct knowledge is compared with each wrong knowledge, and the learning effect is well when the amount of wrong knowledge is relatively small.

3   Datasets

We evaluate our proposed method on two commonsense reasoning tasks. **CommonsenseQA.** [16] consists of commonsense reasoning questions, each of which contains five candidate answers, and the reasoning ability is measured by whether the correct answer can be selected from them. Its training, development, and test set have 9741, 1221, and 1140 questions respectively, and we only validate the development set because its test set is unpublished. **OpenbookQA.** [10] is a question-answering dataset that requires scientific facts and commonsense knowledge. Each of its questions contains 4 candidates. Its training, development, and test set have 4957, 500, and 500 questions respectively, and we do validation on its test set.

4 Experiments

4.1 Experimental Setup

LLM for Knowledge Generation. We use GPT-J with 6B parameters for knowledge generation. We set the temperature to 0.9 to increase randomness, set top_p and top_k to 0.5 and 50 respectively, and set do_sample to true for sample more knowledge, set num_return_sequences to 10 to generate ten pieces of knowledge for each question. For the generated knowledge, we use the exact matching method to deduplicate the knowledge.

Methods for Knowledge Filtering. We use the common T5 model[13] and the Unifiedqa-t5 model[5] fine-tuned on multiple QA datasets to filter the knowledge generated by *Rationalization*, abbreviated as R-T5 and R-UT5, and all models use the version with 3B parameters.

Table 1. Statistics for filtered knowledge

Metric	Dataset	CoT	R-T5	R-UT5
Ratio of correct knowledge to all generated knowledge	CSQA	35.9%	81.5%	88.1%
	OBQA	73.3%	97.5%	98.8%
Ratio of the samples used in the training stage	CSQA	25.2%	54.3%	81.6%
	OBQA	54.3%	89.7%	97.7%

The knowledge generated by CoT is filtered using the method of *FalseRejection*. After filtering with different filtering methods, the ratio of correct knowledge to all generated knowledge is different, as shown in Table 1. Besides, since not all samples have correct knowledge after filtering, we only use samples containing correct knowledge during the Contrastive-Learning, so not all samples participate in the training stage. The ratio of the samples used in the training stage to the training set is shown in Table 1.

Small Model for Knowledge Transfer and Inference Models for Validation. We use T5-Large as a small model of knowledge transfer, use InfoNCE loss (NCE-CL) and Pair loss (PAIR-CL) as loss functions respectively, and study the impact of different loss functions on task performance through the results. In the inference stage, use the small model after transferring the knowledge to generate knowledge based on the question, concatenate question with knowledge and use the inference model for reasoning verification. The effectiveness of knowledge is measured by the improvement of the inference model's ability to answer questions after adding the knowledge.

In order to verify the effectiveness of our proposed method for knowledge transfer, we use the same T5-Large model to perform knowledge transfer on all generated knowledge (Sim-E) and only filtered correct knowledge (Sim-TE).

For fairness, we set the same hyper-parameters, training strategy and knowledge generation strategy in these methods.

4.2 Results

The main results are shown in Table 2. After filtering the knowledge, compared with Sim-E, both Sim-TE and two Contrastive-Learning methods have different degrees of improvement. It proves that the knowledge generated by LLM cannot be simply used in knowledge transfer, and it is necessary to apply filter methods to distinguish the correctness of knowledge. The biggest improvement in CSQA comes from the result of using PAIR-CL to transfer the knowledge filtered by R-UT5 and verifying it with UT5, which is 1.7% higher than SIM-E and SIM-TE, and the biggest improvement in OBQA comes from using NCE-CL to transfer knowledge filtered using R-T5-3b and verifying it with UT5, which is 3.2% higher than SIM-E. After filtering the knowledge, using Contrastive-Learning based method for knowledge transfer performs better than Sim-TE, which proves that it's useful to compare correct knowledge with wrong knowledge in the process of knowledge transfer, it prevents the model from overfitting and generating wrong knowledge to some extent.

Table 2. After using Sim-E, Sim-TE, NCE-CL and PAIR-CL for knowledge transfer respectively, compare the accuracy(%) of answering questions using the knowledge generated by the small model, and mark the best result in bold.

| | CommonsenseQA | | | | | | OpenbookQA | | | | | |
| | CoT | | R-UT5 | | R-T5 | | COT | | R-UT5 | | R-T5 | |
	UT5	T5	UT5	T5	UT5	T5	UT5	T5	UT5	T5	UT5	T5
Sim-E	55.3	41.1	60.8	51.4	60.8	51.4	35.8	22.2	43.4	27.0	42.4	28.2
Sim-TE	56.6	42.3	60.8	51.4	60.2	50.6	39.0	25.4	45.2	**27.2**	41.6	32.6
PAIR-CL	55.8	**43.2**	**62.5**	**52.1**	**61.5**	**51.8**	37.8	25.8	46.0	24.2	40.8	31.8
NCE-CL	**57.0**	42.3	57.4	52.1	57.3	50.5	**39.6**	**28.2**	**46.4**	24.2	**45.6**	**33.2**

4.3 Analysis

The Effect of Different LLMs on the Results. Our method which using GPT-J(6B) to generate knowledge achieved improvement, but whether this improvement can be shown by using a more powerful LLM? Due to the limited budget, we only conduct the same experiment on the CSQA dataset using the newly released ChatGPT[12], the results is shown in Table 3.

It can be seen from the result that LLM's performance has a positive correlation on knowledge transfer, by using the knowledge which generated by the transferred small model can boost the task around 10%. Our proposed filtering and Contrastive-Learning methods are also effective, especially on CoT(about 2% improvement), which further proves the necessity for the effectiveness of discriminative knowledge in transfer learning.

Knowledge-Aware Capabilities of Inference Models Used to Filter Knowledge Generated by _Rationalization_. Use the UT5 model for knowledge filtering and for validation as an inference model, the performance improvement is about 10% comparing with the ordinary T5 model. This is due to the fact that UT5 has been fine-tuned on many QA tasks and has a stronger knowledge perception for question answering. Therefore, a good filtering method can distinguish knowledge more accurately, thereby helping knowledge transfer using Contrastive-Learning.

Table 3. Results of experiments using Chatgpt to generate knowledge

	CoT		R-UT5		R-T5	
	UT5	T5	UT5	T5	UT5	T5
Sim-E	61.5	52.6	61.0	52.1	60.7	53.2
Sim-TE	62.5	53.3	62.0	53.8	61.6	53.7
PAIR-CL	63.6	54.5	**62.7**	**54.7**	61.7	53.6
NCE-CL	**64.0**	**55.9**	61.1	54.4	**61.9**	**53.8**

Impact of Loss Function in Contrastive-Learning on Performance. Compared with T5, UT5(Unifiedqa-t5) has better knowledge perception ability, and the ratio of correct knowledge in its filtering results is higher. Using PAIR-CL can better compare the correct knowledge with all the wrong knowledge pairwise, but when the amount of wrong knowledge increases, a piece of correct knowledge is compared with a large number of wrong knowledge, which will lead to poor learning performance. At this time, it is more effective to use NCE-CL to compare the correct knowledge with the average representation of wrong knowledge. The same result can also be found on OBQA, because the questions and answers are more complicated, there are more wrong knowledge in the generated knowledge, so the method using NCE-CL is much better than the method of PAIR-CL.

5   Conclusion

In this paper, we first make use of LLM's in-context learning ability to generate knowledge, then design different methods to filter knowledge, and finally use Contrastive-Learning to transfer this knowledge to a small model. We explore the impact of various filter methods and what kind of loss function in Contrastive-Learning is more effective under different ratios of correct knowledge. Meanwhile, we used the latest ChatGPT for knowledge generation, the boost is also shown on this more powerful LLM. Our proposed method effectively distinguishes the correctness of the knowledge generated by LLM and successfully transfers it to small models, improving its ability to generate knowledge. Compared with the simply fine-tuned methods, it has improved by up to 1.7% on the CommonsenseQA and 3.2% on the Openbook.

Acknowledgment. This work was supported by the Science and Technology Commission of Shanghai Municipality (No. 21511100302).

References

1. An, C., Feng, J., Lv, K., Kong, L., Qiu, X., Huang, X.: Cont: contrastive neural text generation. arXiv preprint arXiv:2205.14690 (2022)
2. Brown, T., et al.: Language models are few-shot learners. Adv. Neural. Inf. Process. Syst. **33**, 1877–1901 (2020)
3. Chen, T., Kornblith, S., Norouzi, M., Hinton, G.: A simple framework for contrastive learning of visual representations. In: International Conference on Machine Learning, pp. 1597–1607. PMLR (2020)
4. He, K., Fan, H., Wu, Y., Xie, S., Girshick, R.: Momentum contrast for unsupervised visual representation learning. In: Proceedings of the IEEE/CVF Conference on Computer Vision and Pattern Recognition, pp. 9729–9738 (2020)
5. Khashabi, D., et al.: Unifiedqa: crossing format boundaries with a single qa system. arXiv preprint arXiv:2005.00700 (2020)
6. Li, S., et al.: Explanations from large language models make small reasoners better. arXiv preprint arXiv:2210.06726 (2022)
7. Liu, J., Shen, D., Zhang, Y., Dolan, B., Carin, L., Chen, W.: What makes good in-context examples for gpt-3? arXiv preprint arXiv:2101.06804 (2021)
8. Liu, J., et al.: Generated knowledge prompting for commonsense reasoning. arXiv preprint arXiv:2110.08387 (2021)
9. Marasović, A., Beltagy, I., Downey, D., Peters, M.E.: Few-shot self-rationalization with natural language prompts. arXiv preprint arXiv:2111.08284 (2021)
10. Mihaylov, T., Clark, P., Khot, T., Sabharwal, A.: Can a suit of armor conduct electricity? a new dataset for open book question answering. arXiv preprint arXiv:1809.02789 (2018)
11. Oord, A.v.d., Li, Y., Vinyals, O.: Representation learning with contrastive predictive coding. arXiv preprint arXiv:1807.03748 (2018)
12. Ouyang, L., et al.: Training language models to follow instructions with human feedback. Adv. Neural. Inf. Process. Syst. **35**, 27730–27744 (2022)
13. Raffel, C., et al.: Exploring the limits of transfer learning with a unified text-to-text transformer. J. Mach. Learn. Res. **21**(1), 5485–5551 (2020)
14. Rajani, N.F., McCann, B., Xiong, C., Socher, R.: Explain yourself! leveraging language models for commonsense reasoning. arXiv preprint arXiv:1906.02361 (2019)
15. Sutskever, I., Vinyals, O., Le, Q.V.: Sequence to sequence learning with neural networks. In: Advances in Neural Information Processing Systems 27 (2014)
16. Talmor, A., Herzig, J., Lourie, N., Berant, J.: Commonsenseqa: a question answering challenge targeting commonsense knowledge. arXiv preprint arXiv:1811.00937 (2018)
17. Wei, J., et al.: Chain of thought prompting elicits reasoning in large language models. arXiv preprint arXiv:2201.11903 (2022)
18. Wiegreffe, S., Hessel, J., Swayamdipta, S., Riedl, M., Choi, Y.: Reframing human-ai collaboration for generating free-text explanations. arXiv preprint arXiv:2112.08674 (2021)
19. Ye, X., Durrett, G.: The unreliability of explanations in few-shot prompting for textual reasoning. In: Advances in Neural Information Processing Systems (2022)

Diversified Contrastive Learning
For Few-Shot Classification

Guangtong Lu and Fanzhang Li[✉]

School of Computer Science and Technology, Soochow University, Suzhou, China
gtlu@stu.suda.edu.cn, lfzh@suda.edu.cn

Abstract. We argue that the current few-shot learning, which only uses contrastive learning as an auxiliary task, cannot fully realize the potential of contrastive learning. In this paper, we take a deeper exploration of how to combine contrastive learning and few-shot classification better. We use a two-stage training paradigm called pre-training and meta-training, respectively. During the pre-training phase, we differ from previous work that only extracted global features of images for contrastive learning. We extract the global features of the image and local features for contrastive learning, where the local feature contrastive loss is called the maximum matching local contrastive loss. To better integrate contrastive learning with few-shot learning, we propose a prototype contrastive module in the meta-training stage. During the meta-training phase, we record the feature vector representations of all base class prototypes and conduct class-level contrastive learning between K-way class prototypes obtained from the current task and all base class prototypes. Meanwhile, we dynamically update all stored base class prototypes as the training progresses. We validate our model on mimiImagenet and tiredImagenet datasets. Our experimental results show meaningful improvements in few-shot classification and therefore demonstrate the usefulness of our model.

Keywords: Deep learning · Few-shot learning · Meta-learning · Contrastive learning

1 Introduction

With the development of deep learning, it has achieved remarkable success in computer vision, including image classification [26] and more. For all its strengths, deep learning also has some limitations and challenges. One of the main challenges is the requirement for large amounts of labeled data for training, which can be difficult and expensive to obtain. Few-shot learning can effectively overcome the limitations of requiring many labeled samples for training. Currently, the favored approach for few-shot learning [6,12,14,20,22,24], is mainly based on meta-learning methods. Meta-learning can be divided into metric-based [20], optimization-based [6], and model-based [25] approaches depending on how the model works. The metric-based methods are one of the most widely studied

© The Author(s), under exclusive license to Springer Nature Switzerland AG 2023
L. Iliadis et al. (Eds.): ICANN 2023, LNCS 14254, pp. 147–158, 2023.
https://doi.org/10.1007/978-3-031-44207-0_13

directions, which mainly learn a feature extractor to obtain feature representations of images and then calculate the distance between feature representations of samples for classification. Thus it requires image features with strong discrimination and generalization. Unfortunately, features extracted based on very little data often do not have these capabilities and can cause a degree of overfitting problems. Recently, the powerful feature extraction capabilities of contrastive learning have received widespread interest, the core idea of contrastive learning is mapping positive sample pairs to a close vector space while mapping negative sample pairs to a far away vector space. To enhance the generalization and discrimination of meta-learning, we combine metric-based meta-learning with contrastive learning in our work. It is well known that the local features of images also play a crucial role in the discriminative process. Inspired by this, in the training phase, we use the image's global features for contrastive learning and propose a maximum matching local feature contrastive learning to learn the features of the image comprehensively. Meanwhile, to better align with the paradigm of few-shot learning, we proposed a prototype contrastive module in the meta-training stage. In the meta-training stage, we save the vector representations of all base class prototypes. We conduct contrastive learning for each task between the generated N-way class prototypes and the saved base class prototypes. Moreover, we argue that the model generates class prototypes with better representational capabilities as the training process proceeds. Therefore, we dynamically update all saved base class prototypes to ensure the effectiveness of prototype contrastive module. Integrating the above approach, we propose a method called Diversified Contrast Learning (DCL) for few-shot. In summary, the contribution of our study can be described as follows:

- A contrastive learning algorithm using global and maximum matching local features of image data is proposed to improve the ability of the feature extractor.
- To better fit the paradigm of few-shot learning, a prototype contrastive module is proposed in the meta-training phase, which can let the model obtain features that better fit the metric-based method.
- A class prototype dynamic update mechanism is proposed to ensure the validity and discriminatory nature of the prototype contrastive module.
- We experimentally demonstrate that our method DCL reaches competitive accuracy on two popular benchmark datasets.

2   Related Work

2.1   Meta Learning

Meta-learning is born with the expectation of human-like "learning ability." Meta-learning aims to learn new tasks based on their existing knowledge quickly. Meta-learning can be primarily divided into three categories: metric-based methods, model-based methods, and optimization-based methods. Metric-based methods learn a metric space that can efficiently compare similarities between examples and adapt to new tasks quickly. Prototypical networks [20] learn a metric space where examples from the same class are closer together. It is achieved by mapping inputs to a low-dimensional embedding space, where class prototypes are defined as the mean embeddings of examples in each class. Matching Network [24] is achieved by using an attention mechanism to weigh the contributions of the support examples. Model-based methods learn a model that can be conditioned on new inputs to generate desired outputs. such as MMAML [25]. It is achieved by training a model on the distribution of tasks across different modalities and updating the shared representation using gradient descent on a small set of examples from a new task. Optimization-based methods, such as MAML [6] and TAML [10], learn a set of initial model parameters that can be fine-tuned quickly and effectively to new tasks with few examples. These methods use gradient-based optimization to update the model parameters and learn to adapt quickly to new tasks. Although meta-learning has achieved good results in few-shot learning, limited data can still result in overfitting and prevent extracting more discriminative and generalizable features. Therefore, we use contrastive learning to learn more discriminative features for images.

2.2 Contrastive Learning

Contrastive learning [1,2,8,9,23] is powerful for learning representations by contrasting positive and negative sample pairs of instances with various data augmentation and contrasting pairs of samples in a high-dimensional space. The main idea behind contrastive learning is to encourage positive samples to be closer and negative samples to be farther away from each other in the learned representation space. By doing so, contrastive learning can effectively learn discriminative features that capture the underlying structure of the data. Thus, contrastive learning has shown great potential in addressing the problem of data scarcity in few-shot learning. MOCO [8] uses an online encoder to encode input images and a fixed encoder to generate a fixed "memory bank." Then, contrastive learning is performed by comparing the output of the online encoder with the vectors in the "memory bank." SimCLR [2] is a representation learning method that utilizes contrastive loss in the latent space to maximize the consistency between different augmented views of the same data example to learn meaningful representations. Previous work combining few-shot learning with contrastive learning [4,7,21] mainly use the powerful unsupervised learning ability of contrastive learning as an auxiliary task. Although they achieve better results, they do not fully exploit the advantages of contrast learning in few-shot learning. In addition to using contrastive learning as an auxiliary task, we tried combining contrastive learning into a few-shot learning paradigm.

3 Methods

3.1 Problem Definition

In the Few-shot classification, two categories databases are given to us, which are named base dataset D_{base} and novel dataset D_{novel} respectively, $D_{base} =$

$\{(x_b^i, y_b^i)\}_{i=0}^{n_{base}}$, where $y_b^i \in C_{base}$ and the $D_{novel} = \{(x_n^i, y_n^i)\}_{i=0}^{n_{novel}}$, where $y_n^i \in C_{novel}$. The categories in them are disjoint ($D_{base} \cap D_{novel} = \varnothing$) and each category in the base category dataset has sufficient labeled training data, while each category in the novel dataset has only a small amount of labeled training data. Instead of sampling image data to train, in few-shot learning, we sample tasks to train. The task is usually called N-way K-shot which we should classify the N classes sampled with K labeled data in each category correctly. Meanwhile, the task is composed by support set $S = (x_n^i, y_n^i)\}_{i=0}^{N \times K}$ and query set $Q = (x_n^i, y_n^i)\}_{i=N \times K}^{N \times K + N \times Q}$, where Q is the number of images in each category in query set, and they also be sampled from the N categories in each task.

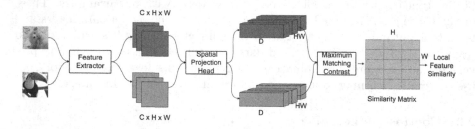

Fig. 1. The framework of the maximum matching local contrastive module.

3.2   Global Contrastive Loss

In our pre-training phase, we apply two different forms of data enhancement to each image in a batch $\{x_i, y_i\}_{i=1}^B$, so that our batch size changes from B to 2B. The two images obtained from the same image with two types of data enhancement form a positive sample pair and form negative sample pairs with other 2B-2 samples. We then define a feature extractor f_θ to extract the feature map of the image data. The feature map $\bar{x}_i = f_\theta(x_i) \in \mathbb{R}^{C \times H \times W}$ becomes the global feature $g_i \in \mathbb{R}^C$ after an adaptive averaging pooling (AdaptiveAvgPool). To improve the extraction power of the feature extractor f_θ, we use a fully-connected layer as mentioned in [2] to project the global feature vector to $h_i \in \mathbb{R}^D$. Finally, the global contrastive loss in the pre-training phase is then shown as follows:

$$L_{\text{global}} = -\sum_{i=1}^{2B} \log \frac{\exp\left(\mathbf{h}_i \cdot \mathbf{h}_i'/\tau_1\right)}{\sum_{j=1}^{2B} \mathbb{1}_{j \neq i} \exp\left(\mathbf{h}_i \cdot \mathbf{h}_j/\tau_1\right)}. \tag{1}$$

In the above equation, $\mathbf{h}_i$ and $\mathbf{h}_i'$ represent the global features of different views of an image data after the two data enhancements while the operation $\cdot$ represents the inner product operation between two vectors and the $\mathbb{1}$ is an indicator function. τ_1 is a temperature parameter.

3.3   Maximum Matching Local Contrastive Loss

We believe that using only the global features of an image for contrastive learning without considering the local features of the image cannot fully utilize the powerful self-supervised learning capability of contrast learning. Because in some images, the subject only accounts for a small part of the image, and the majority of the rest is background noise. Inspired by [4,15,30], we add local feature contrast loss of images in the pre-training phase to improve our model's robustness and generalization ability. Unlike previous work that directly compare feature vectors at corresponding positions of paired images, we consider different positions and poses of image subjects. When an image undergoes random rotation, the position and posture of the main object in the same image will significantly change. If only local feature similarity calculation is conducted based on corresponding positions, positive sample pairs may have extremely low local feature similarity. Therefore, we propose a maximum matching local contrastive loss. Specifically, let the local feature vector of one image perform similarity calculation with all the local feature vectors of another image and then take the maximum value as the similarity between the local position of the current image and the local position of another image. We use a spatial projection head to act on the feature map $\bar{x}_i$ to get the local feature map of the image $z_i \in \mathbb{R}^{HW \times D}$. This means that we divide the entire image data into HW local blocks, and each local block is a D-dimensional vector. The struct of the module is shown in Fig'. 1. The local feature similarity of two image data can be calculated as $sim(z_i, z_j) = \frac{1}{HW} \sum_{k=1}^{HW} \max_{1<=l<=HW}(v_{ik} \cdot v_{jl})$. Where the $v_{ij} \in \mathbb{R}^D$ represents the j th local block in image i. In our work, we take the sum of the local block similarities between images and take the average as the local feature similarity, thus our maximum matching local contrast loss can be computed as follows:

$$L_{\text{local}} = -\sum_{i=1}^{2B} \log \frac{\exp\left(sim(z_i, z_i')/\tau_2\right)}{\sum_{j=1}^{2B} \mathbb{1}_{j \neq i} \exp\left(sim(z_i, z_j)/\tau_2\right)}, \tag{2}$$

where z_i and z_i' represent the local features of different views of an image data after the two data enhancements, τ_2 is a temperature parameter.

3.4   Prototype Contrastive Loss

The contrast learning in the pre-training stage only judges the similarity between the positive and negative sample pairs we have constructed without considering the image category information. We argue that under the few-shot learning paradigm with a small amount of data, we should make full use of all the information of data. We can alleviate the overfitting problem of few-shot learning with all the information in the data. The DCL is based on prototype network [20], so we first compute the class prototype in the current task using the global feature vector g_i as follows:

$$\mathbf{c}_k = \frac{1}{|S_k|} \sum_{(g_i, y_i) \in S_k} g_i, \tag{3}$$

where S_k represents the set of sample data with category k. To effectively

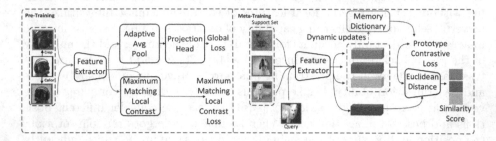

Fig. 2. The framework of the Diverse Contrastive Learning Network.

compare the class prototypes in the meta-training stage, inspired by [8], we use a "memory dictionary" M to store the class prototypes of all base classes, and dynamically update the stored base class prototypes as the training process progresses. The build process for M is as follows:

$$\mathbf{M}[k] = \begin{cases} c_k & M[k] == NULL \\ \lambda M[k] + (1 - \lambda)c_k & otherwise \end{cases}. \tag{4}$$

We use the category as the key of M and the class prototype corresponding to it as the value of M. For a class prototype c_k obtained inside a task, if the category k can be found in the memory dictionary, then the class prototype of the category k in the dictionary is dynamically updated. Otherwise, the current c_k is added to M as a new dictionary item and λ is a weight hyperparameter. Thus the prototype contrast loss can be expressed as follows:

$$L_{\text{prototype}} = -\sum_{i=1}^{N} \log \frac{\exp\left(c_i \cdot M[i]/\tau_3\right)}{\sum_{j=1}^{|M|} \exp\left(c_i \cdot M[j]/\tau_3\right)}, \tag{5}$$

where N represents the number of categories within a task, and M is a memory dictionary that stores prototypes of all base classes meanwhile τ_3 is a temperature parameter.

Our network consists of two training phases called the pre-training phase and the meta-training phase, and the overall network structure is shown in Fig. 2. In the pre-training phase, we perform self-supervised contrastive learning using global features of the image and more fine-grained local features. So the loss in our training phase is defined as $L_{\text{pre}} = \lambda_1 L_{\text{global}} + \lambda_2 L_{\text{local}}$. Besides, our method is a metric-based discriminant, so we also have a metric-based discriminant loss in the meta-training phase as follows:

$$L_{\text{ed}} = \sum_{i=1}^{NQ} -\log\left(\frac{\exp\left(-d\left(g_i, c_k\right)\right)}{\sum_{j=1}^{N} \exp\left(-d\left(g_i, c_j\right)\right)}\right). \tag{6}$$

where g_i represents the global feature vector of x_i and $d(\cdot)$ denotes the Euclidean Distance. So the total loss function of our meta-training phase can be defined as $L_{\text{meta}} = \lambda_3 L_{\text{prototype}} + \lambda_4 L_{\text{ed}}$.

Table 1. Few-shot classification accuracies on mini-imagenet and tiered-imagenet. average 5-way accuracy (%) is reported with 95% confidence interval. ('-' not reported)

Module	Backbone	mini-ImageNet		tirerd-ImageNet	
		1-shot	5-shot	1-shot	5-shot
Optimization-based					
MAML[6]	ConvNet-4	47.78 1.75	64.31 1.10	52.07 0.91	71.10 1.67
MetaOptNet[11]	ResNet-12	62.64 0.61	78.63 0.46	65.99 0.72	81.56 0.53
LEO[18]	WRN-28-10	61.76 0.08	77.59 0.12	66.33 0.05	81.44 0.09
MetaFun-DFP[28]	WRN-28-10	64.13 0.13	80.82 0.17	67.72 0.14	82.81 0.15
Model-based					
Meta-SGD[13]	ConvNet-4	54.24 0.03	70.86 0.04	62.95 0.03	79.34 0.06
Meta-learner[16]	ConvNet-4	43.44 0.77	60.60 0.71	-	-
Metrics					
ProtoNet [20]	ConvNet-4	49.42 0.78	68.20 0.66	53.31 0.89	72.69 0.74
MatchingNet [24]	ConvNet-4	43.56 0.84	55.31 0.73	-	-
RelationNet [22]	ConvNet-4	50.44 0.82	65.32 0.70	54.48 0.93	71.32 0.78
TADAM [14]	ResNet-12	58.05 0.30	76.07 0.30	-	-
DSMNet[29]	ConvNet-4	52.33 0.62	70.48 0.52	-	-
COOPERATE[5]	ResNet-12	62.72 0.41	71.24 0.33	59.51 0.43	73.78 0.34
Meta-OLE[27]	ResNet-12	**67.04 0.72**	82.23 0.67	68.82 0.71	85.51 0.59
CC+rot [7]	WRN-28-10	62.93 0.45	79.87 0.33	62.93 0.45	79.87 0.33
PSST [4]	WRN-28-10	64.16 0.44	80.64 0.32	-	-
Baselines					
Meta-Baseline[3]	ResNet-12	63.17 0.23	79.26 0.17	68.62 0.27	83.29 0.18
Prototypical Network	ResNet-12	60.76 0.39	78.44 0.21	66.25 0.34	80.11 0.91
Ours(Correspond)	ResNet-12	62.14 0.14	80.02 0.43	68.22 0.43	80.87 0.61
Ours(Maximum)	ResNet-12	65.21 0.50	**82.31 0.14**	**69.49 0.34**	**85.63 0.43**

4 Experiments

4.1 Datasets

We selected two data sets that are more mainstream in few-learning.

Mini-Imagenet. [24] is a popular dataset used to test few-shot learning algorithms. It contains 60,000 images from Imagenet, divided into 100 classes with 600 images each. It is usually divided into three subsets: the train set contains 64 classes, the validation set contains 16 classes and the test set contains 20 classes. They do not overlap with each other.

Tiered-Imagenet. [17] is an advanced version of Mini-Imagenet, it consists of 608 classes with 779,165 images. Out of these, 351 categories were used for the training set, 97 categories were used for the validation set, and 8 categories were used for the test set.

4.2   Implementation Details

In both the pre-training phase and the meta-training phase, we used ReNet-12 as the backbone model and Adam as the optimizer. The Adam optimizer for both stages with a momentum of 0.9, the learning rate starts from 0.001 and the weight decay is 0.0006.

Pre-Training Phase. During the pre-training stage, the model was trained for 500 epochs with batch size 64. Meanwhile, we applied cropping with rotation and color jittering with rotation as data augmentations. The temperature parameter $\tau_{1,2}$ were set to 0.5 and 0.3. Meanwhile, The parameters $\lambda_{1,2}$ for balancing global and local contrastive losses were both set to 0.5.

Meta-Training Phase. During the meta-learning stage, the model was trained for 400 epochs, and each epoch contains 100 sampled tasks. In the 5-way 5-shot tasks, we set the value of N to 5, the value of K to 5, and the value of Q to 16. In 5-way 1-shot tasks only the value of K was changed to 1. The hyperparameters τ_3 were set to 0.5 and $\lambda_{3,4}$ were both set to 0.5. The λ used to adjust the update frequency of the memory dictionary is set to 0.01.

Evaluation Metric. We followed the standard setting of few-shot learning, experimenting 5-way 1-shot and 5-way 5-shot on mini-ImageNet and tiered-ImageNet. Our model is evaluated with 600 randomly sampled test tasks and reports the average accuracy with 95% confidence intervals.

4.3   Results on Benchmark Datasets

Following the standard setting, we conducted 5-way 1-shot and 5-way 5-shot experiments on mini-ImageNet and tiered-ImageNet, with the outcomes presented in Table 1. We first compared our model with various mainstream works: Compared with optimization-based methods [6,11,18,28], our method avoided the problem of extra effort to adjust due to the sensitivity of the initial value of the parameters while obtaining superior performance. Compared to metric-based methods [14,20,22,24], we used contrastive learning in both training phases to better extract features from the images, achieving better results while mitigating the overfitting problem caused by the scarcity of data in metric-based methods. In addition, the core idea of our work is based on the prototype network, so we reimplemented it using ResNet-12 as our baseline. Besides, we also used [3] as our baseline, which is a more reliable benchmark in the few-shot classification. Finally, to illustrate the advantages of our maximum matching local comparison, we implemented our DCL with the local comparison of the corresponding position, denoted as Maximum and Correspond, respectively. It could be seen that our proposed method had obvious advantages over the Correspond and baseline. This demonstrates the feasibility of combining contrastive learning with few-shot learning and confirms that our proposed maximum matching local pairwise contrastive algorithm can extract more discriminative features from images without being confused by similar pairs of samples with low similarity. Finally, our method also outperformed PSST [4] and CC+rot [7], which also uses contrastive learning in few-shot learning. In summary, the above comparison experiments could strongly confirm that our model achieves state-of-the-art performance.

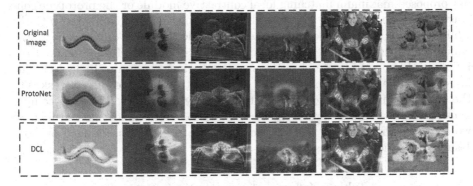

Fig. 3. The Grad-CAM visualization of samples in the mini-ImageNet dataset.

4.4   Ablation Study

To illustrate the validity of the different components of our model. We will use the ResNet-12 as the backbone to conduct 5-way 1-shot and 5-way 5-shot experiments on the mini-ImageNet dataset.

Table 2. Ablation Experiments On DCL. (✓WITH; - Without)

DCL			mini-ImageNet			DCL			mini-ImageNet	
	global	local	prototype	1-shot	5-shot		global	local	prototype	1-shot	5-shot
(a)	–	–	–	60.76	78.44	(e)	✓	✓	-	63.78	80.52
(b)	✓	–	–	61.32	79.56	(f)	✓	–	✓	63.67	80.44
(c)	–	✓	–	63.26	80.02	(g)	–	✓	✓	64.64	81.75
(d)	–	–	✓	63.19	80.12	(h)	✓	✓	✓	65.21	82.31

Influence on Our Module. Table 2 showed the ablation analysis of different components in our model, in which global, local, and prototype represented the global feature contrastive module, the maximum matching local contrastive module, and the prototype contrastive module, respectively. Without considering (h), the combination of local and prototype in the (g) worked best on mini-ImageNet with an improvement of nearly 4% on the 5-shot problem and nearly 3% on the 1-shot problem. This showed that our proposed maximum matching local contrastive module and prototype contrastive module were able to extract better features of the images. Meanwhile, the combination of global and local, represented by (e), and the combination of global and prototypical, represented by (f), also had an improvement of nearly 3% both on 5-shot and nearly 2% on 1-shot. By observing (b),(c), and (d), we could see that removing each component could cause a drop in performance, especially when removing our proposed maximum matching local contrastive module or the prototype contrastive module, there was a drop of almost 4% on the 5-shot compared with (h) while removing only the global contrastive module there was only a drop of 2%, which confirmed the effectiveness of our proposed module. Table 3 showed the influence of hyperparameter λ in the memory dictionary on mini-ImageNet. The larger the value of λ, the more similar a class prototype of the current task is to the corresponding class prototype in the memory dictionary. Thus the component could get a shallow prototype comparison loss with almost no learning. So we could see that when $\lambda = 0.01$, the best performance was obtained on both 1-shot and 5-shot problems.

Table 3. Influence of λ on the mini-imagenet

λ	1-shot	5-shot
0.1	62.79 0.34	80.01 0.54
0.01	**65.21 0.50**	**82.31 0.14**
0.001	62.31 0.72	80.61 0.23

Visualization Analysis. We performed a Grad-CAM [19] visualization of some samples in the novel class of the mini-ImageNet dataset to illustrate our validity model further. In Fig. 3, we can see that our model is more focused on the content of the corresponding category of images than the prototype network. For instance, in the third column, the ProtoNet focuses on only part of the target class, while our model focuses on the entirety of the target class. In the fifth column, the ProtoNet does not correctly focus on the target category due to human interference in the image's background. In contrast, our DCL correctly focuses on the target category. In the last column, our DCL achieves better results than the ProtoNet even when there are multiple target classes in the image, which is a good indication of the effectiveness of our model.

5   Conclusion

In this paper, we deeply explore the effects of the complementarity of contrastive learning and few-shot learning. In the pre-training phase, we propose using the maximum matching local contrast loss module to learn the features of the image more comprehensively. Besides, to better combine contrastive learning with the few-shot learning paradigm, we propose a class-prototype contrastive module in the meta-training phase. The experimental results on benchmark datasets and ablation experiments demonstrate the validity of our method and the competitiveness compared with the state-of-the-art.

Acknowledgement. This work is Supported by the National Key Research and Development Program of China (No. 2018YFA0701700; No. 2018YFA0701701) and National Natural Science Foundation of China (62002253, 62176172, 61672364).

References

1. Bachman, P., Hjelm, R.D., Buchwalter, W.: Learning representations by maximizing mutual information across views. In: Advances in Neural Information Processing Systems 32 (2019)
2. Chen, T., Kornblith, S., Norouzi, M., Hinton, G.: A simple framework for contrastive learning of visual representations. In: International Conference on Machine Learning, pp. 1597–1607. PMLR (2020)
3. Chen, Y., Wang, X., Liu, Z., Xu, H., Darrell, T., et al.: A new meta-baseline for few-shot learning, vol. 2(3), p. 5. arXiv preprint arXiv:2003.04390 (2020)
4. Chen, Z., Ge, J., Zhan, H., Huang, S., Wang, D.: Pareto self-supervised training for few-shot learning. In: Proceedings of the IEEE/CVF Conference on Computer Vision and Pattern Recognition, pp. 13663–13672 (2021)
5. Dai, L., Feng, L., Shang, X., Su, H.: Cross modal adaptive few-shot learning based on task dependence. Chin. J. Electron. **32**(1), 85–96 (2023)
6. Finn, C., Abbeel, P., Levine, S.: Model-agnostic meta-learning for fast adaptation of deep networks. In: International Conference On Machine Learning, pp. 1126–1135. PMLR (2017)
7. Gidaris, S., Bursuc, A., Komodakis, N., Pérez, P., Cord, M.: Boosting few-shot visual learning with self-supervision. In: Proceedings of the IEEE/CVF International Conference on Computer Vision, pp. 8059–8068 (2019)
8. He, K., Fan, H., et al.: Momentum contrast for unsupervised visual representation learning. In: 2020 IEEE/CVF Conference on Computer Vision and Pattern Recognition, Seattle, WA, USA, 13–19 June 2020, pp. 9726–9735. Computer Vision Foundation/IEEE (2020). https://doi.org/10.1109/CVPR42600.2020.00975
9. Hjelm, R.D., et al.: Learning deep representations by mutual information estimation and maximization. arXiv preprint arXiv:1808.06670 (2018)
10. Jamal, M.A., Qi, G.J.: Task agnostic meta-learning for few-shot learning. In: Proceedings of the IEEE/CVF Conference on Computer Vision and Pattern Recognition, pp. 11719–11727 (2019)
11. Lee, K., Maji, S., et al.: Meta-learning with differentiable convex optimization. In: IEEE Conference on Computer Vision and Pattern Recognition, Long Beach, CA, USA, 16–20 June 2019, pp. 10657–10665. Computer Vision Foundation/IEEE (2019). https://doi.org/10.1109/CVPR.2019.01091
12. Li, G., Zheng, H., Liu, D., Wang, C., Su, B., Zheng, C.: Semmae: semantic-guided masking for learning masked autoencoders. arXiv preprint arXiv:2206.10207 (2022)
13. Li, Z., Zhou, F., Chen, F., Li, H.: Meta-sgd: learning to learn quickly for few-shot learning. arXiv preprint arXiv:1707.09835 (2017)
14. Oreshkin, B., Rodríguez López, P., Lacoste, A.: Tadam: task dependent adaptive metric for improved few-shot learning. In: Advances in Neural Information Processing Systems 31 (2018)
15. Ouali, Y., Hudelot, C., Tami, M.: Spatial contrastive learning for few-shot classification. In: Oliver, N., Pérez-Cruz, F., Kramer, S., Read, J., Lozano, J.A. (eds.) ECML PKDD 2021. LNCS (LNAI), vol. 12975, pp. 671–686. Springer, Cham (2021). https://doi.org/10.1007/978-3-030-86486-6_41

16. Ravi, S., Larochelle, H.: Optimization as a model for few-shot learning. In: 5th International Conference on Learning Representations, ICLR 2017, Toulon, France, 24–26 April 2017, Conference Track Proceedings. OpenReview.net (2017)

17. Ren, M., et al.: Meta-learning for semi-supervised few-shot classification. arXiv preprint arXiv:1803.00676 (2018)

18. Rusu, A.A., et al.: Meta-learning with latent embedding optimization. In: 7th International Conference on Learning Representations, New Orleans, LA, USA, 6–9 May 2019. OpenReview.net (2019)

19. Selvaraju, R.R., et al.: Grad-cam: visual explanations from deep networks via gradient-based localization. In: IEEE International Conference on Computer Vision, Venice, Italy, 22–29 October 2017, pp. 618–626. IEEE Computer Society (2017). https://doi.org/10.1109/ICCV.2017.74

20. Snell, J., Swersky, K., Zemel, R.: Prototypical networks for few-shot learning. In: Advances in Neural Information Processing Systems 30 (2017)

21. Su, J.-C., Maji, S., Hariharan, B.: When does self-supervision improve few-shot learning? In: Vedaldi, A., Bischof, H., Brox, T., Frahm, J.-M. (eds.) ECCV 2020. LNCS, vol. 12352, pp. 645–666. Springer, Cham (2020). https://doi.org/10.1007/978-3-030-58571-6_38

22. Sung, F., et al.: Learning to compare: relation network for few-shot learning. In: 2018 IEEE Conference on Computer Vision and Pattern Recognition, Salt Lake City, UT, USA, 18–22 June 2018, pp. 1199–1208. Computer Vision Foundation / IEEE Computer Society (2018). https://doi.org/10.1109/CVPR.2018.00131

23. Tian, Y., Krishnan, D., Isola, P.: Contrastive multiview coding. In: Vedaldi, A., Bischof, H., Brox, T., Frahm, J.-M. (eds.) ECCV 2020. LNCS, vol. 12356, pp. 776–794. Springer, Cham (2020). https://doi.org/10.1007/978-3-030-58621-8_45

24. Vinyals, O., Blundell, C., Lillicrap, T., Wierstra, D., et al.: Matching networks for one shot learning. In: Advances in Neural Information Processing Systems 29 (2016)

25. Vuorio, R., Sun, S.H., Hu, H., Lim, J.J.: Multimodal model-agnostic meta-learning via task-aware modulation. In: Advances in Neural Information Processing Systems 32 (2019)

26. Wang, X., Zheng, Z., He, Y., Yan, F., Zeng, Z., Yang, Y.: Soft person reidentification network pruning via blockwise adjacent filter decaying. IEEE Trans. Cybern. **52**(12), 13293–13307 (2021)

27. Wang, Z., Lu, Y., Qiu, Q.: Meta-ole: meta-learned orthogonal low-rank embedding. In: Proceedings of the IEEE/CVF Winter Conference on Applications of Computer Vision (WACV), pp. 5305–5314 (January 2023)

28. Xu, J., Ton, J.F., Kim, H., Kosiorek, A., Teh, Y.W.: Metafun: meta-learning with iterative functional updates. In: International Conference on Machine Learning, pp. 10617–10627. PMLR (2020)

29. Yan, L., Li, F., Zhang, L., Zheng, X.: Discriminant space metric network for few-shot image classification. In: Applied Intelligence, pp. 1–16 (2023)

30. Yang, Z., Wang, J., Zhu, Y.: Few-shot classification with contrastive learning. In: Computer Vision-ECCV 2022: 17th European Conference, Tel Aviv, Israel, 23–27 October 2022, Proceedings, Part XX, pp. 293–309. Springer (2022). https://doi.org/10.1007/978-3-031-20044-1_17

Enhancing Cross-Lingual Few-Shot Named Entity Recognition by Prompt-Guiding

Yige Wang, Yucheng Huang, Tieliang Gong, and Chen Li[✉]

School of Computer Science and Technology, Xian Jiaotong University, Xian, China
{jihejue039,huangyucheng}@stu.xjtu.edu.cn, {gongtl,cli}@xjtu.edu.cn

Abstract. The cross-lingual named entity recognition task has attracted significant attention from researchers. Previous work has demonstrated that incorporating unlabeled data with potential entities in the target language can enhance cross-lingual model performance. However, unlabeled data for the target language is not always available, and the entity types may not share the same label space as the source language. To address this issue, we introduce a new NER task called cross-lingual few-shot NER. Distance metric learning has emerged as a popular solution for low-resource scenarios without semantic information for the target language. Inspired by few-shot metric learning and prompt learning, we propose a novel method called Cross-lingual Prompt-guiding Named Entity Recognition (CroPoNER) for this task. We use prompts from different languages to serve as 1) supervisory guidance for conveying unseen entity type information to the language model; 2) metric referents for predicting target language entity types; 3) a bridge between different languages that mitigates the language gap. Our experiments on several widely-used cross-lingual NER datasets (CoNLL, WikiAnn) in the few-shot setting demonstrate that our method outperforms state-of-the-art models by a significant margin in most cases for cross-lingual few-shot NER.

Keywords: Named Entity Recognition · Few-shot Learning · Cross-lingual · Metric Referent

1 Introduction

Named Entity Recognition (NER) is a key task in NLU, involving the extraction and categorization of entities in unstructured text. Deep learning has shown impressive potential for NER [2,12,23], but requires large-scale labeled data. Annotating data for minority languages like Dutch is costly and time-consuming. To address the zero-shot cross-lingual NER problem [1,31], studies have explored semi-supervised approaches such as knowledge distillation [28,29] and translation-based augmentation [9,17], which require substantial target language data or a translation model.

© The Author(s), under exclusive license to Springer Nature Switzerland AG 2023
L. Iliadis et al. (Eds.): ICANN 2023, LNCS 14254, pp. 159–170, 2023.
https://doi.org/10.1007/978-3-031-44207-0_14

In the real-world scenario, acquiring labeled data is relatively straightforward for high-resource languages such as English and Chinese, allowing models to perform well. However, in low-resource languages like Dutch, annotating specific domains, such as sentiment analysis or medical terminology, may prove challenging. For these target language domains, procuring substantial annotated data is difficult, while obtaining a small quantity of data necessitates minimal effort and is easily achievable. In such situations, the expectation is for the model to effectively transfer from the source language to the target domain within the target language. Consequently, we introduce a novel task termed cross-lingual few-shot Named Entity Recognition (NER). The complexity of this task lies in the model's capacity to transfer knowledge not only to the target language but also across various domains.

Contemporary Few-shot Learning (FSL) and prompt learning approaches have demonstrated effectiveness in performing Natural Language Understanding (NLU) tasks [10,14] in monolingual, low-resource settings. FSL, leveraging prior knowledge, rapidly generalizes to new tasks with limited samples and supervision. Recent research on distance metrics [22,26,27] reveals their potential for FSL, as they train models to learn a metric space surrounding a single prototype guided by language models like BERT [5] in monolingual contexts. Named Entity Recognition (NER), however, is a token-level task, posing additional challenges. Ding et al. and Yang et al. [7,32] employ nearest neighbor inferences for monolingual test sample predictions. Nonetheless, our experiments indicate that applying distance metrics in the source language without target language knowledge yields unsatisfactory results.

Prompt-based learning, an alternative strategy, exploits language model knowledge via task-specific templates containing task-related information, enabling models to handle similar tasks with less data. This approach has achieved promising results for few-shot problems [11,15,20]. In the NER task, Cui et al. [4] utilize templates for all possible spans to determine entity types, but inefficiencies arise due to span enumeration and potential result disturbances from span overlaps. These methods primarily focus on monolingual settings and prove challenging to transfer to cross-lingual contexts. Transitioning to cross-lingual settings could enhance models' generalization capabilities across various languages.

To address the cross-lingual few-shot Named Entity Recognition (NER) challenge, we introduce a novel method called **CroPoNER** (**C**ross-lingual **Pro**mpt-guided **N**amed **E**ntity **R**ecognition), which combines the strengths of prompt-guided learning and few-shot metric learning. CroPoNER aims to bridge the gap between the source and target languages through prompt guidance and enhance representation via metric learning. Manually designed prompts for target entity types are input to the model to facilitate knowledge acquisition of the target entity type within the language model. The model is provided with target language prompts to convey both language- and entity-specific knowledge. As depicted in Fig. 1, cross-lingual prompt guidance reduces the embedding distance of the same entity type, enabling CroPoNER to better capture language-independent information for target entities. Leveraging prompts eliminates the need for substantial target language unlabeled data or translation models.

We perform experiments on a general English dataset and assess our method on two prevalent cross-lingual datasets in the few-shot context. We examine existing approaches for both few-shot and cross-lingual scenarios within the NER task and compare our method against these techniques. Our experimental results indicate that our method surpasses the state-of-the-art in the majority of cases. In summary, our contributions are as follows:

- We introduce a novel NER task, termed cross-lingual few-shot NER, which better reflects real-world situations where acquiring sufficient target language data in a specific domain is challenging.
- We present a new cross-lingual few-shot method, CroPoNER, that leverages the strengths of prompt and metric learning. By incorporating prompt sentences from different languages, CroPoNER acquires enhanced target language representations in low-resource settings.
- We carry out experiments on widely-used cross-lingual NER datasets within a low-resource context. The results demonstrate that our approach attains state-of-the-art performance compared to prior methods.

2   Task Formulation

The NER task is predominantly approached as a sequence tagging task. Given an input sequence $X = \{x_1, x_2, \cdots, x_l\}$, the NER model is trained to generate a label $y \in \mathcal{C}$ for each word x_i, where $\mathcal{C}$ represents a predefined entity set for the task. The NER task assumes that the input sequences in both the training stage (X_{train}) and evaluation stage (X_{test}) belong to the same language, where $\mathcal{U}_{train} = \mathcal{U}_{test}$.

2.1   Cross-Lingual NER

In the cross-lingual setting, X_{train} and X_{test} are from different language $\mathcal{U}_{train} \cap \mathcal{U}_{test} = \varnothing$ or X_{test} containing more language $\mathcal{U}_{train} \subset \mathcal{U}_{test}$, requiring the model to have the ability for transferring knowledge from the source language $\mathcal{U}_{train}$ to the target language $\mathcal{U}_{test}$.

2.2   Few-Shot NER

For the few-shot NER task, there is a rich source dataset $\mathbb{H}$ for training and a low-resource dataset $\mathbb{L}$ for testing. The label set between $\mathbb{L}$ and $\mathbb{H}$ is not equal, where $\mathcal{C}_L \neq \mathcal{C}_H$, which requires the model to have the ability to fast adjust to a new entity type.

2.3   Cross-Lingual Few-Shot NER

In this paper, we define a new task named cross-lingual few-shot NER. For the training stage, there is a rich source dataset $X_{train} \in \mathbb{H}$ in source language

$X_{train} \in \mathcal{U}_{train}$, on which the model is trained. For the evaluating stage, a low resource dataset $X_{test} \in \mathcal{U}_{test}$ in the target language $X_{test} \in U_{test}$ is provided, and the language type between the source and the target is totally different. The label set between training and testing is not equivalent $\mathcal{C}_L \neq \mathcal{C}_H$, which means we only have a few labeled data in the target language for the new entity type. The model is transferred from X_{train} and is evaluated on X_{test}. In this setting, we can test the model's ability of cross-lingual ability and few-shot ability.

3   Methodology

In this section, we introduce our methodology and its detailed implementation. As shown in Fig. 1, our framework consists of four parts. For only the training stage, few shot sampling is used to reduce the difference between training and evaluation. Secondly, for both training and evaluation, prompts are manually designed for each entity type for each language, and thirdly the prompted sentence is fed to the pre-trained language model (PLM) to encode. For the loss calculation, novel three losses are adopted for model adapting, where the metric losses $\mathcal{L}_{src}$ from the source language and $\mathcal{L}_{tgt}$ from the target language aim to calculate the similarity between each word in text and entity type referents. For referents from different languages, $\mathcal{L}_{sim}$ is calculated additionally to catch the common semantic for both languages.

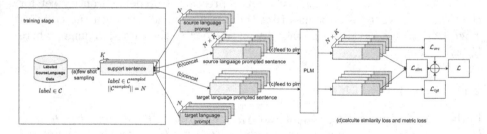

Fig. 1. The architecture of CroPoNER framework with Prompt guiding. For each training step, we (a) use few-shot sampling to sample K' shot the same as evaluating stage. (b) concatenate monolingual and target language prompts with original sentences. (c) feed concatenated sentences to PLM to get sentence embedding. (d) calculate similarity loss between both language embedding and tagging loss for each language. For evaluating stage, we use few-shot samples directly to process (b), following the same path from (b) to (d)

3.1   Few Shot Sampling

For the evaluating phrase, our model is evaluated on a low-resource dataset $\mathbb{L}$, but in the training stage, the model is trained on a rich source dataset $\mathbb{H}$. We want to alleviate the difference between the two stages. For each training episode, several few-shot samples are sampled to imitate the evaluating stage.

For each episode, N entity types are randomly selected from training predefined entity label set $\mathcal{C}^{train}$ where $N = N_{test}$ as $\mathcal{C}^{sampled}$ where $||\mathcal{C}^{sampled}|| = N$. And then, K' sentences are selected that include K shots for each entity type from randomly selected entity types where the number of entity types N is equal to the evaluating phrase dataset's entity type number N_{test}. A greedy-including approach is utilized to achieve this sampling step. As shown in Algorithm 1, with the sampling algorithm, it can be easy to get various different few-shot training samples for models to learn to adapt swiftly.

Algorithm 1. Training Greedy Sample Algorithm

Require: Dataset $\mathcal{X}$, Train Label set $\mathcal{C}^{train}$, shot number K, entity types number N

Ensure: Sampled Episode Data $\mathcal{S}$

1: $\mathcal{S} \leftarrow \varnothing$
2: **for** $i = 1$ to N **do**
3:    $Count[i] = 0$
4: **end for**
5: **while** exists $Count[i] < K$ **do**
6:    Randomly select a pair $(\boldsymbol{x},\boldsymbol{y}) \in \mathcal{X}$
7:    Count entity numbers in $(\boldsymbol{x},\boldsymbol{y})$ $Count_{new}$
8:    $Add \leftarrow true$
9:    **for** $i = 1$ to N **do**
10:      **if** $Count[i] + Count_{new}[i] > K$ **then**
11:        $Add \leftarrow false$
12:      **end if**
13:    **end for**
14:    **if** Add **then**
15:      $\mathcal{S} = \mathcal{S} \cup (\boldsymbol{x},\boldsymbol{y})$
16:      Update Count
17:    **end if**
18: **end while**

3.2 Prompt Engineering

For each unknown entity type, we provide the model with several candidate prompts. We collect the entity descriptions from dataset introduction, Oxford English dictionary [6] and self annotation for English. We asked two questions to two crowd workers in arbitrary order: (1) which prompt can better describe the entity type? (2) which prompt contains more information? This investigation assists us in selecting a better prompt for representing the knowledge from the entity type. In the majority of cases, the test label set $||\mathcal{C}^{test}|| < 10$, which means the manual effort to be made is extremely smaller than getting more annotated data. For the target language, we invited language specialists to translate the selected prompt into the target language. Also, due to the limit of entity label set $\mathcal{C}^{test}$, this procedure requires little manual effort. By this approach, we can get a prompt set $\mathbb{P}$.

3.3   Model Structure

Prompt Construction: Our model will start by constructing prompts. Suppose there is a sampled episode S from few-shot sampling, and its label set is $C^{sampled}$. Prompt $\boldsymbol{p}= \{p_1, p_2, \cdots, p_N\} \in \mathbb{P}$ is selected equal to the label set $C^{sampled}$. As shown in Fig. 1, suppose input sentences are $\boldsymbol{Se}= \{Se_1, Se_2, \cdots, Se_{K'}\}$, concatenated prompt sentence can be acquired by the following equation

$$Concat(\boldsymbol{Se}, \boldsymbol{p}) = \{Sep_1, Sep_2, \cdots, Sep_{N \times K'}\} \tag{1}$$

For each sentence word x in Se_i, where $Se_i = \{x_1, x_2, \cdots, x_{slen}\}$, and for each prompt $p_j = \{x_1^{p_j}, x_2^{p_j}, \cdots, x_{plen}^{p_j}\}$ with prompt word x^{p_j}, concatenated sequence can be provided by $Sep_k = \{[CLS], x_1, x_2, \cdots, x_{slen}, [SEP], x_1^{p_j}, x_2^{p_j}, \cdots, x_{plen}^{p_j}\}$. The [CLS] and [SEP] token is the special token for PLM to notify [5]. In this way, each sentence will be concatenated to N prompted sentence.

Word Encoder: Since this is the cross-lingual NER task, multilingual mBERT [30] is unitized as a word encoder to extract the prompted sentence embedding. The model network structure can be formulated as follows:

$$\boldsymbol{h} = \mathrm{mBERT}(\boldsymbol{Sep}) \tag{2}$$

where $\boldsymbol{h} = \{h\}_{i=1}^{L}$ represents the output of the pre-trained mBERT that corresponds to the input token Sep_i, and the output is the hidden representation of the input sequence. The former part $\{h\}_{i=1}^{slen}$ is the hidden states of the original sentence and the later part $\{h\}_{i=slen+1}^{plen}$ is the hidden states of the prompt sentence.

Referents Calculation: For each sentence Se_i, its corresponding prompted sentence is $Sep_{j=(i-1)N}^{iN-1}$, For each Sep_j, the distance between [SEP] and each word $\boldsymbol{x}$ is calculated by

$$d_j = \mathrm{dot}(\boldsymbol{h}_j^x, h_j^{[Sep]}) \tag{3}$$

where $\boldsymbol{h}_j^x$ represents the original word in the Se_i. And the distance function dot is dot multiplication of matrix. Suppose the original label is (x,y), and contrastive loss [13] of each word as $l(x)$ can be calculated by

$$l(x) = -\log \frac{\exp\left(-d_x^y\right)/\tau}{\sum_{q=1}^{N} \exp\left(-d_x^{y^q}\right)/\tau} \tag{4}$$

where τ is the temperature hyper-parameter for training. And for the whole sentence, the total tagging loss $\mathcal{L}_{src}$ of a sample S in the source language is

$$\mathcal{L}_{src} = \frac{1}{|S|} \sum_{x_i \in S \,\wedge\, p \in \mathcal{U}_{train}} l(x) \tag{5}$$

For the target tagging loss $\mathcal{L}_{tgt}$, the same procedure from equation (1) to equation (5) is adopted. The only change is the prompt's language, which means translated prompt is utilized to concatenate sentences in the target language $\mathcal{U}_{test}$.

$$\mathcal{L}_{tgt} = \frac{1}{|\mathcal{S}|} \sum_{x_i \in \mathcal{S} \wedge p \in \mathcal{U}_{test}} l(x) \tag{6}$$

Similarity Loss Calculation: In this part, inspired by [18], we put forward a hypothesis that is for prompts that represent the same entity type have a higher possibility of having similar embedding. Suppose hidden representations for source language $h_{src}^{[SEP]}$ and target language $h_{tgt}^{[SEP]}$ are given, and cosine similarity between them is calculated by

$$\text{Sim}(h_{src}^{[SEP]}, h_{tgt}^{[SEP]}) = \frac{h_{src}^{[SEP]} \cdot h_{tgt}^{[SEP]}}{\max(||h_{src}^{[SEP]}||_2, ||h_{tgt}^{[SEP]}||_2)} \tag{7}$$

We expect the similarity to get higher. In this section, the BCE loss function is adopted. The similarity loss can be formulated as

$$\mathcal{L}_{sim} = \sum_{i=1}^{N} \mathcal{L}_{BCE}(\text{Sim}_i(h_{src}^{[SEP]}, h_{tgt}^{[SEP]}), 1) \tag{8}$$

And then for the whole model training part, the sum of the above losses is weighed by

$$\mathcal{L} = \alpha_1 \mathcal{L}_{src} + \alpha_2 \mathcal{L}_{tgt} + \beta \mathcal{L}_{sim} \tag{9}$$

where $\alpha_1, \alpha_2, \beta$ are set to adjust manually. Finally, the accumulated loss is used for the training stage in order to optimize the model.

4 Experiment

4.1 Dataset

We test our experiments on three widely used cross-lingual datasets: CoNLL2002 [24], CoNLL2003 [25], WikiAnn [19]. CoNLL2002 has two languages, which are Spanish (**es**) and Dutch (**nl**). And for CoNLL2003, it includes English (**en**) and German (**de**). For WikiAnn, it includes 282 languages, for which we select the three languages equivalent to CoNLL to conduct our experiment from the English (**en**) source language. For the training stage, OntoNotes 5.0 [21] are utilized as a rich source dataset in English. For the test stage, we give few-shot samples for the test dataset to test the ability to transfer knowledge in the cross-lingual few-shot NER task.

4.2 Baselines

In our experiments, we compare the following models:

- TSL [29]: an approach that proposes a teacher-student semi-supervised model for cross-lingual NER.
- AdvPicker [3]: a **distillation-based** cross-lingual NER model, by training a teacher model in the source language to conduct student model training on the target language unlabeled data with pseudo labels. We provide 50 extra sentences for each entity type for the distillation step.
- UniTrans [28]: a **translation augmentation-based** NER model, which translates the source language dataset into the target language word by word.
- COPNER [8]: a **prompt-based** metric referents model for few-shot NER, using label words to represent the label stage, and reached SOTA for few shot NER.

4.3 Implementation Details

We use PyTorch 1.9.1 to construct our model. For PLM, we adopt mBERT [30] as our word encoder in the hugging face transformer.

We set the max sentence length to 70, and the excess part is truncated as the following sentence. We use AdamW [16] as the model optimizer with default hyperparameters except learning rates to 1×10^{-4}. We set the weight parameter $\alpha_1 = 1$, $\alpha_2 = 1$, $\beta = 0.8$, and the temperature τ the same as [13].

5 Results and Discussion

In this section, we report the performance on the mentioned datasets and analyze the reason for unsatisfactory performance in the cross-lingual few-shot NER task.

Table 1. The results on CoNLL

Model Name	Extra Data	5-shot			3-shot			1-shot			Average
		de	nl	es	de	nl	es	de	nl	es	
TSL	w/	0.28	0.45	0.06	0.27	0.37	0.06	0.25	0.43	0.06	0.25
AdvPicker	w/	0.8	0.44	0.52	0.12	0.32	0.12	0.13	0.32	0.12	0.32
UniTrans	w/	1.198	0.16	0.107	1.72	0.0813	0.0814	1.68	0.0812	0.081	0.66
COPNER	w/o	4.38	3.36	7.29	4.29	2.98	3.68	4.03	2.38	2.82	3.91
CroPoNER(ours)	w/o	**5.67**	**11.79**	**8.5**	**4.96**	**9.06**	**5.19**	**4.46**	**5.27**	**3.45**	**6.48**

Table 2. The results on WikiAnn

Model Name	Extra Data	5-shot			3-shot			1-shot			Average
		de	nl	es	de	nl	es	de	nl	es	
TSL	w/	0.19	0.24	0.39	0.18	0.24	0.34	0.18	0.22	0.31	0.25
Advpicker	w/	0.12	0.33	0.23	0.12	0.24	0.13	0.13	0.23	0.15	0.19
UniTrans	w/	1.1	1.45	7.28	1.19	1.3	6.81	1.1	1.24	6.75	3.14
COPNER	w/o	5.72	9.77	11.54	5.37	**9.75**	6.99	2.04	6.24	4.5	6.88
CroPoNER(ours)	w/o	**11.51**	**11.95**	**17.48**	**9.33**	9.69	**11.48**	**5.98**	**7.11**	**9.18**	**10.41**

5.1   Overall Results

Table 1 and Table 2 report the result of experiments on two datasets with 1-shot, 3-shot, and 5-shot data pieces for three languages.

The experiment results demonstrate the effectiveness of our framework. Compared with the traditional tagging model, the traditional BERT-tagger model cannot solve this problem at all. Compared with the former cross-lingual model AdvPicker and Unitrans, our design structure doesn't require much target language unlabeled data with the latent entity. Furthermore, our model obtains significant and consistent improvements in F1-score. Also, our structure doesn't need a language model translating from source language to target language.

For the few-shot NER model, we import knowledge of the target language by prompted sentence. Compared with COPNER, with sentence-level prompts, we improve F1-score by around 2% for the cross-lingual setting.

5.2   Ablation Study

We perform an ablation study on the following settings to demonstrate our model's effectiveness on the 5-shot WikiAnn dataset in three languages, with the results presented in Table 3.

- w/o similarity: In this setting, we disregard $\mathcal{L}sim$ and set it to zero to assess the importance of extracting similarity between two prompts from both languages. This leads to a decrease in performance due to the absence of information sharing between the languages.
- w/o target language: In this setting, we omit $\mathcal{L}tgt$ and set it to zero to minimize the information regarding the target language. The model relies solely on $\mathcal{L}_{sim}$ for target language information, resulting in diminished performance.

The above results show the effectiveness of the cross-lingual part of our model.

5.3   Embedding Distribution

In this section, we perform experiments on the WikiAnn dataset, utilizing one hundred samples for each entity type. We evaluate the settings without similarity (w/o similarity), without target language (w/o target language), and the original setting, applying t-SNE dimensionality reduction to one dimension in three languages. The results are depicted in Fig. 2.

Table 3. Ablation Study

Model	de	nl	es
CroPoNER	**11.51**	**11.95**	**17.48**
w/o similarity	8.2(−3.31)	9.42(−2.53)	16.67(−0.81)
w/o target language	7.69(−3.82)	10.29(−1.66)	15.43(−2.05)

Our analysis reveals that, for the original approach, the embeddings for each entity type are more compact compared to the settings without target language or the original configuration, indicating that the original approach can yield a superior representation of the entity type.

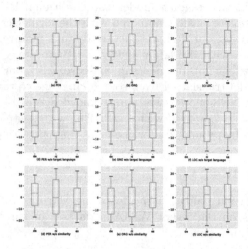

Fig. 2. The embedding distribution for each entity type in WikiAnn. (a)-(c) is the embedding distribution of original CroPoNER, (d)-(f) is the embedding distribution of CroPoNER w/o target language, and (h)-(i) is the embedding distribution of CroP-oNER w/o similarity

6   Conclusion

In this paper, we introduce a novel task termed cross-lingual few-shot Named Entity Recognition (NER) and discuss its application scenarios. We present a model called CroPoNER to address this challenge, extracting information on unknown entity types from both languages and utilizing similarity loss $\mathcal{L}_{sim}$ to determine the similarity between entity types across languages. To enhance understanding of the unknown entity type, we incorporate prompts to guide the model in acquiring both entity-specific and language-specific knowledge. Additionally, we propose a weighting strategy to account for three different losses. While the task is inherently difficult, resulting in relatively low performance, our experiments demonstrate that our model outperforms existing NER models in both few-shot and cross-lingual settings.

References

1. Bari, M.S., Joty, S.R., Jwalapuram, P.: Zero-resource cross-lingual named entity recognition. In: The Thirty-Fourth AAAI Conference on Artificial Intelligence, AAAI, pp. 7415–7423 (2020)

2. Bekoulis, G., Deleu, J., Demeester, T., Develder, C.: Joint entity recognition and relation extraction as a multi-head selection problem. In: Expert Systems with Applications, pp. 34–45 (2018)
3. Chen, W., Jiang, H., Wu, Q., Karlsson, B., Guan, Y.: AdvPicker: effectively leveraging unlabeled data via adversarial discriminator for cross-lingual NER. In: Proceedings of ACL, pp. 743–753 (2021)
4. Cui, L., Wu, Y., Liu, J., Yang, S., Zhang, Y.: Template-based named entity recognition using BART. In: Findings of the Association for Computational Linguistics: ACL-IJCNLP 2021, pp. 1835–1845 (2021)
5. Devlin, J., Chang, M.W., Lee, K., Toutanova, K.: BERT: pre-training of deep bidirectional transformers for language understanding. In: Proceedings of NAACL-HLT, pp. 4171–4186 (2019)
6. Dictionary, O.E.: Oxford english dictionary. Ja & Weiner, Esc, Simpson (1989)
7. Ding, N., et al.: Few-NERD: a few-shot named entity recognition dataset. In: Proceedings of ACL, pp. 3198–3213 (2021)
8. Huang, Y., et al.: COPNER: contrastive learning with prompt guiding for few-shot named entity recognition (2022)
9. Jain, A., Paranjape, B., Lipton, Z.C.: Entity projection via machine translation for cross-lingual NER. In: Proceedings of EMNLP, pp. 1083–1092 (2019)
10. Kang, B., Liu, Z., Wang, X., Yu, F., Feng, J., Darrell, T.: Few-shot object detection via feature reweighting. In: 2019 International Conference on Computer Vision, ICCV, pp. 8419–8428 (2019)
11. Lester, B., Al-Rfou, R., Constant, N.: The power of scale for parameter-efficient prompt tuning. In: Proceedings of EMNLP, pp. 3045–3059 (2021)
12. Li, X., Feng, J., Meng, Y., Han, Q., Wu, F., Li, J.: A unified MRC framework for named entity recognition. In: Proceedings of ACL, pp. 5849–5859 (2020)
13. Lin, Q., et al.: Contrastive graph representations for logical formulas embedding. In: TKDE (2021)
14. Liu, X.. et al.: P-tuning: prompt tuning can be comparable to fine-tuning across scales and tasks. In: Proceedings of ACL, pp. 61–68 (2022)
15. Liu, X., Zheng, Y., Du, Z., Ding, M., Qian, Y., Yang, Z., Tang, J.: Gpt understands, too. ArXiv preprint (2021)
16. Loshchilov, I., Hutter, F.: Decoupled weight decay regularization. In: Proceedings of ICLR (2019)
17. Mayhew, S., Tsai, C.T., Roth, D.: Cheap translation for cross-lingual named entity recognition. In: Proceedings of EMNLP, pp. 2536–2545 (2017)
18. Mikolov, T., Chen, K., Corrado, G., Dean, J.: Efficient estimation of word representations in vector space. arXiv preprint arXiv:1301.3781 (2013)
19. Pan, X., Zhang, B., May, J., Nothman, J., Knight, K., Ji, H.: Cross-lingual name tagging and linking for 282 languages. In: Proceedings of the 55th Annual Meeting of the Association for Computational Linguistics (Volume 1: Long Papers), pp. 1946–1958 (Jul 2017), aclanthology.org/P17-1178
20. Raffel, C., et al.: Exploring the limits of transfer learning with a unified text-to-text transformer. J. Mach. Learn. Res. **140**, 1–67 (2020)
21. Ralph Weischedel, S.P.: Ontonotes release 5.0. LDC2011T03, Philadelphia, Penn.: Linguistic Data Consortium (2011)
22. Snell, J., Swersky, K., Zemel, R.S.: Prototypical networks for few-shot learning. In: Advances in Neural Information Processing Systems 30: Annual Conference on Neural Information Processing Systems 2017, 4–9 December 2017, Long Beach, CA, USA, pp. 4077–4087 (2017)

23. Souza, F., Nogueira, R., Lotufo, R.: Portuguese named entity recognition using bert-crf. ArXiv preprint (2019)

24. Tjong Kim Sang, E.F.: Introduction to the CoNLL-2002 shared task: Language-independent named entity recognition. In: COLING-02: The 6th Conference on Natural Language Learning 2002 (CoNLL-2002) (2002), aclanthology.org/W02-2024

25. Tjong Kim Sang, E.F.: Introduction to the CoNLL-2002 shared task: language-independent named entity recognition. In: COLING-02: The 6th Conference on Natural Language Learning 2002 (CoNLL-2002) (2002)

26. Wang, Y., Yao, Q., Kwok, J.T., Ni, L.M.: Generalizing from a few examples: a survey on few-shot learning. ACM Comput. Surv. (csur) **3**, 1–34 (2020)

27. Wiseman, S., Stratos, K.: Label-agnostic sequence labeling by copying nearest neighbors. In: Proceedings of ACL, pp. 5363–5369 (2019)

28. Wu, Q., Lin, Z., Karlsson, B.F., Huang, B., Lou, J.: Unitrans: unifying model transfer and data transfer for cross-lingual named entity recognition with unlabeled data. In: Proceedings of the Twenty-Ninth International Joint Conference on Artificial Intelligence, IJCAI 2020, pp. 3926–3932 (2020)

29. Wu, Q., Lin, Z., Wang, G., Chen, H., Karlsson, B.F., Huang, B., Lin, C.: Enhanced meta-learning for cross-lingual named entity recognition with minimal resources. In: The Thirty-Fourth AAAI Conference on Artificial Intelligence, AAAI, pp. 9274–9281 (2020)

30. Wu, S., Dredze, M.: Beto, bentz, becas: the surprising cross-lingual effectiveness of BERT. In: Proceedings of EMNLP, pp. 833–844 (2019)

31. Xie, J., Yang, Z., Neubig, G., Smith, N.A., Carbonell, J.: Neural cross-lingual named entity recognition with minimal resources. In: Proceedings of EMNLP, pp. 369–379 (2018)

32. Yang, Y., Katiyar, A.: Simple and effective few-shot named entity recognition with structured nearest neighbor learning. In: Proceedings of EMNLP, pp. 6365–6375 (2020)

FAIR: A Causal Framework for Accurately Inferring Judgments Reversals

Minghua He[1], Nanfei Gu[2], Yuntao Shi[1], Qionghui Zhang[3], and Yaying Chen[1(✉)]

[1] College of Computer Science and Technology, Jilin University, Changchun, China
2328276309@qq.com
[2] School of Law, Jilin University, Changchun, China
[3] Gould School of Law, University of Southern California, Los Angeles, USA

Abstract. Artificial intelligence researchers have made significant advances in legal intelligence in recent years. However, the existing studies have not focused on the important value embedded in judgments reversals, which limits the improvement of the efficiency of legal intelligence. In this paper, we propose a causal **F**ramework for **A**ccurately **I**nferring case **R**eversals (FAIR), which models the problem of judgments reversals based on real Chinese judgments. We mine the causes of judgments reversals by causal inference methods and inject the obtained causal relationships into the neural network as a priori knowledge. And then, our framework is validated on a challenging dataset as a legal judgment prediction task. The experimental results show that our framework can tap the most critical factors in judgments reversal, and the obtained causal relationships can effectively improve the neural network's performance. In addition, we discuss the generalization ability of large language models for legal intelligence tasks using ChatGPT as an example. Our experiment has found that the generalization ability of large language models still has defects, and mining causal relationships can effectively improve the accuracy and explain ability of model predictions.

Keywords: Legal Intelligence · Causal Inference · Language Processing

1 Introduction

Legal intelligence is dedicated to assist legal tasks through the application of artificial intelligence. Data resources in the legal field are mainly presented in the form of textual documents, and China has the world's largest database of judgment documents, which can be further explored for its significant value through natural language processing(NLP). In recent years, with the increase of computing power and data scale, deep learning algorithms have developed rapidly and gradually become the mainstream technology of legal intelligence. ChatGPT is a typical large language model(LLM) that has triggered intense discussions, and its generalization ability in the legal field also needs to be studied.

M. He and N. Gu—Contribute equally to this work.

© The Author(s), under exclusive license to Springer Nature Switzerland AG 2023
L. Iliadis et al. (Eds.): ICANN 2023, LNCS 14254, pp. 171–182, 2023.
https://doi.org/10.1007/978-3-031-44207-0_15

Artificial intelligence researchers have put forth many fruitful efforts in advancing the use of deep learning in legal intelligence. Several works in recent years have contributed very rich legal data resources to the natural language processing community [2,20,21], and these datasets together form the basis of legal intelligence research. Based on these datasets, researchers have designed diverse legal AI tasks based on the practical needs of the legal domain, among which representative tasks include legal judgment prediction (LJP) [16], legal case matching [22], legal entity extraction [2], etc. Based on natural language processing techniques, researchers have developed corresponding solutions for these tasks and applied them in judicial practice.

However, the established work neglects the issue of judgments reversals, which is the area most closely linked to the application of law. According to our statistics, the percentage of revision of judgments reaches 14.63% of all judgments in China, which is a non-negligible part. The problem of judgments reversals is directly related to the direction of application of AI techniques and the effect of models. In the LJP task, extracting the causal relationship in judgments reversals as a priori knowledge helps to improve the accuracy as well as interpretability of model prediction.

Although the problem of judgments reversals has important theoretical and practical value, there are major challenges in the research. 1) It is more difficult to model the actual situation of reversals of judgments with high quality. The difficulty of this part of the work is that it is difficult to uncover all the factors that influence the judgment, and it is difficult to quantify and analyze factors such as judges' subjective will. 2) It is difficult to directly apply the prior knowledge to the improvement of neural networks. How to make neural networks efficiently use prior knowledge from different domains has been one of the challenges of research in artificial intelligence.

In this paper, we propose a causal **F**ramework for **A**ccurately **I**nferring judgments **R**eversals (FAIR), which mines why revisions occur based on causal inference, which is the process of exploring how one variable T affects another variable Y. In the construction of FAIR, first, the causal graph is initially modeled with the help of legal experts by training an encoder to remove the redundant constraints in the graph. Then, the causal effects between different variables are estimated quantitatively using a causal inference algorithm. Finally, the obtained causal knowledge is injected into the neural network model of the downstream task, which can effectively improve the performance of the model.

While the recent rise of Large Language Models (LLMs) has had a huge impact on the natural language processing community, we are also interested in the generalization ability of LLMs on legal intelligence tasks. We design challenging experiments to explore the knowledge exploitation ability and reasoning power of LLMs in the legal domain, and add LLMs as comparisons in the evaluation experiments of the FAIR framework. The experiments reveal some current limitations of LLM and demonstrate that the generalization ability of LLM can be enhanced by causal knowledge mining and injection.

Our main contributions are as follows: 1) We propose FAIR, a causal Framework for Accurately Inferring judgments Reversals, and better mine the causal relationships in complex legal judgments based on causal inference to uncover the reasons for judgments reversals. 2)The results obtained from performing the LJP task on a real legal dataset indicate that it is effective to improve the performance of neural networks by injecting prior knowledge. 3) We explore the knowledge utilization capability and inference capability of LLM in the legal domain. By comparing our framework with LLM, we reveal some limitations of LLM currently existing and proposed ways to improve its generalization ability.

2   Related Work

2.1   Legal Intelligence

Legal Intelligence focuses on applying natural language processing techniques to the legal domain, for which researchers have designed diverse tasks and provided rich data resources. CAIL2018 [20] is a large-scale Chinese legal dataset designed for the LJP task, focusing on LJP in the criminal law domain. LEVEN [21] considers the legal event detection task. FSCS [12] provides multilingual data for the LJP task and studies the legal differences in different regions. LeSICiN [13] designed the law and regulation identification task, using graphs to model the citation network between case documents and legal texts. MSJudge [10] describes a courtroom argument scenario with multi-actor dialogues for the LJP task. Some work has attempted to provide solutions to the above tasks using natural language processing techniques, and Lawformer [19] has designed a pre-training model for legal text training. EPM [5] considers implicit constraints between events in the LJP task. NSCL [6] attempts to use contrast learning to capture the subtle differences between legal texts in the LJP task. QAjudge [23] uses reinforcement learning to provide interpretable predictions for LJP. However, these works have not taken into account the issue of judgments reversals, which is directly related to the application of the law.

2.2   Causal Inference for Legal Domain

Recent work has attempted to use causal inference to provide more reliable explanations and greater robustness for legal intelligence. Liepina [8] introduces a semi-formal causal inference framework to model factual causality arguments in legal cases. Chockler [3] investigates the problem of legal attribution of responsibility using causal inference to capture complex causal relationships between multiple parties and events. GCI [9] designs a causal inference framework for unlabeled legal texts, using a graph-based approach to construct causal graphs from factual descriptions. Evan [7] uses causal inference to provide explanations for binary algorithms in legal practice. Law-Match [17] considers the influence of legal provisions in legal case-matching tasks and incorporates them as instrumental variables in causal graphs. Chen et al [1] investigated the problem of pseudo-correlation error introduced by pre-trained models and eliminated this error by learning the underlying causal knowledge in legal texts.

3 Methodology

Our framework FAIR consists of three main parts, including causal graph modeling, estimating causal effects on the modeled causal graph, and injecting causal effects into the neural network. Figure 1 illustrates the structure of FAIR.

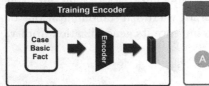 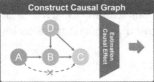 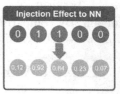

Fig. 1. Overall structure of FAIR

3.1 Modeling Causal Graph

Preliminary Modeling and Analysis. Before conducting a quantitative analysis of causal effects, we need to model the problem based on prior knowledge to ensure the clarity of causal assumptions, and the modeling results are given in the form of a causal graph. We describe the possible causal relationships in the judgment with the help of legal experts as Fig. 2(a). However, in Fig. 2(b), we cannot directly estimate the causal relationship between "Judgment Basis" and "Case Basic Fact" because there are multiple causal paths between them, and we need to block the paths that are not directly connected. Considering the presence of unobserved confounders in Fig. 2(a), we choose the instrumental variable method to block the paths through the confounders, which means that "Case Basic Fact" will be used as an instrumental variable, and it needs to satisfy the correlation and exogeneity. To ensure exogeneity, we need to block the direct path from the instrumental variable to the outcome, which means we need to extract the part of the instrumental variable that is relevant to the treatment and not relevant to the outcome, and we do this using a law article prediction task.

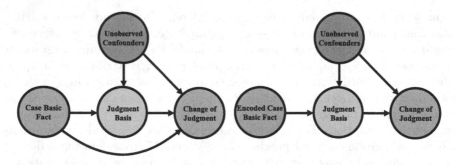

(a) Preliminary Causal Graph   (b) Target Causal Graph

Fig. 2. Preliminary and Target Causal Graph.

Task Definition. Given a factual description of the judgment containing n tokens $X = \{x1, x2, ..., x_n\}$ and a set $L = \{l1, l2, ..., lm\}$ containing m legal entries, we want the model to find a many-to-one mapping F from set X to a subset of L, and the result of the mapping is denoted as an m-dimensional multi-hot vector. This task can be understood as a multi-label classification task.

Encoder. We use the pre-trained model Lawformer as an encoder and fine-tune it in the law article prediction task as a way to capture the features we need. First, we use Lawformer to encode $X = \{x1, x2, ..., x_n\}$.

$$H = Encoder(x_i) \tag{1}$$

Then, the encoded representation H is fed into a linear layer and the dimension of *Output* is m, as same as the number of labels.

$$Output = \{out_1, out_2, ...out_m\} = Linear(H) \tag{2}$$

Considering the possible data imbalance of the real labels, we use ZLPR [15] as the loss function.

$$L_{zlpr} = log(1 + \sum_{i \in \Omega_{pos}} e^{-out_i}) + log(1 + \sum_{j \in \Omega_{neg}} e^{out_j}) \tag{3}$$

where Ω_{pos} is the set of positive samples and Ω_{neg} is the set of negative samples. After extracting the features by Encoder, Fig. 2(b) shows the causal graph we finally obtained.

3.2   Causal Effects Estimation

The estimation of causal effects requires controlling for confounders to ensure the accuracy of the results, which we discuss in detail in Sect. 3.1, where we use "Encoded Case Basic Fact" as an instrumental variable to ensure this.

We use Average Treatment Effect (ATE) as a quantitative criterion for the causal effect. Suppose T is the intervention variable, $p(Y|do(T = a))$ is the interventional distribution, and Y is the target variable. Then, under the reference condition $T = b$, the ATE after imposing the intervention $T = a$ is described as

$$ATE(a, b) = E_p(Y|do(T = a)) - E_p(Y|do(T = b)) \tag{4}$$

Under the condition that instrumental variables are used, the computation of ATE can be described in the following form. We let U be the confounder and Z be the instrumental variable, and suppose that $Y = \delta T + \alpha U$, we have $YZ = \delta TZ + \alpha UZ$, and since Z is not affected by U, the above equation is equivalent to $YZ = \delta TZ$, then the causal estimator $\delta = YZ * (TZ)^{-1}$, it is easy to find that δ is exactly the unbiased estimate of ATE, i.e.

$$ATE(a, b) = \frac{E(Y|Z = a) - E(Y|Z = b)}{E(T|Z = a) - E(T|Z = b)} \tag{5}$$

3.3   Causal Smoothing

In this subsection, we propose a method called Causal Smoothing to inject the causal effects estimated by FAIR into a neural network. We draw inspiration from the widely used Label Smoothing [18]. If y_i is the label of the classification task, y_i is 0 or 1 in the hard label case. Label Smoothing replaces the hard label y_i with a soft label

$$p_i = (1 - \epsilon)y_i + \frac{\epsilon}{K} \tag{6}$$

where K is the number of categories of labels and ϵ is the hyperparameter, which is the same for all samples in training. Causal Smoothing modifies ϵ to $\epsilon_i = \omega \sum_{j=1}^{m} ATE(t_{ij}, 0)$, where t_{ij} is the value of the jth treatment in the ith sample, m is the number of treatments, and ω is the hyperparameter. In Causal Smoothing, the soft label can be expressed as

$$p_{i+causal} = (1 - \omega \sum_{j=1}^{m} ATE(t_{ij}, 0))y_i + \frac{\omega \sum_{j=1}^{m} ATE(t_{ij}, 0)}{K} \tag{7}$$

4   Experiments and Evaluation

In this section, we apply FAIR to a specific legal scenario and test the inference results of the framework in a downstream task of legal intelligence. We have chosen the determination of labor relationship for over-aged labors as the legal issue for the experiment, and the legal judgment prediction task as the downstream task. Our experimental results have shown the superiority of FAIR in this context.

4.1   Dataset

Currently, published datasets do not consider our research topic of judgments reversals and are too coarse-grained to meet the needs of fine-grained tasks. They do not differentiate between initial and appellate judgments in legal cases, and we cannot obtain the required labels for FAIR. Therefore, we construct a dataset of unstructured judgments from the internet and used regular expressions to extract the labels for our experiment. We used this method because Chinese judgments have a relatively fixed structure, and it is fairly accurate for us to extract the required labels. We download and extract all of the judgments on the determination of labor relationships for over-aged labors issues from the pkulaw[1] website. These judgments are real and challenging, as they involve complex legal issues and difficult factual determinations. The number of training sets is 5785, the number of validation sets is 883, and the number of test sets is 416. We choose the challenging second trial data as the test set, in which the number of judgments reversals is 98.

---

[1] https://www.pkulaw.com.

4.2   Experimental Setup

Causal Acquisition. We first design a law article prediction task to train the feature encoder, and selected the most important four law articles related to the determination of labor relationship for over-aged labors as the labels. The encoder was initialized by the pre-trained model Lawformer, and ZLPR was used as the loss function during training. We use the encoded inputs as instrumental variables to construct causal graphs, using the instrumental variables approach provided by the dowhy [14] framework for inference.

Legal Judgement Prediction. In the legal field, LJP task requires the model to predict the outcome of a decision based on the basic fact of the input case. We chose the mainstream LJP models as the baseline, including Lawformer, Longformer, Bert [4], and Bi-LSTM, which were trained under the condition of no causal knowledge and injected causal knowledge respectively. Since Bert only accepts inputs up to 512 tokens in length, we adopt a truncated input and max-pooling approach to obtain the input for the classification layer.

Causal Knowledge Injection. We used Causal Smoothing, introduced in Sect. 3, to inject causal knowledge into the model, and the hyperparameter ω was set to 0.1 for the experiments. We used Label Smoothing as a control, and the hyperparameter ϵ was set to 0.1. in addition to the mainstream models described above, we also explored the performance of large language models for the LJP task, and we chose OpenAI's ChatGPT as the experimental subject and provided it with a priori causal knowledge through different prompts. All the above experiments use Adam as the optimizer, and the Learning rate is set to 1e-4.

4.3   Main Result

Table 1 shows the experimental results of FAIR on the mainstream model of the LJP task. From it, we find that the causal knowledge obtained by inference of FAIR improves all baselines, with significant improvements on both F1 values and Acc. Specifically, for F1 values, the improvements on baselines reach 1.92, 4.88, 1.02, and 12.82, respectively; for Acc, the improvements on baselines reach 4.81, 0.96, 11.54, and 2.41, respectively.

The Bi-LSTM model has the most significant improvement in F1 values, which we believe is because the Bi-LSTM model is not capable of capturing features for long texts, and it is difficult to learn effective knowledge during the training process, so the injection of causal knowledge is a very significant improvement for Bi-LSTM. The Bert model has the largest improvement in Acc, which we believe is because the transformer model can make good use of causal knowledge. Lawformer has the best overall performance without injecting causal knowledge, which proves the advantage of legal text pre-training. In addition, we can find that LLM still has some gaps with supervised learning models in downstream tasks of legal intelligence, which we discuss in detail in Sect. 6.

Table 1. Experimental results of FAIR on LJP task.

Models	P	R	F1	Acc
Lawformer	48.97	**65.75**	56.14	63.94
Lawformer + Causal	**54.87**	61.64	**58.06** (↑ 1.92)	**68.75** (↑ 4.81)
Longformer	44.44	71.23	54.73	58.65
Longformer + Causal	**45.92**	**84.93**	**59.61** (↑ 4.88)	**59.61** (↑ 0.96)
Bert	46.03	**79.45**	58.29	60.09
Bert + Causal	**59.72**	58.90	**59.31** (↑ 1.02)	**71.63** (↑ 11.54)
Bi-LSTM	38.70	16.43	23.07	61.53
Bi − LSTM + Causal	**47.72**	**28.76**	**35.89**(↑ 12.82)	**63.94**(↑ 2.41)
ChatGPT	39.69	**71.23**	**50.98**	51.92
ChatGPT + Prior	39.44	58.90	47.25	53.84
ChatGPT + Prior*	**41.23**	54.79	47.05	**56.73**(↑ 4.81)

5   Analysis

5.1   Robustness of Inference Results

To make our inference results more reliable, we conduct sensitivity tests to analyze the robustness of the results. Specifically, we use the counterfactual sample provided by Dowhy to generate counterfactual samples, and we use three counterfactual methods for testing. 1) Bootstrap Sample Dataset: Replacing a given dataset with bootstrap samples from the same dataset, it ideally does not show significant changes in causal effects. 2) Placebo Treatment: The real intervention variables were replaced with independent random variables, and the new ATE should be zero for the significant causal relationship that should not be exhibited between the variables in this condition. 3) Subset of Data: Replace the given dataset with a subset of data from the same dataset, ideally, the new ATE should remain the same as the previous one. The results of our sensitivity test are shown in Fig. 3. This demonstrates the significant robustness of our inference results. In addition, our inference results are agreed upon by legal experts.

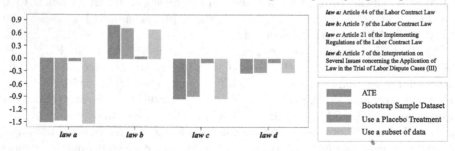

Fig. 3. Test results using three counterfactual methods.

5.2   Effect of Causal Smoothing

FAIR injects the causal knowledge obtained by the inference into the neural network model by Causal Smoothing and achieves significant improvement in downstream tasks. We believe this is because Causal Smoothing is closer to real judgment scenarios than Label Smoothing controlled by the hyperparameter ϵ, which can simulate the judge's thoughts when deciding. For difficult judgments, Causal Smoothing makes its Soft Label closer to the judge's critical value, and the model is not overconfident in its prediction, which enhances the generalization of the model. To verify our conjecture, we select the output of the last hidden layer of the Lawformer model in the LJP experiment, downscale it using t-SNE [11], and projected it onto a two-dimensional plane, and Fig. 4 shows our results. We can find that Label Smoothing reduces the intra-class distance to some extent compared to the Hard Label case, while Causal Smoothing shows the superiority of Causal Smoothing as the intra-class distance is more compact and the inter-class distance is pulled apart compared to the Label Smoothing case.

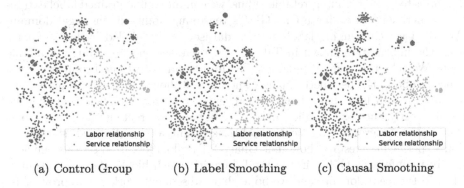

(a) Control Group   (b) Label Smoothing   (c) Causal Smoothing

Fig. 4. The t-SNE plots of feature representations.

6   Limitations of Large Language Model

With the development of LLM, we become interested in the generalization capabilities of LLM in specific domains. In this section, we explore the capabilities of ChatGPT[2] for legal intelligence downstream tasks and discuss its limitations. Our experiments have shown that improving the generalization ability of the LLM through the injection of causal knowledge can be achieved.

Knowledge Utilization Capability. In the experiments shown in Table 1, we conducted LJP experiments with the legal scenario of over-age labors issues and

---

[2] https://openai.com/blog/chatgpt.

compared it to our supervised training model. The results reveal that Chat-GPT performs poorly without prior knowledge, with F1 values and accuracy both around 50. It suggests that ChatGPT struggles to utilize the knowledge of the over-age labors issues during training, and we believe this is because the LJP task is too challenging for a model trained without labels. Furthermore, it is difficult for the model to establish correlations between input facts and the laws learned during training without any additional cues. To investigate further, we incorporated judgment-related laws as prompts in the dialogue. Specifically, we add "you should pay attention to the use of the law x" (x=a, b, c, d) as prior knowledge in the prompt. The greater the influence of x in our inference results, the higher the level of the prompt. We find that ChatGPT's performance improved with different levels of prompts, but it still differed significantly from our supervised model. This indicates that ChatGPT can utilize input knowledge to some degree, but the prompt's design limits its utilization. Therefore, for legal intelligence downstream tasks, we require a supervised model tailored to the legal domain.

Reasoning Ability. To utilize LLM in legal practice, we require the model's decisions to be highly interpretable. Thus, we conduct a fine-grained label extraction experiment to evaluate ChatGPT's reasoning ability in the legal domain. We select six challenging labels from a dataset finely labeled by legal experts with the information shown in Table 2. This dataset will be publicly available soon. We take the original judgments as input and adjust the prompts several times to obtain the best performance, and Table 3 shows the results of our experiments. We can find that ChatGPT can extract better for labels that may be given directly, such as C, while ChatGPT can barely extract effectively for labels that require inference from contextual descriptions to be obtained, such as F. Our experimental results show that ChatGPT still suffers from serious deficiencies in its inference ability in the legal domain, which blocks the application of LLM in the legal domain, and we hope that subsequent work can improve this.

Table 2. The challenging labels we select

A Labor gender 劳动者性别
B When do labors to reach the mandatory age for retirement 劳动者何时达到法定退休年龄
C Whether have a written contract 有无书面合同
D Whether enjoy the benefits of the old-age insurance 有无享受养老保险待遇
E Kind of old-age insurance 养老保险待遇类型
F Whether recognized of the basic old-age insurance 是否认定为基本养老保险待遇

Table 3. Results on ChatGPT

Label	Acc	P	R	F1
A	56.25	56.40	56.73	55.77
B	63.05	63.14	63.32	62.95
C	70.84	72.40	72.06	70.82
D	62.41	58.95	60.46	58.75
E	61.53	38.25	42.20	35.07
F	50.61	42.59	45.93	40.78

7   Conclusion

We propose FAIR, a causal framework for accurately inferring judgment reversals, and we also introduce Causal Smoothing, a technique for incorporating causal knowledge into neural networks. In the context of predicting labor relationships of over-age labors, we demonstrate how the inferred causal effects enhance the model's performance. Our analysis examines the inferred outcomes' quality and sheds light on Causal Smoothing's role. Moreover, we undertake various tasks to evaluate large language models' capabilities in the legal domain. While acknowledging that LLM is not yet adequate for legal intelligence and cannot replace traditional supervised models. However, mining and injecting causal relationships can effectively enhance the generalization ability of the model, and improve the accuracy and fairness of legal result prediction.

Ethical Statement. We utilize a dataset sample sourced from publicly available judgment documents on the China Judgment Network, which is a platform that complies with relevant legal and regulatory requirements and authorizes the use of documents for research purposes. Our objective is to support legal services through FAIR principles and aid judges in their decision-making process rather than replace them. However, crucial information pertaining to over-age labors is often absent or ambiguous due to privacy concerns. This can result in the dataset being incomplete, potentially impacting the final analysis results. In certain cases, our model may generate erroneous judgments; hence users must exercise caution when interpreting the model's inference results. Nevertheless, on the whole, our model can assist judges in identifying pertinent legal articles and aid in ensuring judicial consistency throughout China.

References

1. Chen, H., Zhang, L., Chen, F., Yu, Y.: Knowledge is power: understanding causality makes legal judgment prediction models more generalizable and robust. arXiv preprint arXiv:2211.03046 (2022)
2. Chen, Y., Sun, Y., Yang, Z., Lin, H.: Joint entity and relation extraction for legal documents with legal feature enhancement. In: Proceedings of the 28th International Conference on Computational Linguistics, pp. 1561–1571 (2020)
3. Chockler, H., Fenton, N., Keppens, J., Lagnado, D.A.: Causal analysis for attributing responsibility in legal cases. In: Proceedings of the 15th International Conference on Artificial Intelligence and Law, pp. 33–42 (2015)
4. Devlin, J., Chang, M.W., Lee, K., Toutanova, K.: Bert: Pre-training of deep bidirectional transformers for language understanding. arXiv preprint arXiv:1810.04805 (2018)
5. Feng, Y., Li, C., Ng, V.: Legal judgment prediction via event extraction with constraints. In: Proceedings of the 60th Annual Meeting of the Association for Computational Linguistics (Volume 1: Long Papers), pp. 648–664 (2022)
6. Gan, L., Li, B., Kuang, K., Yang, Y., Wu, F.: Exploiting contrastive learning and numerical evidence for improving confusing legal judgment prediction. arXiv preprint arXiv:2211.08238 (2022)

7. Iatrou, E.: A normative model of explanation for binary classification legal ai and its implementation on causal explanations of answer set programming (2022)
8. Liepina, R., Sartor, G., Wyner, A.: Causal models of legal cases. In: Pagallo, U., Palmirani, M., Casanovas, P., Sartor, G., Villata, S. (eds.) AICOL 2015-2017. LNCS (LNAI), vol. 10791, pp. 172–186. Springer, Cham (2018). https://doi.org/10.1007/978-3-030-00178-0_11
9. Liu, X., Yin, D., Feng, Y., Wu, Y., Zhao, D.: Everything has a cause: leveraging causal inference in legal text analysis. In: Proceedings of the 2021 Conference of the North American Chapter of the Association for Computational Linguistics: Human Language Technologies, pp. 1928–1941 (2021)
10. Ma, L., et al.: Legal judgment prediction with multi-stage case representation learning in the real court setting. In: Proceedings of the 44th International ACM SIGIR Conference on Research and Development in Information Retrieval, pp. 993–1002 (2021)
11. Van der Maaten, L., Hinton, G.: Visualizing data using t-sne. J. Mach. Learn. Res. **9**(11) (2008)
12. Niklaus, J., Chalkidis, I., Stürmer, M.: Swiss-judgment-prediction: a multilingual legal judgment prediction benchmark. arXiv preprint arXiv:2110.00806 (2021)
13. Paul, S., Goyal, P., Ghosh, S.: Lesicin: a heterogeneous graph-based approach for automatic legal statute identification from indian legal documents. In: Proceedings of the AAAI Conference on Artificial Intelligence, vol. 36, pp. 11139–11146 (2022)
14. Sharma, A., Syrgkanis, V., Zhang, C., Kıcıman, E.: Dowhy: addressing challenges in expressing and validating causal assumptions. arXiv preprint arXiv:2108.13518 (2021)
15. Su, J., Zhu, M., Murtadha, A., Pan, S., Wen, B., Liu, Y.: Zlpr: A novel loss for multi-label classification. arXiv preprint arXiv:2208.02955 (2022)
16. Şulea, O.M., Zampieri, M., Vela, M., van Genabith, J.: Predicting the law area and decisions of french supreme court cases. In: Proceedings of the International Conference Recent Advances in Natural Language Processing, RANLP 2017, pp. 716–722 (2017)
17. Sun, Z., Xu, J., Zhang, X., Dong, Z., Wen, J.R.: Law article-enhanced legal case matching: a model-agnostic causal learning approach. arXiv preprint arXiv:2210.11012 (2022)
18. Szegedy, C., Vanhoucke, V., Ioffe, S., Shlens, J., Wojna, Z.: Rethinking the inception architecture for computer vision. In: Proceedings of the IEEE Conference On Computer Vision and Pattern Recognition, pp. 2818–2826 (2016)
19. Xiao, C., Hu, X., Liu, Z., Tu, C., Sun, M.: Lawformer: a pre-trained language model for Chinese legal long documents. AI Open **2**, 79–84 (2021)
20. Xiao, C., et al.: Cail 2018: a large-scale legal dataset for judgment prediction. arXiv preprint arXiv:1807.02478 (2018)
21. Yao, F., et al.: Leven: a large-scale chinese legal event detection dataset. arXiv preprint arXiv:2203.08556 (2022)
22. Yu, W., et al.: Explainable legal case matching via inverse optimal transport-based rationale extraction. In: Proceedings of the 45th International ACM SIGIR Conference on Research and Development in Information Retrieval, pp. 657–668 (2022)
23. Zhong, H., Wang, Y., Tu, C., Zhang, T., Liu, Z., Sun, M.: Iteratively questioning and answering for interpretable legal judgment prediction. In: Proceedings of the AAAI Conference on Artificial Intelligence, vol. 34, pp. 1250–1257 (2020)

FeatEMD: Better Patch Sampling and Distance Metric for Few-Shot Image Classification

Shisheng Deng[1,2], Dongping Liao[3], Xitong Gao[1], Juanjuan Zhao[1],
and Kejiang Ye[1(✉)]

[1] Shenzhen Institute of Advanced Technology, Chinese Academy of Sciences,
Shenzhen 518000, China
{ss.deng,xt.gao,jj.zhao,kj.ye}@siat.ac.cn
[2] University of Chinese Academy of Sciences, Beijing 100049, China
[3] University of Macau, Macau SAR 999078, China
yb97428@umac.mo

Abstract. Few-shot image classification (FSIC) studies the problem of
classifying images when given only a few training samples, which presents
a challenge for deep learning models to generalize well on unseen image
categories. To learn FSIC tasks effectively, recent metric-based methods leverage the similarity measures of deep feature representations with
minimum matching costs, introducing a new paradigm in addressing
the FSIC challenge. Recent metric-learning techniques, *e.g.*, DeepEMD,
measure the distance between features with the earth mover's distance
(EMD), and it is currently the state-of-the-art (SOTA) approach for
FSIC. In this paper, we however identify two fundamental limitations in
DeepEMD. First, it brings high computational cost, as it randomly samples image patches to extract features. This process is often wasteful due
to suboptimal sampling strategies. Second, its accuracy is also limited by
the use of optimal-transport costs based on cosine similarity, which only
measures directional discrepancies. To mitigate the above shortcomings,
we propose an improved method, which we call FeatEMD. First, it introduces a feature saliency-based cropping (FeatCrop) to construct image
patches that concentrates computations on object-salient regions. Second, it proposes a Direction-Distance Similarity (DDS) a more effective
distance criterion in capturing subtle differences in latent space features.
We conduct comprehensive experiments and ablations to validate our
method. Experimental results show FeatEMD establishes new SOTA on
two mainstream benchmark datasets. Remarkably, when compared with
DeepEMD, FeatEMD reduces up to 36% computational costs. Our code
is available at https://github.com/SethDeng/FeatEMD.

Keywords: Few-shot image classification · metric learning ·
saliency-based cropping

S. Deng and D. Liao—Contributed equally to this work.

© The Author(s), under exclusive license to Springer Nature Switzerland AG 2023
L. Iliadis et al. (Eds.): ICANN 2023, LNCS 14254, pp. 183–194, 2023.
https://doi.org/10.1007/978-3-031-44207-0_16

1   Introduction

Recent ground-breaking deep learning techniques rely on training on large-scale data [1–3]. In cost- and privacy-sensitive scenarios such as healthcare and public safety, collecting massive high-quality samples is however impractical and prohibitive for various reasons, impeding the direct application of existing data-driven deep learning paradigm. This prompts few-shot learning (FSL) techniques to improve rapidly in recent years. Amongst a broad variety of applications, few-shot image classification (FSIC) which aims to learn classifiers that can generalize to unseen categories with only a handful of labeled training samples, provides a pivotal benchmark for evaluating the effectiveness of few-shot learning algorithms. Recent years have thus observed a rise of FSIC methods, forming three categories of approaches, namely augmentation-based [4], optimization-based [5,6] and metric-based methods [3,7–13].

In particular, metric-based methods demonstrate great success on pushing the current state-of-the-art (SOTA) of FSIC further. These methods, in general, extract feature representations through deep neural networks, and then compute the distances between pairs of representations of prototypes (condensed features of each class in the support set) and queries (features belonging to images that require classification). Notably, current metric-based learning method (*e.g.*, DeepEMD [13]) further samples multiple patches from input images by *random sampling* to enrich the object representation and thus extract diverse features from the source image for distance evaluation. Such repeated random sampling is proven an effective strategy to achieve SOTA accuracies on FSIC.

While being effective, the naïve random sampling approach may demand a high degree of wasted computational effort. From an intuitive perspective, random sampling is prone to frequently sample background regions when the scale of the salient object is small (Fig. 1). Such crops may not contain necessary information to accurately evaluate the distance metrics between the prototypes and queries. Existing baselines thus requires many random crops to ensure sampled patches to reliably contain the object. This allows it to form effective matches between salient features of the prototypes and queries, and attain high task accuracies. Doing so, however, incurs substantial potentially wasted computation. As certain patches contain only uninformative background, they contribute little to the evaluation of the distance metric and could hence be detrimental to the task performance.

To mitigate the computational costs of metric-based learning by random sampling, it is desirable to introduce a frequency bias in the random sampling procedure. We thus propose FeatCrop, a new sampling algorithm that seeks to sample salient regions in images, allowing patches to concentrate sampling effort to regions containing the object, while retaining feature diversity allowed by random sampling. To summarize, FeatCrop saves computational resources in metric-based few-shot learning by generating semantic embeddings from sampled patches that are balanced in terms of diversity and accuracy for their categorical representations.

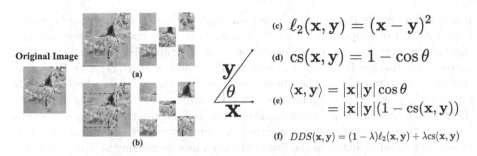

(a)

(b)

Original Image

(c) $\ell_2(\mathbf{x}, \mathbf{y}) = (\mathbf{x} - \mathbf{y})^2$

(d) $\mathrm{cs}(\mathbf{x}, \mathbf{y}) = 1 - \cos\theta$

(e) $\langle \mathbf{x}, \mathbf{y} \rangle = |\mathbf{x}||\mathbf{y}| \cos\theta$
$= |\mathbf{x}||\mathbf{y}|(1 - \mathrm{cs}(\mathbf{x}, \mathbf{y}))$

(f) $DDS(\mathbf{x}, \mathbf{y}) = (1 - \lambda)\ell_2(\mathbf{x}, \mathbf{y}) + \lambda \mathrm{cs}(\mathbf{x}, \mathbf{y})$

Fig. 1. (a) In DeepEMD, image patches are sampled randomly. This approach may lead to the sampling of background patches that are irrelevant to representing the object, and computationally wasteful. (b) Our FeatCrop, in contrast, focuses on semantic sub-regions that contain the foreground objects. For two embedding vectors, (c) The ℓ_2 distance measures magnitude. (d) The cosine similarity measures direction. (e) The inner product multiplies magnitudes with cosine similarity, and $\mathbf{x} = \mathbf{y}$ does not correspond to the minimum. (f) The proposed DDS combines directional and distance similarities between two vectors.

Moreover, existing works [12,13] commonly employ either the cosine similarity (cs), the L2 distance (ℓ_2), or the inner product ($\langle \cdot, \cdot \rangle$), as the distance metrics for evaluating the associated distances between extracted feature vectors. As shown in Fig. 1, none of the ℓ_2, cs or $\langle \cdot, \cdot \rangle$ distance metrics can simultaneously represent both the distance and directional similarity between a pair of vectors. To this end, we take one step forward by proposing a novel distance metric, namely the direction-distance similarity (DDS) to improve the distance criterion. The main contributions of this paper can be summarized as follows:

– To our knowledge, we demonstrate, for the fist time, patch sampling strategies play a critical role in FSIC. We show that the proposed FeatCrop, which introduces saliency-based patch sampling for metric-based FSIC, achieves significant computational cost reduction without sacrificing accuracy.
– We propose the Direction-Distance Similarity (DDS) for the EMD transportation cost matrices. This new metric can notably improve transportation cost estimation and in turn FSIC task accuracies.
– Experiments on mainstream FSIC benchmark datasets (*mini*-ImageNet and *tiered*-ImageNet) show that our algorithm, FeatEMD, achieves SOTA performance and simultaneously reduce up to 36% computational effort when compared against the current best competitors.

2   Related Works

2.1   Metric-Based FSIC Methods

Recently, **metric-based few-shot learning methods** gain notable traction as they can learn a similarity metric that can generalize to new classes with only a few labeled examples. This provides the necessary criterions for the accurate classification of query images from unseen categories. With similar spirits,

many recent works thus employ novel methods to improve the distance metric
between pairs of support and query features, such as the covariance pooling [11],
divergences between multivariate Gaussian distributions [10], optimal transport
in discrete distributions [13], bi-directional random walks [14] and Brownian
distance covariances [12]. The above-mentioned methods achieve better results
either by improving the expressiveness of the features, or by exploiting the (joint)
distribution information of the sample classes. To measure the distances between
features, these methods compute either the inner product, Euclidean distance
or cosine similarity between the final extracted metric-bearing vectors. Our proposed DDS notably differentiates itself from these metrics as it takes distance
and direction jointly into consideration.

2.2 Image Patch Sampling

Image patch sampling is the process of sampling a number of cropped patches
from an original image. Previous researches show that sampling patches from
images can help prevent model overfitting and make models generalize better [15,16]. It has a wide range of applications in computer vision. For example,
in image denoising [17], contrastive learning [18] and high resolution image recognition [19]. In particular for metric-based learning in FSIC, grid-based sampling
and random sampling are often used to crop patches from an image [13]. However, they are prone to selecting irrelevant areas containing the background or
noise, yielding adverse impact on the final feature representation. Therefore, we
propose FeatCrop, which selects informative image patches based on semantic
saliency, allowing important objects to be sampled with higher probabilities.

3 The FeatEMD Method

3.1 Preliminaries

The **few-shot image classification** task can be defined as:

$$\mathcal{D}_{\text{meta}} = \{\mathcal{D}_{\text{train}}, \mathcal{D}_{\text{test}}\}, \text{where}$$
$$\{y \mid (\mathbf{x}, y) \in \mathcal{D}_{\text{train}}\} \cap \{y \mid (\mathbf{x}, y) \in \mathcal{D}_{\text{test}}\} = \emptyset, \tag{1}$$

i.e. the test and train datasets do not contain common classes.

Most recent works on FSIC employ the standard *N-way K-shot (M-query)*
episode task learning introduced in [20]. Specifically, for each meta-task, we
sample n episode tasks $\{T_1, \ldots, T_n\}$ from $\mathcal{D}_{\text{train}}$ as training episodes, and m
episode tasks $\{T_1, \ldots, T_m\}$ from $\mathcal{D}_{\text{test}}$ as testing episodes. Each episode task T_i
consists of a support set T_i^S and a query set T_i^Q. From a dataset, each support or
query set randomly samples N or M categories respectively, with each category
sampling K image-label pairs $(\mathbf{x}, y)$, namely, $T_i^S = \{(\mathbf{x}_k, y_k)\}_{k=1}^{N \times K}$. Both $\mathcal{D}_{\text{train}}$
and $\mathcal{D}_{\text{test}}$ samples the support and query sets following the above configuration,
except the $\mathcal{D}_{\text{test}}$ provides no labels for the query sets, *i.e.* $T_i^Q = \{(\mathbf{x}_k)\}_{k=1}^{N \times M}$.

Given a pair of images, DeepEMD [13] first samples image patches from original image. Then it computes the cost matrix and subsequently the optimal matching flows, using the Earth Mover's Distance (EMD), between pairs of features extracted from image patches. Finally, based on the optimal matching flows, the distance between two images could be computed. In addition, for the *N-way K-shot* setting, when $K > 1$, DeepEMD employs a learnable embedding for each class, namely the Structured Fully Connected Layer (SFC), which represents the prototype of the class. The current SOTA on FSIC is a DeepEMD model that samples 25 patches uniformly from each image, along with cosine similarity as the transportation cost between features (Fig. 2).

3.2 Feature-Based Image Patch Sampling

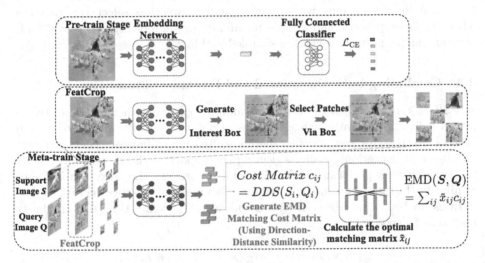

Fig. 2. An overview of our proposed FeatEMD. In the pre-training stage, we first learn an embedding network on the training set, then use it to select image patches for the entire training set by FeatCrop module. In both meta-training and meta-testing stages, we use the learned image patch selection to extract multiple feature vectors from images. The proposed DDS distance metric evaluates the EMD transport costs

In previous FSIC algorithms, grid-based and random sampling are the most common sampling methods for image patch selection. As we mentioned earlier, they would easily select the noise and background areas that contain little relevant information and contribute little to the accurate classification of the query images. Inspired by [18], we propose the FeatCrop module, which uses the backbone model to first localize the salient object by using the extracted feature maps. Specifically, we propose a function L which returns the smallest bounding box B that encloses values in $\mathbf{z} > l$ within the box. Here, norm(reduce($f(\mathbf{x})$)) denotes the heatmap of the input image $\mathbf{x}$, which is obtained by summing across channels (with reduce) the final extracted feature maps $f(\mathbf{x})$ and normalizing the result to be within $[0, 1]$. Formally,

$$B = L(\text{norm}(\text{reduce}(f(\mathbf{x}))) > l), \tag{2}$$

where the constant $l \in (0, 1)$ controls the threshold of activation values to be bounded. In all experiments, we set $l = 0.5$. To introduce diversity in sampling, we then use a Beta distribution $\beta(\alpha, \alpha)$ with a single hyperparameter α to generate crop centers, and additionally sample height and width of patches with a uniform distribution. This enables us to control how patches are sampled within the box B. Notably, the Beta distribution with $\alpha = 1$ corresponds to random sampling.

In our experiments, we find that it is not always desirable to select all patches within the outer bounding box B, as B may occasionally not contain the object to be classified. Assuming we sample n patches, we thus select $\lfloor rn \rfloor$ patches with the above process, and sample remaining ones uniformly, where $r \in [0, 1]$ controls the proportion of patches sampled within B.

3.3 Combining both Directional and Distance Similarities

In FSIC, metric-based methods aim at finding a good distance metric to calculate the distance between image features in order to classify images of unseen labels correctly. However, existing methods often target improvements in image features representations, while neglecting the impact of the distance metric on the few-shot task performance. To this end, we propose the Direction-Distance Similarity (DDS) to measure the distances between two feature vectors as similarities on both the direction and magnitude. We define the DDS similarity metric as follows:

$$\text{DDS}(\mathbf{x}, \mathbf{y}) \triangleq (1 - \lambda)\frac{1}{2}\|\mathbf{x} - \mathbf{y}\|_2^2 + \lambda \text{cs}(\mathbf{x}, \mathbf{y}), \tag{3}$$

where $\mathbf{x}, \mathbf{y}$ are two feature vectors, and λ is a hyperparameter that trades off the L2 distance $\|\mathbf{x} - \mathbf{y}\|_2^2$ with the cosine similarity $\text{cs}(\mathbf{x}, \mathbf{y})$. The details of FeatCrop and the overall FeatEMD algorithm are in Algorithms 1 and 2 respectively.

4   Experiments

We evaluate our FeatEMD on two FSIC benchmark datasets, *mini*-ImageNet [3] and *tiered*-ImageNet [21], and compare it with our baseline, DeepEMD, the current SOTA on FSIC.

Algorithm 1. The FeatCrop method.

1: **function** FEATCROP(Image $\mathbf{x}$, Model f, Activation threshold l, Number of sampled patches n, Proportion r, Beta distribution hyperparameter α)

2:    $S \leftarrow \{\mathbf{x}\}$ ▷ Original image $\mathbf{x}$ as a patch.

3:    $B \leftarrow L(\mathrm{norm}(f(\mathbf{x})) > l)$ ▷ Bounding box from (2).

4:    **for** $i \in \{0, 1, 2, \ldots, n-1\}$ **do**

5:        $(\mu, \sigma) \sim U(0,1)^2$ ▷ Uniform height and width.

6:        $h \leftarrow \mathrm{h}(\mathbf{x})\mu$ ▷ h($\mathbf{x}$): height of image x; h: height of the patch.

7:        $w \leftarrow \mathrm{w}(\mathbf{x})\sigma$ ▷ w($\mathbf{x}$): width of image x; w: width of the patch.

8:        **if** $i \leq \lfloor rn \rfloor$ **then**   ▷ Sample crop center (x,y) in B.

9:            $(u, v) \sim \beta(\alpha, \alpha)^2$

10:           $x = B_{x0} + (B_{x1} - B_{x0}) * u$

11:           $y = B_{y0} + (B_{y1} - B_{y0}) * v$

12:        **else**

13:           $(x, y) \sim U(0,1)^2$ ▷ Traditional random sampling.

14:        **end if**

15:        $S \leftarrow S \cup \{\mathrm{crop}(\mathbf{x}, x, y, h, w)\}$

16:    **end for**

17:    **return** S ▷ Return sampled image patches.

18: **end function**

Algorithm 2. The FeatEMD algorithm.

1: **function** FEATEMD(Images $\mathbf{x}_1, \mathbf{x}_2$, FEATCROP arguments f, l, n, r, α)

2:    $F_1 \leftarrow \{f(\mathbf{s}) \mid \mathbf{s} \in \mathrm{FEATCROP}(\mathbf{x}_1)\}$ ▷ Extract patch features in $\mathbf{x}_1$,

3:    $F_2 \leftarrow \{f(\mathbf{s}) \mid \mathbf{s} \in \mathrm{FEATCROP}(\mathbf{x}_2)\}$ ▷ ... and also in $\mathbf{x}_2$.

4:    **for** $(\mathbf{f}_i, \mathbf{f}_j)$ in $F_1 \times F_2$ **do**

5:        $\mathbf{C}_{ij} \leftarrow \mathrm{DDS}(\mathbf{f}_i, \mathbf{f}_j)$ ▷ Computes the cost matrix with DDS.

6:    **end for**

7:    **return** $\mathrm{EMD}(\mathbf{C})$.   ▷ Evaluates the EMD cost between $\mathbf{x}_1$ and $\mathbf{x}_2$.

8: **end function**

4.1 Implementation Details

For a fair comparison, we use ResNet-12 [22] as the backbone network for the competing methods. In addition, we conduct experiments in both 5-way 1-shot and 5-way 5-shot cases on the two FSIC benchmark datasets. Our code is implemented in PyTorch, and all experiments are performed on NVIDIA V100 GPUs.

4.2 Experimental Results and Analysis

In our study, all experiments on *mini*-ImageNet contains three stages as mentioned above, yet meta-train stage is not obligatory for *tiered*-ImageNet, since its domain differences among train-set, val-set and test-set are larger than *mini*-ImageNet. Table 1 shows the performance of DeepEMD and FeatEMD on *mini*-ImageNet and *tiered*-ImageNet. From Table 1, we can conclude that our method outperforms DeepEMD by a clear margin on two datasets. Remarkably, when

Table 1. Comparison results on *mini*-ImageNet and *tiered*-ImageNet. We report 95% confidence intervals for 5,000 episodes evaluation on DeepEMD and FeatEMD. Results with * are reproduced with the official implementation.

Model	Sampling Method	Distance Metric	Patch Count	*mini*-ImageNet		*tiered*-ImageNet	
				1-shot	5-shot	1-shot	5-shot
MCL [14]	Grid	cs	25	67.51	83.99	72.01	86.02
	Grid	cs	34	67.85	**84.47**	72.13	86.32
DeepEMD [13]	Grid	cs	25	67.83 ± 0.29	83.14 ± 0.57	$71.19 \pm 0.75^{*}$	$85.04 \pm 0.60^{*}$
	Random	cs	25	68.77 ± 0.29	84.13 ± 0.53	$73.60 \pm 0.75^{*}$	$86.92 \pm 0.60^{*}$
FeatEMD	FeatCrop	cs	**16**	68.85 ± 0.54	84.10 ± 0.45	73.63 ± 0.54	86.91 ± 0.44
	FeatCrop	DDS	**16**	$\mathbf{69.36} \pm 0.54$	84.36 ± 0.45	$\mathbf{73.78} \pm 0.54$	$\mathbf{87.14} \pm 0.44$

the number of patches is 16, FeatEMD is competitive against a DeepEMD model that samples 25 patches, which translates to a reduction in computational effort $\approx 36\%$.

FeatCrop dominates under a varying number of patches. We first compare FeatCrop with random sampling under a varying number of selected patches per image, as shown in Fig. 3. Note that for both random sampling and FeatCrop, the total computational cost for inference is directly proportional to the number of patches n, as we need to extract features from each patch using the backbone model. We also highlight that for all n ranging from 4 to 25, FeatCrop dominates random sampling in terms of task accuracies. In contrast, DeepEMD requires 24 patches to obtain similar accuracy. As the number of patches increases, the advantage of FeatCrop may diminish, this is also expected as random sampling is also more likely to select object-relevant patches when given more sampling opportunities.

Varying the Proportion of Patches Sampled within the Bounding Boxes. B. As Fig. 4 shows, FeatCrop outperforms the DeepEMD baseline under the majority of feasible choices of sampling proportions r. Here, larger r corresponds to more patches sampled within the bounding boxes. It shows that it is often useful to include uniform sampling to allow occasional patches outside B, which may also contain relevant information.

Varying α in the Beta Distribution for Crop Center Sampling. In Fig. 3(b), we tweak the hyperparameter α to figure out how different cropping strategies may influence the classification performance. Interestingly, we find cropping in the center ($\alpha = 1.2$), or around the object boundary ($\alpha = 0.4$) yield better results than cropping in the box uniform randomly ($\alpha = 1.0$). This corroborates our observation in Fig. 1 that random sampling could be detrimental to object representation due to frequent sampling of noisy background patches.

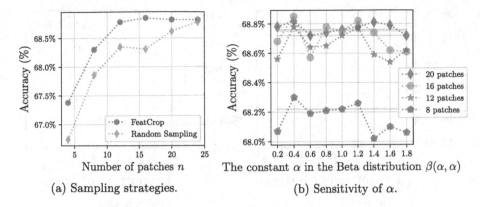

(a) Sampling strategies.   (b) Sensitivity of α.

Fig. 3. (a) Comparing the sampling strategies under the 5-way 1-shot classification task. (b) Sensitivity of α under different numbers of patches. The straight lines denote baseline accuracies reproduced from the random crop used in DeepEMD.

Table 2. Ablation study on the distance metrics. The 95% confidence intervals are all below 0.54 for the 5,000 episodes evaluation.

Distance Metric	*mini*-ImageNet		*tiered*-ImageNet	
	1-shot	5-shot	1-shot	5-shot
$\langle \cdot, \cdot \rangle$	64.70	78.86	71.68	82.80
ℓ_2	61.72	83.00	68.74	86.78
cs	68.85	84.10	73.63	86.91
DDS	**69.36**	**84.36**	**73.78**	**87.14**

***Sensitivity Analysis of* DDS.** Table 2 shows that DDS is substantially better than other competing distance metrics in both 1-shot and 5-shot tasks. As Fig. 5 illustrates, classification accuracies peak at $\lambda = 0.8$ in the 1-shot task, and when $\lambda = 0.6$ in the 5-shot case. The importance values of both the ℓ_2 distance and direction between feature vectors extracted in both 1- and 5-shot tasks are thus different. Such differences can be attributed to the computation of the structured fully-connected layers (SFC) used in the baseline. Namely, the 5-shot case requires additional iterative steps to optimize for the feature prototypes.

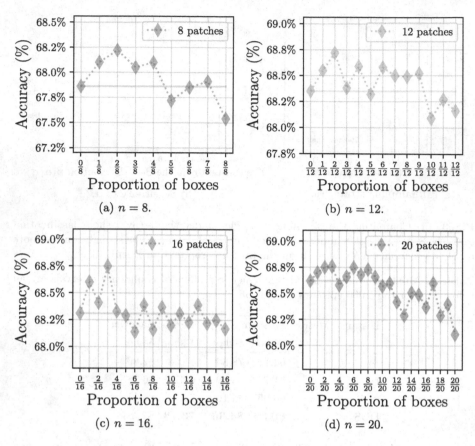

Fig. 4. Ablation results on r for varying numbers of patches. The dashed lines represent baseline accuracy

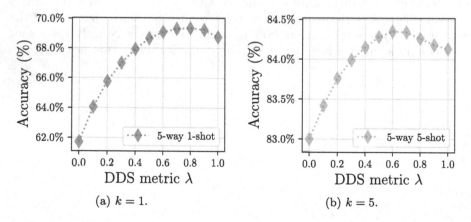

Fig. 5. Sensitivity analysis of the λ interpolation constant in DDS for 5-way k-shot tasks.

5   Conclusion

In this paper, we proposed an improved FSIC method based on DeepEMD. The resulting approach, FeatEMD, reduces up to 36% computational effort and achieve SOTA results across two mainstream benchmark datasets, *mini*-ImageNet and *tiered*-ImageNet. FeatEMD incorporates two novel components, namely FeatCrop and DDS. The former substantially reduces the computational effort by concentrating cropped patches to object relevant regions, and DDS improves the model's performance with a new distance metric. Finally, we hope this work could inspire future research, in particular, to motivate computational efficient FSIC methods while maintaining task performance.

Acknowledgement. This work is supported in part by Science and Technology Development Fund of Macao S.A.R (FDCT) under Nos. 0015/2019/AKP, 0123/2022/AFJ, and 0081/2022/A2, Guang-Dong Basic and Applied Basic Research Foundation (No. 2020B1515130004), and Shenzhen Science and Technology Innovation Commission (Nos. JCYJ20190812160003719, JCYJ20220818101610023). It was carried out in part at SICC, which is supported by SKL-IOTSC, University of Macau.

References

1. He, K., Zhang, X., Ren, S., Sun, J.: Deep residual learning for image recognition. In: IEEE Conference on Computer Vision and Pattern Recognition (2016)
2. Oreshkin, B., Rodríguez López, P., Lacoste, A.: TADAM: task dependent adaptive metric for improved few-shot learning. In: Bengio, S., Wallach, H., Larochelle, H., Grauman, K., Cesa-Bianchi, N., Garnett, R.(eds.) Advances in Neural Information Processing Systems, vol. 31. Curran Associates Inc (2018). https://proceedings.neurips.cc/paper_files/paper/2018/file/66808e327dc79d135ba18e051673d906-Paper.pdf
3. Vinyals, O., Blundell, C., Lillicrap, T., kavukcuoglu, K., Wierstra, D.: Matching networks for one shot learning. In: Lee, D., Sugiyama, M., Luxburg, U., Guyon, I., Garnett, R. (eds.) Advances in Neural Information Processing Systems, vol. 29. Curran Associates Inc. (2016). https://proceedings.neurips.cc/paper/2016/file/90e1357833654983612fb05e3ec9148c-Paper.pdf
4. Yu, X., Aloimonos, Y.: Attribute-based transfer learning for object categorization with zero/one training example. In: Daniilidis, K., Maragos, P., Paragios, N. (eds.) ECCV 2010. LNCS, vol. 6315, pp. 127–140. Springer, Heidelberg (2010). https://doi.org/10.1007/978-3-642-15555-0_10
5. Finn, C., Abbeel, P., Levine, S.: Model-agnostic meta-learning for fast adaptation of deep networks. In: International Conference On Machine Learning. PMLR, pp. 1126–1135 (2017)
6. Antoniou, A., Edwards, H., Storkey, A.: How to train your MAML. In: International Conference on Learning Representations (2018)
7. Snell, J., Swersky, K., Zemel, R.: Prototypical networks for few-shot learning. In: Guyon, I., Luxburg, U.V., Bengio, S., Wallach, H., Fergus, R., Vishwanathan, S., Garnett, R. (eds.) Advances in Neural Information Processing Systems, vol. 30. Curran Associates Inc. (2017). https://proceedings.neurips.cc/paper/2017/file/cb8da6767461f2812ae4290eac7cbc42-Paper.pdf

8. Sung, F., Yang, Y., Zhang, L., Xiang, T., Torr, P.H., Hospedales, T.M.: Learning to compare: Relation network for few-shot learning. In: IEEE Conference on Computer Vision and Pattern Recognition (CVPR) (2018)

9. Ye, H.-J., Hu, H., Zhan, D.-C., Sha, F.: Few-shot learning via embedding adaptation with set-to-set functions. In: IEEE/CVF Conference on Computer Vision and Pattern Recognition (CVPR) (2020)

10. Li, W., Wang, L., Huo, J., Shi, Y., Gao, Y., Luo, J.: Asymmetric distribution measure for few-shot learning

11. Wertheimer, D., Hariharan, B.: Few-shot learning with localization in realistic settings. In: IEEE/CVF Conference on Computer Vision and Pattern Recognition, pp. 6558–6567 (2019)

12. Xie, J., Long, F., Lv, J., Wang, Q., Li, P.: Joint distribution matters: deep brownian distance covariance for few-shot classification. In: IEEE/CVF Conference on Computer Vision and Pattern Recognition, pp. 7972–7981 (2022)

13. Zhang, C., Cai, Y., Lin, G., Shen, C.: DeepEMD: differentiable earth mover's distance for few-shot learning. IEEE Trans. Pattern Anal. Mach. Intell. (2022)

14. Liu, Y., Zhang, W., Xiang, C., Zheng, T., Cai, D., He, X.: Learning to affiliate: mutual centralized learning for few-shot classification. IEEE/CVF Conference on Computer Vision and Pattern Recognition, 14411–14420 (2022)

15. Chen, J., Bai, G., Liang, S., Li, Z.: Automatic image cropping: a computational complexity study. In: IEEE Conference on Computer Vision and Pattern Recognition, pp. 507–515 (2016)

16. Takahashi, R., Matsubara, T., Uehara, K.: RICAP: random image cropping and patching data augmentation for deep CNNs. In: Asian Conference on Machine Learning, PMLR, pp. 786–798 (2018)

17. Oh, G., Choi, D.-W., Moon, B.: Similar patch selection in embedding space for multi-view image denoising. IEEE Access **9**, 98581–98589 (2021)

18. Peng, X., Wang, K., Zhu, Z., Wang, M., You, Y.: Crafting better contrastive views for siamese representation learning. In: IEEE/CVF Conference on Computer Vision and Pattern Recognition, pp. 16031–16040 (2022)

19. Cordonnier, J.-B., Mahendran, A., Dosovitskiy, A., Weissenborn, D., Uszkoreit, J., Unterthiner, T.: Differentiable patch selection for image recognition. In: IEEE/CVF Conference on Computer Vision and Pattern Recognition, pp. 2351–2360 (2021)

20. Lake, B.M., Salakhutdinov, R., Tenenbaum, J.B.: Human-level concept learning through probabilistic program induction. Science **350**(6266) (2015)

21. Ren, M., et al.: Meta-learning for semi-supervised few-shot classification. In: International Conference on Learning Representations (2018)

22. Mishra, N., Rohaninejad, M., Chen, X., Abbeel, P.: A simple neural attentive meta-learner. In: International Conference on Learning Representations (2018)

FFTRL: A Sparse Online Kernel Classification Algorithm for Large Scale Data

Changzhi Su, Li Zhang$^{(\boxtimes)}$, and Lei Zhao

School of Computer Science and Technolgy, Soochow University, Suzhou 215006, China
20205227057@stu.suda.edu.cn, {zhangliml,zhaol}@suda.edu.cn

Abstract. Online kernel learning is an efficient way when dealing with nonlinearly large-scale data. The training speed of online kernel learning is improved by Fourier online gradient descent (FOGD). However, FOGD has a high space complexity when the number of features is relatively high because FOGD lacks of sparsity. In this paper, we propose a new sparse online kernel classification algorithm for large-scale data, called Fourier follow-the-regularized-leader (FFTRL). Existing budget (sparse) online kernel learning methods attempt to bound the number of support vectors through some budget maintenance strategies; however, budget maintenance strategies are unsuitable for FOGD. By introducing the proximal algorithm, follow-the-regularized-leader, FFTRL achieves sparsity in a different way. By applying random Fourier features as the kernel approximation schemes, FFTRL finds the optimal sparse solution in a linear manner. The regret bound analysis shows the feasibility of FFTRL in theory. Comprehensive experiments were carried out on public datasets to compare the performance of FFTRL with related online kernel algorithms. Promising results show that our proposed method enjoys both high accuracy and time efficiency and still produces sparse models, opening a window for obtaining sparsity in online kernel learning.

Keywords: Online learning · Kernel approximation · Sparsity · Online graident descent

1 Introduction

It has been proven that online learning is successful for building accurate and reliable models from a sequence of data elements efficiently. Different from regular batch machine learning algorithms that suffer from massive training time and memory consumption, online learning models often enjoy the properties of fast construction, highly scalable and memory saving. Due to these advantages, online learning algorithms have been successfully used in many real-world applications, such as online advertising [14], weather condition prediction [11], and computational finance [10].

© The Author(s), under exclusive license to Springer Nature Switzerland AG 2023
L. Iliadis et al. (Eds.): ICANN 2023, LNCS 14254, pp. 195–206, 2023.
https://doi.org/10.1007/978-3-031-44207-0_17

Various algorithms have been developed to tackle online binary classification tasks, which can be simply divided into two types: linear and kernel methods. The linear methods are able to construct linear predictive models at an amazing speed. Some well-known examples include online gradient descent (OGD) [18], forward backward splitting (FOBOS) [7], regularized dual averaging (RDA) [19] and follow-the-regularized-leader (FTRL) [13,14]. However, linear models are not always the right choice. Linear online algorithms may fail to produce effective outcomes when faced with linearly non-separable inputs, which is more common in real-world applications. To overcome this issue, researchers invited kernel functions into online learning methods and came up with field of online kernel learning. Kernel-based estimators avoid the non-separable property in the input space by mapping the instances to a high dimensional feature space implicitly. One key limitation of classical online kernel methods is that the functional representation of the produced estimator will become more complex as the observations grows. To be more specific, the learner is asked to maintain a support vector (SV) set during the online learning process. Whenever a newly arrived instance is misclassified, it will be added to the SV set immediately. Thus the complexity of the estimator and memory resource it demands will increase linearly over time, causing memory overflow for a potentially infinite input data sequence.

Several approaches have been proposed to handle the extension issues of online kernel learning. One interesting aspect, which is usually referred to as "budget online kernel learning" [5], tries to bound the number of SVs within a fixed size during the training process. Two major wildly acknowledged budget maintenance strategies are removal and projection. The former simply evicts a selected SV when the number of SVs overflows. It is adopted by many algorithms, such as Forgetron [6], randomized budget perceptron (RBP) [3], and naive online R_{reg} minimisation algorithm (NORMA) [9]. The latter further projects the selected SV onto the remaining ones, which is explored in algorithms like Projectron [15] and online manifold regularization (OMR) [2], Budget strategies do release the pressure to some extent, but the existing budget online kernel methods are either too simple to achieve promising results or just too slow to perform. The other promising aspect is to use the functional approximation scheme [20]. Unlike the budget maintenance strategy, this kind of scheme tackles the problem in a mathematically elegant way. A certain explicit mapping can be derived by approximating a kernel function, making it possible to project data from the input space to a computable highly dimensional feature space. Combining with linear online learning algorithms like OGD, nonlinear kernel-based algorithms are then trained in an efficient linear manner. As far as we known, Fourier online gradient descent (FOGD) has achieved a success in reducing time cost following this idea [12]. To reduce the required memory, the final model should be stored sparsely, or the number of non-zero coefficients in the final model parameter should be small. However, even employing the L_1 penalty, FOGD can hardly produce sparse models. Similarly, it may cause the memory usage problem when the dimension of the feature space becomes too high.

In order to take the advantages of linear online models and produce sparsity simultaneously, we propose a Fourier follow-the-regularized-leader (FFTRL) algorithm in this paper. FFTRL adopts the random Fourier feature technique to approximate shift-invariant kernels and introduces sparsity using the FTRL algorithm. Theoretical analysis and experiments on FFTRL are also provided in this paper.

The rest of the paper is organized as follows. Section 2 details the proposed method. Experimental results and analysis are presented in Sect. 3 and the conclusion is given in Sect. 4.

2 Proposed Method

2.1 Algorithm Description

The proposed FFTRL is a online kernel learning method for binary classification tasks. The goal of FFTRL is to learn a final mapping or hypothesis $f : \mathbb{R}^n \to \mathbb{R}$ from a sequence of data elements $\{(\mathbf{x}_1, y_1), (\mathbf{x}_2, y_2), \ldots, (\mathbf{x}_T, y_T)\}$, where $\mathbf{x}_t \in \mathbb{R}^n$ is the tth training instance, and $y_t \in \{+1, -1\}$ is the corresponding class label, n and T are the number of features and samples, respectively. Generally, a convex loss function $l(f(\mathbf{x}), y) : \mathbb{R} \times \mathbb{R} \to \mathbb{R}$ is used to penalize the deviation of the estimation $f(\mathbf{x})$ from the exact class label y. Further, we assume $\mathcal{H}_k$ is a reproducing kernel Hilbert space (RKHS). Thus, the function $k(\cdot, \cdot) : \mathbb{R}^n \times \mathbb{R}^n \to \mathbb{R}$ is defined as the reproducing kernel of $\mathcal{H}_k$ if and only if it implements the inner product $\langle \cdot, \cdot \rangle$ such that

1. $k(\mathbf{x}, \cdot) \in \mathcal{H}_k$ for $\forall \mathbf{x} \in \mathbb{R}^n$;
2. $\langle f, k(\mathbf{x}, \cdot) \rangle = f(\mathbf{x})$ for $\forall \mathbf{x} \in \mathbb{R}^n$ and $\forall f \in \mathcal{H}_k$.

In classical online kernel learning, the computation of kernel functions improves the complexity of algorithms. Inspired by FOGD, FFTRL represents a kernel mapping in a linear manner. Namely,

$$k(\mathbf{x}_j, \mathbf{x}_m) \approx \mathbf{z}(\mathbf{x}_j)^\mathsf{T} \mathbf{z}(\mathbf{x}_m), \tag{1}$$

where the superscript T means the operation of a vector or matrix transpose, $\mathbf{x}_j$ and $\mathbf{x}_m$ are arbitrary instances in the sequence, and $\mathbf{z}(\mathbf{x}_j)$ is an approximate image of $\mathbf{x}_j$ in the feature space.

Let $f(\mathbf{x}) = \mathbf{w}^\mathsf{T} \mathbf{z}(\mathbf{x})$, where $\mathbf{w}$ is the weight vector. Then the loss function can be represented as $l(\mathbf{w}, \mathbf{z}(\mathbf{x}), y)$. To find $\mathbf{z}(\mathbf{x})$ related to $k(\cdot, \cdot)$, we introduce random Fourier features [16], which is a kernel functional approximation technique that works for shift-invariant kernels like Gaussian and Laplacian kernels. Such kernels have the form of $k(\mathbf{x}_j, \mathbf{x}_m) = k(\Delta \mathbf{x})$, where $\Delta \mathbf{x} = \mathbf{x}_j - \mathbf{x}_m$ is the divergence between the two instances. Bochner's theorem implies that a positive definite kernel function $k(\Delta\mathbf{x})$ is the Fourier transform of a proper probability density function $p(\mathbf{u})$ with a random variable $\mathbf{u} \in \mathbb{R}^n$ [17]. Namely,

$$k(\Delta\mathbf{x}) = \int p(\mathbf{u})e^{i\mathbf{u}^\mathsf{T}\Delta\mathbf{x}}\,d\mathbf{u}, \tag{2}$$

where i is the imaginary unit. By contrary, assume we have the right kernel here. By calculating the inverse Fourier transform of the kernel $k(\Delta\mathbf{x})$, we can obtain

$$p(\mathbf{u}) = \left(\frac{1}{2\pi}\right)^n \int e^{-i\mathbf{u}^\mathsf{T}(\Delta\mathbf{x})}k(\Delta\mathbf{x})\,d(\Delta\mathbf{x}). \tag{3}$$

For example, given a Gaussian kernel $k(\mathbf{x}_j, \mathbf{x}_m) = \exp(-\|\mathbf{x}_j - \mathbf{x}_m\|_2^2/2\sigma^2)$ with the kernel parameter $\sigma > 0$, we have the corresponding distribution $p(\mathbf{u}) = \mathcal{N}(\mathbf{0}, \sigma^{-2}\mathbf{I})$ with the identify matrix $\mathbf{I}$. According to (2), we can see that the kernel function can be expressed as the expectation of $\mathbf{u}$ drawn from the distribution $p(\mathbf{u})$. In other words, we have

$$\int p(\mathbf{u})e^{i\mathbf{u}^\mathsf{T}\Delta\mathbf{x}}\,d\mathbf{u} = E_\mathbf{u}[e^{i\mathbf{u}^\mathsf{T}\mathbf{x}_j}e^{-i\mathbf{u}^\mathsf{T}\mathbf{x}_m}], \tag{4}$$

where the function $E_\mathbf{u}[\cdot]$ is to find the expectation of $\mathbf{u}$. Using Euler's formula, we can rewrite (4) as

$$E_\mathbf{u}[\cos(\mathbf{u}^\mathsf{T}\mathbf{x}_j)\cos(\mathbf{u}^\mathsf{T}\mathbf{x}_m) + \sin(\mathbf{u}^\mathsf{T}\mathbf{x}_j)\sin(\mathbf{u}^\mathsf{T}\mathbf{x}_m)]$$
$$= E_\mathbf{u}\left[[\sin(\mathbf{u}^\mathsf{T}\mathbf{x}_j), \cos(\mathbf{u}^\mathsf{T}\mathbf{x}_j)][\sin(\mathbf{u}^\mathsf{T}\mathbf{x}_m), \cos(\mathbf{u}^\mathsf{T}\mathbf{x}_m)]^\mathsf{T}\right]. \tag{5}$$

According to (5), we can make $\mathbf{z}(\mathbf{x}) = [\sin(\mathbf{u}^\mathsf{T}\mathbf{x}), \cos(\mathbf{u}^\mathsf{T}\mathbf{x})]^\mathsf{T}$ that is a new representation (image) of instance $\mathbf{x}$. Since the kernel function $k(\Delta\mathbf{x})$ equals the expectation of inner productor of $\mathbf{z}(\mathbf{x}_j)$ and $\mathbf{z}(\mathbf{x}_m)$, we can draw D samples $\mathbf{u}_1, \ldots, \mathbf{u}_D$ independently from the distribution p and construct the image of $\mathbf{x}$ as

$$\mathbf{z}(\mathbf{x}) = \left[\sin(\mathbf{u}_1^\mathsf{T}\mathbf{x}), \cos(\mathbf{u}_1^\mathsf{T}\mathbf{x}), \ldots, \sin(\mathbf{u}_D^\mathsf{T}\mathbf{x}), \cos(\mathbf{u}_D^\mathsf{T}\mathbf{x})\right]^\mathsf{T} \in \mathbb{R}^{2D}. \tag{6}$$

Now, we can ignore the computation of kernel function because we get the explicit images in the high-dimensional feature space that is induced by the corresponding kernel function. If the number of samples D is large enough, the error brought by approximation can be omitted reasonably. Thus, the online kernel learning in the original space is transformed into the linear online learning in a high dimensional feature space.

To produce sparsity in the online process, we introduce FTRL that comprehensively considers the differences between FOBOS and RDA on regularization terms and model parameter $\mathbf{w}$. In the tth round, FFTRL performs the update of the weight vector $\mathbf{w}_{t+1}$ as follows:

$$\mathbf{w}_{t+1} = \arg\min_\mathbf{w}\left\{\mathbf{w}^\mathsf{T}\left(\sum_{s=1}^t \mathbf{g}_s\right) + \frac{1}{2}\sum_{s=1}^t \|\sqrt{\sigma_s} \odot (\mathbf{w} - \mathbf{w}_s)\|_2^2 + \lambda\|\mathbf{w}\|_1\right\}, \tag{7}$$

where $\mathbf{g}_s = \nabla_{\mathbf{w}_s} l(\mathbf{w}_s, \mathbf{z}(\mathbf{x}_s), y_s)$ is the gradient in the sth iteration, $\odot$ is the element-wise multiplication operator, $\boldsymbol{\sigma}_s = [\sigma_{s,1}, \ldots, \sigma_{s,2D}]^\top \in \mathbb{R}^{2D}$ is the parameter related to the current learning rate, and λ is a positive regularization parameter. We discuss $\boldsymbol{\sigma}_s$ later.

The basic idea behind FTRL is to minimize the loss cumulated in the online training process, which will get a low-regret solution in the current round. Therefore, FFTRL uses a cumulative gradient to approximately estimate the cumulative loss, or the first term of (7). The second term in (7) works as a stabilization penalty to avoid $\mathbf{w}$ from vibrating extensively in iterations, while the third term is an L_1 penalty. With $\lambda > 0$, FFTRL does an excellent job in producing sparsity.

Moreover, we thought that if a feature variable varies more rapidly than the other, then it is reasonable that the learning rate on this feature variable should decline faster. Thus, FFTRL uses the per-coordinate learning rate instead of a global learning rate like setting $\eta_t = \frac{1}{\sqrt{t}}$ $(t > 0)$ for all features. In other words, the learning rate is calculated independently for each feature. Let $\boldsymbol{\eta}_t = [\eta_{t,1}, \ldots, \eta_{t,2D}] \in \mathbb{R}^{2D}$ be the learning rate used in FFTRL. We reflect the rate of change using the gradient component in a certain dimension. Without loss of generality, let $g_{t,h}$ be the hth entry in $\mathbf{g}_t$. Then, the corresponding learning rate in the hth dimension can be expressed as

$$\eta_{t,h} = \frac{\alpha}{\beta + \sqrt{\sum_{s=1}^{t} g_{s,h}^2}} \tag{8}$$

for $t > 0$, where both $\alpha > 0$ and $\beta > 0$ are two parameters needed to be tuned for good performance. When $t = 0$, $g_{s,t} = 0$. Then, $\eta_{0,h} = \alpha/\beta$ for all h. For $\boldsymbol{\sigma}_s$, its hth component can be defined as

$$\sigma_{s,h} = \frac{1}{\eta_{t,h}} - \frac{1}{\eta_{t-1,h}}. \tag{9}$$

The detail algorithm description of FFTRL is summarized in Algorithm 1. For training data arriving sequentially, we first construct the new representation of an instance using the explicit mapping $\mathbf{z}(\mathbf{x})$ in (6) and then perform a sparse linear online learning using FTRL. The overall time complexity of FTRL in one update round is $O(D)$.

2.2   Theoretical Analysis

We further analyze the theoretical property of our proposed method. For the purpose of simplicity, $l_t(f)$ represents $l(f(\mathbf{x}_t), y_t)$, and $l_t(\mathbf{w})$ is $l_t(\mathbf{w}_t, \mathbf{z}(\mathbf{x}_t), y_t)$. In the following, we show that the regret of our algorithm is sub-linear, which indicates the effectiveness of FFTRL .

Theorem 1. *Assume that the original data is contained by a ball in $\mathbb{R}^n$ of diameter $\tilde{R}$. Let $k(\mathbf{x}, \mathbf{x}') = k(\Delta \mathbf{x})$ be a positive definite and shift-invariant kernel, and $l(f(\mathbf{x}), y) : \mathbb{R} \times \mathbb{R} \to \mathbb{R}$ be a convex loss function that is Lipschitz continuous*

Algorithm 1 Training process of FFTRL.

Input: Kernel function $k(\cdot,\cdot)$, parameters α, β, and λ, and the number of samples D.
Initialize: $\mathbf{w}_1 = \mathbf{0}$; $m_h = 0$, $q_h = 0$ ($\forall h \in \{1,2,\dots,2D\}$).
  Calculate $p(\mathbf{u})$ of kernel $k(\cdot,\cdot)$ using (3);
  Draw D independent and identically distributed samples $\mathbf{u}_1,\dots,\mathbf{u}_D$ from $p(\mathbf{u})$;
  for $t = 1,2,\dots,T$ **do**
    Receive $(\mathbf{x}_t, y_t)$;
    Construct the new representation $\mathbf{z}(\mathbf{x}_t)$ using (6);
    Predict $\hat{y}_t = \mathrm{sgn}(\mathbf{w}_t^\mathsf{T}\mathbf{z}(\mathbf{x}_t))$;
    Calculate $\mathbf{g}_t = \nabla_{\mathbf{w}_t} l(\mathbf{w}_t, \mathbf{z}(\mathbf{x}_t), y_t)$;
    for $h = 1,2,\dots,2D$ **do**
      $\sigma_{t,h} = \frac{1}{\alpha}\sqrt{q_h + g_{t,h}^2} - \sqrt{q_h}$; // which is equivalent to (9).
      $q_h \leftarrow q_h + g_{t,h}^2$;
      $m_h \leftarrow m_h + g_{t,h} - \sigma_{t,h}\mathbf{w}_{t,h}$;
      $\mathbf{w}_{t+1,h} = \begin{cases} 0 & if\ |m_h| < \lambda, \\ \frac{\alpha}{\beta+\sqrt{q_h}}(\lambda\,\mathrm{sgn}(m_h) - m_h) & otherwise. \end{cases}$
    end for
  end for

---

with Lipschitz constant L. Assume that $\mathbf{w}_1,\dots,\mathbf{w}_T$ is the sequence of model parameters generated by FFTRL (Algorithm 1) under the mild condition that the learning rate $\eta_{t,h} = \eta_t$ for every dimension in the same iteration, where $\|\mathbf{w}_t\|_2 \le R$. With probability at least $1 - 2^8(\frac{\varsigma_p\tilde{R}}{\epsilon})^2 \exp(\frac{-D\epsilon^2}{4(n+2)})$, the following inequality

$$\sum_{t=1}^T l_t(\mathbf{w}_t) - \sum_{t=1}^T l_t(f^*) \le \frac{(1+\epsilon)\|f^*\|_1^2}{2\eta_T} + L^2\sum_{t=1}^T \eta_t + \frac{3R^2}{2\eta_T} + \sqrt{2D}\lambda R + \epsilon LT\|f^*\|_1$$

holds true for any $f^*(\mathbf{x}) = \sum_{t=1}^T \alpha_t^* k(\mathbf{x}_t,\mathbf{x})$, where $\|f^*\|_1 = \sum_{t=1}^T |\alpha_t^*|$, $\varsigma_p^2 = E_p[\mathbf{u}^\mathsf{T}\mathbf{u}]$ is the second moment of the Fourier transform of the kernel function $k(\cdot,\cdot)$ given that $p(\mathbf{u})$ is the probability density function calculated by (3), and ϵ is a small positive constant.

Proof. Given $f^*(\mathbf{x}) = \sum_{t=1}^T \alpha_t^* k(\mathbf{x}_t,\mathbf{x})$ as the optimal solution of FFTRL, we have the corresponding linear model $\mathbf{w}^* = \sum_{t=1}^T \alpha_t^* \mathbf{z}(\mathbf{x}_t)$. First of all, we have to bound the regret of the sequence $\mathbf{w}_1,\dots,\mathbf{w}_T$ learned by FFTRL with respect to the optimal linear model $\mathbf{w}^*$ in the new feature space. According to the regret analysis of the FTRL algorithm with strongly convex regularizers (Lemma 2.3.) [18], we have:

$$\sum_{t=1}^T (l_t(\mathbf{w}_t) - l_t(\mathbf{w}^*)) \le L^2\sum_{t=1}^T \eta_t + r_{1:T}(\mathbf{w}^*) + \psi(\mathbf{w}^*), \tag{10}$$

where $r_{1:T}(\mathbf{w}^*) = \sum_{t=1}^{T} r_t(\mathbf{w}^*)$. Let $r_t(\mathbf{w}) = \frac{\sigma_t}{2}\|\mathbf{w} - \mathbf{w}_t\|_2^2$ and $\psi(\mathbf{w}) = \lambda\|\mathbf{w}\|_1$. Then, the cumulative sum of regularizers becomes

$$r_{1:T}(\mathbf{w}^*) + \psi(\mathbf{w}^*) = \frac{1}{2}\sum_{t=1}^{T}\sigma_t\|\mathbf{w}^* - \mathbf{w}_t\|_2^2 + \lambda\|\mathbf{w}^*\|_1, \tag{11}$$

which is exactly the same as the regularization term in (7).

For $r_{1:T}(\mathbf{w}^*)$, we can infer that

$$r_{1:T}(\mathbf{w}^*) = \frac{1}{2}\sum_{t=1}^{T}\sigma_t\|\mathbf{w}^* - \mathbf{w}_t\|_2^2$$

$$\leq \frac{1}{2}\sum_{t=1}^{T}\sigma_t(\|\mathbf{w}^*\|_2^2 - 2\langle\mathbf{w}^*, \mathbf{w}_t\rangle + \|\mathbf{w}_t\|_2^2)$$

$$\leq \frac{1}{2}\sum_{t=1}^{T}\sigma_t(\|\mathbf{w}^*\|_2^2 + 3R^2) = \frac{1}{2\eta_T}(\|\mathbf{w}^*\|_2^2 + 3R^2). \tag{12}$$

For $\psi(\mathbf{w}^*)$, it is upper-bounded by $\sqrt{2D}\lambda R$ according to the arithmetic-geometric mean inequality (AGMI). The regret bound (10) now becomes

$$\sum_{t=1}^{T}(l_t(\mathbf{w}_t) - l_t(\mathbf{w}^*)) \leq L^2\sum_{t=1}^{T}\eta_t + \frac{\|\mathbf{w}^*\|_2^2 + 3R^2}{2\eta_T} + \sqrt{2D}\lambda R \tag{13}$$

Next, we examine the difference between $\sum_{t=1}^{T} l_t(\mathbf{w}^*)$ and $\sum_{t=1}^{T} l_t(f^*)$. According to the uniform convergence of random Fourier features (Claim 1 in [16]), with probability at least $1 - 2^8(\frac{s_p \tilde{R}}{\epsilon})^2 \exp(\frac{-D\epsilon^2}{4(n+2)})$, we have

$$\forall j, m, \quad |\mathbf{z}(\mathbf{x}_j)^\mathsf{T}\mathbf{z}(\mathbf{x}_m) - k(\mathbf{x}_j, \mathbf{x}_m)| < \epsilon. \tag{14}$$

In other words, the more we sample, the smaller the probability that the difference between approximated kernel value and real kernel value is greater than the constant ϵ we will get. We further assume $k(\mathbf{x}_j, \mathbf{x}_m) \leq 1$, then we have $\mathbf{z}(\mathbf{x}_j)^\mathsf{T}\mathbf{z}(\mathbf{x}_m) \leq 1 + \epsilon$ that leads to

$$\|\mathbf{w}^*\|_2^2 \leq (1+\epsilon)\|f^*\|_1^2. \tag{15}$$

With (14), we have:

$$\left|\sum_{t=1}^{T}l_t(\mathbf{w}^*) - \sum_{t=1}^{T}l_t(f^*)\right| \leq \sum_{t=1}^{T}|l_t(\mathbf{w}^*) - l_t(f^*)|$$

$$\leq L\sum_{t=1}^{T}\sum_{j=1}^{T}|\alpha_j^*||\mathbf{z}(\mathbf{x}_j)^\mathsf{T}\mathbf{z}(\mathbf{x}_t) - k(\mathbf{x}_j, \mathbf{x}_t)|$$

$$\leq \epsilon L\sum_{t=1}^{T}\sum_{j=1}^{T}|\alpha_j^*| = \epsilon LT\|f^*\|_1. \tag{16}$$

Combing (13), (15) and (16) leads to the completion of the proof.

Table 1. Information of eight publicly available datasets used in experiments.

Datasets	#Instances	#Features
Titanic	2201	3
Spambase	4597	57
Banana	5300	2
Phoneme	5404	5
Coil2000	9822	85
W7a	24,692	300
A7a	32,561	123
Ijcnn1	141,691	22

3 Experiments

3.1 Description of Data and Algorithms Involved

To validate the performance of our proposed algorithm, we conducted extensive experiments on the tasks of online binary classification. We first introduced the datasets used in our experiments and then described the algorithms for comparison.

Table 1 shows the details of eight publicly available datasets where the first five datasets can be downloaded from KEEL dataset repository [1] and the rest three are available at LIBSVM website [4]. We followed the common setting of online binary classification tasks that each dataset should be divided into training and test sets. We adopted the original splits of training and test sets for datasets downloaded from the LIBSVM website. For KEEL datasets, a random split of 4 : 1 training–test was performed.

In experiments, our proposed method was first compared with NORMA and ACCOSVM for regular online kernel classification, which are solved in primal and dual spaces, respectively.

- "NORMA" [9]: Online gradient descent for kernel SVM without budget.
- "ACCOSVM" [8]: An accelerator for online SVM combing quadratic programming and window techniques.

Further, we invited three state-of-the-art budget online kernel learning algorithms to compare with FFTRL. Namely,

- "BNORMA" [9]: The budgeted version of NORMA using removal strategy.
- "Forgetron" [6]: Budget perceptron using the removal strategy.
- "Projectron" [15]: Budget perceptron using the projection strategy.

Finally, we introduced an algorithm sharing the similar idea with our proposed method:

- "FOGD" [12]: Online gradient descent using random Fourier features for kernel approximation.

3.2 Experimental Setting

All the experiments were carried out in Python 3.6 on a PC running Windows 10 with a 2.9GHz Intel Core i7 processor and 16 GB RAM. To make a fair comparison, all algorithms adopted the following same setups. The Gaussian kernel was used as the kernel function $k(\cdot, \cdot)$, and the hinge loss was taken as the convex loss function. Since the hinge loss is a non-smooth function, subgradient was adopted instead of gradient, which counts only when $yf(\mathbf{x}) < 1$.

The budget size in budget online learning algorithms and the number of samples in FOGD and our proposed method were set to 100 and 200, respectively, following the same setups in [12]. The learning rate related parameter β in our algorithm was set to 1 according to the instruction from [14]. Other hyper-parameters were selected by a standard 5-fold cross validation on the training set, including the kernel bandwidth σ, the learning rate related parameter α for FFTRL, the regularization parameter λ for FFTRL, NORMA and BNORMA, the initial learning rate η_0 for FGD, NORMA, and BNORMA, and C for ACCOSVM. Then, the training set was refitted using the best model five times, where at each run the instances were shuffled differently. The mean and standard deviation of mistake rate on the training set, training time, accuracy on the test set, and test time were reported as the final results.

3.3 Results and Analysis

Table 2 summarizes the evaluation results on the eight datasets, where the best results are in bold. Note that the test process of NORMA on the Ijcnn1 dataset was early stopped after 10,000 s, and the instances being tested at the time of early stopping was reported in italic. From Table 2, we can draw the following conclusions.

First, we found that budget online kernel classification algorithms run much faster than the regular ones (say, NORMA and ACCOSVM) in both training and test process. That means scalable online kernel methods are more practical in terms of time efficiency. However, budget online kernel classification algorithms generally make more mistakes on the training set and then get lower accuracy on the test set. Potentional loss of information is occurred when adopting budget strategies, validating the importance of exploring effective techniques for budget online kernel learning algorithms. The same phenomenon happens inside the family of budget online algorithms too. We notice that Projectron takes more time in training and test but obtains more promising results than both BNORMA and Forgetron in five out of eight datasets since the projection strategy is more complex than just simply remove an SV. The trade-offs between accuracy and time efficiency should be analyzed in specific situations.

Second, we compared the two kernel approximation methods (FOGD and FFTRL) with the budget online kernel classification algorithms. As is listed in Table 2, FOGD takes the least time in training, and our proposed method FFTRL shows competitive results too. Both algorithms achieve amazing speed in training, far exceeding any budget online kernel algorithms. We inferred that

Table 2. Comparison of online kernel algorithms on 8 benchmark binary classification datasets.

Algorithm	Titanic				Spambase			
	Mistake Rate (%)	Train (s)	Accuracy (%)	Test (s)	Mistake Rate (%)	Train (s)	Accuracy (%)	Test (s)
NORMA	**22.54 ± 0.57**	10.97 ± 0.02	77.65 ± 1.22	5.47 ± 0.02	12.96 ± 0.51	49.44 ± 0.44	91.10 ± 0.81	24.54 ± 0.29
ACCOSVM	23.33 ± 0.50	137.56 ± 0.54	78.67 ± 1.00	6.36 ± 0.04	12.05 ± 0.88	150.47 ± 3.03	**91.80 ± 0.39**	17.68 ± 0.27
BNORMA	22.86 ± 0.40	1.34 ± 0.01	76.65 ± 1.26	0.33 ± 0.00	18.76 ± 0.33	2.78 ± 0.05	83.77 ± 2.98	0.67 ± 0.01
Forgetron	31.13 ± 0.34	1.78 ± 0.01	76.83 ± 2.77	0.35 ± 0.00	17.19 ± 0.54	3.17 ± 0.04	83.47 ± 1.62	0.70 ± 0.00
Projectron	30.14 ± 0.54	0.24 ± 0.01	77.69 ± 1.62	0.05 ± 0.00	15.44 ± 0.43	10.67 ± 0.44	87.21 ± 1.44	3.94 ± 0.11
FGD	25.03 ± 0.55	**0.02 ± 0.00**	78.15 ± 1.80	0.01 ± 0.00	11.75 ± 0.24	**0.06 ± 0.00**	90.08 ± 1.20	0.01 ± 0.00
FFTRL	22.56 ± 0.29	1.76 ± 0.10	**79.03 ± 1.05**	**0.01 ± 0.00**	**11.21 ± 0.41**	5.63 ± 0.03	91.56 ± 0.49	**0.01 ± 0.00**

Algorithm	Banana				Phoneme			
	Mistake Rate (%)	Train (s)	Accuracy (%)	Test (s)	Mistake Rate (%)	Train (s)	Accuracy (%)	Test (s)
NORMA	11.62 ± 0.36	65.46 ± 0.27	89.08 ± 0.58	34.52 ± 3.74	23.67 ± 0.33	67.29 ± 1.06	77.28 ± 0.91	33.66 ± 0.37
ACCOSVM	**11.11 ± 0.24**	134.27 ± 4.69	89.23 ± 0.62	11.86 ± 0.30	**16.44 ± 0.27**	412.58 ± 17.45	**85.75 ± 0.65**	19.26 ± 0.18
BNORMA	15.89 ± 0.27	3.33 ± 0.11	83.06 ± 1.70	0.80 ± 0.03	23.74 ± 0.39	3.32 ± 0.06	77.17 ± 0.92	0.79 ± 0.01
Forgetron	18.64 ± 0.49	3.67 ± 0.05	80.38 ± 2.23	0.79 ± 0.01	25.80 ± 0.14	4.14 ± 0.07	73.61 ± 2.34	0.82 ± 0.01
Projectron	14.56 ± 0.33	13.14 ± 2.97	85.38 ± 1.82	4.37 ± 0.59	20.38 ± 0.21	11.34 ± 0.46	80.94 ± 2.05	3.46 ± 0.09
FOGD	15.48 0.34	**0.06 0.00**	85.08 1g.13	0.01 0.00	18.02 0.23	**0.07 0.01**	83.62 0.57	0.01 0.00
FFTRL	11.92 0.20	5.26 0.15	**89.81 0.39**	**0.01 0.00**	17.48 0.23	6.68 0.29	84.70 0.53	**0.01 0.00**

Algorithm	Coil2000				W7a			
	Mistake Rate (%)	Train (s)	Accuracy (%)	Test (s)	Mistake Rate (%)	Train (s)	Accuracy (%)	Test (s)
NORMA	7.68 ± 0.17	231.33 ± 1.39	91.81 ± 1.05	114.43 ± 0.20	2.95 ± 0.02	2021.10 ± 248.08	97.14 ± 0.05	4003.87 ± 477.64
ACCOSVM	7.13 ± 0.09	2592.71 ± 59.48	92.89 ± 0.17	118.06 ± 0.74	2.03 ± 0.02	4927.57 ± 318.12	**98.48 ± 0.01**	1770.59 ± 78.54
BNORMA	7.59 ± 0.11	5.94 ± 0.03	91.19 ± 1.52	1.41 ± 0.01	4.27 ± 0.11	21.40 ± 1.34	96.11 ± 0.69	22.63 ± 1.34
Forgetron	11.19 ± 0.15	6.42 ± 0.04	92.34 ± 1.73	1.52 ± 0.01	4.36 ± 0.06	13.98 ± 1.04	96.69 ± 0.67	13.25 ± 0.07
Projectron	10.75 ± 0.16	25.96 ± 0.30	91.67 ± 2.14	10.53 ± 0.17	2.74 ± 0.03	45.78 ± 1.08	98.33 ± 0.10	64.99 ± 1.46
FOGD	7.27 ± 0.04	**0.11 ± 0.00**	92.80 ± 0.12	0.02 ± 0.00	3.47 ± 0.08	**0.37 ± 0.01**	96.67 ± 0.04	0.29 ± 0.02
FFTRL	**6.90 ± 0.06**	10.59 ± 10.4	**93.55 ± 0.93**	0.02 ± 0.01	3.36 ± 0.05	25.86 ± 0.29	96.92 ± 0.01	**0.27 ± 0.01**

Algorithm	A7a				Ijcnn1			
	Mistake Rate (%)	Train (s)	Accuracy (%)	Test (s)	Mistake Rate (%)	Train (s)	Accuracy (%)	Test (s)
NORMA	17.99 ± 0.22	951.63 ± 18.63	82.42 ± 0.02	1958.85 ± 48.16	9.67 ± 0.16	4558.52 ± 104.74	90.26 ± 0.01	*48542.60*
ACCOSVM	**16.34 ± 0.15**	4473.56 ± 192.07	83.63 ± 0.05	1172.24 ± 24.88	**6.15 ± 0.01**	3382.09 ± 338.19	**94.63 ± 0.05**	2997.05 ± 50.54
BNORMA	20.54 ± 0.20	12.82 ± 0.40	80.91 ± 0.48	12.51 ± 0.40	13.03 ± 0.05	45.91 ± 1.22	87.07 ± 2.34	16.86 ± 0.85
Forgetron	24.57 ± 0.22	16.97 ± 0.86	78.23 ± 0.45	13.51 ± 0.27	16.60 ± 0.14	20.22 ± 0.25	86.96 ± 3.68	44.39 ± 0.96
Projectron	20.51 ± 0.37	366.03 ± 15.12	80.47 ± 0.92	372.86 ± 3.45	7.64 ± 0.07	162.50 ± 1.63	94.31 ± 0.90	454.11 ± 2.73
FOGD	18.77 ± 0.14	**0.23 ± 0.01**	82.48 ± 1.04	0.16 ± 0.00	9.33 ± 0.02	**0.43 ± 0.01**	91.46 ± 0.40	0.77 ± 0.01
FFTRL	16.84 ± 0.13	25.12 ± 0.49	**84.15 ± 0.19**	**0.15 ± 0.00**	9.35 ± 0.02	49.27 ± 0.44	91.90 ± 0.20	**0.75 ± 0.01**

the extraordinary time efficiency of kernel approximation methods should be attributed to the linear online learning framework. Moreover, both FOGD and FFTRL also show better mistake rate and accuracy in most cases, which demonstrates that kernel approximation scheme is suitable for large scale online learning.

Finally, we analyzed the performance of FFTRL. It seems surprising to find that FFTRL gets the lowest mistake rate or highest accuracy, even outperforms NORMA in some datasets (such as, Spambase, Coil2000, A7a and Ijcnn1). The reasons may lie in two aspects. The first reason is the appropriate choice of sample number D. According to the conclusions from [12], choosing a too large value of D will result in under-fitting for small datasets, and choosing a too small value of D will result in over-fitting. The second reason is the well-designed per-coordinate learning rate. Except from FFTRL, all the gradient-based algorithms adopt the global learning rate schedule. However, we need to use the learning rate to reflect our confidence of each dimension in online setting, which indicates the global learning rate schedule is not the optimal choice. Besides, FFTRL also produces a sparser model than FOGD as expected. Unfortunately, the benefits of sparsity brought to FFTRL are largely obscured by the efficiency of linear learning framework since the test time of FOGD and FFTRL are generally the

Table 3. Sparsity promotion of FFTRL against FOGD.

	Titanic	Spambase	Banana	Phoneme
FOGD	Baseline	Baseline	Baseline	Baseline
FFTRL	+272.80	+176.40	+193.40	+118.60
	Coil2000	W7a	A7a	Ijcnn1
FOGD	Baseline	Baseline	Baseline	Baseline
FFTRL	+143.00	+203.40	+76.40	+102.20

same. To validate the advantage of our proposed method over FOGD, we listed the number of zero components in the weight vector $\mathbf{w}$ in Table 3, where the number of zero coefficients in FOGD is taken as the baseline. From Table 3, we can obviously see that the model generated by FFTRL is much sparser than that of FOGD.

4   Conclusion

In this paper, we present a novel sparse algorithm FFTRL for solving large-scale online kernel binary classification tasks. The basic idea of FFTRL is to approximate a kernel function via functional approximation technique, which enables us to transform the original online kernel learning task into an approximate linear online learning task. Random Fourier features are used as the kernel approximation scheme, and then a new high dimensional feature space is induced in this process. We further adopt FTRL to find a sparse solution in the new feature space. In theory, we analyze the regret bound of our proposed algorithm.

We performed extensive experiments to evaluate the performance of FFTRL and other state-of-the-art online kernel learning methods. Our promising results show that FFTRL enjoys both time efficiency and accuracy. Moreover, the sparsity produced by FFTRL fits the need of high dimensional and large-scale data scenarios, making FFTRL suitable for real-world applications. In future work, we plan to extend our work by exploring the field of multi-label online classification tasks.

References

1. Alcalá-Fdez, J., et al.: KEEL data-mining software tool: data set repository, integration of algorithms and experimental analysis framework. J. Multiple Valued Logic Soft Comput. **17**, 255–287 (2011)
2. Belkin, M., Niyogi, P., Sindhwani, V.: Manifold regularization: a geometric framework for learning from labeled and unlabeled examples. J. Mach. Learn. Res. **7**(11) (2006)
3. Cavallanti, G., Cesa-Bianchi, N., Gentile, C.: Tracking the best hyperplane with a simple budget perceptron. Mach. Learn. **69**(2), 143–167 (2007)

4. Chang, C.C., Lin, C.J.: LIBSVM: a library for support vector machines. ACM Trans. Intell. Syst. Technol. (TIST) **2**(3), 1–27 (2011)
5. Crammer, K., Kandola, J., Singer, Y.: Online classification on a budget. In: Advances in Neural Information Processing Systems, vol. 16 (2003)
6. Dekel, O., Shalev-Shwartz, S., Singer, Y.: The forgetron: A kernel-based perceptron on a budget. SIAM J. Comput. **37**(5), 1342–1372 (2008)
7. Duchi, J., Singer, Y.: Efficient online and batch learning using forward backward splitting. J. Mach. Learn. Res. **10**, 2899–2934 (2009)
8. Guo, H., Zhang, A., Wang, W.: An accelerator for online SVM based on the fixed-size KKT window. Eng. Appl. Artif. Intell. **92**, 103637 (2020)
9. Kivinen, J., Smola, A.J., Williamson, R.C.: Online learning with kernels. IEEE Trans. Signal Process. **52**(8), 2165–2176 (2004)
10. Li, B., Zhao, P., Hoi, S.C., Gopalkrishnan, V.: PAMR: passive aggressive mean reversion strategy for portfolio selection. Mach. Learn. **87**(2), 221–258 (2012)
11. Li, X., Plale, B., Vijayakumar, N., Ramachandran, R., Graves, S., Conover, H.: Real-time storm detection and weather forecast activation through data mining and events processing. Earth Sci. Inf. **1**(2), 49–57 (2008)
12. Lu, J., Hoi, S.C., Wang, J., Zhao, P., Liu, Z.Y.: Large scale online kernel learning. J. Mach. Learn. Res. **17**(47), 1 (2016)
13. McMahan, B.: Follow-the-regularized-leader and mirror descent: Equivalence theorems and l1 regularization. In: Proceedings of the Fourteenth International Conference on Artificial Intelligence and Statistics. pp. 525–533. JMLR Workshop and Conference Proceedings (2011). ¡!– Wrong Number: [l]1 –¿
14. McMahan, H.B., et al.: Ad click prediction: a view from the trenches. In: Proceedings of the 19th ACM SIGKDD International Conference on Knowledge Discovery and Data Mining, pp. 1222–1230 (2013)
15. Orabona, F., Keshet, J., Caputo, B.: The projectron: a bounded kernel-based perceptron. In: Proceedings of the 25th International Conference on Machine Learning, pp. 720–727 (2008)
16. Rahimi, A., Recht, B.: Random features for large-scale kernel machines. In: Advances in Neural Information Processing Systems 20 (2007)
17. Rudin, W.: Fourier Analysis on Groups. Courier Dover Publications (2017)
18. Shalev-Shwartz, S., et al.: Online learning and online convex optimization. Found. Trends® Mach. Learn. **4**(2), 107–194 (2012)
19. Xiao, L.: Dual averaging method for regularized stochastic learning and online optimization. In: Advances in Neural Information Processing Systems 22 (2009)
20. Zhang, K., Lan, L., Wang, Z., Moerchen, F.: Scaling up kernel SVM on limited resources: a low-rank linearization approach. In: Artificial Intelligence and Statistics, pp. 1425–1434. PMLR (2012)

Fusing Hand and Body Skeletons
for Human Action Recognition
in Assembly

Dustin Aganian[(✉)] [ID], Mona Köhler, Benedict Stephan, Markus Eisenbach,
and Horst-Michael Gross

Ilmenau University of Technology, Neuroinformatics and Cognitive Robotics Lab,
98693 Ilmenau, Germany
dustin.aganian@tu-ilmenau.de

Abstract. As collaborative robots (cobots) continue to gain popularity in industrial manufacturing, effective human-robot collaboration becomes crucial. Cobots should be able to recognize human actions to assist with assembly tasks and act autonomously. To achieve this, skeleton-based approaches are often used due to their ability to generalize across various people and environments. Although body skeleton approaches are widely used for action recognition, they may not be accurate enough for assembly actions where the worker's fingers and hands play a significant role. To address this limitation, we propose a method in which less detailed body skeletons are combined with highly detailed hand skeletons. We investigate CNNs and transformers, the latter of which are particularly adept at extracting and combining important information from both skeleton types using attention. This paper demonstrates the effectiveness of our proposed approach in enhancing action recognition in assembly scenarios.

Keywords: Action Recognition · Skeleton-based · Fusion · Body Skeletons · Hand Skeletons · 3D/2D Skeletons · Assembly · Deep Learning

1 Introduction

Collaborative robots are playing an increasingly important role in the course of Industry 4.0 [9]. In order for the robot to collaborate with a human worker and assist in assembly processes, it first needs to visually perceive its environment, the current assembly state, and human actions [6, 15, 18]. For human action recognition, often RGB-based approaches are utilized in the state of the art, as they achieve the best results. However, RGB-based approaches face major difficulties when the target scenario deviates from the training scenario. They tend

---

This work has received funding from the Carl-Zeiss-Stiftung as part of the project engineering for smart manufacturing (E4SM).

L. Iliadis et al. (Eds.): ICANN 2023, LNCS 14254, pp. 207–219, 2023.
https://doi.org/10.1007/978-3-031-44207-0_18

to overfit to the environment and the persons seen, especially when the training dataset lacks diversity [15]. This limitation frequently applies to assembly datasets [2,3], which are often small and recorded at only a few locations. In contrast, skeleton-based approaches do not face these limitations, as they only process skeletons and, thus, can generalize much better to different environments.

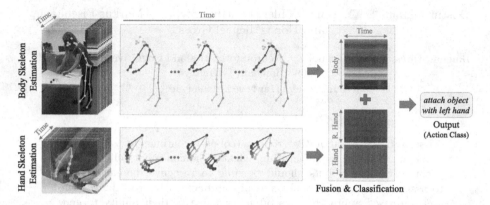

Fig. 1. We combine body skeletons with hand skeletons for human action recognition. Some actions can be recognized primarily by the movement of the hands. The encoding of the skeleton sequences to images is explained in Sect. 4.1. Example frames from [2].

However, as shown in Fig. 1, some actions are difficult to recognize by the body skeleton alone. For example, the action of attaching a small object is mainly characterized by the object movement, as utilized in [1], and how the worker's hands interact with it. For this assembly step, it is therefore also useful to utilize finer hand skeletons. This is already done for other assembly datasets such as Meccano [12] or Assembly101 [14], which are recorded in first-person view. However, using hand skeletons alone might not be sufficient for actions such as turning, rotating or pushing of workpieces. During these actions, the fingers are mostly rigid, and most of the movement takes place in the upper body.

Therefore, in this paper, we want to investigate how highly detailed hand skeletons can be combined with less detailed body skeletons to enhance the recognition of assembly actions on the ATTACH [2] and IKEA ASM [3] datasets. By doing so, we aim to recognize both types of actions.

Our study examines both 2D and 3D body skeletons. While 3D skeletons offer a more comprehensive representation of the person's actions, 2D skeletons are more widely available in practical applications. In this paper, we demonstrate how 2D and 3D hand skeletons can be integrated with various body skeletons. One of the key challenges is that the hands are often occluded, either partially or entirely, which can complicate the estimation of hand positions and the fusion with body skeletons. We also explore the challenges associated with differently detailed skeletons. Specifically, a body skeleton typically has 18–32 joints, while two hand skeletons have most often 42 joints. Although, there are typically more hand joints than body joints, the latter contains significantly more crucial information for many assembly actions. Therefore, in this paper, we describe how to address this dimension imbalance. Our contributions are as follows:

1. We investigate the use of hands in conjunction with body skeletons in both 2D and 3D to improve action recognition for assembly tasks.
2. We predict hand skeletons on the ATTACH and the IKEA ASM datasets and employ a selection process to identify the appropriate hands.
3. To the best of our knowledge, we are the first to employ the SwinV2 transformer [10] for skeleton-based action recognition.

2 Related Work

In the following, we first present the state of the art of action recognition with skeleton sequences, before going into more detail about differences between hand and body skeleton action recognition and possibilities of fusing skeletons.

2.1 Methods for Skeleton-Based Action Recognition

Human action recognition encompasses various subfields, but in this paper, we focus on the action classification task of pre-trimmed video clips of human skeleton sequences, as this task serves as a foundation for other related problems, such as action segmentation or action detection. For skeleton-based action recognition, recently, 2D convolutional neural networks (CNNs) such as VA-CNN [20], 3D CNNs like PoseConv3D [5], graph convolution networks (GCNs) , and transformers like AcT [11] have been used.

In our paper, we adopt the skeleton encoding of [4] and use it like VA-CNN, which employs a ResNet50 backbone, as it has demonstrated superior or comparable results on the ATTACH Dataset [2] compared to GCN methods. In this approach, the skeleton sequence is encoded as an image so that typical image based classifiers can be used. The image encoding also provides the ability to weight the different skeletons based on their occupied image space which will be explained in Sect. 4.

Moreover, we are able to replace the CNN backbone with the SwinV2-T transformer [10], which has demonstrated excellent results in image-based pattern recognition.

2.2 Hand and Body Skeleton-Based Action Recognition

The idea of fusing less detailed body skeletons with highly detailed hand skeletons for action recognition has only been briefly addressed in the literature, and is still a new area of research. For instance, in NTU-X [17] body skeletons from NTU-RGBD 60/120 were extended to include highly detailed hand skeletons and facial features. In [16] a model was trained for every skeleton type to build an ensemble for classifying actions. It was demonstrated in [16,17] that additional hand skeletons from the NTU dataset for everyday and domestic actions (such as eating or blowing one's nose) are helpful to the classification task.

In contrast, during assembly, the hand is often occluded by the object being worked on, and the quality of the estimated hand skeletons varies significantly. Typically, the state of the art for action recognition with hands focuses on gesture recognition, where the hands are usually unoccluded. For action recognition during assembly, hand skeletons have only been used in fine motor assembly (e.g., Meccano [12], Assembly101 [14]), where cameras are mounted either on the worker's head or above the table and focus on the worker's arms and hands. For instance, in the application scenario of fine-motor toy assembly, which is similar to ours, [14] demonstrated that estimated hand skeletons can be utilized for action recognition. This indicates that our approach of fusing body skeletons with hand skeletons shows promise for action recognition in general assembly tasks. Such tasks involve a combination of coarse actions, where the movement of the body is relevant, and fine motor actions (as in Fig. 1), where hand skeletons are primarily important. Therefore, in this paper, our goal is to explore how these differently detailed body and hand skeletons can be combined optimally.

3   Hand and Body Skeleton Dataset Preparation

Below, we first present the datasets we used. Afterwards, we explain how we estimated the hand skeletons and what to consider when processing them.

3.1   Datasets

To show our approach, we utilize two datasets that contain both small-grained assembly actions that can be mainly recognized by the hands movement as well as coarse assembly actions that involve the whole body, namely the ATTACH [2] and the IKEA ASM [3] datasets. Both datasets are captured from multiple views (three) and consist of assembly actions, where IKEA furniture are assembled. The action names for the action recognition task are composed of verb-object pairs. Below, we shortly discuss each dataset characteristics in detail.

ATTACH. The ATTACH dataset [2] provides different training splits, we focus on the person split in this paper as it is the most commonly used split for action recognition. Skeleton data are available in 3D from the Azure Kinect framework. Since the state of the art typically deals with 2D skeletons, we have also transformed the 3D skeletons into the 2D frame of the RGB camera. In our experiments, we consider both 3D and 2D body skeletons for combination with hand skeletons.

It is worth noting that actions are labeled for each hand independently. Moreover, some actions involve the use of tools such as wrenches, hammers or screwdrivers, where most of the movement occurs in the hand and fingers. Intuitively, this suggests that incorporating additional hand skeletons could potentially enhance the performance of skeleton-based action recognition methods.

IKEA ASM. We use the official splits provided in [3]. The dataset provides 2D skeletons for all views estimated by Keypoint R-CNN [8]. Unlike the Kinect skeleton, Keypoint R-CNN only predict one single wrist joint per hand. There-fore, incorporating additional hand skeletons might also be useful for action recognition on the IKEA ASM dataset.

However, it should be noted that some actions are difficult to recognize even with hand skeletons. For example, actions such as *pick up back panel*, *pick up front panel*, and *pick up side panel* can only be distinguished by the object used [1], which is not present in the skeleton data.

3.2   Hand Skeleton Estimation

For estimating hand skeletons, the hands need to be clearly visible in the current frame. However, due to their small size in the IKEA ASM dataset, we first cropped a 300×300 patch of the RGB image around the wrist joint of the body skeleton. For the ATTACH dataset, we can skip this first step.

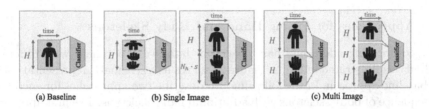

(a) Baseline   (b) Single Image   (c) Multi Image

Fig. 2. Overview of our different fusion approaches. (a) As a baseline we train models with only the body skeleton. H is the height of the input image. (b) As a simple way of fusing both skeleton types we merge them into a single image while investigating different ratios between body and hand skeletons. N_h is the number of hand joints (42 in our case) and s is a scaling factor. (c) We treat both skeletons types as different modalities and apply them as distinct input images.

To detect hands and estimate hand skeletons, we used MediaPipe [19]. How-ever, since the predictions can be rather noisy, we filtered the hands by discarding all hands where the distance between the wrist joints of the predicted hand skele-ton and the body skeleton exceeded a certain threshold. We kept at most two hands per image. In cases where hand skeletons were missing, we simply took skeletons from past frames to attribute for the missing data.

MediaPipe predicts both 2D and 3D hand skeletons with 21 joints each. While 2D hand skeletons are represented in the image plane, the 3D hand skeletons are represented in a metric space, where the origin is located on the surface of each hand. Therefore, when working with 3D data, we transformed the 3D hands into the frame of the 3D body skeletons.

4   Approach

In the following, we describe our approach to action recognition of pre-trimmed skeleton sequences. In Sect. 4.1, we first present our baseline with body skeletons, before discussing different variations for incorporating hand skeletons in Sect. 4.2.

4.1   Baseline: Body Skeleton Approach

For our baseline, we only use the body skeleton, without incorporating additional hand skeletons[1]. For this, we encode the skeletons from a trimmed action sequence into one single RGB image, similar to [4,20]. One column of the image represents one frame, where the skeleton joints are stacked in a fixed order. To transform a joint to RGB, the XYZ coordinates are normalized and scaled.[2] For 2D skeleton data, we have just two channels. These images (see Fig. 1 for a visualization) can then be used as input to typical image-based classification architectures such as ResNet50 (ResNet).

Furthermore, while ResNet is typically used in the state of the art [2,20], we additionally use a SwinV2-T transformer (Swin) [10] for the first time to classify skeleton sequences. Moreover, Swin offers another possibility for fusing hand and body skeleton data, which we will describe in the following.

4.2   Approaches for Fusing Hand and Body Skeletons

For incorporating additional hand skeleton data, we experiment with different methods, as illustrated in Fig. 2. Figure 2a serves as a schematic representation of our baseline approach. In the following, we describe two approaches for encoding the sequence of body skeletons with additional hand skeletons. The first approach involves encoding the hand and body skeletons in a single image, while the second approach creates multiple images that are then combined in the network, similar to multimodal networks that integrate color data with depth data [7,13].

Single Image Fusion. Figure 2b illustrates our single image fusion approach. Naively, the hand skeleton joints could be appended below the body skeleton joints in the skeleton encoded image. For example, for a Kinect Azure skeleton and MediaPipe hands, the first 32 rows would contain the body skeleton, followed by the right hand and the left hand, each with 21 rows. In this way, however, the body skeleton would account for just under 43% of the input, while the hands would account for the remaining 57%. Such a division, in which the number of hand joints of both hands is predominant, is typical for the relevant skeletons used in the state of the art. This example is shown on the left side of Fig. 2b.

However, for recognizing assembly actions, the body skeleton provides more relevant information than the fine hand skeletons, which should only serve as support. With such a naive partitioning of the image, the classifier is given a bias by devoting a larger input space to the hand skeletons.

To address this issue, we investigate another option to fuse the skeletons into one image, which is shown on the right side of Fig. 2b. Here, we keep the original scaling resolution of the body skeleton as in the baseline (see Fig. 2a).

---

[1] Our preliminary experiments on the ATTACH dataset using hand skeletons solely showed far inferior results compared to body skeletons solely and are thus not investigated further.

[2] For ResNet, the image is resized to 224×224 with pixel values ranging from 0–255. For Swin, we use a resolution of 256×256 with pixel values from 0-1.

The body skeleton is scaled up to the original input resolution of the classifier, and subsequently, another image with upscaled hand skeletons is stacked below. We investigate scaling factors $s \in [1, 8]$, where we scale the height of the encoded hand skeleton images (i.e., $N_h = 42$ for MediaPipe skeletons), where $s=8$ resembles the scaling of the body skeleton image.

Multiple Image Input. As an alternative to the previous approach, the skeleton data can be split into different images, and the resulting features can be fused in the network. Recent work on the EMSAFormer [7] has shown that the SwinV2 transformer is particularly suitable for multimodal processing. In their study, the Swin transformer was extended in such a way that RGB and depth images of a scene are fed into the same Swin network as two different images.

We propose a similar approach for processing the encoded body skeleton images and the encoded hand skeleton images. Figure 2c (left) shows how we create two images, one for the body skeleton and one for both hands. The first image is encoded on the first 64 channels of the feature map in the patch embedding, and the second image is encoded on the last 32 channels. After the first attention block, the network combines the information and passes it on to the subsequent blocks, whereby the Swin architecture was not changed.

Alternatively, we can split the skeletons into three images, as shown in Fig. 2c (right). In this case, three images are created, and each is embedded on 32 channels and given to the respective attention head. With this approach, the network itself can decide how to further use the combined information.

5   Experiments

Below we present the results of our experiments on fusing body skeletons with hand skeletons. In Sect. 5.2, we show experiments with 3D body skeletons, before moving on to 2D body skeletons in Sect. 5.3. First, we describe our training setup.

5.1   Setup

Our networks were trained for 100 epochs using the Adam optimizer and a one cycle learning rate scheduler with 10% of epochs as warmup and several maximum learning rates ranging from $5 \cdot 10^{-3}$ to $5 \cdot 10^{-5}$. We validated after each epoch and chose the best epoch for testing. The performances of our trained networks are evaluated using mean class accuracy (mAcc) and top-1 accuracy (top1), two widely used metrics in action recognition literature [2,12,14,17].

Our networks are initialized with ImageNet weights, which improves performance, although the encoded images generated from skeleton data differ a lot from real images. However, performance is still fluctuating, which is why we trained with at least five well-functioning learning rates and repeated training three times for each setup. We present our result using box plots, where each box plots summarizes at least 15 trainings.

5.2 Experiments with 3D Body Skeletons

In the following, we present results solely on the ATTACH dataset [2]. While the IKEA ASM dataset [3] also includes 3D skeletons, they are only available for one camera perspective and captured at a very low frame rate, which makes them rather unsuitable for skeleton-based action recognition.

Baseline – 3D Body Skeletons This subsection serves as a benchmark for our experiments with fused inputs, as we optimize hyperparameters to create a strong baseline using body skeletons solely. On the left side of Fig. 3, we present the results of the baseline experiments with 3D body skeletons on the ATTACH dataset. We compare the performance of two models with similar complexity, namely the SwinV2-T transformer (Swin) and the ResNet50 CNN (ResNet). Our results demonstrate that Swin outperforms ResNet, with a median improvement of more than six percentage points and a maximum improvement of more than four percentage points. Even the worst performing Swin model performs better than the best ResNet model, indicating that Swin is a suitable model for processing skeleton sequences encoded as images.

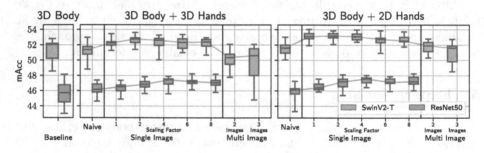

Fig. 3. Results using 3D body skeletons on the ATTACH dataset for our baseline models as in Fig. 2a and our different fusion methods: Naive concatenation as in Fig. 2b left, image concatenation with scaling of encoded hand skeleton image as in Fig. 2b right, multi image input as in Fig. 2c. Best results are listed in Table 1.

However, we want to emphasize that training with Swin is significantly more challenging than with ResNet, which is usually very robust regarding hyperparameters. With Swin, it is crucial to select an appropriate learning rate schedule, as training can fail with even slightly too high learning rates. Conversely, slightly too low learning rates do not produce significant improvements over ResNet. We found that the best results were achieved with learning rates only marginally smaller than the ones that caused training to fail.

Fusion of Hand Skeletons with 3D Body Skeletons Figure 3 illustrates the results of our fusion experiments using our transformed 3D hand skeletons from MediaPipe in the middle, and 2D hand skeletons on the right.

3D Hands: Overall, an improvement of the median and variance can be observed when using the single image fusion approach with the correct scaling factor. While no improvement of the maximum for ResNet is observable, for Swin the incorporation of 3D hands increased performance by about one percentage point. This shows that there is relevant information in the hand skeletons that helps making the training more consistent or even improves the general quality of the models. Moreover, it shows that Swin is significantly better at combining the relevant information from the estimated hand skeletons with the full body skeletons. However, since the 3D hand skeletons in MediaPipe are estimated on 2D color images, a poor estimation of the hand joints may have led to only slight improvements. Therefore, we explore to combine the 3D body skeleton with 2D hand skeletons in the following.

2D Hands: The results of fusing 2D hand skeletons with 3D body skeletons are shown in the right half of Fig. 3. First and foremost, this fusion can be challenging due to the different frames of reference. The 3D skeletons exist in a metric space while the 2D skeletons are given in image coordinates. This means that the different parts of the input image for the single image fusion approach need to be normalized independently.

For ResNet, using the 2D hands results in similar performance compared to 3D hand skeletons. On the other hand, Swin demonstrates that this fusion works very well, and in some cases, it performs even better than the fusion with 3D hands. In fact, the maximum improvement over the baseline is more than one percentage point. This highlights Swin's ability to handle the challenges of using disparate input spaces.

These results also confirm our assumption that the estimated 3D hand skeletons from MediaPipe are less accurate than the 2D hand skeletons.

Fusion Variations: When comparing the different fusion approaches that we examined, both ResNet and Swin yielded similar results. The naive approach, which involves stacking the hand and body skeleton joints and then scale the encoded skeleton image (Fig. 2b left), produced inferior results compared to stacking the encoded images for hand and body skeleton joints (Fig. 2b right). This highlights the importance of scaling up the body skeleton image with a higher upscaling factor, similar to the body skeleton baseline (Fig. 2a).

However, we observed different results when comparing how much the hand skeleton joints need to be upscaled. Swin performed better with a smaller scale factor, while ResNet achieved better results with a larger scale factor. This could possibly be attributed to the different convolutions in the first layer of the respective networks - ResNet uses a 7×7 convolution with stride 2, while Swin's patch embedder is a 4×4 convolution with stride 4.

We also compared single image fusion approaches to multiple image approaches in the Swin transformer. Unfortunately, the multiple image approaches were inferior to all other approaches. The median and maximum results were significantly worse, and the variance was much larger. This suggests that this approach for multimodal input to a Swin network cannot be easily applied.

The lower performance of the multiple image approaches in Swin could potentially be attributed to the patch embedding process. This involves splitting the convolutions to different images to obtain the feature maps with the needed channel sizes. Furthermore, we experimented with larger patch embeddings as in [7], where the body skeleton image is processed into 96 channels of the feature map and the hands into 32 or both into 64. Although this improved the models and made them perform similarly to the single image approaches, it significantly increased the needed computational power and training time. In [7], it was shown that appropriate pre-training can be crucial. However skeleton-based pre-training is not typical in literature and also not the focus of this paper.

5.3 Experiments with 2D Body Skeletons

Most datasets and state-of-the-art approaches utilize 2D skeletons. Therefore, we also experiment with 2D skeletons and show results on the ATTACH [2] and the IKEA ASM [3] dataset. First, we present results of our body only baseline and afterwards the fusion with hand skeletons.

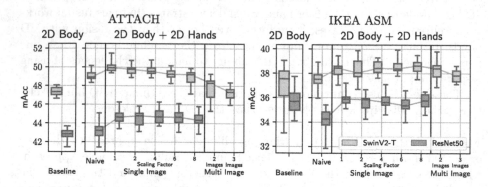

Fig. 4. Results using 2D body skeletons on the ATTACH and IKEA ASM datasets for our baseline models as in Fig. 2a and our different fusion methods: Naive concatenation as in Fig. 2b left, image concatenation with scaling of encoded hand skeleton image as in Fig. 2b right, multi image input as in Fig. 2c. Best results are listed in Table 1.

Baseline – 2D Body Skeletons In Fig. 4, we present the results of the baseline experiments with 2D body skeletons for each dataset. Firstly, it is important to note that the 2D body skeleton baseline results are worse compared to the 3D skeleton baseline results. This can be attributed to the loss of depth information when using 2D skeletons.

As observed in the previous section on using 3D skeletons, Swin outperforms ResNet on both datasets. However, as explained in Sect. 3.1 the skeleton-based action recognition problem is very challenging on IKEA ASM due to a differentiation of actions by objects, which are not encoded in skeleton data. This could explain the smaller improvement in accuracy on IKEA ASM than on ATTACH.

Fusion of Hand Skeletons with 2D Body Skeletons Right to the respective baseline results in Fig. 4, we present the results of the fusion experiments with 2D hand and body skeletons. The comparison between the 2D body skeleton baseline and the fusion approaches reveals a notable improvement in classification performance for both the ATTACH and IKEA ASM datasets. Thus, the inclusion of hand skeletons in addition to body skeletons emerges as a highly effective strategy to elevate the accuracy of action recognition in assembly applications. Below, we go into more detail on the results for each dataset individually.

ATTACH: A closer look on the results on the ATTACH dataset and the comparison with 3D body skeletons reveals that hand skeletons are crucial for achieving improved performance with 2D body skeletons, as indicated by the greater improvement over the corresponding baseline. This holds true for both Swin and ResNet models, highlighting the significance of hand skeletons in mitigating the loss of depth information when only 2D body skeletons are available.

IKEA ASM: The results on the IKEA ASM dataset are less conclusive. Although the addition of hand skeletons generally leads to better medians and smaller variances, the improvement is not as clear as on the ATTACH dataset. Specifically, while the Swin and EMSAFormer models show clear improvement with the addition of hand skeletons, the ResNet only shows improvement in median. One possible explanation for this difference is that predicting hand skeletons on the IKEA ASM dataset is more challenging due to the small size of the hands, which often results in missing hand skeleton estimations. The attention mechanisms in the Swin transformer may be better suited to handle this issue of jumps in the temporal sequence, while the ResNet struggles with it and therefore processes the information contained in the hand skeletons less effectively.

Table 1. Best results of our experiments. We report the mean class accuracy mAcc and in parentheses the top-1 accuracy for the ATTACH [2] and IKEA ASM [3] datasets.

	ATTACH					IKEA ASM	
	3D Body (Baseline)	3D Body 3D Hand	3D Body 2D Hand	2D Body(Baseline)	2D Body 2D Hand	2D Body (Baseline)	2D Body 2D Hand
ResNet50	48.2 (56.5)	48.2 (55.7)	**48.3** (55.9)	43.7 (52.3)	**46.3** (54.6)	**37.7** (70.3)	37.2 (72.6)
SwinV2-T	52.8 (60.3)	53.6 (61.0)	**54.1** (61.7)	48.1 (56.0)	**51.5** (58.9)	39.1 (72.6)	**39.9** (73.9)

6   Conclusion

Our work demonstrates a successful fusion of hand and body skeletons, which improves assembly action recognition notably. While hand skeletons contain important information, they are often prone to noise and misinformation due to difficulties in estimation, such as occlusion or object/tool manipulation. To avoid this issue, our approach specifically handles the importance of the body skeletons to prevent the hand skeletons from dominating the input representation.

Furthermore, our approach demonstrates improved action recognition for two state-of-the-art assembly datasets, not only with 3D body skeletons but also with more commonly available 2D body skeletons. We have demonstrated a successful approach for preparing hand skeletons for action recognition and provided guidance on the key considerations for successful training with the Swin transformer. Overall, our work makes an important contribution to the field of action recognition in mobile robotics and collaborative robots.

References

1. Aganian, D., Köhler, M., Baake, S., Eisenbach, M., Gross, H.M.: How object information improves skeleton-based human action recognition in assembly tasks. In: IEEE International Joint Conference on Neural Networks (IJCNN) (2023)
2. Aganian, D., Stephan, B., Eisenbach, M., Stretz, C., Gross, H.M.: ATTACH dataset: annotated two-handed assembly actions for human action understanding. In: IEEE International Conference on Robotics and Automation (ICRA) (2023)
3. Ben-Shabat, Y., et al.: The IKEA ASM dataset: understanding people assembling furniture through actions, objects and pose. In: IEEE Winter Conference on Applications of Computer Vision (WACV) (2021)
4. Du, Y., Fu, Y., Wang, L.: Skeleton based action recognition with convolutional neural network. In: IEEE IAPR Asian Conference on Pattern Recognition (ACPR) (2015)
5. Duan, H., Zhao, Y., Chen, K., Lin, D., Dai, B.: Revisiting skeleton-based action recognition. In: IEEE Conference on Computer Vision and Pattern Recognition (CVPR) (2022)
6. Eisenbach, M., Aganian, D., Köhler, M., Stephan, B., Schröter, C., Gross, H.M.: Visual scene understanding for enabling situation-aware cobots. In: IEEE International Conference on Automation Science and Engineering (CASE) (2021)
7. Fischedick, S., Seichter, D., Schmidt, R., Rabes, L., Gross, H.M.: Efficient multitask scene analysis with RGB-D transformers. In: IEEE International Joint Conference on Neural Networks (IJCNN) (2023)
8. He, K., Gkioxari, G., Dollár, P., Girshick, R.: Mask R-CNN. In: IEEE International Conference on Computer Vision (ICCV) (2017)
9. Inkulu, A.K., Bahubalendruni, M.R., Dara, A., SankaranarayanaSamy, K.: Challenges and opportunities in human robot collaboration context of industry 4.0 - a state of the art review. Ind. Robot: Int. J. Robot. Res. Appl. 49(2) (2021)
10. Liu, Z., et al.: Swin transformer v2: scaling up capacity and resolution. In: IEEE Conference on Computer Vision and Pattern Recognition (CVPR) (2022)
11. Mazzia, V., Angarano, S., Salvetti, F., Angelini, F., Chiaberge, M.: Action transformer: a self-attention model for short-time pose-based human action recognition. Pattern Recogn., 124 (2022)
12. Ragusa, F., Furnari, A., Livatino, S., Farinella, G.M.: The MECCANO dataset: understanding human-object interactions from egocentric videos in an industrial-like domain. In: IEEE Winter Conference on Applications of Computer Vision (WACV) (2021)

13. Seichter, D., Köhler, M., Lewandowski, B., Wengefeld, T., Gross, H.M.: Efficient RGB-D semantic segmentation for indoor scene analysis. In: International Conference on Robotics and Automation (ICRA) (2021)
14. Sener, F., et al.: Assembly101: a large-scale multi-view video dataset for understanding procedural activities. In: IEEE Conference on Computer Vision and Pattern Recognition (CVPR) (2022)
15. Terreran, M., Lazzaretto, M., Ghidoni, S.: Skeleton-based action and gesture recognition for human-robot collaboration. In: International Conference on Intelligent Autonomous Systems (IAS). Springer (2022). https://doi.org/10.1007/978-3-031-22216-0_3
16. Trivedi, N., Sarvadevabhatla, R.K.: PSUMNet: unified modality part streams are all you need for efficient pose-based action recognition. In: ECCV Workshop and Challenge on People Analysis (WCPA). Springer (2022). https://doi.org/10.1007/978-3-031-25072-9_14
17. Trivedi, N., Thatipelli, A., Sarvadevabhatla, R.K.: NTU-X: an enhanced large-scale dataset for improving pose-based recognition of subtle human actions. In: Indian Conference on Computer Vision, Graphics and Image Processing (ICVGIP). ACM (2021)
18. Wang, L., et al.: Symbiotic human-robot collaborative assembly. CIRP annals 68(2) (2019)
19. Zhang, F., et al.: MediaPipe hands: on-device real-time hand tracking. In: Workshop on Computer Vision for AR/VR (CV4ARVR) (2020)
20. Zhang, P., Lan, C., Xing, J., Zeng, W., Xue, J., Zheng, N.: View adaptive neural networks for high performance skeleton-based human action recognition. IEEE Transactions on Pattern Analysis and Machine Intelligence (TPAMI) (2019)

Gaze Behavior Patterns for Early Drowsiness Detection

Hongfei Gao, Ruimin Hu$^{(\boxtimes)}$, and Zijun Huang

National Engineering Research Center for Multimedia Software (NERCMS), School
of Computer Science, Wuhan University, Wuhan, China
{gaohongfei,hrm,huangzijun}@whu.edu.cn

Abstract. Early drowsiness detection could be crucial for some occupations such as drivers and monitors, as it can greatly improve safety and efficiency. However, most existing drowsiness detection methods do not consider the early stages of drowsiness or the practical feasibility of detection. To address this issue, we propose a gaze behavior pattern-based drowsiness detection model that effectively distinguishes early drowsiness. First, we extract the gaze behavior features of subject from the video, which is composed of eye aspect ratio, head pose and gaze direction. Then we perform a preliminary analysis of the correlation between the gaze behavior features and different stages of drowsiness and propose a multi-stream Transformer model to obtain the classification result from the feature sequences. Our proposed model uses two encoders to encode the temporal and channel information respectively from the gaze behavior features. We conducted experiments on the largest publicly available multi-stage drowsiness video dataset RLDD. Preliminary analysis of the dataset showed the distribution of the features of our selected gaze behavior patterns over different drowsiness stages had relatively significant differences. For early drowsiness detection problem, experiments on real dataset demonstrate the effectiveness of our approach compared to state-of-the-art methods.

Keywords: Early drowsiness detection · Gaze behavior patterns · Transformer · Deep learning

1 Introduction

Drowsiness detection is an important and difficult problem, successful solutions could be used in occupations such as drivers and monitors. Based on careful analysis, experts believe the real number of annual fatalities due to drowsy driving in the U.S. may be closer to 6,000. This would mean drowsiness is involved in approximately 21% of fatal crashes every year. Between hospital admissions, property damage, and other costs, the estimated societal cost of drowsy driving in the U.S. may be anywhere between \$12.5 billion and \$109 billion per year. In addition, studies show that, when driving for a long period of time, drivers lose their self-judgment on how drowsy they are [17], and this can be

L. Iliadis et al. (Eds.): ICANN 2023, LNCS 14254, pp. 220–231, 2023.
https://doi.org/10.1007/978-3-031-44207-0_19

one of the reasons that many accidents occur close to the destination. Research has also shown that sleepiness can affect workers' ability to perform their work safely and efficiently [15]. These troubling facts above prompted us to look for a method to detect and alert people before they fall into drowsiness completely. It is commonly recognized [11,13] that there are three main types of sources of information in drowsiness detection: Performance measurements, physiological measurements, and the behavioral measurements.

Performance measurements focus on subjects' performance of work. For instance, in the driving domain, it is reflected as steering wheel movements, driving speed, brake patterns, and lane deviations, etc. An example is the Autopilot system of Tesla, by measuring the grip on the steering wheel or directly using the lane departure warning system (LDWS) driving data it can obtain the time and degree of vehicle deviation from the lane, and then analyze and project the driver's drowsiness level or whether the driver is distracted. In addition to being expensive, the similar kind of solutions are difficult to redeploy to different workplaces. Some other performance measurements at workplace can be obtained by testing workers' reaction time and short-term memory [3]. Many of these methods can also not be used in other workplaces and the measurement itself can have an impact on the results.

Physiological measurements can use heart rate, electrocardiogram (ECG), electromyogram (EMG), electroencephalogram (EEG) [6,8,14] and electrooculogram (EOG) [8] to monitor drowsiness. However, these methods are intrusive and not practical to deploy in the car or workspace even though they have higher accuracy. Some wearable and convenient devices like hats and watches have been proposed as an alternative for such measurements, but they are still not practical to be used for long time.

Behavioral measurements are mostly obtained from subject's facial movements and expressions which could be captured non-intrusively by a single camera. This data acquisition method not only require lower cost but also is highly versatile, and can be used in almost any workplace, including the field of driver drowsiness detection. And with the rapid development of deep learning and computer vision techniques, behavioral measurements method will play a more important role in the field of drowsiness detection.

Comparing the above three types of methods, the most potential and practicable is the drowsiness detection based on behavioral measurements. However, it is rather difficult to detect early drowsiness in generic workplace using only the behavioral data recorded by the video. The challenges for the recognition are mainly in the early stage. Early drowsiness in real workplace is not evident externally and is highly susceptible to be misclassified into normal or drowsy stage. Most of the existing methods for drowsiness detection are based on videos of pretend drowsiness in laboratory scenarios and most of them are aimed for drowsiness driving only. And in some researches, the early drowsiness stage is often ignored directly.

Thus, in this paper, we propose a vision-based early drowsiness recognition method that aims to extract the behavior patterns of the different drowsiness stages of the subjects in the video to detect early drowsiness in real workplace scenarios. In summary, this paper makes the following contributions:

– We extracted sequences data of eye aspect ratio (EAR), gaze direction, and head posture data for the RLDD dataset. By analyzing the distribution and correlation between these feature sequences, we verified that the sequences of these features in different drowsiness states express different behavioral patterns of the subjects, which can be used for early drowsiness detection better.
– We design a multi-stream transformer model for early drowsiness detection, which learns the gaze behavior patterns of the subjects in the videos by the channel and temporal information from the feature sequences to classify different drowsiness states.
– The experimental results show that our method has a strong advantage in early drowsiness detection in real workplace scenarios based on video. And our model significantly outperforms the baseline method of the RLDD dataset and other multivariate time series classification methods.

2   Preliminary

In this section, we first present the RLDD dataset and our preprocessing operation of it. Then we perform an exploratory analysis to disclose the gaze behavior patterns and further demonstrate the motivation for our proposed model.

2.1   Dataset

The RLDD dataset proposed by Ghoddoosian et al. [5] is the largest to date realistic drowsiness dataset. It was created for the task of multistage drowsiness

Table 1. KSS drowsiness scale and drowsiness state categories

Drowsiness State	Description	Score
Normal	Extremely alert	1
	Very alert	2
	Alert	3
Early Drowsy	Rather alert	4
	Neither alert nor sleepy	5
	Some signs of sleepiness	6
	Sleepy, no difficulty remaining awake	7
Drowsy	Sleepy, some effort to keep alert	8
	Extremely sleepy, fighting sleep	9

detection, targeting not only extreme and easily visible cases, but also subtle cases of drowsiness. The RLDD dataset consists of around 30 h of RGB videos of

60 healthy participants. For each participant they obtained one video for each of three different classes: alertness, low vigilance, and drowsiness, for a total of 180 videos. Subjects were undergraduate or graduate students and staff members who were from different ethnicities and ages. Videos were taken from roughly different angles in different real-life environments and backgrounds. Each video was self-recorded by the participant, using their cell phone or web camera. We reclassified the videos in the dataset into the three categories in Table 1. based on the KSS table [1] and the original labels. Our exploratory analysis and the experimental part are all performed on this RLDD dataset.

2.2 Preprocessing and Feature Extraction

The motivation behind using gaze behavior features: eye aspect ratio, gaze direction, and head pose, was to capture temporal patterns that appear naturally in human gaze behavior and could easily be overlooked by spatial feature detectors like CNNs. We used dlib's pre-trained face detector based on a modification to the standard Histogram of Oriented Gradients + Linear SVM method for object detection [4]. Then we calculate eye aspect ratio with the six facial landmarks per eye (Fig. 1), and use the average value of two eyes as the EAR. For each eye, we denote:

$$EAR = \frac{\overline{AE} + \overline{BD}}{2\overline{FC}} \qquad (1)$$

where $\overline{AE}$, $\overline{BD}$ and $\overline{FC}$ is the length of the line segment connecting the corresponding points in the Fig. 1.

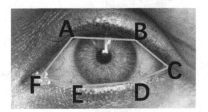

Fig. 1. The eye landmarks to define EAR for each eye.

In contrast to the blink features of Ghoddoosian et al. [5], we used original eye aspect ratio of each frame of videos to preserve the continuity of the time series so that it could be able to form multidimensional time series with other features of gaze behavior.

For the head pose and gaze direction, we use the preprocessing pipeline from [12] to obtain 3D head pose since the dataset does not provide camera parameters and we plug ResNet50 [7,19] to the PnP-GA framework [10] to obtain 3D gaze direction. Both of the extracted head pose and gaze direction are presented by pitch and yaw angle. All angles are converted to the camera-based coordinate system so that they can be used together for drowsiness detection. A visual representation of these two features is shown in Fig. 2 and Fig. 3.

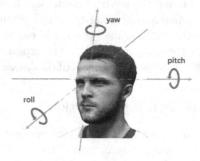

Fig. 2. The pitch, yaw and roll angle of head pose.

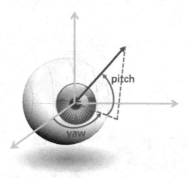

Fig. 3. The pitch and yaw angle of gaze direction

It is worth noting that for head pose and gaze direction, their pitch angle and yaw angle could be corresponded one by one in that they are both used to express the direction to which the head or the eye is directing. As for the roll angle of head pose, because the head can be tilted, for example, with the palm of the hand propped up diagonally, we need a roll angle to measuring its degree of inclination. And obviously, this angle could be significantly different in different drowsiness phrase. For the direction of gaze, we do not consider the complex eye structure here, we simply treat the eye as a sphere or a point, so the direction of gaze does not need a roll angle.

For each frame of the videos of RLDD dataset, we have a 6-dimention feature: $\{EAR,\ pitch_h,\ yaw_h,\ roll_h,\ pitch_g,\ yaw_g\}$, in which EAR means the average eye aspect ratio, $pitch_h$, yaw_h and $roll_h$ means the pitch angle, yaw angle and roll angle of head pose, $pitch_g$ and yaw_g means the pitch angle and yaw angle of gaze direction. These are the gaze behavior features that we use as the input of our early drowsiness detection model.

2.3   Exploratory Analysis

Given the real-world early drowsiness dataset, we next convey several exploratory analyses on all subjects from different perspectives to distinguish different drowsiness state.

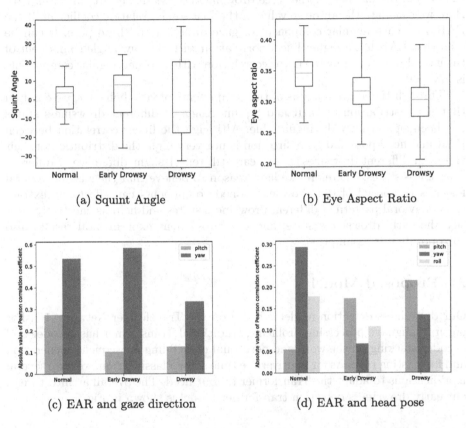

(a) Squint Angle

(b) Eye Aspect Ratio

(c) EAR and gaze direction

(d) EAR and head pose

Fig. 4. Feature comparison between different drowsiness states

From $\{pitch_g,\ yaw_g\}$ and $\{pitch_h,\ yaw_h\}$, the squint angle θ_s of gaze direction and head pose can be calculated. In general, when a person looks at someplace, the head will also turns to the direction of looking accordingly, so the direction of a person's gaze direction and the direction of the head pose should be basically the same, that is, the θ_s is not large. But if a person is in a drowsy state, then he is likely to lean on the chair or tilt the body to look at the screen, when the squint angle of gaze direction and head pose could be larger. We made a statistic of the squint angle under different drowsiness states for all subjects in the dataset, as shown in Fig. 4(a). The distribution of the data fits well with our assumption: Gradual increase in squint angle with increasing drowsiness.

As for EAR, it is a widely used feature in drowsiness detection. Here we show its distribution over 3.24 M frames of the dataset in the Fig. 4(b). Even though there is some individual variability in the value of EAR, it is still possible to see a certain degree of differentiation in its distribution across the different drowsiness phases. As drowsiness increases, the eye aspect ratio tends to decrease. Then we show visualization of EAR in relation to gaze direction and head posture for all subjects in the dataset for the three drowsiness states in Fig. 4(c) and Fig. 4(d). Here we calculate the absolute value of the Pearson correlation coefficient of the EAR with each angular component of gaze direction and head pose. It can be seen that EAR has a higher linear correlation with the yaw angle component of the gaze direction, while the linear correlation with all other angular components is low (<0.3).

Through the above analysis of the components of gaze behavior, we can find that the distribution of EAR and Squint Angle at different drowsiness states has been significantly distinguishable. Although the linear correlation between EAR and head pose and gaze direction is not very high, the distribution of their values in different drowsiness states can still reflect slight difference of different drowsiness states. Therefore, we have reason to believe that the gaze behavioral features composed of the above-mentioned components can effectively extract the behavioral pattern of different drowsiness states and help us effectively classify the early drowsiness state, and our subsequent experimental results also corroborate our assumption.

3   Proposed Model

Our drowsiness detection model is based on the Transformer Network [16]. For natural language processing problems, traditional Transformer has encoder and decoder stacking on the word and positional embedding for sequence generation and forecasting task. As for multivariate time series classification, we have several modifications to adapt the Transformer for our need. The overall architecture of our early drowsiness detection transformer model is shown in Fig. 5.

3.1   Embedding

We use the gaze behavior feature extracted from the video in the preprocessing section as the input of our early drowsiness detection model, it's a 6-dimensional time series. We divide the input into temporal stream feature and channel stream feature by time step and channel.

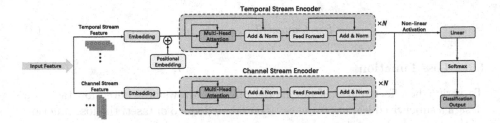

Fig. 5. Overview of our multi-stream transformer model

In the original Transformers [16], all the tokens are projected to an embedding layer. For the time series data is continuous, we replace the embedding layer with fully connected layer. Instead of the linear projection, we use a non-linear activation $tanh$. The positional encoding is added with the temporal stream feature to encode the temporal information to utilize the sequential correlation of time step better.

3.2   Multi-stream Encoder

Gaze behavior features we extract has multiple channels where each channel is a multi-variate time series. The common assumption is that there exists some hidden correlation between different channels. Capturing both the temporal and channel information is the key for our early drowsiness detection.

One of the usual approaches is to apply convolutions, that is, the reception field integrates both channel and temporal feature by the 2D kernels or the 1D kernels with fixed parameter sharing. We design a multi-stream extension where the encoders in each stream explicitly capture the channel and temporal correlation by attention and masking, as shown in Fig. 5.

Different from the natural language processing task, our task in this step is actually a multi-variate time series classification task, so we do not need the decoder [16] part of traditional Transformer.

Then, to merge the information of the two streams which encodes temporal and channel correlations respectively, we use a fully connect layer after out put of both encoders with the non-linear activation as T and C. Then we use a linear projection layer to get h:

$$h = W \cdot Concat(T, C) + b \tag{2}$$

Through the softmax function, the streaming weight of each stream are computed as s_T and s_C:

$$s_T, \ s_C = Softmax(h) \tag{3}$$

Each streaming weight is attending on the corresponding stream's output and we get the final feature vector f:

$$f = Concat(T \cdot s_T, \ C \cdot s_C) \tag{4}$$

3.3   Loss Function

To verify the effectiveness of our model on early drowsiness detection task, we design a supervised leaning framework on labeled video dataset. the loss function of this framework is as follows:

$$y_{pre} = \sigma(W' f + b') \tag{5}$$

$$Loss = -\frac{1}{N} \sum_{N} \sum_{i=0}^{2} y_i ln(p_i) \tag{6}$$

It's the loss function for our triple classification task. y_{pre} is classification probability of model output: $y_{pre} = [p_0, \ p_1, \ p_2]$, p_i is predictive probability of category i. And y_i is the onehot representation of the sample y: $y = [y_0, \ y_1, \ y_2]$, when the sample y belongs to category i, $y_i = 1$, otherwise $y_i = 0$.

4   Experiment

4.1   Implementation Details

We used one fold of the RLDD dataset as our test set, and the remaining four folds for training. After repeating this process for each fold, the results were averaged across the five folds. All experiments are carried out with 6-dimensional time series with a window length of 256 frames on the server, the step size of the window movement is set to 128 frames and the batch sizes are 128. The optimizer is uniformly used Adam, the learning rate is $4e - 5$, the experiments were conducted on a server with two NVIDIA A40 GPUs.

4.2   Evaluation Metrics

Accuracy, *Precision*, *Recall*, and *F1-score* are used to evaluate models. Four evaluation indexes are computed as follows:

$$Accuracy = \frac{TP + TN}{TP + TN + FP + FN} \tag{7}$$

$$Precision = \frac{TP}{TP + FP} \tag{8}$$

$$Recall = \frac{TP}{TP + FN} \tag{9}$$

$$F1 - score = \frac{2 \times Precision \times Recall}{Precision + Recall} \tag{10}$$

For our target of early drowsiness detection problem, we choose *Accuracy* and *Precision*, *Recall*, and *F1-score* of early drowsy category to evaluate our model.

4.3 Results

We used SVM [2], HM-LSTM [5], and two state-of-the-art multivariate time series classification methods: LSTM-FCNs [9] and TapNet [18] as our comparison methods. The overall metrics of the RLDD dataset are shown in Table 2. From this table, we observe that our method achieves significant results in the overall *accuracy* and *Precision*, *Recall*, and *F1-score* of early drowsiness state respectively, proving that our multi-stream Transformer model has good performance on early drowsiness drowsiness detection problem. Compared with the baseline HM-LSTM, all other methods using our proposed gaze behavior features performer much better on early drowsiness classification, and this indicates that our proposed gaze behavior features have a large contribution in early drowsiness detection. Among all methods using gaze behavior features for classification, our proposed model have the best performance in overall accuracy and three metrics of early drowsiness classification.

Table 2. Performance of early drowsiness detection using different classification methods on the RLDD dataset.

Method	Accuracy	Precision*	Recall*	F1-score*
HM-LSTM	0.6522	0.5105	0.3233	0.3959
SVM	0.6333	0.5112	0.5333	0.5220
LSTM-FCNs	0.7311	0.7213	0.6900	0.7053
TapNet	0.7411	0.6698	0.7033	0.6861
Ours	**0.7833**	**0.7309**	**0.7333**	**0.7321**

* The matrics of the early drowsy category

4.4 Ablation Study

We study the effectiveness of the channel stream encoder and each part of our proposed gaze behavior features:1)**Channel Stream Encoder:**We remove the channel stream encoder from the model and use the same gaze behavior features for training and classification. The results in Table 3 show that there is large reduction in the overall metrics of the model after the removal of channel stream encoder. This result indicates that the Channel stream Encoder part of our model plays a significant role in our early drowsiness detection model. 2)**Gaze Behavior Features:** Our proposed gaze behavior features is composed of EAR, gaze direction and head pose. To discover the extent to which each of these features contributes to the final classification result, we remove 1 or 2 of the three input features and get the corresponding classification results. The results show a drop in classification results when either 1 or 2 features are removed which means each part of the gaze behavior features contributes to the final classification result, of these, EAR is the most important, followed by gaze direction and head pose.

Table 3. Performance after removing channel stream encoder or parts of gaze behavior features on the RLDD dataset

Method	Accuracy	Precision*	Recall*	F1-score*
Ours	0.7833	0.7309	0.7333	0.7321
Ours(remove channel stream encoder)	0.6188	0.5570	0.5700	0.5634
Ours(EAR)	0.6511	0.5980	0.6000	0.5990
Ours(head pose)	0.5889	0.4685	0.5200	0.4929
Ours(gaze direction)	0.6289	0.5710	0.5767	0.5738
Ours(EAR + head pose)	0.6933	0.6063	0.6367	0.6211
Ours(EAR + gaze direction)	0.6922	0.5868	0.6533	0.6183
Ours(head pose + gaze direction)	0.7244	0.6495	0.6733	0.6612

5   Conclusion

This paper addressed the problem of early drowsiness detection, and found an approach to early drowsiness detection on gaze behavior feature sequence learning by learning the variability of subjects of different drowsiness state in gaze behavior through data analysis. Based on the found variability in features of gaze behaviors between subjects of different drowsiness state, we propose a new variant model of Transformer by changing the internal structure of it to consider gaze behaviors of subjects in combination with drowsiness state and using an channel stream encoder a spatial stream encoder to better recognize gaze behavior patterns which can improve the accuracy of early drowsiness detection effectively. Experiments on real dataset demonstrate the effectiveness of the gaze behavior features and model we proposed compared to state-of-the-art methods, especially for the early drowsiness state. Our research may provide a reference for the drivers and monitors' drowsiness monitoring and warning system.

References

1. Åkerstedt, T., Gillberg, M.: Subjective and objective sleepiness in the active individual. Int. J. Neurosci. **52**(1–2), 29–37 (1990)
2. Burges, C.J.: A tutorial on support vector machines for pattern recognition. Data Min. Knowl. Disc. **2**(2), 121–167 (1998)

3. Caldwell, J.A., Caldwell, J.L., Thompson, L.A., Lieberman, H.R.: Fatigue and its management in the workplace. Neurosci. Biobehav. Rev. **96**, 272–289 (2019)
4. Dalal, N., Triggs, B.: Histograms of oriented gradients for human detection. In: 2005 IEEE Computer Society Conference On Computer Vision And Pattern Recognition (CVPR'05), vol. 1, pp. 886–893. IEEE (2005)
5. Ghoddoosian, R., Galib, M., Athitsos, V.: A realistic dataset and baseline temporal model for early drowsiness detection. In: Proceedings of the IEEE/CVF Conference on Computer Vision and Pattern Recognition Workshops, pp. 178–187 (2019)
6. Guarda, L., Tapia, J., Droguett, E.L., Ramos, M.: A novel capsule neural network based model for drowsiness detection using electroencephalography signals. Expert Syst. Appl., 116977 (2022)
7. He, K., Zhang, X., Ren, S., Sun, J.: Deep residual learning for image recognition. In: Proceedings of the IEEE Conference On Computer Vision and Pattern Recognition, pp. 770–778 (2016)
8. Jiao, Y., Deng, Y., Luo, Y., Lu, B.L.: Driver sleepiness detection from EEG and EOG signals using GAN and LSTM networks. Neurocomputing **408**, 100–111 (2020)
9. Karim, F., Majumdar, S., Darabi, H., Harford, S.: Multivariate LSTM-FCNS for time series classification. Neural Netw. **116**, 237–245 (2019)
10. Liu, Y., Liu, R., Wang, H., Lu, F.: Generalizing gaze estimation with outlier-guided collaborative adaptation. In: Proceedings of the IEEE/CVF International Conference on Computer Vision, pp. 3835–3844 (2021)
11. Ngxande, M., Tapamo, J.R., Burke, M.: Driver drowsiness detection using behavioral measures and machine learning techniques: a review of state-of-art techniques. In: 2017 pattern recognition Association of South Africa and Robotics and mechatronics (PRASA-RobMech), pp. 156–161 (2017)
12. Park, S., Mello, S.D., Molchanov, P., Iqbal, U., Hilliges, O., Kautz, J.: Few-shot adaptive gaze estimation. In: Proceedings of the IEEE/CVF International Conference On Computer Vision, pp. 9368–9377 (2019)
13. Reddy, B., Kim, Y.H., Yun, S., Seo, C., Jang, J.: Real-time driver drowsiness detection for embedded system using model compression of deep neural networks. In: Proceedings of the IEEE Conference On Computer Vision And Pattern Recognition Workshops, pp. 121–128 (2017)
14. Reddy, T.K., Behera, L.: Driver drowsiness detection: an approach based on intelligent brain-computer interfaces. IEEE Syst. Man Cybern. Mag. **8**(1), 16–28 (2022)
15. Sadeghniiat-Haghighi, K., Yazdi, Z.: Fatigue management in the workplace. Ind. Psychiatry J. **24**(1), 12 (2015)
16. Vaswani, A., et al.: Attention is all you need. In: Advances Neural Information Processing Systems, vol. 30 (2017)
17. Wheaton, A.G., Shults, R.A., Chapman, D.P., Ford, E.S., Croft, J.B.: Drowsy driving and risk behaviors–10 states and Puerto Rico, 2011–2012. Morb. Mortal. Wkly Rep. **63**(26), 557 (2014)
18. Zhang, X., Gao, Y., Lin, J., Lu, C.T.: TapNet: multivariate time series classification with attentional prototypical network. In: Proceedings of the AAAI Conference on Artificial Intelligence, vol. 34, pp. 6845–6852 (2020)
19. Zhang, X., Park, S., Beeler, T., Bradley, D., Tang, S., Hilliges, O.: ETH-XGaze: a Large scale dataset for gaze estimation under extreme head pose and gaze variation. In: Vedaldi, A., Bischof, H., Brox, T., Frahm, J.-M. (eds.) ECCV 2020. LNCS, vol. 12350, pp. 365–381. Springer, Cham (2020). https://doi.org/10.1007/978-3-030-58558-7_22

GH-QFL: Enhancing Industrial Defect Detection Through Hard Example Mining

Xianjing Xiao[1], Yan Du[1], Rui Yang[1], Runze Hu[2], and Xiu Li[1(✉)]

[1] Tsinghua Shenzhen International Graduate School,
Tsinghua University, Shenzhen, China
{xxj21,duy21,r-yang20}@mails.tsinghua.edu.cn, li.xiu@sz.tsinghua.edu.cn
[2] School of Information and Electronics,
Beijing Institute of Technology, Beijing, China

Abstract. In the manufacturing sector, industrial defect detection technology has become a crucial component for substantial improvements in both product quality and production efficiency. However, the accuracy of deep learning-based defect detection methods can be compromised by uneven training data, which could result in a bias towards over-represented classes. To address this issue, some hard example mining (HEM) methods have been developed to balance the contribution of different classes during training. Nonetheless, on the custom dataset, these methods still inherit the hyper-parameters predefined on the COCO dataset. We thereby propose a novel loss function, called Gradient Harmonized Quality Focal Loss (GH-QFL), to weight hard examples dynamically based on gradient statistics. The proposed approach is evaluated on a defect detection dataset: NEU-DET. The results demonstrate that our method outperforms the detection method using other loss functions by 3.1% mean average precision (mAP).

Keywords: Hard example mining · Defect detection · Loss function

1 Introduction

Industrial defect detection [1,2,5] is a critical aspect of the production process, as it plays a vital role in ensuring the quality and safety of the end product. With the rapid growth of deep learning in recent years, the use of convolutional neural networks (CNN) [4] and the Vision Transformer (ViT) [3,28] has emerged as a promising approach for defect detection tasks. Most deep learning-based defect detection methods follow the same procedure as general object detection methods. As illustrated in Fig. 1, the features are first extracted by the backbone and feature pyramid networks (FPN) [17]. Then, two independent branches classify and regress the extracted features separately. Finally, the generated bounding boxes are filtered and merged using methods such as Non-Maximum Suppression (NMS). The localization quality estimation and classification score are

---

X. Xiao and Y. Du - Equal contribution.

L. Iliadis et al. (Eds.): ICANN 2023, LNCS 14254, pp. 232–243, 2023.
https://doi.org/10.1007/978-3-031-44207-0_20

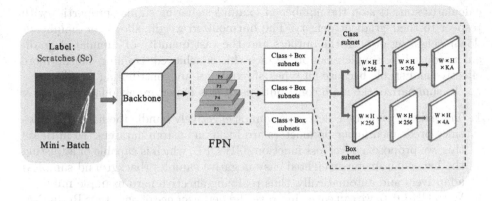

Fig. 1. The overview of detection framework.

usually trained independently but compositely utilized during inference [16]. In most existing defect detection methods, classification scores are used to rank the prediction frames. However, this may induce the problem of classification-localization imbalance. Specifically, samples with high classification scores but low localization quality are more likely to be kept at NMS, whereas samples with low classification scores but good localization quality are more likely to be suppressed.

To address the above issue, the classical generalized focal loss (GFL) [16] introduces a joint representation between localization quality (IoU score) and classification score. GFL takes the IoU score between the positive bounding box and its ground-truth box as the target of the classification branch. For negative bounding boxes, their IoU score equals 0. As a result, the outputs of the classification branch can represent the location quality, thus alleviating the inconsistency between the classification and regression branches. Nonetheless, the class imbalance problem still occurs in one-stage detectors. Generally, it can be alleviated by hard example mining. Similar to focal loss [18], a scaling factor with some hyper-parameters is introduced to make the detector attend more to hard examples. These hyper-parameters are usually tuned on the COCO dataset [19] and then directly applied to other defect detection datasets, wherein these hyper-parameters remain unchanged throughout the entire training process. However, fixed hyper-parameters cannot be the ideal choice for different inputs.

In order to mine hard examples automatically and adaptively, we herein propose a gradient harmonized quality focal loss, termed GH-QFL, to avoid manually-adjusted hyper-parameters. GH-QFL is a novel loss function that attenuates the loss from the perspective of the example number with a certain range of the gradient norm. This loss function not only inherits the advantage of the QFL but also automates finding hard examples and weighing them. It can dynamically adjust the base loss dependent on the gradient statistics of the current batch to handle the imbalance problem in the training examples. To assign a harmonizing weight to each example's gradient, the GH-QFL first calculates statistics on the number of examples sharing similar properties with respect to their gradient density. The harmonized weight allows for significant down-weighting of both the outliers and the vast quantity of cumulated gradient produced by simple examples. Once this is achieved, training can be more effective and stable because all types of examples are contributing equally.

To summarize, the main contributions of this paper are as follows:

1. The existing one-stage detectors cannot effectively handle the hard examples since predefined hyper-parameters are fixed on custom datasets. To mitigate this, we propose a novel loss function, GH-QFL, which is capable of adjusting the hyper-parameters weighted easy negative samples (background samples) adaptively and automatically, thus realizing effective hard example mining.
2. With GH-QFL, we can easily improve the performance of one-stage RetinaNet on the custom dataset, e.g., NEU-DET.

2   Related Work

The issue of imbalance in object detection datasets is a well-recognized problem, which has been addressed by various techniques proposed in the literature. However, most of the current one-stage object detection frameworks [20, 22–24] fail to tackle this issue effectively, as they often assume a balanced distribution of positive and negative examples. Furthermore, in real-world scenarios, certain instances of object classes might be rare, which further exacerbates the problem of imbalance [6, 7, 29]. Many datasets have a skewed distribution of classes, where only a few dominant classes are accounted for the majority of the data while the rest of the classes have very few examples. This poses a significant challenge in effectively learning the characteristics of the underrepresented classes, which may lead to poor detection performance for these classes.

The problem of accurately mining difficult examples based on RoIs is addressed by the online difficulty example mining (OHEM) [26] approach. This method involves selecting positive and negative examples based on a fixed threshold and calculating the loss for all prediction boxes. The candidate boxes are then sorted based on the size of the loss, and the first K boxes with the highest loss are selected as difficult examples. During backpropagation, only the gradient of these K examples is computed, while the gradient of other candidate boxes is set to 0 and no backpropagation is performed. This results in a targeted difficult example mining approach that can be used to improve the accuracy and robustness of object detection models.

However, one of the drawbacks of the OHEM method is that it prioritizes retaining only the examples with high losses, while completely ignoring simple examples. Therefore, further research is needed to explore alternative techniques that can overcome these limitations.

While Balanced Cross Entropy solves the problem of positive and negative example imbalance, it does not distinguish between simple and difficult examples. When there are too many easily distinguishable negative examples, the whole training process will be carried out around them, and then flood the positive examples, causing great losses [11]. So Lin et al. [18] introduced a modulation factor, named focal loss, which is a dynamically scaled cross-entropy loss used to focus on difficult-to-distinguish examples. Through it, the weight of difficult-to-distinguish examples can be dynamically reduced during the training process, so that the center of gravity can quickly focus on those difficult-to-distinguish examples (which may be positive examples or negative examples, but are all helpful to the training network).

Due to a fact that the initial focal loss only supported discrete labels, Li et al. developed Quality Focal Loss (QFL) [16] based on the concept of focal loss and modified its form to allow continuous labels and be suitable for one-stage target identification.

In addition, traditional loss functions such as cross-entropy and smooth L1 loss treat each object equally, without considering differences in difficulty and complexity [12]. In contrast, QFL incorporates the quality and difficulty of each object and extends the idea of focal loss to the range of object qualities. It introduces a quality factor that assigns higher weights to difficult-to-detect objects, allowing the model to focus more on challenging objects and improve detection performance.

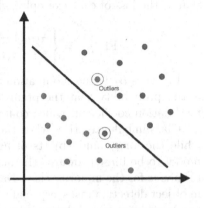

Fig. 2. Outliers are data points that are significantly different from the majority of the other data points in a dataset.

Moreover, focal loss has been found to cause the model to over-emphasize examples that are particularly difficult to distinguish, potentially leading to reduced performance on other examples. As a result, the model might converge, but outliers in the examples would still be wrongly classified [13,30,31]. To address this issue, Li et al. [15] argue that attention should not only be paid to easily separable examples but also to particularly difficult examples(outliers), as shown in Fig. 2. To this end, they proposed Gradient Harmonizing Mechanism (GHM) to attenuate loss from the perspective of the example number within a certain range of confidence. GHM is designed to effectively balance the contribution of each example to the total loss, taking into account the example distribution and the degree of difficulty. This allows the model to give more attention to challenging examples while preventing the loss from being dominated by the easy examples.

3   Approach

With the advent of deep learning in the field of defect detection, the number of defect regions and non-defect regions in images is extremely unbalanced, which can lead to poor detection performance. In industrial settings, the hard example mining technique improves the detection accuracy of the model by preferentially selecting difficult-to-identify defect examples during the training process. In this paper, we propose the Gradient Harmonized Quality Focal Loss (GH-QFL) method to address this issue of mining hard examples during training.

3.1 Focal Loss

By providing different weights for different examples, focal loss can dynamically reduce the loss of easy examples while increasing the loss of challenging ones.

$$\text{FL}\,(p_t) = \begin{cases} -\alpha_t\,(1 - p_t)^\gamma \log\,(p_t)\,, & \text{if } y = 1 \\ -(1 - \alpha_t)\,p_t^\gamma \log\,(1 - p_t)\,, & \text{otherwise} \end{cases} \tag{1}$$

In (1), $-\alpha_t$ is the modulation factor of positive and negative examples; p_t is the probability that the prediction is a positive example ($y = 1$); γ is the modulation coefficient, which controls the attention to the example.

Class imbalance arises when the majority of the image contains background, while the foreground objects of interest are relatively sparse. This causes the model to be biased towards the majority class, resulting in poor detection performance for the minority class. Designed to address the issue of class imbalance in object detection tasks, especially for one-stage object detection networks, focal loss introduces a modulating factor that down-weights the loss contribution from easy examples and focuses more on hard examples. By doing so, the network can effectively mine the hard samples that are previously ignored and improve the detection performance for the minority class [10]. With this mechanism, focal loss has been shown to achieve state-of-the-art performance on many popular object detection datasets.

3.2 Soft Label

The original focal loss had a misalignment of classification and regression branches and only supported discrete labels. Therefore, based on GFL [16], an implicit joint representation is designed to align the classification branch and the regression branch, named Quality Focal Loss (QFL).

As shown in the Fig. 3, we take the detection box of the regression branch prediction and the IoU (Intersection over Union) that corresponds to the true value as the target of branch classification when we are going through the training process, where its supervision softens the standard one-hot category label and result in a float target for the corresponding category. So the classification loss is changed as follows:

$$\text{QFL}\,(p_t) = \begin{cases} -\,(q_t - p_t)^\gamma \left[(1 - q_t)\log\,(1 - p_t) + q_t \log\,(p_t)\right], & \text{if } y = 1, q_t > 0 \\ -p_t{}^\gamma \log\,(1 - p_t)\,, & \text{otherwise} \end{cases} \tag{2}$$

where q_t is the IoU between the prediction box and its true value; γ is the modulation coefficient. Similar to focal loss, the weighting method of corresponding examples is employed here to improve focus on hard samples. $(q_t - p_t)$ close to 0 indicates an easy sample, while $(q_t - p_t)$ is larger signifies a harder one.

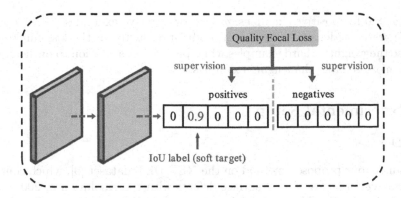

Fig. 3. The combined representation of classification scores and positioning quality estimates is efficiently learned by the Quality Focal Loss.

3.3 GH-QFL

The above-mentioned methods share the same issue with focal loss, which requires manual adjustment of hyper-parameters on different datasets in order to achieve efficient mining of difficult samples. Inspired by gradient-based method [15], we have designed "GH-QFL", a classification loss function that is self-adjusting based on the gradient norm.

Specifically, this gradient-based method firstly constructs a histogram of gradients based on the current batch, and then uses the histogram to estimate the gradient frequency and the gradient range of each bin. Next, it calculates a weight for each example based on the gradient frequency and the gradient range of its corresponding bin, and finally applies the example weight to adjust the gradient of the example during backpropagation.

$GD\left(g_t\right)$ denotes the gradient density of the region where the gradient of the t-th example lies, as shown in the following equation:

$$GD(g) = \frac{\sum_{k=1}^{N} \delta_\varepsilon \left(g_{k'} g\right)}{l_\varepsilon(g)} \tag{3}$$

$$\delta_\epsilon(x, y) = \begin{cases} 1 & \text{if } y - \frac{\epsilon}{2} <= x < y + \frac{\epsilon}{2} \\ 0 & \text{otherwise} \end{cases} \tag{4}$$

$$l_\epsilon(g) = \min\left(g + \frac{\epsilon}{2}, 1\right) - \max\left(g - \frac{\epsilon}{2}, 0\right) \tag{5}$$

where $\sum_{k=1}^{N} \delta_\varepsilon \left(g_{k'} g\right)$ indicates the number of gradient magnitudes falling within the interval of $(g - \varepsilon/2, g + \varepsilon/2)$, g is a point previously partitioned within the interval $(0,1)$, and $|q_k - p_k|$ represents the gradient magnitude of the k-th example corresponding to g_k; $l_\varepsilon(g)$ denotes the length of the interval being computed.

$$L\left(p_t\right) = \frac{\left(1 - q_t\right)\log\left(1 - p_t\right) + q_t \log\left(p_t\right)}{GD\left(g_t\right)} \tag{6}$$

where $q_t > 0$ for positive examples, $q_t = 0$ for negative examples.

The gradient density is used as a modulation factor of the loss function to increase the weight of hard examples while paying less attention to outliers, thus mining more reliable challenging examples.

4   Experimental Setup

4.1   Dataset

We evaluate our proposed method on the NEU-DET dataset [9], which contains 1800 grayscale images of steel surface defects with the resolution of 200 × 200. As shown in Fig. 4, the NEU-DET dataset consists of six kinds of surface defects of the hot-rolled steel strip, i.e., crazing (Cr), inclusion (In), patches (Pa), pitted surface (PS), rolled-in scale (RS) and scratches (Sc). In the experiments, the dataset is randomly split into a training set and a test set with a ratio of 8:2.

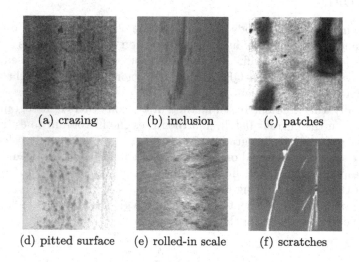

(a) crazing   (b) inclusion   (c) patches

(d) pitted surface   (e) rolled-in scale   (f) scratches

Fig. 4. Examples of NEU-DET dataset

4.2   Configuration Setup

To train the defect detection model, we used the framework of PyTorch. All the experiments are conducted on NVIDIA Geforce RTX 3090 GPU. RetinaNet is used as the baseline. The initial learning rate is set to 0.1, and the batch size is 8 with 50 epochs. The stochastic gradient descent(SGD) is used to optimize the training process. To improve the robustness of the model, data augmentation such as random flipping, adjusting contrast, clipping, and scale change are used in the training process.

4.3 Evaluation Metrics

The average precision (AP) metric, a trade-off between precision and recall, is used to evaluate the effectiveness of the detection approach. The definition of these indices is as follows:

$$\text{Precision} = \frac{TP}{TP + FP} \tag{7}$$

$$\text{Recall} = \frac{TP}{TP + FN} \tag{8}$$

$$\text{AP} = \frac{\text{Precision} + \text{Recall}}{2}, \tag{9}$$

where TP, FP, and FN represent the number of true positives, false positives, and false negatives, respectively. In order to assess overall performance, the mean AP (mAP) across all classes, is also calculated.

5 Experimental Results

5.1 Performance Comparison

Table 1 shows the performance of our proposed method on NEU-DET dataset. We compare our method with one-stage object detection algorithms RetinaNet [18] and EfficientDet [27] and two-stage object detection algorithm Faster R-CNN [25]. RetinaNet surpasses Faster R-CNN by 4.1 mAP and EfficientDet by 5.1 mAP with a mAP of 75.2. With the same backbone ResNet-50, our proposed method outperforms RetinaNet by 3.1 points, achieving a mAP of 78.3. This outcome shows that RetinaNet performed better in the defect detection tasks when GH-QFL was used. Furthermore, our proposed method receives the highest AP in four of the six categories, inclusion, patches, rolled-in scale and scratches.

Table 1. Detection results on NEU-DET dataset.

Method	AP(%)						mAP(%)
	crazing	inclusion	patches	pitted surface	rolled-in scale	scratches	
Faster R-CNN [25]	39.5	77.3	85.2	81.6	64.5	78.2	71.1
EfficientDet [27]	45.9	62.0	83.5	**85.5**	70.7	73.1	70.1
RetinaNet [18]	**49.3**	81.5	94.5	81.4	65.2	79.1	75.2
RetinaNet *w/* GH-QFL(Ours)	48.4	**85.5**	**94.7**	84.2	**71.4**	**85.4**	**78.3**

Figure 5 compares the visualization results of the proposed method with original RetinaNet on NEU-DET dataset. It can be noticed that the proposed method gives improved detection results for various examples that RetinaNet finds difficult to identify.

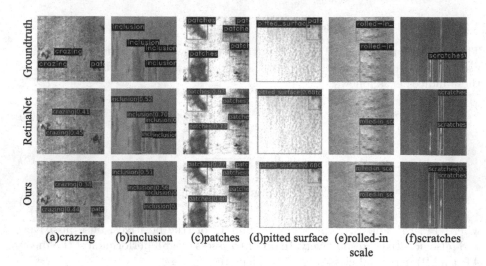

(a)crazing   (b)inclusion   (c)patches   (d)pitted surface   (e)rolled-in scale   (f)scratches

Fig. 5. Visualization of detection results on NEU-DET dataset

5.2 Ablation Study

To evaluate the effectiveness of GH-QFL, ablation experiments are carried out to analyze the results of detection as well as hard examples mining. We compare the performance of RetinaNet using different loss functions: (1) Focal Loss [18], (2) GHM Loss [15], (3) Quality Focal Loss [16], (4) GH-QFL. Except for the loss function, the architecture and parameters of the detector remain unchanged.

Table 2. Detection results of RetinaNet using different loss functions on NEU-DET dataset.

Loss function	AP(%)						mAP(%)	FN-TP	TP-FN
	crazing	inclusion	patches	pitted surface	rolled-in scale	scratches			
Focal [18]	**49.3**	81.5	94.5	81.4	65.2	79.1	75.2	–	–
GHM [15]	42.9	85.4	91.4	80.7	64.1	87.4	75.3	52	46
QFocal [16]	38.0	85.0	93.9	84.1	68.6	**90.1**	76.6	54	43
GH-QFL	48.4	**85.5**	**94.7**	**84.2**	**71.4**	85.4	**78.3**	**67**	**21**

Detection Results. Table 2 displays the detection results of RetinaNet using different loss functions on the NEU-DET dataset. Although the detection results are improved when GHM Loss and Quality Focal Loss are employed independently, our method achieved the highest mAP of 78.3, which was 3 points higher than GHM Loss and 1.7 points higher than Quality Focal Loss. The experimental results highlights the positive impact of introducing the GHM mechanism into Quality Focal Loss.

Table 3. Detection results on different backbones.

Backbone	Loss function	AP(%)						mAP(%)
		crazing	inclusion	patches	pitted surface	rolled-in scale	scratches	
ResNet-50 [8]	Focal Loss [18]	49.3	81.5	94.5	81.4	65.2	79.1	75.2
	GH-QFL	48.4	85.5	**94.7**	84.2	**71.4**	85.4	78.3
ResNet-101 [8]	Focal Loss [18]	47.1	85.1	91.6	**88.1**	68.9	82.5	77.2
	GH-QFL	**49.7**	**87.7**	94.3	86.0	71.2	86.3	**79.2**
Swin-T [21]	Focal Loss [18]	41.5	85.0	92.1	78.5	66.7	86.9	75.1
	GH-QFL	46.2	86.2	92.6	79.9	67.1	**89.8**	77.0

Hard Example Mining Results. Since we do not predetermine the set of hard examples, we define the defective examples that cannot be detected on baseline RetinaNet, i.e., FN examples, as hard examples. If method B can detect examples overlooked by method A, i.e., convert FN to TP, and has less error output for TP of method A, it is reasonable to conclude that method B is superior to method A in detecting hard examples. [14] By comparing the quantity of FN-TP pairs and TP-FN pairs, we can validate the proposed method's capacity to mine hard examples.

FN-TP pairs are examples that are misidentified as FN by RetinaNet and correctly identified as TP by the other approach. In the same approach, the TP-FN pairs are defined. A good hard example mining approach should have a higher number of FN-TP pairs and less TP-FN pairs.

According to the results which are presented in Table 2, our proposed method converts 67 FN samples into TP, which is superior to GHM Loss with 52 FN-TP pairs and Quality Focal Loss with 54 FN-TP pairs. Moreover, in comparison to the original RetinaNet, only 21 TP samples are lost using GH-QFL, which is almost half of that of GHM Loss or Quality Focal Loss. These experimental findings show that the our proposed loss function works well for hard example mining.

Different Backbones. Transformer-based backbones [21,28] are widespread recently. Therefore, to make results more convincing, we compare the performance of Focal Loss and GH-QFL by conducting experiments with different backbones. As is demonstrated in Table 3, our proposed method achieves a highest mAP of 79.2 with ResNet-101 [8], which is higher than that of ResNet-50 [8] and Swin Transformer [21]. With all of the above-mentioned backbones, GH-QFL outperforms Focal Loss with higher mAP.

6 Conclusion

This paper elaborates on a challenging yet often overlooked task in the defect detection field, called hard example mining. We propose an effective loss function, namely GH-QFL, to realize an effective hard example mining, and thus facilitating further research on the defect detection task. The experiments presented in this paper demonstrate the effectiveness of our proposed method for detecting defects in industrial applications. However, defect detection is an area that requires continued research and attention. Our future work will focus on the accurate localization of a wider range of defect styles, as well as improving the computational efficiency of our proposed method to better meet the needs of practical applications.

Acknowledgment. This research was supported by the National Key R&D Program of China (Grant No. 2020AAA0108303), Shenzhen Science and Technology Project (Grant No. JCYJ20200109143041798), Shenzhen Stable Supporting Program (WDZC20200820200655001), the National Natural Science Foundation of China (No. 62192712), and Beijing Institute of Technology Research Fund Program for Young Scholars.

References

1. Chen, Y., Ding, Y., Zhao, F., Zhang, E., Wu, Z., Shao, L.: Surface defect detection methods for industrial products: a review. Appl. Sci. **11**(16), 7657 (2021)
2. Czimmermann, T., et al.: Visual-based defect detection and classification approaches for industrial applications–a survey. Sensors **20**(5), 1459 (2020)
3. Dosovitskiy, A., et al.: An image is worth 16×16 words: transformers for image recognition at scale. arXiv preprint arXiv:2010.11929 (2020)
4. Fukushima, K.: A self-organizing neural network model for a mechanism of pattern recognition unaffected by shift in position. Biol. Cybern. **36**, 193–202 (1980)
5. Han, H., Yang, R., Li, S., Hu, R., Li, X.: SSGD: a smartphone screen glass dataset for defect detection. In: ICASSP 2023–2023 IEEE International Conference on Acoustics, Speech and Signal Processing (ICASSP), pp. 1–5 (2023)
6. He, C., et al.: Camouflaged object detection with feature decomposition and edge reconstruction. In: Proceedings of the IEEE/CVF Conference on Computer Vision and Pattern Recognition, pp. 22046–22055 (2023)
7. He, C., et al.: Weakly-supervised concealed object segmentation with SAM-based pseudo labeling and multi-scale feature grouping. arXiv preprint arXiv:2305.11003 (2023)
8. He, K., Zhang, X., Ren, S., Sun, J.: Deep residual learning for image recognition. In: Proceedings of the IEEE Conference on Computer Vision and Pattern Recognition, pp. 770–778 (2016)
9. He, Y., Song, K., Meng, Q., Yan, Y.: An end-to-end steel surface defect detection approach via fusing multiple hierarchical features. IEEE Trans. Instrum. Meas. **69**(4), 1493–1504 (2020)
10. Hu, R., Liu, Y., Gu, K., Min, X., Zhai, G.: Toward a no-reference quality metric for camera-captured images. IEEE Trans. Cybernet. (2021)
11. Hu, R., Liu, Y., Wang, Z., Li, X.: Blind quality assessment of night-time image. Displays **69**, 102045 (2021)
12. Hu, R., Monebhurrun, V., Himeno, R., Yokota, H., Costen, F.: An adaptive least angle regression method for uncertainty quantification in FDTD computation. IEEE Trans. Antennas Propag. **66**(12), 7188–7197 (2018)
13. Hu, R., Monebhurrun, V., Himeno, R., Yokota, H., Costen, F.: A general framework for building surrogate models for uncertainty quantification in computational electromagnetics. IEEE Trans. Antennas Propag. **70**(2), 1402–1414 (2021)

14. Koksal, A., Tuzcuoglu, O., Ince, K.G., Ataseven, Y., Alatan, A.A.: Improved hard example mining approach for single shot object detectors. arXiv preprint arXiv:2202.13080 (2022)
15. Li, B., Liu, Y., Wang, X.: Gradient harmonized single-stage detector. In: Proceedings of the AAAI Conference on Artificial Intelligence, vol. 33, pp. 8577–8584 (2019)
16. Li, X., et al.: Generalized focal loss: learning qualified and distributed bounding boxes for dense object detection. Adv. Neural. Inf. Process. Syst. **33**, 21002–21012 (2020)
17. Lin, T., Dollár, P., Girshick, R.B., He, K., Hariharan, B., Belongie, S.J.: Feature pyramid networks for object detection. In: Conference on Computer Vision and Pattern Recognition, CVPR, pp. 936–944 (2017)
18. Lin, T.Y., Goyal, P., Girshick, R., He, K., Dollár, P.: Focal loss for dense object detection. In: Proceedings of the IEEE International Conference on Computer Vision, pp. 2980–2988 (2017)
19. Lin, T.Y., et al.: Microsoft COCO: Common objects in context. Corr, vol. abs/1405.0312. arXiv preprint arxiv:1405.0312 (2014)
20. Liu, W., et al.: SSD: single shot multibox detector. Corr, vol. abs/1512.02325. arXiv preprint arxiv:1512.02325 (2015)
21. Liu, Z., et al.: Swin transformer: hierarchical vision transformer using shifted windows. In: Proceedings of the IEEE/CVF International Conference on Computer Vision, pp. 10012–10022 (2021)
22. Redmon, J., Divvala, S., Girshick, R., Farhadi, A.: You only look once: unified, real-time object detection. In: Proceedings of the IEEE Conference on Computer Vision and Pattern Recognition, pp. 779–788 (2016)
23. Redmon, J., Farhadi, A.: YOLOv3: an incremental improvement. Corr, vol. abs/1804.02767, 2018 (1804)
24. Redmon, J., Farhadi, A.: YOLO9000: better, faster, stronger. In: Proceedings of the IEEE Conference on Computer Vision and Pattern Recognition, pp. 7263–7271 (2017)
25. Ren, S., He, K., Girshick, R., Sun, J.: Faster R-CNN: towards real-time object detection with region proposal networks. In: Advances in Neural Information Processing Systems, vol. 28 (2015)
26. Shrivastava, A., Gupta, A., Girshick, R.: Training region-based object detectors with online hard example mining. In: Proceedings of the IEEE Conference on Computer Vision and Pattern Recognition, pp. 761–769 (2016)
27. Tan, M., Pang, R., Le, Q.V.: EfficientDet: scalable and efficient object detection. In: Proceedings of the IEEE/CVF Conference on Computer Vision and Pattern Recognition, pp. 10781–10790 (2020)
28. Yang, R., Ma, H., Wu, J., Tang, Y., Xiao, X., Zheng, M., Li, X.: Scalablevit: rethinking the context-oriented generalization of vision transformer. In: European Conference on Computer Vision, pp. 480–496 (2022)
29. Yang, R., Song, L., Ge, Y., Li, X.: BoxSnake: polygonal instance segmentation with box supervision. In: International Conference on Computer Vision (2023)
30. Zhang, Y., Li, Z., Xie, Y., Qu, Y., Li, C., Mei, T.: Weakly supervised semantic segmentation for large-scale point cloud. In: Proceedings of the AAAI Conference on Artificial Intelligence, vol. 35, pp. 3421–3429 (2021)
31. Zhang, Y., Qu, Y., Xie, Y., Li, Z., Zheng, S., Li, C.: Perturbed self-distillation: Weakly supervised large-scale point cloud semantic segmentation. In: Proceedings of the IEEE/CVF International Conference on Computer Vision, pp. 15520–15528 (2021)

HaarStyle:Revision Style Transfer Based on Multiple Resolutions

Hongwei Chen, Mengjie Li[✉], and Yupeng Lei

Hubei University of Technology, Wuhan, China
102101024@hbut.edu.cn, rum_naive@163.com, love@hbut.edu.cn

Abstract. Image style transfer aims to obtain content images with corresponding styles by migrating style information to content images, but transfer models in recent years have certain application limitations, for which good image quality and transfer speed of the model cannot be guaranteed at the same time, and it's common that clear edges cannot be maintained when stylizing. This paper proposes a new feed-forward model Haar Based Network (HaarStyle), which uses different resolution modules to complement the edge information and content features of the image to improve its quality. It is experimentally demonstrated that HaarStyle can ensure a certain transmission speed with fewer artifacts, avoiding the problem of over stylization.

Keywords: Style Transfer · Image Quality · Deep Learning · VGG-19 · AdaIN

1 Introduction

With the development of deep learning, image style transfer has gradually become one of the research hotspots in the field of computer vision. By transferring the style of the style image to the content image, the image with both style image pattern and content image is obtained, which method has been widely researched in industry and academia.

PhotoNAS [1] proposed that skip connections will invalidate the transmission module at the bottleneck of the autoencoder, and autoencoders with skip connections generally lose the ability to generate stylized images.DRLN [2] employs cascading residual on the residual structure to allow the flow of low-frequency information to focus on learning high and mid-level features. Xia [20] proposed a feed-forward neural network that learns local edge-aware affine transforms that automatically obey the photorealism constraint.PhotoWCT [14] improves the network of WCT [13] to get a preliminary synthetic image with target style, and then smoothing operation is performed on the synthetic image, which improves the image quality and solves the problem of identical space but inconsistent stylization within the image.WCT^2 [21] further improves the ability to grasp the details of the content image by using filtering instead of upsampling and downsampling operations, which completely retains the detailed information of

© The Author(s), under exclusive license to Springer Nature Switzerland AG 2023
L. Iliadis et al. (Eds.): ICANN 2023, LNCS 14254, pp. 244–255, 2023.
https://doi.org/10.1007/978-3-031-44207-0_21

the image and speeds up the process. STROTSS [9] improves the image quality by modifying the loss function and relaxing the EMD calculation to expand the application of the loss function, while its slow optimization process hampers its practical application. LapStyle [16] proposed to obtain high quality images by Draft-Revision to add detailed modifications gradually from low-quality images, but the images obtained suffer from certain artifacts and over styling. Ensuring the overall stylization of the image while preserving the detailed features of the image is still a major difficulty in image style transfer. The goal of this paper is to achieve a higher stylized image quality with a certain style transfer speed.

The contribution of this paper is shown as follows. A new feed-forward model is proposed, which first performs style transfer through low-resolution images, then incorporates high-resolution image features on this basis. This method enhances the understanding of content features when stylizing the model by adding filtering, which ensures the speed of model transfer while reducing the image quality problems of artifacts and over styling.

2 Related Work

Style Transfer. The main deep learning-based image style transfer methods currently include two types. One of image based iterations and the other of model based iterations. The goal of image based iterations is to make the white noise image match both the content feature representation of the content image as well as the style feature representation of the style image, and the stylized synthetic image is obtained thereafter. The methods based on image iterations are divided into three main ways: maximum mean difference based, Markov random field based, and depth image analogy based. Gatys [5] was able to extract abstract content representations from arbitrary images based on maximum mean difference by reconstructing the abstract feature representations in the middle layer of the VGG network [19], and the stylistic feature representations of arbitrary images can be extracted by constructing Gram matrices; Li et al. [10] proposed a combination of Markov random fields and deep convolution neural networks to partition the image feature mapping into many region blocks. Combining the concept of image depth analogy with deep learning, Liao [15] proposed a deep image analogy method optimized with iterative region block matching. The image iteration based approach can produce stylized images with high and excellent effect quality without data training. However, it takes longer computation time due to the need for multiple iterations and it relies greatly on pretrained models. The model iteration based approach is a good solution to the above problem, thus it can also be combined with the image iteration based approach to achieve better image results. The style transfer based on model iteration can be divided into Per-Style-Per-Model, Multi-Style-Per-Model and Arbitrary-Style-Per-Model according to the number of style transfer that the model can achieve. Per-Style-Per-Model method are featured by pre-trained feed-forward neural networks to generate a stylized resultant graph [7], Li et al. [11] were inspired by MRF-based neural style transfer algorithms that utilize GAN to solve the efficiency problem of Markov forward networks. Benefiting from an effective block design, it can ensure texture information in complex images, but it lacks semantic considerations. Multi-Style-Per-Model method fuses multiple styles into one model, increasing the flexibility of the model for more application scenarios. Its two main implementations are as follows: Dumoulin et al. [4] kept the same convolution parameters in a convolution neural network and only affined transformations of the parameters in the IN layer to simulate different styles. Li et al. [12] first produced the desired stylized results by linking stylized encoding features and image content encoding features together for input into the decoder module in a stylized transfer neural network. Schmidt [3] achieves arbitrary style transfer by finding content blocks that match the style blocks, exchanging and rebuilding with reconstruction algorithm for fast reconstruction. Belongie [6], inspired by Dumoulin [4] and others, proposed AdaIN in the IN layer using the mean as well as variance statistics information of content and style features to achieve arbitrary stylization operations.

Picture Quality Improvement. WCT^2 [21] uses filtering to decompose the whole image into one low-frequency feature and three high-frequency features. And by filtering instead of upsampling and downsampling, the original image can be fully restored without losing feature information. LapStyle [16] employs coarse to fine strategy to further process the image through the Revision network, transforming the image at lower solution. PhotoWCT [14] adds manifold ranking to correct the local content similarities of images into a consistent style, but its grasp of detailed features is insufficient compared to that of WCT^2 [21] and LapStyle [16]. The HaarStyle in this paper outperforms the above models in terms of detailed features as it can effectively reduce artifacts and blurring of content edges.

3   Introduced Approach

In order to make the generated image content closer to the content image, it is necessary to grasp the image details of the content processing. Image styles are transferred at low-resolution first. Due to the large receiving field, and less local details, global styles are easier to transfer at low-resolutions. Haar filtering is used to decompose the picture into low-frequency features and high-frequency features, where high-frequency features are used to repair the image details.

3.1   Network Architecture

The overall structure is shown in Fig. 1. The model consists of two main parts: one is the low-resolution style transfer module, and the other is the high-resolution module, which adds high-frequency image features to obtain a better feature representation by performing style transfer at low-frequencies. Besides, the loss function part of the model is also included in this part.

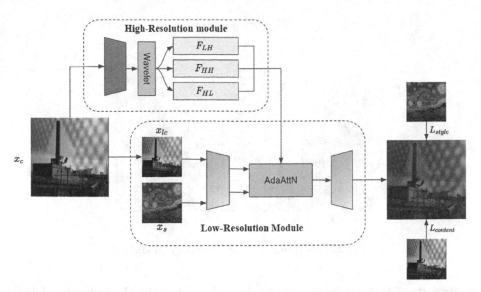

Fig. 1. Overview of HaarStyle Framework, the model consists of two main parts: the Low-resolution style transfer module, and the High-resolution module

3.2 Low-Resolution Module

The low-resolution module is designed to transfer the target style of the image to the content image at a low-resolution. Firstly, the low-resolution image x_{lc} of the content image is obtained by downsampling the original image x_c. The image of low resolution will have less details and thus can be transferred better compared to the original image, accelerating the computational efficiency of transfer to a certain extent to obtain a faster transfer model.

Some content features of the remaining low-frequency features may be lost after the high-resolution module separation, and compared with WCT [13], AdaIN [6] prefers to learn the complete image distribution rather than just a part of the content image, so the low-frequency features filtered by direct Haar filtering are not used here.

The whole low-resolution module mainly includes encoder, AdaIN, and decoder parts, and the overall structure is shown in Fig. 2. Multi-level links are adopted, the features of layer4 are taken as the input of AdaIN, and the three layer-level features obtained are acquired into decoder as the repair part of the image. In the final model, the Revision Network [16] is added to further improve the image quality.

3.3 High-Resolution Module

The high-resolution module is taken from the first 4 layers of VGG-19 [19], and the original content image x_c is input to the network to get the content features F_c, where F_c is the feature information of each layer, which is decomposed into

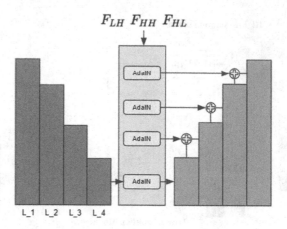

Fig. 2. Illustration of Low Frequency Module.

three parts of high-frequency features F_{LH}, F_{HL}, F_{HH} by Haar filtering. These features are incorporated into the low-resolution module for feature fusion, and the low-frequency images are given high-frequency features in this way.

Haar filtering is mainly divided into three convolution kernels, corresponding to the three high-frequency image parts of F_{LH}, F_{HL}, and F_{HH}. The specific composition of the three convolution kernels is shown in (1).

$$F_{LH} = \frac{1}{2}\begin{bmatrix} -1 & 1 \\ -1 & 1 \end{bmatrix}, F_{HL} = \frac{1}{2}\begin{bmatrix} -1 & -1 \\ 1 & 1 \end{bmatrix}, F_{HH} = \frac{1}{2}\begin{bmatrix} 1 & -1 \\ -1 & 1 \end{bmatrix} \tag{1}$$

Three separate high-pass filters are used to extract vertical, horizontal and diagonal edge like information, which corresponds to the detailed information in the image and is used to fill in the detailed features lost in low-frequency images, ensuring that the image is generated with a good grasp of the detailed part.

3.4   Loss Function

During the training process, The encoder uses part of the VGG-19 network [19] and the parameters are fixed, and decoder parameters update through parameters training. The loss mainly contains two parts, namely content loss and style loss. Therefore the loss function is introduced through these two aspects.

Content Loss. The content loss mainly adopts the widely used perceptual loss, with the self similarity loss proposed in STROTSS [9] taken into consideration. By comparing the feature value of the image to be generated after convolution with that of the target image after convolution, perceptual loss makes the image to be generated more semantically similar to the target image. The specific formula is shown in (2).

$$l_p = \|\text{norm}\,(F_c) - \text{norm}\,(F_{cs})\|_2 \tag{2}$$

where $norm$ is the normalization operation for feature F, F_c is the content image feature after CNN, and F_{cs} is the corresponding image feature after stylization. Self similarity loss preserves the correlation between content image and target image, which have the same content and the same self similarity or emergence. Self similarity loss is calculated as in (3).

$$l_{ss} = \frac{1}{(hw)^2} \sum_{i,j} \left| \frac{D_{cs}}{\sum_i D_{ij}^{cs}} - \frac{D_c}{\sum_i D_{ij}^c} \right| \tag{3}$$

where D_{ij}^c and D_{ij}^{cs} are the (i,j) elements of matrix D_c and matrix D_{cs}, while Dij here is the pairwise cosine similarity $< F_i, F_j >$

Style Loss. The style loss uses mean-variance loss and relaxed Earth Mover Distance (rEMD). rEMD is relaxed in STROTSS to enable it to comply with the requirements of gradient descent for style transfer, which aims to capture the distance between two sets. The feature vectors in the style loss are extracted from each layer of the encoder. rEMD loss is calculated as shown in (4).

$$l_r = \max \left(\frac{1}{h_s w_s} \sum_{i=1} \min_j C_{ij}, \frac{1}{h_{cs} w_{cs}} \sum_{j=1} \min_i C_{ij} \right) \tag{4}$$

C_{ij} represents the cosine distance between the feature vectors, which is shown in (5).

$$C_{ij} = 1 - \frac{F_{s,i} . F_{cs,j}}{\|F_{s,i}\| \, \|F_{cs,j}\|} \tag{5}$$

However, the cosine distance ignores the size of the feature vector. In practice, this leads to visual bias in the output, so the usual mean-variance loss is added to this part, where μ and σ are the mean and variance of the distribution, respectively. The formula is shown in (6).

$$l_m = \|\mu(F_s) - \mu(F_{cs})\|_2 + \|\sigma(F_s) - \sigma(F_{cs})\|_2 \tag{6}$$

Loss of Network. The high-resolution module uses VGG-19 [19] with fixed parameters, so it is not involved in the loss calculation. In the low-resolution module, the input is the content image and style image, and the output is the stylized target image. The network calculates the loss function from the target image and the input content image and style image. And the overall loss function of the whole network is shown in (7).

$$L_{loss} = (l_p + \omega_1 \times l_{ss}) + \alpha(l_m + \omega_2 \times l_r) \tag{7}$$

The weights ω_1 and ω_2 as well as α are set for each part and are mainly used to control the balance of each part and to make adjustments, l_p, l_{ss}, l_m, l_r are mentioned in (2), (3), (6) and (5) respectively.

4 Experiment

4.1 Dataset

The "COCO2017" from MS-COCO [17] is used as the content images during training. The overall size of the content image is 18.2G, and the validation set is also the validation set from COCO2017, which contains about 5,000 images, and a number of distinctive art style images are selected as the data source of style images.

The devices used for the experiments are Intel(R) Xeon(R) Silver 4110 CPU @ 2.10 GHz and RTX 2080 Ti, and all experiments are carried out with a single GPU. For the training of the network as a whole, the Adam [8] optimizer is used. The initial learning rate is set at 1e−4, while the batch-size is set to 5 images, with 30,000 iterations for training and every 500 iterations for validation of the validation set. The initial settings of each weight ω_1 and ω_2 and α in the loss function are 16, 3, 3.

4.2 Qualitative Comparison

As is shown in Fig. 3, the LapStyle [16] model is Per-Style-Per-Model with fast style transfer, which can generate high quality images at a guaranteed fast speed. But over-styling features may occur in the processing of images. For example, in the stylized image in row 6, column 2, LapStyle [16] generates certain noise content (excessive yellow spots) while stylizing, while the building in the stylized image in row 6, column 1 has certain edge distortion. AdaIN [6], WCT [13], SANet [18] of the Arbitrary-Style-Per-Model have certain advantages over Per-Style-Per-Model in processing styles, but the performance of image quality in transfer for a specific style is not as high as that of Per-Style-Per-Model. Specifically, the performance is poor when converting for larger content features in images. And in some cases, the conversion style fails. At the same time, the content has some edge blurring and does not effectively retain the content features of the content images. Among them, WCT [13] performs slightly lower than the other two of the Arbitrary-Style-Per-Model in the retention of content features and cannot guarantee the contours of content image features. In this regard, our model performs better than the Arbitrary-Style-Per-Model in generating images with higher quality, and better preserves the content features of the images while ensuring the stylization. AdaIN [6] showed sensitivity to color distribution when stylizing, with regard to the fact that the color distribution of the original content image is still retained in the stylized image. Being of the Per-Style-Per-Model, our modle has some advantages over others in terms of the quality of the stylized transferred image performance.

We also compared HaarStyle with the image based iterative model [5, 9], shown in Fig. 4. Gatys et al. [5] used Gram matrix for image stylization, which was not suitable enough for stylization of local details and distribution of stylization to the overall picture, let alone the overall picture style conversion.

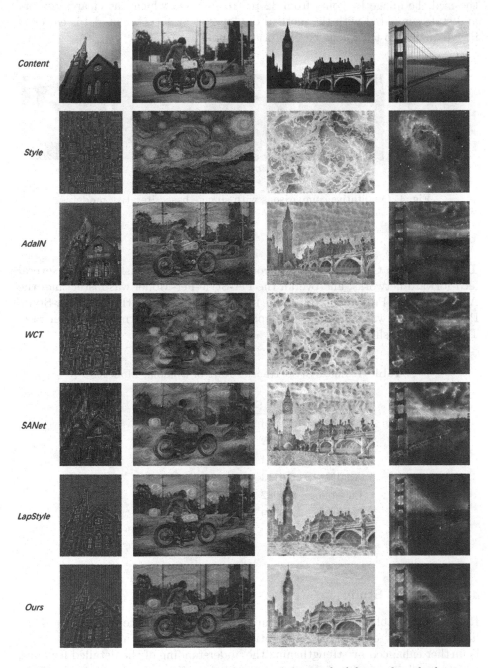

Fig. 3. Qualitative comparisons with state-of-the-art feed forward methods.

STROTSS [9] used a relaxed EMD distance for stylized loss function and synthesized the image by going from 32 pix to 512 pix, which has clearer texture and style compared with the method of Gatys et al. [5]. Our model is closer in image quality to the image based iterative model.

| Content | Style | Ours | STROTSS | Gatys et al. |

Fig. 4. Qualitative comparisons with simage based iterative model.

Transfer Rate Comparison. We compared the style transfer rates of several feed-forward networks, and overall the Per-Style-Per-Model was faster than the Arbitrary-Style-Per-Model. HaarStyle model was faster than the other Per-Style-Per-Model, and was similar to the LapStyle [16] model in terms of transfer rate. The details are shown in Table 1.

Table 1. Image Style Transfer Rate of Different Models.

Method	Time (256pix)	Time(512pix)
Gatys et al	15.863	50.804
WCT	0.6892	0.9974
SANet	0.0174	0.0553
AdaIN	0.0113	0.0392
LapStyle	0.0082	0.0091
Ours	0.0079	0.0089

4.3   Ablation Study

Results of the ablation experiments are shown in Fig. 5. After adding the Harr filter, the ability of the image generation to depict the original image elements is further enhanced by strengthening the understanding of the detailed features, which is reflected in Fig. 5 as a more detailed depiction of the contours of the clouds.

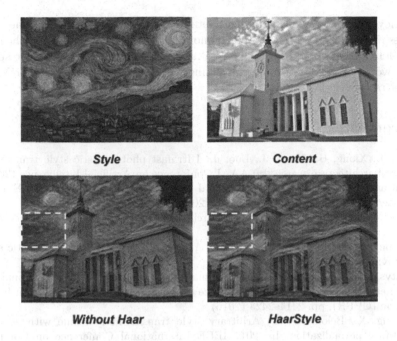

Style   **Content**

Without Haar   **HaarStyle**

Fig. 5. Ablation Study.

Content-Style Tradeoff. When training, we control the degree of stylization of the model by changing the size of α. As is shown in Fig. 6, when α is low, the model as a whole tends to retain a lot of detailed features without enough stylization, and when α is high, the model has higher stylization but less content information.

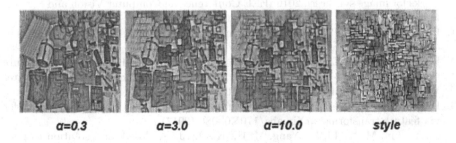

$\alpha=0.3$ $\alpha=3.0$ $\alpha=10.0$ **style**

Fig. 6. Content-style Tradeoff.

5   Conclusion

In this paper, we propose a feed-forward Per-Style-Per-Model, HaarStyle, which performs fast style transfer by a low resolution module, while adding high-frequency features for enhancing the detailed features of the image. The effectiveness of our proposed structure is demonstrated experimentally, and the overall model can guarantee the image quality with a certain style transfer speed. Future work will revolve around converting the model from Per-Style-Per-Model to Arbitrary-Style-Per-Model.

References

1. An, J., Xiong, H., Huan, J., Luo, J.: Ultrafast photorealistic style transfer via neural architecture search. In: AAAI Conference on Artificial Intelligence (2019)
2. Anwar, S., Barnes, N.: Densely residual Laplacian super-resolution. IEEE Trans. Pattern Anal. Mach. Intell. **44**, 1192–1204 (2019)
3. Chen, T.Q., Schmidt, M.W.: Fast patch-based style transfer of arbitrary style. arXiv:abs/1612.04337 (2016)
4. Dumoulin, V., Shlens, J., Kudlur, M.: A learned representation for artistic style. arXiv:abs/1610.07629 (2016)
5. Gatys, L.A., Ecker, A.S., Bethge, M.: Image style transfer using convolutional neural networks. In: 2016 IEEE Conference on Computer Vision and Pattern Recognition (CVPR), pp. 2414–2423 (2016)
6. Huang, X., Belongie, S.J.: Arbitrary style transfer in real-time with adaptive instance normalization. In: 2017 IEEE International Conference on Computer Vision (ICCV), pp. 1510–1519 (2017)
7. Johnson, J., Alahi, A., Fei-Fei, L.: Perceptual losses for real-time style transfer and super-resolution. arXiv:abs/1603.08155 (2016)
8. Kingma, D.P., Ba, J.: Adam: a method for stochastic optimization. CoRR, abs/1412.6980 (2014)
9. Kolkin, N.I., Salavon, J., Shakhnarovich, G.: Style transfer by relaxed optimal transport and self-similarity. In: 2019 IEEE/CVF Conference on Computer Vision and Pattern Recognition (CVPR), pp. 10043–10052 (2019)
10. Li, C., Wand, M.: Combining Markov random fields and convolutional neural networks for image synthesis. 2016 IEEE Conference on Computer Vision and Pattern Recognition (CVPR), pp. 2479–2486 (2016)
11. Li, C., Wand, M.: Precomputed real-time texture synthesis with Markovian generative adversarial networks. arXiv:abs/1604.04382 (2016)
12. Li, Y., Fang, C., Yang, J., Wang, Z., Lu, X., Yang, M.-H.: Diversified texture synthesis with feed-forward networks. In: 2017 IEEE Conference on Computer Vision and Pattern Recognition (CVPR), pp. 266–274 (2017)
13. Li, Y., Fang, C., Yang, J., Wang, Z., Lu, X., Yang, M.-H.: Universal style transfer via feature transforms. arXiv:abs/1705.08086 (2017)
14. Li, Y., Liu, M.-Y., Li, X., Yang, M.-H., Kautz, J.: A closed-form solution to photorealistic image stylization. arXiv:abs/1802.06474 (2018)
15. Liao, J., Yao, Y., Yuan, L., Hua, G., Kang, S.B.: Visual attribute transfer through deep image analogy. ACM Trans. Graph. (TOG) **36**, 1–15 (2017)
16. Lin, T., et al.: Drafting and revision: Laplacian pyramid network for fast high-quality artistic style transfer. In: 2021 IEEE/CVF Conference on Computer Vision and Pattern Recognition (CVPR), pp. 5137–5146 (2021)
17. Lin, T.-Y., et al.: Microsoft COCO: common objects in context. In: Fleet, D., Pajdla, T., Schiele, B., Tuytelaars, T. (eds.) ECCV 2014. LNCS, vol. 8693, pp. 740–755. Springer, Cham (2014). https://doi.org/10.1007/978-3-319-10602-1_48

18. Park, D.Y., Lee, K.H.: Arbitrary style transfer with style-attentional networks. In: 2019 IEEE/CVF Conference on Computer Vision and Pattern Recognition (CVPR), pp. 5873–5881 (2018)
19. Simonyan, K., Zisserman, A.: Very deep convolutional networks for large-scale image recognition. CoRR, abs/1409.1556 (2014)
20. Xia, X., et al.: Joint bilateral learning for real-time universal photorealistic style transfer. arXiv:abs/2004.10955 (2020)
21. Yoo, J., Uh, Y., Chun, S., Kang, B., Ha, J.-W.: Photorealistic style transfer via wavelet transforms. In: 2019 IEEE/CVF International Conference on Computer Vision (ICCV), pp. 9035–9044 (2019)

Semi-Supervised Learning Classifier for Misinformation Related to Earthquakes Prediction on Social Media

Or Elroy[1,2] and Abraham Yosipof[1,2]([envelope])

[1] Faculty of Information Systems and Computer Science, College of Law and Business,
Ramat-Gan, Israel
aviyo@clb.ac.il
[2] International Institute for Applied Systems Analysis, Laxenburg, Austria

Abstract. Social media is a fertile ground for the growth and distribution of misinformation. The belief in misinformation can have devastating consequences, and may lead to unnecessary loss of life. Properly identifying and countering misinformation on social media is therefore necessary for the fight against misinformation. In this research, we developed an Adjusted Semi-Supervised Learning for Social Media (ASSLSM) method to classify and analyze tweets regarding misinformation related to earthquakes prediction. The ASSLSM method adjusts the pseudo-labeling constraints based on assumptions related to metadata of the tweets and users, with the goal of providing better information to the underlying models. We collected a dataset of 82,129 tweets related to the subject of earthquakes prediction. Expert seismologists manually labeled 4,157 tweets. We evaluated and compared the performance of ASSLSM, supervised learning, and semi-supervised learning (SSL) methods on the dataset. We found that the ASSLSM methodology provides better and more consistent performance in comparison to supervised learning and SSL. Finally, we used an ASSLSM classifier to classify the full dataset and analyzed the classified dataset.

Keywords: Semi-Supervised Learning · Misinformation · RoBERTa · NLP · Earthquakes · Social Media

1 Introduction

Social media has a key role in the expression and distribution of authoritative as well as speculative information on different subjects in recent times, primarily because of its massive adoption, audience, and accessibility.

Social media platforms reach different sectors of the population and are often accessed multiple times a day, or even continuously throughout the day, for recreational purposes as well as for receiving important information. Considering its reachability and instantaneous nature, social media inevitably became a viable channel of communication for information, such as warnings about upcoming and ongoing emergencies and disasters.

L. Iliadis et al. (Eds.): ICANN 2023, LNCS 14254, pp. 256–267, 2023.
https://doi.org/10.1007/978-3-031-44207-0_22

During the COVID-19 pandemic, social media served as a communication channel for news and updates about the spread of the virus throughout the world, as well as medical recommendations [1].

It is important to acknowledge that social media is also a ground for the growth and dissemination of misinformation. Misinformation is false or inaccurate information according to the best factual evidence that is available at a given point in time, regardless of an intention to mislead or deceive [2].

Misinformation and the belief therein are driven by a natural need to rationalize unexplained or unexpected emergencies and disasters. The lack of authoritative sources with reliable information regarding emergencies and disasters, such as an outbreak of a virus or an earthquake, combined with circumstantial evidence, promotes misinformation [3, 4]. The belief in misinformation can have devastating consequences, and even lead to unnecessary loss of life.

Earthquakes prediction is one of the topics of misinformation that is being discussed on social media. According to the current state of research, earthquakes cannot be predicted. The exact location, time and magnitude of future events cannot be specified [5, 6]. However, misinformation regarding earthquakes prediction or advance warnings is constantly spread on social media [5, 7]. Earthquakes contribute to anxiety, shock, and panic of the population, which consequently make the population more vulnerable to misinformation [8]. A population that frequently encounters misinformation regarding earthquake predictions may hesitate to take necessary actions to protect itself when a real earthquake alert is issued. Misinformation regarding earthquake predictions causes a variety of symptoms, such as confusion, anxiety, or misguided beliefs that further lead to unnecessary actions like evacuation. Misinformation on social media is a commonly researched topic in general and on Twitter specifically [1, 9, 10].

In this research, we developed a new semi-supervised classifier to classify and analyze tweets regarding misinformation related to earthquake predictions. This methodology presents several challenges, including the collection of enough relevant data, labeling the data as misinformation or not-misinformation, and the development of a classifier to detect tweets that spread misinformation. Finally, the classified tweets are analyzed to gain knowledge and insights on how to support the fight against misinformation regarding earthquakes prediction.

We address these challenges and provide the following contributions. We collected 82,129 tweets according to a specific search query that expert seismologists curated. A key task in analyzing tweets related to misinformation is to label and classify the tweets [1]. Collecting a large amount of data is often efficient and fast, whereas labeling the data can be a lengthy, costly, and complicated process. Therefore, a relatively small amount of labeled data is often used to classify a relatively large amount of unlabeled data. In this work, expert seismologists labeled 4,157 tweets. The labeled dataset constitutes about five percent of the dataset.

Training a classifier where only five percent of data is labeled can provide a good model for the training set. However, applying the model on the rest of the data may be problematic regardless of how representative the training set and classifier are [11]. Semi-Supervised Learning (SSL) methods address this concern by making assumptions about the actual labels of the unlabeled data based on the confidence levels of the predictions.

In this work, we eased the confidence level assumption and introduced new assumptions that are more robust when labeling data from social media.

Classification models depend on features that represent samples in the dataset. For textual data, the features are often derived from Natural Language Processing (NLP) word embedding algorithms. The outcome is that two semantically-similar texts are likely to be classified as having the same label.

However, classification models based on word embedding features do not account for valuable metadata of social media posts, such as the classification of other posts of the same users, the number of followers a user has, or the time the user has existed on the platform. While semantically similar tweets share similar embeddings, the actual classification of other tweets posted by the same user can be even more useful than the classification of more semantically similar tweets from other users.

In this work, we present the Adjusted Semi Supervised Learning for Social Media (ASSLSM) method. ASSLSM takes into consideration different metadata of the users who posted the tweets, as well as metadata of the tweets. This approach is more robust and adapted to the environment of social media in general, and to misinformation regarding earthquake predictions specifically. To the best of our knowledge, this work is the first to consider features derived from social media metadata in the process of SSL.

2 Related Work

Twitter is a valuable and frequently used source of information for research regarding misinformation on social media. Erokhin et al. [9] analyzed the behavior of different conspiracy theories related to the COVID-19 pandemic. Batzdorfer et al. [12] investigated the dynamics of tweets that discuss COVID-19 conspiracy theories, by comparing tweets from a group of users that talked about conspiracy theories and a group of users that participated in the general discussion on the virus. Darwish et al. [13] created a fake news detection system and built a dataset of fake and real tweets about the Russian-Ukrainian conflict using deep-learning and machine learning methods.

NLP methodologies such as Bidirectional Encoder Representations from Transformers (BERT) [14], provide superior results for different NLP tasks, including word embedding [15, 16]. Micallef et al. [17] used BERT embeddings to investigate and counter misinformation in tweets related to COVID-19 over a period of five months. Elroy and Yosipof [1] transformed BERT word embeddings to sentence embedding using Sentence-BERT [18] to train a classifier and classify a dataset of over 300K tweets related to the COVID-19 5G conspiracy theory.

RoBERTa is a Robustly Optimized BERT Pretraining Approach model based on BERT, that was pretrained with different design decisions, leading to improved performance and state of the art results [19–21].

Sentence-BERT is a modification of the pre-trained BERT network that uses Siamese and triplet network structures on top of the BERT model and fine-tuned based on high quality sentence interface data to learn more sentence level information [18]. Sentence-BERT can also be applied on RoBERTa's embeddings to transform the word embeddings into a single sentence embedding, resulting in 768 features per tweet when used with RoBERTa-base.

In addition to embeddings, training a classifier for misinformation on social media also requires a labeled set. The labeled set is traditionally gathered through a lengthy process of manual labeling and often results in a relatively small number of labeled samples out of a relatively large amount of data. SSL addresses this issue by enhancing the labeled dataset with pseudo-labels based on assumptions regarding the appropriate labels for some of the unlabeled dataset.

Multiple SSL approaches exist, such as consistency training, proxy-label methods, generative methods, and graph-based methods [22]. SSL models operate under certain assumptions, such as that two samples that are close enough to each other in terms of distance should share the same labels [22]. Another possible common assumption is that two samples in the same cluster share the same label [22]. Depending on the task, these assumptions can be more or less strict, which is reflected in the size and quality of the pseudo-labeled dataset.

SSL proxy-label methods leverage a model that was trained on the labeled dataset to label samples of the unlabeled dataset using heuristic approaches. A common requirement that the prediction meets a certain threshold of confidence level is typical for proxy-label methods [22]. In this case, a label is considered a proxy label if the prediction probability is greater than a certain threshold.

Metadata and characteristics of social media posts, as well as their authors, were proven to be useful for classification tasks of tweets and were used to enhance classification models in previous works [1, 23–25]. These include the number of users who follow the author and the number of users the author follows as an indication of the author being a robot [23], or URLs, mentions, retweets, and tweet length as indicators for credibility [24, 25]. Balaanand et al. used tweets metadata in graph-based semi-supervised learning to detect fake users on Twitter [26]. Jan et al. used tweets metadata as features for the underlying classifier in a SSL methodology [27].

3 Workflow

To achieve the research objective, we developed the following workflow. Figure 1 describes the workflow used in this work. The workflow consists of four stages, namely data collection and preprocessing, models evaluation, results, and analysis.

The data collection and preprocessing phase involves the collection of tweets related to the discussion of earthquakes prediction misinformation on Twitter, the computation of the embedding for each tweet, and the hand-labeling of tweets.

The evaluation process of the models consists of testing and comparing the performance of different models using different techniques, namely supervised learning, SSL, and ASSLSM.

Following the evaluation, the complete dataset is classified using the model that provides the best performance, and the classified dataset is analyzed.

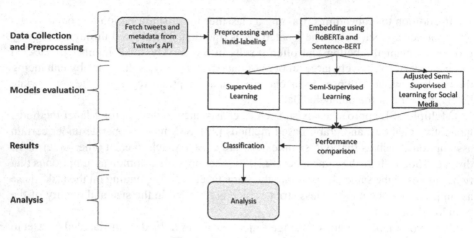

Fig. 1. Research workflow.

4 Dataset

We collected 82,129 tweets related to the subject of earthquakes prediction, forecasts, and notifications, and metadata of the users that posted the tweets, over a period of about two years, from March 1, 2020, to March 31, 2022. The data was collected using a Twitter API that is limited to academic research and provides access to Twitter's full archive. The search query used in this study was defined by expert seismologists as [[predict OR forecast OR warn OR updates OR alert] AND [earthquake OR quake OR [seismic AND event] OR seismicity OR shaking OR EQ]].

The data includes the tweets themselves as well as metadata such as the number of retweets, likes, and replies a tweet received. Metadata of the users who posted the tweets was also collected, such as the total number of tweets the user posted on the platform, the number of followers they have, and the number of other users they follow.

Expert seismologists manually labeled 4,157 tweets into three categories in accordance with the Communication Guide [6]. The three categories are misinformation, not-misinformation, and irrelevant tweets (see Table 1). Tweets claiming to be able to predict future earthquakes were labeled as misinformation (835 tweets, Table 1). Tweets notifying about current earthquakes, rejecting others' ability to predict future earthquakes, or explaining how certain services work, were labeled as not-misinformation (1,416 tweets, Table 1). Other tweets that are not directly related to earthquakes, such as secondary hazards, were labeled as irrelevant (1,906 tweets, Table 1).

We used RoBERTa-base to calculate the word embeddings of each tweet in the dataset, and transformed the word embeddings of each tweet to a sentence embedding using Sentence-BERT [18], yielding a vector of 768 features per tweet.

Table 1. Categories of the manually labeled dataset with examples, number of tweets and proportion of each category.

Category	Example	# of Tweets	% of Tweets
Misinformation	"24 h WARNING: 5.5 + earthquake is likely in the Mammoth Lakes - Bridgeport area and 5.0 + earthquake is likely within 50 miles of Santa Clarita - NW of Los Angeles during the next 24 h."	835	20.09
Not misinformation	"No one can accurately predict earthquakes. The USGS issues long term earthquake forecasts for certain areas."	1,416	34.06
Irrelevant	"Could end in 5 billion gallons of lava or nothing will happen. Hard to say. *[link]*"	1,906	45.85

5 ASSLSM: Adjusted Semi-Supervised Learning for Social Media

SSL based on proxy-method uses an underlying supervised learning model to predict the labels for the unlabeled data. Predictions that meet certain criteria are assigned as pseudo-labels to the labeled dataset for the purpose of training a model. A common assumption in SSL is that predictions with a confidence level above a certain threshold are correct.

ASSLSM implements additional constraints for the pseudo-labels, based on features of the metadata of the tweets and the users who posted them.

The ASSLSM methodology provides better information to the models by adjusting the constraints used in SSL, to achieve more consistent performance across different underlying models. The constraints used in the ASSLSM methodology require all of the following:

(A) The prediction matches most of the existing labels for that user in the labeled dataset.
(B) The user who posted the tweet has >=100 tweets in the dataset.
(C) The confidence level of the prediction is above threshold T.

Constraint A is based on the presumption that a new tweet by a user who mostly posted tweets belonging to a certain category is very likely to also belong to the same category. Constraint B reduces the number of exceptions to the previous presumption by ignoring users without enough samples in the dataset. Constraint C uses a lower threshold than basic SSL methods, to compensate for the lower number of samples due to constraints A and B.

6 Results

According to the workflow previously described, we evaluated three methodologies, namely supervised learning, semi-supervised learning, and ASSLSM with two different confidence thresholds. Each evaluation phase tested the performance of five different machine learning models, namely k-NN with k = 3, Random Forest with 100 trees, Gaussian Naïve-Bayes, Logistic Regression, and a Voting Ensemble classifier of all previous models with soft voting. We used 5-fold cross-validation for each model. Table 2 presents the weighted F1, precision, and recall scores of the models using supervised learning, SSL, and ASSLSM.

First, we tested traditional supervised learning using the labeled dataset. The results of the supervised learning performance are presented in Table 2, Supervised Learning.

Second, we tested a proxy-method based SSL model by calculating the prediction probability for the sentence embedding of each unlabeled tweet using each model at a time. Predictions with a confidence level over a threshold of 0.9 were added to the labeled dataset as pseudo-labels (Table 2, Semi-Supervised Learning). For the SSL method, we used a single constraint that requires the confidence level of the prediction to be greater than a fixed threshold of 0.9.

Finally, we tested the ASSLSM method (Table 2, ASSLSM) using a confidence level threshold of >0.7, and a confidence level threshold of >0.8.

The supervised learning models provided an average F1 score of 0.752 with a standard deviation of 0.04, using a dataset of only 4,157 labeled samples.

The SSL models with a confidence threshold of >0.9 presented a much higher average F1 score of 0.938 and a slightly higher standard deviation than the supervised learning models. These results represent an increase of almost 25% in the average F1 over the average F1 of the supervised learning models. The SSL approach significantly increased the number of samples in the labeled dataset by hundreds of percent with pseudo-labeled samples.

ASSLSM provided even better results with average F1, precision, and recall scores of 0.961, 0.971, and 0.958, respectively, using a confidence level threshold of >0.7; and 0.956, 0.969, and 0.953, respectively, using a confidence level threshold of >0.8. ASSLSM also provided a significantly lower standard deviation. The additional constraints introduced in the ASSLSM method enable the use of a lower threshold for the confidence level of the predictions while achieving better F1 scores than those of the SSL method. The ASSLSM methodology performed better on average than the SSL methods, using a lower average number of samples because of the tighter constraints in ASSLSM.

The SSL methodology provided an average of 42,598 labeled and pseudo-labeled samples. ASSLSM provided a lower number of labeled and pseudo-labeled samples, with an average of 27,819 and 29,990, using a threshold of > 0.7 and >0.8, respectively. The standard deviation of the number of labeled and pseudo-labeled samples in the different models is also significantly larger in SSL (21,890) compared to ASSLSM (3,468 and 1,967). The results show that more samples do not necessarily imply better performance of the models. For example, the SSL Naïve Bayes model (80,423 labeled samples, mean F1 of 0.853) and the SSL k-NN model (49,600 labeled samples, mean F1 of 0.967) with a relatively larger number of samples, performed worse than the SSL logistic regression (36,552 labeled samples, mean F1 of 0.979) and the SSL voting ensemble (31,191 labeled samples, mean F1 of 0.968) models.

Table 2. Supervised, Semi-Supervised, and ASSLSM classification performance metrics.

Model	Labeled	F1	Precision	Recall
Supervised Learning				
k-NN	4,157	0.742 ± 0.053	0.756 ± 0.047	0.748 ± 0.050
Random Forest	4,157	0.763 ± 0.075	**0.812 ± 0.047**	0.780 ± 0.065
Naïve Bayes	4,157	0.681 ± 0.100	0.683 ± 0.098	0.688 ± 0.100
Logistic Regression	4,157	**0.799 ± 0.056**	0.812 ± 0.046	**0.804 ± 0.051**
Voting Ensemble	4,157	0.773 ± 0.066	0.785 ± 0.056	0.781 ± 0.060
Average ± Std	*4,157 ± 0*	*0.752 ± 0.04*	*0.770 ± 0.048*	*0.760 ± 0.04*
Semi-Supervised Learning with threshold >0.9				
k-NN	49,600	0.967 ± 0.024	0.967 ± 0.024	0.967 ± 0.024
Random Forest	15,222	0.923 ± 0.072	0.950 ± 0.037	0.922 ± 0.083
Naïve Bayes	80,423	0.853 ± 0.054	0.875 ± 0.047	0.843 ± 0.057
Logistic Regression	36,552	**0.979 ± 0.037**	**0.980 ± 0.035**	**0.978 ± 0.038**
Voting Ensemble	31,191	0.968 ± 0.043	0.971 ± 0.040	0.969 ± 0.043
Average ± Std	*42,598 ± 21,890*	*0.938 ± 0.047*	*0.949 ± 0.038*	*0.936 ± 0.05*
ASSLSM with threshold >0.7				
k-NN	28,151	0.959 ± 0.036	0.966 ± 0.025	0.958 ± 0.041
Random Forest	27,126	0.961 ± 0.044	0.976 ± 0.021	0.958 ± 0.052
Naïve Bayes	32,010	0.947 ± 0.045	0.960 ± 0.025	0.943 ± 0.053
Logistic Regression	31,546	0.968 ± 0.038	0.976 ± 0.024	0.965 ± 0.045
Voting Ensemble	31,116	**0.969 ± 0.040**	**0.979 ± 0.021**	**0.966 ± 0.047**
Average ± Std	*29,990 ± 1967*	*0.961 ± 0.008*	*0.971 ± 0.007*	*0.958 ± 0.008*
ASSLSM with threshold >0.8				
k-NN	27,793	0.958 ± 0.036	0.966 ± 0.025	0.957 ± 0.041
Random Forest	21,473	0.945 ± 0.057	0.968 ± 0.028	0.944 ± 0.063
Naïve Bayes	31,996	0.948 ± 0.045	0.961 ± 0.025	0.943 ± 0.053
Logistic Regression	28,931	0.964 ± 0.044	0.974 ± 0.026	0.961 ± 0.051
Voting Ensemble	28,902	**0.966 ± 0.042**	**0.977 ± 0.022**	**0.962 ± 0.050**
Average ± Std	*27,819 ± 3468*	*0.956 ± 0.008*	*0.969 ± 0.006*	*0.953 ± 0.008*

The results show that applying the ASSLSM methodology optimized the data provided to the models, resulting in more consistent performance results between the different models.

The dataset contains 82,129 tweets posted by 34,219 unique users. Only 42 users had 100 or more tweets in the labeled and unlabeled dataset, hence meeting constraint B, according to which the user who posted the predicted tweet has $>=100$ tweets in the labeled and unlabeled datasets. These 42 users are responsible for 33,084 tweets (about a third of the dataset). It may therefore be presumed that participants in the discussion of a certain domain of misinformation are likely to be repeating actors, and therefore more predictions could be pseudo-labeled.

7 Analysis

We applied the ASSLSM methodology with a confidence level threshold of >0.7, which provided the best performance, to train a Voting Ensemble model and classify the unlabeled dataset. Table 3 presents the distribution of tweets in each classification label. The results show that tweets in both the misinformation and not-misinformation groups are posted by a relatively small number of authors (2,644 and 2,760 users, respectively). On the other hand, authors who posted tweets that are classified as irrelevant, typically quit the discussion after posting a little more than a single tweet on average.

Table 3. Distribution of tweets in each label.

Label	# of Tweets	% of Tweets	# of Unique Authors	Tweets/Author
Misinformation	7,412	9.0	2,644	2.803
Not misinformation	32,539	39.6	2,760	11.789
Irrelevant	42,178	51.4	30,530	1.382

We analyzed the time series of the tweet frequency in both groups. Figure 2 presents the daily tweet frequency of the misinformation and not-misinformation groups. Certain peaks are immediately visible and can be attributed to actual earthquakes that happened at the time. For instance, the highest peaks on February 10, 2021 and March 4, 2021 (Fig. 2, annotations 1–2), correlate with a Mw 7.7 earthquake near Loyalty Islands and a Mw 8.1 earthquake near Keramedac Islands. The peak on August 14, 2021 (Fig. 2, annotation 3) correlates with a Mw 7.2 earthquake near Haiti.

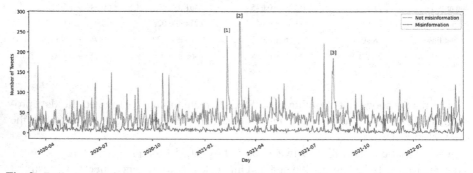

Fig. 2. Daily tweets frequency per category. The blue line represents the not-misinformation tweets, and the red line represents the misinformation tweets.

The cross correlation between the daily tweet frequency of the misinformation and the not-misinformation groups examines how one group dynamics depending on the dynamics of the other group. The results show a positive correlation of r = 0.36 between the daily tweet frequency in the misinformation and not-misinformation groups at time

t. This finding means that the tweet frequency of either group is associated with the tweet frequency of the other group on the same day.

8 Conclusion

In this study, we introduced the Adjusted Semi-Supervised Learning for Social Media methodology for the classification of misinformation tweets related to earthquakes prediction. ASSLSM takes into consideration useful metadata from social media that is not directly related to the text of the posts. We compared the performance of ASSLSM to the performance of supervised learning and SSL. We found that ASSLSM achieves significantly better results than supervised learning, and a model that is much more fit with more consistent results than SSL.

The results show that the additional constraints introduced in ASSLSM helped achieve better performance on average, while using a lower average number of samples than SSL. The variance of the results also decreased significantly when using ASSLSM. This finding suggests that using constraints that are more relevant to the data improves the performance and consistency of the models, despite reducing the number of pseudo-labels.

We used ASSLSM to classify the complete dataset of tweets related to earthquakes prediction into three categories, namely misinformation, not-misinformation, and irrelevant, and analyzed the resulting labeled dataset.

The analysis of the classified dataset shows that relatively small groups of authors are responsible for most tweets in the misinformation and not-misinformation groups. In the group of irrelevant tweets, however, more authors participate in the discussion but typically quit the conversation after a little more than one post in average. We also found that the daily tweet frequencies of the misinformation and not-misinformation groups are positively correlated and peak during an earthquake.

Valid information regarding ongoing events and the effective spread thereof, especially in case of potentially hazardous events, is important for public safety [28]. At the same time, the prevention of misinformation is of similar importance. As such, it can be recommended to communicate authoritative and correct information in a timely manner as an effective measure against misinformation on social media.

Future works can extend the ASSLSM to classify misinformation of other disaster and emergencies events in social media, by fine-tuning the constraints to better fit other datasets, as well as generalize the constraints to fit a wider variety of datasets, either on different topics or from different social media platforms.

Acknowledgements. This research has received funding from the European Union's Horizon 2020 research and innovation program under grant agreement No. 101021746, CORE (science and human factor for resilient society).

References

1. Elroy, O., Yosipof, A.: Analysis of COVID-19 5G conspiracy theory tweets using sentence-BERT embedding. In: Artificial Neural Networks and Machine Learning–ICANN 2022: 31st International Conference on Artificial Neural Networks, Bristol, UK, 6–9 September 2022, Proceedings, Part II, pp. 186–196 (2022)
2. Komendantova, N., et al.: A value-driven approach to addressing misinformation in social media. Human. Soc. Sci. Commun. **8**, 1–12 (2021)
3. Aschwanden, A., Demir, C., Hinselmann, R., Kasser, S., Rohrer, A.: Zika and travel: public health implications and communications for blood donors, sperm donors and pregnant women. Travel Med. Infectious Disease (2018)
4. Ortiz-Martínez, Y., Garcia-Robledo, J.E., Vásquez-Castañeda, D.L., Bonilla-Aldana, D.K., Rodriguez-Morales, A.J.: Can Google® trends predict COVID-19 incidence and help preparedness? the situation in Colombia. Travel Med. Infect. Dis. **37**, 101703 (2020)
5. Fallou, L., Corradini, M., Bossu, R., Cheny, J.-M.: Preventing and debunking earthquake misinformation: insights into EMSC's practices. Front. Commun. **7**, 287 (2022)
6. Fallou, L., Marti, M., Dallo, I., Corradini, M.: How to fight earthquake misinformation: a communication guide. Seismol. Res. Lett. **93**, 2418–2422 (2022)
7. Cochran, E.S., et al.: Research to improve ShakeAlert earthquake early warning products and their utility. US Geological Survey (2018)
8. Huang, Y.L., Starbird, K., Orand, M., Stanek, S.A., Pedersen, H.T.: Connected through crisis: Emotional proximity and the spread of misinformation online. In: Proceedings of the 18th ACM Conference on Computer Supported Cooperative Work and Social Computing, pp. 969–980 (2015)
9. Erokhin, D., Yosipof, A., Komendantova, N.: COVID-19 conspiracy theories discussion on Twitter. Social Media + Soc. **8**, 20563051221126051 (2022)
10. Elroy, O., Erokhin, D., Komendantova, N., Yosipof, A.: Mining the discussion of monkeypox misinformation on Twitter using RoBERTa. In: IFIP International Conference on Artificial Intelligence Applications and Innovations, pp. 429–438 (2023)
11. Yosipof, A., Senderowitz, H.: Optimization of molecular representativeness. J. Chem. Inf. Model. **54**, 1567–1577 (2014)
12. Batzdorfer, V., Steinmetz, H., Biella, M., Alizadeh, M.: Conspiracy theories on Twitter: emerging motifs and temporal dynamics during the COVID-19 pandemic. Int. J. Data Sci. Anal. pp. 1–19 (2021)
13. Darwish, O., et al.: Identifying fake news in the russian-ukrainian conflict using machine learning. In: Barolli, L. (eds.) Advanced Information Networking and Applications. AINA 2023. Lecture Notes in Networks and Systems, vol. 655. Springer, Cham (2023). https://doi.org/10.1007/978-3-031-28694-0_51
14. Devlin, J., Chang, M.-W., Lee, K., Toutanova, K.: Bert: pre-training of deep bidirectional transformers for language understanding. arXiv preprint arXiv:1810.04805 (2018)
15. Piskorski, J., Haneczok, J., Jacquet, G.: New benchmark corpus and models for fine-grained event classification: to BERT or not to BERT? In: Proceedings of the 28th International Conference on Computational Linguistics, pp. 6663–6678 (2020)
16. González-Carvajal, S., Garrido-Merchán, E.C.: Comparing BERT against traditional machine learning text classification. arXiv preprint arXiv:2005.13012 (2020)
17. Micallef, N., He, B., Kumar, S., Ahamad, M., Memon, N.: The role of the crowd in countering misinformation: a case study of the COVID-19 infodemic. In: 2020 IEEE International Conference on Big Data (Big Data), pp. 748–757 (2020)
18. Reimers, N., Gurevych, I.: Sentence-bert: sentence embeddings using siamese bert-networks. arXiv preprint arXiv:1908.10084 (2019)

19. Adoma, A.F., Henry, N.-M., Chen, W.: Comparative analyses of bert, roberta, distilbert, and xlnet for text-based emotion recognition. In: 2020 17th International Computer Conference on Wavelet Active Media Technology and Information Processing (ICCWAMTIP), pp. 117–121 (2020)

20. Naseer, M., Asvial, M., Sari, R.F.: An empirical comparison of bert, roberta, and electra for fact verification. In: 2021 International Conference on Artificial Intelligence in Information and Communication (ICAIIC), pp. 241–246 (2021)

21. Tarunesh, I., Aditya, S., Choudhury, M.: Trusting roberta over bert: insights from checklisting the natural language inference task. arXiv preprint arXiv:2107.07229 (2021)

22. Ouali, Y., Hudelot, C., Tami, M.: An overview of deep semi-supervised learning. arXiv preprint arXiv:2006.05278 (2020)

23. Beskow, D.M., Carley, K.M.: Bot-hunter: a tiered approach to detecting and characterizing automated activity on twitter. In: Conference paper. SBP-BRiMS: International Conference on Social Computing, Behavioral-Cultural Modeling and Prediction and Behavior Representation in Modeling and Simulation, vol. 3, p. 3 (2018)

24. ODonovan, J., Kang, B., Meyer, G., Höllerer, T., Adalii, S.: Credibility in context: an analysis of feature distributions in Twitter. In: 2012 International Conference on Privacy, Security, Risk and Trust and 2012 International Conference on Social Computing, pp. 293–301 (2012)

25. Gupta, A., Kumaraguru, P., Castillo, C., Meier, P.: Tweetcred: real-time credibility assessment of content on Twitter. In: International Conference on Social Informatics, pp. 228–243 (2014)

26. Balaanand, M., Karthikeyan, N., Karthik, S., Varatharajan, R., Manogaran, G., Sivaparthipan, C.: An enhanced graph-based semi-supervised learning algorithm to detect fake users on Twitter. J. Supercomput. 75, 6085–6105 (2019)

27. Jan, T.G., Khurana, S.S., Kumar, M.: Semi-supervised labeling: a proposed methodology for labeling the twitter datasets. Multimedia Tools Appl. 81, 7669–7683 (2022)

28. Yosipof, A., Woo, G., Komendantova, N.: Persistence of risk awareness: manchester arena bombing on 22 May 2017. Int. J. Disaster Risk Reduction 103805 (2023)

SkinDistilViT: Lightweight Vision Transformer for Skin Lesion Classification

Vlad-Constantin Lungu-Stan[1(✉)], Dumitru-Clementin Cercel[1],
and Florin Pop[1,2]

[1] Faculty of Automatic Control and Computers, University Politehnica of Bucharest,
Bucharest, Romania
vlad.lungu@stud.acs.upb.ro, {dumitru.cercel,florin.pop}@upb.ro
[2] National Institute for Research and Development in Informatics - ICI Bucharest,
Bucharest, Romania

Abstract. Skin cancer is a treatable disease if discovered early. We provide a production-specific solution to the skin cancer classification problem that matches human performance in melanoma identification by training a vision transformer on melanoma medical images annotated by experts. Since inference cost, both time and memory wise is important in practice, we employ knowledge distillation to obtain a model that retains 98.33% of the teacher's balanced multi-class accuracy, at a fraction of the cost. Memory-wise, our model is 49.60% smaller than the teacher. Time-wise, our solution is 69.25% faster on GPU and 97.96% faster on CPU. By adding classification heads at each level of the transformer and employing a cascading distillation process, we improve the balanced multi-class accuracy of the base model by 2.1%, while creating a range of models of various sizes but comparable performance. We provide the code at https://github.com/Longman-Stan/SkinDistilVit.

Keywords: Skin Lesion Diagnosis · Vision Transformer · Knowledge Distillation

1 Introduction

Skin cancer classification is a crucial problem because health complications can be avoided through early detection and treatment. Deep learning can shine here because both medics and machine learning solutions base their decision on the same information, namely medical images. Since this is important for all humankind, no matter the available computing power, this paper proposes a lightweight, production-ready algorithm that classifies eight types of skin lesions. The algorithm not only provides high performance, but it is also inexpensive to run.

Since 2017, the mechanism that has revolutionized natural language processing, attention [20], has shown its prowess for image processing with the vision transformer (ViT) [5]. We opt for an attention-based model because of its versatility and performance. However, a problem with the transformer [20] models is their size. Therefore, we use the knowledge distillation technique [8] to obtain great performance with a smaller model. We also compare the ViT to convolutional neural networks (CNNs) [10], the traditional solution for image processing tasks.

The difficulty of gathering medical data leads to small datasets being publicly available. Training transformers require huge amounts of data; thus, training one for our melanoma classification task requires extra consideration. Luckily, there are works that train transformer models with considerable data and whose weights are publicly available [22]. These models make transfer learning [15] possible, enabling the adoption of the ViT for our task.

By training a ViT-based solution for the skin lesion classification problem, we match human performance on melanoma identification and obtain a precision of 91.53% and a recall of 86.73% for cancer identification in skin lesion images. Through knowledge distillation, we boost the speed considerably (97.96%) while reducing the number of parameters almost by half (49.60%). We also study three ways of producing a series of models of increasing sizes: introducing classification heads after each layer, adding classification heads and forcing their probability distributions to match, and cascading distillation, a technique of gradually distilling away one transformer layer at a time. These techniques boost the base model's performance while creating a range of models that preserve the teacher's performance well.

The rest of this paper is organized as follows. In the next section, we present current approaches to our goals. Section 3 details our models, while Sect. 4 presents the experimental setup. Then, Sect. 5 describes our results. Lastly, Sect. 6 concludes the paper.

2 Related Work

EfficientNets. Image classification is traditionally solved using CNNs. One prominent set of CNN architectures is the EfficientNet [18]. This family of models is the result of a grid search that aims to produce efficient and easy-to-scale models. The authors obtained state-of-the-art (SOTA) performance while drastically reducing the models' size. EfficientNets are the go-to models for competitive image classification tasks on online platforms like Kaggle[1]. These reasons make EfficientNet a good baseline for our task.

ISIC 2019 Challenge. The International Skin Imaging Collaboration (ISIC)[2] is an initiative aimed at alleviating this problem and increasing the performance of melanoma detection systems. State of the art for the ISIC 2019 competition [1] is dominated by ensembles of EfficientNets. The first position [7] in the contest was obtained by an ensemble of EfficientNet-B0 to B6, while the second place [24] was obtained with an ensemble of EfficientNet-B3 to B4. While ensembles

---

[1] https://www.kaggle.com/, last visited March 2023.
[2] https://www.isic-archive.com, last visited March 2023.

are known to behave better than single models, their performance gain of several points is not outstanding, considering the additional computing resources needed for inference. We are interested in high-speed and memory needs, so ensembles are unattractive.

Knowledge Distillation. Since we aim for a practical approach, even a single model might be too big. One solution to tackle this problem is the technique called knowledge distillation. A noteworthy example of transformer distillation is DistilBERT [17], a distilled version of BERT [9]. DistilBERT is impressive because it maintains most of the parent's performance, 97%, while reducing the size by 40%. In the process, it also gains a 60% speed boost by eliminating half of the blocks, copying the weights of the rest, and using soft labels according to the probability distribution of the teacher.

Transformers , a family of attention-centric models, represent a milestone in the evolution of deep learning. Originally designed for text, they have over-taken recurrent neural networks [6] due to their superior context awareness [9]. Transformers have also shown themselves capable of handling images using the ViT by matching or exceeding SOTA performance [12]. The idea is to con-sider patches of 16×16 pixels, which are embedded into standard transformer encodings and treated like word embeddings. Since images are inherently two-dimensional, unlike text, special care is given to the positional encodings so that they relay correct information about the positioning of the patch in the image. We choose ViT because a good solution to our problem must localize the skin lesion and ignore the rest, which suits the attention mechanism perfectly.

3   Method

3.1   Vanilla SkinDistilViT

Teacher Model. To the best of our knowledge, there is no vanilla ViT trained for the ISIC 2019 challenge and with publicly available weights. Therefore, we train one ourselves. The ViT is one of the models supported by the Huggingface library [23], a popular open-source project for experimenting with and running transformer models. Although it is also available through the vanilla PyTorch[3], we opt for the Huggingface library version[4] to train our models because of its user-friendliness and training optimizations.

Training transformers from scratch without considerable data is a bad idea since their scale and attention mechanism make training unstable [16]. Since we have a fairly limited dataset, we rely on transfer learning from the existing ViT trained on ImageNet [4]. Because it is not a tiny dataset (25k images), we fine-tune all parts of the model and follow the standard training procedure, with the default hyperparameters provided by the framework.

---

[3] https://pytorch.org/, last visited March 2023.
[4] https://huggingface.co/google/vit-base-patch16-224, last visited March 2023.

Student Model. Since transformers are highly modular, we follow the example of DistilBERT and eliminate half of the encoder blocks to create the student model. Out of the 12 blocks of the original ViT, we keep only blocks 0, 2, 4, 7, 9, and 11. We perform this by altering the state dictionary of the bigger model. We keep all non-transformer block parameters. We solve the weight initialization problem by copying the weights of the selected transformer blocks of the teacher model. We also copy all the other trainable weights.

Loss Functions. Similar to DistilBERT, we use a mix of losses for fine-tuning our distilled model. Besides the original training objective, we use a cross-entropy loss between the teacher's and the student's outputs and a cosine loss between their hidden states. We also experiment with a mean square error (MSE) loss between the logits of the two networks. These losses are combined linearly to obtain the final loss, with their weights representing training hyperparameters.

3.2 Full Distillation

We are interested in providing models of different sizes and levels of performance. Therefore, we propose three techniques to obtain models ranging from a full configuration of twelve transformer blocks to models with only a few, even one. We call the process full distillation.

First, we study a ViT model that outputs a prediction for the class at every stage by adding an independent prediction head at each of them. We try two approaches. In the first case, we use the hidden states of each classification layer independently. We use the usual cross-entropy loss at every layer and combine them linearly. We call this **Full Classification ViT (FCViT)**. This approach injects gradient at each level and forces the model to find the best features for our task early. In the second case, we link the classification heads of each level by pushing the resulting probability distribution to match the one of the next level by employing a Kullback-Leibler divergence loss [11] while keeping the cross-entropy loss only for the topmost layer. We call this **Full Classification ViT with Probabilities (FCViTProbs)**. For convergence, we employ a multi-step training approach in which we train only the final classification head for M epochs, then add the classification heads one by one every N epochs, starting from the last but one downwards and finishing by fine-tuning the whole stack for another P epochs. This creates an implicit distillation process in the same model without separate training. Both solutions make an implicit stack of models that can be used standalone for classifying the result, all with a single training.

The second approach is to progressively distill the model, eliminating one transformer block at a time. The idea is to let the model concentrate the information as well as possible by eliminating minimal capacity, unlike SkinDistil-ViT's case, where we eliminate half the capacity from the start. We name this process **Cascading Distillation ViT**. The idea is similar to FCViTProbs, but we ensure that all the possible knowledge is kept from one layer to the next by forcing both the probability distribution matching and the correct task predictions. In this case, for a model with k layers, the teacher is the model with

$k + 1$ layers. For the full model, we use the full FCViT as a teacher but keep the same size. The subsequent students are initialized from the previous student by stripping it of the last transformer block. We do this for the whole stack until only one transformer layer is kept.

4   Experimental Setup

4.1   Dataset

The ISIC 2019 challenge proposed a hefty set of 33,569 high-quality dermoscopic images of skin lesions, classified into eight categories, as follows: Melanoma, Melanocytic nevus, Basal cell carcinoma, Actinic keratosis, Benign keratosis, Dermatofibroma, Vascular lesion, and Squamous cell carcinoma. This dataset is split into 25,331 annotated images (i.e., the training set) and 8,238 images without public annotations (i.e., the test set). The whole dataset is a combination of three corpora, namely BCN_20000 [3], HAM1000 [19], and MSK [2]. We use this dataset for training our models.

Since the official test set of ISIC 2019 is not available, we split the existing labeled data into 80% training and 20% test, taking class imbalance into account. The class imbalance problem is major, with the most populated class having more than ten thousand samples and the least populated one having only several hundred samples.

Data Augmentation. A downside of small datasets is that they do not provide sufficient variety. This can lead to models that have a hard time generalizing. Since no two melanoma are the same, this is a dangerous shortcoming. We address this problem by employing augmentation techniques. All images of the dataset have the lesion close to the center. To avoid this bias, we use random cropping but keep the target size large enough so that the lesion is still fully present. We also apply: (i) basic spatial transformations, like shift, scale, and rotate, and (ii) color augmentations, like RGB shift and randomly changing the brightness or contrast.

4.2   Compared Methods

CNN Models. We train two CNN baselines. For the first baseline, we choose the EfficientNet-B4 because it stands in the middle of the EfficinetNet-B0 to B7 family and is part of the ensembles of the top two best-performing solutions from the competition. For the second baseline, we train the EfficientNet-B6 because it has roughly the same number of parameters as our SkinDistilViT. We train the EfficientNets using Pytorch Lightning[5]. For fairness, we employ the same augmentations as ViT.

---

[5] https://www.pytorchlightning.ai/, last visited March 2023.

ViT. The official results of the ISIC 2019 challenge are incompatible with our experiments. On the one hand, they lack public labels, so we cannot compute our performance on them. On the other hand, we cannot submit our models to the competition because the official test set contains images from categories never seen at train time, which should be labeled as "unknown". This task is of no interest to our use case, so we omit it. Thus, we rely on training a baseline ViT ourselves.

SkinDistilViT. It is initialized by transferring the weights from the ViT model trained on our task. SkinDistilViT is trained with both the task loss and the cross-entropy loss, combined with weights 1 and 0.5, respectively. Unlike Distil-BERT, SkinDistilViT did not benefit from adding either the hidden cosine loss or the MSE logit loss; therefore, we omit those results for brevity.

SkinDistilViT Variants. We study the importance of weight initialization by training four versions of SkinDistilViT, all starting from the same architecture but with different initializations, as follows:

- DistiViT_fs -from scratch- has its parameters initialized randomly, so it does not benefit from pre-training.
- SkinDistilViT_fi -from ImageNet- has its parameters extracted from the original, pre-trained on ImageNet, ViT.
- SkinDistilViT_nt is an untrained version whose weights are just copied from its teacher.
- SkinDistilViT_t is a version trained only with the task loss.

4.3 Evaluation Metrics

Because of the inherent imbalance of the real data in medical scenarios, we resort to the balanced multi-class accuracy (BMA) as a metric for comparing results, as suggested in the ISIC 2019 challenge. We also employ the standard metrics for classification tasks, namely accuracy, precision, recall, and the F1-score, in their weighted form. We compute all these metrics using the official TorchMetrics implementation of PyTorch.

4.4 Implementation Details

We have done all experiments on a machine with an i5-13600K paired to a 3090 Ti with 32 GB RAM. All models are trained on the same training set, with the same augmentations, for 20 epochs. The batch size is 64 for all transformer models. The EfficientNets require more memory at training time, and therefore, we use a batch size of 32 for EfficientNet-B4 and 8 for EfficientNet-B6.

5 Results

5.1 Performance Comparisons

Table 1 depicts the comparison between the models. SkinDistilViT obtains great results, the best of all SkinDistilViT variants, proving the importance of teacher guidance. All fine-tuned SkinDistilViTs beat both CNNs in all metrics. The untrained SkinDistilViT does surprisingly well, too, considering many connections from its parent have been cut. We argue that this is due to the skip connections of the transformer block.

Table 1. Model performance comparison. The top part compares ViT to EfficientNets, while the bottom part compares SkinDistilViT variants. Bold indicates the best score for each metric, per comparison.

Model	BMA (%)	Accuracy (%)	Precision (%)	Recall (%)	F1-score (%)
EfficientNet-B4	27.64	71.60	67.95	71.62	67.80
EfficientNet-B6	31.51	81.62	86.25	81.62	82.21
ViT	**83.73**	**89.18**	**89.04**	**89.18**	**89.06**
SkinDistilViT_nt	42.00	66.60	64.25	66.60	64.24
SkinDistilViT_fs	39.88	66.79	63.67	66.79	64.03
SkinDistilViT_fi	80.23	86.68	86.49	86.68	86.51
SkinDistilViT_t	80.96	87.80	87.60	87.80	87.61
SkinDistilViT	**82.34**	**88.51**	**88.34**	**88.51**	**88.37**

The behavior of the ViTs in the case of imbalanced classes is interesting when compared to CNNs. While the CNNs are greatly affected by the imbalance, as seen in the BMA score, the ViTs seem unfazed. We suspect this stems from the filter-based nature of the CNNs, which makes them more reliant on the image's texture.

Since all images contain skin, they can get more easily confused. The better behavior of ViT can be explained by the attention mechanism, which only ensures the processing of the relevant part of the image. The attention mechanism in action can be observed in Fig. 1, where the model only pays attention to the skin lesion. The class imbalance problem, although alleviated, is still present because the BMA score is several points lower than all the others.

5.2 Full Distillation Results

We train the three full distillation experiments. The results of all three approaches can be observed in Table 2. FCViT and FCViTProbs are trained starting from the original ViT trained on ImageNet, just like our ViT baseline. For the cascading distillation process, we use as a teacher the best-performing

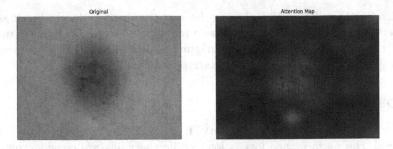

Fig. 1. Attention map visualization with BertViz [21]: original image without and with the attention map applied.

full model we had obtained that far, FCViTProbs, which has a BMA of 85.13% compared to the 83.73% BMA of the base ViT. We do not start from the same model because we are more interested in the loss of performance rather than actual numbers.

Table 2. Full distillation results in terms of BMA. Lx represents the classification layer we computed the result from. Bold indicates the best score for each line.

Last Layer	FCViT (%)	FCViTProbs (%)	Cascading Distillation ViT (%)	ViT (%)	SkinDistilViT (%)
L0	31.23	12.26	**42.86**	–	–
L1	50.42	13.69	**65.18**	–	–
L2	63.53	12.30	**75.71**	–	–
L3	74.19	17.70	**80.90**	–	–
L4	79.16	27.72	**81.75**	–	–
L5	82.27	40.52	**83.39**	–	82.34
L6	83.46	52.77	**84.33**	–	–
L7	84.27	61.26	**84.74**	–	–
L8	84.20	66.18	**85.16**	–	–
L9	84.57	73.70	**85.16**	–	–
L10	84.66	82.50	**85.54**	–	–
L11	84.68	85.13	**85.83**	83.73	–

Training everything on one go behaves well in the FCViT case. Thus, it is stable, and its performance is more than adequate. This approach matches the SkinDistilViT in terms of performance, without extra training and guidance from a teacher model, while surpassing the SkinDistilViT_t considerably. However, at lower dimensions, the performance greatly diminishes. Thus, the cascading distillation approach is more suitable for tiny models. The probability distribution matching ViT behaves rather badly, not managing to give good classifiers, especially at lower levels. However, the approach seems to help with training the network because the performance of the full model surpasses both the ViT and the FCViT, respectively.

Cascading Distillation ViT obtains the best results at all levels, but it shines in preserving the performance at a lower number of layers. All full-size models surpass the original ViT model. The original SkinDistilViT is still competitive, behaving slightly better than the similarly sized FCViT.

5.3 Distillation Trade-off

A trade-off analysis between SkinDistilViT and ViT can be observed in Table 3. In general, the performance loss is low, while the gains are considerable. The loss is greater in BMA's case, which indicates that the smaller model loses more nuances.

Regarding speed, we run the same scenario for both CPU and GPU. We measure the speed by dividing the number of test samples by the inference time of the model, ignoring batching and data loading. Interestingly, the speed gain on the CPU is larger. This is explainable by the differences in the design of the two processing units. Thus, GPUs are designed for matrix multiplications and deal with great deals of data in parallel, so the speed does not double. Instead, CPUs are more general, which translates into the expected double speed.

Table 3. Distillation trade-off.

	BMA (%)	Recall (%)	Speed CPU (it/s)	Speed GPU (it/s)	#Params (Millions)
ViT	83.73	89.10	10.79	206.31	85.85
SkinDistilViT	82.43	88.51	21.36	349.20	43.27
Gain	−1.57%	−0.60%	97.96%	69.25%	49.60%

Regarding the speed comparison between ViT and CNNs, EfficientNet-B6 has a speed of 64.67 items/second on GPU, while the similarly sized SkinDistilViT sits at 349.2 items/second, 5.4 times faster. Training the SkinDistilViT took 81 min for 20 epochs, while training the EfficientNet-B6 took 364 min for the same number of epochs, 4.49 times more. The convolution operation explains the difference because it uses the same parameters for many operations. This means the EfficientNet does more operations than the ViT for the same number of parameters, hence the lower speed.

A comparison of the expressiveness between the embeddings of the teacher and the student can be observed in Fig. 2. We use the t-distributed stochastic neighbor embedding (t-SNE) technique [13] to project the high-dimensional embedding provided by the ViT to a two-dimensional space. The teacher model separates the eight classes well, with clearly defined clusters, regardless of the class imbalance. The student model, albeit noisier, keeps the same performance.

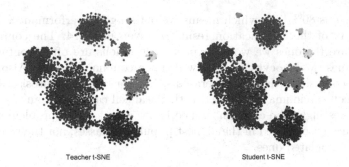

Teacher t-SNE   Student t-SNE

Fig. 2. Visualizations of two-dimensional t-SNE embeddings for the teacher (i.e., ViT) and student (i.e., SkinDistilViT) models. The student embeddings are noisier but keep the separation of the teacher classes well.

5.4   Cancer Detection Performance

Another performance metric is how well the model determines whether a lesion is cancer or not. This metric is not directly computed through the dataset. We compute it by separating the classes into cancer classes (i.e., Melanoma, Basal cell carcinoma, and Squamous cell carcinoma) and benign classes (i.e., Melanocytic nevus, Actinic keratosis, Benign keratosis, Dermatofibroma, and Vascular lesion). When analyzing the results based on this split, we obtain an accuracy of 92.8%, a precision of 91.53%, a recall of 86.73%, and an F1-score of 89.06%. The confusion matrix for this problem can be found in Fig. 3.

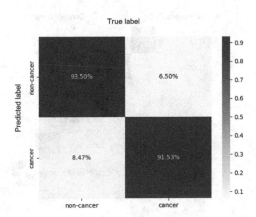

Fig. 3. The confusion matrix for our Cascading Distillation ViT on cancer versus non-cancer problem.

Our best-performing model classifies melanoma correctly in 80.64% of the cases. The human baseline for this operation, i.e., dermatologists with ten years of experience, is 80% [14], which means we obtain good performance. The confusion matrix of the classification results is given in Fig. 4. The confusions of our model are the ones we would expect. The lesions are often confused with common moles (Melanocytic nevus), which is a common mistake. Also, Actinic keratosis is confused with Benign keratosis, another type of keratosis. Moreover, Squamous cell carcinoma is confused with Basal cell carcinoma, another type of cancer. Interestingly, the class imbalance is not necessarily a problem since the top scores are not obtained in the highest populated classes, nor the worst scores in the least populated ones.

6   Conclusions and Future Work

In this work, we provided a model for the skin lesion classification that is lightweight, yet performant. The resulting distilled network is strong, keeping most of the performance while considerably increasing speed and decreasing memory consumption. Due to the attention mechanism, it has also proven superior to CNNs in terms of performance, especially considering class imbalance.

Careful weight initialization is critical to a good model. Training a distilled model from scratch provides worse results than simply copying weights from the bigger model. ImageNet initialization is good, but starting from the fine-tuned ViT is better. Teacher guidance completes the distillation by providing a good performance increase.

By forcing a consistency loss between layers and employing cascading distillation on top of the resulting model, we were able to boost the performance

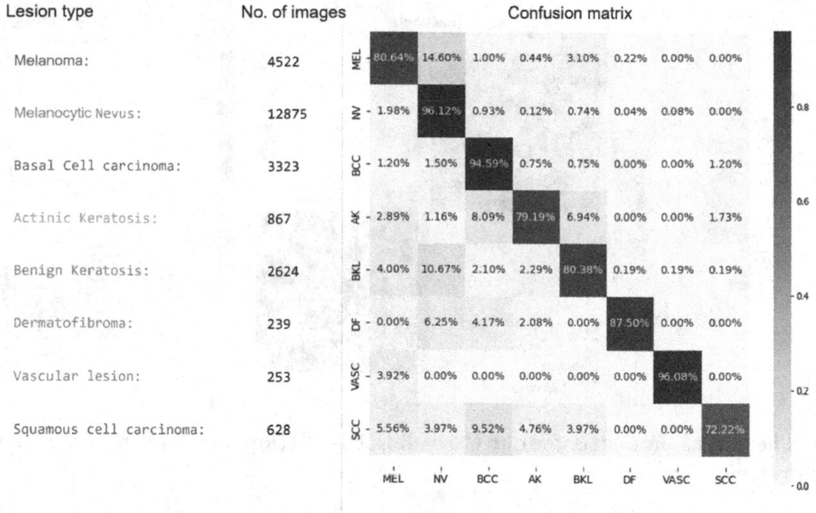

Fig. 4. The confusion matrix of the Cascading Distillation ViT (full size, 12 layers). Red represents malignant classes, green represents benign classes, and orange represents benign classes that can turn malignant. (Color figure online)

across all numbers of layers compared with the standard ViT and SkinDistilViT. Moreover, this technique creates a family of well-performing models of different sizes.

Last, our full-size models surpass the human baseline on melanoma identification and almost match it in the distilled form, while providing solid results for the skin cancer identification problem.

As future work, we propose combining the three full distillation techniques. We can add all the classification heads and train them as in FCViT but also force the probability distributions of their outputs to match, then apply the cascading distillation process. Another next step would be to study the impact of class imbalance. Although robust to it, SkinDistilViT might benefit from a balanced dataset.

Acknowledgments. This research has been funded by the University Politehnica of Bucharest through the PubArt program.

References

1. International skin imaging collaboration (ISIC) challenge 2019. https://github.com/rwightman/pytorch-image-models (2019)
2. Codella, N.C., et al.: Skin lesion analysis toward melanoma detection: a challenge at the 2017 international symposium on biomedical imaging (ISBI), hosted by the international skin imaging collaboration (ISIC). In: 2018 IEEE 15th International Symposium on Biomedical Imaging (ISBI 2018), pp. 168–172. IEEE (2018)
3. Combalia, M., et al.: BCN20000: dermoscopic lesions in the wild. arXiv preprint arXiv:1908.02288 (2019)
4. Deng, J., et al.: ImageNet: a large-scale hierarchical image database. In: 2009 IEEE Conference on Computer Vision and Pattern Recognition, pp. 248–255. IEEE (2009)
5. Dosovitskiy, A., et al.: An image is worth 16×16 words: Transformers for image recognition at scale. arXiv preprint arXiv:2010.11929 (2020)
6. Elman, J.L.: Distributed representations, simple recurrent networks, and grammatical structure. Mach. Learn. **7**, 195–225 (1991)
7. Gessert, N., Nielsen, M., Shaikh, M., Werner, R., Schlaefer, A.: Skin lesion classification using ensembles of multi-resolution EfficientNets with meta data. MethodsX **7**, 100864 (2020)
8. Hinton, G., Vinyals, O., Dean, J.: Distilling the knowledge in a neural network. Stat **1050**, 9 (2015)
9. Kenton, J.D.M.W.C., Toutanova, L.K.: Bert: pre-training of deep bidirectional transformers for language understanding. In: Proceedings of NAACL-HLT, pp. 4171–4186 (2019)
10. Kim, Y.: Convolutional neural networks for sentence classification. In: Proceedings of the 2014 Conference on Empirical Methods in Natural Language Processing (EMNLP), pp. 1746–1751. Association for Computational Linguistics, Doha, Qatar, October 2014
11. Kullback, S., Leibler, R.A.: On information and sufficiency. Ann. Math. Stat. **22**(1), 79–86 (1951)

12. Liu, Z., et al.: Swin transformer: Hierarchical vision transformer using shifted windows. In: Proceedings of the IEEE/CVF International Conference on Computer Vision, pp. 10012–10022 (2021)
13. van der Maaten, L., Hinton, G.E.: Visualizing data using t-SNE. J. Mach. Learn. Res. **9**, 2579–2605 (2008)
14. Morton, C., Mackie, R.: Clinical accuracy of the diagnosis of cutaneous malignant melanoma. Br. J. Dermatol. **138**(2), 283–287 (1998)
15. Pan, S.J., Yang, Q.: A survey on transfer learning. IEEE Trans. Knowl. Data Eng. **22**(10), 1345–1359 (2009)
16. Popel, M., Bojar, O.: Training tips for the transformer model. Prague Bull. Math. Linguist. **110**, 43–70 (2018)
17. Sanh, V., Debut, L., Chaumond, J., Wolf, T.: Distilbert, a distilled version of bert: smaller, faster, cheaper and lighter. arXiv preprint arXiv:1910.01108 (2019)
18. Tan, M., Le, Q.: EfficientNet: rethinking model scaling for convolutional neural networks. In: International Conference on Machine Learning, pp. 6105–6114. PMLR (2019)
19. Tschandl, P., Rosendahl, C., Kittler, H.: The ham10000 dataset, a large collection of multi-source dermatoscopic images of common pigmented skin lesions. Sci. Data **5**(1), 1–9 (2018)
20. Vaswani, A., et al.: Attention is all you need. In: Advances in Neural Information Processing Systems, vol. 30 (2017)
21. Vig, J.: A multiscale visualization of attention in the transformer model. In: Proceedings of the 57th Annual Meeting of the Association for Computational Linguistics: System Demonstrations, pp. 37–42 (2019)
22. Wightman, R.: PyTorch image models. https://github.com/rwightman/pytorch-image-models (2019). https://doi.org/10.5281/zenodo.4414861
23. Wolf, T., et al.: Transformers: state-of-the-art natural language processing. In: Proceedings of the 2020 Conference on Empirical Methods in Natural Language Processing: System Demonstrations, pp. 38–45 (2020)
24. Zhou, S., Zhuang, Y., Meng, R.: Multi-category skin lesion diagnosis using dermoscopy images and deep CNN ensembles. Technical Report, DysionAI (2019)

Sparse Block DETR: Precise and Speedy End-to-End Detector for PCB Defect Detection

JiXuan Hong[1], JingJing Xie[1], and ChenHui Yang[2]([✉])

[1] Department of Computer Science and Technology, Information College, Xiamen University, Fujian, China
[2] Information College, Xiamen University, Fujian, China
chyang@xmu.edu.cn

Abstract. The trade-off between high detection accuracy and fast detection speed is a major challenge for printed circuit board (PCB) defect detection. In this paper, a Sparse Block DETR method is proposed, which can achieve precise and speedy PCB defect detection. First, based on Deformable DETR, an object set reinforcement method is designed. This method trains a set map prediction module, extracts the feature of the target region, and adds the original encoder tokens to obtain the reinforcement encoder tokens, which significantly enhance the saliency of PCB defects. Second, an encoder queries sparsification method is designed, which trains an object centers prediction module, extracts object regions, and maps the object regions to reinforcement encoder tokens to form sparse block tokens, which are used as new input to the deformable encoder. Finally, the two proposed methods are combined for validation on the enhancement PCB dataset.

Keywords: Sparse Block Attention · Object Set Reinforcement · PCB Defect Detection

1 Introduction

With the rapid development of electronic technology and electronic manufacturing, electronic products are also becoming increasingly compact and lightweight. The quality of printed circuit board(PCB) plays a vital role in the stable operation of electronic products. Even minor PCB defects may potentially cause complete product failure. Therefore, PCB defect detection, including the detection of weld defects and component issues, is of utmost importance. This paper primarily focuses on six common defect types in weld defect detection in actual industrial scenarios: Missing Hole, Mouse Bite, Open Circuit, Short, Spur, Spurious Copper. See Fig. 1

Traditional machine vision inspection systems, such as Automatic Optical Inspection(AOI), use cameras to obtain PCB image data for analysis, which improves detection accuracy, reduces detection costs, and is more efficient than

L. Iliadis et al. (Eds.): ICANN 2023, LNCS 14254, pp. 281–292, 2023.
https://doi.org/10.1007/978-3-031-44207-0_24

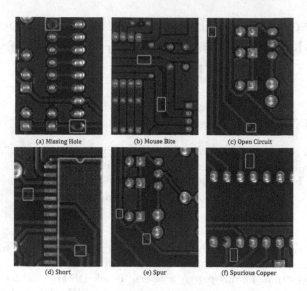

(a) Missing Hole   (b) Mouse Bite   (c) Open Circuit

(d) Short   (e) Spur   (f) Spurious Copper

Fig. 1. Six types of defects of PCB

manual inspection methods. However, their false detection rate and missed detection rate are still high, making them unable to meet industrial requirements. In addition, the detection effect is easily affected by factors including lighting conditions, occlusion, angle changes, etc. during image acquisition. At the same time, conventional detection algorithms [3,13,19] generally have problems such as poor anti-interference performance, time-consuming calculation, and poor real-time detection ability.

In recent years, deep learning plays an increasingly significant role in object detection, and a variety of object detection algorithms have been proposed. At present, the mainstream algorithms can be divided into two categories: two-stage method and single-stage method. The two-stage object detectors put forward proposals first, and then predict boxes w.r.t. proposals. While this type of detector has relatively high veracity, its real-time performance is not up to par. Typical algorithms include R-CNN [8], SPP-Net [9], Fast R-CNN [7], FaserR-CNN [21], etc. The single-stage detectors proposes anchors [15] and then performs classification and refinement, which greatly improves the inference speed. Typical algorithms include SSD [17], RetinaNet [14], YOLO [20], etc. However, these algorithms require non-maximum suppression (NMS) post-processing of near-repeated predictions, and the final performance of these algorithms heavily depends on the exact way these initial guesses are set.

To eliminate the hand-crafted process of previous algorithms, a fully end-to-end detector DETR [4] that uses a set-based predictive approach to eliminate the need for NMS post-processing is proposed. This algorithm uses the Hungarian algorithm for object classification and regression with favorable performance. However, due to the characteristics of small and low contrast of PCB defects, the accuracy and inference speed of DETR in PCB defect detection cannot achieve satisfactory results. To solve this problem, Deformable DETR [26] inspired by the deformable convolution [5] is proposed, which adds multi-scale features to better detect small targets. Meanwhile, the deformable attention mechanism sparsifies the attention modules in the DETR, reducing the quadratic complexity to linear complexity. Deformable DETR solves the problems of slow convergence and high complexity of DETR. However, adopting multi-scale features as encoder input will increase the number of encoder tokens to be processed by about 20 times, leading to the overall inference speed of the model extremely reduced.

In actual industrial scenarios, high detection accuracy and fast detection speed are required for PCB defect detection. Based on the insights mentioned above, we take Deformable DETR as baseline and propose a Sparse Block DETR method to achieve a balance of fast inference speed and high detection accuracy. The main contributions of this paper are summarized as follows:

- We design an object set reinforcement module to extract the feature regions that may include small targets for enhancement, making small objects more conspicuous in the process of computing attention.
- We put forward an encoder queries sparsification method to reduce the number of encoder tokens, further cut down the computational complexity and improve the inference speed of the model.
- We propose a sparse block attention mechanism to select encoder tokens, thinning out the attention span and avoiding mass meaningless attention calculations.

2   Method

As illustrated in Fig. 2, we put forward a precise and speedy end-to-end detector, called Sparse Block DETR, for PCB defect detection. Based on the baseline, two portions are mainly altered, one is object set reinforcement, and the other is encoder queries sparsification. Before describing the details, we review briefly Transformer [24], DETR [4] and Deformable DETR [26].

2.1   Review

Transformer. Transformer is a deep learning model based entirely on self-attention, which is suitable for parallel computing and could promote the speed of model training. It is widely used in the field of Natural Language Processing(NLP). Transformer is mainly composed of encoder and decoder, which specifically consists of self-attention and feedforward neural network(FFN). The input of self-attention is the embedding, and query Q, key K, and value V are obtained through embedding. The calculation of self-attention is as follows:

$$Attention(Q, K, V) = softmax(\frac{QK^T}{\sqrt{d_k}})V \tag{1}$$

where d_k represents the dimension of K, $softmax$ represents activation function.

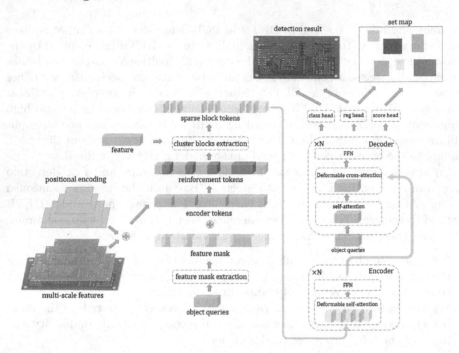

Fig. 2. Sparse Block DETR architecture

DETR. DETR has applied Transformer to the visual field with remarkable success. It extracts the input feature $x \in \mathbb{R}^{L \times D}$ from the Convolutional Neural Networks (CNN) backbone ResNet [10], and converts the input feature into the feature of the object queries through the standard Transformer [24] encoder-decoder framework, where L represents the number of encoder tokens and D represents the dimension of encoder tokens. The object queries are then processed by a 3-layer feedforward neural network(FFN), which is referred to as the regression head, and a linear projection, referred to as the classification head, to detect objects. Finally predict bounding boxes coordinate $b \in [0,1]^4$ and classification score $c \in [0,1]^C$, where C denotes the number of object classes.

Deformable DETR. Replacing dense attention with deformable attention ameliorates the convergence speed and reduces the computational complexity of the model by sparsifying encoder keys. Suppose there is a query collection and a key collection of the same size, denoted Φ_q and Φ_k respectively, $|\Phi_q| = |\Phi_k| = L$, for each pair $\{(q,k) : q \in \Phi_q, k \in \Phi_k\}$. The complexity of calculating attention weight A_{qk} using traditional dense attention is $O(L^2)$. The computational complexity of deformable attention is $O(LK)$, where K is the number of keys selected. $K \ll L$. At the same time, Deformable DETR adopts multi-scale features to extract multi-layer input features from the backbone, and converts these features into the same dimension through convolution. Then concatenate the features as encoder tokens, which can significantly elevate the accuracy of small targets. However, the citation of multi-scale features increases the number of encoder tokens while elevating the model performance, resulting in a greatly increased overall computational complexity of the model.

2.2 Object Set Reinforcement

Since PCB defects, such as Open Circuit and Short, are extremely small, the model is prone to feature disappearance when using the down-sampling operations to extract features, resulting in low accuracy of defect detection. To address the challenge of the low accuracy of small object detection, this section designs an object set reinforcement module, inspired by QueryDet [25], to strengthen the saliency of target features.

First, with the object queries as the input, the target region and confidence of each target region is predicted through the set map prediction module. In this way we acquire object set map, which includes the target region coordinate $\hat{b} \in [0,1]^4$ and the confidence $\hat{c} \in \{0,1\}$ of each target region. Subsequently, the object set map is mapped into multi-scale features, the top $\lambda\%$ confidence are assigned a value of 1, and the rest are assigned a value of 0 to form a feature mask. The feature mask extraction module is shown in Fig. 3. Add the obtained feature mask to the original encoder tokens to produce reinforcement tokens. Secondly,

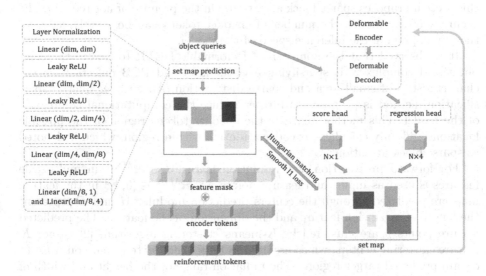

Fig. 3. Feature Mask Extraction. Each box of set map in the figure represents a prediction target region, the color of the box represents the confidence level of the region, and N represents the length of the object queries. The parameters in parentheses of the linear layer are the input and output dimensions of the layer

a score head is added after the model decoder, which predicts the confidence of the decoder object set. The score head is trained using FocalLoss [15]. The decoder object set map is obtained by combining the score head and regression head. The decoder object set map includes the target region coordinate $b \in [0,1]^4$ and the confidence $c \in \{0,1\}$ of each target region. The predicted object set map is updated by using the decoder object set map as the pseudo ground-truth.

Finally, the set map prediction module consists of two parts: target region confidence prediction and target region prediction. Each prediction module consists of five linear layers and a Layer Normalization [1], except for the last linear layer, all of the other layers are followed by a Leaky ReLU [18] activation layer. Set map prediction module is trained by minimizing the SmoothL1 loss [7] between b and $\hat{b}$, and also minimizing the SmoothL1 loss between c and $\hat{c}$ after matching each region by Hungarian algorithm [12].

2.3   Encoder Queries Sparsification

Due to the relatively high real-time requirement of PCB defect detection in the industry, Deformable DETR far exceeds DETR in detection accuracy, but Deformable DETR uses multi-scale features, the number of encoder tokens has increased significantly, leading to the reduction of model inference speed. In order to solve this problem, Roh et al. proposed Sparse DETR [22], which uses decoder cross-attention map predictor to sparsify encoder tokens. Building on this work, this section proposes sparse block attention. On the premise of not reducing the accuracy of the model, the number of encoder tokens can be greatly reduced, thereby improving the inference speed of the model.

It is observed that the approach of Deformable DETR to reduce the computational complexity is sparsifying encoder keys and PCB defects have the characteristics of small area and sparse distribution. An encoder queries sparsification method is proposed to further reduce the computational complexity of the model. This method extracts the encoder tokens region of the possible locations and only calculates encoder attention within region, which is denoted as sparse block attention.

For forward propagation, low resolution feature $l \in \mathbb{R}^{M \times D}$ in multi-scale features is used as input, and feature points $\hat{p} \in \mathbb{R}^{M \times 2} \in [0,1]^2$ in the feature map are predicted through the centers prediction module. M and D represent the length of expansion feature and the dimension of the feature. The predicted feature points $\hat{p}$ are clustered by K-means clustering algorithm [2] to get K feature clustering centers, which are used as target centers to radiate outward to obtain predicted target regions. The radiation range of the height and width of the target region is one tenth of the original feature height and width respectively. The extraction process of cluster blocks is shown in Fig. 4. Extract and integrate target regions corresponding to center coordinates $\hat{p}$ in encoder tokens to form encoder sparse block tokens, which are used as new encoder tokens for deformable encoder and decoder operations. If $K = 10$, the number of encoder sparse block tokens is 10% of the original encoder tokens.

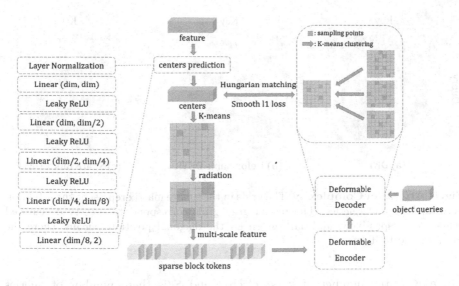

Fig. 4. Cluster Blocks Extraction. The parameters in parentheses of the linear layer are the input and output dimensions of the layer

For backpropagation, after the deformable decoder, the sampling points corresponding to each encoder token will be obtained. All sampling points are clustered by K-means to obtain K sampling points clustering centers $p \in \mathbb{R}^{K \times 2} \in [0,1]^2$, which are used as the pseudo ground-truth of the feature points $\hat{p}$. The Hungarian algorithm for binary matching is used to match the sampling points clustering centers p and the predicted feature points $\hat{p}$. Centers prediction module is trained by minimizing the SmoothL1 loss [7] between p and $\hat{p}$. Among them, the centers prediction module is composed of a Layer Normalization and five linear layers. All but the last layer, all the other linear layers are followed by a Leaky RELU activation.

2.4 Attention Complexity

Suppose there is the same size of a collection of a query and a collection of key, denoted Φ_q and Φ_k respectively, $|\Phi_q| = |\Phi_k| = L$, for each pair (q,k) : $q \in \Phi_q, k \in \Phi_k$, calculating attention weight A_{qk} complexity. *Dense*, *Deform* and *Sparse_Block* respectively represent the attention weights of traditional dense attention, deformable attention and sparse block attention proposed in this paper. The computational complexity of attention weight A_{qk} for different types of attention is as follows.

$$O(Dense) = O(L^2) \qquad (2)$$

$$O(Deform) = O(LK) \qquad (3)$$

$$O(Sparse\_Block) = O(SK) \qquad (4)$$

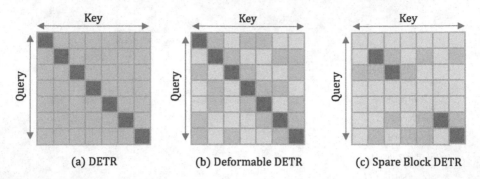

Fig. 5. Attention Complexity. The grids in the square matrix represent the attention between keys and queries. The reseda/gray grids correspond to preserved/removed connection respectively, and dark green on the diagonal positions means where the token attend to itself

where K is the number of keys selected and S is there number of queries selected. $K \ll L$, $S \ll L$, thus $O(Sparse\_Block) \ll O(Deform) \ll O(Dense)$. Deformable DETR reduces the attention complexity through encoder keys sparsification, and we further reduce the attention complexity through encoder queries sparsification, as shown in Fig. 5.

3 Experiments

3.1 Datasets and Implementation Details

Datasets. The dataset [23] comes from the public dataset provided by the Open Laboratory of Intelligent Robots at Peking University. The dataset has a total of 693 images, including six common types of defects: Missing Hole, Mouse bite, Open Circuit, Short, Spur, and Spurious Copper.

In this experiment, the dataset is made into the standard COCO [16] dataset format, but the amount of data in the original dataset is relatively few, which easily leads to the occurrence of overfitting during the training process. Therefore, the offline data enhancement method is adopted to increase the richness and diversity of the dataset. That includes cropping, rotating the image, adjusting the contrast etc. Increase the total number of images in the dataset to 6930, denoted PCB enhancement dataset. In the experiment, 90% of the images are randomly used as the training set and the remaining 10% as the test set.

Implementation Details. We implement our approach based on the PyTorch platform. All models are trained on 2 GTX 1080 Ti GPUs. ImageNet[6] pre-trained ResNet-50 [10] is utilized as backbone. Following Deformable DETR, we train our model using Adam optimize r[11] with base learning rate of 0.0002, $\beta_1 = 0.9$, $\beta_2 = 0.999$, and weight decay of 0.0001. We train Sparse Block DETR with a total batch size of 2, for 50 epochs, where the learning rate is decayed at the 40th by a factor of 0.1. As for the object set reinforcement module, the loss coefficient of SmoothL1 loss and FocalLoss added by us both are 1. As for the centers prediction module, the loss coefficient of SmoothL1 loss is 2. The negative slope of the Leaky RELU activation is 0.1. We use other same hyperparameters as in Deformable DETR.

3.2 Comparison Studies

As shown in Table. 1, we compare Sparse Block DETR with Faster R-CNN [21], RetinaNet [14], DETR [4] and Deformable DETR [26]. To ensure the reliability of the experiments, all methods are trained and tested on the PCB enhancement dataset with the same configuration. In Sparse Block DETR, encoder tokens are sparsified with cluster centers of 10, 20, 30, and 40 categories, using the cluster blocks extraction method. The $\lambda\%$ of the object set reinforcement module in all Sparse Block DETR is 30%. We demonstrate detection performance average precision(AP) and inference speed frames per second(FPS) on the PCB enhancement dataset.

Table 1. Comparison of different methods on PCB enhancement test set. K represents the clustering category using K-means clustering, and Ψ represents the ratio of sparse encoder queries to original encoder queries

Method	Epochs	K	Ψ	AP	AP_{50}	AP_{75}	AP_S	AP_M	AP_L	FPS
Faster-RCNN	100	-	-	30.8	78.7	14.7	15.0	30.9	32.6	26
RetinaNet	100	-	-	32.3	80.3	15.2	16.8	32.1	33.6	22
DETR	300	-	-	20.8	64.2	7.1	2.3	20.8	24.6	28
Deformable DETR	50	-	-	38.7	90.3	20.2	18.8	39.3	32.3	19
Sparse Block DETR	50	10	10%	37.0	89.6	17.4	10.0	36.3	32.8	**25**
	50	20	20%	40.8	91.1	20.7	20.0	38.5	30.4	23
	50	30	30%	**55.1**	**97.3**	**56.2**	**25.1**	**54.8**	**50.7**	22
	50	40	40%	52.6	96.8	49.9	23.3	52.1	49.3	20

The experimental results show that the proposed method achieves the highest detection accuracy when the encoder queries only account for 30% of the original one. Compared with Deformable DETR, AP and AP_S increase by 16.4 and 6.3 respectively, and FPS increase by 15.8%.

3.3 Ablation Studies

As shown in Table 2, ablation studies are conducted on the PCB enhancement dataset to analyze how each component affected the accuracy and speed of detection. All the ablation experiments are conducted under the condition that the number of clustering categories is 30. Besides, the hyper-parameters keep consistent.

Table 2. Ablation studies for Sparse Block DETR on PCB enhancement test set. OSR indicates object set reforcement module, and EQS indicates encoder queries sparsification module. $\lambda\%$ indicates the percentage of object set map selected

baseline	OSR	EQS	$\lambda\%$	AP	AP_{50}	AP_{75}	AP_S	AP_M	AP_L	FPS
✓			-	38.7	90.3	20.2	18.8	39.3	32.3	19
✓	✓		10%	43.3	94.8	28.9	16.9	40.9	38.3	18
✓	✓		20%	45.9	95.4	33.3	20.4	46.5	43.6	18
✓	✓		30%	52.6	96.8	49.9	23.3	52.1	49.3	18
✓	✓		40%	42.1	92.9	27.9	25.0	42.6	37.1	18
✓		✓	-	46.8	92.6	30.3	7.1	46.5	49.1	**23**
✓	✓	✓	30%	**55.1**	**97.3**	**56.2**	**25.1**	**54.8**	**50.7**	22

When the OSR module whose $\lambda\%$ is 30% is added separately, AP and AP_S increase by 13.9 and 4.5 respectively. When the EQS module whose K is 30 is added separately, AP and AP_{75} increase by 8.1 and 10.1 respectively, simultaneously FPS increase by 21.1%. Obviously, each module significantly contributes to the predicted objects, which confirmed the effectiveness of each proposed component.

4   Conclusion

On the one hand, we propose an encoder queries sparsification method to reduce the computational cost of the encoder, which promotes the inference speed of the model without sacrificing the accuracy. On the other hand, we propose an object set reinforcement method, which can effectively alleviate the phenomenon of feature disappearance in the downsampling operation of small targets, and effectively improve the detection accuracy of the model. Experiments show that the combination of these two methods achieves state-of-the-art performance.

References

1. Ba, L.J., Kiros, J.R., Hinton, G.E.: Layer normalization. CoRR abs/1607.06450 (2016)
2. Bock, H.H.: Clustering methods: a history of k-means algorithms. Selected Contrib. Data Anal. Classif. 161–172 (2007). https://doi.org/10.1007/978-3-540-73560-1_15
3. Bonello, D.K., Iano, Y., Neto, U.B.: A new based image subtraction algorithm for bare PCB defect detection. Int. J. Multimed. Image Process. **8**(3), 438–442 (2018)
4. Carion, N., Massa, F., Synnaeve, G., Usunier, N., Kirillov, A., Zagoruyko, S.: End-to-end object detection with transformers. In: Vedaldi, A., Bischof, H., Brox, T., Frahm, J.-M. (eds.) ECCV 2020. LNCS, vol. 12346, pp. 213–229. Springer, Cham (2020). https://doi.org/10.1007/978-3-030-58452-8_13
5. Dai, J., et al.: Deformable convolutional networks. In: IEEE International Conference on Computer Vision, ICCV 2017, Venice, Italy, October 22–29, 2017, pp. 764–773. IEEE Computer Society (2017). http://orcid.org/10.1109/ICCV.2017.89

6. Deng, J., Dong, W., Socher, R., Li, L., Li, K., Fei-Fei, L.: Imagenet: a large-scale hierarchical image database. In: 2009 IEEE Computer Society Conference on Computer Vision and Pattern Recognition (CVPR 2009), 20–25 June 2009, Miami, Florida, USA, pp. 248–255. IEEE Computer Society (2009). http://orcid.org/10.1109/CVPR.2009.5206848

7. Girshick, R.: Fast r-CNN. In: 2015 IEEE International Conference on Computer Vision (ICCV), pp. 1440–1448 (2015). http://orcid.org/10.1109/ICCV.2015.169

8. Girshick, R., Donahue, J., Darrell, T., Malik, J.: Rich feature hierarchies for accurate object detection and semantic segmentation. In: 2014 IEEE Conference on Computer Vision and Pattern Recognition, pp. 580–587 (2014). http://orcid.org/10.1109/CVPR.2014.81

9. He, K., Zhang, X., Ren, S., Sun, J.: Spatial pyramid pooling in deep convolutional networks for visual recognition. IEEE Trans. Pattern Anal. Mach. Intell. **37**(9), 1904–1916 (2015). http://orcid.org/10.1109/TPAMI.2015.2389824

10. He, K., Zhang, X., Ren, S., Sun, J.: Deep residual learning for image recognition. In: 2016 IEEE Conference on Computer Vision and Pattern Recognition, CVPR 2016, Las Vegas, NV, USA, June 27–30, 2016, pp. 770–778. IEEE Computer Society (2016). http://orcid.org/10.1109/CVPR.2016.90

11. Kingma, D.P., Ba, J.: Adam: A method for stochastic optimization. In: Bengio, Y., LeCun, Y. (eds.) 3rd International Conference on Learning Representations, ICLR 2015, San Diego, CA, USA, May 7–9, 2015, Conference Track Proceedings (2015)

12. Kuhn, H.W.: The hungarian method for the assignment problem. In: Jünger, M., (eds.) 50 Years of Integer Programming 1958-2008 - From the Early Years to the State-of-the-Art, pp. 29–47. Springer (2010)

13. Kumar, M., Singh, N.K., Kumar, M., kumar Vishwakarma, A.: A novel approach of standard data base generation for defect detection in bare PCB. In: International Conference on Computing, Communication & Automation, pp. 11–15. IEEE (2015)

14. Lin, T.Y., Goyal, P., Girshick, R., He, K., Dollár, P.: Focal loss for dense object detection. In: Proceedings of the IEEE International Conference On Computer Vision, pp. 2980–2988 (2017)

15. Lin, T., Goyal, P., Girshick, R.B., He, K., Dollár, P.: Focal loss for dense object detection. In: IEEE International Conference on Computer Vision, ICCV 2017, Venice, Italy, October 22–29, 2017, pp. 2999–3007. IEEE Computer Society (2017). http://orcid.org/10.1109/ICCV.2017.324

16. Lin, T.-Y., et al.: Microsoft COCO: common objects in context. In: Fleet, D., Pajdla, T., Schiele, B., Tuytelaars, T. (eds.) ECCV 2014. LNCS, vol. 8693, pp. 740–755. Springer, Cham (2014). https://doi.org/10.1007/978-3-319-10602-1_48

17. Liu, W., et al.: SSD: single shot multibox detector. In: Leibe, B., Matas, J., Sebe, N., Welling, M. (eds.) ECCV 2016. LNCS, vol. 9905, pp. 21–37. Springer, Cham (2016). https://doi.org/10.1007/978-3-319-46448-0_2

18. Maas, A.L., Hannun, A.Y., Ng, A.Y., et al.: Rectifier nonlinearities improve neural network acoustic models. In: Proceedings of ICML. vol. 30, p. 3. Atlanta, Georgia, USA (2013)

19. Raj, A., Sajeena, A.: Defects detection in PCB using image processing for industrial applications. In: 2018 Second International Conference on Inventive Communication and Computational Technologies (ICICCT), pp. 1077–1079. IEEE (2018)

20. Redmon, J., Divvala, S., Girshick, R., Farhadi, A.: You only look once: Unified, real-time object detection. In: Proceedings of the IEEE Conference On Computer Vision And Pattern Recognition, pp. 779–788 (2016)

21. Ren, S., He, K., Girshick, R., Sun, J.: Faster r-CNN: Towards real-time object detection with region proposal networks. IEEE Trans. Pattern Anal. Mach. Intell. **39**(6), 1137–1149 (2017). http://orcid.org/10.1109/TPAMI.2016.2577031
22. Roh, B., Shin, J., Shin, W., Kim, S.: Sparse DETR: efficient end-to-end object detection with learnable sparsity. In: The Tenth International Conference on Learning Representations, ICLR 2022, Virtual Event, April 25–29, 2022. OpenReview.net (2022)
23. Unicersity, P.: PCB defect dataset. www.robotics.pkusz.edu.cn/resources/dataset/
24. Vaswani, A., et al.: Attention is all you need. In: Guyon, I., (eds.) Advances in Neural Information Processing Systems 30: Annual Conference on Neural Information Processing Systems 2017, December 4–9, 2017, Long Beach, CA, USA, pp. 5998–6008 (2017),
25. Yang, C., Huang, Z., Wang, N.: Querydet: Cascaded sparse query for accelerating high-resolution small object detection. In: IEEE/CVF Conference on Computer Vision and Pattern Recognition, CVPR 2022, New Orleans, LA, USA, June 18–24, 2022, pp. 13658–13667. IEEE (2022). http://orcid.org/10.1109/CVPR52688.2022.01330
26. Zhu, X., Su, W., Lu, L., Li, B., Wang, X., Dai, J.: Deformable DETR: deformable transformers for end-to-end object detection. In: 9th International Conference on Learning Representations, ICLR 2021, Virtual Event, Austria, May 3–7, 2021. OpenReview.net (2021),

SWP:A Sliding Window Prompt for Emotion Recognition in Conversation

Hanlin Zhao[1], Yan Chen[1], Jiajian Xie[1], and Kangshun Li[2(✉)]

[1] College of Mathematics and Informatics, South China Agricultural University, Guangzhou, China
[2] School of Artificial Intelligence, Dongguan City University, Dongguan, China
likangshun@sina.com

Abstract. Emotion Recognition in Conversation(ERC), also referred to as sentiment mining in dialogues, aims at analyzing the speaker's state and recognizing their emotions during conversation. The study of emotion recognition has attracted increasing interest in recent years due to its wide range of applications, such as customer service analysis, medical consulting, and intelligent robot conversations. However, the weak correlation between emotion and semantics has posed several challenges to emotion recognition in dialogues. Even for semantically similar utterances, their emotions may differ greatly because of contextual or speaker differences. To address this, we propose a new method for recognizing emotions in dialogues called adjustable sliding chat window context modeling, which uses prompt learning templates to focus on the speaker's emotional changes. Moreover, we introduce curriculum learning technique in the training stage to alleviate the impact of extreme samples on the training process. We achieved state-of-the-art performance on three widely used public datasets. To demonstrate the effectiveness of our proposed curriculum learning strategy and adversarial training, we conducted an ablation study.

Keywords: Context Modeling · Prompt Learning · Curriculum Learning

1 Introduction

With the development of online social networks, emotion recognition in conversation has received increasing attention from the research community. It is extremely important in many social network scenarios, such as sentiment mining on WeChat chat records, Weibo public opinion analysis, and medical healthcare applications on social media. The purpose of dialogue emotion recognition task is to identify different emotions based on the content in each turn of the conversation. A dialogue usually involves several speakers and several rounds, so the

This work is supported by the Key Field Special Project of Guangdong Provincial Department of Education with No.2021ZDZX1029.

speaker's emotions may vary greatly during the conversation. Unlike traditional text classification tasks, understanding the speaker's emotions requires not only one turn of text dialogue, but also contextual information. Figure 1 shows an example of ERC.

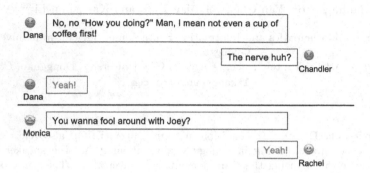

Fig. 1. Examples of emotion recognition in conversation. The same utterance "Yeah!" can express different emotions in different contexts

ERC is a completely different task from traditional text classification tasks, posing new challenges for researchers, with three issues worth solving:

(1) In ERC, similar utterances within a dialogue may express different meanings depending on the context. Therefore, it is significant to explore contextual cues to optimize emotion recognition tasks.

(2) To guide pre-trained models using prompt learning, a manual template is required. However, each template varies significantly in performance, and finding the optimal one is expensive. Hence, developing a robust and quickly implementable suite of prompt learning templates is critical to effectively guide pre-trained models for emotion recognition.

(3) Dialogue emotion recognition datasets commonly include multiple modalities. However, some text data in these dialogues may not provide enough information to distinguish emotions. Training a text-based emotion recognition model using these high difficulty samples can result in reduced performance.

Regarding the first issue, we developed a sliding chat window module that models context and speaker information to effectively capture the appropriate cues for emotion recognition. The size of the chat window can be adjusted according to different datasets as they may require different amounts of contextual information. For the second issue, we created a set of prompt templates that randomly generate examples to improve the robustness of template learning. To mitigate the decrease in performance caused by extreme samples, we used a curriculum learning strategy [1] by creating a distance-based difficulty measurement function and training scheduler to sort the training data and schedule model learning. Experimental findings support the efficacy of our proposed curriculum learning strategy. The main contributions of this paper are summarized as follows:

- We designed a sliding chat window to model contexts that include both the speaker's information and background information so that the conversation's context information can be fully utilized.

- We designed a set of multi-prompt learning training strategies to quickly integrate prompts, which can use the complementary advantages of different prompts and reduce the cost of prompt design. Because choosing the best-performing prompt is challenging, stabilizing the downstream task's performance allows the PLM to pay more attention to the speaker's emotional changes in a specified context.

- We introduced curriculum learning and designed a difficulty measure function based on inter-class distance and a training scheduling strategy based on probability distribution. According to curriculum learning, the training dataset can be sorted by the difficulty scores, allowing the PLM to learn from easy to hard.

- We achieved state-of-the-art results on three widely used multi-modal public datasets using text features. The experimental results further demonstrate the effectiveness of our proposed multi-prompt learning and curriculum learning strategies.

2   Related Work

Most previous dialogue emotion recognition models were achieved by encoding the dialogue text into semantic embeddings, and then treating each round of dialogue as a step or node. Then they use recurrent neural networks [11] or graph neural networks [6] to obtain the corpus representation for final emotion prediction. The dialogue text encoders in earlier models included Glove [14] and Word2Vec [12]. In recent years, inspired by pre-trained language models' (PLM) ability to encode text semantic aspects, pre-trained models have also been used as encoders to achieve higher recognition performance [16]. Although some achievements have been made, previous PLM-based ERC models have rarely made full use of the potential knowledge of PLM, resulting in limited performance improvements. Recently, some researchers have proposed prompt-based learning paradigms to use PLM in various downstream NLP tasks: designing appropriate prompts to guide PLM to better use knowledge related to downstream tasks. As a result, PLM's performance on downstream tasks has been improved. Inspired by the rich semantic and emotional knowledge related to utterances in human dialogues contained in PLM during the pre-trained phase, we use prompts about this knowledge to guide PLM to perform emotion recognition tasks. However, applying prompt-based learning paradigm on pre-trained models to implement ERC is still challenging.

3   Methodology

3.1   Task Definition

The goal of emotion recognition in conversation is to identify the emotion in each sentence of a dialogue from several predefined emotions **E** based on the dialogue records and information on each speaker. Specifically, an input sequence of **N** utterances is given as $[(u_1, s_1),(u_2, s_2),(u_3, s_1)...,(u_N, s_M)]$, where $s_i \in S$ is the speaker in utterance i, **M** denotes the total number of speakers, and $u_i \in U$ represents the utterance in the i_{th} turn. The objective is to predict the emotion label $e_i \in E$ for each utterance u_i.

3.2   Context Modeling

We developed a prompt-based scenario encoder that employs the BERT pre-trained model [4] to represent emotions, capturing both contextual information and speaker information. The architecture of the scenario encoder is depicted in Fig. 2. We computed the representation of u_t by incorporating the most recent **k** rounds of dialogue as background information, with **k** being variable window size.

$$C_t = [(u_{t-k/2}, s_{t-k/2}), .., (u_t, s_t), .., (u_{t+k/2}, s_{t+k/2})] \tag{1}$$

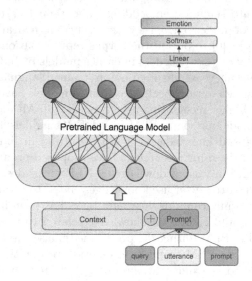

Fig. 2. The architecture of our proposed scenario encoder

Kim and Vossen [8] pointed out that pre-trained language models have difficulty distinguishing between "context" represented by C_t and the target utterance (i.e., (s_t, u_t)). Inspired by prompt learning, and taking into account the difficulty of selecting the best-performing prompts during prompt learning, and the significant differences in the performance of different templates, we have constructed a set of Multi-Prompt, a rapid integration of multiple prompts at the t_{th} turn, as shown below:

$$query = random[query_1, query_2, ..., query_n] \tag{2}$$

$$prompt = random[prompt_1, prompt_2, ..., prompt_n] \tag{3}$$

$$P_t = query + u_t, s_t + prompt \tag{4}$$

3.3 Prompt Ensembling

Prompt ensembling is a technique used to predict inputs during reasoning that have not received responses by using multiple prompts, whether discrete or continuous. This type of integration can leverage the complementary advantages of different prompts, reduce the cost of prompt design, and stabilize the performance of downstream tasks. Figure 3 shows the architecture of the discrete prompts used in this study.

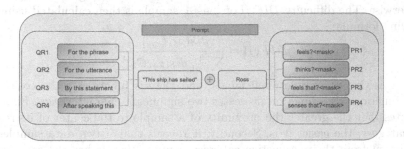

Fig. 3. The architecture of our proposed scenario encoder

In this paper, we constructed the query and prompt sets separately. By randomly extracting queries and prompts from the set, we concatenate them with the emotion recognition statements to create Prompt.

3.4 Curriculum Learning

Curriculum learning (CL) has become increasingly popular in recent years. Bengio [1] first proposed the concept of CL, which advocates that models start learning from easy samples and gradually advance to complex samples and knowledge, mimicking the process of human learning. The CL strategy has demonstrated powerful ability in improving the generalization ability and convergence rate of models in various scenarios, such as computer vision and natural language processing. The focus of CL is that it requires appropriate difficulty measure function and training schedulers, which are usually determined based on prior knowledge of human experts.

Multi-modal collection is the usual way of gathering existing ERC datasets. The lack of adequate emotional information can affect the effectiveness of a purely text-based ERC model during development. Including these extreme data points during training can noticeably decrease performance. This paper aims to utilize curriculum learning as a solution to this issue.

Difficulty Measure Function. We have incorporated a difficulty measurement function based on inter-class distance from [18] into our research. Our approach involves calculating the emotional representation of each data sample z_i and its corresponding label y_i. Before each training epoch, we calculate the centers of each emotion C_k based on the emotional representations. Specifically, for the k_{th} emotion, we calculate its center as follows:

$$C_k = \frac{1}{|\{z_i | \forall i, y_i = k\}|} \sum_{i=1}^{L} z_i \cdot \mathbb{I}(y_i = k) \tag{5}$$

where $\mathbb{I}()$ is the indicator function, which outputs **1** if the argument is true and **0** otherwise. The difficulty $DIF(j)$ of the j_{th} sample is then calculated using the following formula:

$$DIF(j) = \frac{dis(z_j, C_{y_j})}{\sum_{k=1}^{|\varepsilon|} dis(z_j, C_k)} \tag{6}$$

where ε is the set of emotional labels, and the dis function is the cosine distance function. This function possesses two significant characteristics. Firstly, it indicates that the greater the proximity of a sample to the center of its respective category, the easier it is. Secondly, it reveals that if two data samples are equidistant from their respective category centers, the farther the samples are from the centers of other categories, the easier they will be.

Training Scheduling Strategy. The present study proposes a technique to construct a range of training subsets, gradually increasing in difficulty, by sorting the complete training set according to a difficulty measure function. Specifically, an arithmetic sequence a of length **L**, is calculated to train the model in the k_{th} epoch.

$$a_1 = 1 - k/R \tag{7}$$

$$a_n = a_1 + (n-1) * d \tag{8}$$

$$d = \frac{2k/R - 1}{L - 1} \tag{9}$$

where **R** represents the total number of training epochs. The initial term in the arithmetic sequence is a_1, and d is the common difference. The Bernoulli distribution is initialized using a, and a binary random array R_B is generated from it. Subsequently, we use R_B to extract a subset, D_{sub-k}, from the training set of the present training epoch, defined as $D_{sub-k} \equiv \{x_i \in D_{train}|R_{B_i} = 1\}$. Consequently, D_{sub-0} mainly comprises simple samples, while D_{sub-R} mainly consists of difficult samples. This approach results in a more consistent progression of difficulty for the model.

Adversarial Training. The implementation of curriculum strategies in our model has led to the reduction of emotional representation in each training epoch. Nonetheless, we aim to provide adequate training to the model even when training becomes more challenging. To this end, we introduce adversarial training to augment the emotional representation. In this approach, we employ fast gradient sign method (FGM), as proposed by [13], to introduce perturbations to the word embeddings in the recurrent neural network as opposed to the raw input. Consequently, we observe significant improvement in the quality of the learned word embeddings and reduction in overfitting during training, as demonstrated in our experimental results.

3.5 Training and Evaluation

Training. Initially, we perform context modeling on the training set, followed by using pre-trained language models to generate emotional representation for all samples. Subsequently, we leverage these emotional representations to assess the difficulty level of each sample. Based on the estimated difficulty scores, we sort the training set in order. Then sample a training subset D_{sub-k} and train it using cross-entropy loss.

3.6 Evaluation

After obtaining the emotional representation z_i of the current utterance using the scenario encoder, we added a linear fully connected layer to input z_i into the layer. The final probability of emotion prediction is obtained by applying the softmax operation. Subsequently, we calculate the loss using the cross-entropy function based on the actual emotion label and perform backpropagation.

$$p^i = W \cdot z_i + b \tag{10}$$

$$L = -\frac{1}{N} \sum_{i=1}^{N} \sum_{c=1}^{\varepsilon} y_{ic} \cdot log(p_{ic}) \tag{11}$$

where $W \in \mathbb{R}^{dim \times |\varepsilon|}$ is a trainable parameter and b is the matrix bias value.

4 Experiments

4.1 Experimental Setup

For the pre-trained model, we utilized the code framework and initial weights that were provided by Huggingface's Transformers [21]. Our backbone was "sup-simcse-roberta-large". The model was trained using the AdamW optimizer and a cosine learning rate schedule approach. Training samples were limited to a maximum of 256 in length. Hyperparameters were fine-tuned on the development set. The best checkpoint on the development set was chosen and utilized to report results on the test set. The entire experiment was conducted using a GeForce RTX 3090 GPU.

4.2 Datasets

We conducted experiments on three widely used benchmarks: IEMOCAP [2], MELD [15], and EmoryNLP [22].

IEMOCAP. This dataset consists of 151 video clips featuring 2 speakers each, for a total of 302 clips. Each segment is annotated as one of 9 emotions (anger, excitement, fear, sadness, surprise, frustration, happiness, disappointment, and neutral). The dataset was recorded in 5 conversations with 5 pairs of speakers.

MELD. This dataset has over 1,400 dialogues and 13,000 utterances from the television series Friends. Multiple speakers are involved in these conversations. Each utterance in the dialogue is tagged as one of the seven emotions: anger, disgust, sadness, joy, neutral, surprise, and fear.

EmoryNLP. This dataset includes 97 plots, 897 scenes, and 12,606 utterances, with each utterance annotated as one of the seven emotions borrowed from the six primary emotions in the Willcox's feeling wheel [20]: sadness, anger, fear, potency, peace, happiness, and the default neutral emotion.

4.3 Metrics

From Fig. 4, we observe that there is class imbalance in the three datasets. Therefore, weighted F1 score is used as the evaluation metric in our experiments. Weighted-F1 considers the importance of different categories by using the sample quantity of each class as the weight and calculates the weighted F1 score. The statistical numbers of these datasets are listed in Table 1. No. Dials represents the number of dialogues, while No. Uttrs represents the total number of data in the dataset. No. CLS is the number of different emotions in the dataset.

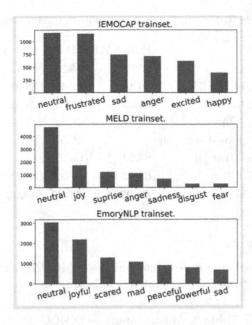

Fig. 4. Emotion distributions of the three datasets

Table 1. Statistics of the three datasets

	IEMOCAP	MELD	EmoryNLP
No.Dials	151	1,432	827
Train	100	1,038	659
Dev	20	114	89
Test	31	280	79
No.Uttrs	7,333	13,708	9,489
Train	4,810	9,989	7,551
Dev	1,000	1,109	954
Test	1,523	2,610	984
No.CLS	6	7	7

4.4 Main Results

We conducted a comparative study between our proposed SWP method and state-of-the-art text-based ERC methods. The results are presented in Table 2, which demonstrate that by combining context modeling and curriculum learning strategy, we achieved superior performance on all three benchmarks, with enhancements of 0.25%(S+PAGE on IEMOCAP), 0.81%(CoMPM on MELD), and 0.79%(S+PAGE on EmoryNLP) over the previous state-of-the-art methods.

Table 2. Performance comparisons on three datasets

Models	IEMOCAP	MELD	EmoryNLP
COSMIC [5]	65.28	65.21	38.11
DialogueCRN [7]	66.46	63.42	38.91
DAG-ERC [17]	68.03	63.65	39.02
CoMPM [9]	66.61	66.52	37.37
EmotonFlow-Large [19]	-	66.50	-
M2FNet-Text [3]	66.20	66.23	-
S+PAGE [10]	68.72	63.32	39.14
SWP(Ours)	**68.97**	**67.33**	**39.93**

4.5 Ablation Study

While conducting ablation experiments on the IEMOCAP dataset, Table 3 displays the results obtained throughout this ablation study.

Table 3. Ablation study on IEMOCAP

Model	IEMOCAP
SWP	**68.97**
SWP w/o CL	68.28
SWP w/o FGM	68.38
SWP w/o CL+FGM	68.01

We discovered that both the curriculum learning and adversarial training strategies can independently improve our model's performance effectively. Implementing the curriculum learning strategy alone resulted in a performance gain of 0.37%, while the adversarial training strategy alone resulted in a gain of 0.27%. Curriculum learning guides the model to learn from easy to hard, enabling the model to find the global optimum more efficiently. Additionally, the adversarial training introduces a perturbation variable to the word embeddings during each training epoch, improving the model's generalization abilities. Combining these two methods generated a significant improvement (0.96%) in the model's training, further proving the viability of using adversarial training to compensate for the emotional representation information loss caused by the curriculum learning strategy.

5 Conclusion

In this paper, we propose a new contextual modeling method called Sliding Window Prompt(SWP) for emotion recognition in conversation tasks. Compared with the traditional method of contextual modeling using the previous utterances, we can freely select the relevant dialogue records with the current utterance because the dialogues in different datasets have different lengths, and the size of the chat window should be adjusted accordingly. Properly reducing or increasing the contextual information of the current speaker's speech can help capture their emotional states. Meanwhile, in order to guide the backbone to focus on the speaker's emotional changes, we design an integrated prompt template, which can leverage the advantages of different templates while reducing the cost of design and maintaining the stability of downstream tasks. Finally, we introduced curriculum learning to reduce the impact of outliers. Since we construct an easy-to-hard training subset based on sampling, we lose some emotional information in each training epoch, and therefore we increase the adversarial training to compensate for this loss. We conducted experiments on three widely used benchmarks: IEMOCAP, MELD, and EmoryNLP. The results show that our method achieved state-of-the-art performance on all three datasets.

References

1. Bengio, Y., Louradour, J., Collobert, R., Weston, J.: Curriculum learning. In: Proceedings of the 26th Annual International Conference On Machine Learning, pp. 41–48 (2009)
2. Busso, C., et al.: Iemocap: interactive emotional dyadic motion capture database. Lang. Resour. Eval. **42**, 335–359 (2008)
3. Chudasama, V., Kar, P., Gudmalwar, A., Shah, N., Wasnik, P., Onoe, N.: M2fnet: multi-modal fusion network for emotion recognition in conversation. In: Proceedings of the IEEE/CVF Conference on Computer Vision and Pattern Recognition, pp. 4652–4661 (2022)
4. Devlin, J., Chang, M.W., Lee, K., Toutanova, K.: Bert: Pre-training of deep bidirectional transformers for language understanding. arXiv preprint arXiv:1810.04805 (2018)
5. Ghosal, D., Majumder, N., Gelbukh, A., Mihalcea, R., Poria, S.: Cosmic: Commonsense knowledge for emotion identification in conversations. arXiv preprint arXiv:2010.02795 (2020)
6. Ghosal, D., Majumder, N., Poria, S., Chhaya, N., Gelbukh, A.: Dialoguegcn: A graph convolutional neural network for emotion recognition in conversation. arXiv preprint arXiv:1908.11540 (2019)
7. Hu, D., Wei, L., Huai, X.: Dialoguecrn: Contextual reasoning networks for emotion recognition in conversations. arXiv preprint arXiv:2106.01978 (2021)
8. Kim, T., Vossen, P.: Emoberta: Speaker-aware emotion recognition in conversation with roberta. arXiv preprint arXiv:2108.12009 (2021)
9. Lee, J., Lee, W.: Compm: Context modeling with speaker's pre-trained memory tracking for emotion recognition in conversation. arXiv preprint arXiv:2108.11626 (2021)
10. Liang, C., Yang, C., Xu, J., Huang, J., Wang, Y., Dong, Y.: S+ page: A speaker and position-aware graph neural network model for emotion recognition in conversation. arXiv preprint arXiv:2112.12389 (2021)
11. Majumder, N., Poria, S., Hazarika, D., Mihalcea, R., Gelbukh, A., Cambria, E.: Dialoguernn: An attentive RNN for emotion detection in conversations. In: Proceedings of the AAAI conference on artificial intelligence. vol. 33, pp. 6818–6825 (2019)

304 H. Zhao et al.

12. Mikolov, T., Chen, K., Corrado, G., Dean, J.: Efficient estimation of word repre-
    sentations in vector space. arXiv preprint arXiv:1301.3781 (2013)
13. Miyato, T., Dai, A.M., Goodfellow, I.: Adversarial training methods for semi-
    supervised text classification. arXiv preprint arXiv:1605.07725 (2016)
14. Pennington, J., Socher, R., Manning, C.D.: Glove: Global vectors for word repre-
    sentation. In: Proceedings of the 2014 Conference on Empirical Methods in Natural
    Language Processing (EMNLP), pp. 1532–1543 (2014)
15. Poria, S., Hazarika, D., Majumder, N., Naik, G., Cambria, E., Mihalcea, R.: Meld:
    A multimodal multi-party dataset for emotion recognition in conversations. arXiv
    preprint arXiv:1810.02508 (2018)
16. Qin, L., Che, W., Li, Y., Ni, M., Liu, T.: Dcr-net: A deep co-interactive relation
    network for joint dialog act recognition and sentiment classification. In: Proceedings
    of the AAAI Conference on Artificial Intelligence, vol. 34, pp. 8665–8672 (2020)
17. Shen, W., Wu, S., Yang, Y., Quan, X.: Directed acyclic graph network for conver-
    sational emotion recognition. arXiv preprint arXiv:2105.12907 (2021)
18. Song, X., Huang, L., Xue, H., Hu, S.: Supervised prototypical contrastive learning
    for emotion recognition in conversation. arXiv preprint arXiv:2210.08713 (2022)
19. Song, X., Zang, L., Zhang, R., Hu, S., Huang, L.: Emotionflow: Capture the dia-
    logue level emotion transitions. In: ICASSP 2022-2022 IEEE International Confer-
    ence on Acoustics, Speech and Signal Processing (ICASSP), pp. 8542–8546. IEEE
    (2022)
20. Willcox, G.: The feeling wheel: a tool for expanding awareness of emotions and
    increasing spontaneity and intimacy. Trans. Anal. J. **12**(4), 274–276 (1982)
21. Wolf, T., et al.: Transformers: State-of-the-art natural language processing. In:
    Proceedings of the 2020 Conference on Empirical Methods in Natural Language
    Processing: System Demonstrations, pp. 38–45 (2020)
22. Zahiri, S.M., Choi, J.D.: Emotion detection on tv show transcripts with sequence-
    based convolutional neural networks. arXiv preprint arXiv:1708.04299 (2017)

VDCNet: A Vulnerability Detection and Classification System in Cross-Project Scenarios

Dongping Zhang[1], Hequn Xian[1,2(✉)], Jiyang Chen[3,4], and Zhiguo Xu[3]

[1] College of Computer Science and Technology, Qingdao University, Qingdao, China

[2] Institute of Cryptography and Cyberspace Security(Huangpu), Guangzhou, China
xianhq@126.com

[3] Shandong Zhengzhong Information Technology Co., LTD, Jinan 250014, China
chenjy@sdas.org, xuzhg@sdas.org

[4] Shandong University, Qingdao 266237, China

Abstract. The existence of software vulnerabilities is the primary cause of most security incidents in cyberspace. Timely detection of potential vulnerabilities from source code during the software development stage is a critical issue for developers. With the increasing scale of open-source projects, traditional static analysis tools are becoming more and more unreliable and stagnant in their development. Meanwhile, approaches for vulnerability detection based on deep learning are being investigated. This paper introduces a novel deep learning-based vulnerability detection system, VDCNet, to identify and classify multiple vulnerabilities more effectively. We extract advanced semantic information from AST representations of source code and capture patterns of vulnerable functions by training neural networks. VDCNet constructs a BERT model for embedding and a Bi-LSTM network for prediction. The experimental results on a comprehensive dataset demonstrate that our method is more efficient in binary vulnerability detection than other deep learning-based methods, with outstanding multi-classification performance in cross-project scenarios.

Keywords: Vulnerability detection · Code representation · Deep learning · Feature extraction

1 Introduction

Vulnerability detection [16] is the primary technology to identify potential security vulnerabilities in software systems, particularly in the early stages of software development. In recent years, the annual number of security vulnerabilities disclosed by the National Vulnerability Database (NVD) has shown an upward trend. However, traditional static analysis approaches that rely on manual feature definition and code audit have proven inefficient [8,12]. There exists an

L. Iliadis et al. (Eds.): ICANN 2023, LNCS 14254, pp. 305–316, 2023.
https://doi.org/10.1007/978-3-031-44207-0_26

urgent need for automated approaches to vulnerability detection with high efficiency and accuracy.

Guided by manually defined rules, static analysis achieves high coverage-code audit without compiling source code [1]. However, with the increasing complexity of open-source projects, these rules are gradually unable to cope with the diversity of source code, and the cost of rule definition is also increasing. Encouraged by the success of deep learning in Natural Language Processing (NLP), many security researchers have turned to deep learning as a solution to the bottleneck problem of static analysis [3]. Firstly, programming language and natural language share certain homogeneity, as both can be considered serialized symbols with semantic information. Additionally, deep learning is suitable for automatically extracting features from big data without human intervention.

Existing approaches based on deep learning still have some limitations despite their advantages over traditional static analysis methods. Firstly, existing methods lack the capability or have a poor capability for cross-project vulnerability detection [11]. This limitation is evident in the model's poor performance when the training and testing datasets come from different projects. Secondly, classifying detected vulnerabilities according to Common Weakness Enumeration (CWE) types is of great reference value for the subsequent bug fixes. Unfortunately, there is a complete lack of approaches with multi-classification capability for vulnerabilities and datasets suitable for such tasks.

In this paper, we present VDCNet, a framework for more efficient C/C++ vulnerability detection and classification. The main contributions of this paper can be summarized as follows:

- We improve the code representation method based on Abstract Syntax Tree (AST) to provide better semantic information retention and project dependency reduction.
- We propose a vulnerability detection and classification system, VDCNet, based on neural networks. VDCNet can perform detection in cross-project scenarios. And to the best of our knowledge, it is the first system to classify the detected vulnerabilities.
- Evaluated on a comprehensive dataset including real-world vulnerability samples, VDCNet outperforms other binary classification systems, achieving satisfactory performance in multi-classification.

2 Related Work

Static analysis tools analyze code properties such as syntax, data flow, and control flow to detect potential vulnerabilities. For instance, Flawfinder [12] detects vulnerabilities based on its built-in high-risk function database, while KLEE [1] calculates all possible program paths through mathematical operations. Some other tools review the source code to detect vulnerabilities based on pre-defined rules [8,16]. However, these detection systems ignore the semantic information of the source code to varying degrees, resulting in a high false positive rate in practice.

VulDeePecker [9] was an early successful application of deep learning for vulnerability detection, achieving higher precision than static analysis. Feng et al. [6] mapped the AST pre-order sequences into vector space and trained a Gated Recurrent Unit (GRU) for semantic information extraction. However, these models do not consider vulnerability classification and have poor cross-project detection ability. Lin et al. [11] combined a Long Short-Term Memory (LSTM) and a random forest classifier to enhance the ability of cross-project vulnerability detection. Nevertheless, their method relies on human experts to determine vulnerabilities in the model's output.

As for vulnerability detection granularity, some researchers identifies vulnerabilities within source code files [2,11], which is not conducive to locating vulnerabilities owing to the possible presence of multiple vulnerabilities in one file. In other methods, vulnerabilities are detected in single statements [3,16], often resulting in poor performance, as most vulnerabilities are caused by multiple statements.

Inspired by the research above, we propose an efficient vulnerability detection system that can operate in cross-project scenarios and classify the vulnerabilities detected while identifying vulnerable functions.

3   Method

VDCNet aims to analyze C/C++ source code input and predict the existence of vulnerable functions and their possible vulnerability types. In this paper, we define functions with no vulnerabilities as benign functions. The general workflow of VDCNet is shown in Fig. 1.

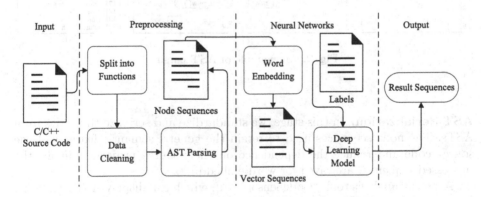

Fig. 1. An overview of VDCNet

Firstly, we parse the source code files into ASTs [10], and process semantically related AST nodes to construct node sequences. Next, we perform further pretraining on a Bidirectional Encoder Representation from Transformers (BERT) with code corpus for word embedding [4]. Finally, we construct an LSTM [15] model to capture semantic features of vulnerabilities for classification.

3.1   Preprocessing

Data Cleaning and AST Parsing. VDCNet identifies vulnerabilities within function boundaries. For each input file, VDCNet removes components unrelated to the code semantics (such as header files and comments.). In contrast, the main part of source files, function definitions, must be reserved and divided. After code segmentation, each function will be labeled as one record with its type (vulnerability type or benign) in the dataset and parsed into AST.

AST is an intermediate result in the process of programming language compilation, which implies lexical units stream and syntax information of the source code organized in a tree structure. Taking the function in the first part of Fig. 2 for example, its AST representation is demonstrated in the second part. Each node in AST contains rich syntax information but does not exhibit every detail of the actual syntax. For instance, nested brackets are concealed in the tree structure and not explicitly shown in nodes. Therefore, converting code into AST reduces data redundancy significantly while preserving semantic information in a great measure.

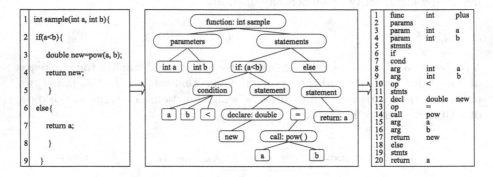

Fig. 2. An example of AST parsing

AST Serialization. In this stage, we standardize and serialize the nodes from ASTs. The node sequences need to retain the general semantic features of the source code and reduce the dependence on their source projects. Finally, the processed sequences are saved for word embedding.

A syntax analysis tool, "CodeSensor" [14], which can display AST as a table, is selected as the AST parser of VDCNet. As demonstrated in the third part of Fig. 2, "Codesensor" presents the ASTs in a table structure. Each row in the table represents a node from the AST and its possible semantic information. Values in the first column of the table denoting node types (nt), while the subsequent two columns provide specific semantic values of nodes.

In order to obtain semantic information as the original order of statements, we successively process each row, which is equivalent to performing an in-order traversal of the AST. Three sets are defined to simplify the serialization:

- **NT**: Including values in the first column (nt) of the table.
- **ST**: Including the first semantic values of those nodes with two semantic values and "op" nodes, denoting the semantic types (st) of nodes.
- **SN**: Including other semantic values denoting the semantic names (sn) of nodes.

During serialization, $nt \in \mathbf{NT}$ and $st \in \mathbf{ST}$ need to be directly retained, as they have no relation to the dependency of projects. On the other hand, $sn \in \mathbf{SN}$ may come from specific projects and have dependencies on their source projects. Directly retaining semantic names will lead to excessive sensitivity of the trained model to specific vulnerable function names. Completely anonymizing them into "$func1$," "$var1$," "$var2$," and so on ignores many frequently used vulnerable function calls in standard libraries.

VDCNet either retains or anonymizes $sn \in \mathbf{SN}$ depending on whether they come from standard libraries or specific projects. We use the C99 and C++11 standard library as the reference for C and C++ functions, respectively. All function and variable names other than these libraries are treated as project-specific names. To sum up, the node sequence generation method can be described as Algorithm. 1.

Algorithm 1. Node Sequence Generation Method

Input: Source Files: SF^1, SF^2, ..., SF^t, ... , SF^T, C99 and C++11 Libraries: L
Output: Node Sequences for Each Function: $N(1, 2, ..., s, ..., S)$
1: Initialize $s = 0$
2: **for** each t in $(1, T)$ **do**
3:    Clean and split the SF^t into functions: FT_1^t, FT_2^t, ..., FT_i^t, ...
4:    **for** each i **do**
5:       $s = s + 1$.
6:       Obtain $Row_i^t(1, 2, ..., r)$ by feeding FT_i^t into **CodeSensor**
7:       **for** each $j(nt \in \mathbf{NT}, st \in \mathbf{ST}, sn \in \mathbf{SN})$ in $Row_i^t(1, r)$ **do**
8:          Append nt and st into N_s
9:          **if** $sn \in L$ **then**
10:             Anonymize and append the sn into N_s
11:          **else**
12:             Append the sn into N_s
13:          **end if**
14:       **end for**
15:    **end for**
16: **end for**

For the example function in Fig. 2, the node sequence after serialization is [$func$, int, $func1$, $params$, $param$, int, $var1$, ..., if, $cond$, ..., arg, int, $var2$, op, $<$, ..., $call$, pow, ..., $return$, $var1$].

3.2 Neural Networks

In this stage, two tasks are solved with neural networks. First, we perform further pre-training on a bert-base-cased model [4] to map the node sequences into vector space. Next, a Bi-Directional LSTM (Bi-LSTM) network is trained for vulnerability classification. The detailed workflow of VDCNet is shown in Fig. 3.

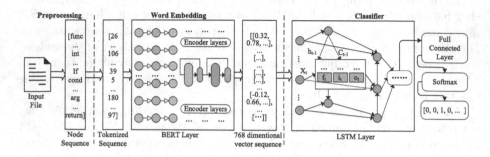

Fig. 3. Detailed workflow of VDCNet

Word Embedding from Pre-trained Weight Matrix. Given a node sequence $N[word_1, word_2, ..., word_s]$, word embedding aims to map N into a vector sequence $V[vector_1, vector_2, ..., vector_s]$, where the relative position of vectors represents the semantic similarity between words.

Traditional Word2vec models [13] perform CBOW or Skip-gram training and extract their hidden layer output as a weight matrix $W \in \mathbb{R}^{s \times m}$ for word embedding. In sequence N, the word vector of N_i, $V^i \in \mathbb{R}^m$ can be calculated as:

$$V^i_{1 \times m} = O^i_{1 \times s} \times W_{s \times m} \quad i = 1 \cdots s, \tag{1}$$

where m is the dimension of the word vectors we have preset and $O^i \in \mathbb{R}^s$ is the one-hot vector of the N_i.

Word Vectors Generated by BERT. VDCNet regards the last hidden layer output of the bert-base-cased model as word vectors to map node sequence N into vector sequence V. Compared with the static word vectors generated by Word2vec, word vectors dynamically generated by BERT using the bidirectional information of sentences have richer contextual semantic information [4].

BERT takes the token sequence of N as initial input. The embedding layer of BERT is composed of token embedding $T \in \mathbb{R}^d$, segment embedding $S \in \mathbb{R}^d$ and position embedding $P \in \mathbb{R}^d$, where d is the dimension of word vector in bert-base model, namely 768. For a word input x in node sequence N, its word vector H_x that will be input into the classifier can be computed following the calculation of the hidden layer in BERT:

$$H_x = E_n(E_{n-1}(\cdots E_1(LN(T_x + S_x + P_x)))), \tag{2}$$

where E and LN represent encoder layer and linear normalization computations. The number of encoders that the bert-base model has is n, namely 12.

BERT Further Pre-training. BERT models were pre-trained on the English text datasets. However, the semantic knowledge of initial BERT needs to be more specific [7]. To make BERT provide a better semantic feature extraction in code context, we further pre-trained a bert-base-cased model before word embedding.

The training task and dataset selected for pre-training are Masked Language Modeling (MLM) and our whole dataset. Unlike natural language sentences, functions in programming language lack the semantic relationship similar to "next sentence." Hence, we did not consider the Next Sentence Prediction (NSP) task. The MLM training script released by Hugging Face, with default settings, was utilized for training.

Vulnerability Classifier. The classifier we designed consists of Bi-LSTM layers and a fully connected layer. It takes vector sequences of functions as input.

LSTM addresses the limitation of Recurrent Neural Network (RNN) in capturing long-term dependencies of time series [15]. As the length of word sequences of functions is often longer than that of natural language sentences, and vulnerability patterns are often associated with statements in different lines with long distances, the model must have a better ability to handle long sequences. LSTM introduces the cell state mechanism based on RNN. For each LSTM unit t, the information it passes to later units includes hidden state h_t and cell state c_t. The cell state, which decides information that needs to be saved or forgotten in the training process, is calculated using three gates: forget gate f_t, input gate i_t, and output gate o_t.

In VDCNet, we build two Bi-LSTM layers. Compared with LSTM with a single direction, Bi-LSTM can learn the patterns and extract advanced semantic features of vulnerabilities from both front and back directions. The output of the hidden layer with dropout is connected to the dense layer for linear transformation. After SoftMax activation, the model outputs a one-hot vector representing the predicted result of input.

4   Experiment

4.1   Environment and Metrics

We construct VDCNet on a Windows server with Intel Xeon W-2133 CPU and NVIDIA GeForce RTX 2080Ti GPU.

Some widely used metrics are selected for evaluation: Accuracy ($Accuracy = \frac{TP}{TP+FP+TN+FN}$), Precision ($Precision = \frac{TP}{TP+FP}$), False Positive Rate ($FPR = \frac{FP}{FP+TN}$), False Negative Rate($FNR = \frac{FN}{FN+TP}$), Recall ($Recall = \frac{TP}{FN+TP}$), and F1 score ($F1 = \frac{2 \times Recall \times Precision}{Recall+Precision}$).

4.2   Datasets

We select six CWE types of vulnerability for classification, three of which are among the 2022 CWE Top 25 list. Our dataset is divided into two categories according to where the source code comes from: manually built code and code from real-world open-source projects. Both datasets satisfy the requirement of comprising common vulnerability types. The following is the split:

- SARD: This dataset is part of the Juliet Test Suite 1.3 released by the Software Assurance Reference Dataset (SARD). This suite is a manually built vulnerability reference manual for software developers.
- RW: We constructed this dataset from source code in real-world open-source projects.

Most detection systems in previous research conducted their experiments on part of the SARD dataset, lacking evaluation of real-world vulnerabilities. To fill the gap of real-world code data for vulnerability multi-classification, we collected the RW dataset by supplementing and re-categorizing the dataset released by Lin et al. [11]. Their dataset comes from six open-source projects: *Asterisk, FFmpeg, LibPNG, LibTIFF, Pidgin,* and *VLC*. We collected additional samples from other projects such as *Wireshark, Firefox,* and *OpenSSL*. Each function in the RW dataset has a unique Common Vulnerabilities and Exposures (CVE) ID, and all functions in both datasets have a CWE ID representing their CWE type. The detail of our dataset is presented in Table 1.

Table 1. Details of the datasets

Source and CWE Type	Vulnerability Brief	Vulnerable functions
SARD-119	Memory Buffer Error	9148
SARD-125	Out-of-bounds Read	2824
SARD-787	Out-of-bounds Write	1792
SARD-189	Numeric Errors	6201
SARD-399	Resource Management Errors	1527
RW-119	Memory Buffer Error	195
RW-125/787	Out-of-bounds Read/Write	107
RW-20	Improper Input Validation	84
RW-189/369	Numeric Errors	116
RW-399	Resource Management Errors	78

Overall, there exist 41094 and 3500 functions (including benign ones) in the SARD and RW datasets, respectively. To label functions, we assign numeric values starting from 0 and incrementing by 1 to denote non-vulnerable functions and functions with specific vulnerability types. In the experimental stage, we divide the dataset into training, validation, and test sets with a ratio of 6: 2: 2.

4.3 Settings

We conducted three groups of experiments. The first group performs binary vulnerability detection on the Buffer Error (CWE-119) dataset (part of the SARD dataset) to compare the binary classification capability of VDCNet with the baseline. The second and third groups use the complete RW and SARD datasets, respectively, to evaluate the multi-classification performance of VDCNet. We list the fine-tuned parameters of VDCNet in Table 2.

Table 2. Parameters in the vulnerability classifier

Parameter	Description
Word Embedding dimension	768 for each word vector
Input sequence length	Variable length using pack-padded-sequence
LSTM neurons	256 (hidden size: 64)
Training epoch	100
Batch size	32
Optimizer	Adam
Learning rate	0.001 for group 1 and group 2. 0.005 for group 3
Loss function	Cross Entropy Loss
Dropout	0.5 for group 2 and group 3

4.4 Results

In the first group, we select six vulnerability detection systems as the baseline. These systems comprise two static analysis tools, RATS [8] and Flawfinder [12], and four popular deep learning-based systems, Deepsim [17], VulSniper [5], VulDeePecker [9] and the system proposed by Feng et al. [6]. The experimental results of the first group are presented in Table 3. In vulnerability binary classification, VDCNet outperformed the baseline in most metrics, indicating its superiority in distinguishing between benign and vulnerable functions.

The performance of RATS and Flawfinder reflect the defect of the high false positive rate of traditional static analysis tools. These tools cannot comprehend the semantics of source code at all. While Deepsim and VulSniper use data flow, control flow, and code property graphs as intermediate code representations, this process results in the truncation of code semantics. VulDeePecker transforms the source code into code gadgets similar to the AST sequence, but this representation lacks information on variables' relationships. Feng et al. use AST sequences as the code representation and employ the Word2vec model for word embedding. In contrast, word vectors of BERT can more effectively represent the semantic information in the code context.

Table 3. Binary vulnerability detection performance of VDCNet on SARD-119 dataset compared with the baseline

System	Precision	Recall	FPR	FNR	F1 Score
RATS	40.5	68.7	67.2	31.3	51.0
Flawfinder	39.9	55.2	56.6	44.8	46.3
Deepsim	71.6	58.4	16.1	41.6	64.4
VulSniper	88.7	73.8	6.4	26.2	80.6
VulDeePecker	91.7	82.0	**2.9**	18.0	86.6
Feng et al. [6]	93.8	73.5	3.0	26.5	82.4
VDCNet	**94.2**	**84.6**	4.7	**15.4**	**88.6**

Experiment results of the second and third groups are presented in Fig. 4. These two groups perform vulnerability multi-classification on RW and SARD datasets, respectively. To the best of our knowledge, no previous research has ever conducted experiments on vulnerability multi-classification, leading to a lack of comparative experiments. Generally, VDCNet achieved a high accuracy of 90.7% and 93.9% on the RW and SARD datasets, respectively.

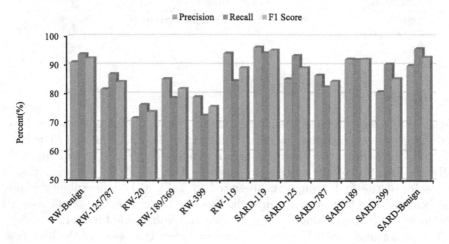

Fig. 4. The performance of VDCNet in classifying each CWE type of vulnerabilities in multi-classification

The figure reflects the performance of VDCNet for detecting each type of function in multi-classification tasks. Overall performance on the SARD dataset is better than that of the RW dataset. For the SARD dataset, all classes achieved high and balanced scores. However, classes with more training samples, such as SARD-119 and SARD-Benign, tend to have slightly higher scores, and this imbalance is more evident in the RW dataset. Although the classifier demonstrates high average accuracy on the RW dataset, the performance in detecting RW-20 and RW-399 functions is obviously worse than other functions due to the scarcity of training samples.

It is worth noting that collecting source code of CVE vulnerabilities from real-world projects is a challenging task, as CVE database only provides an introduction without corresponding source code for each CVE ID. The primary source of vulnerable functions is the source code in the historical version of open-source projects. To provide a vulnerability multi-classification system with better and more balanced performance, the data augmentation method for real-world vulnerability data may have significant research value.

5   Conclusions

In this paper, we propose a method to improve the performance of deep learning-based vulnerability detection in cross-project scenarios and a model to detect vulnerability by CWE types. We first refine the AST-based code representation method and then apply word vectors generated by the BERT model to our classifier. Finally, we demonstrate the superiority of VDCNet over the baseline and the feasibility of vulnerability multi-classification through experiments. However, there are still limitations to our detection system. Our model has a lower performance on RW dataset than SARD dataset. The deficiency of vulnerable samples from real-world projects limits VDCNet's performance to detect some classes of vulnerabilities. Compared with the manually built vulnerabilities, the semantic distinction between different types of real-world vulnerable samples is more complicated to be caught.

Acknowledgment. This work was supported in part by the National Natural Science Foundation of China under Grant 62102212, and in part by the Open Project of the State Key Laboratory of Information Security under Grant 2020-MS-09.

References

1. Cadar, C., Dunbar, D., Engler, D.: Klee: Unassisted and automatic generation of high-coverage tests for complex systems programs. In: Proceedings of the 8th USENIX Conference on Operating Systems Design and Implementation, pp. 209–224. OSDI'08 (2008)
2. Cao, D., Huang, J., Zhang, X., Liu, X.: FTCLNet: Convolutional LSTM with Fourier transform for vulnerability detection. In: 2020 IEEE 19th International Conference on Trust, Security and Privacy in Computing and Communications (TrustCom), pp. 539–546 (2020). https://doi.org/10.1109/TrustCom50675.2020.00078
3. Chakraborty, S., Krishna, R., Ding, Y., Ray, B.: Deep learning based vulnerability detection: are we there yet? IEEE Trans. Softw. Eng. **48**(9), 3280–3296 (2022). https://doi.org/10.1109/TSE.2021.3087402
4. Devlin, J., Chang, M.W., Lee, K., Toutanova, K.: BERT: pre-training of deep bidirectional transformers for language understanding. arXiv preprint arXiv:1810.04805 (2018)

5. Duan, X., Wu, J., Ji, S., Rui, Z., Luo, T., Yang, M., Wu, Y.: VulSniper: focus your attention to shoot fine-grained vulnerabilities. In: Proceedings of the 28th International Joint Conference on Artificial Intelligence, pp. 4665–4671. AAAI Press (2019)

6. Feng, H., Fu, X., Sun, H., Wang, H., Zhang, Y.: Efficient vulnerability detection based on abstract syntax tree and deep learning. In: 2020 IEEE Conference on Computer Communications Workshops (INFOCOM WKSHPS), pp. 722–727 (2020). https://doi.org/10.1109/INFOCOMWKSHPS50562.2020.9163061

7. Guo, D., Lu, S., Duan, N., Wang, Y., Zhou, M., Yin, J.: UniXcoder: unified cross-modal pre-training for code representation. In: Proceedings of the 60th Annual Meeting of the Association for Computational Linguistics (Volume 1: Long Papers), pp. 7212–7225. Association for Computational Linguistics (2022). https://doi.org/10.18653/v1/2022.acl-long.499

8. Kaur, A., Nayyar, R.: A comparative study of static code analysis tools for vulnerability detection in C/C++ and java source code. Procedia Comput. Sci. **171**, 2023–2029 (2020). https://doi.org/10.1016/j.procs.2020.04.217, third International Conference on Computing and Network Communications (CoCoNet'19)

9. Li, Z., et al.: VulDeePecker: a deep learning-based system for vulnerability detection. In: 25th Annual Network and Distributed System Security Symposium, NDSS 2018 (2018)

10. Lin, C., Ouyang, Z., Zhuang, J., Chen, J., Li, H., Wu, R.: Improving code summarization with block-wise abstract syntax tree splitting. In: 2021 IEEE/ACM 29th International Conference on Program Comprehension (ICPC), pp. 184–195 (2021). https://doi.org/10.1109/ICPC52881.2021.00026

11. Lin, G., et al.: Cross-project transfer representation learning for vulnerable function discovery. IEEE Trans. Ind. Inform. **14**(7), 3289–3297 (2018). https://doi.org/10.1109/TII.2018.2821768

12. Lipp, S., Banescu, S., Pretschner, A.: An empirical study on the effectiveness of static c code analyzers for vulnerability detection. In: Proceedings of the 31st ACM SIGSOFT International Symposium on Software Testing and Analysis, pp. 544–555. ISSTA 2022 (2022). https://doi.org/10.1145/3533767.3534380

13. Mikolov, T., Chen, K., Corrado, G., Dean, J.: Efficient estimation of word representations in vector space. In: 1st International Conference on Learning Representations, ICLR 2013, Scottsdale, Arizona, USA, May 2–4, 2013, Workshop Track Proceedings (2013). https://arxiv.org/abs/1301.3781

14. Moonen, L.: Generating robust parsers using island grammars. In: Proceedings Eighth Working Conference on Reverse Engineering, pp. 13–22 (2001). https://doi.org/10.1109/WCRE.2001.957806

15. Yu, Y., Si, X., Hu, C., Zhang, J.: A review of recurrent neural networks: LSTM cells and network architectures. Neural Comput. **31**(7), 1235–1270 (2019). https://doi.org/10.1162/neco_a_01199

16. Zhang, B., Li, J., Ren, J., Huang, G.: Efficiency and effectiveness of web application vulnerability detection approaches: a review. ACM Comput. Surv. **54**(9) (2021). https://doi.org/10.1145/3474553

17. Zhao, G., Huang, J.: DeepSim: deep learning code functional similarity. In: Proceedings of the 2018 26th ACM Joint Meeting on European Software Engineering Conference and Symposium on the Foundations of Software Engineering, pp. 141–151. ESEC/FSE 2018 (2018). https://doi.org/10.1145/3236024.3236068

CFNet: Point Cloud Upsampling via Cascaded Feedback Network

Xuan Wang[1][iD], Yi Li[2], Linna Wang[1], and Li Lu[1]([✉])

[1] College of Computer Science,Sichuan University,Chengdu, China
{wangxuan8,lenawang,luli}@stu.scu.edu.cn
[2] National Key Laboratory of Fundamental Science on Synthetic Vision,Sichuan
University,Chengdu, China
liyi_ws@scu.edu.cn

Abstract. The rapid development of point cloud processing has ushered in a new era of point cloud upsampling. However, most existing methods for point cloud upsampling focus on designing feed-forward cascaded networks based on a coarse-to-fine pipeline to enhance the network's performance. Unfortunately, these methods overlook the potential benefits of incorporating higher-level information to improve low-level feature learning. To address this issue, we propose a novel architecture called Cascaded Feedback Network (CFNet), which differs from previous methods by incorporating both feed-forward and feedback mechanisms. The feedback mechanism in our CFNet can enhance the feature learning of the low-level layer by fusing the information from the high-level layer. Additionally, we propose a novel Feedback Upsampling (FU) module to construct our CFNet. Through extensive experiments on synthetic datasets such as PU1K and PU-GAN datasets, we demonstrate that our proposed CFNet architecture, along with the FU module, outperforms existing methods in point cloud upsampling, indicating the effectiveness of our proposed approach.

Keywords: Point Cloud Upsampling · Cascaded Feedback Network · Feedback Upsampling module

1 Introduction

Point clouds are widely used in 3D reconstruction and computer vision applications, including autonomous driving, augmented reality, and robotics. However, point clouds acquired by scanning devices often suffer from limitations and noise problems that result in irregular and sparse data with varying densities and sampling intervals. These irregularities can significantly impede the effectiveness of point cloud processing and analysis, as observed in public benchmark datasets such as KITTI and ScanNet. Thus, it is crucial to process these sparse and irregular point clouds into dense and regular point sets to improve their quality.

Point cloud upsampling is a technique utilized to convert irregular point clouds into regular point clouds. The pioneering method, PU-Net [24], achieves

L. Iliadis et al. (Eds.): ICANN 2023, LNCS 14254, pp. 317–329, 2023.
https://doi.org/10.1007/978-3-031-44207-0_27

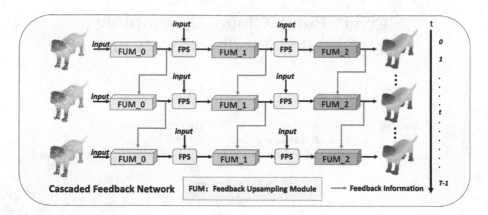

Fig. 1. The architecture of proposed Cascaded Feedback Network (CFNet). The CFNet contains several Feedback Upsampling (FU) modules based on parameter sharing, which aims to reconstruct dense point clouds from sparse input across time steps. We use FPS to initialize the input of feedback upsampling modules, which can provide the prior information to the module

this by learning multi-scale features and expanding the number of points through multi-branch Multi-layer Perceptrons (MLP). Subsequently, numerous methods [7,10,14,16] have adopted a single-stage network to generate dense points. More recently, based on the coarse-to-fine pipeline, cascaded networks [3] have been proposed to upsample point clouds, leading to impressive performance improvements. It is worth noting that these methods are all feed-forward networks where information only flows from the low-level to the high-level layers.

The aim of this paper is to introduce a feedback mechanism that can incorporate information from high-level layers into low-level layers for point cloud upsampling. To achieve this objective, we propose a novel approach named Cascaded Feedback Network (CFNet), which is composed of three cascaded Feedback Upsampling (FU) modules, as depicted in Fig. 1. The parameters of these FU modules are shared with the iteration of the time step. The FU module is utilized to upsample the input with the feedback connection, where the high-level information is fed back to the low-level layers through the feedback connection in each FU module. With the progression of time steps, the upsampling process of the FU module is progressively refined by fusing feedback features. We conduct extensive experiments on synthetic datasets, such as PU1K and PU-GAN, to evaluate the effectiveness of our proposed method. Our experimental results demonstrate that CFNet significantly outperforms the state-of-the-art methods.

The main contributions are listed as follows:

- We propose a novel Cascaded Feedback Network (CFNet) for point cloud upsampling. The proposed network can easily refine sparse point clouds across time steps. To the best of our knowledge, the proposed CFNet is the first feedback-based network for point cloud upsampling task.

- We propose a Feedback Upsampling (FU) module to upsample the point cloud. Based on the feedback mechanism, the FU module fuses the feedback information to guide the current model to learn an impressive shape.
- Our network achieves leading performance on some widely adopted benchmarks including the PU1K dataset and PU-GAN dataset compared to state-of-the-art methods. Moreover, the complexity of our model remains comparable to other existing point cloud upsampling methods.

2 Related Work

2.1 Point Cloud Upsampling

Point cloud processing methods [12,13,18,21] have accelerated the development of point cloud upsampling techniques. PU-Net [24] proposed a classic framework consisting of three parts: feature extraction, feature expansion, and coordinate reconstruction. Subsequent works [1,7,10,14,15] related to point cloud upsampling, mostly adopted this framework. For example, PU-GCN [14] applied graph convolution network to feature extraction, while its upsampling module was based on NodeShuffle, which experimentally demonstrated superior performance compared to PU-GAN [7]. PU-EVA [10] introduced the Edge-vector based approximation upsampling module, utilizing neighborhood points and max-pooling to ensure point uniformity. Very recently, PUCRN [3] proposed a cascaded refinement network for point cloud upsampling, featuring a transformer-based feature extraction module to learn both global and local shape context. However, all of these methods are feed-forward networks. To address this limitation, in this paper, we propose a feedback mechanism to fuse high-level layer information with low-level layer information, achieving impressive point cloud shape reconstruction.

2.2 Feedback Methodology

The feedback mechanism is a technique that adjusts the output of the feed-forward by integrating information from high-level layers. It has been extensively used in 2D images in computer vision [2,4,6,9,17,25], leading to improved accuracy and robustness of models. Recently, the feedback mechanism has been applied in point cloud processing, and FBNet [22] is the pioneering work in this area. The Cross-Transformer module proposed by FBNet [22] overcomes the feature mismatching problem and selectively enhances low-level features by adaptively selecting valuable information from feedback features. In this paper, we adopt the feedback mechanism in the point cloud upsampling task and achieve state-of-the-art performance.

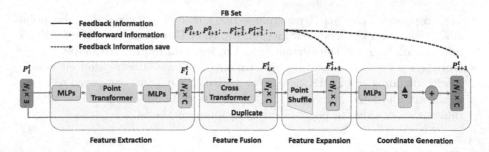

Fig. 2. The detailed architecture of each Feedback Upsampling (FU) module. Each FU module consists of four parts: Feature Extraction, Feature Fusion, Feature Expansion, and Coordinate Generation. FB module Set denotes the points and features reflowed from the $t-1$ step

3   Method

3.1   Cascaded Feedback Network (CFNet)

In this paper, we propose a Cascaded Feedback Network (CFNet) for point cloud upsampling. CFNet contains several Feedback Upsampling (FU) modules, as shown in Fig. 1. CFNet aims to refine the sparse input point cloud to the dense point cloud. From the left to right in Fig. 1, we use three FU modules to generate the feed-forward feature information. Each FU module takes the output of the previous module as a part of the input. It should be noted that we concatenate the original input and the feedforward output of the $i-1$-th module. Then we downsample concatenated point cloud by using the Farthest Point Sampling (FPS) algorithm to the fixed scale. In this way, the input of the current module is fused with the prior information of the original data, which is more conducive to obtaining a favorable output. In particular, the input of the 0-th module is the pure original point cloud.

Apart from the feedforward information, CFNet also contains feedback information flowing from the higher layer to the lower one. Hence, we introduce the feedback mechanism via the time iterations, as shown in Fig. 1 (top to down). With the time steps, the feedback information from the $t-1$ step reflow to the t step. We infer that the output of the high layer at the $t-1$ step has fine information, which can help the low layer feature to generate a more fine-grained super-resolution point cloud at the t step. Across time steps and the feedforward information flows, FU modules gradually refine their output and we will get representative and fine point cloud via our CFNet. This is also confirmed in our subsequent experiments.

3.2   Feedback Upsampling (FU) Module

The proposed Feedback Upsampling (FU) module aims to refine the sparse point cloud to fine-gained ones through the upsampling and feedback mechanism. Since we need to fuse the feedback information, our FU module consists of four parts: Feature Extraction, Feature Fusion, Feature Expansion, and Coordinate Generation, as shown in Fig. 2. In the following, we will introduce each part in detail.

Feature Extraction. Previous methods [7,8,24] usually use the MLP-based feature extraction to learn features of the input. However, the MLP-based methods are not able to capture the local and context features. Therefore, we introduce the Transformer in 3D vision [3,5,11,26] to our network.

Specifically, we denote the input of i-th FU module at t time step is $P_i^t = \{p_j\}_{j=1}^{N}$ of three channels, the output of the feature extraction is the corresponding point cloud feature $F_i^t = \{f_j\}_{j=1}^{N}$ with channel C, where N is the number of points. We first perform MLPs on the original point P_i^t to obtain the original point features. We then utilize max-pooling on the obtained point features to obtain the global features. We can get the final features F' via a fusion operation $\mathcal{K}$ between point features and global features. F' can be formulated as:

$$F' = \mathcal{K}([\mathcal{A}(\mathcal{M}(P_i^t)), \mathcal{M}(P_i^t)]), \tag{1}$$

where $\mathcal{M}$ and $\mathcal{A}$ denotes MLPs and max-pooling operation, respectively. $[\cdot]$ is the operation of concatenation.

In the second stage, we use the Point Transformer [26] to extract the local and context features F'' by building the relation between points. F'' can be calculated as:

$$F'' = \vartheta\left(F', P_i^t\right), \tag{2}$$

where ϑ is the point-transformer function [26].

Finally, we aggregate the global features again like in the first stage to generate the final point features F_i^t. This process is roughly the same as Eq. 1.

Feature Fusion. The feature fusion is used to aggregate the feed-forward features and the feedback features. Cross-layer feature fusion strategies are widely used in point cloud completion methods [19,20,22] in the field of point cloud processing. Feedforward information flows from the lower layer to the upper layer, and the output reflows to the next step as feedback information for fusion. However, the premise of cross-layer feature fusion is that the resolutions of the two are consistent. In the field of point cloud processing, both point cloud completion and upsampling involve upsampling rate, which will lead to unequal resolutions of features we need to fuse. FBNet [22] proposed the Cross Transformer method to fuse features from two point clouds with different resolutions. FBNet [22] also proved its effectiveness through a series of experiments. Therefore, we directly apply Cross Transformer to the feature fusion module of our network.

We denote the feed-forward point cloud and its features of the i-th FU module in the t step as P_i^t, F_i^t, the corresponding feedback point cloud and its features as

P_{i+1}^{t-1}, F_{i+1}^{t-1}. The fusion operation based on Cross Transformer can be formulated as the following:

$$F_{i,r}^t = \mathcal{R}(F_{i+1}^{t-1}, F_i^t, P_{i+1}^{t-1}, P_i^t), \tag{3}$$

where $\mathcal{R}$ denotes the Cross Transformer.

Specifically, the Cross Transformer build the relation between feed-forward features F_i^t and feedback feature F_{i+1}^{t-1} via the attention mechanism. Therefore, the Cross Transformer can query the useful information from the feedback point cloud to enrich the current point cloud and obtain more valuable features. Note that, when the feedback information is None (e.g., $t = 0$), the Cross Transformer degenerates into the point transformer.

Feature Expansion. Similar to the pixel shuffle, we use the point shuffle to expand the aggregated point feature $F_{i,r}^t$. We first apply a series of fully-connection layers to obtain the high-dimension feature with the scale of $rC \times N$, where r is the upsampling rate. Then, the expanded features are reshaped to the low-dimension but high-resolution feature F_{i+1}^t with the scale of $C \times rN$. Our feature expansion module is time-saving and relatively saves some computing resources.

Coordinate Generation. The purpose of coordinate generation is to generate a new set of points $P_{i+1}^t = \{p_j\}_{j=1}^{rN}$ from the upsampled point features F_{i+1}^t. A common method for coordinate reconstruction is to directly regress the 3D point coordinates, but it is difficult to generate high-fidelity coordinates in a noise-free environment. We choose to utilize both the original point cloud and the upsampled point features for the coordinate generation to solve this problem. The output of the coordinate generation module can be calculated as:

$$P_{i+1}^t = \mathcal{V}(F_{i+1}^t) + \mathcal{D}\left(P_i^t, r\right) \tag{4}$$

where $\mathcal{V}$ denotes MLP, and $\mathcal{D}$ denotes duplicated operation. The r is the upsampling rate of the current FU module. This method alleviates learning conflicts between multiple stages in a coarse-to-fine framework. In this way, we can generate reliable point coordinates through the stacked FU blocks.

3.3   Training Loss

We use Chamfer Distance (CD) as the loss function during our end-to-end training. The loss function can be formulated as:

$$\mathcal{L}_{CD}\left(P, P'\right) = \frac{1}{|P|} \sum_{x \in P} \min_{y \in P'} \|x - y\|^2 + \frac{1}{|P'|} \sum_{y \in P'} \min_{x \in P} \|y - x\|^2. \tag{5}$$

where P and P' are different point clouds, and x and y are the points belonging to P and P' respectively.

Table 1. The quantitative results on **PU1K** dataset (×4 upsampling rate) in terms of CD (10^3) and HD (10^3). There are different numbers of points of the input, including 512 (sparse), 1024 (medium), and 2048 (dense)

Methods	512 points		1024 points		2048 points	
	CD ($\downarrow$)	HD ($\downarrow$)	CD ($\downarrow$)	HD ($\downarrow$)	CD ($\downarrow$)	HD ($\downarrow$)
PU-Net [24]	2.990	35.403	1.920	24.181	1.157	15.297
MPU [23]	2.727	30.471	1.268	16.088	0.861	11.799
Dis-PU [8]	2.130	25.471	1.210	16.518	0.731	9.505
PU-GAN [7]	2.089	22.716	1.151	14.781	0.661	9.238
PU-GCN [14]	1.975	22.527	1.142	14.565	0.635	9.152
PU-EVA [10]	1.942	20.980	1.065	13.376	0.649	8.870
PUCRN [3]	1.594	17.733	0.808	10.750	0.471	7.123
CFNet (Ours)	**1.500**	**16.639**	**0.783**	**10.002**	**0.450**	**5.918**

Table 2. The quantitative results on **PU-GAN** dataset (×4 upsampling rate) in terms of CD (10^3) and HD (10^3). The number of points of input is 1024

Methods	CD($\downarrow$)	HD($\downarrow$)
PU-Net [24]	0.883	7.132
MPU [23]	0.589	6.206
Dis-PU [8]	0.527	5.706
PU-GAN [7]	0.566	6.932
PU-GCN [14]	0.584	5.257
PU-EVA [10]	0.571	5.840
PUCRN [3]	0.520	6.102
CFNet (Ours)	**0.497**	**4.676**

The loss function of our network is joint because each Feedback Upsampling (FU) module has its own predicted output. So our joint loss function can be defined as the following:

$$\mathcal{L} = \sum_{t=0}^{T} \sum_{i=0}^{n} \mathcal{L}_{CD}\left(P_i^t, GT\right) \tag{6}$$

where t denotes the step times, and n denotes the number of FU modules in the same step. Obviously, P_i^t is the output point cloud in the i-th module at t step. GT denotes the corresponding ground truth of P_i^t. In our paper, we set $n = 3$, $T = 3$, so the total loss function consists of 9 parts.

4   Experiment

We demonstrate the effectiveness of our proposed network by conducting experiments on publicly available datasets in the field of point cloud upsampling. The datasets we selected are PU1K and PU-GAN. Detailed parameter settings will be introduced in Sects. 4.1 and 4.2. The number of time steps in our CFNet is set to 3. The methods compared with our CFNet contain seven existing point cloud upsampling methods, including PU-Net [24], MPU [23], PU-GAN [7], Dis-PU [8], PU-GCN [14], PU-EVA [10] and PUCRN [3]. The model's performance is evaluated by Chamfer Distance (CD) and Hausdorff Distance (HD). Smaller values for these metrics indicate better performance. We set the upsampling rate of the first FU module to 1, and the rest to 2, to reach ×4 upsampling. The experimental results of other methods are referenced in the PUCRN method [3].

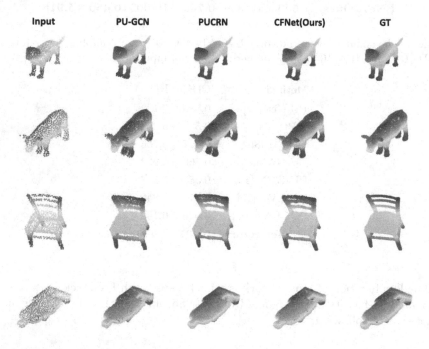

Fig. 3. The visualized results on PU-GAN dataset (×U4 upsampling) with the input of 1024 points

4.1   Evaluation on PU1K Dataset

Dataset. PU1K is a large-scale dataset for point cloud upsampling proposed by PU-GCN [14]. PU1K contains 1,147 3D models divided into 1020 training samples and 127 test samples. For inference, we follow the general settings [3, 7,

Table 3. The ablation study of **feedback mechanism** on PU-GAN dataset with the input of 1024. The values of CD and HD are multiplied by 10^3

Feedback	CD($\downarrow$)	HD($\downarrow$)
False	0.502	4.891
True	**0.497**	**4.676**

Table 4. The ablation study on effect of **time step**. Conducted on PU-GAN dataset with the input of 1024. The values are multiplied by 10^3

Time-step	CD($\downarrow$)	HD($\downarrow$)
1	0.504	5.209
2	0.501	5.099
3	**0.497**	**4.676**

14,24] and divide the input point cloud into point patches according to the seed points. Therefore, PU1K is composed of 69000 training patches.

Setting. Our model is trained with 200 epochs on the PU1K dataset, and the batch size is set to 64. The initial learning rate is set to 0.001 and drops by a decay rate of 0.7 every 15 epochs. During training, the points of each training patch's ground truth are 1024, and the input contains 256 points randomly sampled from the ground truth.

Results. We take the input of 256 points to train our model on the PU1K dataset. The output of the predicted point cloud contains 1024 points after $\times 4$ upsampling. We conduct experiments to test the performance of our model on different input sizes of points, including 512 (sparse), 1024 (medium), and 2048 (dense). The quantitative results is shown in Table 1. Compared with the current state-of-the-art models, our method achieves the best performance on all of the resolutions in the metrics of CD and HD.

4.2 Evaluation on PU-GAN Dataset

Dataset. PU-GAN dataset is a smaller dataset than PU1K, proposed by PU-GAN [7]. It is collected from the released datasets of PU-Net and MPU, composed of 147 3D models. Different from PU1K, PU-GAN only contains 24000 training patches collectd from 120 3D models and the rest for testing. Each training patch has 256 points and each ground truth has 1024 points as well as PU1K.

Setting. The batch size of PU-GAN is set to 32, and the rest of the experimental settings are the same as PU1K. Following PUCRN [3], we test our model on the input of 1024 points, which is migrated from PU1K's test set with the input of 1024 points, as well as the ground truth with 4096 points.

Results. Following the abovementioned settings, we conduct experients on PU-GAN dataset with $\times 4$ upsampling rate. Table 2 shows our quantitative results. In general, our methods can achieve the best results of all metrics. In particular, our results on the HD metric received a significant boost, decreasing from 6.102 of PUCRN [3] to 4.676, also exceeding the current best PU-GCN [14]. Moreover, we visualize the results of PU-GCN [14], PUCRN [3] and our method in Fig. 3. In contrast to PU-GCN [14] and PUCRN [3], our CFNet exhibits superior performance in generating point clouds with a high degree of uniformity and detail, while also minimizing the presence of outliers.

Table 5. The Complexity Analysis

Methods	Params (M)	CD ($\downarrow$)	HD ($\downarrow$)
PU-Net [24]	0.812	0.883	7.132
MPU [23]	**0.076**	0.589	6.206
Dis-PU [8]	1.047	0.527	5.706
PU-GAN [7]	0.542	0.566	6.932
PU-GCN [14]	**0.076**	0.584	5.257
PU-EVA [10]	2.869	0.571	5.840
PUCRN [3]	0.847	0.520	6.102
CFNet ($T = 1$)	1.252	0.504	5.209
CFNet ($T = 2$)	1.252	0.501	5.099
CFNet ($T = 3$)	1.252	**0.497**	**4.676**

5   Ablation Study

In order to demonstrate the effectiveness of the core components and settings in our model, we design ablation experiments to quantitatively evaluate them. The ablation study mainly tests the feedback mechanism and the time step.

5.1   The Effect of Feedback Mechanism

Compared to the previous work based on the feed-forward network, we introduce the feedback mechanism into our model. To demonstrate the effectiveness of the feedback mechanism for point cloud upsampling, we conduct our ablation experiments on the PU-GAN dataset with the input of 1024. The results are shown in Table 3, from which we can see the model with feedback connections is better than the model without one.

5.2   The Effect of Time Step

Our proposed network can achieve refined point clouds across time steps. Hence, we set different values of t to conduct experiments on the PU-GAN dataset with 1024 input to demonstrate the effectiveness of the time step. As shown in Table 4, the value of t is bigger, and the performance of our network is better.

6   Complexity Analysis

In this section, we analyze the complexity of our proposed model and compare it with the existing point cloud upsampling methods. We test all methods on the PU-GAN dataset with the input of 1024 points. As shown in Table 5, Compared with PU-EVA [10], our method has fewer parameters but significantly improves the performance. Compared with PU-Net [24], Dis-PU [8], and the latest upsampling method PUCRN [3], we achieve the best performance with small parameter growth. Overall, our cascaded feedback network (CFNet) not only achieves significant performance gains but also achieves comparable model complexity to other networks.

7   Conclusion

In this paper, we propose a cascaded feedback upsampling network (CFNet) for point cloud upsampling. To the best of our knowledge, we are the first to apply the feedback mechanism to the field of point cloud upsampling. The CFNet is composed of three Feedback Upsampling (FU) modules. The FU module achieves the upsampling rate distributedly, making the network structure more flexible. By introducing feedback connections in the FU module, CFNet can learn more representative and informative low-level features with the help of rerouted high-level information and achieve impressive super-resolution point clouds as time steps. Experiments on public datasets including PU1K and PU-GAN show that our method outperforms the current state-of-the-art methods.

References

1. Atzmon, M., Maron, H., Lipman, Y.: Point convolutional neural networks by extension operators. arXiv preprint arXiv:1803.10091 (2018)
2. Chen, C., Li, H.: Robust representation learning with feedback for single image deraining. In: Proceedings of the IEEE/CVF Conference on Computer Vision and Pattern Recognition, pp. 7742–7751 (2021)
3. Du, H., Yan, X., Wang, J., Xie, D., Pu, S.: Point cloud upsampling via cascaded refinement network. In: Proceedings of the Asian Conference on Computer Vision, pp. 586–601 (2022)
4. Feng, M., Lu, H., Ding, E.: Attentive feedback network for boundary-aware salient object detection. In: Proceedings of the IEEE/CVF Conference on Computer Vision and Pattern Recognition, pp. 1623–1632 (2019)
5. Guo, M.H., Cai, J.X., Liu, Z.N., Mu, T.J., Martin, R.R., Hu, S.M.: PCT: point cloud transformer. Comput. Vis. Media 7, 187–199 (2021)
6. Li, Q., Li, Z., Lu, L., Jeon, G., Liu, K., Yang, X.: Gated multiple feedback network for image super-resolution. arXiv preprint arXiv:1907.04253 (2019)
7. Li, R., Li, X., Fu, C.W., Cohen-Or, D., Heng, P.A.: PU-GAN: a point cloud upsampling adversarial network. In: Proceedings of the IEEE/CVF International Conference on Computer Vision, pp. 7203–7212 (2019)

8. Li, R., Li, X., Heng, P.A., Fu, C.W.: Point cloud upsampling via disentangled refinement. In: Proceedings of the IEEE/CVF Conference on Computer Vision and Pattern Recognition, pp. 344–353 (2021)

9. Li, Z., Yang, J., Liu, Z., Yang, X., Jeon, G., Wu, W.: Feedback network for image super-resolution. In: Proceedings of the IEEE/CVF Conference on Computer Vision and Pattern Recognition, pp. 3867–3876 (2019)

10. Luo, L., Tang, L., Zhou, W., Wang, S., Yang, Z.X.: PU-EVA: an edge-vector based approximation solution for flexible-scale point cloud upsampling. In: Proceedings of the IEEE/CVF International Conference on Computer Vision, pp. 16208–16217 (2021)

11. Pan, X., Xia, Z., Song, S., Li, L.E., Huang, G.: 3D object detection with point-former. In: Proceedings of the IEEE/CVF Conference on Computer Vision and Pattern Recognition, pp. 7463–7472 (2021)

12. Qi, C.R., Su, H., Mo, K., Guibas, L.J.: PointNet: deep learning on point sets for 3D classification and segmentation. In: Proceedings of the IEEE Conference on Computer Vision and Pattern Recognition, pp. 652–660 (2017)

13. Qi, C.R., Yi, L., Su, H., Guibas, L.J.: PointNet++: deep hierarchical feature learning on point sets in a metric space. In: Advances in Neural Information Processing Systems, vol. 30 (2017)

14. Qian, G., Abualshour, A., Li, G., Thabet, A., Ghanem, B.: PU-GCN: point cloud upsampling using graph convolutional networks. In: Proceedings of the IEEE/CVF Conference on Computer Vision and Pattern Recognition, pp. 11683–11692 (2021)

15. Qian, Y., Hou, J., Kwong, S., He, Y.: PUGeo-Net: a geometry-centric network for 3D point cloud upsampling. In: Vedaldi, A., Bischof, H., Brox, T., Frahm, J.-M. (eds.) ECCV 2020. LNCS, vol. 12364, pp. 752–769. Springer, Cham (2020). https://doi.org/10.1007/978-3-030-58529-7_44

16. Qiu, S., Anwar, S., Barnes, N.: Pu-transformer: point cloud upsampling transformer. In: Proceedings of the Asian Conference on Computer Vision, pp. 2475–2493 (2022)

17. Sam, D.B., Babu, R.V.: Top-down feedback for crowd counting convolutional neural network. In: Proceedings of the AAAI Conference on Artificial Intelligence, vol. 32 (2018)

18. Spata, D., Grumpe, A., Kummert, A.: End-to-end on-line multi-object tracking on sparse point clouds using recurrent convolutional networks. In: Farkaš, I., Masulli, P., Otte, S., Wermter, S. (eds.) ICANN 2021. LNCS, vol. 12894, pp. 407–419. Springer, Cham (2021). https://doi.org/10.1007/978-3-030-86380-7_33

19. Wen, X., Li, T., Han, Z., Liu, Y.S.: Point cloud completion by skip-attention network with hierarchical folding. In: Proceedings of the IEEE/CVF Conference on Computer Vision and Pattern Recognition, pp. 1939–1948 (2020)

20. Xiang, P., et al.: SnowflakeNet: point cloud completion by snowflake point deconvolution with skip-transformer. In: Proceedings of the IEEE/CVF International Conference on Computer Vision, pp. 5499–5509 (2021)

21. Yan, H., Wu, Z., Lu, L.: Low-level graph convolution network for point cloud processing. In: Pimenidis, E., Angelov, P., Jayne, C., Papaleonidas, A., Aydin, M. (eds.) Artificial Neural Networks and Machine Learning-ICANN 2022: 31st International Conference on Artificial Neural Networks, Bristol, UK, 6–9 September 2022, Proceedings, Part II, pp. 557–569. Springer, Cham (2022). https://doi.org/10.1007/978-3-031-15931-2_46

22. Yan, X., et al.: FBNet: feedback network for point cloud completion. In: Avidan, S., Brostow, G., Cissé, M., Farinella, G.M., Hassner, T. (eds.) Computer Vision-ECCV

2022: 17th European Conference, Tel Aviv, Israel, 23–27 October 2022, Proceedings, Part II, pp. 676–693. Springer, Cham (2022). https://doi.org/10.1007/978-3-031-20086-1_39

23. Yifan, W., Wu, S., Huang, H., Cohen-Or, D., Sorkine-Hornung, O.: Patch-based progressive 3D point set upsampling. In: Proceedings of the IEEE/CVF Conference on Computer Vision and Pattern Recognition, pp. 5958–5967 (2019)

24. Yu, L., Li, X., Fu, C.W., Cohen-Or, D., Heng, P.A.: PU-Net: point cloud upsampling network. In: Proceedings of the IEEE Conference on Computer Vision and Pattern Recognition, pp. 2790–2799 (2018)

25. Zeng, Yu., Lin, Z., Yang, J., Zhang, J., Shechtman, E., Lu, H.: High-resolution image inpainting with iterative confidence feedback and guided upsampling. In: Vedaldi, A., Bischof, H., Brox, T., Frahm, J.-M. (eds.) ECCV 2020. LNCS, vol. 12364, pp. 1–17. Springer, Cham (2020). https://doi.org/10.1007/978-3-030-58529-7_1

26. Zhao, H., Jiang, L., Jia, J., Torr, P.H., Koltun, V.: Point transformer. In: Proceedings of the IEEE/CVF International Conference on Computer Vision, pp. 16259–16268 (2021)

DA-TSD: Double Attention Two-Stage 3D Object Detector from Point Clouds

Xinyi Zhao, Yong Li$^{(\boxtimes)}$, Rui Tian, and Yunli Chen

Faculty of Information Technology, Beijing University of Technology, Beijing, China
zxy20210903@emails.bjut.edu.cn, {li.yong,rui.tian,yunlichen}@bjut.edu.cn

Abstract. In this paper, we focus on the problem of small and long-range object misses in 3D object detection on point clouds. We observed that in challenging situations, especially for hard objects such as small objects, the performance of the detector remains unsatisfactory. To address these issues, this paper proposes a voxel-based two-stage 3D object detector, named DA-TSD, which mainly includes a Double Attention (DA) module and a Pyramid Sampling (PS) module. The DA module comprehensively considers point-wise and channel-wise excitation attention, which can effectively enhance the crucial information of the object and suppress irrelevant noise. In addition, the stacked DA module utilizes not only the current level feature but also the multi-level feature attention. The PS module provides cross-layer feature mappings to obtain more comprehensive feature representations. The experimental results on the *val* set of the KITTI dataset demonstrate the superiority and effectiveness of DA-TSD. DA-TSD provides higher detection accuracy while maintaining real-time frame processing rate, running at a speed of 28.5 FPS on an NVIDIA GeForce RTX 3090 Ti GPU.

Keywords: 3D Object Detection · Point Clouds · Autonomous driving

1 Introduction

In recent years, 3D object detection using point clouds has received extremely wide attention in areas such as autonomous driving and augmented reality where point clouds provide more reliable geometric information and accurate depth. Although a large amount of researches [17] have contributed to significant advances in 2D object detection, which can indicate the position and category of each object in an image, applying these methods to 3D point clouds is still difficult. In addition, the sparsity and unstructured properties of point clouds pose more significant challenges for accurate object detection.

To address these challenges, many 3D object detection methods for point clouds have emerged, which can be roughly divided into two categories: point-based and voxel-based. Point-based methods [16,21] operate directly on the raw point clouds from which features are extracted and 3D bounding boxes are generated. The methods of using raw point clouds have problems such as high time

© The Author(s), under exclusive license to Springer Nature Switzerland AG 2023
L. Iliadis et al. (Eds.): ICANN 2023, LNCS 14254, pp. 330–343, 2023.
https://doi.org/10.1007/978-3-031-44207-0_28

costs for sampling and nearest neighbor search. Voxel-based methods usually divide the point clouds into more regular voxel grids and generate 3D bounding boxes on this basis to achieve 3D object detection. Compared with point-based methods that have higher time costs, voxel-based methods have more efficient sparse convolution [27] and can achieve SOTA detection performance. Sparse convolution is most commonly used in voxel-based network structures.

Small object detection is crucial for safe driving in the field of autonomous vehicles, especially the pedestrians and cyclists can easily appear in blind spots of the driver's vision and be overlooked. We identify two reasons for the poor performance of existing methods on challenging objects, especially small objects: 1) a low foreground point ratio results in fewer points being scanned on small objects by LiDAR; 2) quantization leads to information loss during feature extraction of 3D sparse convolution backbone. Although there have been some studies [8,22,28] on this subject, these methods either perform high-density feature extraction on objects, which is still a very difficult task and has poor portability, or are susceptible to noise.

This paper proposes two modules aimed at mitigating the impact of the aforementioned factors. We draw inspiration from Voxel R-CNN [3] and adopt a voxel-based framework to aggregate 3D structural contexts from 3D voxel features. To enhance point recognition and reduce the impact of diverse background information on voxel feature extraction, the Double Attention (DA) module is introduced in the 3D backbone network. Specifically, the DA module contains point-wise and channel-wise excitation attention, and these two types of attention are combined through element-wise multiplication.

The feature extraction process of the 3D sparse convolution backbone may result in the loss of some information due to quantization. Considering the small receptive field of the low-level network and its strong ability to represent geometric detail information, we propose a Pyramid Sampling (PS) method to provide voxel feature maps across layers.

In summary, the key contributions of the proposed method lie in:

- We introduce a novel Double Attention (DA) module that considers point-wise and channel-wise excitation attention, and then obtains multi-level feature attention via stacking.
- We propose a new feature sampling method that provides cross-layer voxel feature maps.
- Experimental results on the KITTI object detection benchmark [4] show that DA-TSD boosts the baseline model more significantly for Pedestrian and Cyclist, proving that DA-TSD is effective for small object detection.

2   Related Work

Recently, the rapid development of computer vision technology has led to a wide range of research on 3D object detection from point clouds. A large number of methods adopt point-based or voxel-based detection frameworks. Point-based methods [1,13,16,21,24] utilized abstract set of points to detect objects.

CenterPoint [31] provided a simple and effective anchor-free framework for 3D detection. 3DSSD [29] improved point-based methods by adopting a new feature-distance-based sampling strategy. STD [28] further extended proposal refinement by converting sparse point features to dense voxel representations. SPG [26] generated semantic points to recover missing parts of foreground objects. Although these methods have better detection results, they suffer from time-consuming processes of sampling and feature aggregation from irregular points, resulting in a slower running speed. Another category of methods is the voxel-based approach [2,23,25,33], which aimed to improve computational efficiency by voxelizing unstructured point clouds into regular 2D or 3D grids and encoding only the non-empty voxels. SECOND [27] proposed a sparse convolutional operation instead of dense 3D convolution to speed up 3D convolutional network inference. Pioneering work [2] encoded point clouds into 2D BEV (Bird's-Eye View) feature maps to generate highly accurate 3D candidate boxes, and inspired many efficient BEV-based methods. Sparse2Dense [22] boosted small object detection performance by learning to densify point clouds in latent space, but high-density feature extraction is a difficult task. We used a two-stage voxel-based detection pipeline in our approach. However, the traditional voxel-based approaches tend to ignore and obfuscate the details and texture information of small objects. To address this issue, we consider the channel-wise and point-wise excitation attention on point clouds to learn more robust representations for each voxel, highlight key features and lead to better detection results.

3   DA-TSD Design

This section provides a detailed presentation of DA-TSD, a two-stage voxel-based 3D object detector. As shown in Fig. 1, our innovation mainly lies in two parts, namely, the DA module and the PS module. The former adaptively learns the importance between point-wise and channel-wise feature maps, highlights key feature information, while the latter provides cross-layer feature maps to reduce the impact of information loss caused by quantization of sparse convolution.

3.1   Double Attention

Assuming that the point clouds $\mathbf{P}$ in 3D space is divided into a set of fixed-size voxels, with each voxel having a size of v_W, v_H, v_D, the size of the voxel grid can be calculated by division. It should be noted that, inspired by [10], we do not perform voxel grid division on the Z-axis.

Previous studies have shown that random sampling methods employed in SECOND [27] can be unstable in the vicinity of the LiDAR sensor. To mitigate this issue, we adopt the sampling method proposed in [30]. A sampling point is considered valid if it satisfies the condition that all $Dist > M$, where $Dist$ can be represented using Euclidean distance and M is a fixed value, and in our experiments we set $M = 3$. The sampling process is accelerated using the absolute value distance, i.e.:

$$Dist = |x - x_{val}| + |y - y_{val}| + |z - z_{val}|, \tag{1}$$

where $x_{val}, y_{val}, z_{val}$ denote the coordinates of the existing valid sample points.

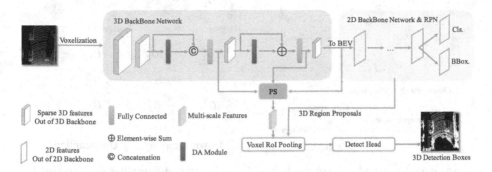

Fig. 1. An overview of DA-TSD. The raw point clouds are first divided into regular voxels and feature extraction is performed using a 3D backbone network, where the DA module processes each voxel separately to obtain more representative features. The features processed by DA are sampled using PS to obtain features with stronger geometric details. Then the 3D features are transformed into a Bird's Eye View (BEV) representation, and 2D backbone network and Region Proposal Network (RPN) are applied on the BEV to generate 3D region proposals. Finally Region of Interest (RoI) features are extracted using Voxel RoI Pooling and fed into the detection subnet for further box refinement.

A set of voxels V consisting of K voxels can be denoted as $V = \{V^1, V^2, ..., V^K\}$, where $V^k \in \mathbb{R}^{N \times C}$ represents the k-th voxel.

Point-Wise Excitation Attention. Given a voxel V^k, global average pooling is used to aggregate point features across the channel-wise dimension, resulting in a per-voxel point-wise response $Z^k \in \mathbb{R}^{N \times 1}$. To exploit the aggregated information generated in the previous step and to capture the dependencies of points in space, in the second step, two fully connected layers (FC) are used to encode the global response to limit the complexity of the model and help generalize it, and a simple gating mechanism with sigmoid activation [7] is used to normalize the values of the attention matrix to the range $[0, 1]$, i.e.:

$$S^k = \sigma\Big(g(Z^k, W_1, W_2)\Big) = \sigma\Big(W_2\delta(W_1 Z^k)\Big), \qquad (2)$$

where δ is the ReLU [14] function, σ is the sigmoid function, $W_1 \in \mathbb{R}^{r \times N}, W_2 \in \mathbb{R}^{N \times r}$ are the weight parameters of the reduced-dimensional FC and the increased-dimension FC respectively, indicating the importance of point-level features for each voxel. $S^k \in \mathbb{R}^{N \times 1}$ is the point-wise excitation attention of V^k. As shown in Fig. 2(a), the upper branch of the attention module is used to describe the spatial dependencies between points within each voxel.

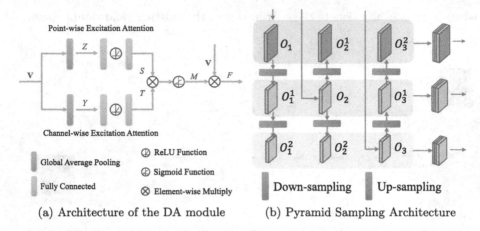

(a) Architecture of the DA module   (b) Pyramid Sampling Architecture

Fig. 2. Architecture of the DA module (a) and Pyramid Sampling Architecture (b).

Channel-Wise Excitation Attention. The channel-wise excitation attention is similar to the point-wise excitation attention, as shown in Fig. 2(a). The global average pooling operation of the channel-wise excitation attention is to aggregate the channel features in the point dimension, such that a channel-wise response $Y^k \in \mathbb{R}^{1 \times C}$ for a voxel is obtained. Then, we compute $T^k = \sigma(g((Y^k)^T, W_1', W_2')) = \sigma(W_2'\delta(W_1'(Y^k)^T))$, where $W_1' \in \mathbb{R}^{r \times C}$ and $W_2' \in \mathbb{R}^{C \times r}$ represent the importance of channel-level features to each voxel.

Given a voxel V^k, we perform element-wise multiplication on point-wise spatial attention S^k and channel-wise attention T^k to obtain an attention matrix $M^k \in \mathbb{R}^{N \times C}$, i.e.:

$$M^k = S^k \times T^k. \tag{3}$$

Therefore, a feature with attention can be expressed as $F^k = M^k \odot V^k \in \mathbb{R}^{N \times C}$, which weights the importance of all points within a voxel in the point-wise and channel-wise dimensions.

Through the above two operation steps, the feature representation F^k reinforces the key features. It has a positive effect on our task, and also suppresses irrelevant noise features. We name the module that integrates these two types of attention Double Attention (DA).

As shown in Fig. 1, in our approach, two DA modules are used so that multiple levels of feature attention can be used. For each DA module, in order to incorporate more features, we concatenate/sum its input and output. High-dimensional feature representations are then obtained through fully connected layers.

3.2 Pyramid Sampling

In order to reduce the effect of lost information during convolutional quantization, a PS module is used to obtain cross-layer feature mapping, as illustrated in Fig. 2(b). The features processed by the two DA blocks are denoted as O_1 and

O_2, and the features processed by the last sparse convolution block are denoted as O_3. The shapes are $(C', H/2, W/2), (2C', H/4, W/4)$ and $(2C', H/8, W/8)$, respectively. Based on O_1, a feature pyramid $\{O_1, O_1^1, O_1^2\}$ is constructed, where O_1^1 and O_1^2 are obtained by down-sampling O_1 twice. Similarly, the $\{O_2, O_2^1, O_2^2\}$ is obtained by up-sampling and down-sampling O_2. Two up-sampling operations are performed on O_3 to get $\{O_3, O_3^1, O_3^2\}$. In these three pyramids, O_1^1 has the same size as O_2, while O_1^2 has the same size as O_3. After obtaining the three feature pyramids, features with the same scale are concatenated horizontally to obtain $PS = \{PS_1, PS_2, PS_3\}$, which will serve as a part of the input to Voxel RoI Pooling.

3.3   Backbone and Region Proposal Networks

The backbone network of DA-TSD is similar to the architecture of [20,27]. The 3D backbone network extracts features from voxelized inputs and stacks along the Z-axis to generate BEV feature maps. The 2D backbone network consists of a top-down feature extraction sub-network and a multi-scale feature fusion sub-network, where the former contains two 3×3 convolutional layer blocks, and the latter involves up-sampling and concatenating top-down features. Finally, the output of the 2D backbone network is convolved using two 11 convolutional layers to generate 3D region proposals.

3.4   Voxel RoI Pooling and Detect Head

Voxel RoI Pooling introduced in Voxel R-CNN is utilized in DA-TSD. First we group a set of neighboring voxels using voxel queries, then aggregate the neighboring voxel features using [16]. The voxel features are processed through an MLP (Multilayer Perceptron) and channel-wise max pooling to obtain aggregated features. Finally, we concatenate the aggregated features from different stages to obtain the RoI features, which are used as input for the detect head. In the detect head, MLP converts RoI features into feature vectors. After flattening it is fed into two branches, one for bounding box regression that is used to predict the residuals between 3D region proposals and ground truth boxes and the other for prediction confidence, which is used to predict the IoU-related confidence score.

3.5   Loss Function

Losses of RPN. The loss function of Region Proposal Network (RPN) comprises of both classification loss and bounding box regression loss. Due to the extreme imbalance between foreground and background points during training, we apply Focal Loss [11] as classification loss:

$$\mathcal{L}_{clS} = -\alpha_t (1 - p_t)^{\gamma_t} \log(p_t),$$

$$p_t = \begin{cases} p, & y = 1, \\ 1 - p, & otherwise, \end{cases} \tag{4}$$

where p is the estimated probability of the model for the class with label $y = 1$. α_t and γ_t are the parameters of Focal Loss, and in our experiments, we set $\alpha_t = 0.25$ and $\gamma_t = 2$.

For the regression target, the positive anchor is parameterized as $*_a$ and Δ^* is used to represent the corresponding residual. Then the offset between the prior anchor a and the ground-truth box g in bounding box regression can be expressed as Eq. 5, and the regression loss is computed using the SmoothL1 [18] function.

$$\Delta x = \frac{x_g - x_a}{d_a}, \Delta y = \frac{y_g - y_a}{d_a}, \Delta z = \frac{z_g - z_a}{h_a},$$

$$\Delta l = \log\left(\frac{l_g}{l_a}\right), \Delta w = \log\left(\frac{w_g}{W_a}\right), \Delta h = \log\left(\frac{h_g}{h_a}\right), \quad (5)$$

$$\Delta\theta = \sin(\theta_g - \theta_a).$$

The 3D ground-truth bounding box is defined as $x_g, y_g, z_g, l_g, w_g, h_g, \theta_g$, where x, y, z is the center position, l, w, h represent the length, width, and height of the 3D bounding box, and θ is the yaw rotation around the Z-axis. $d_a = \sqrt{l_a^2 + w_a^2}$ is the diagonal length of the bottom of anchor box base.

The total loss function for RPN can be defined as:

$$\mathcal{L}_{RPN} = \frac{1}{N_{pos}}\left[\sum_i \mathcal{L}_{cls}(p_i^a, c_i^a) + \mathbb{1}(c_i^* \geq 1)\sum_i \mathcal{L}_{reg}(\delta_i^a, t_i^*)\right], \quad (6)$$

where N_{pos} represents the number of positive anchors, p_i^a is the output of the classification branch, c_i^a is the classification label, δ_i^a is the output of the regression branch, and t_i^* is the regression target. The term $\mathbb{1}(c_i^* \geq 1)$ indicates that only the regression loss of positive anchors is calculated.$\mathcal{L}_{reg}$ and $\mathcal{L}_{cls}$ denote the regression and classification loss functions, respectively, as described earlier.

Losses of Detect Head. The confidence scores are measured using IoU as follows:

$$l_i^*(IoU_i) = \begin{cases} 0, & IoU_i < \theta_L, \\ \frac{IoU_i - \theta_L}{\theta_H - \theta_L}, & \theta_L \leq IoU_i < \theta_H, \\ 1, & IoU_i > \theta_H, \end{cases} \quad (7)$$

where IoU_i is the IoU between the i-th predicted proposal and the ground truth box. If IoU_i is less than θ_L, the anchor is assigned as background (negative), and if IoU_i is greater than θ_H, the anchor is assigned as foreground (positive). Binary Cross-Entropy is used for confidence prediction, while SmoothL1 is used to calculate the loss for the box regression branch. The total loss function of the detect head can be defined as:

$$\mathcal{L}_{head} = \frac{1}{N_p}\left[\sum_i \mathcal{L}_{cls}(p_i, l_i^*(IoU_i)) + \mathbb{1}(IoU_i \geq \theta_{reg})\sum_i \mathcal{L}_{reg}(\delta_i, t_i^*)\right], \quad (8)$$

where N_p is the number of region proposals during training, and $\mathbb{1}(IoU_i \geq \theta_{reg})$ indicates that only region proposals with $IoU_i \geq \theta_{reg}$ are considered for computing the regression loss.

4 Experiments

4.1 Datasets

DA-TSD was trained on the KITTI dataset [4], which contains 7481 training samples and 7518 test samples. For experimental studies, the training samples are usually divided into a *training* set of 3712 samples and a *val* set of 3769 samples. We report the performance of our model on the KITTI *val* set. According to the KITTI official evaluation protocol, mAP is used as evaluation metric. If the datasets in general need to use our method, the data format needs to be changed to the storage format of the KITTI.

4.2 Implementation Details

For data augmentation, 15, 10, and 10 ground truth samples of Cars, Pedestrians, and Cyclists, respectively, are randomly selected and "pasted" into the current point clouds to increase the number of objects. Secondly, points in the ground truth boxes are randomly rotated from $[-\pi/4, \pi/4]$. Thirdly, the scale noise is extracted from the uniform distribution $[0.95, 1.05]$.

For cars, we use an anchor with dimensions of $w = 1.6 \times l = 3.9 \times h = 1.56$ m, centered at $z = -1.0$ m. For pedestrians, we use an anchor with dimensions of $w = 0.6 \times l = 0.8 \times h = 1.73$ m, and for cyclists, the anchor has dimensions of $w = 0.6 \times l = 1.76 \times h = 1.73$ m; both are centered at $z = -0.6$ m.

The network setup of DA-TSD is similar to the baseline model Voxel R-CNN, with four Conv. blocks in 3D backbone, and all three blocks contain three sparse Conv. layers except the first one with one sparse Conv. layer, and the number of filters are 16, 32, 64, and 64, respectively. The 2D backbone network consists of two blocks, where the first block has the same resolution as the output of the 3D backbone network on the X and Y axis, and the second block has half the resolution of the first block. The number of Conv. layers in both blocks is set to 5. The network is optimized end-to-end using the Adam optimizer with an initial learning rate of 0.01, and cosine annealing strategy is used for updating. The network is trained for 80 epochs with a batch size of 4. In the detect head, θ_H is set to 0.75, θ_L is set to 0.25, and θ_{reg} is set to 0.55.

During the inference stage, NMS (Non-Maximum Suppression) is first applied on the RPN with an IoU threshold of 0.7, and the top 100 region proposals are kept as input for the detect head. Subsequently, NMS is applied again with an IoU threshold of 0.1 to refine the predictions and eliminate redundant detections.

4.3 Comparison with State-of-the-Arts

In this section, we evaluate our approach on the KITTI *val* set according to a common protocol to report the performance of the model with an IoU threshold of 0.7 for Car class and 0.5 for Pedestrian class and Cyclist class. The mAP was calculated with the AP setting of recall 40 positions and 11 positions, respectively. Experimental inference was conducted using NVIDIA GeForce RTX 3090 Ti GPU.

Table 1. Performance comparisons with state-of-the-art methods on the KITTI *val* set. All results are reported by the average precision with 0.7 IoU threshold and 11 recall positions

Method	Modality	Car 3D AP			3D mAP
		Easy	Mod.	Hard	
MV3D [2]	LIDAR+RGB	71.29	62.68	56.56	**63.51**
F-PointNet [15]	LIDAR+RGB	83.76	70.92	63.65	**72.78**
AVOD-FPN [9]	LIDAR+RGB	84.41	74.44	68.65	**75.83**
PointRCNN [21]	LIDAR	88.26	77.73	76.67	**80.89**
SECOND [27]	LIDAR	87.43	76.48	69.1	**77.67**
STD [28]	LIDAR	89.70	79.80	79.30	**82.93**
VoxelNet [33]	LIDAR	81.97	65.46	62.85	**70.09**
PV-RCNN [20]	LIDAR	89.35	83.69	78.70	**83.91**
TANet [12]	LIDAR	87.52	76.64	73.86	**79.34**
SASSD [5]	LIDAR	90.15	79.91	78.78	**82.95**
SVGA-Net [6]	LIDAR	**90.59**	80.23	79.15	**83.32**
Voxel R-CNN [3]	LIDAR	89.41	84.52	78.93	**84.59**
DA-TSD (Ours)	LIDAR	90.32	**85.95**	**80.46**	**85.55**

As shown in Table 1 and Table 2, DA-TSD outperforms previous methods in the key metrics, moderate Car 3D (R11) and Car 3D (R40). Specifically, DA-TSD improves the baseline Voxel R-CNN [3] by 1.43% and 2.06% on the two recall positions, and outperforms the SOTA SVGA-Net [6] by 5.72% and SE-SSD [32] by 1.23%, respectively. For hard Car 3D (R11) and hard Car 3D (R40), the baseline Voxel R-CNN [3] is improved by 1.53% and 1.97% on the two recall positions, and outperforms the SOTA SVGA-Net [6] by 1.31% and CT3D [19] by 1.37%, respectively. Regarding the result of SVGA-Net [6] in easy Car 3D (R11), which is slightly higher than our method, we speculate that our method weakens the relationship between local point sets. The next step in establishing relationships between local point sets will be attempted to improve this situation.

Table 2. All results are reported by the average precision with 0.7 IoU threshold and 40 recall positions

Method	Modality	Car 3D AP			3D mAP
		Easy	Mod.	Hard	
PV-RCNN [20]	LIDAR	92.57	84.83	82.69	**86.70**
CT3D [19]	LIDAR	92.85	85.82	83.46	**87.38**
SE-SSD [32]	LIDAR	93.19	86.12	83.31	**87.54**
Voxel R-CNN [3]	LIDAR	92.38	85.29	82.86	**86.84**
DA-TSD (Ours)	LIDAR	**93.58**	**87.35**	**84.83**	**88.59**

Table 3. Performance of the Pedestrian and Cyclist for 3D object detection on the KITTI *val* set compared to several state-of-the-art methods. All results are reported by the average precision with 0.5 IoU threshold and 11 recall positions

Method	Modality	Pedestrian 3D AP			Cyclist 3D AP		
		Easy	Mod.	Hard	Easy	Mod.	Hard
PointRCNN [21]	LIDAR	65.62	58.57	51.48	82.76	62.83	59.62
VoxelNet [33]	LIDAR	57.86	53.42	48.87	67.17	47.65	45.11
PointPillars [10]	LIDAR	66.73	61.06	56.50	83.65	63.40	59.71
DA-TSD (Ours)	LIDAR	**67.90**	**63.50**	**59.33**	**85.44**	**72.75**	**70.48**

Table 4. Performance comparison of BEV object detection for Car and 3D object detection for Pedestrian and Cyclist on KITTI *val* set at 40 recall positions with baseline

Method	Modality	Car BEV AP			Pedestrian 3D AP			Cyclist 3D AP		
		Easy	Mod.	Hard	Easy	Mod.	Hard	Easy	Mod.	Hard
Voxel R-CNN [3]	LIDAR	95.52	91.25	**88.99**	63.18	55.06	49.34	88.12	68.81	64.28
DA-TSD (Ours)	LIDAR	**95.57**	**92.08**	88.78	**69.96**	**65.91**	**61.77**	**89.71**	**75.39**	**70.92**

Table 3 shows the performance of 3D object detection in the Pedestrian and Cyclist on the KITTI *val* set at 11 recall positions compared to several SOTA methods. For moderate Pedestrian 3D (R11) and hard Pedestrian 3D (R11), a performance improvement of 2.44% and 2.83% was achieved, by the proposed method over PointPillars [10]. And for moderate Cyclist 3D (R11) and hard Cyclist 3D (R11), the proposed method demonstrates improvements of 9.35% and 10.77%, respectively, compared to the baseline Voxel R-CNN [3]. The improvement for the Pedestrian and Cyclist is more pronounced. The performance improvement mainly comes from the DA, which allows better learning of important features of the objects, resulting in better detection performance. In addition, the performance is shown comparing the proposed approach with the baseline Voxel R-CNN in Table 4.

4.4   Ablation Study

In this section, extensive ablation experiments are conducted in order to analyze the effectiveness of each component of our approach. All modules were trained on the Car class *train* split of the KITTI dataset and evaluated on the *val* split.

Table 5. "P.E." and "C.E." represent point-wise and channel-wise excitation attention, respectively. The results were evaluated by calculating the mAP of the Car class with 40 recall positions

Method	P.E	C.E	Concat	DA module	Car mAP_{3D} (%)
Baseline					86.84
(a)	✓				87.22
(b)		✓			87.10
(c)	✓	✓	✓		87.51
(d)	✓	✓		✓	87.97

Table 6. Experimental results on the effectiveness of the proposed PS. "P.S." stands for pyramid sampling. The results were evaluated by calculating the mAP of the Car class with 40 recall positions

Method	P.S	DA module	Car mAP_3D (%)
Baseline			86.84
(a)	✓		87.09
(b)		✓	87.97
(c)	✓	✓	88.59

Analysis of the Attention Mechanisms. Table 5 shows the ablation study on the proposed attention mechanism. The baseline method used in this study is Voxel R-CNN. By using only the point-wise excitation attention (a) and channel-wise excitation attention (b), the performance is improved to 87.22% and 87.10%. DA module employs a parallel fusion mechanism of P.E. and C.E., and when the two are combined, the 3D mAP of (d) improves to 87.61%, outperforming the baseline model by 1.13%. We also used the Concat operation to concatenate the outputs of these two types of attention along the channel direction (c). It can be observed that method (d) outperforms method (c), indicating that the DA module can better utilize spatial and channel information in a more reasonable way.

Effect of the Pyramid Sampling. We further investigated the effect of pyramid sampling (see Table 6). We compared two settings based on the baseline: with or without the DA module. In the absence of the DA module (a), the improvement of PS was not so obvious. It is worth noting that with the DA module (c), the improvement of PS is significant. This suggests that with the help of the DA module, PS can better utilize the different scale information of the data to improve detection performance. This indicates that the two methods complement each other well. The DA module can provide more robust feature representations, while PS can provide more informative cross-layer voxel features.

5   Conclusion

In this paper, we propose a voxel-based two-stage 3D object detector called DA-TSD. The core modules of DA-TSD are mainly the Double Attention (DA) module and the Pyramid Pampling (PS) module. The former can encode the critical features of the object and suppress the noisy features. The latter provides cross-layer feature maps and obtains more comprehensive feature representations. Experimental results on the KITTI dataset demonstrate the effectiveness of the DA and PS modules. Compared with previous methods, our method shows a significant improvement in detecting small objects.

References

1. Chen, C., Chen, Z., et al.: SASA: semantics-augmented set abstraction for point-based 3D object detection. In: Proceedings of the AAAI Conference on Artificial Intelligence, vol. 36, pp. 221–229 (2022)
2. Chen, X., Ma, H., et al.: Multi-view 3D object detection network for autonomous driving. In: Proceedings of the IEEE Conference on Computer Vision and Pattern Recognition, pp. 1907–1915 (2017)
3. Deng, J., Shi, S., et al.: Voxel R-CNN: towards high performance voxel-based 3D object detection. In: Proceedings of the AAAI Conference on Artificial Intelligence, vol. 35, pp. 1201–1209 (2021)
4. Geiger, A., Lenz, P., et al.: Are we ready for autonomous driving? The KITTI vision benchmark suite. In: 2012 IEEE Conference on Computer Vision and Pattern Recognition, pp. 3354–3361. IEEE (2012)
5. He, C., Zeng, H., et al.: Structure aware single-stage 3D object detection from point cloud. In: Proceedings of the IEEE/CVF Conference on Computer Vision and Pattern Recognition, pp. 11873–11882 (2020)
6. He, Q., Wang, Z., et al.: SVGA-Net: sparse voxel-graph attention network for 3D object detection from point clouds. In: Proceedings of the AAAI Conference on Artificial Intelligence, vol. 36, pp. 870–878 (2022)
7. Hu, J., Shen, L., et al.: Squeeze-and-Excitation networks. In: Proceedings of the IEEE Conference on Computer Vision and Pattern Recognition, pp. 7132–7141 (2018)
8. Hu, J.S., Kuai, T., et al.: Point density-aware voxels for LiDAR 3D object detection. In: Proceedings of the IEEE/CVF Conference on Computer Vision and Pattern Recognition, pp. 8469–8478 (2022)

9. Ku, J., Mozifian, M., et al.: Joint 3D proposal generation and object detection from view aggregation. In: 2018 IEEE/RSJ International Conference on Intelligent Robots and Systems (IROS), pp. 1–8. IEEE (2018)

10. Lang, A.H., Vora, S., et al.: PointPillars: fast encoders for object detection from point clouds. In: Proceedings of the IEEE/CVF Conference on Computer Vision and Pattern Recognition, pp. 12697–12705 (2019)

11. Lin, T.Y., Goyal, P., et al.: Focal loss for dense object detection. In: Proceedings of the IEEE International Conference on Computer Vision, pp. 2980–2988 (2017)

12. Liu, Z., Zhao, X., et al.: TANet: robust 3D object detection from point clouds with triple attention. In: Proceedings of the AAAI Conference on Artificial Intelligence, vol. 34, pp. 11677–11684 (2020)

13. Mao, J., Niu, M., et al.: Pyramid R-CNN: towards better performance and adaptability for 3D object detection. In: Proceedings of the IEEE/CVF International Conference on Computer Vision, pp. 2723–2732 (2021)

14. Nair, V., Hinton, G.E.: Rectified linear units improve restricted Boltzmann machines. In: Proceedings of the 27th International Conference on Machine Learning (ICML-2010), pp. 807–814 (2010)

15. Qi, C.R., Liu, W., et al.: Frustum PointNets for 3D object detection from RGB-D data. In: Proceedings of the IEEE Conference on Computer Vision and Pattern Recognition, pp. 918–927 (2018)

16. Qi, C.R., Su, H., et al.: PointNet: deep learning on point sets for 3D classification and segmentation. In: Proceedings of the IEEE Conference on Computer Vision and Pattern Recognition, pp. 652–660 (2017)

17. Redmon, J., Divvala, S., et al.: You only look once: unified, real-time object detection. In: Proceedings of the IEEE Conference on Computer Vision and Pattern Recognition, pp. 779–788 (2016)

18. Ren, S., He, K., et al.: Faster R-CNN: towards real-time object detection with region proposal networks. In: Advances in Neural Information Processing Systems, vol. 28 (2015)

19. Sheng, H., Cai, S., et al.: Improving 3D object detection with channel-wise transformer. In: Proceedings of the IEEE/CVF International Conference on Computer Vision, pp. 2743–2752 (2021)

20. Shi, S., Guo, C., et al.: PV-RCNN: point-voxel feature set abstraction for 3D object detection. In: Proceedings of the IEEE/CVF Conference on Computer Vision and Pattern Recognition, pp. 10529–10538 (2020)

21. Shi, S., Wang, X., et al.: PoinTRCNN: 3D object proposal generation and detection from point cloud. In: Proceedings of the IEEE/CVF Conference on Computer Vision and Pattern Recognition, pp. 770–779 (2019)

22. Wang, T., Hu, X., Liu, Z., Fu, C.W.: Sparse2Dense: learning to densify 3D features for 3D object detection. In: Koyejo, S., Mohamed, S., et al. (eds.) Advances in Neural Information Processing Systems, vol. 35, pp. 38533–38545. Curran Associates, Inc. (2022)

23. Wu, H., Wen, C., et al.: Transformation-equivariant 3D object detection for autonomous driving. arXiv preprint arXiv:2211.11962 (2022)

24. Wu, H., Wen, C., et al.: Virtual sparse convolution for multimodal 3D object detection. arXiv preprint arXiv:2303.02314 (2023)

25. Wu, X., Peng, L., et al.: Sparse fuse dense: towards high quality 3D detection with depth completion. In: Proceedings of the IEEE/CVF Conference on Computer Vision and Pattern Recognition, pp. 5418–5427 (2022)

26. Xu, Q., Zhou, Y., et al.: SPG: unsupervised domain adaptation for 3D object detection via semantic point generation. In: Proceedings of the IEEE/CVF International Conference on Computer Vision, pp. 15446–15456 (2021)
27. Yan, Y., Mao, Y., Li, B.: SECOND: sparsely embedded convolutional detection. Sensors **18**(10), 3337 (2018)
28. Yang, Z., Sun, Y., et al.: STD: sparse-to-dense 3D object detector for point cloud. In: Proceedings of the IEEE/CVF International Conference on Computer Vision, pp. 1951–1960 (2019)
29. Yang, Z., Sun, Y., et al.: 3DSSD: point-based 3D single stage object detector. In: Proceedings of the IEEE/CVF Conference on Computer Vision and Pattern Recognition, pp. 11040–11048 (2020)
30. Ye, Y., Chen, H., et al.: SARPNET: shape attention regional proposal network for lidar-based 3D object detection. Neurocomputing **379**, 53–63 (2020)
31. Yin, T., Zhou, X., et al.: Center-based 3D object detection and tracking. In: Proceedings of the IEEE/CVF Conference on Computer Vision and Pattern Recognition, pp. 11784–11793 (2021)
32. Zheng, W., Tang, W., et al.: SE-SSD: self-ensembling single-stage object detector from point cloud. In: Proceedings of the IEEE/CVF Conference on Computer Vision and Pattern Recognition, pp. 14494–14503 (2021)
33. Zhou, Y., Tuzel, O.: VoxelNet: end-to-end learning for point cloud based 3D object detection. In: Proceedings of the IEEE Conference on Computer Vision and Pattern Recognition, pp. 4490–4499 (2018)

Enhanced Point Cloud Interpretation via Style Fusion and Contrastive Learning in Advanced 3D Data Analysis

Ruimin Zhou⬤ and Chung-Ming Own$^{(\boxtimes)}$⬤

Tianjin University, Tianjin, China
`chungming.own@tju.edu.cn`

Abstract. Point clouds, as the most prevalent representation of 3D data, are inherently disordered, unstructured, and discrete. Feature extraction from point clouds can be challenging, as objects with similar styles may be misclassified, and uncertain backgrounds or noise can significantly impact the performance of traditional classification models. To address these challenges, we introduce StyleContrast, a novel contrastive learning algorithm for style fusion. This approach effectively fuses styles of point clouds belonging to the same category across different domain datasets at the feature level, thus fulfilling the need for data enhancement. By aligning point clouds with their corresponding style-fused point clouds in the feature space, StyleContrast allows the feature extractor to learn style-independent invariant features. Moreover, our method incorporates category-centric contrastive loss to differentiate between similar objects from different categories. Experimental results demonstrate that StyleContrast achieves superior performance on Modelnet40, Shapenet-Part, and ScanObjectNN, surpassing all existing methods in terms of classification accuracy. Ablation experiments further confirm that our approach excels in point cloud feature analysis.

Keywords: Point cloud · Contrastive learning · Style fusion

1 Introduction

In recent years, the growing presence of 3D data represented by point clouds has prompted more in-depth exploration of the 3D domain and advancements in point cloud feature extraction [18,19,24,25]. This phenomenon has led to an increase in applications for classification [18,19,24], detection [31], and semantic segmentation [3,19,24]. However, models that excel in CAD-based datasets may underperform in real-world scenes with ambient backgrounds or uncertain noise interference. Additionally, 3D point cloud datasets' volume and diversity are significantly smaller than their 2D counterparts. For example, ModelNet40 [27], a widely-used 3D point cloud classification benchmark, contains only 12311 CAD models across 40 categories, while ImageNet [5], a standard benchmark for 2D classification, boasts around 1.2 million images covering 1000 categories. Therefore, it is crucial

L. Iliadis et al. (Eds.): ICANN 2023, LNCS 14254, pp. 344–355, 2023.
https://doi.org/10.1007/978-3-031-44207-0_29

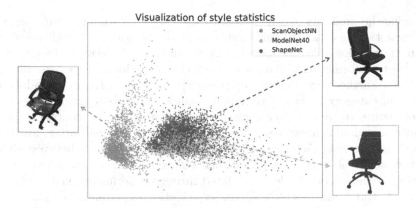

Fig. 1. The 2D t-SNE [10] visualization of style statistics on ModelNet40, ShapeNet, and ScanObjectNN.

to address the challenge of learning class-invariant features unrelated to style from limited data while avoiding misclassification in realistic scenarios.

Contrastive learning methods [4,7], which leverage correlations and differences between data to learn the nature of objects, have experienced great success in the 2D domain. Recently, 3D contrastive learning models [2,9,28] have also emerged. These methods require robust data augmentation to create positive sample pairs [4]. Researchers have attempted to adapt augmentation techniques from the 2D domain to 3D tasks. As style transfer tasks in 2D continue to evolve [8], similar approaches for transferring geometric properties between target and source shapes have emerged in the 3D domain [1,26,29]. However, the concept of 3D style still needs further clarification, with only one study [15] proposing stylistic similarities among 3D objects based on their geometric shapes. We observed that the generation method for different point clouds can also influence their style. For instance, both Modelnet40 and Shapenet [3] utilize CAD models to generate point clouds, while ScanObjectNN [23] employs actual scene sampling. To verify this observation, we use the first residual block of DGCNN [24] to extract point cloud features from the point set through a dynamically updated local graph structure. The style feature is then calculated using the Gram matrix and downscaled to 2D using t-SNE [10]. As illustrated in Fig. 1, the three images represent the same semantic concept (a chair) but possess distinct styles. The feature statistics capture these styles, as evidenced by the separable clusters. Our StyleFusion method is designed to efficiently synthesize novel styles by combining these instance-level feature statistics. Notably, there has been limited research on using style transfer to construct positive sample pairs in 3D contrastive learning.

In this study, we propose StyleContrast, a contrastive learning method based on style transfer. After feature extraction, we introduce a self-supervised contrastive learning branch to complement supervised learning. For each input point cloud, the style features of target and source shapes are fused in the feature space, leveraging the similarity of content feature distribution within the same category while maintaining a more distinct style feature distribution. The addition of contrastive learning enables the model to better distinguish between the structural and stylistic information of the point cloud, thereby enhancing its generalization capability. Furthermore, inspired by prototype networks [21], we introduce the concept of category centers and employ confidence levels to guide the generation of feature vectors for each category center, ensuring they contain sufficient semantic information about the corresponding category. StyleContrast learns the intrinsic character of each category by minimizing the distance between all feature vectors in the feature space and their respective category-centered vectors. The effectiveness of our model is validated through experiments on ModelNet40, ShapeNet, and ScanObjectNN. Moreover, ablation experiments emphasize the importance of both StyleFusion and contrastive learning modules. The main contributions of this submission can be summarized as follows:

- We introduce StyleContrast, a pseudo label guidanced contrastive learning based on style transfer, which enables the model to focus more on the structural information of the point cloud while minimizing the influence of style information on model performance.
- We develop a confidence category-centric contrastive learning method that allows the model to learn the essential properties of each category.
- We present a novel approach to enhance stylistic diversity by combining CAD-generated point clouds with real scene sampled point clouds.
- We apply our StyleContrast method to a wide range of downstream tasks, achieving improved results compared to the original supervised learning approach.

2   Related Works

2.1   Contrastive Learning on Point Cloud

Contrastive learning methods maximize consistency among different augmented views of the same data instance to learn representations, which has achieved remarkable results in 2D tasks [4,7]. Typically, contrastive loss employs InfoNCE [17], which measures similarity through a dot product. Recent research has attempted to learn representations for tasks in the 3D domain, such as classification [2,13,20], segmentation [9,28], object detection tasks [31], and shape completion [16]. PointContrast [28] introduces PointInfoNCE loss to handle similarity between matched points. CrossPoint [2] enhances the representation of 3D point clouds by employing 3D-2D consistency along with 2D image feature correspondence. Another study [16] supplements the training set with additional human-set RGB information. In contrast to most 3D contrastive learning methods that rely on 2D images, our approach focuses on learning the point cloud itself without requiring auxiliary information.

2.2   Data Augmentation on Point Cloud

Point clouds are characterized by their irregular arrangement, permutation invariance, and rotation invariance. These unique properties render conventional geometric transformations used in 2D data augmentation (such as flipping, rotating, and scaling) inapplicable to point clouds. For laser point clouds, commonly used data augmentation methods include downsampling, random rotation around the gravity axis, random scaling, random jittering [18,19], random deletion, and random swapping [31]. While these methods have fixed parameters in the model, they have not achieved optimal augmentation. Some studies have explored point or color transformations to address these limitations [11,13], but they primarily focus on the instance level of the point cloud. Data augmentation at the feature level still needs to be explored. In this paper, we leverage the distributional properties of content and style features to adaptively mix style information from different samples within the same category, achieving style migration at the feature level.

3   Proposed Method

3.1   Preliminaries

This section outlines the network structure of our proposed StyleContrast method, as illustrated in Fig. 2. First, the source input consists of a random batch containing N point clouds. For each point cloud, a point cloud pair (p_i^s, p_i^t) is constructed by randomly selecting another point cloud from the same category i. Second, the model extracts features using a feature extractor and adjusts the model parameters with pseudo label guided contrastive learning joint cross-entropy loss, as discussed in Sect. 3.2. Finally, the aggregation of features across categories is enhanced through confidence category-centric contrastive learning, introduced in Sect. 3.3. To improve contrastive learning, we propose a new data augmentation scheme called StyleFusion, with details provided in Sect. 3.4.

3.2   Pseudo Label Guidanced Contrastive Learning

For the point cloud pair, p_i^s is considered the source style sample, while p_i^t is the target style sample. As per the StyleFusion method proposed in Sect. 3.4, content features extracted by the first layer are combined with style features to generate augmented samples p_i^{aug} and construct positive sample pairs (p_i^s, p_i^{aug}). The feature pairs (f_i^s, f_i^{aug}) are extracted by the subsequent network, and the pseudo labels (y_i^s, y_i^{aug}) are generated using the classifier (Mlp blocks). In this study, the extracted feature pairs (f_i^s, f_i^{aug}) are treated as positive sample pairs. In contrast, all feature vectors from the remaining $2N - 2$ vectors with a different pseudo-label are considered negative samples. A non-linear mapping layer maps each feature vector, obtaining the feature vectors (pro_i^s, pro_i^{aug}) to enhance the feature representation before calculating the contrastive loss. We use cosine

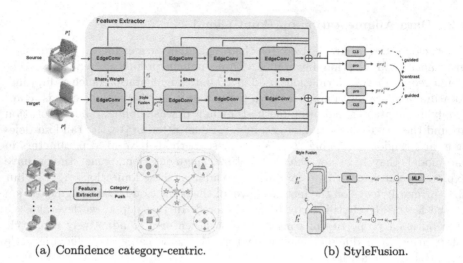

(a) Confidence category-centric.   (b) StyleFusion.

Fig. 2. The overall structure and partial details of StyleContrast, where $\oplus$ indicates concatenation and $\odot$ indicates element-wise product. The EdgeConv block is consistent with that used in DGCNN. The KL block in (b) performs the divergence operation.

similarity as the similarity metric. The contrastive loss for each mapped pair of feature vectors is computed as follows,

$$l_{s,aug} = -log \frac{exp(sim(pro_i^s, pro_i^{aug})/\tau)}{\sum\limits_{k=1}^{2N} \mathbb{I}_{(y_i^s \neq y_i^k)} exp(sim(pro_i^s, pro_i^k)/\tau)}, \quad (1)$$

$$l_{aug,s} = -log \frac{exp(sim(pro_i^s, pro_i^{aug})/\tau)}{\sum\limits_{k=1}^{2N} \mathbb{I}_{(y_i^{aug} \neq y_i^k)} exp(sim(pro_i^{aug}, pro_i^k)/\tau)}, \quad (2)$$

where y_i^s and y_i^{aug} represent the categories to which the mappings pro_i^s and pro_i^{aug} belong, respectively, and τ is the temperature coefficient. The indicator function, $\mathbb{I}(y_i^s \neq y_i^k)$, equals one when y_i^s is not equal to y_i^k and zero in all other cases.

3.3 Confidence Category-Centric Contrastive Learning

In the prototype network [21], the category centroid vector M_c is obtained by calculating the mean of all same-category feature vectors f_c. To obtain a more representative vector of category centroids, weights are assigned to all correctly classified samples based on their classification confidence. Generally, samples with higher classification confidence within the same category contain more stylistic information. Conversely, samples with lower classification confidence feature vectors contain more invariant features for classification. Therefore, we

use $C_i^c = Softmax(f_i^c)$ to calculate the confidence C_i^c and express its importance as $1 - C_i^c$. The f_i^c refers to the features for the ith sample in category c.
The category centers are generated as follows,

$$M_c = \frac{1}{N^c}\sum_{i=1}^{N^c}(1 - C_i^c)f_i^c, \tag{3}$$

where N_c denotes the total number of samples within category c.

We aim to map feature vectors to be more similar to their corresponding
category centroid vectors in the feature space while being less similar to other
categories. The cosine similarity measures the similarity between each feature
vector f_i^c and its respective category centroid vector. The category centroid
alignment loss is then defined and calculated as follows,

$$l_{f_i^c} = -log\frac{exp(sim(f_i^c, M_c)/\tau)}{\sum\limits_{k=1}^{L}\mathbb{I}_{(k\neq c)}exp(sim(f_i^c, M_k)/\tau)}, \tag{4}$$

where c represents the category to which the feature vector f_i^c belongs. L denotes
the total number of categories in the dataset, and τ is the temperature coefficient.

3.4   StyleFusion

In this approach, we consider the features of each channel as individually distributed data samples. The point cloud's category information should exhibit
minor variations within the same category. Consequently, we calculate the distribution relationship between the source style feature and the target style feature
channels to filter the channels corresponding to the category information. We
employ divergence values to extract the differences between the distribution of
the source and target channels. Channels with smaller difference values are considered category information, while those with larger values are treated as style
information. The divergence values are mapped to the interval $[0, 1]$, allowing for
shifting style information with more significant divergence differences. We define
these inter-channel differences as W_{dif},

$$W_{dif}^l(f_s^l, f_t^l) = f_s^l log\frac{f_s^l}{f_t^l}, \tag{5}$$

where f_s^l and f_t^l represents the channel l features of the source style and the
target style.

The channels of features are not independent; instead, they have a specific
correlation. To extract the relationship between the target style features' channels, we calculate the inner product of the feature matrix and its transpose. This
represents the inter-channel correlation, denoted as W_{rel},

$$W_{rel}^l = f_t^{l^T} \cdot f_t^l. \tag{6}$$

The weights W^l_{imp} of each channel, where the target style feature is added to the source style feature, are calculated as the dot product of the inter-channel relationships (learned through full connectivity) and the inter-channel differences. The process of StyleFusion is shown below,

$$f^l_{aug} = (1 - W^l_{imp})f^l_s + W^l_{imp}f^l_t, \tag{7}$$

where f^l_{aug} denotes the feature of the channel l after data enhancement.

4 Experiments

In this section, we thoroughly evaluate the performance of our proposed Style-Contrast method on several benchmarks, following standard protocols. For a fair comparison with existing methods, we use DGCNN as a point cloud feature extractor. Our StyleContrast is implemented in PyTorch, experimenting with an NVIDIA GeForce RTX 3090 graphics processing unit.

4.1 Classification on Modelnet40

The ModelNet40 dataset, the most commonly used benchmark for 3D point cloud classification, contains 12311 CAD models across 40 classes (9843 for training and 2468 for testing). We report class-average accuracy (mAcc) and overall accuracy (OA) on the testing set. All models are trained for 200 epochs with a batch size of 24.

Table 1. Classification results for ModelNet40.

Method	Inputs	$mAcc(\%)$	$OA(\%)$
Pointnet [18]	1024	86.0	89.2
PointNet++ [19]	1024	-	91.9
DGCNN [24]	1024	90.2	92.9
PCT [6]	1024	-	93.2
PosPool [14]	5000	-	93.2
PointCutmix [30]	1024	-	93.4
DGCNN + MD [22]	1024	90.26	93.39
StyleContrast (Ours)	1024	**90.6**	**93.5**

Results. Table 1 compares our StyleContrast method with previous approaches. Among these methods, StyleContrast uses only 1024 points and achieves an overall accuracy significantly higher than the baseline DGCNN method by 0.6% (93.5% vs. 92.9%). This improvement is due to the method's focus on the invariant features of categories and its ability to avoid style interference. StyleContrast

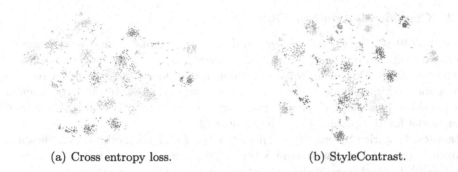

(a) Cross entropy loss.   (b) StyleContrast.

Fig. 3. Visualization results for ModelNet40 are presented, where each point represents a sample, and the same color is used to indicate instances of the same category.

performs better by at least 0.1% without relying on attention mechanisms like PCT [6], pre-training as in DGCNN + MD [22], or adding location information to the pooling layer like PosPool [14]. Additionally, our method outperforms PointCutmix [30], which employs data augmentation during training.

Visualization of Learned Feature. To gain a deeper understanding of the representations learned by StyleContrast, we visualized the features of each sample in the ModelNet40 test set using t-SNE. The results are displayed in Fig. 3(a), which relies solely on cross-entropy loss supervision. Some samples are mixed, leading to an unclear distinction between categories and increasing the classification difficulty for the model. By introducing StyleContrast, as shown in Fig. 3(b), point cloud features of the same category are better clustered together, ultimately enhancing the ability to distinguish between classes.

Table 2. Classification results for ScanObjectNN. We tested all methods on the most challenging variant (PB T50 RS).

Category	Pointnet [18]	PointNet++ [19]	DGCNN [24]	PointCNN [12]	BGA-DGCNN [16]	StyleContrast (Ours)
$OA(\%)$	68.2	77.9	78.1	78.5	79.7	**80.4**
$mAcc(\%)$	63.4	75.4	73.6	75.1	75.7	**77.6**
Bag	36.1	49.4	49.4	57.8	48.2	**62.7**
Bin	69.8	84.4	82.4	82.9	81.9	**86.4**
Box	10.5	31.6	33.1	33.1	30.1	**42.9**
Cabinet	62.6	77.4	83.9	83.6	**84.4**	77.4
Chair	89	91.3	91.8	**92.6**	**92.6**	90.5
Desk	50	74	63.3	65.3	**77.3**	67.3
Display	73	79.4	77	78.4	80.4	**83.3**
Door	**93.8**	85.2	89	84.8	92.4	90.5
Shelf	72.6	72.6	79.3	84.2	80.5	**86.3**
Table	67.8	72.6	**77.4**	67.4	74.1	73.3
Bed	61.8	75.5	64.5	80	73.6	**81.8**
Pillow	67.6	**81**	77.1	80	80	78.1
Sink	64.2	80.8	75	72.5	77.5	**82.5**
Sofa	76.7	90.5	91.4	**91.9**	**91.9**	90.5
Toilet	55.3	**85.9**	69.4	71.8	**85.9**	80.0

4.2   Classification on ScanObjectNN

ModelNet40 is a synthetic dataset, and as a result, many models struggle to perform well on perturbed scenes. To address this, we validated our approach using ScanObjectNN, a dataset containing 15000 real-world samples across 15 categories, which include background, noise, and occlusion. In our experiments, we considered the most challenging perturbation variant (PB T50 RS), training our model for 200 epochs with a batch size 32.

Results. Empirically, our StyleContrast outperforms all methods, significantly improving both mean class accuracy (mAcc) and overall accuracy (OA), as shown in Table 2. For instance, StyleContrast achieved a 4.0% higher mAcc and a 2.3% higher OA compared to DGCNN, outperforming both BGA-based methods [16] and other approaches [12] that focus on local structures of point clouds. Our method excels in 7 out of 15 categories, and for challenging categories like boxes and bags, we see accuracy improvements of 5% and 10%, respectively. The performance improves for objects with similar geometric properties, such as sofas and beds. Our model can accurately classify samples with background information interference, like a display with information about a table. Additionally, our method has a small gap between average class precision and overall precision, indicating that StyleContrast is not biased towards a specific class and demonstrates robustness.

4.3   Ablation Study and Analysis

In this subsection, we conduct a comprehensive ablation study to demonstrate the effectiveness of StyleContrast both quantitatively and qualitatively, using the ModelNet40 dataset as a basis for analysis.

Table 3. Different methods for constructing positive sample pairs on ModelNet40.

Method	$mAcc(\%)$	$OA(\%)$
DGCNN [24]	90.2	92.9
StyleContrast (normal)	90.2	93.0
StyleContrast (fix)	90.1	92.8
StyleContrast (StyleFusion)	**90.4**	**93.3**

The Impact of Style Fusion. We conducted experiments to assess the effectiveness of the proposed StyleFusion model. Specifically, the baseline method employs a cross-entropy (CE) loss function for pixel-level supervision. StyleContrast (normal) represents enhancement using only random rotation, scaling, or dithering. StyleContrast (fix) denotes the fixed fusion parameter ($W_{imp} = 0.5$). As demonstrated in Table 3, StyleContrast (fix) results suggest that data augmentation generates poor positive sample pairs because the fusion parameters require adaptive adjustment. Closing the distance of these poor positive sample pairs harms the model's performance. StyleContrast (normal) also underperforms due to the simplicity of the constructed positive sample pairs. However, StyleContrast continually improves upon the baseline, and its performance is further enhanced as the style fusion of point clouds provides more robust positive sample pairs for contrastive learning.

Table 4. Different category center construction methods on ModelNet40.

Method	$mAcc(\%)$	$OA(\%)$
DGCNN [24]	90.2	92.9
Direct Averaging	90.1	93.1
Confidence-guided	**90.3**	**93.2**

The Impact of Confidence-Based Category Center. Further experiments confirm the efficacy of the confidence-guided approach in constructing category centers. Table 4 presents various construction methods, with "Direct Averaging" representing the average method and "Confidence-guided" denoting our approach. As demonstrated by rows 2 and 3 in the table, the confidence-guided method effectively manages the unique features of individual categories and generates a more robust representation of category centers.

5 Conclusion

In this study, we introduce a simple yet effective point cloud analysis architecture called StyleContrast. This approach employs contrastive learning combined with StyleFusion, reducing the impact of style and encouraging the model to learn invariant features unrelated to style. By migrating the styles of CAD-generated point clouds with real scene-sampled point clouds, we enhance the stylistic diversity of the samples. Additionally, incorporating category-centered contrastive learning leads to a more compact distribution of features within the same category, further improving the model's performance. Our experimental results demonstrate that StyleContrast surpasses related work on various benchmarks. This method successfully applies contrastive learning to point clouds, offering novel insights and solutions for future 3D point cloud feature understanding.

References

1. Abhinav, U., Alpana, D., Kuriakose, S.-M., Mahato, D.: 3DSTNet: neural 3D shape style transfer. In: 2022 IEEE International Conference on Multimedia and Expo Workshops (ICMEW), pp. 1–6. IEEE (2022)
2. Afham, M., Dissanayake, I., Dissanayake, D., Dharmasiri, A., Thilakarathna, K., Rodrigo, R.: CrossPoint: self-supervised cross-modal contrastive learning for 3D point cloud understanding. In: The IEEE/CVF Conference on Computer Vision and Pattern Recognition (CVPR), pp. 9892–9902. IEEE (2022)

3. Chang, A.-X., et al.: ShapeNet: an information-rich 3D model repository. CoRR abs/1512.03012 (2015). arxiv.org/abs/1512.03012

4. Chen, T., Kornblith, S., Norouzi, M., Geoffrey, H.: A simple framework for contrastive learning of visual representations. In: The 37th International Conference on Machine Learning, pp. 1597–1607 (2020)

5. Deng, J., Dong, W., Socher, R., Li, L.-J., Kai, L., Li, F.-F.: ImageNet: a large-scale hierarchical image database. In: The IEEE Conference on Computer Vision and Pattern Recognition (CVPR), pp. 248–255. IEEE (2009)

6. Guo, M., Cai, J., Liu, Z., Mu, T., Martin, R., Hu, S.: PCT: point cloud transformer. Comput. Vis. Media **7**(2), 187–199 (2021)

7. He, K.-M., Fan, H.-Q., Wu, Y.-X., Xie, S.-N., Girshick, R.-B.: Momentum contrast for unsupervised visual representation learning. In: The IEEE/CVF Conference on Computer Vision and Pattern Recognition (CVPR), pp. 9726–9735. IEEE (2020)

8. Isola, P., Zhu, J.-Y., Zhou, T.-H., Efros, A.-A.: Image-to-image translation with conditional adversarial networks. In: The IEEE/CVF Conference on Computer Vision and Pattern Recognition (CVPR), pp. 1125–1134. IEEE (2017)

9. Jiang, L., et al.: Guided point contrastive learning for semi-supervised point cloud semantic segmentation. In: 2021 IEEE/CVF International Conference on Computer Vision (ICCV), pp. 6403–6412. IEEE (2021)

10. Laurens, V.-M., Geoffrey, E.-H.: Visualizing data using t-SNE. J. Mach. Learn. Res. **9**, 2579–2605 (2021)

11. Li, R.-H., Li, X.-Z., Heng, P.-A., Fu, C.-W.: PointAugment: an auto-augmentation framework for point cloud classification. In: The IEEE/CVF Conference on Computer Vision and Pattern Recognition (CVPR), pp. 6377–6386. IEEE (2020)

12. Li, Y., Bu, R., Sun, M., Wu, W., Di, X., Chen, B.: PointCNN: convolution on X-transformed points. In: NeurIPS, vol. 31. Curran Associates (2018)

13. Lin, M.-X., et al.: Single image 3D shape retrieval via cross-modal instance and category contrastive learning. In: 2021 IEEE/CVF International Conference on Computer Vision (ICCV), pp. 11385–11395. IEEE (2021)

14. Liu, Z., Hu, H., Cao, Y., Zhang, Z., Tong, X.: A closer look at local aggregation operators in point cloud analysis. In: Vedaldi, A., Bischof, H., Brox, T., Frahm, J.-M. (eds.) ECCV 2020. LNCS, vol. 12368, pp. 326–342. Springer, Cham (2020). https://doi.org/10.1007/978-3-030-58592-1_20

15. Lun, Z.-L., Kalogerakis, E., Sheffer, A.: Elements of style: learning perceptual shape style similarity. ACM Trans. Graph. (TOG) **34**(4), 1–14 (2015)

16. Nazir, D., Afzal, M.-Z., Pagani, A., Liwicki, M., Stricker, D.: Contrastive learning for 3D point clouds classification and shape completion. Sensors **21**(21), 7392 (2021)

17. Oord, A., Li, Y.-Z., Vinyals, O.: Representation learning with contrastive predictive coding. CoRR abs/1807.03748 (2018). arxiv.org/abs/1807.03748

18. Qi, C.-R., Su, H., Mo, K., Guibas, L.-J.: PointNet: deep learning on point sets for 3D classification and segmentation. In: The IEEE/CVF Conference on Computer Vision and Pattern Recognition (CVPR), pp. 77–85. IEEE (2017)

19. Qi, C.-R., Yi, L., Su, H., Guibas, L.-J.: PointNet++: deep hierarchical feature learning on point sets in a metric space. In: NIPS, vol. 30, pp. 5099–5108 (2017)

20. Sanghi, A.: Info3D: representation learning on 3D objects using mutual information maximization and contrastive learning. CoRR abs/2006.02598 (2020). arxiv.org/abs/2006.02598

21. Snell, J., Swersky, K., Zemel, R.-S.: Prototypical networks for few-shot learning. CoRR abs/1703.05175 (2017). arxiv.org/abs/1703.05175

22. Sun, C., Zheng, Z., Wang, X., Xu, M., Yang, Y.: Self-supervised point cloud representation learning via separating mixed shapes. IEEE Trans. Multimedia, 1–11 (2022)
23. Uy, M.-A., Pham, Q.-H., Hua, B.-S., Nguyen, D.-T., Yeung, S.K.: Revisiting point cloud classification: a new benchmark dataset and classification model on real-world data. In: 2019 IEEE/CVF International Conference on Computer Vision (ICCV), pp. 1588–1597. IEEE (2019)
24. Wang, Y., Sun, Y.-B., Liu, Z.-W., Sarma, S.-E., Michael, M.-B., Justin, M.-S.: Dynamic graph CNN for learning on point clouds. ACM Trans. Graph. (TOG) **38**(5), 1–12 (2019)
25. Wu, W.-X., Qi, Z.-G., Li, F.-X.: PointConv: deep convolutional networks on 3D point clouds. In: The IEEE/CVF Conference on Computer Vision and Pattern Recognition (CVPR), pp. 9613–9622. IEEE (2019)
26. Wu, Z.-J., Wang, X., Lin, D., Lischinski, D., Cohen-Or, D., Huang, H.: Structure-aware generative network for 3D-shape modeling. ACM Trans. Graph. (TOG) **38**(4), 1–14 (2019)
27. Wu, Z.-R., et al.: 3D ShapeNets: a deep representation for volumetric shapes. In: The IEEE/CVF Conference on Computer Vision and Pattern Recognition (CVPR), pp. 1912–1920. IEEE (2015)
28. Xie, S.-N., Gu, J.-T., Guo, D.-M., Qi, C., Guibas, L.-J., Litany, O.: PointContrast: unsupervised pre-training for 3D point cloud understanding. CoRR abs/2007.10985 (2020). arxiv.org/abs/2007.10985
29. Yin, K., Chen, Z.-Q., Huang, H., Cohen-Or, D., Zhang, H.: LOGAN: unpaired shape transform in latent overcomplete space. ACM Trans. Graph. (TOG) **38**(6), 1–13 (2019)
30. Zhang, J., et al.: PointCutMix: regularization strategy for point cloud classification. Neurocomputing **505**, 58–67 (2022)
31. Zheng, W., Tang, W.-L., Jiang, L., Fu, C.-W.: SE-SSD: self-ensembling single-stage object detector from point cloud. In: The IEEE/CVF Conference on Computer Vision and Pattern Recognition (CVPR), pp. 14489–14498. IEEE (2021)

PoinLin-Net: Point Cloud Completion Network Based on Geometric Feature Extraction and Linformer Structure

Dejie Li$^{(\boxtimes)}$ [ID], Kejin Huang [ID], Yinchu Wang [ID], and Haijiang Zhu [ID]

Beijing University of Chemical Technology, Beijing 100000, China
lidejie@buct.edu.cn, {huangkj,zhuhj}@mail.buct.edu.cn,
wangyinchuncut@outlook.com

Abstract. Existing 3D sensors can collect only incomplete and sparse point cloud data because of object self-occlusion. Therefore, a method for completing the missing point cloud and obtaining a high-quality point cloud is of great significance. Current transformers model the point cloud completion problem as a set-to-set conversion problem. However, due to the high time and space complexity, it is impossible to effectively convert the known point cloud information to obtain the missing part of it. To this end, this paper proposes a point cloud completion network based on the encoder-decoder structure of Linformer and Connect-DGCNN structure (PoinLin-Net). First, the linear complexity attention mechanism is introduced to reduce the amount of calculation of the proposed model, and it maximizes the proposed model's performance. After that, a new feature extraction network structure Connect-DGCNN, which combines original and local geometric information, is designed to minimizes effectively the loss of geometric information during feature extraction. From experimental results, we can find that the proposed method is superior to current best-performing methods in ShapeNet-55 and ShapeNet-34. Furthermore, our model reduces a burden of computation by 66.7%.

Keywords: point cloud completion · linear complexity attention · feature extraction

1 Introduction

With the rapid development of visual hardware, a series of depth perception devices such as Lidar and RGBD cameras are available to obtain objects' depth information directly. As the three-dimensional data closest to the original sensor, the point cloud has a compact and straightforward representation. Point cloud data easily and comprehensively captures 3D shapes, so researchers favor it. However, in practical applications, data on actual scanned objects are often incomplete due to the limitations of a single viewing angle, occlusion, and the

Supported by National Key R&D Program of China (Grant No. 2022YFF0607503).

environment. This leads directly to the incompleteness of the collected point cloud data [15], causing point cloud geometry and semantic information loss, which greatly limits the perception capabilities of vision and AI. Thus, restoring the missing point cloud shape information to complete the object shape information is challenging for researchers.

Following the success of transformers [11] in natural language processing (NLP), the ability of transformers to learn local structural features and determine long-term correlations has been demonstrated. Some studies convert point cloud completion into a sequence generation problem, thus applying transformers to the tasks of point cloud completion and long-sequence prediction through an internal self-attention mechanism. For example, PoinTr [20] predicts missing point cloud sequences by setting the point proxy input into the transformer encoder-decoder. However, because the computational complexity of the transformer's self-attention layer is proportional to the sequence length, the computation of long sequences is very time-consuming, influencing the model's performance and making the completion accuracy low.

In response to this problem, our study adopted a self-attention mechanism of linear complexity in the Linformer [12] model to optimize the self-attention mechanism in the transformer model and avoid secondary operations. This mechanism can reduce the complexity of the self-attention layer from $O(n^2)$ to $O(n)$ in time and space. The time efficiency of the Linformer model is significantly higher than the standard transformer model, so we replaced the transformer in the PoinTr network to form a new network structure: PoinLin-Net. We successfully conducted experiments using PoinLin-Net on several different datasets, and its performance proved superior to that of PoinTr. Multiple indicators on the ShapeNet-55 [20] and ShapeNet-34 datasets have surpassed the current best-performing methods. Furthermore, the number of calculations needed for the model is the lowest.

The main contributions are summarized as follows:

- This work proposes a point cloud completion network based on the encoder-decoder structure of Linformer and Connect-DGCNN structure, and it is called as PoinLin-Net.
- A new feature extraction network structure Connect-DGCNN is designed to minimizes effectively the loss of geometric information through combining original and local geometric information.
- The linear complexity attention mechanism is introduced to decrease the computational expense and maximize the proposed model's performance.

2 Related Work

Researchers have tried many methods over many years to solve the problem of point cloud completion using deep learning. Early research on this applied methods commonly used in 2D completion tasks to 3D point clouds through voxel localization and 3D convolution. For example, GRNet [18] reconstructs full 3D voxels coarse-to-finely. The network first uses a 3D convolutional neural network to predict a rough shape. Then it selects similar parts from the full-shape dataset [2] for fine output or reconstructs a dense point cloud from the output voxels. However, these methods incur an increasingly higher computational cost as the spatial resolution increases and lose many details.

Researchers have gradually begun to pay more attention to the representation of unstructured point clouds as 3D objects. This is because the storage and processing requirements are much less computationally expensive than voxels, and this approach can represent fine-grained details. Since the commonly used convolutional network is no longer suitable for unstructured point cloud data, researchers use encoders such as PointNet [7] or PointNet++ [8] to extract global features from incomplete point cloud data and use decoders to generate a complete point cloud based on the extracted features. For example, PCN [21] was the first learning-based shape completion method to directly manipulate 3D point clouds without the intermediate voxelization to generate dense, complete point clouds in a coarse-to-fine manner. After PCN, TopNet [10] improved the structure of the decoder, which could generate structured point clouds by implicitly modifying the point cloud structure in the root tree. In addition, some methods based on the transformer structure have emerged. For example, PointTr [20] used the transformer encoder-decoder to predict the center point of the missing part of the point cloud. SeedFormer [23] designed an upsample transformer structure to learn the spatial and semantic relationship between adjacent points. These methods all pursue the generation of 3D shapes for more detailed structures, higher resolution, and stronger robustness.

3   Our Approach

3.1   PoinLin-Net Architecture

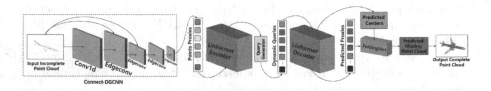

Fig. 1. The overall structure of PoinLin-Net.

The overall structure of PoinLin-Net is shown in the Fig. 1. First, Connec-DGCNN is used to extract the input point cloud features. Then the point cloud center and the point proxy for predicting the missing part are generated through the Linformer decoder and the existing point cloud is encoded. Finally, Fold-ingNet [19] is used to obtain the local point cloud corresponding to the point proxy and complete the restoration of the point cloud from coarse to fine. The following is a detailed introduction to the PoinLin-Net process.

Extract Features. First, perform the farthest sampling method on the input point cloud to obtain a fixed number of N point centers in part of the point cloud. Then use DGCNN [14] to extract features from a local area of the point cloud to obtain N local area features, which correspond to the area features that are the center points. But this method is easy to ignore part of original geometric features. Connect-DGCNN connects features of different layers, making the output global geometric information more perfect. Finally, an MLP network extracts the positional embeddings of each local feature, which are summed to obtain a point proxy for the input to the Linformer encoder.

Predict Centers. The global feature is obtained from the output of the Linformer encoder, and then the rough coordinate of the center point of the incomplete point cloud is predicted by the Linformer encoder, where M represents the number of predicted point proxies. After splicing the center point coordinates with the global features, a multi-layer perceptron generates the query feature, which is the dynamic point proxy.

Generate Points. The decoder converts the dynamic point proxy into a predicted point proxy corresponding to the centered local point cloud. Then FoldingNet is used to reconstruct the offset coordinates of the point proxy to obtain a detailed local shape centered on the predicted point proxy. Finally, the input point cloud is spliced with the predicted result to generate a complete point cloud.

3.2   Connect-DGCNN

DGCNN utilizes EdgeConv to capture the local geometric structure while maintaining alignment invariance, and adds FPS (farthest point sampling) to extract the key points of the point cloud. With n points as input, let each point be $X = \{ x_i | i = 1, 2, ..., n \}$ on the EdgeConv layer to compute the edge features of each point x_i and its k neighbors, which constitute the edge feature set. These feature sets are aggregated and output by aggregation functions such as MaxPooling to update the value of x_i. Finally, a global geometric feature is generated. The local features extracted in this way will make some of the important original features lost, so that the complete global geometric information cannot be obtained. In order to solve this problem, this paper links the hierarchical features of the first two EdgeConv layers on the basis of DGCNN, and combines the current features with the original features splicing, with FPS to form a new point cloud feature extraction network Connect-DGCNN, whose structure is shown in Fig. 2.

3.3   Linear Attention Mechanism

In the PoinTr network, the transformer encoder-decoder is used for the input point cloud to predict the missing part of the point cloud. However, the complexity of $O(n^2)$ time and space is used in the transformer's self-attention, affecting

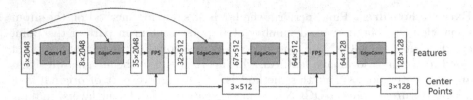

Fig. 2. Structure of Connect-DGCNN.

the correlation information between points in the point cloud. We applied the linear self-attention mechanism to the Linformer model in the computation to solve this problem. The principal advantage of the linear self-attention mechanism is adding two linear projection matrices $E_i, F_i \in R^{k \times n}$ when calculating the key layer K and value layer V so that the n-order self-attention is reduced to a fixed k-dimensional matrix, $E_i QW_i^Q, F_i KW_i^K \in R^{k \times d_k}$. The specific formula of each head is as follows:

$$f(QW_i^Q, E_i KW_i^K, F_i VW_i^V)$$
$$= softmax[\frac{QW_i^Q(E_i KW_i^K)^T}{\sqrt{d_k}}]F_i VW_i^V \quad (1)$$

At this time, the calculation in the SoftMax function is given by

$$QW_i^Q(E_i KW_i^K)^T = n \times d_k \times (k \times d_k)^T = n \times k \quad (2)$$

The calculation of the entire attention layer is

$$QW_i^Q(E_i KW_i^K)^T F_i VW_i^V = n \times k \times k \times d_v = n \times d_v \quad (3)$$

Calculating the query layer and key layer of linear attention only needs O(kn) time complexity, which effectively improves the efficiency of model operation. The original (n×d)-dimensional key and value layers and the projection to (k×d)-dimensional key and value layers are shown in Fig. 3.

4   Experiments

4.1   Implementation

The PoinLin-Net proposed in this paper is implemented in Pytorch [6]. An 8-head attention is used in all Linformer modules, and their hidden dimensions are set to 384. At the same time, the AdamW optimizer [5] trains the network, with the initial learning rate set to 0.00025 and the weight decay set to 0.0005. The models using the ShapeNet-55 and ShapeNet-34 datasets take 2,048 points as input and predict the other 6,144 points. We set the batch size to 32 and 64, respectively, and trained for 300 epochs. The learning rate decayed by 0.76 every 20 epochs. With the PCN dataset, the model takes 2,048 points as input and predicts the other 14,336 points. We set the batch size to 32 and trained for 400 epochs. The learning rate decayed by 0.9 every 20 epochs. And all models were trained on a GeForce RTX 3090 Ti GPU.

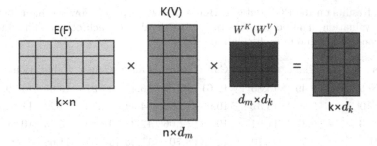

Fig. 3. Example of projection process for value and key layers.

4.2 Evaluation Metric

Our study utilized the most-used chamfering distance in point cloud completion as an evaluation index that can calculate the average shortest point distance between the generated point cloud P and the actual point cloud G and the distance between the generated point cloud and the real point cloud. The formula used in the computation is

$$d_{CD}(P,G) = \frac{1}{|P|} \sum_{p \in P} \min_{g \in G} \|p - g\| + \frac{1}{|G|} \sum_{g \in G} \min_{p \in P} \|g - p\| \qquad (4)$$

The first term is the minimum distance between each point in the generated point cloud and the closest point of the real point cloud. The second term represents the coverage of the real point cloud in the generated point cloud. Following the previous method [4,10,18,21], our study used two versions of the chamfering distance as evaluation indices to compare the performance of the existing point cloud completion network. $CD - l_1$ uses the L1-norm to calculate the distance between two points, while $CD - l_2$ uses the L2-norm. According to the literature [9], the F-Score is used as a comprehensive evaluation index to determine the quality of point cloud completion results.

4.3 Results on the PCN Dataset

This paper reports using synthetic CAD models from ShapeNet [1] to create a large-scale dataset consisting of partial and complete point cloud pairs, namely the PCN dataset. This is also one of the most used benchmark datasets in point cloud completion tasks. It contains eight categories: airplanes, cabinets, cars, chairs, lamps, sofas, tables, and ships. The residual point cloud used in this paper has 2,048 points, and the real and complete point cloud has 16,384 points. As shown in Table 1, we compared $CD - l_1$ with other methods and achieved optimal results in the Car category, with overall reached sub-optimal levels. Compared with PoinTr, the average CD was reduced by 14.43% (down from 8.38 to 7.17).

Table 1. Results on the PCN dataset. Here $CD-l_1$ ($\times 10^3$) (a lower value is better) is used for evaluation. The bold font is the optimal value in each column.The underline is the second best value in each column.

Methods	Plane	Cabinet	Car	Chair	Lamp	Couch	Table	Boat	Avg
FoldingNet [19]	9.49	15.80	12.61	15.55	16.41	15.97	13.65	14.99	14.31
TopNet [10]	7.61	13.31	10.90	13.82	14.44	14.78	11.22	11.12	12.15
AtlasNet [3]	6.37	11.94	10.10	12.06	12.37	12.99	10.33	10.61	10.85
PCN [21]	5.50	22.70	10.63	8.70	11.00	11.34	11.68	8.59	9.64
GRNet [18]	6.45	10.37	9.45	9.41	7.96	10.51	8.44	8.04	8.83
PMP-Net [16]	5.65	11.24	9.64	9.51	6.95	10.83	8.72	7.25	8.73
CRN [13]	4.79	9.97	8.31	9.49	8.94	10.69	7.81	8.05	8.51
PoinTr [20]	4.75	10.47	8.68	9.39	7.75	10.93	7.78	7.29	8.38
NSFA [22]	4.76	10.18	8.63	8.53	7.03	10.53	7.35	7.48	8.06
SnowflakeNet [17]	4.29	<u>9.16</u>	8.08	7.89	<u>6.07</u>	<u>9.23</u>	<u>6.55</u>	6.40	7.21
SeedFormer [23]	**3.85**	**9.05**	<u>8.06</u>	**7.06**	**5.21**	**8.85**	**6.05**	**5.85**	**6.74**
PoinLin-Net	<u>4.08</u>	9.28	**7.88**	<u>7.70</u>	6.18	9.25	6.63	<u>6.32</u>	<u>7.17</u>

Table 2 compares the number of parameters, number of calculations, and $CD - l_1$ ($\times 10^3$) index of different models, while the inference times of different models are given in Table 3. The number of calculations in the proposed method is lower than other methods, the reasoning speed of the model is faster (the average inference time is shortened from 73ms to 63ms), and compared with PoinTr, the number of parameters is also reduced by 10.25%.

Table 2. Comparison of model parameters and the number of calculations

Methods	Params (M)	FLOPs (G)	$CD - l_1$
FoldingNet [19]	**2.41**	27.65	14.31
PCN [21]	6.84	14.69	9.64
GRNet [18]	76.71	25.88	8.83
PoinTr [20]	30.90	10.41	8.38
SnowflakeNet [17]	19.32	10.32	7.21
SeedFormer [23]	3.20	29.61	**6.74**
PoinLin-Net	27.73	**9.86**	7.17

Table 3. Comparison of inference time in no-load state and load state of the model

Methods	Average (ms)	No-load (ms)	Load (ms)
FoldingNet [19]	71	53	89
PCN [21]	**60**	43	**76**
GRNet [18]	72	49	95
PoinTr [20]	73	56	90
SnowflakeNet [17]	85	**42**	126
SeedFormer [23]	262	118	296
PoinLin-Net	63	44	82

4.4 Ablation Study on PCN Dataset

To verify the effectiveness of the method in this section, we conducted ablation experiments on the PCN dataset, and the results are shown in Table 4. Model A indicates that only Linformer is used. From the results in Table 4, we can see that the complementation effect of Model A has been significantly improved compared with PoinTr. PoinLin-Net indicates that Connect-DGCNN is added to A, and the model performance is further improved, but the improvement is not significant. Figure 4 gives a comparison of the complementation effect of our study's method with other methods under several categories, and the complementation result of PoinLin-Net is more refined.

Table 4. Ablation experiments under $CD - l_1$ ($\times 10^3$) and $CD - l_2$ ($\times 10^4$) contrast

Model	Linformer	Connect-DGCNN	$CD - l_1$	$CD - l_2$
PoinTr [20]	-	-	8.38	3.35
A	✓	-	7.41	2.34
PoinLin-Net	✓	✓	**7.17**	**2.22**

4.5 Results on the ShapeNet-55 Dataset

The ShapeNet-55 dataset [20] uses all objects in the 55 categories in ShapeNet. Since real 3D objects are more diverse, we had to consider a richer category to evaluate the point cloud completion model so that the model's performance with a more diverse dataset could be more comprehensively tested. The training set of this dataset is a random sample of 80% of the objects from each category, and the rest are used for testing. The test samples are divided into three difficulty levels by setting the number of missing point clouds n, where n is 2,048, 4,096, and 6,144, corresponding to simple, medium, and challenging difficulty levels. These account for 25%, 50%, and 75% of the total point cloud. By comparing

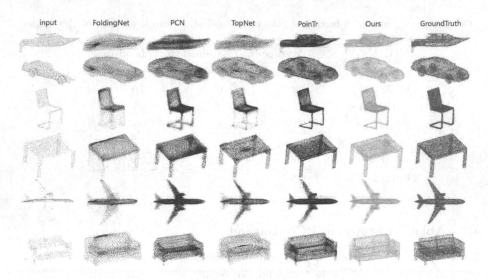

input   FoldingNet   PCN   TopNet   PoinTr   Ours   GroundTruth

Fig. 4. Comparison of visualization effects of different models on the PCN dataset.

Table 5. Completion results of the ShapeNet-55 dataset under the evaluation of $CD-l_2$ ($\times 10^3$) (a lower value is better) and F-score@1% (a higher value is better). The value in bold font is the best in each column. The underline is the second best value in each column.

Methods	Table	Chair	Airplane	Car	Sofa	Remote	Key board	Rocket	CD-S	CD-M	CD-H.	CD-Avg	F1
FoldingNet [19]	2.53	2.81	1.43	1.98	2.48	1.44	1.24	1.48	2.67	2.66	4.05	3.12	0.082
PCN [21]	2.13	2.29	1.02	1.85	2.06	1.33	0.89	1.32	1.94	1.96	4.08	2.66	0.133
TopNet [10]	2.21	2.53	1.14	2.18	2.36	1.49	0.95	1.32	2.26	2.16	4.3	2.91	0.126
PFNet [4]	3.95	4.24	1.81	2.53	3.34	2.91	1.29	2.36	3.83	3.87	7.97	5.22	0.339
GRNet [18]	1.63	1.88	1.02	1.64	1.72	1.09	0.89	1.03	1.35	1.71	2.85	1.97	0.238
PoinTr [20]	0.81	0.95	0.44	0.91	0.79	0.53	0.38	0.57	0.58	0.88	1.79	1.09	0.464
SeedFormer [23]	<u>0.72</u>	**0.81**	<u>0.40</u>	<u>0.89</u>	<u>0.71</u>	<u>0.46</u>	<u>0.36</u>	**0.50**	<u>0.50</u>	<u>0.77</u>	**1.49**	<u>0.92</u>	<u>0.472</u>
PoinLin-Net	**0.69**	**0.81**	**0.38**	**0.77**	**0.66**	**0.42**	**0.33**	**0.50**	**0.45**	**0.73**	<u>1.54</u>	**0.91**	**0.479**

the data of each method under these three difficulty levels through experiments, it is possible to judge the ability of each network to handle tasks of different difficulty levels. In addition, this paper uses CD-Avg with three difficulty levels to show the overall performance. From Table 3, we can quantitatively compare our method with other methods on ShapeNet-55. Compared with the SOTA method SeedFormer [23], the model in this paper is better at the simple and medium levels. Furthermore, the mean CD at all three levels is superior to the SOTA method. In terms of performance in the selected eight categories, the proposed method achieves the best performance in seven categories. Compared with PoinTr, the index of the average CD value is reduced by 16.51%, which verifies the superiority of the module proposed in this paper. Figure 5 shows the visualization results of this and other methods on ShapeNet-55 (Table 5).

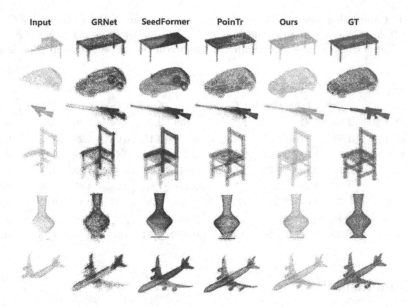

Fig. 5. Comparison of visualization effects of different models on the ShapeNet-55 dataset.

4.6 Results on ShapeNet-34

The ShapeNet-34 dataset [20] primarily evaluates the performance of point cloud completion models on new categories. The dataset divides ShapeNet into two parts: 21 invisible categories and 34 visible categories. In each visible category, 100 objects are randomly selected as the test set of the visible category, and the rest are used as the training set. Also, the dataset uses 2,305 objects from 21 invisible categories to form a test set. The evaluation indicators used in the experiment are the same as those of the ShapeNet-55 experiment. Table 4 shows the comparison between the method proposed in this paper and the other methods. In comparing the ten indicators in the two test sets, eight indicators of the method in this paper reached the optimal state, although two indicators were sub-optimal. The F1 indicators of the two categories improved by 8.2% and 10.9% over the SOTA method (Table 6).

Table 6. Completion results of the ShapeNet-55 dataset under the evaluation of $CD-l_2$ ($\times 10^3$) (a lower value is better) and F-score@1% (a higher value is better). The value in bold font is the best in each column. The underline is the second best value in each column.

Methods	34 seen categories					21 unseen categories				
	CD-S	CD-M	CD-H	CD-Avg	F1	CD-S	CD-M	CD-H	CD-Avg	F1
FoldingNet [19]	1.86	1.81	3.38	2.35	0.139	2.76	2.74	5.36	3.62	0.095
PCN [21]	1.87	1.81	2.97	2.22	0.154	3.17	3.08	5.29	3.85	0.101
TopNet [10]	1.77	1.61	3.54	2.31	0.171	2.62	2.43	5.44	3.50	0.121
PFNet [4]	3.16	3.19	7.71	4.68	0.347	5.29	5.87	13.33	8.16	0.322
GRNet [18]	1.26	1.39	2.57	1.74	0.251	1.85	2.25	4.87	2.99	0.216
PoinTr [20]	0.76	1.05	1.88	1.23	0.421	1.04	1.67	3.44	2.05	0.384
SeedFormer [23]	<u>0.48</u>	<u>0.70</u>	<u>1.30</u>	<u>0.83</u>	<u>0.452</u>	<u>0.61</u>	<u>1.07</u>	**2.35**	**1.34**	<u>0.402</u>
PoinLin-Net	**0.43**	**0.63**	**1.26**	**0.77**	**0.489**	**0.57**	**1.01**	<u>2.50</u>	<u>1.36</u>	**0.451**

5 Conclusion

This paper has described a new point cloud completion network PoLin-Net. The difference from the PoinTr network is that our study has proposed a new point cloud feature extraction network Connect-DGCNN, which combined original features with current local features to obtain more complete global features. Secondly, our network utilized the Linformer encoder-decoder instead of the usual transformer encoder-decoder. The linear attention mechanism in the Linformer was adopted to reduce the complexity of the self-attention layer, thereby improving the overall encoding and decoding performance and ultimately improving the accuracy of the entire point cloud completion. Comprehensive experimental results show that the performance of the proposed method on the ShapeNet-55 and ShapeNet-34 datasets is currently the best method and requires fewer calculations.

References

1. Choy, C.B., Xu, D., Gwak, J.Y., Chen, K., Savarese, S.: 3D-R2N2: a unified approach for single and multi-view 3D object reconstruction. In: Leibe, B., Matas, J., Sebe, N., Welling, M. (eds.) ECCV 2016. LNCS, vol. 9912, pp. 628–644. Springer, Cham (2016). https://doi.org/10.1007/978-3-319-46484-8_38
2. Dai, A., Ruizhongtai Qi, C., Nießner, M.: Shape completion using 3D-encoder-predictor CNNs and shape synthesis. In: Proceedings of the IEEE Conference on Computer Vision and Pattern Recognition, pp. 5868–5877 (2017)
3. Groueix, T., Fisher, M., Kim, V., Russell, B., Aubry, M.: AtlasNet: a papier-mâché approach to learning 3D surface generation. arxiv 2018. arXiv preprint arXiv:1802.05384 (1802)
4. Huang, Z., Yu, Y., Xu, J., Ni, F., Le, X.: PF-Net: point fractal network for 3D point cloud completion. In: Proceedings of the IEEE/CVF Conference on Computer Vision and Pattern Recognition, pp. 7662–7670 (2020)

5. Loshchilov, I., Hutter, F.: Fixing weight decay regularization in Adam (2018)
6. Paszke, A., et al.: PyTorch: an imperative style, high-performance deep learning library. In: Advances in Neural Information Processing Systems, vol. 32 (2019)
7. Qi, C.R., Su, H., Mo, K., Guibas, L.J.: PointNet: deep learning on point sets for 3D classification and segmentation. In: Proceedings of the IEEE Conference on Computer Vision and Pattern Recognition, pp. 652–660 (2017)
8. Qi, C.R., Yi, L., Su, H., Guibas, L.J.: PointNet++: deep hierarchical feature learning on point sets in a metric space. In: Advances in Neural Information Processing Systems, vol. 30 (2017)
9. Tatarchenko, M., Richter, S.R., Ranftl, R., Li, Z., Koltun, V., Brox, T.: What do single-view 3D reconstruction networks learn? In: Proceedings of the IEEE/CVF Conference on Computer Vision and Pattern Recognition, pp. 3405–3414 (2019)
10. Tchapmi, L.P., Kosaraju, V., Rezatofighi, H., Reid, I., Savarese, S.: TopNet: structural point cloud decoder. In: Proceedings of the IEEE/CVF Conference on Computer Vision and Pattern Recognition, pp. 383–392 (2019)
11. Vaswani, A., et al.: Attention is all you need. In: Advances in Neural Information Processing Systems, vol. 30 (2017)
12. Wang, S., Li, B.Z., Khabsa, M., Fang, H., Ma, H.: Linformer: self-attention with linear complexity. arXiv preprint arXiv:2006.04768 (2020)
13. Wang, X., Ang, M.H., Jr., Lee, G.H.: Cascaded refinement network for point cloud completion. In: Proceedings of the IEEE/CVF Conference on Computer Vision and Pattern Recognition, pp. 790–799 (2020)
14. Wang, Y., Sun, Y., Liu, Z., Sarma, S.E., Bronstein, M.M., Solomon, J.M.: Dynamic graph CNN for learning on point clouds. ACM Trans. Graph. (TOG) **38**(5), 1–12 (2019)
15. Wen, X., Li, T., Han, Z., Liu, Y.S.: Point cloud completion by skip-attention network with hierarchical folding. In: Proceedings of the IEEE/CVF Conference on Computer Vision and Pattern Recognition, pp. 1939–1948 (2020)
16. Wen, X., et al.: PMP-Net++: point cloud completion by transformer-enhanced multi-step point moving paths. IEEE Trans. Pattern Anal. Mach. Intell. (2022)
17. Xiang, P., et al.: SnowflakeNet: point cloud completion by snowflake point deconvolution with skip-transformer. In: Proceedings of the IEEE/CVF International Conference on Computer Vision, pp. 5499–5509 (2021)
18. Xie, H., Yao, H., Zhou, S., Mao, J., Zhang, S., Sun, W.: GRNet: gridding residual network for dense point cloud completion. In: Vedaldi, A., Bischof, H., Brox, T., Frahm, J.-M. (eds.) ECCV 2020. LNCS, vol. 12354, pp. 365–381. Springer, Cham (2020). https://doi.org/10.1007/978-3-030-58545-7_21
19. Yang, Y., Feng, C., Shen, Y., Tian, D.: FoldingNet: point cloud auto-encoder via deep grid deformation. In: Proceedings of the IEEE Conference on Computer Vision and Pattern Recognition, pp. 206–215 (2018)
20. Yu, X., Rao, Y., Wang, Z., Liu, Z., Lu, J., Zhou, J.: PoinTr: diverse point cloud completion with geometry-aware transformers. In: Proceedings of the IEEE/CVF International Conference on Computer Vision, pp. 12498–12507 (2021)
21. Yuan, W., Khot, T., Held, D., Mertz, C., Hebert, M.: PCN: point completion network. In: 2018 International Conference on 3D Vision (3DV), pp. 728–737. IEEE (2018)

22. Zhang, W., Yan, Q., Xiao, C.: Detail preserved point cloud completion via separated feature aggregation. In: Vedaldi, A., Bischof, H., Brox, T., Frahm, J.-M. (eds.) ECCV 2020. LNCS, vol. 12370, pp. 512–528. Springer, Cham (2020). https://doi.org/10.1007/978-3-030-58595-2_31

23. Zhou, H., et al.: SeedFormer: patch seeds based point cloud completion with upsample transformer. In: Avidan, S., Brostow, G., Cissé, M., Farinella, G.M., Hassner, T. (eds.) European Conference on Computer Vision, pp. 416–432. Springer, Cham (2022). https://doi.org/10.1007/978-3-031-20062-5_24

Accurate Detection of Spiking Motifs in Multi-unit Raster Plots

Laurent U. Perrinet(✉) ⓘ

INT UMR7289, Aix Marseille Univ, CNRS, 27 Bd Moulin, 13005 Marseille, France
laurent.perrinet@univ-amu.fr

Abstract. Recently, interest has grown in exploring the hypothesis that neural activity conveys information through precise spiking motifs. To investigate this phenomenon, various algorithms have been proposed to detect such motifs in Single Unit Activity (SUA) recorded from populations of neurons. In this study, we present a novel detection model based on the inversion of a generative model of raster plot synthesis. Using this generative model, we derive an optimal detection procedure that takes the form of logistic regression combined with temporal convolution. A key advantage of this model is its differentiability, which allows us to formulate a supervised learning approach using a gradient descent on the binary cross-entropy loss. To assess the model's ability to detect spiking motifs in synthetic data, we first perform numerical evaluations. This analysis highlights the advantages of using spiking motifs over traditional firing rate based population codes. We then successfully demonstrate that our learning method can recover synthetically generated spiking motifs, indicating its potential for further applications. In the future, we aim to extend this method to real neurobiological data, where the ground truth is unknown, to explore and detect spiking motifs in a more natural and biologically relevant context.

Keywords: Neurobiology · spike trains · population coding · spiking motifs · heterogeneous delays · pattern detection

1 Introduction

1.1 The Age of Large-Scale Neurobiological Event-Based Data

Over the past decade, remarkable technological progress across multiple disciplines has expanded the potential for experimental neuroscience research. These cutting-edge methods, such as *in vivo* two-photon imaging, large population recording arrays, optogenetic circuit control tools, transgenic manipulations, and large volume circuit reconstructions, allow researchers to explore neural networks' function, structure, and dynamics with unparalleled precision.

The complexity revealed by these advanced technologies underscores the significance of neurobiological knowledge in bridging the gap between abstract brain

Supported by A*MIDEX grant AMX-21-RID-025 "Polychronies".

function principles and their biological implementation in neural circuits. Consequently, there is a growing need to scale up analysis methods to handle the vast amounts of data generated by these powerful techniques. By meeting this demand, researchers can gain deeper insights into brain function, further our understanding of neural circuits, and make groundbreaking discoveries in neuroscience.

One approach aimed at addressing this challenge is the Rastermap algorithm [24]. This algorithm rearranges neurons in the raster map based on the similarity of their activity and utilizes a deconvolution strategy with a linear model. However, it's worth noting that the Rastermap algorithm's primary testing has been on calcium imaging data, which may introduce some imprecision in the timing of spiking activity observed in Single Unit Activity (SUA) recordings. Another significant contribution is from the work of Williams *et al.* [32]. They propose a point process model that overcomes limitations present in existing models, such as the need for discretized spike times or lack of uncertainty estimates for model predictions and estimated parameters. By incorporating learnable time-warping parameters to model sequences of varying durations, the model effectively captures experimentally observed patterns in neural circuits.

1.2   Decoding Neural Activity Using Spike Distances

Neuroscience research heavily relies on defining appropriate metrics to compute the distance between spike trains, and one well-known measure for this purpose is the Victor-Purpura distance [30]. This metric effectively addresses inconsistencies observed with firing rate-based estimation of spike trains. Another study refines the Victor-Purpura distance by introducing a time constant as a parameter, allowing for interpolation between a coincidence detector and a rate difference counter [27]. Additionally, researchers have extended these distance measures to non-Euclidean metrics and morphological manipulations, enabling the computation of spike train dissimilarity.

Regarding spike timings, various methods have been developed to estimate the latency of neural responses. Bayesian binning [19] is one such method. Unitary event analysis, based on a statistical model of chance detection, has been widely used to detect significant synchronous patterns above chance in neuron pair recordings [11]. Recent extensions of these methods, such as the 3D-SPADE approach [29], enable the identification of reoccurring patterns in parallel spike train data and assess their statistical significance. Incorporating possible temporal dithering in spike timings has been shown to improve performance, particularly in the presence of patterns with varying durations, such as surrogates used to evaluate precisely timed higher-order spike correlations.

However, some of these methods may suffer from computational complexity, block-based implementations, and narrow specialization for specific tasks. To address these challenges, novel methods like SPIKESHIP [28] are being developed. The complexity and diversity of these spike train distance and timing comparison methods demonstrate the growing interest in integrating such measures to understand the neural code. A critical step in testing their potential usefulness is scaling these methods to handle larger amounts of data, enabling broader applications and deeper insights into neural activity patterns and their significance.

1.3   A Novel Hypothesis: Spiking Motifs

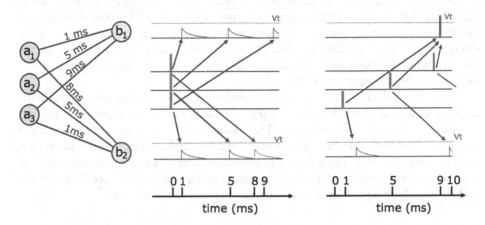

Fig. 1. Core Mechanism of Spiking Motif Detection: In this illustrative example, we consider a scenario involving three presynaptic neurons denoted as a_1, a_2, and a_3, which are fully connected to two postsynaptic neurons b_1 and b_2. The synaptic delays for the connections to b_1 are 1, 5, and 9 ms, while for b_2 they are 8, 5, and 1 ms, respectively. In the middle panel, when the three presynaptic neurons emit synchronous pulses, the postsynaptic potentials generated in b_1 and b_2 reach them asynchronously due to the heterogeneous delays. Consequently, the postsynaptic potentials may not be sufficient to reach the membrane threshold (dashed line) in either of the postsynaptic neurons, and no output spike is generated. In the right panel, the pulses emitted by the presynaptic neurons are arranged in such a way that, taking into account the delays, they reach the postsynaptic neuron b_1 at the same time (at $t = 10$ ms in this example). As a result, the postsynaptic potentials V_t evoked by the three presynaptic neurons sum up, causing the voltage threshold to be crossed. This leads to the emission of an output spike, signaling the detection of a spiking motif in the presynaptic population (highlighted in red color). This core mechanism illustrates how the interplay between heterogeneous delays in the network allows for precise spike timing, enabling the detection of spiking motifs in neural populations. (Color figure online)

In recent studies, the importance of spike timing has been emphasized, especially in the barn owl auditory system, where precise spike timing in response to the sound of a mouse allows the brain to determine the prey's position [7]. This discovery aligns with a growing body of literature suggesting that the brain's dynamics often exhibit stereotyped sequences known as *spiking motifs* [9]. The concept of spiking motifs is a generalization of the patterns observed in the *polychronization* model developed by Izhikevich [16]. This theoretical model comprises a random recurrent network of spiking neurons with biologically realistic synaptic delays and evolving weights governed by Spike-Time Dependent Plasticity (STDP) learning rule.

The interplay between the synaptic delays and STDP leads to the spontaneous organization of neurons into groups called "polychronous groups." Despite neurons in one of these groups firing at different times, the heterogeneous delays enable their spikes to converge synchronously on the postsynaptic neuron. This convergence results in the summation of excitatory postsynaptic potentials, leading to the firing of the postsynaptic neuron (see Fig. 1). The polychronization model allows spiking neurons to self-organize into groups and generate reproducible time-locked spiking motifs. The STDP rule increases synaptic weights selectively for neurons involved in these polychronous groups, thereby consolidating the formation of such groups.

While the polychronization model provides valuable insights into understanding spiking neural networks and their potential role in generating spatio-temporal spiking motifs, it has a limitation. The model's heterogeneous delays are fixed and cannot evolve over time, which may limit its applicability in certain scenarios. However, the underlying mechanism offers valuable implications for studying neural activity motifs and their significance in the brain. To effectively detect spiking motifs, we propose a novel metric inspired by this model.

1.4   The Heterogeneous Delays Spiking Neural Network (HD-SNN)

In this work, we propose to accurately detect spatio-temporal spiking motifs using a feed-forward, single layer heterogeneous delays spiking neural network (HD-SNN). The paper is organized as follows. We develop a theoretically defined HD-SNN for which we can attune both the weights and delays. We first detail the methodology by defining the basic mechanism of spiking neurons that utilize heterogeneous delays. This will allow us to formalize the spiking neuron used to learn the model's parameters in a supervised manner and test its effectiveness. In the results section, we will first evaluate the efficiency of the learning scheme. We will also study the robustness of the spiking motif detection mechanism and in particular its resilience to changing the dimensions of the presynaptic or postsynaptic populations, or the depth in the number of different possible delays. Then, we will explore how the spiking motifs may be learned using supervised learning, and evaluate how the efficiency of the algorithm may depend on the parameters of the HD-SNN architecture. This will allow us to show how such a model can provide an efficient solution which may in the future be applied to neurobiological data. Finally, we will conclude by highlighting the main contributions of this paper, while defining some limitations which will open perspectives for future detection methods.

2   Methods

Let us formally define the HD-SNN model. First, we will define raster plots similar to those obtained from Single Unit Activity (SUA) recordings using an event-based and then binarized setting. We will then derive a generative model for raster plots using a HD-SNN, and derive a model for efficient detection of event-based motifs using a similar HD-SNN with "inverted" delays.

2.1 Raster Plots: From Event-Based to Binarized

In neurobiological recordings, any generic raster plot consists of a stream of *spikes*. This can be formalized as a list of neural addresses and timestamps tuples $\epsilon = \{(a_r, t_r)\}_{r \in [1, N_{ev}]}$ where $N_{ev} \in \mathbb{N}$ is the total number of events in the data stream and the rank r is the index of each event in the list of events. Each event has a time of occurrence t_r (these are typically ordered) and an associated address a_r in the space $\mathcal{A}$ of the neural population. In a neurobiological recording like that of SUAs, this can be the identified set of neurons.

Events are generated by neurons which are defined on the one hand by the equations governing the evolution of its membrane potential dynamics on their soma and on the other hand by the integration of the synaptic potential propagating on their dendritic tree. A classical characterization consists in detailing the synaptic weights of each synaptic contact, the so-called weight matrix. As we saw above, neurons can receive inputs from multiple presynaptic neurons with heterogeneous delays. These delays represent the time it takes for a presynaptic spike to reach the soma of the postsynaptic neuron. In such neurons, input presynaptic spikes ϵ will be multiplexed in time by the dendrites defined by this synaptic set (see Fig. 1).

Let's formalize such a layer of spiking neurons in the HD-SNN model. Each postsynaptic neuron $b \in \mathcal{B}$ connects to presynaptic neurons from a set of addresses in $\mathcal{A}$. In biology, a single cortical neuron has generally several thousands of synapses. Each may be defined by its synaptic weight and also its delay. Note that two neurons may contact with multiple synapses, and thus different delays. Scanning all neurons b, we thus define the set of $N_s \in \mathbb{N}$ synapses as $\mathcal{S} = \{(a_s, b_s, w_s, \delta_s)\}_{s \in [1, N_s]}$, where each synapse is associated to a presynaptic address a_s, a postsynaptic address b_s, a weight w_s, and a delay δ_s.

This defines the full connectivity of the HD-SNN model. The receptive field of a postsynaptic neuron refers to the set of synapses that connect to it. Similarly, the emitting field of a presynaptic neuron refers to the set of synapses it connects to. These fields determine the synaptic inputs and outputs of individual neurons. More formally, the receptive field of a postsynaptic neuron is defined $\mathcal{S}^b = \{(a_s, b_s, w_s, \delta_s) \| b_s = b\}_{s \in [1, N_s]}$, and the emitting field of a presynaptic neuron as $\mathcal{S}_a = \{(a_s, b_s, w_s, \delta_s) \| a_s = a\}_{s \in [1, N_s]}$. Following this definition, an event stream which evokes neurons in the presynaptic address space is multiplexed by the synapses into a new event stream which is defined by the union of the sets generated by each emitting field from the presynaptic space: $\cup_{r \in [1, N_{ev}]} \{(b_s, w_s, t_r + \delta_s)\}_{s \in \mathcal{S}_{a_r}}$. In biology, this new stream of events is naturally ordered in time as events reach the soma of post-synaptic neurons. Synchronous activation of postsynaptic neurons, where multiple spikes converge on the soma simultaneously, will increase the firing probability of those neurons.

From the perspective of simulating such event-based computations on standard CPU- or GPU-based computers, it is useful to transform this event-based representation into a dense representation. Indeed, we may transform any event-based input as the boolean matrix $A \in \{0,1\}^{N \times T}$, where N is the number of presynaptic neurons in $\mathcal{A}$ and T is the number of time bins (see Fig. 2a). In this simplified model, we will consider that heterogeneous delays are integers limited in range between 0 and D (that is, $\forall s \in [1, N_s]$, $0 \le \delta_s < D$) such that the synaptic set can be represented by the dense matrix $K^b \in \mathbb{R}^{N \times D}$ giving for each neuron b the weights as a function of presynaptic address and delay (see Fig. 2b). It is equal to zero except on synapses: $\forall s \in \mathcal{S}^b, K^b(a_s, \delta_s) = w_s$. Equivalently, one may define for each presynaptic neuron a the emitting kernel as the transpose kernel $K_a^T \in \mathbb{R}^{M \times D}$, where M is the number of postsynaptic neurons, whose values are zero except on synapses: $\forall s \in \mathcal{S}_a, K_a^T(b_s, \delta_s) = w_s$.

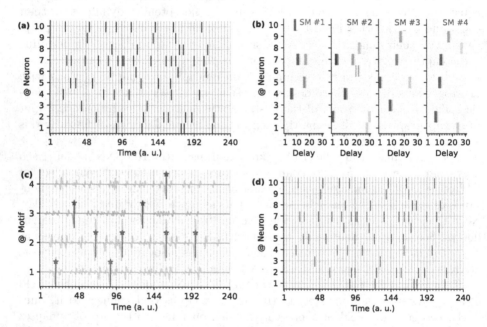

Fig. 2. From generating raster plots to inferring spiking motifs. **(a)** As an illustration for the generative model, we draw a multiunit raster plot synthesized from 4 different spiking motifs and for 10 presynaptic neurons. **(b)** We show these motifs, each identified at the top by a different color. The evidence of activation (red) or deactivation (blue) is assigned to each presynaptic neuron and 31 different possible delays. **(c)** The activation in time of the different motifs (denoted by stars) is drawn at random and then used to generate a raster plot on the multi-unit address space (see panel a). By inverting this model, an inference model can be defined for their efficient detection, outputting an evidence value (continuous line) from which the identity and timing of SMs can be inferred (vertical bars). **(d)** The original raster plot can be annotated with each identified spiking motif (as represented by the respective color assigned to SMs). (Color figure online)

2.2   A Generative Model for Raster Plots

As described in Fig. 1, a spiking motif can be detected using a properly tuned HD-SNN that maximizes spike synchronization at the postsynaptic terminal. Taking the argument the other way around, one may form a generative model for realistic raster plots in which spikes in the presynaptic address space are generated as the conjunction of spiking motifs defined in the postsynaptic space, knowing that both populations are connected by a set of weights and delays whose structure is stable relatively to the coding timescale. When connection weights are strong and sparsely distributed, this firing will robustly cause a specific temporal motif. Overall, these examples show that raster plots may be considered as a mixture of the effects of different elementary causes, and that each event triggers a specific spatio-temporal spiking motif.

Formally, the activation of spiking motifs can occur independently and at random times. The activity is represented as a boolean matrix $B \in \{0,1\}^{M \times T}$, where M is the number of different spiking motifs (see Fig. 2c). Each entry $B(b,t)$ indicates whether a particular motif b is activated at time t. The firing of a neuron a at time t is considered a Bernoulli trial with a bias parameter $p(a,t) \in [0,1]$. This bias is conditioned by the presence of spiking motifs on postsynaptic neurons with corresponding delays. Assuming that this bias is conditioned by the presence of spiking motifs on *all* efferent postsynaptic neurons with the corresponding delays, it can be shown that the logit (inverse of the sigmoid) of this probability bias can be written as the sum of the logit of each of these factors, whose values we will define as the corresponding weights in the kernel. We can thus write the probability bias $p(a,t)$ as the accumulated evidence given these factors as

$$p(a,t) = \sigma\left(K_\mathcal{A}(a) + \sum_{b \in \mathcal{S}_a, 0 \leq \delta \leq D} B(b, t+\delta) \cdot K_a(b, \delta)\right)$$

where σ is the sigmoid function. We will further assume that kernel's weights are balanced (their mean is zero) and that $K_\mathcal{A}$ is a bias such that $\forall a, t, \sigma(K_\mathcal{A}(a))$ is the average background firing rate.

Finally, we obtain the raster plot $A \in \{0,1\}^{N \times T}$ by drawing spikes using independent Bernoulli trials based on the computed probability biases $A \sim \mathcal{B}(p)$. Note that, depending on the definition of kernels, the generative model can model a discretized Poisson process, generate rhythmic activity or more generally propagating waves. This formulation thus defines a simple generative model for raster plots as a combination of independent spiking motifs. This generative model can be easily extented to include a refractory period in order to ensure that there is a minimum time gap between successive action potentials, preventing them from overlapping. This temporal separation allows for discrete and well-defined neural signals, enabling accurate information processing and mitigating signal interference. The refractory period contributes to energy efficiency in neural systems and plays a crucial role in temporal coding by creating distinct time windows between successive spikes.

2.3   Detecting Spiking Motifs

Assuming the spiking motifs (as defined by the kernel K) are known, the generative model allows to determine an inference model for detecting sources $\hat{B}$ when observing a raster plot A. Indeed, by using this forward model, it is possible to estimate the likelihood $p(b,t)$ for the presence of a spiking motif of address b and at time t by using the transpose convolution operator. This consists in using the emitting field $\mathcal{S}_a$ of presynaptic neurons in place of the receptive field $\mathcal{S}^b$ of postsynaptic neurons. It thus comes that when observing A, then one may infer the logit of the probability as the sum of evidences:

$$p(b,t) = \sigma\big(K_{\mathcal{B}}(b) + \sum_{a \in \mathcal{S}^b, 0 \leq \delta \leq D} A(a, t - \delta) \cdot K^b(a, \delta)\big)$$

This also takes the form of a temporal convolution. This assumption holds as long as the kernels are uncorrelated, a condition which is met here numerically by choosing a relatively sparse set of synapses (approximately 1% of active synapses). Finally, we compute $\hat{B}$ by selecting the most likely items, allowing to identify the spiking motifs in the input raster plot (see Fig. 2d).

One may naturally extend this algorithm when the spiking motifs (that is, the weights) are not known, but that we know the timing and identity of the spiking motifs. Indeed, the equation above is differentiable. Indeed, the activation function of our spiking neural is a sigmoid function implementing a form of Multinomial Logistic Regression (MLR) [10]. The underlying metric is the binary cross-entropy, as used in the logistic regression model. In particular, if we consider kernels with similar decreasing exponential time profile, one can prove that this detection model is similar to the method of Berens *et al.* [2]. In our specific case, the difference is that the regression is performed in both dendritic and delay space by extending the summation using a temporal convolution operator.

3   Results

To quantify the efficiency of this operation, we generated raster plots parameterized by $N = 128$ presynaptic inputs and $M = 144$ synthetic spiking motifs as random independent kernels and with $D = 31$ possible delays. We drew random independent instances of B with a length of $T = 1000$ time steps and an average of 1.0 spikes per neuron. This allowed us to generate a large number of synthetic raster plots, which we use to infer $\hat{B}$. We compute accuracy as the rate of true positive detections (both for inferring the address and its exact timing) and observe on average $\approx 98.8\%$ correct detections.

We extended this result by showing how accuracy evolves as a function of the number of simultaneous spiking motifs, holding the frequency of occurrence constant. We show in Fig. 3 (left) that the accuracy of finding the right spiking motif is still above 80% accuracy with more than 1364 overlapping spiking motifs. This observation illustrates quantitatively the capacity of the HD-SNN in representing a high number of simultaneous motifs. Furthermore, we show in

Fig. 3 (middle) that (with $M = 144$ spiking motifs fixed) the accuracy increases significantly with increasing temporal depth D of the spiking motif kernel, quantitatively demonstrating the computational advantage of using heterogeneous delays. These results were obtained under the assumption that we know the spiking motifs through K. However, this is generally not the case, for example, when considering the raster plot of biological neurons.

Finally, we evaluated the performance of the supervised learning scheme in inferring the connection kernel when the address and timing of spiking motifs are known. The kernel was initialized with random independent values, and we used stochastic gradient descent with a learning rate of 1e-4 over 1e4 trials of rasters as defined above ($T = 1000$ and $N = 128$). Qualitatively, the convergence was monotonous, and the correct values of the $M = 144$ spiking motifs were quickly recovered. Quantitatively, the correlation between the true and learned kernel weights showed that all kernels were correctly recovered (see Fig. 3, right). Performing inference with the learned weights was as efficient as with the true kernels, and showed no significant difference (not shown).

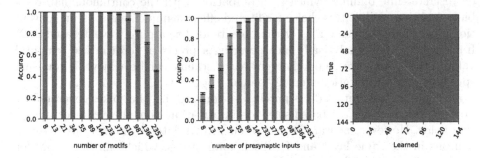

Fig. 3. Detecting spiking motifs using spiking neurons with heterogeneous delays. Accuracy of detection for the classical correlation (red) and the HD-SNN method (blue) as a function of (**Left**) the number M of kernels, (**Middle**) the number of presynaptic neurons, (**Right**) Correlation matrix of true vs learned kernels. (Color figure online)

4 Discussion

4.1 Synthesis and Main Contributions

In this paper, we present a novel Heterogeneous Delays Spiking Neural Network (HD-SNN) model designed for the detection of spiking motifs in synthetic neurobiologically-inspired raster plots.

Our contributions encompass several innovations. Firstly, we formulate the HD-SNN model from first principles, optimizing the detection of event-based spatiotemporal motifs. Unlike previous models like the tempotron, which are evaluated on simplified problems, our model is rigorously tested on realistic data. The results demonstrate that, assuming that the spiking motifs are known, our model accurately detects the identity and timing of spiking motifs, even when multiple motifs are superimposed. Additionally, we show that our method outperforms correlation-based heuristics, such as those used in previous works like [6,33], in terms of efficiency. Secondly, compared to other event-based methods, like HOTS [18], our model's weights are interpretable. These weights are directly related to the logit, which is the inverse sigmoid of the probability of detecting each spatiotemporal spiking motif. Finally, a crucial novelty lies in the simultaneous learning of weights and delays in our model. In contrast, models like the polychronization model [16] only learn weights and delays are frozen. These contributions highlight the significance and effectiveness of our HD-SNN model for detecting spiking motifs, offering insights into the neural mechanisms involved in pattern recognition and information processing.

4.2   Main Limits

The model comes with certain limitations. First, the entire framework is based on discrete time binning, which is incompatible with the continuous nature of biological time. While this choice facilitated efficient implementation on conventional hardware such as GPUs, it can be extended to a purely event-based SNN framework [8]. By analytically incorporating a precision term in the temporal value of the input spikes, a purely event-based scheme can be achieved, promising speedups and computational energy gains.

Second, the current model is purely feed-forward, i.e. the spikes generated by postsynaptic neurons are based solely on information from their classical receptive fields. However, neural systems often involve lateral interactions between neurons in the same layer and feedback connections, which can be crucial for computational principles and modulation of neural information. While our theoretical model can incorporate these recurrent connections by inserting new spikes into the list of spikes reaching presynaptic addresses, it requires proper tuning to avoid perturbations of the homeostatic state. For the implementation of predictive or anticipatory processes, recurrent activity would be essential, especially when dealing with multiple different delays that require temporal alignment. Such recurrent activity has previously been modelled to explain phenomena such as the flash-lag illusion. Implementing this using generalised coordinate and delay operators would allow predictive mechanisms to be incorporated into our proposed HD-SNN model, providing an elegant solution to this problem.

Addressing these limitations and exploring the extension of the HD-SNN model to event-based schemes and recurrent connections would enrich its potential applications and pave the way for a better understanding of neural information processing in complex systems.

4.3   Perspectives

The coding results were obtained under the assumption that we know the spiking motifs by way of K, or using supervised learning by knowing the identity and timing of spiking motifs. However, this is generally not the case, e.g. when observing the neurobiological raster plot of a population of neurons. One perspective would be to extend the model to a fully self-supervised learning paradigm, i.e. without any labeled data [1]. This type of learning is thought to be prevalent in the central nervous system and, assuming the signal is sparse [23], one could extend these Hebbian sparse learning schemes to spikes [22,25].

We expect that this would be particularly adapted for exploring neurobiological data [21]. Indeed, there is a large literature showing that brain dynamics often organize into stereotyped sequences such as synfire chains [15], packets [20], or hippocampal sequences [31] (for a review, see [9]). These motifs are stereotyped and robust, as they can be activated in the same motif from day to day [13]. In contrast to conventional methods used to process neurobiological data, such an event-based model would be able to answer key questions regarding the representation of information in neurobiological data.

References

1. Barlow, H.: Unsupervised learning. Neural Comput. **1**(3), 295–311 (1989)
2. Berens, P., Ecker, A.S., Cotton, R.J., Ma, W.J., Bethge, M., Tolias, A.S.: A fast and simple population code for orientation in primate V1. J. Neurosci. **32**(31), 10618–10626 (2012)
3. Boutin, V., Franciosini, A., Chavane, F.Y., Ruffier, F., Perrinet, L.U.: Sparse deep predictive coding captures contour integration capabilities of the early visual system. PLoS Comput. Biol. (2020)
4. Boutin, V., Franciosini, A., Ruffier, F., Perrinet, L.U.: Effect of top-down connections in hierarchical sparse coding. Neural Comput. **32**(11), 2279–2309 (2020)
5. Chavane, F., Perrinet, L.U., Rankin, J.: Revisiting horizontal connectivity rules in V1: from like-to-like towards like-to-all. Brain Struct. Funct. (2022)
6. Ghosh, R., Gupta, A., Silva, A.N., Soares, A., Thakor, N.V.: Spatiotemporal filtering for event-based action recognition (2019)
7. Goodman, D.F.M., Brette, R.: Spike-timing-based computation in sound localization. PLoS Comput. Biol. **6**(11) (2010)
8. Grimaldi, A., Boutin, V., Ieng, S.H., Benosman, R., Perrinet, L.U.: A robust event-driven approach to always-on object recognition. Neural Netw. (2023)
9. Grimaldi, A., Gruel, A., Besnainou, C., Jérémie, J.N., Martinet, J., Perrinet, L.U.: Precise spiking motifs in neurobiological and neuromorphic data. Brain Sci. **13**(1), 68 (2023)
10. Grimaldi, A., Perrinet, L.U.: Learning heterogeneous delays in a layer of spiking neurons for fast motion detection. Biolog. Cybern. (2023)
11. Grün, S., Diesmann, M., Aertsen, A.: Unitary events in multiple single-neuron spiking activity: II. Nonstationary data. Neural Computat. **14**(1), 81–119 (2002)
12. Gütig, R., Sompolinsky, H.: The tempotron: a neuron that learns spike timing-based decisions. Nat. Neurosci. **9**(3), 420–428 (2006)
13. Haimerl, C., et al.: Internal representation of hippocampal neuronal population spans a time-distance continuum. Proc. Nat. Acad. Sci. **116**(15), 7477–7482 (2019)
14. Hogendoorn, H., Burkitt, A.N.: Predictive coding with neural transmission delays: a real-time temporal alignment hypothesis. eNeuro **6**(2), ENEURO.0412–18.2019 (2019)

15. Ikegaya, Y., et al.: Synfire chains and cortical songs: temporal modules of cortical activity. Science **304**(5670), 559–564 (2004)
16. Izhikevich, E.M.: Polychronization: computation with spikes. Neural Comput. **18**(2), 245–282 (2006)
17. Khoei, M.A., Masson, G.S., Perrinet, L.U.: The flash-lag effect as a motion-based predictive shift. PLoS Comput. Biol. **13**(1), e1005068 (2017)
18. Lagorce, X., Orchard, G., Galluppi, F., Shi, B.E., Benosman, R.B.: HOTS: a hierarchy of event-based time-surfaces for pattern recognition. IEEE Trans. Pattern Anal. Mach. Intell. **39**(7), 1346–1359 (2017)
19. Levakova, M., Tamborrino, M., Ditlevsen, S., Lansky, P.: A review of the methods for neuronal response latency estimation. Biosystems **136**, 23–34 (2015)
20. Luczak, A., Barthó, P., Marguet, S.L., Buzsáki, G., Harris, K.D.: Sequential structure of neocortical spontaneous activity in vivo. Proc. Nat. Acad. Sci. **104**(1), 347–352 (2007)
21. Mackevicius, E.L., et al.: Unsupervised discovery of temporal sequences in high-dimensional datasets, with applications to neuroscience. eLife **8**, e38471 (2019)
22. Masquelier, T., Guyonneau, R., Thorpe, S.J.: Competitive STDP-based spike pattern learning. Neural Comput. **21**(5), 1259–1276 (2009)
23. Olshausen, B.A., Field, D.J.: Emergence of simple-cell receptive field properties by learning a sparse code for natural images. Nature **381**(6583), 607–609 (1996)
24. Pachitariu, M., Stringer, C., Harris, K.D.: Robustness of spike deconvolution for neuronal calcium imaging. J. Neurosci. **38**(37), 7976–7985 (2018)
25. Perrinet, L.U.: Emergence of filters from natural scenes in a sparse spike coding scheme. Neurocomputing **58–60**(C), 821–826 (2004)
26. Perrinet, L.U., Adams, R.A., Friston, K.J.: Active inference, eye movements and oculomotor delays. Biolog. Cybern. **108**(6), 777–801 (2014)
27. van Rossum, M.: A novel spike distance. Neural Comp. **13**(4), 751–763 (2001)
28. Sotomayor-Gómez, B., Battaglia, F.P., Vinck, M.: SpikeShip: a method for fast, unsupervised discovery of high-dimensional neural spiking patterns. bioRxiv Preprint Server Biol., 2020–2026 (2021)
29. Stella, A., Quaglio, P., Torre, E., Grün, S.: 3D-SPADE: significance evaluation of spatio-temporal patterns of various temporal extents. Biosystems **185**, 104022 (2019)
30. Victor, J.D., Purpura, K.P.: Nature and precision of temporal coding in visual cortex: a metric-space analysis. J. Neurophysiol. **76**(2), 1310–1326 (1996)
31. Villette, V., Malvache, A., Tressard, T., Dupuy, N., Cossart, R.: Internally recurring hippocampal sequences as a population template of spatiotemporal information. Neuron **88**(2), 357–366 (2015)
32. Williams, A.H., Degleris, A., Wang, Y., Linderman, S.W.: Point process models for sequence detection in high-dimensional neural spike trains. Technical report, 2010.04875, arXiv (2020)
33. Yu, C., Gu, Z., Li, D., Wang, G., Wang, A., Li, E.: STSC-SNN: spatio-temporal synaptic connection with temporal convolution and attention for spiking neural networks (2022). arXiv:2210.05241

Context-Dependent Computations in Spiking Neural Networks with Apical Modulation

Romain Ferrand, Maximilian Baronig, Thomas Limbacher[ID],
and Robert Legenstein[(✉)][ID]

Institute of Theoretical Computer Science, Graz University of Technology, Graz,
Austria
{ferrand,baronig,limbacher,legenstein}@igi.tugraz.at

Abstract. Neocortical pyramidal neurons integrate two distinct
streams of information. Bottom-up information arrives at their basal dendrites, and resulting neuronal activity is modulated by top-down input
that targets the apical tufts of these neurons and provides context information. Although this integration is essential for cortical computations,
its relevance for the computations in spiking neural networks has so far
not been investigated. In this article, we propose a simple spiking neuron
model for pyramidal cells. The model consists of a basal and an apical
compartment, where the latter modulates activity of the former in a multiplicative manner. We show that this model captures the experimentally
observed properties of top-down modulated activity of cortical pyramidal
neurons. We evaluated recurrently connected networks of such neurons
in a series of context-dependent computation tasks. Our results show
that the resulting novel spiking neural network model can significantly
enhance spike-based context-dependent computations.

Keywords: Spiking neural networks · Dendrites · Context-dependent
computations · Simplified neuron models · Neuromorphic computing

1 Introduction

Spiking neural networks (SNNs) have emerged as a standard model for the investigation of computation and learning in the brain [10]. They have also become
the standard computational paradigm for energy-efficient neuromorphic hardware [8,9,23,24,26]. Typically, SNNs are based on very simple spiking neuron
models that implement the basic computational principle of leaky integration
and thresholding: Input spikes are weighted by synaptic weights, temporally
integrated in a leaky manner, and compared to a firing threshold in order to

Supported by the European Community's Horizon 2020 FET-Open Programme, grant
number 899265, ADOPD and by the CHIST-ERA grant CHIST-ERA-18-ACAI-004,
Austrian Science Fund (FWF) proj. nb. I 4670-N (project SMALL).

382   R. Ferrand et al.

determine whether to spike or not. These neurons are then organized either in feed-forward or recurrently connected networks.

A number of recent advances have improved the computational and learning capabilities of SNNs. New training methodologies have been developed that allow us to optimize SNNs to a degree that is comparable to that of standard artificial neural networks [4,31,38]. Extensions have been proposed that improve their temporal computing capabilities [4] and their utilization of memories [20].

Nevertheless, these models lack essential features of the computational organization of the neocortex. A host of biological evidence suggests that a central computational function of cortical microcircuits is the integration of bottom-up sensory input with top-down contextual information [11,16,30]. In this way, sensory processing in cortex is enriched with behavioral context such as attention, expectations, and task information. Pyramidal neurons in neocortical layers 2/3 and 5 are assumed to play a pivotal role in this computation, since the morphological structure of these cells is well-aligned to integrate the two information streams [11]. Feed-forward input from the thalamus or from areas located lower in the cortical hierarchy are relayed via layer 4 to the basal dendrites of the pyramidal cells. On the other hand, top-down input from higher cortical areas targets mainly neocortical layer 1, where it reaches the apical tufts of these cells. The dendrites of the apical tuft are electrotonically segregated from the basal dendrites, allowing for an independent integration of these two signals [30]. Their integration within the cell is based on a repertoire of nonlinear dendritic processes [18]. In particular, it has been shown that contextual input arriving at the apical tuft of pyramidal cells can modulate the gain of the cell output in response to bottom-up input [17].

In this article, we study a simple extension of the standard SNN model. We include in this network model extended leaky-integrate-and-fire (LIF) neurons that consist of two compartments, a basal and an apical compartment. The basal compartment acts as a standard leaky integrator, which is multiplicatively modulated by the apical activity (see Fig. 1A). We train this model in a number of context-dependent temporal processing tasks and compare its performance to standard recurrent SNN models [4]. We find that multiplicative gain modulation improves learning speed and test accuracy on context-dependent tasks based on the DVS gesture [1] and Spiking Heidelberg Digits (SHD) [7] data sets.

2   Related Work

In recent years, several simplified models for cortical pyramidal cells were proposed and compared to experimental data and to the behavior of detailed compartmental models [5,17,27,34,36]. The simplified models proposed in [17,27] explicitly model interactions between the somatic and dendritic compartments, which makes it hard to optimize them in larger networks with gradient-based optimization techniques. Other models [5,34,36] incorporate a more detailed structure of the dendritic tree, which hinders efficient optimization of large networks and is not in the scope of this study. The computational properties of such a simplified neuron model were studied in [27]. There, it was shown that a three-compartmental model was capable to implement several basic computational operations related to coincidence detection, inhibition of input pathways, logical operations, basic memory, transition detection, and sequence recognition. However, the computational capabilities of dendritic interactions in networks of such neurons have to the best of our knowledge not been studied so far.

The study of the computational capabilities of standard SNNs has a long history. It was proven in [21] that SNNs are strictly more powerful than artificial neural networks in terms of the number of neurons needed to implement functions. See [25] for a review of results and [32] for a more recent review of SNNs in the context of deep learning. A recent study has shown that the specific structure of cortical networks can benefit computations in SNNs [6]. The study however did not investigate the implications of top-down signals and did not consider the important role of pyramidal cells in the integration of these signals with bottom-up input.

3 Results

3.1 Context-Dependent Spiking Neural Networks (cSNNs)

To incorporate top-down modulation of neuron responses, we extended the standard LIF neuron model with an apical compartment, see Fig. 1A. The apical compartment is implemented as a leaky integrator of its synaptic input as in [27] with time constant τ_a. The apical membrane potential is given by

$$V_j^a(t + \Delta t) = \alpha V_j^a(t) + (1 - \alpha)R_m I_j^a(t + \Delta t), \tag{1}$$

where $\alpha = \exp(-\frac{\Delta t}{\tau_a})$, I_j^a is the apical input current, R_m the membrane resistance, and Δt is the discrete time step (we used $\Delta t = 1$ ms). The resulting apical membrane potential is rectified via a rectified linear (ReLu) nonlinearity and multiplicatively modulates the somatic membrane potential

$$V_j(t+\Delta t) = \beta V_j(t)+(1-\beta)\left[R_m I_j(t + \Delta t) \cdot \text{ReLu}\left(V_j^a(t + \Delta t)\right)\right]-V^{th}s_j(t), \tag{2}$$

where $\beta = \exp(-\frac{\Delta t}{\tau_m})$ for membrane time constant τ_m. Note that the rectifying nonlinearity of the apical contribution avoids the inversion of the somatic membrane potential. When the somatic membrane potential crosses threshold V^{th}, the neuron outputs a spike, i.e. $s_j(t) = 1$ ($s_j(t) = 0$ otherwise). In the next time step, the membrane potential is reset by subtraction of Vth. In the following, we refer to this model as the contextual LIF (cLIF) neuron model.

We studied recurrently connected networks of cLIF neurons—referred to as context-dependent SNNs (cSNNs) in the following—in a series of context-dependent processing tasks, see Fig. 1B. Neurons in the network receive bottom-up input at their somatic compartments from a set of spiking input neurons. Another set of spiking input neurons conveys context-information. These neurons are connected to the apical compartments of the cLIF neurons in the network. We studied two variants for recurrent connections in the network. In the

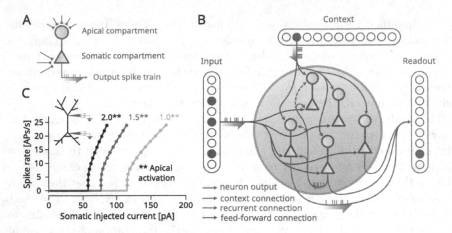

Fig. 1. Context-dependent spiking neural networks (cSNNs). A) Schema of the contextual LIF neuron model. **B)** In a cSNN, bottom-up input (gray) arrives at the somatic and top-down contextual input (blue) at the apical compartment. Recurrent inputs target the somatic (red) and optionally the apical compartment (dashed red). **C)** The input output transformation of the cLIF model captures the basic properties of pyramidal cells under top-down input, compare to Fig. 5 in [17].

first variant, neuron outputs are connected exclusively to the basal compartment of other neurons. In the second variant, recurrent connections to both the basal and the apical compartment exist. Finally, all network neurons project to an output layer that consists of (non-spiking) leaky integrators. The activation of these neurons determines the output of the network. In order to evaluate the computational capabilities of these networks, we trained them with backpropagation through time (BPTT) using the surrogate gradient method [4,38].

3.2 Contextual LIF Neurons Capture the Behavior of Pyramidal Cells Under Top-Down Input

We first asked whether our phenomenological neuron model captures the basic properties of cortical pyramidal cells under the influence of top-down input. Top-down modulation of layer 5 pyramidal cells (L5PCs) was described by Larkum et al. [17]. The authors recorded the firing rate of L5PCs in response to a somatic current ramp under different amplitudes of apical current injection (Fig. 1C inset). They found that apical current injection has two effects on the f/I-curve, that is, the dependence of the firing rate f of the neuron on the somatic injection current I: First, increasing the apical current decreases the rheobase-current, that is, the somatic current necessary to elicit action potentials. Second, the apical current increases the gain of the f/I-curve: above the rheobase current, the firing rate rises faster with increasing input current. Under the assumption of a constant apical activation a, the f/I-curve can be computed analytically in our model, adopting the standard derivation for LIF neurons [10]. This yields

$f(I) = [-\tau_m \ln(1 - \frac{V^{\text{th}}}{aR_m I})]^{-1}$. This relationship is illustrated in Fig. 1C for neuron parameters that are based on experimental results [33], see *Methods*. We observe that the cLIF model exhibits the same behavior in terms of both the decrease in the rheobase current and the gain increase. In contrast, an additive integration of apical activation would only induce a rheobase decrease, but not a gain increase.

3.3 Improved Performance of cSNNs in Context-Dependent Temporal Processing Tasks

In order to evaluate the context-dependent computing capabilities of cSNNs, we defined a principled way to convert multi-class classification tasks into context-dependent tasks of increasing complexity. Consider a K-class classification task for which we have a data set $\mathcal{D} = \langle(\mathbf{x}^{(1)}, t^{(1)}), \ldots, (\mathbf{x}^{(N)}, t^{(N)})\rangle$. In our case, each $\mathbf{x}^{(n)}$ is a multi-dimensional spike train (the inputs to the network) and $t^{(n)} \in \{1, \ldots, K\}$ indicates the classification target for this input. Based on this data set, we define three binary context-dependent tasks: single-sample classification, sequence classification, and sequence memory.

In all variants, we generate a new data set $\tilde{\mathcal{D}} = \langle(\tilde{\mathbf{x}}^{(1)}, c^{(1)}, \tilde{t}^{(1)}), \ldots, (\tilde{\mathbf{x}}^{(N)}, c^{(N)}, \tilde{t}^{(N)})\rangle$. Here, $c^{(n)} \in \{1, \ldots, K\}$ is the context variable that indicates the class to be detected in the input and $\tilde{t}^{(n)} \in \{0, 1\}$ is the binary target output. In the single-sample classification task, each data point $(\tilde{\mathbf{x}}^{(n)}, c^{(n)}, \tilde{t}^{(n)})$ is generated as follows, Fig. 2A. First, $\tilde{\mathbf{x}}^{(n)}$ is given by a randomly chosen input sample $\mathbf{x}^{(s_n)}$ with $s_n \in \{1, \ldots, N\}$. The context variable $c^{(n)}$ is chosen as the corresponding target class in 50% of the cases (then, $\tilde{t}^{(n)} = 1$) and uniformly over the other classes otherwise (then, $\tilde{t}^{(n)} = 0$). In the sequence classification task, each network input $\tilde{\mathbf{x}}^{(n)}$ is given by a concatenation of five randomly chosen input samples $\mathbf{x}^{(s_{n,1})}, \ldots, \mathbf{x}^{(s_{n,5})}$, each from a different class, Fig. 2B. The context variable $c^{(n)}$ indicates one of these classes. The target $\tilde{t}^{(n)}$ is defined here for each presented pattern in the sequence, $\tilde{t}^{(n)} = (\tilde{t}_1^{(n)}, \ldots, \tilde{t}_5^{(n)})$, with $\tilde{t}_k^{(n)}$ being 1 if the k-th input pattern belongs to the indicated class and 0 otherwise. In the sequence memory task, inputs are generated in the same way. The target is defined again for each presented pattern, being 1 if the current or a previous pattern of the sequence did belong to the indicated class and 0 otherwise, Fig. 2C.

These constructions allow us to convert arbitrary classification tasks into context-dependent tasks. The context-input in these tasks can be interpreted as a task-context. Our construction implies K different binary classification tasks, one for each context. The context input defines which of those tasks should be performed by the network. Another interpretation is an attention signal that indicates to which of the classes the network should attend and respond to.

Faster Convergence and Improved Performance of cSNNs in Single-Sample Classification. We first evaluated the performance of cSNNs on the single-sample-task version of the DVS gesture [1] and Spiking Heidelberg Digits

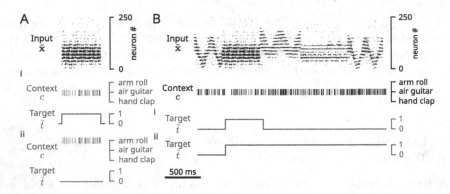

Fig. 2. Context-dependent classification tasks. A) Example for a data point in the single-sample classification task. The same input (right arm clockwise movement from DVS gesture) should be classified as 1 in context i (green) and 0 in other contexts (e.g. ii, red). **B)** Sequence classification task without and with memory. Top: The input consists of a sequence of five gesture patterns and the context indicates the target class (air guitar). The target is 1 when the indicated class is presented (i, dark blue, sequence classification task)/when the indicated class is currently or has been presented (ii, light blue, Sequence memory task). (Color figure online)

(SHD) [7] datasets. DVS gesture consist of samples from 10 classes of hand gestures, recorded using a spiking vision sensor. After preprocessing (see *Methods*), each input $\mathbf{x}^{(n)}$ is a 512-dimensional spike train of a variable length from 196 to 1476 ms. SHD consist of samples from 20 classes of spoken digits from 0 to 9, processed by an artificial cochlea model [7]. Here, after preprocessing, $\mathbf{x}^{(n)}$ is a 350-dimensional spike train, of a variable length from 116 to 684ms.

Example input spike trains for DVS gesture are shown in Fig. 2. In the context-dependent version considered here, the context-input to the network consists of 10 neurons, one for each class. The target-class is indicated by Poisson firing with 200 Hz of the corresponding context-neuron, while other context-neurons remain silent. The target output is 1 if the shown gesture was drawn from the target class and 0 otherwise.

We trained a cSNN consisting of 200 cLIF neurons on this task using BPTT. For this task, recurrent connections in the network were targeting only the somatic compartments of network neurons. As a baseline model, we considered a long-short-term memory spiking neural network (LSNN), which is a state-of-the-art recurrent SNN model for temporal processing tasks [4]. To evaluate the value of multiplicative modulation of somatic activity in our cSNN model, we also compared it to a version where this modulation was replaced by an additive integration of the apical activation, see *Methods*. All networks were trained for 10 epochs for DVS and 20 epochs for SHD. We found that the cSNNs outperformed both baseline models in terms of the final test accuracy on both data sets (**DVS:** cSNN: 89.4 ± 1.0, additive cSNN: 80.4 ± 2.2, LSNN: 75.9 ± 1.4, **SHD:** cSNN: 87.8 ± 0.77, additive cSNN: 72.2 ± 2.0, LSNN: 66.1 ± 1.7; mean±SD for $n = 5$

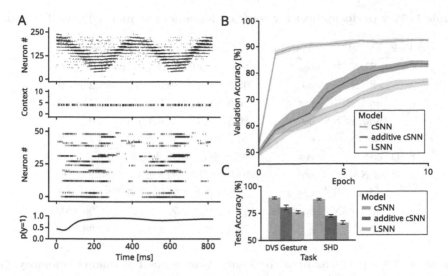

Fig. 3. Improved performance and convergence for single-sample context-dependent classification. A) Input spike trains, context input, network response, and network output for an example inference run on DVS gesture. **B)** Validation accuracy over training epoch for cSNNs and baseline models. **C)** Comparisons of test accuracies for DVS gesture (left) SHD (right) (mean±SD for $n = 5$ training runs).

training runs), see Fig. 3. In addition, when inspecting the training progress, one can observe highly significant faster learning in the cSNN as compared to both baselines. Note that we optimized the learning rate independently for all three models, hence, slower learning in the comparison models cannot be compensated by learning rate adjustments.

Apical Recurrence Improves Performance of cSNNs at Context-dependent Sequence Classification. Next, we considered the sequence classification task on DVS gesture and SHD. In addition to the LSNNs and additive cSNNs baseline models, we also investigated whether recurrent connections to apical compartments may improve the performance of cSNNs. In this task, target classes are imbalanced, we therefore report also precision and recall performance in Table 1, with precision being the most relevant measure. On the sequential version of both data sets, LSNNs performed poorly with respect to precision. Results for additive cSNNs with or without apical recurrence were clearly better. A significant jump in performances can be observed for cSNNs with multiplicative apical integration. The inclusion of apical recurrent connections further improved the performance, achieving a test precision of $88.5 \pm 1.6\%$ on DVS and $89.4 \pm 3.5\%$ on SHD, an improvement of 30–40% over LSNNs on these tasks.

A Variety of Apical Time Constants Improves Performance of cSNNs on Context-Dependent Sequence Memory Tasks. It has been shown that

Table 1. Test performances for context-dependent sequential classification.

Task	Model	Apical Rec	Accuracy	Precision	Recall
DVS	cSNN	yes	**95.1 ± 0.6**	**88.5 ± 1.6**	**86.8 ± 2.0**
	cSNN	no	93.3 ± 0.5	82.5 ± 2.7	85.2 ± 1.9
	add. cSNN	yes	86.9 ± 0.8	64.3 ± 2.0	78.7 ± 5.0
	add. cSNN	no	86.5 ± 0.9	63.0 ± 1.5	79.0 ± 4.0
	LSNN	-	84.8 ± 0.52	58.4 ± 1.1	83.7 ± 2.2
SHD	cSNN	yes	**95.9 ± 0.8**	**89.4 ± 3.5**	**90.49 ± 1.4**
	cSNN	no	93.08 ± 0.5	80.8 ± 1.5	86.2 ± 1.8
	add. cSNN	yes	84.5 ± 3.3	59.0 ± 6.5	81.0 ± 2.2
	add. cSNN	no	84.8 ± 0.3	59.4 ± 0.7	76.96 ± 0.5
	LSNN	-	78.4 ± 0.4	47.8 ± 0.6	77.98 ± 1.7

Table 2. Test performances for context-dependent sequence memory. $\mathcal{U}$ denotes a uniform distribution over the given range. We report mean±SD for $n = 5$.

Model	Apical Recurrence	τ_a	DVS Acc	SHD Acc
cSNN	yes	$\mathcal{U}(0.02, 0.2)$	**83.9 ± 2.9**	**75.7 ± 2.5**
cSNN	yes	0.2	76.5 ± 2.8	66.6 ± 3.2
cSNN	yes	0.02	74.7 ± 2.9	66.2 ± 7.0
cSNN	no	$\mathcal{U}(0.02, 0.2)$	59.6 ± 1.6	53.1 ± 0.6
add. cSNN	yes	$\mathcal{U}(0.02, 0.2)$	51.1 ± 2.3	55.8 ± 1.3
add. cSNN	no	$\mathcal{U}(0.02, 0.2)$	50.1 ± 2.9	53.2 ± 1.2
LSNN	-	-	51.9 ± 1.6	51.0 ± 0.6

separate dendritic compartments can implement a form of short-term memory [27]. This is because dendrites can elicit long-lasting plateau potentials due to the activation of N-methyl-D-aspartate (NMDA) channels which can last on the order of 100 milliseconds and Ca^{2+} spikes that can last for a few hundred milliseconds [2]. The memorizing effect of plateau potentials is further boosted by the electrical segregation of distal dendritic compartments from the soma. Due to this segregation, these compartments are not reset, hence they can retain depolarizations beyond action potential output. This type of memory was termed dendritic memory in [27].

We wondered whether dendritic memory could boost performance of SNNs in context-dependent sequence memory task as described above. To this end, we considered cSNNs with apical recurrence and increased the time constant τ_a of the apical compartment for each neuron from the standard 20 ms to a value from 20 to 200 ms (drawn from a uniform distribution for each neuron). This increased time constant captures the memorizing effect of dendritic plateau potentials in the arguably simplest manner. We compared the test accuracy of this model with the accuracy of LSNNs and several variations of cSNNs, see Table 2. Interestingly, LSNNs and cSNNs without apical recurrence failed on this task, with a test accuracy at chance level. On the other hand, cSNNs with apical recurrence and a variety of apical time constants achieved $83.9 \pm 2.9\%$ and $75.7 \pm 2.5\%$ on DVS and SHD respectively, outperforming all other tested variants. Interestingly, a variety of time constants was crucial for good performance: the performance of cSNNs with homogeneous τ_a of either 20 ms or 200 ms showed a clear reduction of 7-9%. Also, the multiplicative integration of apical activation was necessary for good performance: the additive variant with apical recurrence performed close to chance level.

4   Discussion

Our knowledge about the architecture of the neocortical network suggests that the integration of bottom-up with top-down input is a key feature of cortical computation. In the center of this architecture are pyramidal cells in layers 2/3 and 5 of the cortical column. Experimental results suggest that a main feature of these neurons is a modulation of activity through the apical dendritic compartment that receives top-down input. We have investigated in this article the context-dependent computational capabilities of cSNNs, that are, SNNs based on neurons which implement this modulation in an abstract manner. The main advantage of our model is its simplicity, making it in principle possible to train large networks on large data sets.

Our results show that cSNNs can drastically improve performance on such tasks when compared to state-of-the-art SNN models, hinting at a computational advantage of this architecture. While a detailed analysis of the reasons for this advantage is out of the scope of this article, there are several arguments that can be given. First, it has been recognized that multiplicative interactions enrich the representational capabilities of neural networks [13]. The authors in [13] argue that multiplicative interactions offer a powerful inductive bias when fusing multiple streams of information or when conditional computation is required, which is exactly the case in context-dependent computation tasks considered here. Such interactions can be found in several modern neural network models such as long short-term memory networks (LSTMs) or transformers [12,35]. In SNNs, multiplicative interactions have not been studied extensively so far. LSNNs [4] implement long time constants to mimic longer-lasting memory in LSTMs, but they do not utilize multiplicative interactions as cSNNs do. Multiplicative interactions may also be beneficial for optimization. When the apical activation is combined multiplicatively with the somatic one, gradients for the apical compartment are influenced directly by the somatic activation, which is not the case in the additive case. This might explain why cSNNs exhibit faster training in our single-sample context-dependent classification task, Fig. 3.

Second, as briefly discussed above, segregated apical compartments can implement a form of dendritic memory [27], in particular if longer dendritic time constants are utilized. Since the apical compartment is segregated from the somatic one, action potential output does not reset this memory.

SNNs are a fundamental architecture for energy-efficient neuromorphic hardware [8,22–24,26]. Context-dependent computations have been recognized as an important application area of this technology [3,19,37], and the potential for nonlinear dendritic operations in neuromorphic hardware has been studied [14,29]. Our results show that rather simple spiking architectures can be utilized for context-dependent computations with neuromorphic systems.

5   Methods

cLIF Neuron and Model Parameters: The apical current is given by $I_j^a(t) = \sum_i w_{ji}^{a,in} c_i(t) + \sum_{i \neq j} w_{ji}^{a,rec} s_i(t) + b_j^a$. The somatic current is $I_j(t) = \sum_i w_{ji}^{in} x_i(t) + \sum_{i \neq j} w_{ji}^{rec} s_i(t) + b_j$. Here, $w_{ji}^{a,in}$ denotes the apical weight from contextual input i, $w_{ji}^{a,rec}$ apical recurrent weights, and b^a and b the apical and somatic biases respectively. Weights were initialized as in [28], biases were initialized to zero. Further simulation parameters: $V^{th} = 0.05$, $\tau_m = 20$ ms. R_m was set to $R_m = 1$ for simplicity as in [4]. $\tau_a = 20$ ms for DVS and 40 ms for SHD, unless stated otherwise. For the LSNN, adaptive threshold time-constants drawn from $\mathcal{U}(20, 200)$ ms, with threshold increment coefficient of 1.3. Networks were optimized using surrogate gradients and an upper spike regularization targeting 10 Hz as in [4]. In the additive cSNN, the membrane voltage of neurons evolved as $V_j(t + \Delta t) = \beta V_j(t) + (1 - \beta) \left[R_m I_j(t + \Delta t) + V_j^a(t + \Delta t) \right] - V^{th} s_j(t)$. Parameters for Fig. 1C were $V^{th} = 25.5mV$, $R_m = 220\,M\Omega$ and $C_m = 170$ pF.

Data Pre-processing: In the DVS gesture dataset, events are recorded with a polar DVS camera of sensor size 128×128, which we summed over 8×8 spatial and 5 ms temporal blocks. Binarization was employed, by setting positions to 1 if event sums ≥ 3 within each processed block, and 0 otherwise. As in [9], only the first 40% of transformed gestures were considered, which is sufficient for high accuracy due to the periodicity of recorded gestures. For the SHD dataset [7], events on a 700-dimensional grid were processed with blocks of spatial resolution 2, and temporal resolution of 2 ms. Binarization was employed as before by setting positions to 1 if event sums ≥ 1 for each block, and 0 otherwise.

Network Training: We used the binary cross entropy loss where a unique target is provided for each sampled item (e.g. gesture) in the sequence. For item k of length n in the sequence, prediction is computed as $p(y_k = 1) = \sigma\left(\sum_{t=t_k}^{t_k+n-1} o(t)/n\right)$, where $o(t)$ is the non-spiking leaky integrator readout output at time step t, and t_k the onset time step of item k. Models were trained using Adam [15] with initial learning rate 0.01 and batch size 64. We decayed the learning rate exponentially after each epoch p via $\eta^{(p+1)} = \gamma \eta^{(p)}$ with $\gamma = 0.75$ for DVS and 0.85 for SHD. For DVS gesture, 10 epochs were used for task 1 and 2 and 20 for task 3. For SHD, 20 epochs were used for tasks 1 and 2 and 30 for tasks 3. For task 3, test accuracies were computed with respect to the output at the last shown sample (hence, indicating whether the network correctly memorized the appearance of the target class in the sequence). Training and test examples were generated to balance these targets.

References

1. Amir, A., et al.: A low power, fully event-based gesture recognition system. In: Proceedings of the IEEE Conference on Computer Vision and Pattern Recognition, pp. 7243–7252 (2017)
2. Antic, S.D., Zhou, W.L., Moore, A.R., Short, S.M., Ikonomu, K.D.: The decade of the dendritic NMDA spike. J. Neurosci. Res. **88**(14), 2991–3001 (2010)
3. Asgari, H., Maybodi, B.M.N., Payvand, M., Azghadi, M.R.: Low-energy and fast spiking neural network for context-dependent learning on FPGA. IEEE Trans. Circuits Syst. II Express Briefs **67**(11), 2697–2701 (2020)
4. Bellec, G., Salaj, D., Subramoney, A., Legenstein, R., Maass, W.: Long short-term memory and learning-to-learn in networks of spiking neurons. In: Advances in Neural Information Processing Systems, vol. 31 (2018)
5. Beniaguev, D., Segev, I., London, M.: Single cortical neurons as deep artificial neural networks. Neuron **109**(17), 2727–2739 (2021)
6. Chen, G., Scherr, F., Maass, W.: A data-based large-scale model for primary visual cortex enables brain-like robust and versatile visual processing. Sci. Adv. **8**(44), eabq7592 (2022)
7. Cramer, B., Stradmann, Y., Schemmel, J., Zenke, F.: The Heidelberg spiking data sets for the systematic evaluation of spiking neural networks. IEEE Trans. Neural Netw. Learn. Syst. **33**(7), 2744–2757 (2020)
8. Davies, M., et al.: Loihi: a neuromorphic manycore processor with on-chip learning. IEEE Micro **38**(1), 82–99 (2018)
9. Frenkel, C., Indiveri, G.: ReckOn: a 28 nm sub-mm2 task-agnostic spiking recurrent neural network processor enabling on-chip learning over second-long timescales. In: 2022 IEEE ISSCC, vol. 65, pp. 1–3. IEEE (2022)
10. Gerstner, W., Kistler, W.M., Naud, R., Paninski, L.: Neuronal Dynamics: From Single Neurons to Networks and Models of Cognition. Cambridge University Press, Cambridge (2014)
11. Gilbert, C.D., Li, W.: Top-down influences on visual processing. Nat. Rev. Neurosci. **14**(5), 350–363 (2013)
12. Hochreiter, S., Schmidhuber, J.: Long short-term memory. Neural Comput. **9**(8), 1735–1780 (1997)
13. Jayakumar, S.M., et al.: Multiplicative interactions and where to find them. In: ICLR (2020)
14. Kaiser, J., Billaudelle, S., Müller, E., Tetzlaff, C., Schemmel, J., Schmitt, S.: Emulating dendritic computing paradigms on analog neuromorphic hardware. Neuroscience **489**, 290–300 (2022)
15. Kingma, D.P., Ba, J.: Adam: a method for stochastic optimization (2017)
16. Kreiman, G., Serre, T.: Beyond the feedforward sweep: feedback computations in the visual cortex. Ann. N. Y. Acad. Sci. **1464**(1), 222–241 (2020)
17. Larkum, M.E., Senn, W., Lüscher, H.R.: Top-down dendritic input increases the gain of layer 5 pyramidal neurons. Cereb. Cortex **14**(10), 1059–1070 (2004)
18. Larkum, M.E., Wu, J., Duverdin, S.A., Gidon, A.: The guide to dendritic spikes of the mammalian cortex in vitro and in vivo **489**, 15–33 (2022)
19. Liang, D., Indiveri, G.: A neuromorphic computational primitive for robust context-dependent decision making and context-dependent stochastic computation. IEEE Trans. Circuits Syst. II: Express Briefs **66**(5), 843–847 (2019)
20. Limbacher, T., Özdenizci, O., Legenstein, R.: Memory-enriched computation and learning in spiking neural networks through Hebbian plasticity. arXiv preprint arXiv:2205.11276 (2022)

21. Maass, W.: Networks of spiking neurons: the third generation of neural network models. Neural Netw. **10**(9), 1659–1671 (1997)
22. Merolla, P.A., et al.: A million spiking-neuron integrated circuit with a scalable communication network and interface. Science **345**(6197), 668–673 (2014)
23. Moradi, S., Qiao, N., Stefanini, F., Indiveri, G.: A scalable multicore architecture with heterogeneous memory structures for dynamic neuromorphic asynchronous processors (DYNAPs). IEEE Trans. Biomed. Circuits Syst. **12**(1), 106–122 (2017)
24. Painkras, E., et al.: Spinnaker: a 1-w 18-core system-on-chip for massively-parallel neural network simulation. IEEE J. Solid-State Circuits **48**(8), 1943–1953 (2013)
25. Paugam-Moisy, H., Bohte, S.M.: Computing with spiking neuron networks. Rozenberg, G., Bäck, T., Kok, J.N. (eds.) Handbook of Natural Computing, vol. 1, pp. 1–47 (2012). https://doi.org/10.1007/978-3-540-92910-9_10
26. Pei, J., et al.: Towards artificial general intelligence with hybrid Tianjic chip architecture. Nature **572**(7767), 106–111 (2019)
27. Quaresima, A., Fitz, H., Duarte, R., Broek, D.V.D., Hagoort, P., Petersson, K.M.: The tripod neuron: a minimal structural reduction of the dendritic tree. J. Physiol. (2022)
28. Rossbroich, J., Gygax, J., Zenke, F.: Fluctuation-driven initialization for spiking neural network training. Neuromorphic Comput. Eng. **2**(4), 044016 (2022)
29. Schemmel, J., Kriener, L., Müller, P., Meier, K.: An accelerated analog neuromorphic hardware system emulating NMDA-and calcium-based non-linear dendrites. In: IJCNN, pp. 2217–2226. IEEE (2017)
30. Schuman, B., Dellal, S., Prönneke, A., Machold, R., Rudy, B.: Neocortical layer 1: an elegant solution to top-down and bottom-up integration. Annu. Rev. Neurosci. **44**, 221–252 (2021)
31. Shrestha, S.B., Orchard, G.: Slayer: spike layer error reassignment in time. In: Advances in Neural Information Processing Systems, vol. 31 (2018)
32. Tavanaei, A., Ghodrati, M., Kheradpisheh, S.R., Masquelier, T., Maida, A.: Deep learning in spiking neural networks. Neural Netw. **111**, 47–63 (2019)
33. Tripathy, S.J., Savitskaya, J., Burton, S.D., Urban, N.N., Gerkin, R.C.: NeuroElectro: a window to the world's neuron electrophysiology data. Front. Neuroinform. **8**, 40 (2014)
34. Ujfalussy, B.B., Makara, J.K., Lengyel, M., Branco, T.: Global and multiplexed dendritic computations under in vivo-like conditions. Neuron **100**(3), 579–592 (2018)
35. Vaswani, A., et al.: Attention is all you need. In: Advances in Neural Information Processing Systems, vol. 30 (2017)
36. Wybo, W.A., Jordan, J., Ellenberger, B., Marti Mengual, U., Nevian, T., Senn, W.: Data-driven reduction of dendritic morphologies with preserved dendro-somatic responses. eLife **10**, e60936 (2021)
37. Yang, S., Wang, J., Deng, B., Azghadi, M.R., Linares-Barranco, B.: Neuromorphic context-dependent learning framework with fault-tolerant spike routing. IEEE Trans. Neural Netw. Learn. Syst. **33**(12), 7126–7140 (2021)
38. Zenke, F., Vogels, T.P.: The remarkable robustness of surrogate gradient learning for instilling complex function in spiking neural networks. Neural Comput. **33**(4), 899–925 (2021)

Efficient Uncertainty Estimation in Spiking Neural Networks via MC-dropout

Tao Sun[1], Bojian Yin[1], and Sander Bohté[1,2,3]($\boxtimes$)

[1] CWI, Machine Learning Group, Amsterdam, The Netherlands
{tao.sun,byin,sbohte}@cwi.nl
[2] Rijksuniversiteit Groningen, Groningen, The Netherlands
[3] University of Amsterdam, Amsterdam, The Netherlands

Abstract. Spiking neural networks (SNNs) have gained attention as models of sparse and event-driven communication of biological neurons, and as such have shown increasing promise for energy-efficient applications in neuromorphic hardware. As with classical artificial neural networks (ANNs), predictive uncertainties are important for decision making in high-stakes applications, such as autonomous vehicles, medical diagnosis, and high frequency trading. Yet, discussion of uncertainty estimation in SNNs is limited, and approaches for uncertainty estimation in ANNs are not directly applicable to SNNs. Here, we propose an efficient Monte Carlo(MC)-dropout based approach for uncertainty estimation in SNNs. Our approach exploits the time-step mechanism of SNNs to enable MC-dropout in a computationally efficient manner, without introducing significant overheads during training and inference while demonstrating high accuracy and uncertainty quality.

Keywords: Spiking Neural Network · Uncertainty Estimation · MC-dropout

1 Introduction

Inspired by the brain's event-driven and sparse communication, spiking neural networks (SNNs) are enabling applications with high energy-efficiency in the form of neuromorphic computing [21]. Analogous to biological neurons, spiking neurons in SNNs communicate using discrete spikes, and time stepping is typically used to account for the evolution of these neurons' internal state as a response to impinging and emitted spikes. With recent advances in architectures and training methods, SNNs now achieve performance comparable to their artificial neural network (ANN) counterparts in many tasks [3,25,26].

To employ SNNs in the real-world however, accurate predictions have to be paired with high-quality uncertainty estimation to enable decision-making in high-stakes applications such as autonomous vehicles, medical diagnosis, and high frequency trading [4]: uncertain predictions in these applications may need

L. Iliadis et al. (Eds.): ICANN 2023, LNCS 14254, pp. 393–406, 2023.
https://doi.org/10.1007/978-3-031-44207-0_33

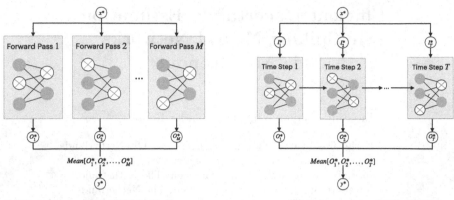

(a) Inference with ANN MC-dropout   (b) Inference in AOT-SNN

Fig. 1. (a) In ANNs, MC-dropout is performed by averaging results for a predefined number (M) of forward passes through a dropout-enabled network. (b) In AOT-SNNs, inference at each time step is taken as functionally equivalent to a forward pass in the MC-dropout method. As the SNN network evaluation requires T time-steps already, only one effective forward pass is needed.

to be reviewed by human experts for final decisions. In ANNs, predictive uncertainties in classification models are commonly represented by predictive distributions [13]. While evidence suggests that the brain performs a form of Bayesian inference based on uncertainty representations [18], the literature on uncertainty in SNNs is relatively limited and primarily concentrates on the sampling of probabilistic distributions, typically from a neuroscience perspective [12,20].

Approaches for uncertainty estimation in classical deep learning models can be divided into two groups: deterministic methods and Bayesian methods [6]. With a deterministic method, a model learned from training data is essentially a point estimate of the model's parameters. In a deterministic deep network, each predictive distribution is estimated by a single forward propagation followed by the softmax function. Yet, although it is feasible to infer uncertainty with deterministic methods, these methods are known to be prone to output overconfident estimation [6,13]. In contrast, a Bayesian network learns the posterior distribution of parameters in the network rather than depending on a single setting of parameters. The probability outputs of a Bayesian method can be analytically obtained by marginalizing the likelihood of the input with the estimated posterior distribution; this however is generally an intractable problem. To tackle this issue, many approximation methods and non-Bayesian methods have been introduced [6]. Example of these methods like Monte-Carlo-dropout (MC-dropout) [5] and deep ensembles [13] achieve excellent performance in terms of uncertainty estimation quality, either by repeatedly carrying out inference for each sample in perturbed versions of the network (Fig. 1a), or by training a collection of networks and then carrying out inference in each network.

Here, we propose an efficient uncertainty estimation approach for SNNs by exploiting their time-step mechanism. Specifically, we apply continual MC-dropout in SNNs by taking their outputs averaged over time steps as predictive distributions, where we train SNNs with a loss function that also involves their time steps: **A**verage-**O**ver-**T**ime-SNNs (AOT-SNNs, Fig. 1b). In AOT-SNNs, we take inference of each time step as functionally equivalent to a forward pass in the classical MC-dropout method. Since only one forward pass is needed in inference, the computational overhead for AOT-SNNs is significantly reduced relative to the MC-dropout method while still allowing effective uncertainty estimation. We compare the performance of AOT-SNNs with more standard SNNs, as well as with SNNs using the classical MC-dropout approach and SNN ensembles, across multiple classification tasks. We demonstrate that for identical network architectures, AOT-SNNs substantially outperform more standard SNNs and achieve comparable accuracy as ensembles and classical MC-dropout SNNs at little cost to uncertainty estimation quality while being much more computationally efficient.

2 Background

2.1 Problem Setup

We assume a training dataset $\mathcal{D}$ that consists of $\mathcal{N}$ i.i.d data points $\mathcal{D} = \{\mathbf{X}, \mathbf{Y}\} = \{\mathbf{x}_n, y_n\}_{n=1}^N$, where $\mathbf{x}_n \in \mathbb{R}^d$ and the true label $y_n \in \mathbf{y} = \{1, \ldots, K\}$. Given a sample $\mathbf{x}_n$, a neural network outputs the probabilistic predictive distribution $p_\omega(y_n|\mathbf{x}_n)$, where ω is the parameters of the network.

A number of non-Bayesian methods achieving excellent performance in term of uncertainty estimation have been proposed, among which are deep ensembles [13] and post-hoc calibration methods [10]. Deep ensembles are considered a "gold standard" for uncertainty estimation [24], while a set of models are trained with a proper scoring rule as the loss function. At inference time, the output of all models are then combined to obtain a predictive distribution. Post-hoc calibration methods, such as temperature scaling [10], involve the re-calibration of probabilities using a validation dataset and achieve excellent calibration performance in the i.i.d test dataset.

2.2 Bayesian Neural Networks and MC-Dropout Approximation

In a Bayesian neural network, the predictive distribution for a sample $\mathbf{x}$ is given by:

$$p(\mathbf{y}|\mathbf{x}, \mathcal{D}) = \int p(\mathbf{y}|\mathbf{x}, \omega)p(\omega|\mathcal{D})d\omega. \tag{1}$$

The posterior distribution, $p(\omega|\mathcal{D})$ or $p(\omega|\mathbf{X}, \mathbf{Y})$, of the parameters ω can be computed by applying Bayes' theorem

$$p(\omega|\mathbf{X}, \mathbf{Y}) = \frac{p(\mathbf{Y}|\mathbf{X}, \omega)p(\omega)}{p(\mathbf{Y}|\mathbf{X})}. \tag{2}$$

Due to the intractability of the normalizer in (2), the posterior distribution $p(\omega|\mathcal{D})$ and the predictive distribution $p(\mathbf{y}|\mathbf{x}, \mathcal{D}))$ usually cannot be evaluated analytically. A variety of approximation methods have been introduced to tackle this issue [9,14]. One such approximation is the MC-dropout method, which is often taken as a baseline model in uncertainty estimation [13,17] due to its feasibility and relatively good performance.

Dropout [22] is a simple but effective technique used in deep learning models to prevent overfitting. In the MC-dropout method, dropout is applied before each weight layer of a neural network in both **training** and **testing**. The predictive distribution calculation with the MC-dropout method is performed by averaging results over a predefined number of forward passes through a dropout-enabled network. Gal & Gharamani [5] showed that neural networks with such configuration can be viewed as an approximation to a Bayesian method in the form of *deep Gaussian processes* [2].

Either MC-dropout models or deep ensembles involves multiple forward propagation passes in inference. As a result, when naively applied to SNNs, the computational and energy costs becomes relatively high due to the necessity of repeatedly running SNNs for multiple times during inference.

2.3   Source and Quality of Predictive Uncertainty

The only source of predictive uncertainty of deterministic methods is from the noisy data. Uncertainty in a Bayesian method comes from both data and defects of the model itself [6]: uncertainty caused by data is referred to as *data uncertainty*, while uncertainty caused by defects of the model itself is referred to as *model uncertainty*.

The quality of predictive uncertainties can be measured from two aspects [13]. The first concerns uncertainty quality on in-distribution data, where test data and training data share the same distribution. The second aspect evaluates generalization of uncertainty on domain-shifted data. While certain post-hoc calibration methods may generate accurate predictive probabilities for i.i.d data, their effectiveness in predicting uncertainty for domain-shifted data is not ensured [17]. For both aspects, model calibration is examined as the indication of uncertainty quality [17]. For classification tasks, accuracy and calibration are two evaluation measures that are mutually orthogonal [13]. Accuracy, defined as the ratio of corrected classified examples to total number of examples, measures how often a model correctly classifies; calibration measures the quality of predictive probability distributions [13] and indicates the extent to which the probability of a predicted class label reflects the real correct likelihood. A class of metrics to measure calibration is referred to as *proper scoring rules* [8], which include the Brier score (BS) and negative log-likelihood (NLL); another calibration metrics is the *Expected Calibration Error* (ECE) [10], which is a scalar summary statistic of calibration that approximates miscalibration. Although the definition ECE is intuitive and thus widely used, it is not a perfect metric for calibration because optimal ECE values can be generated by trivial solutions [17]; see the Appendix for details on proper scoring rules and ECE.

2.4 SNN

SNNs typically work with the same types of network topologies as ANNs, but computation in SNNs is distinct. SNNs use stateful and binary-valued spiking neurons, rather than the stateless and analog valued neurons of ANNs. As a result, unlike synchronous computation in ANNs, inference in SNNs is in a iterative form through multiple time steps $t = 0, 1, ..., T$: in each time step t, the membrane potential of a spiking neuron $U(t)$ is affected by the impinging spikes from connecting neurons emitted at time step $t - 1$, and the past potential $U(t - 1)$. Once the membrane potential $U(t)$ reaches a threshold θ, the neuron itself emits a spike. Such sparse and asynchronous communications between connected neurons is key to enabling SNNs to achieve high energy-efficiency.

LIF Neurons. Various spiking neuron models exist, ranging in complexity from the detailed Hodgkin-Huxley model to the simplified Leaky-Integrated-and-Fire (LIF) neuron model [7]. The latter is widely used in SNNs, as it is interpretable and computationally efficient. Resembling an RC circuit, the LIF neural model is represented as:

$$\tau \frac{dU}{dt} = -U + RI. \tag{3}$$

where I and R are the current and input resistance, and τ is the time constant of the circuit. The discrete approximation of (3) can be written as:

$$u_i^t = \lambda u_i^{t-1} + \sum_j w_{ij} s_j^t - s_i^{t-1} \theta, \tag{4}$$

$$s_i^t = \begin{cases} 1, & \text{if } u_i^t > \theta \\ 0, & \text{otherwise} \end{cases} \tag{5}$$

where u_i is the membrane potential of a neuron i, λ denotes the leaky constant (< 1) for the membrane potential, w_{ij} represents the weight connecting the neuron i and its pre-synaptic neuron j, and s_i indicates whether a neuron spikes.

With the introduction of surrogate gradient methods [16,25] and learnable LIF neurons [3,25], both trainability and performance of SNNs have been improved dramatically.

3 Methods

Here, we present our proposed AOT-SNNs. We first explain how we efficiently apply MC-dropout to SNNs, and then introduce the loss function used in AOT-SNNs, which is based on the mean output values over time steps. Lastly, we explain the network architecture we use to demonstrate AOT-SNNs in practice.

3.1   Efficient MC-dropout in SNNs

As noted, the classical MC-dropout method runs a test sample a specified number (M) times in a model with dropout enabled, and takes the output of these forward passes as the final predictive distribution (Fig. 1a). Thus applied in ANNs, MC-dropout results in satisfactory predictive uncertainty estimation.

In principle, such MC-dropout can be applied directly to SNNs, as *MC-dropout SNN*. This, however, results in computationally expensive inference as an SNN typically has to be run for multiple time steps to perform inference. Naively performing inference of a single sample in an *MC-dropout SNN* would mean running M forward passes of a sample through a network where each individual pass entails the evaluation of T time steps, incurring $M \times T$ time steps in total.

As an alternative, we propose to leverage the SNN time-step mechanism by enabling MC-dropout in AOT-SNNs during a single evaluation. Specifically, we compute predictive distributions in a dropout-enabled AOT-SNN by averaging outputs at multiple time steps. For a sample $\mathbf{x}$, the AOT-SNN computes at each time step t a probability distribution $p_t(\mathbf{y}|\mathbf{x})$. Thus, the probability distribution for the sample $\mathbf{x}$ is calculated as:

$$p(\mathbf{y}|\mathbf{x}) = \frac{1}{T} \sum_{t=1}^{T} p_t(\mathbf{y}|\mathbf{x}).$$

In this view, each time step in an AOT-SNN is weakly equivalent to a single forward pass in the classical MC-dropout method. As such, only one forward pass is required during inference, which requires just T time steps compared to $M \times T$ for the MC-dropout SNN.

3.2   Loss Function

Loss functions in many current high-performing SNN learning algorithms [3, 19, 25, 27] are computed based on the output values of last time step, and we will refer such loss functions as *last-time-step* loss, resulting in Last-Time-Step-SNNs (*LTS-SNNs*). The last-time-step loss can be written as:

$$L = l(T), \tag{6}$$

where $l(T)$ is the loss function computed from the output values of the final time step T.

Since the last-time-step loss is not compatible with the proposed uncertainty estimation approach in AOT-SNNs, we introduce the *average-over-time* loss, which calculates its output by averaging over multiple time steps:

$$L = \frac{1}{T} \sum_{t=1}^{T} l(t). \tag{7}$$

By combining the average-over-time loss with dropout, we expect that the quality of uncertainty estimation for our approach will be improved, as the AOT loss pushes SNNs to correctly classify as much as possible at every time step. This is in contrast to LTS-SNNs, where dropout is not enabled during inference[1] and the predictive distributions output of only the last time step are used.

For $l(t)$, either negative log-likelihood (NLL) loss or the mean squared error (MSE) loss [3] can be used. Here, we use the MSE loss, as we find that in practice the NLL loss causes a disconnect between NLL and accuracy, which is an indication of miscalibration [10].

3.3 Network Architecture

We use AOT-SNNs with a network architecture very similar to the high-performing PLIF networks in [3]. These networks are composed of a *spiking encoder network* and a *classifier network*. The spiking encoder network consists of multiple downsampling modules. Each downsampling module has a certain number of convolution blocks and a pooling layer (*kernel size* = 2, *stride* = 2). The convolution block is composed of a convolution layer (*kernel size* = 3, *stride* = 1, *padding* = 1), a batch normalization layer, and a spiking neuron layer.

Our classifier network is slightly modified from [3] and includes a fully-connected layer, a spiking neuron layer, another fully-connected layer, which is then followed by a readout integrator layer. Unlike the original PLIF networks that classify using relatively coarse summed rate-coding collected from a population of output neurons, probabilities of AOT-SNNs are computed based on the membrane potentials of readout integrator neurons as in [25]. This modification enables AOT-SNNs to achieve better uncertainty estimation performance compared to corresponding standard PLIF networks while obtaining similar accuracy. In the spiking neuron layers, PLIF neurons [3] are used, where the time constants τ are learned and shared by neurons within the same layer. Note that dropout is applied to the neurons' output spikes, and input data is directly injected into the network as current into the input neurons.

4   Experiments

We performed a series of experiments to compare AOT-SNNs to LTS-SNNs, as well as MC-dropout SNNs and also with the 'gold standard' of SNN ensembles, across multiple classification tasks. As a proof of concept, we first applied this approach to the MNIST dataset. Second, we experiment on the CIFAR-10 dataset to compare our models with corresponding LTS-SNNs. Additionally, we reported and analyzed results on the CIFAR-100 dataset. Furthermore, we carried out an ablation study where we characterized the uncertainty properties of AOT-SNNs with regard to dropout rates and dropout types.

---

[1] For LTS-SNNs, dropout is not enabled at inference time as this leads to notably weak performance for LTS-SNNs, similar to that of ANNs.

Table 1. Performance comparisons between the AOT-SNN and its corresponding LTS-SNN on the MNIST dataset (mean±std across 10 models). The numbers after the model names represent time steps.

MODEL	ACCURACY (%) ↑	BS ↓	NLL ↓	ECE ↓
AOT-SNN (8)	99.54 ± 0.030	7.0e-4 ± 4.3E-5	0.0144 ± 7.6E-4	1.2e-3 ± 3.4E-4
LTS-SNN (8)	99.37 ± 0.080	9.8E-4 ± 9.9E-5	0.021 ± 2.5E-3	4E-3 ± 1.1E-3
MC-DROPOUT SNN (8, 10)	99.57 ± 0.033	6.5E-4 ± 5.0E-05	0.0125 ± 9.6E-4	1.1E-3 ± 2.9E-4
SNN ENSEMBLES (8, 10)	99.56	7.5E-4	0.0180	6.7E-3

4.1   Experimental Setup

In our experiments, LTS-SNNs used the same layer structure as their corresponding AOT-SNNs. All the MC-dropout SNNs and SNN ensembles are based on their corresponding LTS-SNNs.

The Adam optimizer was used, with a cosine annealing learning rate scheduler, whose initial learning rate is 0.001 and T_{max} is 64. The default dropout rate used is 0.5. For the MINIST dataset, we used a batch size of 150, while the batch sizes were 60 for CIFAR-10 and 15 for CIFAR-100. The number of epochs used for each dataset were 200 (MNIST), 300 (CIFAR-10), and 300 (CIFAR-100).

4.2   MNIST

The spiking encoder network for the MNIST dataset has two downsampling modules, each of which includes only one convolution block. In Table 1, we compared the AOT-SNNs, its corresponding LTS-SNNs, MC-dropout SNNs, and SNN ensembles, all using best performing models that have eight time steps to evaluate samples. The results demonstrate that the AOT-SNNs outperform the LTS-SNNs in both accuracy and the predictive uncertainty metrics, including Brier score, NLL, and ECE. Furthermore, AOT-SNNs exhibit similar accuracy and uncertainty estimation as both MC-dropout SNNs and SNN ensembles.

4.3   CIFAR-10 and CIFAR-100

The architectures of AOT-SNNs for the CIFAR-10 and CIFAR-100 dataset are similar. They apply the same spiking encoder network, which has two downsampling modules, each with three convolution blocks. Their classifier networks differ only in the last fully-connected layer due to their different number of ground truth classes.

CIFAR-10 Held-Out Test Dataset. Table 2 presents a comparison of AOT-SNNs to LTS-SNNs, MC-dropout SNNs, and SNN ensembles. While each MC-dropout SNN ran five forward passes, each SNN ensemble consisted of five models. We show results for 4 and 8 time steps, corresponding to respective best performing duration (see also Table 3). AOT-SNNs exhibit superior performance

Table 2. Comparison on the CIFAR-10 dataset between AOT-SNNs, LTS-SNNs, MC-dropout models, and deep ensembles (mean± std across 5 models). The digits enclosed in brackets following the model names indicate the number of SNN time steps and the number of forward passes or models used in inference.

MODEL	ACCURACY (%) ↑	BS ↓	NLL ↓	ECE ↓
AOT-SNN (4, 1)	90.2 ± 0.26	0.0153 ± 3.0E-4	0.38 ± 1.2E-2	0.040 ± 3.1E-3
AOT-SNN (8, 1)	90.8 ± 0.23	0.0144 ± 4.0E-4	0.37 ± 2.2E-2	0.043 ± 4.1E-3
LTS-SNN (4, 1)	88.9 ± 0.71	0.017 ± 1.1E-3	0.43 ± 2.8E-2	0.058 ± 4.4E-3
LTS-SNN (8, 1)	88.5 ± 0.60	0.0181 ± 8.1E-4	0.47 ± 1.3E-2	0.067 ± 3.4E-3
MC-DROPOUT SNN (4, 5)	90.53 ± 0.37	0.0140 ± 4.1E-4	0.32 ± 1.0E-2	0.026 ± 3.0E-3
MC-DROPOUT SNN (8, 5)	90.43 ± 0.37	0.0145 ± 5.3E-4	0.35 ± 1.3E-2	0.037 ± 1.4E-3
SNN ENSEMBLES (4, 5)	90.9	0.0134	0.2919	0.012
SNN ENSEMBLES (8, 5)	90.8	0.0135	0.2967	0.016

Table 3. Performance comparisons between AOT-SNNs and LTS-SNNs on CIFAR10 (mean±std across 5 trials).

MODEL	TIME STEPS	ACCURACY (%) ↑	BS ↓	NLL ↓	ECE ↓
AOT-SNN	2	89.4 ± 0.18	0.0168 ± 1.4E-4	0.417 ± 6.1E-3	0.047 ± 2.3E-3
AOT-SNN	3	89.7 ± 0.26	0.0160 ± 2.7E-4	0.40 ± 2.1E-2	0.044 ± 4.2E-3
AOT-SNN	4	90.2 ± 0.26	0.0153 ± 3.0E-4	0.38 ± 1.2E-2	0.040 ± 3.1E-3
AOT-SNN	5	90.4 ± 0.07	0.0150 ± 2.4E-4	0.39 ± 2.6E-2	0.043 ± 3.6E-3
AOT-SNN	6	90.5 ± 0.16	0.0149 ± 2.8E-4	0.38 ± 1.7E-2	0.043 ± 3.0E-3
AOT-SNN	7	90.2 ± 0.34	0.0151 ± 4.3E-4	0.37 ± 1.2E-2	0.043 ± 1.9E-3
AOT-SNN	8	90.8 ± 0.23	0.0144 ± 4.0E-4	0.37 ± 2.2E-2	0.043 ± 4.1E-3
AOT-SNN	9	90.5 ± 0.55	0.0147 ± 7.3E-4	0.37 ± 2.4E-2	0.044 ± 4.1E-3
AOT-SNN	10	90.7 ± 0.41	0.0146 ± 6.2E-4	0.37 ± 2.4E-2	0.044 ± 5.2E-3
LTS-SNN	1	88.2 ± 0.47	0.0168 ± 6.8E-4	0.36 ± 1.3E-2	0.014 ± 3.4E-3
LTS-SNN	2	88.6 ± 0.40	0.0180 ± 3.1E-4	0.46 ± 1.2E-2	0.067 ± 5.5E-3
LTS-SNN	3	88.0 ± 0.56	0.0184 ± 7.6E-4	0.44 ± 2.3E-2	0.060 ± 3.0E-3
LTS-SNN	4	88.9 ± 0.71	0.017 ± 1.1E-3	0.43 ± 2.8E-2	0.058 ± 4.4E-3
LTS-SNN	5	88.4 ± 0.27	0.0181 ± 4.7E-4	0.46 ± 1.6E-2	0.063 ± 3.1E-3
LTS-SNN	7	88.3 ± 1.12	0.018 ± 1.4E-3	0.48 ± 2.6E-2	0.068 ± 6.2E-3
LTS-SNN	8	88.5 ± 0.60	0.0181 ± 8.1E-4	0.47 ± 1.3E-2	0.067 ± 3.4E-3
LTS-SNN	9	88.0 ± 0.52	0.0189 ± 8.2E-4	0.49 ± 2.5E-2	0.069 ± 3.6E-3
LTS-SNN	10	88.0 ± 0.91	0.019 ± 1.5E-3	0.49 ± 4.6E-2	0.069 ± 6.2E-3

compared to LTS-SNNs and achieve comparable accuracy to SNN ensembles while yielding slightly lower results on BS and NLL, only underperforming on ECE. In comparison to the MC-dropout SNNs, AOT-SNNs do deliver superior accuracy and performed almost as well as BS and NLL, with only a slight loss in ECE.

Table 4. Performance comparisons between the AOT-SNN and the corresponding LTS-SNN on the CIFAR-100 dataset.

MODEL	TIME STEPS	ACCURACY (%) ↑	BS ↓	NLL ↓	ECE ↓
AOT-SNN	8	65.15	5.028E-3	1.6749	0.1352
LTS-SNN	8	62.32	5.333E-3	1.7325	0.1665

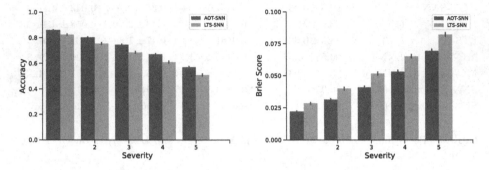

Fig. 2. Comparisons of the AOT-SNN model and its corresponding LTS-SNN on each severity level of CIFAR-10-C.

Table 3 presents the results of AOT-SNNs and LTS-SNNs with time steps smaller or equal to 10. With each model trained five times, the table lists the mean and standard deviation for all the metrics. In this exhaustive comparison, we see that that AOT-SNNs significantly outperform LTS-SNNs, with all models with more than 3 time steps achieving significantly better accuracy and Brier score, with best results for 8 time steps. Moreover, almost all AOT-SNNs achieve better NLL and ECE, except for the model with a single time step (which however has considerably lower accuracy).

CIFAR-100. Comparing the AOT-SNN with time step eight with its corresponding LTS-SNN for CIFAR-100 (Table 4), we similarly find that AOT-SNNs achieve significantly better results than the LTS-SNN, in both accuracy and predictive uncertainty quality.

CIFAR-10-C: Domain-Shifted Test Dataset. As mentioned earlier, the quality of predictive uncertainties needs to be measured on both in-distribution held-out data and domain-shifted data. We evaluated AOT-SNNs on the CIFAR-10-C dataset [11], a domain-shifted test dataset of CIFAR-10. The CIFAR-10-C dataset is designed to evaluate the robustness of image classification models against common corruptions. It contains 19 corruption types that are created by applying a combination of 5 severity levels to the original CIFAR-10 test set. The CIFAR-10-C dataset is commonly used as a benchmark to evaluate the uncertainty estimation in domain-shifted settings [17]. We compared the

Table 5. Performance comparisons between the AOT-SNN with DropConnect and its corresponding LTS-SNN on the CIFAR-10 dataset. The numbers after the model names represent time steps.

MODEL	ACCURACY (%) ↑	BS ↓	NLL ↓	ECE ↓
AOT-SNN (8)	90.8 ± 0.23	0.0144 ± 4.0E-4	0.37 ± 0.022	0.043 ± 4.1E-3
AOT-SNN-DC (8)	90.5 ± 0.37	0.0140 ± 4.1E-4	0.32 ± 0.010	0.026 ± 3.0E-3
LTS-SNN (8)	88.5 ± 0.60	0.0181 ± 8.1E-4	0.47 ± 0.013	0.067 ± 3.4E-3
LTS-SNN-DC (8)	90.2 ± 0.25	0.0161 ± 3.6E-4	0.47 ± 0.035	0.065 ± 4.1E-3

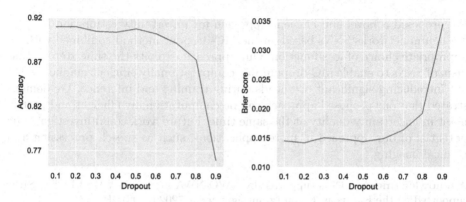

Fig. 3. The impact of dropout rate on performance of AOT-SNNs on the CIFAR-10 dataset. Dropout rates are ranging from 0.1 to 0.9 in increments of 0.1.

performance of the AOT-SNN with eight time steps and its corresponding LTS-SNN on all the severity levels of CIFAR-10-C (Fig. 2). With the AOT-SNN outperforming the LTS-SNN in all severity levels, we conclude that AOT-SNNs also improve uncertainty estimation over LTS-SNNs in domain-shifted settings.

Ablation Study. We further considered the impact of dropout rates and dropout types on the quality of uncertainty estimates of AOT-SNNs.

Dropout Type. We replaced the dropout in the LTS-SNN and our best-performing model, both of which have eight time steps, with DropConnect [23]. Instead of dropping the spikes like the regular dropout, DropConnect randomly drops the weights in each layer before the PLIF neuron layer. As shown in Table 5, despite the slightly better performance of the LTS-SNN-DC compared to the corresponding dropout-based models (LTS-SNN), the AOT-SNN-DC outperform LTS-SNN-DC in terms of both accuracy and uncertainty quality (both models in the table have a dropout rate of 0.5). The observation suggests that DropConnect may fulfill the same function as regular dropout in AOT-SNNs, and in some cases even could be preferable.

Dropout Rate. To investigate the impact of dropout rate on performance, we tested AOT-SNNs with dropout rates ranging from 0.1 to 0.9 in increments of 0.1. These experiments were based on our best-performing model of eight time steps and trained on the CIFAR-10 dataset separately for each amount of dropout. The accuracy and Brier score were plotted in Fig. 3. The trends in accuracy, Brier score are consistent, with models having dropout rates lower than 0.5 producing flat results, followed by a decline in performance.

5   Conclusion

We proposed a novel and efficient approach for uncertainty estimation in spiking neural networks SNNs based on the MC-dropout method combined with an appropriate choice of loss-function. Our approach exploits the time-step mechanism of SNNs to enable MC-dropout in a computationally efficient manner, without introducing significant overheads during training and inference. We demonstrated that our proposed approach can be computationally efficient and performant in uncertainty quality at the same time. Future work could investigate the potential of our approach in more applications, such as speech processing and medical imaging.

Acknowledgments. TS is supported by NWO-NWA grant NWA.1292.19.298. SB is supported by the European Union (grant agreement 7202070 "HBP").

Appendix

Proper Scoring Rules. A *scoring rule* $S(\mathbf{p}, y)$ assigns a value for a predictive distribution $\mathbf{p}$ and one of the labels y. A *scoring function* $s(\mathbf{p}, \mathbf{q})$ is defined as the expected score of $S(\mathbf{p}, y)$ under the distribution $\mathbf{q}$

$$s(\mathbf{p}, \mathbf{q}) = \sum_{y=1}^{K} q_y S(\mathbf{p}, y). \tag{8}$$

If a scoring rule satisfies $s(\mathbf{p}, \mathbf{q}) <= s(\mathbf{q}, \mathbf{q})$, it is called a *proper scoring rule*. If $s(\mathbf{p}, \mathbf{q}) = s(\mathbf{q}, \mathbf{q})$ implies $\mathbf{q} = \mathbf{p}$, this scoring rule is a *strictly proper scoring rule*. When evaluating quality of probabilities, an optimal score output by a proper scoring rule indicates a perfect prediction [17]. In contrast, trivial solutions could generate optimal values for an improper scoring rule [8,17].

The two most commonly used proper scoring rules are Brier score [1] and NLL. Brier score is the squared L_2 norm of the difference between $\mathbf{p}$ and one-hot encoding of the true label y. NLL is defined as $S(\mathbf{p}, y) = -\log p(y|\mathbf{x})$ with y being the true label of the sample $\mathbf{x}$. Among these two rules, the Brier score is more recommendable because NLL can unacceptably over-emphasize small differences between small probabilities [17]. Note that proper scoring rules are often used as loss functions to train neural networks. [8,13].

ECE. The ECE is a scalar summary statistic of calibration that approximates miscalibration [10,15]. To calculate ECE, the predicted probabilities, $\hat{y}_n = \mathrm{argmax}_y \mathbf{p}(y|\mathbf{x_n})$, of test instances are grouped into M equal-interval bins. The ECE is defined as

$$ECE = \sum_{m=1}^{M} f_m |o_m - e_m|, \tag{9}$$

where o_m is the fraction of corrected classified instances in the mth bin, e_m the average of all the predicted probabilities in the mth bin, and f_m the fraction of all the test instances falling into the mth bin. The ECE is not a proper scoring rule and thus optimum ECEs could come from trivial solutions.

References

1. Brier, G.W., et al.: Verification of forecasts expressed in terms of probability. Mon. Weather Rev. **78**(1), 1–3 (1950)
2. Damianou, A., Lawrence, N.D.: Deep gaussian processes. In: Artificial Intelligence and Statistics, pp. 207–215. PMLR (2013)
3. Fang, W., Yu, Z., Chen, Y., Masquelier, T., Huang, T., Tian, Y.: Incorporating learnable membrane time constant to enhance learning of spiking neural networks. In: CVPR, pp. 2661–2671 (2021)
4. Gal, Y.: Uncertainty in Deep Learning. Ph.D. thesis, Department of Engineering, University of Cambridge, Cambridge (2016)
5. Gal, Y., Ghahramani, Z.: Dropout as a bayesian approximation: representing model uncertainty in deep learning. In: ICML, pp. 1050–1059. PMLR (2016)
6. Gawlikowski, J., et al.: A survey of uncertainty in deep neural networks. arXiv preprint arXiv:2107.03342 (2021)
7. Gerstner, W., Kistler, W.M.: Spiking Neuron Models: Single Neurons, Populations, Plasticity. Cambridge University Press, Cambridge (2002)
8. Gneiting, T., Raftery, A.E.: Strictly proper scoring rules, prediction, and estimation. J. Am. Stat. Assoc. **102**(477), 359–378 (2007)
9. Graves, A.: Practical variational inference for neural networks. In: NIPS, vol. 24 (2011)
10. Guo, C., Pleiss, G., Sun, Y., Weinberger, K.Q.: On calibration of modern neural networks. In: ICML, pp. 1321–1330. PMLR (2017)
11. Hendrycks, D., Dietterich, T.: Benchmarking neural network robustness to common corruptions and perturbations. In: ICLR (2019). https://openreview.net/forum?id=HJz6tiCqYm
12. Jang, H., Simeone, O.: Multisample online learning for probabilistic spiking neural networks. IEEE Trans. Neural Netw. Learn Syst. **33**(5), 2034–2044 (2022)
13. Lakshminarayanan, B., Pritzel, A., Blundell, C.: Simple and scalable predictive uncertainty estimation using deep ensembles. In: NIPS, vol. 30 (2017)
14. Mackay, D.J.C.: Bayesian methods for adaptive models. Ph.D. thesis, California Institute of Technology (1992)
15. Naeini, M.P., Cooper, G., Hauskrecht, M.: Obtaining well calibrated probabilities using bayesian binning. In: AAAI (2015)

16. Neftci, E.O., Mostafa, H., Zenke, F.: Surrogate gradient learning in spiking neural networks: bringing the power of gradient-based optimization to spiking neural networks. IEEE Sig. Process. Mag. **36**(6), 51–63 (2019)
17. Ovadia, Y., et al.: Can you trust your model's uncertainty? evaluating predictive uncertainty under dataset shift. In: NIPS, vol. 32 (2019)
18. Pouget, A., Beck, J.M., Ma, W.J., Latham, P.E.: Probabilistic brains: knowns and unknowns. Nat. Neurosci. **16**(9), 1170–1178 (2013)
19. Rathi, N., Srinivasan, G., Panda, P., Roy, K.: Enabling deep spiking neural networks with hybrid conversion and spike timing dependent backpropagation. In: ICML (2020). https://openreview.net/forum?id=B1xSperKvH
20. Savin, C., Deneve, S.: Spatio-temporal representations of uncertainty in spiking neural networks. Adv. Neural Inf. Process Syst. (2014)
21. Schuman, C.D., Kulkarni, S.R., Parsa, M., Mitchell, J.P., Date, P., Kay, B.: Opportunities for neuromorphic computing algorithms and applications. Nat. Comput. Sci. **2**(1), 10–19 (2022)
22. Srivastava, N., Hinton, G., Krizhevsky, A., Sutskever, I., Salakhutdinov, R.: Dropout: a simple way to prevent neural networks from overfitting. J. Mach. Learn. Res. **15**(1), 1929–1958 (2014)
23. Wan, L., Zeiler, M., Zhang, S., Le Cun, Y., Fergus, R.: Regularization of neural networks using dropconnect. In: ICML, pp. 1058–1066. PMLR (2013)
24. Wilson, A.G., Izmailov, P.: Bayesian deep learning and a probabilistic perspective of generalization. NIPS **33**, 4697–4708 (2020)
25. Yin, B., Corradi, F., Bohté, S.M.: Accurate and efficient time-domain classification with adaptive spiking recurrent neural networks. Nat. Mach. Intell. **3**(10), 905–913 (2021)
26. Yin, B., Corradi, F., Bohté, S.M.: Accurate online training of dynamical spiking neural networks through forward propagation through time. Nat. Mach. Intell. (2023)
27. Yue, Y., et al.: Hybrid spiking neural network fine-tuning for hippocampus segmentation. arXiv preprint arXiv:2302.07328 (2023)

QMTS: Fixed-point Quantization for Multiple-timescale Spiking Neural Networks

Sherif Eissa$^{(\boxtimes)}$, Federico Corradi, Floran de Putter, Sander Stuijk, and Henk Corporaal

Eindhoven University of Technology, Eindhoven, Netherlands
s.s.b.eissa@tue.nl

Abstract. Spiking Neural Networks (SNNs) represent a promising solution for streaming applications at the edge that have strict performance and energy requirements. However, implementing SNNs efficiently at the edge requires model quantization to reduce memory and compute requirements. In this paper, we provide methods to quantize a prominent neuron model for temporally rich problems, the parameterized Adaptive Leaky-Integrate-and-Fire (p-ALIF). p-ALIF neurons combine the computational simplicity of Integrate-and-Fire neurons, with accurate learning at multiple timescales, activation sparsity, and increased dynamic range, due to adaptation and heterogeneity. p-ALIF neurons have shown state-of-the-art (SoTA) performance on temporal tasks such as speech recognition and health monitoring. Our method, QMTS, separates SNN quantization into two stages, allowing one to explore different quantization levels efficiently. QMTS search heuristics are tailored for leaky heterogeneous neurons. We demonstrate QMTS on several temporal benchmarks, showing up to 40x memory reduction and 4x sparser synaptic operations with little accuracy loss, compared to 32-bit float.

Keywords: quantization · spiking neural networks · neuromorphic computing

1 Introduction

Spiking Neural Networks (SNNs) are neural networks that integrate temporally sparse events, called *spikes*, over time. Their sparse event-based activity makes them suitable for ultra-low-power streaming applications at the edge. They are considered dynamical systems similar to recurrent networks [1].

Spiking neuron models come in different flavors that vary in complexity and biorealism [2]. In this paper, we focus on computationally simple models that can accurately learn temporally rich tasks on multiple timescales.

ALIF networks with parameterized time constants (Heterogeneous neurons) achieve SoTA performance on challenging temporal tasks [3,4] (see Table 1). They combine the simplicity of LIF neurons, with the advantages of Spike Frequency Adaptation (SFA) and heterogeneity of responses. In this paper, we refer

© The Author(s), under exclusive license to Springer Nature Switzerland AG 2023
L. Iliadis et al. (Eds.): ICANN 2023, LNCS 14254, pp. 407–419, 2023.
https://doi.org/10.1007/978-3-031-44207-0_34

to such models as parameterized ALIF (p-ALIF) models. We introduce QMTS[1], a method for quantizing heterogeneous leaky SNNs. Our contributions are:

1. Two-stage quantization method to effectively traverse the search space;
2. Tailored iterative search algorithms for quantizing p-LIF SNNs;
3. Simplification and full quantization of p-ALIF SNN models;
4. Up to 40x size and 4x activity reduction on SOTA temporal SNN tasks.

Sect. 2 introduces background materials. In Sect. 3, we discuss recent approaches in SNN quantization and motivate our choice to use the p-ALIF neuron. Our methodology, including QMTS, is defined in Sect. 4 and our experiments and results are in Sect. 5. We conclude our study in Sect. 6.

2   Background

The ALIF model extends the LIF model with spiking threshold adaptation. This section introduces the ALIF neuron, by first examining LIF as its subset.

Leaky Integrate-and-Fire (LIF) neuron integrates current into its membrane, which leaks over time. When the membrane reaches a certain threshold voltage (v_{thr}), the neuron fires a spike and resets. The following first-order RC circuit differential equation and firing condition describe this model:

$$\tau_m \frac{du(t)}{dt} = -[u(t) - u_{rest}] + RI(t) \tag{1}$$

$$\text{if } (u(t) > v_{thr}) \rightarrow S(t+1) = 1, \ u(t+1) = u_{rest}. \text{ else} \rightarrow S(t+1) = 0 \tag{2}$$

where τ_m is the leakage time constant, $u(t)$ is the membrane potential over time, $I(t)$ is the summed input current due to pre-synaptic spikes, R is a resistance constant, u_{rest} is the rest membrane potential state, S is the output spike, and v_{thr} is the neuron's firing threshold.

Equation 2 describes the firing and reset behavior. In biology, neuron membranes have a limited voltage range; they fire and reset to u_{rest} immediately upon reaching a threshold voltage. In SNNs, however, membrane potentials can have greater variations. Hence, another way to reset the membrane potentials in SNNs, which preserves information [5], is to subtract their firing threshold at spiking time instead of a hard reset, as we do in Sect. 4.1.

Adaptive Leaky-Integrate-and-Fire (ALIF) Neuron is an extension of the LIF neuron. In addition to leaky integration, the ALIF neuron's firing threshold adapts (increases) in response to an output spike. This adaptive behavior is governed by another time constant which is typically an order of magnitude bigger that the membrane potential's leakage time constant. In addition to Eq. 1, the ALIF neuron can be described by the following equations:

$$B(t) = v_{thr} + b(t) \tag{3}$$

---

[1] QMTS framework is open-sourced at https://github.com/TUE-EE-ES/QMTS .

$$\tau_{adp}\frac{db(t)}{dt} = -b(t) + \beta S(t) \tag{4}$$

$$\text{if } (u(t) > B(t)) \rightarrow S(t+1) = 1, u(t+1) = u_{rest}. \text{ else} \rightarrow S(t+1) = 0 \tag{5}$$

where $B(t)$ is the adaptive firing threshold, $b(t)$ is the adaptation variable, which leaks over time according to τ_{adp} and is incremented by an adaptation constant β whenever the neuron spikes.

3 Related Work

3.1 SNN Quantization

The deployment of deep learning models in embedded devices requires quantization and pruning. Recent studies explore weight quantization and pruning for SNNs [6–8]. Although some use techniques orthogonal to SNNs, such as magnitude-based weight pruning [9], and weight quantization [10], others use spike-based techniques, such as pruning neurons with low activity [11].

In [12], pruning and quantization are integrated into an optimizer. Based on Dale's principle, Deep-R [13] uses Bayesian probability to prune excitatory and inhibitory connections. [14] applies the lottery ticket hypothesis to train pruned SNNs while balancing workloads to preserve hardware utilization. These studies focus only on connections and ignore neuron dynamics.

A few recent studies completely quantize SNNs. Q-SpiNN [6] is an SNN Design-Space Exploration (DSE) quantization framework that demonstrated benchmarks that use variants of LIF neurons. It fixes parameter ranges during exploration and combines weight and membrane exploration together. In our work, we separate their exploration into two stages, and explore range clipping.

In [7], the DECOLLE [15] SNN model is fully quantized to integer, including error and gradient signals. While activations' upper bounds were determined analytically, different ranges and scales were explored as well.

In [8], a simplified DECOLLE model is quantized using hessian traces to determine layer-wise noise sensitivity. Less sensitive layers were more aggressively pruned and quantized. Their study show no parameter exploration.

All these studies quantize LIF-based neuron models. This work is the first to explore full quantization of networks of adaptive parameterized neurons. Our methods apply a simple and effective DSE to find efficient quantized SNNs.

3.2 Multiple Timescale Neurons

Neuron models capture a huge variety of features found in biological neurons. They cover a wide spectrum with different degrees of complexity and biological fidelity. This subsection investigates the role of three features on the ability of SNNs to learn patterns at multiple timescales: Spike Frequency Adaptation (SFA), recurrent connections, and heterogeneous time constants.

SFA leads to higher coding efficiency over a larger dynamic range, it increases sparsity in signal representation [16–18], and it increases the learning capacity of

Table 1. SoTA SNNs on temporal benchmarks.s.

Benchmark	Ref	Model	Architecture	Params (k)	Accuracy	Size.Loss (k)
SHD	[34]	TA-LIAF[1]	128F-128F	109	91.1%	9.7
	[25]	LIF[2]	128F-128F	109	74.0%	28.3
	[22]	p-LIF[2]	3x128F	126	87.0%	16.4
	[25]	r-LIF[2]	256R	250	82.2%	44.5
	[28]	r-LIF[2]	128R	109	71.7%	30.8
	[28]	pr-LIF[2]	128R	109	82.1%	19.5
	[22]	pr-LIF[2]	3x128R	175	89.8%	17.9
	[22]	p-ALIF[2]	3x128F	126	**93.1%**	8.7
	[22]	p-ALIF[2]	3x128F(sparse)	21	91.6%	**1.8**
	[22]	pr-ALIF[2]	3x128R	175	92.9%	12.4
GSC (35	[25]	r-LIF[2]	256R	85	85.3%	12.5
classes)	[23]	r-ALIF[2]	256R	86	**88.5%**	**9.9**
GSC (12	[3]	r-LIF[2]	2048R	4,303	89.0%	473
classes)	[3]	r-ALIF[2]	2048R	4,307	91.2%	379
	[4]	pr-ALIF[2]	300F-300R	220	**92.1%**	**17.4**
S-MNIST	[3]	r-LIF[2]	220R	36	60.9%	14.0
	[3]	r-ALIF[2]	220R (sparse)	9	92.0%	**0.7**
	[4]	pr-ALIF[2]	64R-256R	89	**98.7%**	1.2

[1]Temporal Attention-Leaky Integrate Analogue Fire neuron.
[2]p: trainable time-constants. r: recurrent network. (A)LIF: neuron model.

a network over long timescales [19]. In addition, SFA also provides a high-pass filtering response to the input stimuli [20]. These adaptation features are also visible in biological neural circuits [21]. Moreover, adaptation also leads to significantly higher accuracy for (recurrent) spiking neurons solving temporally rich tasks, compared to non-adapting (recurrent) spiking neurons, by showing much higher learning capacity and more robust generalization [3,4,22,23]. Recurrent connections can help model a working memory, which is useful for sequential problems requiring to recall input patterns over long timescales [24,25].

On the other hand, a neuron's (frequency) response is affected by its time-constant parameters. Neural heterogeneity through the incorporation of train-able (i.e. parameterized) time constants has shown to improve performance, generalization, and temporally-complex pattern detection [26–30].

Table 1 shows the SoTA SNN models' performance in classifying three temporal datasets; the Spiking Heidelberg Digits (SHD) [31], the Google Speech Commands (GSC) [32], and the Sequential MNIST (S-MNIST) [33] datasets. The table shows a comparison between networks using adaptive versus nonadaptive neurons [3,4,22,34], recurrent connections versus feedforward-only connections [3,22], and heterogeneous versus homogeneous time constants [28]. Reported results show more accurate classification from networks composed of adaptive and parameterized neurons over neuron models with nontrainable time constants. This motivates our choice to use p-ALIF SNNs as quantization targets.

4   Methodology

Quantizing p-ALIF SNNs require a tailored strategy that accounts for their dynamic heterogeneous behavior. This section presents our methods for such task. First, we introduce the neuron model's discrete approximate solution and our simplification for more efficient deployment in Sects. 4.1 and 4.2. Finally, we present QMTS for quantizing leaky heterogeneous SNNs in Sect. 4.3.

4.1   (p-)ALIF Discrete Solution

The (p-)ALIF approximate discrete solution is described by:

$$b[t] = \rho b[t-1] + (1-\rho)S[t] \tag{6}$$

$$B[t] = v_{thr} + \beta b[t] \tag{7}$$

$$U[t] = \alpha U[t-1] + (1-\alpha)I[t] - S[t]B[t] \tag{8}$$

$$\text{if } (u[t] > B[t]) \rightarrow S[t+1] = 1 \tag{9}$$

where α and ρ are the neuron decay parameters derived from τ_m and τ_{adp} respectively. α and ρ are typically defined as hyperparamters. However, for p-ALIF, they are defined per neuron. The other terms were defined already in Sect. 2.

The input current ($I[t]$) is the summed post-synaptic current due to spikes from pre-synaptic neurons. Such synaptic connections can be fully-connected, convolutional, recurrent or others. Batch normalization (BN), and $(1-\alpha)$ from Eq. 8, are fused to the synaptic connections for efficient deployment [35].

4.2   Simplifying P-ALIF

In ALIF SNNs, in addition to ρ, $\gamma = \beta(1-\rho)$ is pre-computed and stored as the adaptation constant (see Eqs. 6, 7), to avoid extra computation. For p-ALIF SNNs, this overhead is per neuron. We reduce this requirement by using an average adaptation constant over a population of neurons $\hat{\gamma} = \beta(1 - \hat{\rho})$. Furthermore, we set v_{thr} to 0. Substituting this into Eqs. 6 and 7 leads to:

$$B[t] = \rho B[t-1] + \hat{\gamma}S[t] \tag{10}$$

where $\hat{\gamma}$ is the average adaptation constant per layer or population of neurons.

4.3 QMTS

We start with a 32-bit float baseline model. After simplifying it, we apply quantization. We define a range and scale per parameter and per layer or channel. As SNNs are typically deployed in event-based systems, where input spikes are sporadic and input scheduling is typically unpredictable, we restrict our parameters to uniform fixed-point representation without zero offset, where scales are strictly powers of 2, as in Fig. 1, to avoid computation overhead [35].

We implement Quantization-Aware Training (QAT) using a straight-through estimator [36] to approximate the gradient through quantizers. We separate our method into two stages. First, we quantize parameters that are unchanged after learning, such as layer parameters (weight, external input), and neuron parameters (decay, bias, neuron constant). Then, we quantize neuron activations, which vary dynamically during inference and reflect the network's temporal memory [3], such as the membrane time constant and the adapting spiking threshold. This separation is effective as the quantization of activations is highly dependent to the quantization of parameters, as activations act as accumulators of these parameters. It also reduces our search space as illustrated in Fig. 2.

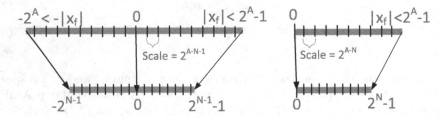

Fig. 1. Uniform Signed (left) and unsigned fixed-point quantization (right) for a maximum range $|x_f|$ and N target bitwidth. Scales are strictly powers of 2.

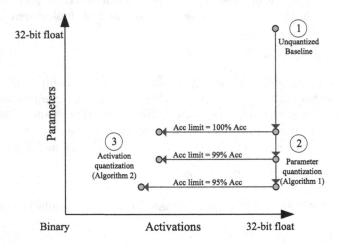

Fig. 2. QMTS efficiently traverses the search space with different accuracy limits.

Weight Quantization (Algorithm 1): For parameter quantization, we apply our tailored search algorithm to p-LIF network weights (see Fig. 3(b)). Heterogeneous leaky neurons can have extremely varying responses. Note in Eq. 8 how LIF time constant ($\alpha = e^{-1/\tau}$) affects memory retention and current response. Relatively smaller time constants create larger current responses that decay quicker and extremely low time constants cause abrupt responses with instant decay. To tackle this issue, QMTS iteratively reduces the fixed-point bitwidth of different weight parameters, while exploring different ranges where such extreme kernel responses of relatively low time constants can be clipped. First, we calculate initial 16-bit quantization parameters that cover the full range of values for each layer/channel (**Pre-process**). Then, we iteratively reduce the number of bits of each layer, by reducing range and/or increasing scale (i.e. removing most and/or least significant bit(s)) according to accuracy (**Range exploration**) until all layers fail successively in reducing their weight bitwidth. The result is used in Algorithm 2 for activations quantization.

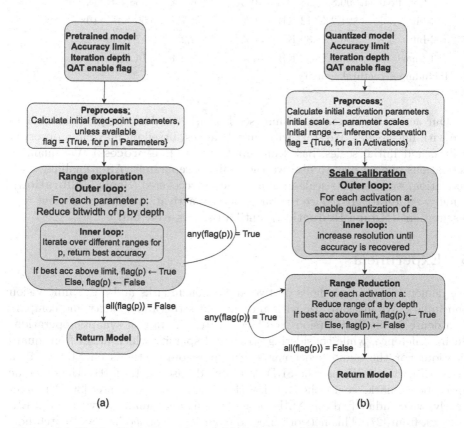

Fig. 3. (a) Weight (Algorithm 1) and (b) Activations (Algorithm 2) quantization.

Activations Quantization (Algorithm 2): Neuron activations in SNNs are comparable to accumulators in Artificial Neural Networks (ANNs). Membrane potentials accumulate weights triggered by spikes, while adaptations accumulate adaptation constants after output spikes. Accumulator bitwidth constraints can be statically analyzed for ANNs [37]. However, neuron activations are non-volatile over time, so we record their ranges during inference.

Like ANN accumulators, an accumulator's scale should not exceed its respective input scale [37]. Hence, a membrane potential scale is tied to its weights (and inputs) scale, while an adaptation variable scale is tied to its adaptation constant ($\hat{\gamma}$) scale. Unlike ANNs, due to decay, having relatively smaller scales might be necessary to model leakage correctly. This is in line with previous research which showed that small leakage (> 0.9) requires more accurate computation [38].

Table 2. SHD model parameters quantization

Model	Acc	Size	W Density	SOP%[1]	Size[1]	Reduction
32-bit float [4]	90.8%	558 KB	100%	6.2%	558 KB	1x
4-bit	91.2%	72 KB	76%	4.7%	56 KB	10x
2-bit	90.6%	39 KB	37%	2.2%	17 KB	32x
Ternary	89.2%	32 KB	37%	2.3%	14 KB	40x

[1]Including structural sparsity.

Our activation search algorithm (see Fig. 3(b)) tackles the problem of leakage with finer scales. We start with initial ranges, based on maximum observed values, and initial scales, based on input scales (**Pre-process**). We quantize activations one by one, to observe their effects separately. After enabling each activation, we reduce its scale until accuracy is recovered (**Scale Calibration**). Finally, we iteratively reduce the range of each activation for more efficient representations (**Range Reduction**), until all successively fail.

5   Experiments

We demonstrate our methods on two audio benchmarks and a dynamic vision benchmark. We measure size with and without structural sparsity and compare to a dense 32-bit float version. SOP% indicates the rate of synaptic operations during inference, while considering structural sparsity which arises from quantization. For the audio benchmarks, we apply our methods on SRNN [4], a pr-ALIF network. We use the SHD and GSC datasets [31,32]. For the dynamic vision benchmark, we use the IBM DVS128 hand gestures dataset [39]. Unfortunately, we couldn't find a p-ALIF model for this benchmark, so we use a p-LIF network from [27]. This network uses convolutional connections and batch normalization (Conv+BN). We use the same training methods as published for each benchmark. We quantize all neuron parameters (α, ρ, and $\hat{\gamma}$) with a scale of 2^{-8}.

5.1   Spiking Heidelberg Digits (SHD) Results

SHD is a spiking audio dataset of spoken words encoded by a cochlea model, consisting of 8156 training and 2264 test samples. Data is pre-processed into spikes with 4 ms timestep window and 250 timesteps. We use SRNN model and framework [4]. The model consists of 2 recurrent layers of 128 pr-ALIF neurons.

Algorithm 1 quantizes the model to 4-bit with no accuracy loss. By lowering accuracy limit, we achieve 2-bit and ternary weights models. Table 3 summarizes weight quantization results. 2-bit quantization results in very high weight sparsity. However, output layer weights are 6-bit wide and are $\approx$ 90% dense. Next, activations are quantized according to Algorithm 2, with scales calibrated to values lower than their respective inputs as shown in Table 3.

Table 3. SHD full quantized model

Model	Acc	S	LS	S^1	LS^1	W_{h1}	U_{h1}	W_{h2}	U_{h2}	$\gamma_{h1,h2}$	$B_{h1,h2}$	W_{out}	U_{out}
4-bit	91.7%	71	6.0	55	4.7	4, −7	10, −7	4, −6	10, −7	3, -8	10, −10	6, −8	10, −8
2-bit	91.3%	37	3.4	15	1.4	2, −5	10, −6	2, −5	10, −6	3, −8	10, −10	6, −8	11, −8
Ternary	89.7%	30	3.2	12	1.3	−4	10, −6	−4	10, −6	−3, −8	10, −10	6, −8	11, −8

x, y: (un)signed fixed point with x bitwidth, 2^y scale. x : $\pm 2^x$ Ternary.
Subscripts: layer id. S: Size, LS: Loss x Size (KB). [1]Including weight sparsity.
W: weights. U: membrane potentials. γ: adaptation constant. B: adaptive threshold.

Table 4. GSC model parameters quantization

Model	Acc	Size(KB)	I rate	W Density	SOP% [1]	Size [1](KB)	Reduct.
32-bit float [4]	92.1%	865	99%	100%	–	865	1x
32-bit float	91.0%	865	99%	100%	23.0%	865	1x
Ternary	91.5%	51	36%	42%	5.1%	23	38x

[1] Including structural sparsity.

5.2   Google Speech Commands Results

GSC consists of 35 spoken words/classes. Raw input is pre-processed as in typical audio applications [4]. We use the SRNN model [4], consisting of 120 inputs, and two layers of 300 p-ALIF neurons. Only the second layer is recurrent. We train using a balanced subset of the GSC dataset, comprising roughly 60K audio recordings with 12 class labels, using hyperparameters and training framework from [4]. We split it into 90% train, 5% test, and 5% validation sets. We use the same test set as in literature to report accuracy [4].

We quantize the external input and hidden layer weights to ternary with no accuracy loss. Table 4 summarizes the results of parameters quantization. Similar to SHD, hidden layer weights are heavily quantized and sparsified, while the output layer weights more resolution and have roughly 90% density. Next, activations are quantized according to Algorithm 2, with scales calibrated to values lower than their respective inputs as shown in Table 5.

5.3   IBM's DVS128 Gesture Dataset

DVS 128 Gesture Dataset [39] consists of 1,500 human gestures recordings with a dynamic vision camera. It comprises 11 classes, 29 subjects, and 3 illumination conditions. The subjects are split into 75% train and 25% test sets. We use the architecture from [27] consisting of 5 Conv+BN layers with 128 filters each and two hidden layers. Each layer is connected to a p-LIF layer with *only one* learned time constant per layer, followed by max pooling for Conv layers. Conv kernels are fused with BN and $(1 - \alpha)$, where BN introduces a bias term to the kernel. Events are pre-processed as in [27], using SpikingJelly [40] to split frames by event count. The 128×128 input frame has two channels, each holding sum of positive and negative events respectively. Hence, inputs are whole numbers. This network consists of about 1.7 M weight parameters and 2.8M neurons in total.

Table 5. GSC full quantized model

Model	Acc	S	LS	S^1	LS^1	Input	W_{h1}	U_{h1}	W_{h2}	U_{h2}	$\gamma_{h1,h2}$	$B_{h1,h2}$	W_o	U_o
Ternary	91.5%	47	4.0	20	1.7	−3	−2	8, −5	−3	8, −3	3, −8	6, −8	5, −1	8, −1

x, y : (un)signed fixed point with x bitwidth, 2^y scale. x: $\pm 2^x$ Ternary.
Subscripts: layer id. S: Size, LS: Loss x Size (KB). ^{1}Including weight sparsity.
W: weights. U: membrane potentials. γ: adaptation constant. B: adaptive threshold.

Table 6. IBM DVS128 model parameters quantization

Model	Acc	Size	W Density	SOP%[1]	Size[1]
32-bit float [27]	97.6%	17 MB	100%	—	17 MB
32-bit float	96.9%	17 MB	100%	7.1%	17 MB
Ternary	96.9%	11 MB	68%	5.2%	11 MB

[1] Including structural sparsity.

Table 7. IBM full quantized model

Model	Acc	S	LS	S^1	LS^1	Input	U_{c1}	U_{c2}	U_{c3}	U_{c4}	U_{c5}	U_{h1}	U_{h2}	Reduction
Ternary	96.9%	3.0	96	2.9	93	uint3	8, 2	8, 2	8, 1	8, 2	7, 1	9, 1	8, 1	6x

x, y: x bitwidth, 2^{-y} membrane scale to weight scale ratio.^{1}Including weight sparsity.
S: Size, LS: Loss x Size (KB). U: membrane potentials. Subscripts: layer id.

For Conv weights, we apply per-channel quantization, where each output channel range and scale are based on their respective maximum absolute values. However, fine-grained search of reduced ranges can be unfeasible, as we have many filter channels (5 layers x 128 channels). Instead, we apply a coarse search per layer. However, unlike others, Algorithm 1 range search did not provide any gain here, as each layer has only one time constant (homogenous). We directly quantize weights and biases to ternary, and inputs to 3-bit unsigned int. Although all weights are ternary, hidden layer weights are significantly denser ($\approx 90\%$) than Conv weights ($\approx 25\%$). Table 6 summarizes our results.

For activations quantization, we follow Algorithm 2 to find proper neuron membrane scales. However, we apply a coarse-grained algorithmic search, per layer instead of per output channel. A layer's quantization is defined by two parameters; its number of bits, and the number of bit shifts between each channel's membrane potential scale and weight scale. Fine-grained algorithmic search may yield more efficient results, but requires more search iterations. Table 7 summarizes our results, showing how scale calibration is useful for leaky neurons.

6 Conclusion and Discussion

In this paper, we present QMTS, a two-step approach and search heuristics to efficiently deploy (adaptive) leaky heterogeneous SNNs. We demonstrated our approach on SoTA temporal benchmarks for spiking neurons, showing a significant reduction in size up to 40x, compared to dense 32-bit float baseline models, with little to no accuracy loss. Although quantization generally increases neuron activity rate [7], the overall rate of synaptic activity was reduced by up to 4x due to structural sparsity in highly quantized connections. While QMTS's two-step iterative approach is applicable to any neural network, the search algorithms are tailored to improve the performance of leaky heterogeneous neurons.

Constrained accumulators trained with QAT may perform as good as unconstrained accumulators. However, restricting accumulators beyond a certain limit leads to accuracy loss. This is in line with ANN quantization, where wide accumulators are necessary to store feature maps prior to applying their nonlinear activation function [37]. Additionally, leakage may require finer scales, and weight clipping can improve quantization for layers of heterogeneous neurons.

Acknowledgement. This work has been funded by the Dutch Organization for Scientific Research (NWO) as part of P16-25 eDL project 7.

References

1. Neftci, E., et al.: Surrogate gradient learning spiking neural networks. CoRR (2019)
2. Gerstner, W., et al.: Neuronal Dynamics: From Single Neurons to Networks and Models of Cognition. Cambridge University Press, Cambridge (2014)
3. Bellec, G., et al.: Long short-term memory and learning-to-learn in networks of spiking neurons. In: Advances in Neural Information Processing Systems (2018)
4. Yin, B., et al.: Accurate and efficient time-domain classification with adaptive spiking recurrent neural networks. Nat. Mach. Intell. **3**(10), 905–913 (2021)
5. Rueckauer, B., et al.: Conversion of continuous-valued deep networks to efficient event-driven networks for image classification. Front. Neurosci. **11** (2017)
6. Putra, R., et al.: Q-SpiNN: a framework for quantizing spiking neural networks. In: 2021 International Joint Conference on Neural Networks (IJCNN), pp. 1–8 (2021)

7. Schaefer, C.J., et al.: Quantizing spiking neural networks with integers. In: International Conference on Neuromorphic Systems. In: ICONS (2020)
8. Lui, H.W., Neftci, E.: Hessian aware quantization of spiking neural networks. In: International Conference on Neuromorphic Systems 2021, pp. 1–5 (2021)
9. Rathi, N., et al.: STDP-based pruning of connections and weight quantization in spiking neural networks for energy-efficient recognition. IEEE Trans. Comput.-Aided Des. Integr. Circ. Syst. **38**(4), 668–677 (2019)
10. Schaefer, C.J., et al.: The hardware impact of quantization and pruning for weights in spiking neural networks. arXiv preprint arXiv:2302.04174 (2023)
11. Yan, Y., et al.: Backpropagation with sparsity regularization for spiking neural network learning. Frontiers Neurosci. **16**, 760298 (2022)
12. Deng, L., et al.: Comprehensive SNN compression using ADMM optimization and activity regularization. IEEE Trans. Neural Netw. Learn. Syst. 1–15 (2021)
13. Bellec, G., et al.: Deep rewiring: training very sparse deep networks. In: International Conference on Learning Representations (2018)
14. Yin, R., et al.: Workload-balanced pruning for sparse spiking neural networks. arXiv preprint arXiv:2302.06746 (2023)
15. Kaiser, J., et al.: Synaptic plasticity dynamics for deep continuous local learning (DECOLLE). Frontiers Neurosci. **14** (2020)
16. Bohte, S.: Efficient spike-coding with multiplicative adaptation in a spike response model. In: Advances in Neural Information Processing Systems, vol. 25 (2012)
17. Huang, C., et al.: Adaptive spike threshold enables robust and temporally precise neuronal encoding. PLOS Comput. Biol. **12**(6), 1–25 (2016)
18. Zambrano, D., et al.: Sparse computation in adaptive spiking neural networks. Frontiers Neurosci. **12** (2019)
19. Kiselev, M., et al.: Comparison of memory mechanisms based on adaptive threshold potential and short-term synaptic plasticity. In: Advances in Neural Computation, Machine Learning, and Cognitive Research V (2022)
20. Brenda, J.: Neural adaptation. Curr. Biol. (2021)
21. Betkiewicz, R., et al.: Circuit and cellular mechanisms facilitate the transformation from dense to sparse coding in the insect olfactory system. eNeuro **7**(2) (2020)
22. Bittar, A., Garner, P.N.: A surrogate gradient spiking baseline for speech command recognition. Front. Neurosci. **16** (2022)
23. Salaj, D., et al.: Spike frequency adaptation supports network computations on temporally dispersed information. eLife **10**, e65459 (2021)
24. Bellec, G., et al.: A solution to the learning dilemma for recurrent networks of spiking neurons. Nat. Commun. (2020)
25. Zenke, F., Vogels, T.P.: The remarkable robustness of surrogate gradient learning for instilling complex function in spiking neural networks. Neural Comput. **33**(4), 899–925 (2021)
26. Chakraborty, B., Mukhopadhyay, S.: Heterogeneous recurrent spiking neural network for spatio-temporal classification. Frontiers Neurosci. **17** (2023)
27. Fang, W., et al.: Incorporating learnable membrane time constant to enhance learning of spiking neural networks. In: Proceedings of ICCV (2021)
28. Perez-Nieves, N., et al.: Neural heterogeneity promotes robust learning. Nat. Commun. (2021)
29. Quax, C., et al.: Adaptive time scales in recurrent neural networks. Sci. Rep. **10**(1), 11360 (2020)
30. Zeldenrust, F., et al.: Efficient and robust coding in heterogeneous recurrent networks. PLOS Comput. Biol. **17**(4), 1–27 (2021)

31. Cramer, B., et al.: The heidelberg spiking data sets for the systematic evaluation of spiking neural networks. IEEE Trans. Neural Netw. Learn. Syst. **33**(7), 2744–2757 (2022)
32. Warden, P.: Speech commands: a dataset for limited-vocabulary speech recognition (2018)
33. Lecun, Y., et al.: Gradient-based learning applied to document recognition. Proc. IEEE **86**(11), 2278–2324 (1998)
34. Yao, M., et al.: Temporal-wise attention spiking neural networks for event streams classification. In: Proceedings of IEEE Conference on Computer Vision (2021)
35. Jacob, B., et al.: Quantization and training of neural networks for efficient integer-arithmetic-only inference (2017)
36. Bengio, Y., et al.: Estimating or propagating gradients through stochastic neurons for conditional computation. CoRR abs/1308.3432 (2013)
37. de Bruin, B., et al.: Quantization of deep neural networks for accumulator-constrained processors. Microprocess. Microsyst. **72**, 102872 (2020)
38. Eissa, S., et al.: Hardware approximation of exponential decay for spiking neural networks. In: IEEE International Conference on AI Circuits and Systems (2021)
39. Amir, A., et al.: A low power, fully event-based gesture recognition system. In: IEEE Conference on Computer Vision and Pattern Recognition (CVPR) (2017)
40. Fang, W., et al.: Spikingjelly.github.com/fangwei123456 (2020)

Self-Organizing Temporally Coded Representation Learning

Adrien Fois[1,2] and Bernard Girau[1,2(✉)]

[1] Université de Lorraine, LORIA, UMR 7503, Vandoeuvre-lès-Nancy 54506, France
{adrien.fois,bernard.girau}@loria.fr
[2] CNRS, LORIA, UMR 7503, Vandoeuvre-lès-Nancy 54506, France

Abstract. The self-organizing map (SOM) is an unsupervised learning algorithm that extracts representations from an input dataset and organizes them in a topographic manner. Nevertheless, the SOM is unable to handle event-based and asynchronous data such as spikes. This work introduces a spiking SOM that consists of a network of leaky integrate and fire neurons. Our spiking model differs from previous ones by demonstrating not only the ability to generate topographically ordered maps, but also the additional capability of vector quantization (VQ). Thus our model replicates for the first time the two key functions of SOM. To do so, we extend the VQ capabilities of a previous model by incorporating a novel neuromodulator, which enables the generation of ordered maps. We demontrate good performances on synthetic and real datasets.

Keywords: Spiking neural networks · self-organizing feature maps · temporal code · representation learning

1 Introduction

Topographically ordered maps are ubiquitous in the sensory cortex [8,9] and are considered to be a fundamental organizational and computational principle. They are characterized by spatially close neurons sharing similar input representations, and they are created by projecting high-dimensional input data onto a low-dimensional surface (the cortex), minimizing the synaptic connections between neurons and enabling local calculations to be performed on nearby data points within the cortex [2]. This principle of local computation between neurons sharing similar representations can potentially be exploited by neuromorphic processors to increase their efficiency. These processors mimic the organization of the cortex by implementing hundreds of neurosynaptic cores, where memory (synapse) and computation (neurons) are co-localized [3]. By exploiting locality, the need for costly long-distance communications between cores can be reduced.

The canonical bio-inspired model for generating a topographically ordered map is Kohonen's SOM [6]. It consists of a vector quantization (VQ) module, which employs competitive learning to represent the current input, and a neighborhood function that enables cooperative learning among the winning neuron and its neighboring neurons. The combination of VQ and topographic self-organization in SOM can have direct applications such as defining neural distances exploited to enable novelty detection by SOM [1].

Hardware implementations of SOM are able to preprocess and categorize the vast amount of digital data collected by embedded systems like IoT and edge computing. Implementing SOM on neuromorphic chips thus sounds promising for several embedded applications. These chips implement 3rd generation neurons [7] that communicate temporally through spikes. However, Kohonen's SOM is not suited for computing and learning with spikes, which are sparse event-based and asynchronous data. As a solution, several spiking models have been developed to replicate the functionalities of SOM [5,11–13]. Although they exhibit some capacity to generate ordered maps, they fail to demonstrate the second crucial function of the SOM: vector quantization aiming for low reconstruction loss. Furthermore, apart from the work of [11], synaptic weights rather than delays are considered as learnable parameters to extract representations from temporal codes. In contrast to synaptic weights, delays intrinsically operate in the temporal domain. Hence, we want to use delays to store representations, as delays appear as a better candidate than weights to process and learn temporal codes.

Our work presents a novel model of spiking SOM, called Self-Organizing Temporally Coded Representation Learning (SO-TCRL). To the best of our knowledge, our model is the first to integrate the two key functionalities of Kohonen's SOM [6], namely, the ability to create topographically ordered maps and the capability of vector quantization (VQ). Our model is based on the VQ capability of [4], extended by our new neuromodulator to produce ordered maps. Neuromodulators in the brain act on sets of synapses to guide learning. Neuromodulators play a crucial role in shaping various essential properties of learning, including but not limited to the learning rate, as well as more intricate properties such as the temporal profile of STDP (Spike-Timing-Dependent Plasticity) [10]. Notably, neuromodulators can be found in neuromorphic processors, often referred to as eligibility traces [3].

Section 2 defines the main components of our model that implements the functionalities of the SOM algorithm in a network of spiking neurons, with a focus on our new neuromodulator. Several components of the model such as the temporal code and the STDP rules are based on the model of [4]. The experimental study is summarized in Sect. 3, using synthetic and natural datasets.

2   Material and Methods

This section depicts the different architectural and algorithmic components that make the neural model designed for learning representations and organizing them topographically. Our model uses a neuromodulator to regulate the learning rate of the STDP rules of [4], and its performance is assessed using both synthetic and real datasets. Emphasis is placed on the differences with the work presented by [4], with a focus on the new neuromodulator. For a more detailed analysis of the common algorithmic components of the two models, see [4].

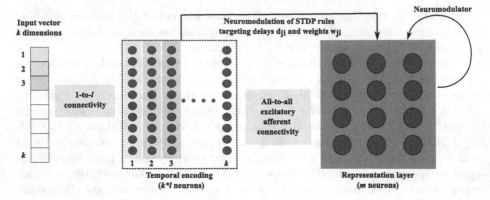

Fig. 1. Block diagram of the SNN architecture. Given a k-dimensional input vector, one dimension of the input vector is encoded by the relative firing latencies of l neurons. The sparse activity of the $k*l$ neurons is transmitted to the representation layer. Delays d_{ji} and synaptic weights w_{ji} (where i represents the index of a presynaptic neuron and j represents the index of a postsynaptic neuron) between these two layers are learned using two distinct STDP rules. Additionally, a novel neuromodulator operates based on the activity of the representation layer and modulates the learning rate of both STDP rules

2.1 Architecture

The spiking neural network consists of two fully connected layers. The first layer encodes the input data into the relative latencies of sets of spiking neurons assigned to each input vector coordinate. The second layer extracts representations from the received spike patterns, while also possessing the ability to generate an ordered map thanks to the introduction of a neuromodulation.

These two layers are fully connected, as illustrated in Fig. 1. Learning occurs between these two layers through the use of two STDP rules. One STDP rule adapts the delays d_{ji} to store representations in the temporal domain, while the other adapts the weights w_{ji} to filter the features based on their temporal variability. The learning rate of these STDP rules are modulated by our new neuromodulator.

2.2 Synapse and Neuron Model

Each synapse has access to one presynaptic trace $x_i(t)$ (with $i = 1, 2, \ldots n$) and a postsynaptic trace $y_j(t)$ (with $j = 1, 2, \ldots m$). The traces are governed by the following equations:

$$x_i(t) \leftarrow 1 \quad \text{if } s_i(t) = 1, \qquad \tau_x \frac{dx_i(t)}{dt} = -x_i(t) \quad \text{otherwise}$$

$$y_j(t) \leftarrow 1 \quad \text{if } s_j(t) = 1, \qquad \tau_y \frac{dy_j(t)}{dt} = -y_j(t) \quad \text{otherwise}$$

where $s(t)$ is an indicator function that returns 1 when a neuron emits a spike at time t, and 0 otherwise.

The neuron model is the Leaky Integrate-and-Fire (LIF). The potential $V_j(t)$ of neuron j is internally governed by a continuous evolution equation (1). Neurons of the encoding layer receive a continuous, time varying input $I_{ext}(t)$ similar to the first retinal coding stage producing analog voltages rather than discrete spikes (see 2.3). Conversely, neurons of the representation layer do not receive analog voltages from the encoding layer, i.e. $I_{ext}(t) = 0$, but are rather subject to instantaneous changes equal to the sum of the received presynaptic activities delayed by transmission delays d_{ji} and weighted by synaptic strengths w_{ji} (2). Firing is triggered when the potential reaches a threshold V_θ (3), and a potential reset is induced during a refractory period T_{refrac}:

$$\tau_m \frac{dV(t)}{dt} \;=\; -V(t) + I_{ext}(t) \tag{1}$$

$$V_j(t) \;\leftarrow\; V_j(t) + \sum_{i=1}^{n} w_{ji} s_i(t - d_{ji}) \tag{2}$$

$$\text{if } V(t) \geq V_\theta, \text{ then } \begin{cases} s(t) = 1 \text{ (else } s(t) = 0) \\ V(u) = 0 \; \forall u \in]t, t + T_{refrac}] \end{cases} \tag{3}$$

2.3   Encoding Input in Spatio-Temporal Spike Patterns

We use the same encoding procedure as presented in [4]. The input is a normalized k-dimensional vector of real numbers, with each dimension distributed across a population of $l = 10$ neurons. Each neuron within the population emits a single spike at a specific time, encoding the input value as a temporal code through a specific spatio-temporal pattern. Each neuron in the population has an associated gaussian receptive field in a circular space in range $[0, 1]$, with a center (or preferential value) μ_i and width σ. The centers are uniformly distributed between 0.05 and 0.95, while the width is constant at $\sigma = 0.6$ so that each gaussian covers the entire input interval. These preferential values used for the encoding process are then used again for decoding as illustrated in Fig. 2.

2.4   From VQ to SOM: Adding a New Spatial Neuromodulator

To address the limitation of [4], which lacks a mechanism for the self-organized generation of topographically ordered maps, we introduce a novel spatial neuromodulator that shapes the learning dynamics in the representation layer.

Each neuron j in the representation layer modulates its own learning rate in an event-driven and local manner based on its activity and the recent activity of the other neurons in the network. When neuron j fires a spike $(s_j(t) = 1)$, it determines the Spiking Best Matching Unit (SBMU) as the index of the first neuron that fired for an input. To identify the SBMU, neuron j uses the postsynaptic traces $y_h(t)$ of all m neurons in the representation layer, where $h = 1, 2, ..., m$. The SBMU is found by identifying the postsynaptic trace with the lowest value

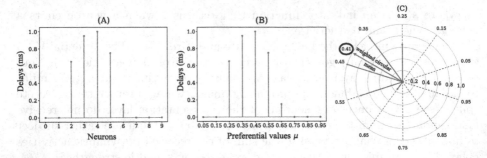

Fig. 2. Decoding process. **(A)** The relative spike timing relationships of the input spike patterns are stored in the delays. **(B)** Each presynaptic neuron has an associated preferential value μ. **(C)** The decoding process involves using a circular mean of the encoding neuron's preferential values, weighted by the delay values, to map the stored temporal representation back to the input space. In this example the value 0.41 was decoded from the delays

within a time window of $3\tau_y$ after a postsynaptic spike, indicated by $y_h(t) > \epsilon$, with a threshold $\epsilon = 0.05 \approx e^{-3\tau_y/\tau_y}$.

$$\text{sbmu} = \underset{h=1,\ldots,m}{\arg\min}\, y_h(t) \quad \text{if } y_h(t) > \epsilon \tag{4}$$

Next, the value of the spatial neuromodulator Θ_j of neuron j is determined by a Gaussian kernel that depends on the normalized Euclidean distance between the SBMU and neuron j in the map. The closer (farther) the neurons are in the map, the higher (lower) the value of the modulation. This allows two spatially close neurons to gradually learn to share similar representations in the input space. The spatial modulation can be interpreted as a static factor imposing a topological constraint on the map.

$$\Theta_j = \exp\left(-\frac{d(j, \text{sbmu})^2}{r^2}\right) \tag{5}$$

where hyperparameter r corresponds to the radius of the neighborhood centered on the position of the SBMU. A large (small) r implies a large (small) neighborhood radius.

2.5 Modulation of Delay Learning

After having introduced our neuromodulator, we now integrate it into the STDP rules of [4], starting with the STDP rule that targets the delays. This rule is based on two modules consisting of a vector quantization module and a regularization module. The vector quantization module is responsible for learning the underlying structure of relative spike timings within the delays, with the goal of minimizing reconstruction loss. The regularization module, on the other hand, aims to promote small delay values in order to prevent the emergence of unnecessary large delays. By integrating the neuromodulator into the STDP rule that adapts the delays, we obtain the following rule with two adaptation cases:

$$\Delta d_{ji} = \begin{cases} \Theta_j \cdot \alpha^+ \left(-\tau_x \ln(x_i(t)) - (d_{ji} + \lambda d_{ji})\right), & \text{if } s_j(t) = 1 \text{ and } x_i(t) > \epsilon \\ -\Theta_j \cdot \alpha^- \left(-\tau_y \ln(y_j(t))\right), & \text{if } s_i(t - d_{ji}) = 1 \text{ and } y_j(t) > \epsilon \end{cases}$$
(6)

As the neuromodulator Θ_j falls in range $]0, 1]$, the learning rates in our STDP rule that adapts delays now vary between $]0, \alpha^+]$ and $[-\alpha^-, 0[$, respectively.

Note that the second adaptation case for a postsynaptic neuron j is triggered if this neuron j has previously emitted a postsynaptic spike in a time window set by $y_j(t) > \epsilon$ relative to the current time t. This implies that the use of the neuromodulator Θ_j is valid because Θ_j has previously been updated in a temporal proximity, at the time of the postsynaptic spike emission by neuron j.

2.6 Modulation of Weights Learning

The other STDP rule assigns relevance weights to the features by estimating the temporal variance of the features. A high (low) temporal variance induces a small (large) relevance weight. We apply the neuromodulator to all adaptative mechanisms in the network. Therefore, by integrating the neuromodulator into the STDP rule adapting the synaptic weights, we obtain the following rule with two adaptation cases:

$$\Delta w_{ji} = \begin{cases} \Theta_j \cdot \beta^+ \left(\exp\left(-\frac{v_{ji}}{\sigma^2}\right) - w_{ji}\right), & \text{if } s_j(t) = 1 \text{ and } x_i(t) > \epsilon \text{ and } e_{ji} \geq 0 \\ -\Theta_j \cdot \beta^- \left(1 - y_j(t)\right), & \text{if } s_i(t - d_{ji}) = 1 \text{ and } y_j(t) > \epsilon \end{cases}$$
(7)

Again, since the neuromodulator Θ_j fall in range $]0, 1]$, the learning rates in our STDP rule that adapts the weights now vary between $]0, \beta^+]$ and $[-\beta^-, 0[$, respectively. The local temporal error $e_{ji} = -\tau_x \ln(x_i(t)) - d_{ji}$ is already calculated and available in Eq. 6.

The use of the neuromodulator in the second adaptation case is valid for the same reasons as in the STDP rule that targets the delays.

When the constraints of the first adaptation case are satisfied, not only is the first adaptation case triggered, but also the online event-based estimation of the temporal variance v_{ji}. The adaptation rate of the exponentially moving variance thus also depends on the neuromodulator. A low value of Θ_j implies a low update of the variance v_{ji}, allowing for relative stability. For example, a neuron spatially distant from the SBMU receives a low neuromodulation value, so that it remains locked onto the region of the input space that it clusters.

$$v_{ji} = (1 - \Theta_j \cdot \alpha^+ \cdot \gamma) \cdot (v_{ji} + \Theta_j \cdot \alpha^+ \cdot \gamma e_{ji}^2)$$
(8)

3 Experiments and Results

In this section, we carry out a set of experiments to assess the expected features of a comprehensive SOM model, which include the ability to generate ordered maps and to perform vector quantization (VQ). In our experiments, we employed a toric topology for the map to suppress border effects.

Hyperparameters are fixed for all experiments except for the firing threshold V_θ of the neurons in the representation layer. We use a simple and effective method to automatically determine its value, as explained below.

We first evaluate the topographic ordering capability of our model using a synthetic dataset by measuring the preservation of distances between data points as distances between the positions of the neurons representing them. Next, we evaluate the model's ability to perform VQ and to preserve local neighborhood relationships between neurons in their code vectors, which promotes sharing of similar representations among neighboring neurons.

3.1 Parameters of the SNN

We propose a generic parameterization of the SO-TCRL model that can be applied to any input vector dimension k. The only dimension-dependent parameter is the neuron spiking threshold V_θ in the representation layer. Since each input dimension is encoded by a population of $l = 10$ neurons, the total number of emitted spikes is $k*l$. To ensure that a neuron fires in the representation layer, its spiking threshold V_θ must be set to $c*k*l$, where $c \in [0,1]$ is a coefficient to be determined. We assume for convenience a linear relationship between $k*l$ and V_θ. Using an optimization method, we found as optimal value $c = 0.44$.

The parameters we use for the SO-TCRL model are provided in Table 1.

3.2 Metrics

We use three metrics to assess the quality of the generated map.

Root Mean Squared Error. We use the Root Mean Squared (RMS) error to quantify the quality of the learned representations. It quantifies the difference between an input vector $\mathbf{a}_p$ and the associated code vector decoded from the synaptic delays of the SBMU $\hat{\mathbf{a}}_p$:

$$\text{RMS} = \frac{1}{P} \sum_{p=1}^{P} \sqrt{\frac{1}{k} \sum_{i=1}^{k} (a_{i,p} - \hat{a}_{i,p})^2} \tag{9}$$

Here, k is the input dimension and P is the number of input patterns, and $a_{i,p}$ is the ith coordinate of a_p.

Table 1. Parameters of SO-TCRL used in all simulations

Neuronal parameters for ...					
... the encoding layer			... the representation layer		
V_θ	τ_m	T_{refrac}	V_θ	τ_m	T_{refrac}
0.5	10.0 ms	6 ms	0.44 kl	5.3 ms	6ms
Synaptic parameters				Neuromodulator parameter	
τ_x	τ_y	d_{min}	d_{max}	r	
4 ms	3 ms	0 ms	10 ms	0.10	

Parameters of the STDP rules							
λ	α^+	α^-	β^+	β^-	γ	σ	ϵ
0.58	0.07	0.042	0.18	0.036	0.24	10.0 ms	0.05

MDN. Like Kohonen's SOM, the SO-TCRL model aims to maintain local neighborhood relations between neurons in their code vectors, creating a kind of local continuity in the map. We use the Mean Distance to Neurons (MDN) to quantify this property, which aggregates distances between a neuron's code vector and its neighboring neurons' code vectors. In our case each neuron has four neighbors. This measure is intrinsic to the map, meaning that it does not require an external reference. The MDN is formulated as follows:

$$\text{MDN} = \frac{1}{m} \sum_{j=1}^{m} \sum_{k=1}^{m} \begin{cases} ||c_k - c_j||^2, & \text{if dist}(j,k) = 1 \\ 0, & \text{otherwise} \end{cases} \tag{10}$$

This formulation is based on code vectors c_j decoded from each neuron j with a weighted circular mean (see Fig 2).

EMDS. The MDN is a local and intrinsic measure based on the code vectors of neurons, whereas the EMDS (expectation of multi-dimensional scaling measure) is a global and extrinsic measure based on the spatial coordinates of neurons on the map. While the MDN evaluates the preservation of neighborhood relations in the code vectors, the EMDS evaluates the ability to preserve distances between input data points on the map. The EMDS metric is based on a calculation of dissimilarity between the distance in input space for two data points and the spatial distance of the two neurons representing them. A value of 0 indicates perfect topological preservation. Distances in input space and on the map are normalized for comparison. The EMDS metric is given by:

$$\text{EMDS} = \frac{2}{P(P-1)} \sum_{p=1}^{P} \sum_{j<p} \left(F(\mathbf{a}_p, \mathbf{a}_j) - G\big(M(\mathbf{a}_p), M(\mathbf{a}_j)\big) \right)^2 \tag{11}$$

where P is the number of input vectors. F and G are similarity measures in input space and map space, respectively. $F(\mathbf{a}_p, \mathbf{a}_j)$ measures the similarity between a pair of input vectors $\mathbf{a}_p$ and $\mathbf{a}_j$ using a normalized Euclidean distance. These two input vectors $\mathbf{a}_p$ and $\mathbf{a}_j$ are represented by two neurons on the map, whose spatial positions are given by $M(\mathbf{a}_p)$ and $M(\mathbf{a}_j)$. $G\big(M(\mathbf{a}_p), M(\mathbf{a}_j)\big)$ measures the similarity between these two positions $M(\mathbf{a}_p)$ and $M(\mathbf{a}_j)$ using a normalized Euclidean distance.

3.3   Numerical Tests

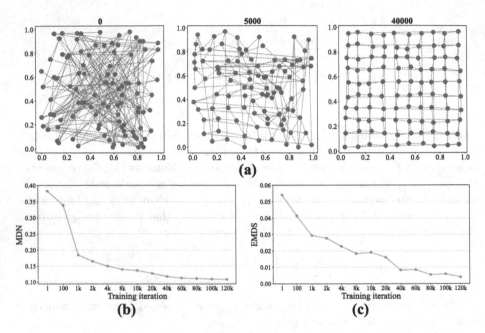

Fig. 3. Results for 2-D input. (a) Generation of an ordered map with a toroidal topology after 0, 5000, 40000 training iterations. The code vectors of the neurons are decoded and projected onto the 2-D input space and displayed as red dots. The connections of the neurons with their four neighboring neurons are depicted using blue dotted lines. (b)-(c) Model performance through training iterations in terms of (b) MDN and (c) EMDS (Color figure online)

2-D Input. First, we evaluate the ability of the model to generate topographically ordered maps using EMDS and MDN metrics. We perform a controlled experiment, based on the one described in [13], which aims to reach a theoretical global minimum of 0 for the EMDS value. We use a 10×10 two-dimensional map with uniformly spaced 10*10 points in the $[0,1]^2$ interval as the dataset. This setup allows us to project any distance between two input points onto the spatial distance between two neurons.

We train the SO-TCRL with 120,000 randomly selected data points. The delays between the encoding layer and the representation layer are randomly initialized within the range of $[0, 0.4]$ ms using a normal distribution centered on 0.2 ms with a standard deviation of 0.1 ms. The synaptic weights are initialized to their maximum values of 1. We evaluate the map quality obtained from 100 independent runs.

The EMDS and MDN measures consistently decrease with the number of training iterations. The EMDS (Fig. 3c) decreases until reaching a plateau after 80,000 iterations around a value of 0.005, indicating that the spatial distance between the two SBMUs selected for two data points converges to the distance between those two points in the input space. This shows that the map learns in a self-organized manner to preserve the distances between data points in the spatial distances of neurons. The mean EMDS after the training phase is 0.00521 ± 0.00663, equivalent to 0.00554 ± 0.00483 as reported by [13] (Table 2).

Table 2. Comparison of mean model performances.

Method	RMS Recon. Error	EMDS
Fois et al. [4]	0.06	–
Rumbell et al. [13]	–	0.00554
SO-TCRL	**0.05**	**0.00521**

At 80,000 iterations, the MDN (Fig. 3b) reaches a plateau at 0.11, revealing that neighboring neurons possess comparable representations. This metric can be related to the global input data distribution, where uniform spacing of 0.10 in each dimension specifies a theoretical ideal MDN value of 0.10 ± 0.00. The achieved MDN value is 0.11 ± 0.01, close to the ideal 0.10 ± 0.00.

Figure 3a shows the successful unfolding of maps during learning iterations. The neurons' code vectors learned not only the uniform data distribution but also shared similar representations when located close to each other in a circular space. The map topology is toric, and encoding neurons have receptive fields located in a circular space, where extremal values are equivalent. The linear representation of Fig. 3a shows that code vectors close to the extremes of one dimension of the input space are also close in a circular space, resulting in connections between opposite sides of the input space.

Natural Image Dataset. We now evaluate the SNN's ability to perform VQ and generate local continuity using non-uniform and higher-dimensional dataset.

For that purpose we use the natural image dataset used in [4]. Input normalization is restricted to $[0.05, 0.95]$ due to the projection of linear input data onto a circular space where extremal values 0 and 1 would become equivalent. Patches of 4×4 pixels extracted from 512×512 natural images are used as input vectors, with 60,000 patches provided during the training phase.

Both the RMS reconstruction error and MDN metric decrease as the SNN learns to compress input data distribution and reduce the distance between code

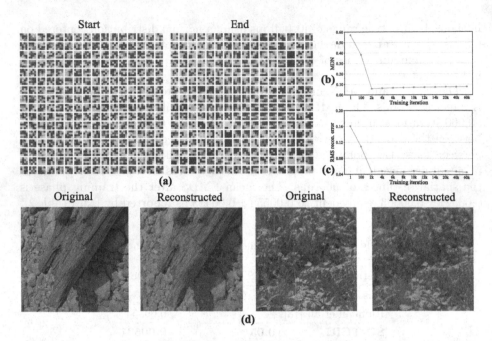

Start   End

(b)

(c)

(a)

Original   Reconstructed   Original   Reconstructed

(d)

Fig. 4. Results for the natural image dataset with $m = 256$ neurons in the representation layer. (a) Code vectors at random initialization and after the training phase. The blue-red gradient represent minimum-maximum values. (b)–(c) Model performance through training iterations in terms of (b) MDN (ideal minimum is 0.10), and (c) RMS reconstruction error. (d) Natural images are presented as input to the network and reconstructed by the decoded code vectors. (Color figure online)

vectors of neighboring neurons. Fig 4c and Fig 4b show the decrease in RMS reconstruction error and MDN respectively.

The code vectors in the representation layer have become selective to various visual orientations, see Fig. 4a. These orientations are arranged in an orderly manner on the map, with spatially close neurons sharing similar orientations.

Finally the reconstruction of natural images from the code vectors of the representation layer produces images of high quality, comparable to the original natural images, as shown in Fig. 4d. Experiments for other databases or network sizes have been carried out and show similar results.

4 Discussion

This paper presents SO-TCRL, a self-organizing model for representation learning based on temporally coded data handled by spiking neurons. To be best of our knowledge, SO-TCRL is the first complete model of spiking self-organizing map able to combine the two key functions of a self-organizing map, vector quantization, and the creation of topographically organized maps on generic datasets.

Furthermore, unlike in [13], our model does not need any manual adjustment of the maximum synaptic weight magnitude based on input data dimension.

Our main contribution is a novel spatial neuromodulator that enhances the VQ capacity of [4] by incorporating the ability to generate ordered maps. Unlike related works that use a lateral excitation-inhibition profile to influence spike timing, our neuromodulator regulates the learning rates of neurons to create orderly maps.

The SO-TCRL model was subjected to an experimental evaluation to test its key functions, and we found that it performed comparably to the state-of-the-art works by [4,13], combining the benefits of both models : a low reconstruction error and a low mapping error. As a future research direction, we now plan to investigate hierarchical architectures based on the SO-TCRL model for clustering hierarchical data.

Acknowledgments. This work has been supported by ANR project SOMA ANR-17-CE24-0036.

References

1. Bernard, Y., Hueber, N., Girau, B.: Novelty detection in images using vector quantization with topological learning. In: IEEE International Conference on Electronics Circuits and Systems (ICECS) (2020)
2. Chklovskii, D.B., Koulakov, A.A.: Maps in the brain: what can we learn from them? Ann. Rev. Neurosci. **27**, 369–392 (2004)
3. Davies, M., Srinivasa, N., Lin, T.H., et al.: Loihi: a neuromorphic manycore processor with on-chip learning. IEEE Micro **38**(1), 82–99 (2018)
4. Fois, A., Rostro-Gonzalez, H., Girau, B.: Unsupervised learning of visual representations using delay-weight spike-timing-dependent plasticity. In: 2022 International Joint Conference on Neural Networks (IJCNN) (2022)
5. Hazan, H., Saunders, D.J., Sanghavi, D.T., Siegelmann, H., Kozma, R.: Lattice map spiking neural networks (LM-SNNs) for clustering and classifying image data. Ann. Math. Artif. Intell. **88**(11), 1237–1260 (2019). https://doi.org/10.1007/s10472-019-09665-3
6. Kohonen, T.: Essentials of the self-organizing map. Neural Netw. **37**, 52–65 (2013)
7. Maass, W.: Networks of spiking neurons: the third generation of neural network models. Neural Netw. **10**(9), 1659–1671 (1997)
8. Moser, E.I., Roudi, Y., Witter, M.P., et al.: Grid cells and cortical representation. Nature Rev. Neurosci. **15**(7), 466–481 (2014)
9. Ohki, K., Chung, S., Kara, P., et al.: Highly ordered arrangement of single neurons in orientation pinwheels. Nature **442**(7105), 925–928 (2006)
10. Pawlak, V., Wickens, J., Kirkwood, A., et al.: Timing is not everything: neuromodulation opens the STDP gate. Front. Synaptic Neurosci. **2**, 146 (2010)
11. Pham, D., Packianather, M., Charles, E.: A self-organising spiking neural network trained using delay adaptation. In: IEEE International Symposium (2007)
12. Ruf, B., Schmitt, M.: Self-organization of spiking neurons using action potential timing. IEEE Trans. Neural Networks **9**(3), 575–578 (1998)
13. Rumbell, T., Denham, S.L., Wennekers, T.: A spiking self-organizing map combining STDP, oscillations, and continuous learning. IEEE Tran. Neural Netw. Learn. Syst. **25**(5), 894–907 (2014)

A System-Level Brain Model for Enactive Haptic Perception in a Humanoid Robot

Kristín Ósk Ingvarsdóttir, Birger Johansson, Trond A. Tjøstheim,
and Christian Balkenius

Lund University Cognitive Science, Lund, Sweden
christian.balkenius@lucs.lu.se

Abstract. Perception is not a passive process but the result of an interaction between an organism and the environment. This is especially clear in haptic perception that depends entirely on tactile exploration of an object. We investigate this idea in a system-level brain model of somatosensory and motor cortex and show how it can use signals from a humanoid robot to categorize different object. The model suggests a number of critical properties that the sensorimotor system must have to support this form of enactive perception. Furthermore, we show that motor feedback during controlled movements is sufficient for haptic object categorization.

Keywords: Enactive perception · Affordances · Haptic perception · Object categorization · Humanoid robot

1 Introduction

Traditional theories of perception emphasize the passive bottom-up reception of sensory information from the environment. According to these theories, perception is a matter of processing sensory inputs and constructing a representation of the world that matches those inputs. In contrast, *enactive* perception is based on the idea that perception arises from the dynamic interaction between the perceiver and their environment. Rather than simply processing sensory inputs, the perceiver actively engages with their environment, exploring and manipulating it in ways that shape their perception. This interaction is characterized by a continuous perception-action loop, in which the perceiver's movements and actions shape and influence their perception, which in turn guides their subsequent actions.

The theory emphasizes the active and embodied nature of perception and how our perception of the shape and texture of an object is influenced by how our body interacts with it during manipulation. We actively explore the surface of an object to learn how rough or smooth it is. Similarly, we weigh the objects with our hand to estimate its weight, and we test how hard an object is by applying force to its surface [3,15,16,22].

Enactive perception is intimately connected to the idea of *affordances*. Gibson [8] described affordances as the link between perception and action. He argued that we as active agents perceive action possibilities (affordances) of objects directly through vision [24]. According to Gibson, the design of a chair affords the action *to sit* and the handle of a coffee cup affords the action *to hold*. Although Gibson's idea of the term affordance usually applies to the geometrical shape of an object, it is reasonable to use the concept also to describe perceived action possibilities based on other object properties than shape. After all, objects do not only come in various geometrical forms, they also come in various types of materials that differ in physical properties. Each of these properties may require a specific type of handling. For instance, a fluffy cube with rounded edges made of synthetic fibres has soft physical properties and would afford the action *to squash*, whereas a similarly shaped wooden cube with hard sharp edges would require a greater force to be deformed. Despite their similarities in geometrical shape, the perceived action possibilities are different due to their different material properties. The shape and material of an object affords different actions, but these different actions also define the physical properties of the object. Softness affords squashing, while the act of squashing is what makes us perceive the object as soft. This has important consequences for models of perceptual processing.

If perception is not separate from action, but a results of the ongoing interaction of objects in the world, it may be necessary to reevaluate many models of information processing and coding in the brain. If perception and action are two sides of the same coin, it does not make sense to look for separate regions for sensation or motor control. Instead, we would expect brain regions involved in tactile manipulation to reflect both sensory and motor aspects of the task.

In the brain, the coding of haptic object properties depends on an interaction between a number of regions (Fig. 1). The main areas are the primary and premotor cortices as well as the primary and secondary somatosensory cortices (S1, S2), together with Brodmann's areas 5 and 7. Although traditionally divided into memory and motor regions, there is now evidence that cortical area S2, as well as area 5 and 7 code for both sensory and motor information.

The primary motor cortex (M1) is located in the frontal lobe. It is responsible for the initiation and control of voluntary movements. Neurons in M1 send signals down the spinal cord to activate the appropriate muscles and produce movements. Different regions of M1 are responsible for controlling different parts of the body, with the motor representation of the body arranged in an ordered topographic manner. Premotor cortex is located anterior to M1 and plays an important role in the control of complex movements such as reaching, grasping, and manipulating objects. While M1 is primarily responsible for generating the basic motor commands that result in muscle contraction, premotor cortex is involved in more complex aspects of motor control, such as sequencing of movements, coordination of multiple muscles, and adaptation of movements to changing conditions. Damage to premotor cortex can result in impairments in motor planning and sequencing.

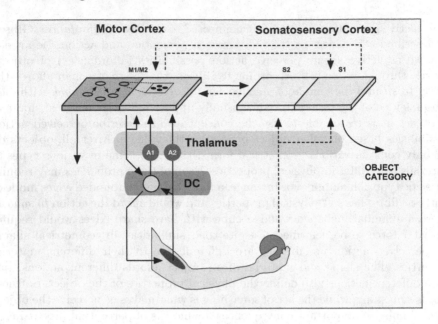

Fig. 1. Regions in the brain involved in haptic perception included in the model. Motor cortex is assumed to contain cells that produce sequences of activations (left) of different motor patterns (right). Secondary somatosensory cortex uses sequences of comparisons between efference copies of motor commands and afferent signals from muscle spindles to recognize objects. A1: alternative model 1. A2: Alternative model 2. See Sect. 2.3. Dotted lines represent connections that are not included in the current simulations.

The primary somatosensory cortex (S1) is located in the parietal lobe and it is responsible for processing sensory information from the body. It receives information about touch, temperature, pressure, and pain sensations. The secondary somatosensory cortex (S2), which is adjacent to the primary somatosensory cortex, is a higher-order processing region that receives and integrates sensory and motor information to create more complex coding of haptic stimuli. Its functions include object recognition by touch, and the processing more complex aspects of somatosensory information, such as the size, shape, texture, and orientation of objects.

Area 5 is also located in the parietal lobe, adjacent to area S2, and together these areas are involved in the processing and integration of somatosensory information from the hand and other body parts. While area S2 is thought to be involved in the perception of the body in space and the recognition of objects based on their physical properties, area 5 is more specifically involved in the planning and execution of fine motor movements, such as grasping and manipulation. This area is also involved in coding the position of the hand. Specifically, area 5 contains neurons that are sensitive to the position and movement of the hand, as well as to the location of tactile stimuli on the hand. These neurons form a body-centered reference frame, which allows for the accurate coding of hand position and movement relative to the body.

Area 7 (which is posterior to area 5 and adjacent to the temporal and occipital lobes is involved in a range of cognitive functions, including sensory integration, attention, and spatial perception. It is divided into two subregions: areas 7a and 7b. Area 7a is primarily involved in the integration of somatosensory and visual information to contribute to spatial perception and movement planning and receives inputs from S1, S2, as well as visual regions of the brain to create a unified perception of the body in space. Area 7b is important for spatial working memory together with Area 7a, and is also associated with attention. It is involved in the selection and manipulation of visual and spatial information, and plays a role in the perception of objects and scenes. Area 7b also integrates visual, and somatosensory information. Lesions in area 7a have been associated with deficits in spatial working memory, while lesions in area 7b have been associated with impairments in visual perception and attention.

The above shows that the brain systems involved in object manipulation are only one step away from systems thought to be involved in higher level cognitive processes. This suggests that to understand how cognition is implemented in the brain, we need to start with the parts that control the physical interaction with the environment.

Already from a young age we learn about the physical properties of the world and incorporate that knowledge into our actions, for example, when picking up a soft toy or a handling hard building block. These motor actions appear effortless, but are nevertheless remarkable, considering the great diversity of physical properties that need to be recognized in order to handle them successfully. Moreover, objects are made from all kinds of materials, all of which have their own specific characteristics. Perceived hardness is based on the compliance of the material from which the object is made, and can be perceived using the ratio of the force applied to the object and its deformation (i.e. indentation depth) [16] [4]. For a study on perceived compliance see e.g. [29]. Hardness and shape differs from visual properties in that they require an active manipulation of the object to be perceivable.

Several studies have investigated how robots can learn affordances by interacting with objects [6,9,20], how a robot could learn about tools use [17] and the dynamic properties of objects [27]. Methododologies includes Bayesian networks [20], convolutional networks [21], and metric learning [10].

Although the shape of an object is usually the primary focus in studies of affordances, a number of techniques have been developed to allow humanoid robots to sense the hardness of manipulated objects. Matsuoka [18] used competitive neural networks to learn the hardness of objects from measurements made using force-sensitive resistors in combination with a potentiometer-based angle sensor in each finger. A similar idea was used to recognize both hardness and texture using self-organizing maps [13,14]. Regoli at al. [23] also used this approach for the iCub that repeatedly squeezed an object to determine its hardness. This can be seen as exploratory movements that serve to obtain information about the object [11]. An alternative method is to use optical techniques to record the deformation of the finger as it touches an object [28]. Common to all these methods is that they look at the sensory signal over time as an object is touched. The change to the sensory signal over time then reflects the hardness of the object. The weight of an object is in principle easier to determine. It can be measured by using piezoelectric sensors directly [5] or by using deflection sensors in the limbs [26].

Below, we present a system-level brain model of haptic perception modelled after the relevant regions of the mammalian brain. System-level models are characterised by a number of interacting components that corresponds to different brain regions. The focus is on the component needed for a particular task and the coding and information processing in each component rather than on the physiological details of the processing in each region. The model was implemented in the Ikaros system [1] and used to categorize objects manipulated by the humanoid robot Epi [12]. The model forms one component of the BAM model that aims at eventually containing integrated models for most parts of the brain.

The central idea that we investigate is that the difference between the motor command and the feedback from the muscle spindles varies over time as a function of the shape of a grasped object. We model this in the robotic set-up in two ways: first using a 'load' signal from the robot servos that corresponds to a rough estimate of the effort exercised by the servo at each time; and second by calculating the difference between the position command sent to the servos and their current position. The first alternative would require that the error signals calculated in the stretch reflex system of the spinal cortex is projected to cortex to be further processed there. The second alternative corresponds to an assumption that the cortex calculates the difference between the efferent motor signals and the signals from the muscle spindles [19,25]. We then test if these signals contain enough information to categorize object using the proposed model.

2   Methods

2.1   The Humanoid Robot Epi

For the experiments, we used the humanoid robot Epi that has been developed at Lund University Cognitive Science [12] (Fig. 2). It has two arms with five degrees of freedom each, three in the shoulder, one in the elbow, and one in the wrist. Each joint is controlled by a Dynamixal MX-106 servo that allows position control and produces a large number of feedback signals that can be read through a serial interface. These include the current position, the current used, temperature etc.

Epi has two hands with a single servo that controls all fingers except for the stationary thumb (Fig. 2 right). Each of the movable digits are controlled by an single tendon. The tendons and joints are made from 3D-printed polyurethane plastic printed as a single component without any seams. The polyurethane design can withstand very strong forces and it is not possible to manually break

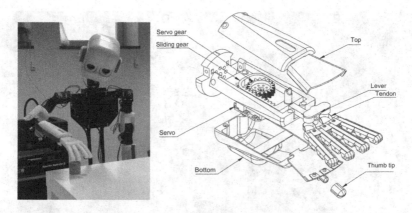

Fig. 2. Left. The robot Epi picking up an object. **Right.** The design of the robot hand used in the experiments. The four movable fingers are controlled by a single servo through a gear rack that drags rubber tendon using a whippletree mechanism within the palm of the hand to distribute the force from the servo to the different fingers

the tendons by dragging or tearing. The joints continue into the tendon that then seamlessly connect to tendon of the next finger [12]. The outer parts of the digits are made from 3D-printed PLA plastic. The force onto each of the tendons is controlled by a whippletree mechanism [7] within the palm of the hand that distributes the forces between the fingers and makes the fingers automatically grasp around objects.

The fingers have no dedicated touch sensors. Instead, the robot uses feedback from the servo controller to determine if the fingers are touching during a grasp.

2.2   Objects

We used 25 objects to test the ability of the model to learn to recognize objects, based on the sensory information from the robot. The object have different shapes, hardness and textures. Some of the objects are very similar (A and B, G and H) while most other object differ in some dimension. The object were selected to be easy to pick up by the robot's hand and to have different visual appearances (although that aspect is not used in this study) (Fig. 3).

2.3   Model

Figure 1 shows an overview of the model. The main components are the motor cortex, somatosensory cortex and the dorsal column of the spinal cord (DC).

The motor cortex consists of two regions with different properties (or alternatively two types of neurons). The right part of the motor cortex in the figure is responsible for controlling movements by sending motor commands to the muscles to move the arm and hand in a particular way. These codes are assumed to be learned, but in the instantiation of the model used here, a fixed set of motor

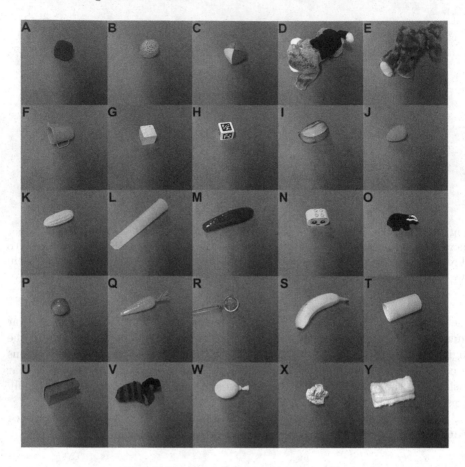

Fig. 3. The 25 objects used in the study

patterns are used. The other part of motor cortex (to the left in the figure) is used to sequence movements by activating different patterns over time. When the robot is about to pick up an object, a sequence is activated that will make the robot hand reach for the object, grasp it, and lift it. Like the motor patterns, we assume that these sequences are learned, but since we are mainly interested in object categorization here, we do not investigate how different motor sequences are learned and selected.

S2 is assumed to receive a time series where each signal corresponds to the difference between the motor command sent by motor cortex and its corresponding proprioceptive input. A central idea of the model is that this feedback will reflect properties of the manipulated object. When no object is present, the feedback will closely follow the movement of the hand, but during haptic exploration, the object will hinder the fingers of the hand which will result in a larger difference between the motor command and the proprioceptive feedback. The profile of this signal over time codes the interaction between the hand and the object in an object-specific way. Our central hypothesis is that this time series will code the identity of the object in a way that could be categorized by S2. To this end, we model S2 as a self-organizing map that learns the different patterns obtained from motor cortex. A 100×100 grid of nodes was used for the map.

If O_i is an output from motor cortex and P is the corresponding input from the muscle spindles,

$$\Delta_i(t) = O_i - P_i. \tag{1}$$

The input to S2 is given by the time series,

$$I_i^{S2}(t) = \langle \Delta_i(t), \Delta_i(t-1), ..., \Delta_i(t-n) \rangle. \tag{2}$$

For the simulations, n=425 and each time step is 40 ms.

To train the self-organizing map that corresponds to S2 to associate each haptic pattern with a specific category, we extended the input vector with a one-hot representation of each object category. This extra input has negligible impact on learning, but allows the category of the best matching unit to be read out during object recognition. The maximum element of this part of the weight vector for the best matching using was considered the detected category. Note that the one-hot category input was not used during testing of the model. While testing, each node of the map is only activated by the other 425 inputs. However, since the category input was present during training, the weight of the winning node will reflect the detected category in this part of its weight vector.

We implemented two versions of the model. In alternative 1, we used the error signals from the servos directly as input to the model of S2. This signal corresponds to error signals from the reflex loops within the dorsal column of the spinal cord. This mechanism is unlikely to be used for object categorization in the real brain, but we tested it as it could be a useful possibility for a robot.

The second alternative was to assume that the difference was instead calculated in cortex between an efference copy of the motor command and the input from the muscle spindles. This is a much more biologically likely mechanism.

3 Results

3.1 Signal Analysis

We analyzed the contents of the signals according to Eqs. 2 for our two alternative hypotheses using principal component analysis on the time series. Figure 4 (top left) shows the explained variance for each of the principal components for alternative 1. Figure 4 (top right) shows the location of the measured objects in the space spanned by the first two principal component of the time series recorded during the squeezing operation (Eq. 2). The first principal component roughly corresponds to the hardness of the objects but the second principal component also appears to differ for the different objects. Subsequent measurement of the same objects are nicely clustered together indicating both that the robot hand shows good repeatability and that different objects can be distinguished based on the load feedback.

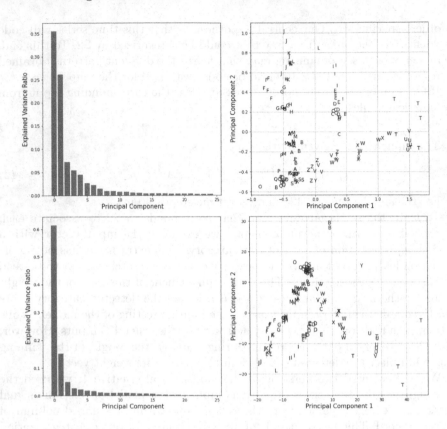

Fig. 4. The variance ratio for the first 25 principal components of the times series during the squeeze operation. See text for explanation

Figure 4 (bottom) shows the same data for the cortical alternative 2. The plots show that both are viable alternatives for haptic object recognition but alternative 1 appears to contain more information than alternative 2, in that the variance is explained by a larger number of principal components. The objects also appear to be more spread out for alternative 1. The separation of the objects is not perfect in either case, but that would not be expected given that some of the objects are rather similar. For example, the two cubes differ only in visual appearance and not in weight, shape or hardness.

3.2   Categorization Performance

The performance of the model was validated using leave-one-out cross-validation of the two alternative models. The cross-validation measured the categorization accuracy for alternative 1 and 2. For the first alternative, the categorization accuracy was 88% while for the second method, the accuracy was 81%. This is consistent with the signal analysis that shows a better spread of the objects for alternative 1.

4 Discussion

We have presented a system-level model of haptic perception in the brain and tested it with a humanoid robot grasping different objects. Using the model, we have shown that both shape and weight can be estimated without any specific sensors by using feedback from the robot servos involved in the manipulation of an object. This is similar to how proprioceptive information could be used in a biological organism. We put forward two hypotheses about where in the brain the necessary discrepancy between motor command and muscle spindle feedback could be calculated, and showed that in principle both could be true. In our experiments, assuming a cortical mechanism gave slightly worse performance compared to using brain stem feedback. We do not claim that this simulation has any bearing on deciding what is actually going on in the brain, but it does show how two mechanisms that are present in the brain could be used to categorize object based on touch.

There do not appear to be any evidence that the alpha motor neurons project back to cortex, which would be needed for our first mechanism. However, it is still a valid method to use in the robot if biological realism is not a factor. On the other hand, it is well known that the muscle spindles project to the motor cortex where the signals could be compared to an efference copy of the motor command [25]. This is likely to be done in motor cortex before the result is sent to somatosensory cortex and integrated with different forms of sensory information.

It is interesting to note that the robot does not directly measure the shape of the different objects; instead it categorises the temporal feedback from the servos as it grasps and lifts each object. The coding of each object depends on the interaction between the body of the robot and the physical properties of the object, including its shape and hardness. Even though we only measure feedback from a single servo in this experiment, the time series of the signal contains information about both shape and hardness. As the robot hand closes around an object, the fingers engage with different parts of the object at different times depending on its shape. The variations in the feedback signal over time is thus an indication of the shape of the object.

In the future we want to further explore the two different alternatives proposed here to investigate if the cortical alternative can be enhanced for better performance, since this is the most likely mechanism in the real brain. We also want to include other haptic modalities in addition to proprioception. In the next iteration, we will include motor exploration and learning in the part of the model corresponding to the motor cortex. Another development will be to include visual categorization of the objects, and investigate how the robot can associate between the visual and haptic modality to select the appropriate motor sequence for the visually localized object. Another goal is to develop models of the somatosensory regions responsible for working memory, and spatial attention and to include the components presented here in our BAM-model to study the interplay between spatial attention, working memory and decision making [2].

In summary, we have shown how an enactive approach to perception fits well with the way the brain interprets signals from the hand during the haptic exploration of an object. We believe that to model cognitive processing in the brain, it is important to start with an accurate view of how sensory information is processed: namely as a result of the interaction between the organism and object in the environment. Our results show that this view is viable both for models of the brain, and for the design of robots.

Acknowledgments. This work was partially supported by the Wallenberg AI, Autonomous Systems and Software Program - Humanities and Society (WASP-HS) funded by the Marianne and Marcus Wallenberg Foundation and the Marcus and Amalia Wallenberg Foundation.

References

1. Balkenius, C., Johansson, B., Tjøstheim, T.A.: Ikaros: A framework for controlling robots with system-level brain models. Int. J. Adv. Robot. Syst. **17**, 1729881420925002 (2020)
2. Balkenius, C., Tjøstheim, T.A., Johansson, B., Wallin, A., Gärdenfors, P.: The missing link between memory and reinforcement learning. Frontiers Psychol. **11**, 560080 (2020)
3. Bergmann Tiest, W.M.: Tactual perception of material properties. Vis. Res. **50**(24), 2775–2782 (2010)
4. Bergmann Tiest, W.M., Kappers, A.: Cues for haptic perception of compliance, pp. 189–199. IEEE Trans Haptics (2009)
5. Choi, B., Lee, S., Choi, H.R., Kang, S.: Development of anthropomorphic robot hand with tactile sensor: Skku hand ii. In: 2006 IEEE/RSJ International Conference on Intelligent Robots and Systems, pp. 3779–3784. IEEE (2006)
6. Fitzpatrick, P., Metta, G., Natale, L., Rao, S., Sandini, G.: Learning about objects through action-initial steps towards artificial cognition. In: 2003 IEEE International Conference on Robotics and Automation (Cat. No. 03CH37422), vol. 3, pp. 3140–3145. IEEE (2003)
7. Fukaya, N., Toyama, S., Asfour, T., Dillmann, R.: Design of the TUAT/Karlsruhe humanoid hand. In: Proceedings. 2000 IEEE/RSJ International Conference on Intelligent Robots and Systems (IROS 2000) (Cat. No. 00CH37113), vol. 3, pp. 1754–1759. IEEE (2000)
8. Gibson, J.J.: The Senses Considered as Perceptual Systems. Allen and Unwin, Crows Nest (1966)
9. Gonçalves, A., Saponaro, G., Jamone, L., Bernardino, A.: Learning visual affordances of objects and tools through autonomous robot exploration. In: 2014 IEEE International Conference on Autonomous Robot Systems and Competitions (ICARSC), pp. 128–133. IEEE (2014)
10. Hjelm, M., Ek, C.H., Detry, R., Kragic, D.: Invariant feature mappings for generalizing affordance understanding using regularized metric learning. arXiv preprint arXiv:1901.10673 (2019)
11. Hoelscher, J., Peters, J., Hermans, T.: Evaluation of tactile feature extraction for interactive object recognition. In: 2015 IEEE-RAS 15th International Conference on Humanoid Robots (Humanoids), pp. 310–317. IEEE (2015)
12. Johansson, B., Tjøstheim, T.A., Balkenius, C.: Epi: an open humanoid platform for developmental robotics. Int. J. Adv. Robot. Syst. **17**(2), 1729881420911498 (2020)

13. Johnsson, M., Balkenius, C.: Experiments with self-organizing systems for texture and hardness perception. Robot. Autonom. Syst. **4**, 53–62 (2009)
14. Johnsson, M., Balkenius, C.: Recognizing texture and hardness by touch. IEEE/RSJ International Conference on Intelligent Robots and Systems, 2008. IROS 2008, pp. 482–487. IEEE (2008)
15. Lederman, S.J.: Tactile roughness of grooved surfaces: The touching process and effects of macro- and microsurface structure. Perception & Psychophysics **16**, 385–395 (1974)
16. Lederman, S.J., Klatzky, R.L.: Hand movements: a window into haptic object recognition. Cogn. Psychol. **19**(3), 342–368 (1987)
17. Mar, T., Tikhanoff, V., Metta, G., Natale, L.: Self-supervised learning of grasp dependent tool affordances on the iCub humanoid robot. In: 2015 IEEE International Conference on Robotics and Automation (ICRA), pp. 3200–3206. IEEE (2015)
18. Matsuoka, Y.: Embodiment and manipulation learning process for a humanoid hand. Technical Report, 1546, MIT Artificial Intelligence Laboratory (1995)
19. Miall, R.C., Wolpert, D.M.: Forward models for physiological motor control. Neural Netw. **9**(8), 1265–1279 (1996)
20. Montesano, L., Lopes, M., Bernardino, A., Santos-Victor, J.: Learning object affordances: from sensory-motor coordination to imitation. IEEE Trans. Robot. **24**(1), 15–26 (2008)
21. Nguyen, A., Kanoulas, D., Caldwell, D.G., Tsagarakis, N.G.: Detecting object affordances with convolutional neural networks. In: 2016 IEEE/RSJ International Conference on Intelligent Robots and Systems (IROS), pp. 2765–2770. IEEE (2016)
22. Okamoto, S., Nagano, H., Yamada, Y.: Psychophysical dimensions of tactile perception of textures. IEEE Trans. Haptics **6**(1), 81–93 (2013)
23. Regoli, M., Jamali, N., Metta, G., Natale, L.: Controlled tactile exploration and haptic object recognition. In: 2017 18th International Conference on Advanced Robotics (ICAR), pp. 47–54. IEEE (2017)
24. Şahin, E., Çakmak, M., Doğar, M.R., Uğur, E., Üçoluk, G.: To afford or not to afford: a new formalization of affordances toward affordance-based robot control. Adapt. Behav. **15**(4), 447–472 (2007)
25. Sperry, R.W.: Neural basis of the spontaneous optokinetic response produced by visual inversion. J. Comp. Physiol. Psychol. **43**(6), 482 (1950)
26. Sugaiwa, T., Fujii, G., Iwata, H., Sugano, S.: A methodology for setting grasping force for picking up an object with unknown weight, friction, and stiffness. In: 2010 10th IEEE-RAS International Conference on Humanoid Robots, pp. 288–293. IEEE (2010)
27. Tikhanoff, V., Pattacini, U., Natale, L., Metta, G.: Exploring affordances and tool use on the iCub. In: 2013 13th IEEE-RAS International Conference on Humanoid Robots (Humanoids), pp. 130–137. IEEE (2013)
28. Yussof, H., Ohka, M., Takata, J., Nasu, Y., Yamano, M.: Low force control scheme for object hardness distinction in robot manipulation based on tactile sensing. In: 2008 IEEE International Conference on Robotics and Automation, pp. 3443–3448. IEEE (2008)
29. Zoeller, A., Lezkan, A., Paulun, V., Fleming, R., Drewing, K.: Integration of prior knowledge during haptic exploration depends on information type. J. Vis. **19**(4), 20 (2019)

Clarifying the Half Full or Half Empty Question: Multimodal Container Classification

Josua Spisak[✉], Matthias Kerzel, and Stefan Wermter

Knowledge Technology, Department of Informatics, University of Hamburg,
Vogt-Koelln-Street 30, 22527 Hamburg, Germany
josua.spisak@uni-hamburg.de
http://www.knowledge-technology.info

Abstract. Multimodal integration is a key component of allowing robots to perceive the world. Multimodality comes with multiple challenges that have to be considered, such as how to integrate and fuse the data. In this paper, we compare different possibilities of fusing visual, tactile and proprioceptive data. The data is directly recorded on the NICOL robot in an experimental setup in which the robot has to classify containers and their content. Due to the different nature of the containers, the use of the modalities can wildly differ between the classes. We demonstrate the superiority of multimodal solutions in this use case and evaluate three fusion strategies that integrate the data at different time steps. We find that the accuracy of the best fusion strategy is 15% higher than the best strategy using only one singular sense.

Keywords: Multimodality · Robotics · Machine Learning

1 Introduction

We constantly receive information and stimuli from all of our senses. Even in simple actions that we perform every day, such as drinking water, we will taste it, touch the bottle or glass holding the water, feel our muscles that help us lift it, and hear how we swallow it or how it moves around. We are processing all of these modalities at once, integrating their features [23]. Robots, on the other hand, are often much more limited in their perception, often only singular senses are used for given tasks or a combination of just two or three senses. For these tasks, a limited diversity of senses is often enough, however, if we want robots to be able to freely interact with their environment, they need to be able to sense more of their environment. To facilitate this, we use three sensory modalities of our robot in this paper vision, tactile and proprioception and look at how to best integrate them. We do this on a task where perception with a single modality can be challenging.

In the theory of affordances [5], the perception of the world and specifically the perception of objects is discussed. The focus lies on perceiving what the

© The Author(s) 2023
L. Iliadis et al. (Eds.): ICANN 2023, LNCS 14254, pp. 444–456, 2023.
https://doi.org/10.1007/978-3-031-44207-0_37

Fig. 1. The seven object classes, from left to right, we have: the empty bottle, the filled bottle, the half filled bottle, the empty spam box, the filled spam box, the empty tomato can and the filled tomato can.

world or objects can afford us. Depending on the observer, objects can have affordances, such as a ball affording to lift or to grasp if the size of the ball relative to the observer fits, if the ball is a bit bigger it might afford sitting on it or leaning against it and so on. The idea is that when we perceive anything, we mainly perceive what it affords us, as that is what we need to perceive in order to interact with it. One group of objects that can be especially flexible when it comes to their affordances are containers. The content of containers can differ widely, changing what the container affords us. An empty container affords space to store things safely, while a container filled with water could afford drinking, washing or cooling. One of the challenges with creating robots that can learn from the world, imitate others, and use that learned knowledge to interact with the world, is that some objects are difficult to correctly perceive [3]. This is a fundamental process on which further steps rely.

Robots tend to have multiple sensors and ways in which they can receive information about the world, so we need to look at how we can use that multimodal data and how to combine it. We want to explore which senses are useful and how to best integrate them to get a more complete concept of the world. In this paper, we use a multimodal system to allow a robot to detect the contents of containers, thereby gaining a deeper understanding of the affordances of containers for the robot. This understanding allows the robot to interact with the world and learn from it, the robot can be helped by having a model of the world. Part of such a model should be the effects of actions. If a robot can understand the effect of actions, it can also predict what will happen after actions are performed. This can allow the robot to interact with others as it can understand the purpose or goal of actions. It can also allow it to learn from others [11,13]. As it can find actions that lead to the same effects as the actions it observes

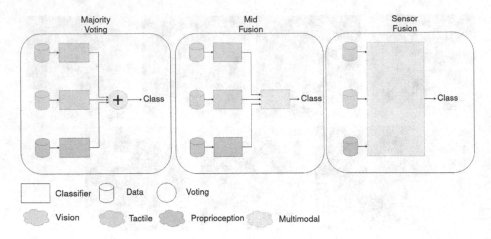

Fig. 2. An overview of the three methods of multimodal fusion we use.

from others. The ability to detect the content of containers can also improve human-robot cooperation [20].

Using multiple strategies for multimodal object recognition has been tried before [1, 21], however, to our knowledge it has never been used for the detection of content inside of containers, where the modalities encounter a higher number of challenges. The containers we use vary more than in other research studies. Where most studies only concern themselves with one type of container such as a glass and different contents [6], we experimented with three containers that differ in size, material and form.

The main contributions of this paper are summarised as follows:

By using a multimodal approach that utilises vision, touch and proprioception to detect the contents of containers, we improve the abilities of robots to interact with their environment and other actors.

We collected multimodal data with a real-world humanoid robot of 3 objects each with different fill levels for a total of 7 classes. Examples of the seven classes can be seen in Fig. 1.

2   Related Work

2.1   Container Content Detection

Detecting the content of containers can be done in many ways, often depending on the kind of container at hand. We can find some separation between them by looking at which modalities are used. Using vision to detect the content of containers is a common approach, where it is possible to look into or through the container to see the content [4, 14, 17]. The vision can consist of just RGB cameras or be improved further with specialised cameras such as depth cameras or CCD cameras. The perceived images can be processed with many kinds of mechanisms such as neural networks, edge detectors or probabilistic models. There are some containers where vision is not quite as useful to detect the content. This applies for instance to cans, where we cannot see anything inside them, or even fruits such as avocados, whose colouring tells us little about their ripeness. A modality that can be used for these containers is the tactile sense [2]. Just like humans would touch an avocado to learn about its ripeness, machine learning mechanisms can use the data gathered by tactile sensors to classify what is inside of an object. Similarly, proprioception can be used to detect the weight of a container and extrapolate from that to information about the content [15].

To use the advantages of more than a single modality, multimodal approaches integrate senses to improve detection. While there is often an imbalance in the performance between senses, the combination of them does improve the overall results [7, 8, 16].

2.2 Multimodal Integration

Of course, using multiple modalities means that we have to integrate them and bring them together. Fusion strategies are often separated into three groups. The three groups are known by multiple terms [10, 18, 19], but tend to be quite similar. The first group of fusion strategies fuses the data gained from the sensors directly before any sort of mapping happens from the data to a desired result. This fusion can be done in many ways depending on the data and often challenges are encountered, such as different sizes of the data or other ways in which the data is hard to match between senses [10]. Another group of fusion strategies only fuses the information at the very end of the process. Here, the senses are handled individually until they finish mapping from the information to the result, and the results from the senses are then fused to form a consensus. Some exemplary methods are majority voting, weighted majority voting, behaviour knowledge space, and Naive-Bayes classification [12]. The last group is somewhat in between, here the data is first processed individually but fused before coming to clear results. The later we integrate the information, the easier this integration tends to be, with lesser training requirements or data requirements. The downside of later fusions is that it is easier to miss cross-modal interaction, as some information about how the modalities interact with each other can be lost [22].

3   Multimodal Data Set for Container Content Classification

We propose a multimodal data set including three modalities, vision, proprioception and tactile perception. We recorded this data set with the NICOL (Neuro-Inspired COLlaborator) [9]. We started recording data from the cameras hosted in the head of NICOL, the effort of its joints and the data from the tactile sensors of the fingers. We put the container onto the table in front of NICOL, where the robot moves its arm to grasp the container. Then the robot lifts the container briefly, moving it around before putting it back in place. We filtered out the data where the robot was not holding the container for the tactile and

Fig. 3. Exemplary images recorded with the fish eye lens camera from the NICOL robot.

proprioception data later on. The modalities are recorded at different frequencies depending on the robot's capabilities. We used three kinds of containers, a water bottle, and, from the YCB Object and Model set, the spam box as well as the tomato can. For the water bottle, we had three possible fill levels, empty, halfway filled and filled. The other objects could either be filled or empty. The bottle and the tomato can be grasped using a side grasp, while we used a top grasp for the spam box. In total, we recorded around 77000 samples from the joints, 95000 samples from the tactile sensors and around 57000 images.

For the vision, the robot recorded images at a resolution of 1920 × 1080 with a fish eye camera lens. We record 30 images per second. Which is quite high regarding the movement in the images. This means that the difference between two sequential images can be insignificant, so we only used every tenth image. The containers only take up a small part of the image. Some exemplary images are shown in Fig. 3. We annotated the data by hand, drawing bounding boxes around the containers and labelling them.

The tactile data was recorded from the tactile sensors that NICOL has in its five fingers. We used the values representing the directional forces relative to the fingertips, so the force that is measured along the x, the y and the z-axis. The tactile data is recorded at 50 samples per second. The tactile data does depend on the grip that the robot has on the container. Throughout the lifting attempts, the way each finger is positioned can change and impact the values we receive from the tactile sensors.

The proprioceptive data was gathered from the joints of NICOL. For each joint, we receive three values describing the position of the joint, the velocity of the joint and the effort of the joint. Similar to the tactile data, the proprioception data is impacted by the way in which the robot grasps the container. The proprioception data is recorded at a frequency of 40 samples per second. By proprioception data, we refer to the data we get from the joint motors of the robot, in our case, we have 23 joints.

Throughout the data collection, we used two ways of grasping the object, for the spam box we used a top grasp while we used a side grasp for the other objects.

4 Approach

We have used three ways of integrating our modalities, they are depicted in Fig. 2. The first strategy is majority voting, where we have individual classifiers for vision, proprioception and tactile data. We further have two voting mechanics to combine the output of these classifiers. The first one is hard voting, where we take the classification from each classifier as one value. So, this classification will either be filled, unfilled or half filled. Each classifier is counted as one voter. The option that was voted for by the majority of the classifiers is chosen. If there is no clear majority and there are multiple classifications with the highest number of votes, we declare the vote as undecided and count it as a false classification. Secondly, we have soft majority voting. Instead of taking a clear classification from each classifier, we use the whole output from each classifier. This means that each classifier provides us with an array that has seven values, one value for each possible classification. We add the arrays together, forming a new array also with three values. To form a final classification, we simply look at the highest of the three values and the class it correlates to.

Apart from the majority voting, we also used a neural network to fuse the modalities. We used the output from our classifiers as the input for another classifier, fusing the modalities and providing a classification. Finally, we fused the data at the beginning and created a NN that uses the fused data to directly classify the fill level. So, we have three strategies as to when the fusion happens in relation to the mapping from the data to the class.

To allow any of this, we first have to synchronise the data. The modalities are recorded in different frequencies, and we want the samples to match for each of the modalities. To avoid having a sample multiple times, we took the vision data as our lead, as it had the lowest frequency. We then synchronised the data from all modalities so that the samples would match each other across the modalities. Like this, we compose a data set that has data from all modalities. This is the data set that we use in our experiments. This way, the individual classifiers are also looking at the same time frame.

We preprocessed the visual data, inverted the colours, and cut down the image so that the container is a larger part of the image and in the centre of the image. We used the images with a resolution of 256×256 for our CNN, which worked as our visual classifier. The inversion of colour was done, so that parts of the images that are important to the detection of the content become easier to see [14]. For example, the border where water meats air in the bottles. We cut down the image because the original images had a lot of background with only a small part being the container we wanted to focus on. This meant, that often the classifier had problems finding the container in the first place, not even getting to the task of identifying the contents.

In our mid fusion strategy, we create a classifier to fuse the output from the classifiers for each of the modalities. This classifier is a dense NN which consists of 4 layers with the activation function relu and an output layer with the sigmoid function and three neurons which provide three output values corresponding to the possible fill levels. We use Adam as our optimiser and the categorical cross-entropy loss function. We trained this network for 10 epochs with a batch size of 5. This strategy allows us to process more cross-modal information, as the classifier providing the final output has access to some information about each modality. It also means that it would still be possible to judge the quality of the individual modalities and gain information from them. This could be useful for evaluating the modalities or judging how trustworthy the results are.

In the sensor fusion strategy, the classifier we create needs to be able to process both visual data as well as data from the tactile sensors or the joints. To facilitate this, there are two input arms, one consisting of convolutional layers while the other one uses dense layers. The convolutional arm has 4 convolutional blocks of a convolutional layer and a max pooling layer, each before a dense layer. The dense arm has four dense layers with 100 neurons each. Both arms then lead into a dense layer with 100 neurons, followed by three more dense layers before the output layer with three neurons and the sigmoid activation function which produced our output. The model can be seen in Fig. 4. The output is the same as with the other models and has one value correlating to each possible fill level. This strategy allows us to use a lot of cross-modal information. The model has direct sensory data from each of the modalities and can gain a deeper understanding of how they relate to each other and the desired output. However, the model also has to deal with more complex data, so its task is more difficult. We also lose some understanding about the model itself, as it would be a lot harder to tell afterwards how important which modality was to the result and whether or not we need all modalities or how to improve the data collection.

To gain a deeper understanding of each of our modalities, we further researched how classifiers, that only depend on one of the modalities, perform. Starting with the vision, we used the classifier that is also used for the majority voting. We have a CNN with eight convolutional blocks, each consisting of one convolutional layer with a relu activation function and max pooling layer. After the convolutional blocks, we have one dense layer with 64 neurons, which also uses the relu activation function. Finally, we have our output layer which has three neurons and uses the sigmoid activation function to produce our output which consists of three values, each corresponding to one possible fill level of the container. We used the Adam optimiser and the categorical cross-entropy loss function. We trained the network for 10 epochs and used an 80:20 split for the training and validation set. The training data is a subset of the data set introduced in Sect. 3.

For the other modalities, we used a dense neural network consisting of four dense layers with the relu activation function and one output layer with three neurons, which has the sigmoid function as its activation function. The only difference between the tactile classifier and the proprioception classifier is, that

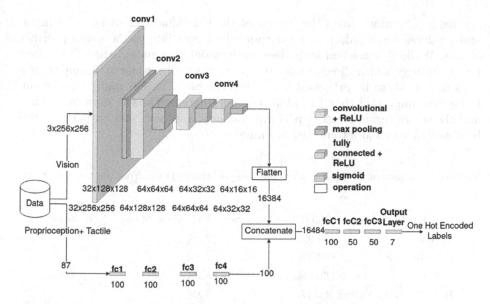

Fig. 4. This figure displays the architecture of the neural network, that is utilised in our sensor fusion strategy. The sensory data, gathered from the robot's vision, joints and tactile sensors, is used as the input. The outputs are one-hot encoded labels corresponding to the seven possible classes we have. The number below the layers denotes their output shape

the tactile classifier has 15 input values which are the force directions along the x, y and z axis for each of the five fingers while the proprioception model has 69 input values which are the velocity, position and effort of each of the 23 joints. Both of these models use the Adam optimiser and the categorical cross-entropy loss function. We did, however, find that the proprioceptive model needs significantly more epochs to converge than the tactile model; therefore, the tactile model is trained for 10 epochs while the proprioception model is trained for 50 epochs.

5   Results and Discussion

Table 1 shows the results of our fusion strategies, as well as the results of using only singular modalities. The results are averaged from ten training runs. The data used changed in between runs but stayed the same in one run for each classification method. The only way of fusing our data that performs worse than any of the individual modalities is the hard majority fusion. Here the negative impact of the more inaccurate modalities can be seen. As the other fusion strategies use more sophisticated approaches to fuse the data, they can find more nuances and be less impacted by the less accurate modalities. With most fusion strategies performing better than even the best modality, we show the benefits of multimodality. The best-performing fusion strategy is the mid Fusion, in which we created a NN, which takes the output of the individual classifiers as its input and produces seven values as its output which correlate to the seven possible classes. While this method keeps less cross-modal information than the sensor fusion strategy which directly takes the data from all sensors as its input, the data that needs to be processed is also less complex. This advantage turns out to be more important than the additional information. The soft majority voting and the sensor fusion strategy perform similarly, and both still outperform the best modality by more than 0.07 accuracy.

Table 1. Comparison of the classifiers on the synchronised data from ten training runs.

Classification Method	Validation Accuracy	Validation Standard Deviation
Tactile	74.9%	2.2%
Proprioception	43.3%	1.4%
Vision	60.9%	8.2%
Hard Majority Voting	65.4%	5.8%
Soft Majority Voting	83.5%	4.9%
Mid Fusion	**90.6%**	3.7%
Sensor Fusion	82.8%	6.8%

Out of the individual modalities, the classifier using the tactile data performs the best, followed by the classifier using the visual data and finally the classifier using the proprioception data. The tactile sensors can tell us a lot about the weight of the object, and the different forms of the object also make it so that they are grasped differently. Combining this information with the tactile data allows the classifier to be able to accurately differentiate between the classes. For the visual data, there are more obstacles to overcome, for some of the recorded samples it is almost impossible to tell whether a given container is filled or not with the hand of the robot occluding the content of the container. Another hindrance is the transparent nature of the bottles and the water they are filled with, which can also make it hard to detect the fill level. These factors lead to the visual data, leading to a less accurate classifier. The classifier using the proprioception data had the lowest accuracy. While it was able to have a far better idea about the container than could be gained from simply guessing, the data from the motors is quite noisy, especially with the grasping and lifting process differing with each attempt.

While each of the modalities has its challenges, we have already seen that the combination of them improves the results, to gain a deeper understanding of the benefit that the combination of modalities provides, we compare how each classification method performs for each class in Table 5. The results in the table are averaged over ten runs. The first thing that comes to note is that all of the best results for the classes come either from the mid fusion strategy, the sensor fusion strategy or, in one case, the Classifier using only tactile data. While the mid fusion strategy is not surprising here as we had already seen in Table 1 that it produced the best results overall, it is unexpected that for two of the seven classes, the sensor fusion strategy is the most accurate. The soft majority voting had a better overall accuracy, but also ends up being less volatile, having higher lows and lower highs than the sensor fusion strategy. With the main difference between the fusion strategies being the amount of cross-modal information available, it appears that for the classes "Bottle Half Filled" and "Can Full", this information is more important than for other classes. The other possible explanation is that the sensor fusion strategy does not make use of the classifiers for the individual modalities. So, it could be possible that the mid fusion and the soft majority voting perform worse for these three classes than the sensor fusion because the individual classifiers are less sure about these classes, so they could have high values for the class as well as a secondary class. With the class "Bottle Half Filled", we can easily imagine that the classifiers see a larger similarity to the classes "Bottle Filled" and "Bottle Empty" than they see between these two classes directly. Similarly, the classes "Can Empty" and "Can Full" could be quite close to each other as they do look quite similar, and the container is less prone to be deformed during the grasp regardless of its fill level.

We can also see some peculiarities with individual modalities, The visual classifier seems to be particularly challenged by the classes "Bottle Empty" and

	Bottle Filled	Bottle Empty	Bottle Half Filled	Spam Empty	Spam Filled	Can Empty	Can Filled
Tactile	66.4	88.5	58.2	45.1	86.0	94.7	76.9
Proprioception	40.6	35.7	32.7	41.3	65.1	45.6	25.3
Vision	83.1	12.0	26.0	70.9	82.5	77.7	60.7
Hard Majority Voting	86.5	43.0	32.9	55.1	88.3	84.2	56.0
Soft Majority Voting	81.9	74.3	78.3	84.6	91.6	92.0	73.1
Mid Fusion	90.6	89.2	83.5	86.4	95.9	93.6	91.7
Sensor Fusion	74.6	62.3	85.4	85.9	79.5	93.9	94.9

Fig. 5. Comparison of the average results of the Classifiers per class over ten runs in percent.

	Bottle Filled	Bottle Empty	Bottle Half Filled	Spam Empty	Spam Filled	Can Empty	Can Filled
Bottle Filled	0.72	0.28	0	0	0	0	0
Bottle Empty	0.83	0.15	0	0	0	0.026	0
Bottle Half Filled	0.99	0.01	0	0	0	0	0
Spam Empty	0	0	0	0.57	0.43	0	0
Spam Filled	0	0	0	0.025	0.97	0.0062	0
Can Empty	0	0	0	0.0076	0	0.99	0
Can Filled	0	0	0	0	0	0.79	0.21

Fig. 6. Confusion Matrix for the vision classifier from a single run.

"Bottle Half Filled". If we look further at the individual runs, we can see that there is always one bottle label that performs very well, most of the time that is the "Bottle Filled" but on some runs, it is one of the others, the problem seems to be to differentiate between the fill levels of bottles and not in detecting the bottle. We can also see this in the confusion matrix shown in Fig. 6, where the classifier has a strong bias towards the "Bottle Filled" class whenever any of the bottle classes should be predicted. The tactile data finds the class "Spam Empty" to be the hardest to detect. Of course, the tactile data also provides the best result for the class "Can Empty". That the visual classifier has such difficulties with two of the bottle classes could be explained by the challenge of transparency, why the tactile sensors performed worse on the "Spam Empty" class would need to be researched further.

6   Conclusion

In this paper, we present multiple ways of classifying containers and their content, integrating up to three modalities. Our experiments compare different fusion strategies and showcase their strengths and weaknesses on data collected by a new robot. We evaluate the results and find that the best-performing fusion strategy utilises an NN to combine the results of individual classifiers for each of the modalities. We find an NN that can accurately classify multiple containers and their content, which improves the ability of the robot to perceive the world and learn about the objects in said world, which is necessary to discern self from others. The large variance in shape appearance and material of the containers in our data sets lets us find strengths and weaknesses of the sensory modalities, as well as how we can overcome them by fusing the modalities. Future work can include expanding the data set with more containers.

Acknowledgment. The authors gratefully acknowledge support from the DFG (CML, MoReSpace, LeCAREbot), BMWK (SIDIMO, VERIKAS), and the European Commission (TRAIL, TERAIS).

References

1. Castellini, C., Tommasi, T., Noceti, N., Odone, F., Caputo, B.: Using object affordances to improve object recognition. IEEE transactions on autonomous mental development **3**(3), 207–215 (2011)
2. Chitta, S., Piccoli, M., Sturm, J.: Tactile object class and internal state recognition for mobile manipulation. In: 2010 IEEE International Conference on Robotics and Automation. pp. 2342–2348. IEEE (2010)
3. Cui, Z.J., Wang, Y., Shafiullah, N.M.M., Pinto, L.: From play to policy: Conditional behavior generation from uncurated robot data. arXiv preprint arXiv:2210.10047 (2022)
4. Do, C., Schubert, T., Burgard, W.: A probabilistic approach to liquid level detection in cups using an rgb-d camera. In: 2016 IEEE/RSJ International Conference on Intelligent Robots and Systems (IROS). pp. 2075–2080. IEEE (2016)

5. Gibson, J.J.: The theory of affordances. Hilldale, USA **1**(2), 67–82 (1977)
6. Güler, P., Bekiroglu, Y., Gratal, X., Pauwels, K., Kragic, D.: What's in the container? classifying object contents from vision and touch. In: 2014 IEEE/RSJ International Conference on Intelligent Robots and Systems. pp. 3961–3968. IEEE (2014)
7. Hall, D.L., Llinas, J.: An introduction to multisensor data fusion. Proceedings of the IEEE **85**(1), 6–23 (1997)
8. Jonetzko, Y., Fiedler, N., Eppe, M., Zhang, J.: Multimodal object analysis with auditory and tactile sensing using recurrent neural networks. In: International Conference on Cognitive Systems and Signal Processing. pp. 253–265. Springer (2020)
9. Kerzel, M., Allgeuer, P., Strahl, E., Frick, N., Habekost, J.G., Eppe, M., Wermter, S.: Nicol: A neuro-inspired collaborative semi-humanoid robot that bridges social interaction and reliable manipulation. arXiv preprint arXiv:2305.08528 (2023)
10. Lahat, D., Adali, T., Jutten, C.: Multimodal data fusion: an overview of methods, challenges, and prospects. Proceedings of the IEEE **103**(9), 1449–1477 (2015)
11. Lopes, M., Melo, F.S., Montesano, L.: Affordance-based imitation learning in robots. In: 2007 IEEE/RSJ international conference on intelligent robots and systems. pp. 1015–1021. IEEE (2007)
12. Mangai, U.G., Samanta, S., Das, S., Chowdhury, P.R.: A survey of decision fusion and feature fusion strategies for pattern classification. IETE Technical review **27**(4), 293–307 (2010)
13. Montesano, L., Lopes, M., Bernardino, A., Santos-Victor, J.: Learning object affordances: from sensory-motor coordination to imitation. IEEE Transactions on Robotics **24**(1), 15–26 (2008)
14. Pau, D., Kumar, B.P., Namekar, P., Dhande, G., Simonetta, L.: Dataset of sodium chloride sterile liquid in bottles for intravenous administration and fill level monitoring. Data in Brief **33**, 106472 (2020)
15. Piacenza, P., Lee, D., Isler, V.: Pouring by feel: An analysis of tactile and proprioceptive sensing for accurate pouring. In: 2022 International Conference on Robotics and Automation (ICRA). pp. 10248–10254. IEEE (2022)
16. Pieropan, A., Salvi, G., Pauwels, K., Kjellström, H.: Audio-visual classification and detection of human manipulation actions. In: 2014 IEEE/RSJ International Conference on Intelligent Robots and Systems. pp. 3045–3052. IEEE (2014)
17. Pithadiya, K.J., Modi, C.K., Chauhan, J.D.: Selecting the most favourable edge detection technique for liquid level inspection in bottles. International Journal of Computer Information Systems and Industrial Management Applications (IJCISIM) ISSN pp. 2150–7988 (2011)
18. Ross, A., Jain, A.: Information fusion in biometrics. Pattern recognition letters **24**(13), 2115–2125 (2003)
19. Sanderson, C., Paliwal, K.K.: Identity verification using speech and face information. Digital Signal Processing **14**(5), 449–480 (2004)
20. Sciutti, A., Mara, M., Tagliasco, V., Sandini, G.: Humanizing human-robot interaction: On the importance of mutual understanding. IEEE Technology and Society Magazine **37**(1), 22–29 (2018)
21. Toprak, S., Navarro-Guerrero, N., Wermter, S.: Evaluating integration strategies for visuo-haptic object recognition. Cognitive computation **10**, 408–425 (2018)
22. Turk, M.: Multimodal interaction: A review. Pattern recognition letters **36**, 189–195 (2014)
23. Zmigrod, S., Hommel, B.: Feature integration across multimodal perception and action: a review. Multisensory research **26**(1–2), 143–157 (2013)

CycleIK: Neuro-inspired Inverse Kinematics

Jan-Gerrit Habekost[✉], Erik Strahl, Philipp Allgeuer, Matthias Kerzel,
and Stefan Wermter

Knowledge Technology, Department of Informatics, University of Hamburg,
Hamburg, Germany
{jan-gerrit.habekost,stefan.wermter}@uni-hamburg.de

Abstract. The paper introduces CycleIK, a neuro-robotic approach
that wraps two novel neuro-inspired methods for the inverse kinematics
(IK) task—a Generative Adversarial Network (GAN), and a Multi-Layer
Perceptron architecture. These methods can be used in a standalone fashion, but we also show how embedding these into a hybrid neuro-genetic
IK pipeline allows for further optimization via sequential least-squares
programming (SLSQP) or a genetic algorithm (GA). The models are
trained and tested on dense datasets that were collected from random
robot configurations of the new Neuro-Inspired COLlaborator (NICOL),
a semi-humanoid robot with two redundant 8-DoF manipulators. We
utilize the weighted multi-objective function from the state-of-the-art
BioIK method to support the training process and our hybrid neuro-
genetic architecture. We show that the neural models can compete with
state-of-the-art IK approaches, which allows for deployment directly to
robotic hardware. Additionally, it is shown that the incorporation of the
genetic algorithm improves the precision while simultaneously reducing
the overall runtime.

Keywords: Neuro-inspired Inverse Kinematics · Humanoid Robots ·
Genetic Algorithms · Generative Adversarial Networks

1 Introduction

The inverse kinematics task searches for suitable joint configurations for a kinematic chain in order to achieve a specified end-effector Cartesian pose. Recent
collaborative and humanoid robot designs often rely on redundant manipulators
with more than six degrees of freedom (DoF). The complexity of the inverse
kinematics task is therefore increased, as the problem is then under-determined
and a set of redundant solutions for a single pose can be found, referred to as the
nullspace. The Python-based genetic IK solver Gaikpy [10], originally developed
for the child-sized NICO robot [11] with 6-DoF arms, requires a long runtime
in order to deal with the 8-DoF manipulators of the recently developed Neuro-
Inspired COLlaborator [9], pictured in the top-left image in Fig. 1.

© The Author(s) 2023
L. Iliadis et al. (Eds.): ICANN 2023, LNCS 14254, pp. 457–470, 2023.
https://doi.org/10.1007/978-3-031-44207-0_38

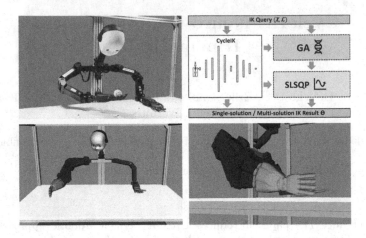

Fig. 1. CycleIK deployed to physical NICOL hardware (top-left). CycleIK hybrid neuro-genetic inverse kinematics pipeline (top-right). Visualization of the nullspace manifold from the CycleIK Generative Adversarial Network (bottom).

Traditionally, Jacobian-based methods are utilized for the IK task, such as KDL [17] and Trac-IK [5] which are popular plug-ins in the MoveIt [7] framework and can currently be seen as the industry standard. Both analytical solvers require a high runtime when deployed to NICOL, and have a higher error than Gaikpy [9]. We initially configured BioIK [18] to be the default solver, a popular state-of-the-art genetic approach, which was also deployed via Moveit. MoveIt, however, does not return a solution for an IK query, when the error is higher than the internal threshold, leaving the control cycle of the robot with no action.

Neural inverse kinematics is a field that unites a wide range of neuro-robotic applications that control the configuration space of a robotic system. The inverse kinematics task is fundamentally embodied in every action-generating neural architecture that takes data from Cartesian space as input. Explicit neural approaches to the task, however, rarely show results with high precision and are distributed over the different application domains of inverse kinematics ranging from robotics to character animation.

Two neural architectures, an auto-regressive Multi-Layer Perceptron (MLP) and a normalizing flow-based Generative Adversarial Network, are proposed in this work. The models solve the inverse kinematics task for a given pose in the reachability space of NICOL and can be deployed directly to robotic hardware, or alternatively be optimized with Gaikpy. The MLP returns exactly one solution for the IK task, while the GAN allows for the exploration of the nullspace manifold. The method is inspired by CycleGAN [20], which trains a dual-GAN architecture in an unsupervised fashion, to transform between two image domains. The positional and rotational errors are measured in Cartesian space by calculating the forward kinematics (FK) for a set of IK solutions that are inferred from the neural models. The FK function calculates the end-effector pose from a given robot configuration and has a short runtime of below $1ms$. Consequently, a second generator as in the original dual-GAN setup of CycleGAN, that approximates the FK function to transform from configuration to Cartesian space, is not necessarily needed for this application.

2   Related Work

The most similar normalizing flow-based approaches to ours are IKFlow from Ames et al. [3] and the work of Kim and Perez [12]. IKFlow is a recent and promising neural IK approach. The authors propose a conditional normalizing flow network for the inverse kinematics task, a form of Invertible Neural Network (INN) [4], introduced by Ardizzone et al. for invertible problems. Samples from a simple normal distribution are transformed into valid solution manifolds in the configuration domain through coupling layers that consist of multiple simple invertible functions. The solution manifold can optionally be further optimized with Trac-IK[5].

The approach of Kim and Perez [12] has a very similar architecture to IKFlow. Compared to IKFlow, which calculates the error with analytical forward kinematics, Kim and Perez use a second neural network to approximate the FK function in an autoencoder architecture. The approach of Kim and Perez has a comparably high error in the centimeter range and requires further optimization with the Jacobian, while IKFlow reaches a millimeter range of error.

Lembono et al. [14] present an ensemble architecture in which multiple GAN generators learn to sample from disjunct patches of the configuration space. A single forward kinematics discriminator is used that also checks for further constraints, e.g. minimal displacement of the arms. A more detailed investigation of GANs in the context of IK is given by Ren and Ben-Tzvi [16]. The paper modifies four different types of GAN architectures to solve the inverse kinematics problem. The discriminator produces binary output, while most GAN designs perform regression and calculate the continuous error to the target pose.

Bensadoun et al. [6] introduce a Gaussian Mixture Model (GMM) ensemble to calculate multiple solutions for the IK problem. A GMM is created for every joint in the kinematic chain. A hypernet parameterizes the GMMs conditioned to the target pose. Volinski et al. [19] utilize Spiking Neural Networks (SNN) to solve the inverse kinematics problem. The approach trains three different variations of simple SNN architectures. ProtoRes [15] was introduced by Oreshkin et al. to reconstruct natural body poses from sparse user input for animation tasks. The framework consists of a pose encoder that creates a latent embedding from the user input and then solves the IK task with a pose decoder.

3   Method

We propose CycleIK, a neuro-inspired
inverse kinematics solver that makes
use of the cyclic dependency between
the transformation from configuration
to Cartesian space and its inverse.
An overview of the architecture is
given in Fig. 2. The framework enables
either training a single-solution autoregressive Multi-Layer Perceptron or a
normalizing flow-based GAN architecture that allows the parallel inference
of multiple redundant solutions within
1 ms. Furthermore, the approach can
be utilized as a neuro-kinematic toolbox. The default networks can be sub-

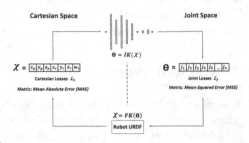

Fig. 2. CycleIK neuro-inspired training
and architecture overview. A batch of
Cartesian poses $\mathcal{X}$ is inferred by the network to predict a set of valid robot configurations Θ under constraints $\mathcal{L}$.

stituted by any end-to-end or multi-stage robotic control architecture that predicts joint angles and provides a Cartesian pose as a label. CycleIK is implemented in PyTorch, to be as openly available as possible. Most IK solvers are
implemented in C++ and generally rely on iterative numerical methods for the
optimization process, often leading to a higher runtime compared to the inference
of a neural network.

CycleIK treats the joint space as a semi-hidden domain, and calculates positional and rotational losses only in Cartesian space, by inferring a full cycle back
to Cartesian space, as shown in the following equations (Eq. 1 and 2):

$$\hat{\mathcal{X}} = FK(IK(\mathcal{X})) \tag{1}$$

$$e_{IK} = \|\hat{\mathcal{X}} - \mathcal{X}\| \tag{2}$$

where $\mathcal{X}$ is a batch of an arbitrary natural number of target poses, and e_{IK} is
the linear Cartesian error. While learning a one-to-one mapping between data
from Cartesian space and corresponding joint angles θ can work for lower-DoF
manipulators [10], the approach shows a high error for redundant manipulators
like on the NICOL robot [9], as these manipulators have a one-to-many mapping
in the form of the redundant nullspace manifold Θ. Thus, we minimize the linear
Cartesian error e_{IK} instead, which in our experience learns and generalizes more
smoothly.

Similar to neuro-inspired multi-solution solvers like IKFlow and CycleIK,
genetic algorithms produce multiple solutions for an IK query, and have shown
good results for the IK task [1,10,18]. The most popular genetic IK approach is
BioIK [18], which is available in both MoveIt and Unity. The method supports
genetic algorithms by hybridization with particle swarm optimization (PSO).
The architecture allows generic IK queries through a weighted partial cost func-
tion $\phi(\Theta, \mathcal{L})$ that is applied to the set of IK solutions Θ under the constraints $\mathcal{L}$.
The constraints can be reformulated at every IK query, so complex dynamic tasks

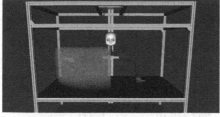 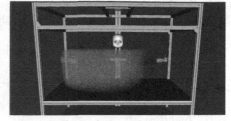

$Small_{1000}$ dataset front view $Full_{1400}$ dataset front view

Fig. 3. Visualization of NICOL's right arm workspace, with the $Small_{1000}$ dataset on the left and the $Full_{1400}$ dataset on the right.

such as collision avoidance in motion planning can be performed. Different goal types can be set for either the links or joints of the robot. We adapt the weighted partial cost function from BioIK for both of our models. CycleIK's single-solution model optionally makes use of a set of weighted constraints $\mathcal{L} = \mathcal{L}_C \cup \mathcal{L}_J$, that consists of specified goals, either in Cartesian or joint space. The constraints are applied by the multi-objective function in every training step. Both, the single-solution MLP as well as the multi-solution GAN, can optionally be further optimized by the Python-based genetic IK Gaikpy [10] or non-linear sequential least squares quadratic programming [13], where again a partial weighted cost function can be used to select the optimal solution. An overview of the neuro-genetic IK pipeline is given in the top-right image of Fig. 1.

3.1 Dataset

Three datasets were collected from NICOL's workspace: $Small_{1000}$, $Full_{1000}$ and $Full_{1400}$. Uniform random collision-free robot configurations were sampled. The $Small_{1000}$ and $Full_{1400}$ dataset are shown in Fig. 3. The $Small_{1000}$ dataset contains 1,000,000 samples and is limited to the right side of the tabletop, which is located 80cm above the ground. The $Full_{1000}$ and $Full_{1400}$ datasets with $1,000,000$ and $1,400,000$ poses are sampled from the whole workspace of the right arm over the tabletop. We built test sets with 10% size and validation sets with 1% size for each of the training datasets. In all datasets, a 20cm safety margin was included at the back of the workspace on the x-axis, as well as a 10cm safety margin on the y-axis on the right-hand side of the robot workspace. All properties of the datasets can be seen in Table 1. A convex hull was generated around the data points to approximate the Cartesian volume of each dataset.

Table 1. Overview of the training datasets and the corresponding 10% test sets ($Small_{100}$, $Full_{100}$ and $Full_{140}$) and 1% validation sets ($Small_{10}$, $Full_{10}$ and $Full_{14}$).

Dataset	Workspace [x, y, z] (m)	Samples	Volume (cm^3)	Sample Density $(samples\ per\ cm^3)$
$Small_{1000}$		10^6	$295.56 \cdot 10^3$	3.383
$Small_{100}$	$\begin{bmatrix} 0.2 & -0.9 & 0.8 \\ 0.85 & 0.0 & 1.4 \end{bmatrix}$	10^5	$293.34 \cdot 10^3$	0.341
$Small_{10}$		10^4	$287.11 \cdot 10^3$	0.035
$Full_{1000}$		10^6	$420.11 \cdot 10^3$	2.38
$Full_{100}$	$\begin{bmatrix} 0.2 & -0.9 & 0.8 \\ 0.85 & 0.48 & 1.4 \end{bmatrix}$	10^5	$415.13 \cdot 10^3$	0.241
$Full_{10}$		10^4	$401.75 \cdot 10^3$	0.025
$Full_{1400}$		$1.4 \cdot 10^6$	$420.43 \cdot 10^3$	3.33
$Full_{140}$	$\begin{bmatrix} 0.2 & -0.9 & 0.8 \\ 0.85 & 0.48 & 1.4 \end{bmatrix}$	$1.4 \cdot 10^5$	$416.09 \cdot 10^3$	0.336
$Full_{14}$		$1.4 \cdot 10^4$	$405.07 \cdot 10^3$	0.035

3.2   Architecture

The basic network architecture is very similar for both models. The pose is encoded as a 7-dimensional vector, i.e. the 3-dimensional position $[x_p, y_p, z_p]^T$ concatenated with the rotation represented as a 4-dimensional unit quaternion $[x_r, y_r, z_r, w_r]^T$, as shown in Fig. 2. The output of the network has the same dimension as the robot DoF, so every field of the output vector corresponds to a motor position in the kinematic chain. The GAN additionally concatenates the pose with a second input, a random uniform noise vector that is utilized to sample from the nullspace manifold. The models utilize two different activation functions. While Gaussian-Error Linear Units [8] (GELU) are generally used for all the layers, the Tanh activation is applied to the last one to three layers of the network, as this highly improves the results. The data is normalized to lie in the interval $[-1, 1]$, which is equivalent to the limits of the network input and output. Thus, the method cannot push the joint angles through their joint limits, which is a shortcoming of a lot of Jacobian-based IK solvers. Visualizations of the two network architectures for the NICOL robot can be found in Fig. 4.

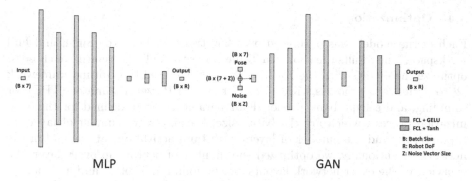

Fig. 4. Neural architectures optimized for the $Small_{1000}$ dataset, Multi-Layer Perceptron (left) and Generative Adversarial Network (right).

3.3   Training

In every training step, a batch of poses $\mathcal{X}$ is inferred by the network. For the single-solution network, the training step is straightforward—after inference, forward kinematics are applied to the batch of solutions Θ to determine the reached poses $\hat{\mathcal{X}}$ and then apply the multi-objective loss function, as in Eq. 3:

$$loss_{\mathcal{L}} = \phi(\Theta, \hat{\mathcal{X}}, \mathcal{L}) \tag{3}$$

Here, $\mathcal{L}$ holds at least the positional and rotational error. For the NICOL robot, we applied a zero-controller goal that minimizes the displacement of the motor position from the zero position of the selected subset of redundant joints in the kinematic chain. Our preliminary experiments showed the best performance by using the mean absolute error for Cartesian space losses and mean squared error for the joint space losses, as the error increased for all other evaluated error terms. The learning rate is decreased linearly at the end of each epoch.

The training process for the multi-solution GAN extends the training process of the MLP. After calculation of the positional and rotational loss for a batch of Cartesian samples from the training set, one of the poses is randomly chosen from the batch. A tensor of the same size as the training batch is created and filled with the chosen pose. Random uniform noise $\mathcal{Z}$ of the required batch size and noise vector size is then generated and used for the forward pass. The training aims to maximize the variance in the solution batch Θ. The normalizing flow method is applied, as the network is not being forced to regress to only one solution, but instead fit the nullspace distribution Θ to the noise $\mathcal{Z}$, as in Eq. 4:

$$loss_{var} = MSE(var(\Theta) - var(\mathcal{Z})) \tag{4}$$

The method can produce multiple valid solutions for the NICOL robot with millimeter-level accuracy. One possible extension would be to combine Kullback-Leibler divergence for the loss and normally distributed noise in the input, as done by IKFlow [3] and Kim and Perez [12].

3.4 Optimization

Each of the models was optimized over 250 trials for both the Small and Full workspace. The results are shown in Table 2. For the Full workspace, we chose to optimize the models with the $Full_{1400}$ dataset. We used the Optuna framework [2] to optimize the models with a Tree-structured Parzen Estimator (TPE) for sampling, and a hyperband pruner. Four parameters were defined for the optimization process, which are the batch size, learning rate, number of layers in the network, and the number of layers with tanh activations at the end of the network. Additionally, we optimized the number of neurons in every layer. An overview of the exact network layouts can be found in Table 3, and a visualization of the network structures for the Small workspace is shown in Fig. 4. For the GAN only, we also optimized the size of the input noise vector.

Table 2. Training parameters for the different network types, optimized for the $Small_{1000}$ and $Full_{1400}$ datasets.

Parameter	MLP		GAN		Parameter	Limits
	Small	Full	Small	Full	min./max.	step size
Batch Size	150	300	350	300	100 / 600	50
Learning Rate	$1.6 \cdot 10^{-4}$	10^{-4}	$2.1 \cdot 10^{-4}$	$1.9 \cdot 10^{-4}$	10^{-5} / 10^{-3}	10^{-5}
Number Layers	8	8	8	8	7 / 9	1
Number Tanh Layers	3	3	3	2	1 / 3	1
Noise Vector Size	–	–	8	10	3 / 10	1

Table 3. Network structures of the different network types optimized for the $Small_{1000}$ and $Full_{1400}$ workspace.

Model	Workspace	Neurons per Layer
MLP	Small	[3380, 2250, 3240, 2270, 1840, 30, 60, 220]
	Full	[2200, 2400, 2400, 1900, 250, 220, 30, 380]
GAN	Small	[790, 990, 3120, 1630, 300, 1660, 730, 540]
	Full	[1180, 1170, 2500, 1290, 700, 970, 440, 770]

4 Results

The application of the weighted partial cost function on the MLP network and the variance loss on the GAN created stability issues in the training process of differing severity for the two models. The MLP rarely shows stability issues during the training process, but they sometimes occur when trained for more

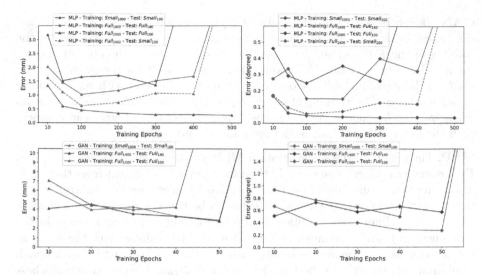

Fig. 5. Average positional and rotational error of the MLP and GAN model under training for varying numbers of epochs.

than 100 epochs, and can be dealt with using gradient clipping. The GAN suffers more severe stability issues, and could not be trained for more than 50 epochs in our experiments. We hypothesize it is due to the competition of maximizing the nullspace manifold variance while maintaining precise IK regression. Gradient clipping cannot be applied as easily in the case of the GAN because it prevents learning proper minimization of the variance loss.

4.1 Optimal Number of Epochs

To determine the optimal number of epochs for the training process, we trained both presented models for each of the three datasets that were generated, so that six models in total were evaluated under different epoch configurations. A standalone training was performed for every individual model and number of epochs. To handle the stability issues of the models, we gave every evaluated epoch configuration a number of restarts in case stability issues occur. Each choice of maximum epochs was allowed two restarts for the MLP and nine for the GAN. If exploding gradients occurred in every observed training, the combination was considered to have failed. The results of our experiments are shown in Fig. 5. We calculated the positional and rotational error for the MLP by first taking the average over the three corresponding axes of the 6-DoF pose error, and then averaging the results for the whole 10% test sets. For the multi-solution GAN, we first calculated the average error over single batches of nullspace solutions, before taking the mean over the whole test set. We take the success definition for the inverse kinematics task from Kerzel et al. [10], which allows $10mm$ positional and 20-degree rotational error.

GAN. It can be seen that the training process of the $Small_{1000}$ dataset had the lowest error for most of the epoch configurations when compared to the training of the $Full_{1000}$ and $Full_{1400}$ datasets. For a higher number of epochs, the positional error of the GAN models behaves similarly for the $Small_{1000}$ and $Full_{1400}$ datasets. Instabilities occur for short training and with regard to the rotational error. The training of the $Full_{1000}$ GAN model already starts to fail when training for more than 40 epochs, while the rotational error can compete with the loss of the $Full_{1400}$ model for a lot of configurations.

MLP. The results of the single-solution MLP for the training on the $Small$ and $Full$ workspace differ more strongly than for the GAN. Different from the GAN, where the exact same loss is used for both workspaces, the zero-controller goal that we set for the training of the MLP has to be tuned for a specific workspace and therefore differs. The additional joint space goal can therefore explain the differences in training behavior to some degree. The training with the $Full_{1000}$ dataset can also for the MLP compete with the $Full_{1400}$ training for some epoch configurations. Overall, the best model for the $Full_{1400}$ dataset exceeds the best model for the $Full_{1000}$ dataset.

The training with the $Small_{1000}$ dataset proceeded the smoothest, and we did not experience any stability issues. In contrast to the GANs, where the smallest positional error is achieved after 50 epochs for both workspaces, with slightly below $3mm$ average error, the MLP models differ in the ideal training length as well as in the smallest error. While the lowest positional error for the Full workspace is achieved after 100 epochs, the best results for the Small workspace are found after 300 training epochs. The best results for the $Full_{1000}$ dataset are also achieved with 300 training epochs, but cannot compete with the best model of the $Full_{1400}$ dataset. We evaluated the performance of the different models for the $Full_{1400}$ dataset on the $Small_{100}$ test set to make the $Small_{1000}$ and $Full_{1400}$ models directly comparable. It can be seen from the green dotted line in Fig. 5 that the $Full_{1400}$ models perform very similarly when evaluated on the same test data as the $Small_{1000}$ models. Positional and rotational errors only show small differences until 100 training epochs are exceeded.

Overall, we focus more on the positional error rather than the rotational error, as the rotational error is far below our success limit of 20 °C in almost all cases. Especially the models that were only trained for 10 or 20 epochs can show up to 5 mm average positional error, and therefore a lot of solutions around the upper bound of the error exceed the limit of 1 cm.

4.2   Precision Analysis

From the previous experiment, the best-performing models were selected and evaluated for the $Small_{100}$ and $Full_{140}$ test sets. We seeded 50% of Gaikpy's initial population with solutions from the neural models in a follow-up experiment and filled the other half of the population with uniform random robot configurations within the joint limits. As a baseline, errors for standalone BioIK and Gaikpy were evaluated. The results of our IK experiments on the Small and Full workspace can be seen in Table 4. The framework offers SLSQP for further optimization but we did not use it in the experiments, as the solutions are already precise enough to be deployed to the physical hardware.

The performance of BioIK on the test sets was measured via MoveIt. Since MoveIt reports an exception for solutions whose error lies over a specified threshold, as this threshold cannot be influenced, no solution can be evaluated for the failed requests. This behavior is different from all other methods that are utilized in this work, as they always report at least some kind of solution. For the failed MoveIt requests, we calculated the distance between the initial rest end-effector pose and the target pose, which increases the average positional and rotational error in comparison to the other methods. The positional error lies around 0.02 to $0.05mm$ for the successful requests and would therefore outperform the presented Python-based methods.

For the GAN, 500 solutions for the same pose were generated, and the average error for every pose was calculated before the mean was taken over the whole test set. For all other methods, we only analyzed the error of the best solution for every test pose. For the GAN results, the average error of the best solution for every test pose is the average minimum error reported in Table 4.

It can be seen that the GAN model performs better for the Full workspace, while the MLP performs better for the Small workspace. The average error of the GANs is between three to ten times higher than for the MLPs. However, it was possible to improve the solutions of the GANs as well as the MLPs through optimization with Gaikpy. In general, the orientation errors of the MLPs increased while the positional errors decreased. Moreover, while the average maximum error of the GANs is near the upper limit we defined for the error, which is generally good as it indicates that most solutions are within the error limit, the success rate of the GANs can only compete with BioIK and the CycleIK MLP model through the genetic optimization. Both the MLP and GAN models can be deployed directly to real hardware without further optimization, as the positional error stays far below 1 cm on average.

The standalone Gaikpy method shows a lower average positional error than BioIK and a similar to slightly lower rotational error. The divergent success definition of BioIK is the reason that its success rate of over 98% outperforms the success rate of Gaikpy by about 3–5%, while the average error of BioIK is tremendously higher. When Gaikpy is seeded with the neural models from CycleIK, the error of the solutions can be reduced by around 60% to 90% while the timeout of the genetic algorithm can be reduced by over 98%, enabling the neuro-genetic method to directly compete with BioIK regarding success rate as well as average error. The standalone Gaikpy method overcomes both neuro-only architectures as well as the Gaikpy variant that was seeded with the GAN solutions with regard to the positional error. In contrast, Gaikpy's orientation error is higher than for all CycleIK setups, which indicates that the seeding with neural solutions increases Gaikpy's performance with regard to the orientation.

Table 4. Results of different CycleIK variants and standalone Gaikpy and BioIK on the $Small_{100}$ and $Full_{140}$ test set.

Model	Work-space	Position (mm) Avg.	Position (mm) Min./Max.	Orientation (°) Avg.	Orientation (°) Min./Max.	Success Rate (%)	Timeout (ms)
CycleIK$_{MLP}$	Small	0.295	$5.36 \cdot 10^{-4}$ / 143.56	0.033	$2.39 \cdot 10^{-4}$ / 85.73	99.48	0.242
	Full	1.022	$1.12 \cdot 10^{-3}$ / 376.39	0.152	$3.92 \cdot 10^{-4}$ / 127.41	98.49	0.243
CycleIK$_{MLP}$ w. Gaikpy	Small	0.074	$4.83 \cdot 10^{-6}$ / 245.57	0.089	$2.74 \cdot 10^{-4}$/ 93.43	99.85	19.589
	Full	0.163	$3.44 \cdot 10^{-6}$ / 271.33	0.308	$1.59 \cdot 10^{-4}$ / 128.11	99.38	19.603
CycleIK$_{GAN}$	Small	2.892	0.602 / 11.87	0.266	0.046 / 2.82	92.07	0.458
	Full	2.795	0.7 / 10.84	0.563	0.134/ 3.56	94.77	0.448
CycleIK$_{GAN}$ w. Gaikpy	Small	0.525	$6.84 \cdot 10^{-6}$ / 169.33	0.308	$4.22 \cdot 10^{-4}$ / 127.27	98.46	19.922
	Full	0.4	$9.34 \cdot 10^{-6}$ / 366.22	0.407	$7.58 \cdot 10^{-4}$ / 133.89	98.97	19.572
Gaikpy	Small	0.113	$5.16 \cdot 10^{-6}$ / 62.83	8.066	0.09 / 139.45	93.33	1022.534
	Full	0.062	$3.19 \cdot 10^{-6}$ / 100.83	5.969	0.03 / 143.06	96.06	1106.849
BioIK	Small	33.487	$1.24 \cdot 10^{-6}$ / 654.83	7.625	$1.39 \cdot 10^{-6}$ / 142.48	98.72	1
	Full	41.468	$9.93 \cdot 10^{-6}$ / 575.57	8.349	$1.54 \cdot 10^{-6}$ / 147.08	98.05	1

5 Conclusion

This work presented two novel neuro-inspired architectures for the inverse kinematics task that deliver state-of-the-art performance when compared to other bio-inspired methods. We showed that the neuro-only architectures are precise enough to be directly deployed to real-world robots. It was also shown that the solutions from the GAN, as well as the MLP architecture, can additionally be used as seeds for a genetic algorithm. The results showed that seeding the GA with the CycleIK output did not only improve the Cartesian precision of the neural solutions, but also reduced the runtime of the GA by over 98%. The weighted multi-objective function that was applied during the training of the

MLP proved to successfully support the training and made it possible to influence the kinematic behavior of the model. Finally, the importance of the presented normalizing-flow method for the IK task is underlined, as the GAN model reaches a similar precision as IKFlow and therefore has better performance than most neuro-inspired IK approaches. CycleIK will be utilized for more sophisticated experimental setups in the future, such as collision-free motion planning in human-robot interaction and multi-modal grasping.

Acknowledgements. The authors gratefully acknowledge support from the DFG (CML, MoReSpace, LeCAREbot), BMWK (SIDIMO, VERIKAS), and the European Commission (TRAIL, TERAIS).

References

1. Aguilar, O.A., Huegel, J.C.: Inverse kinematics solution for robotic manipulators using a CUDA-based parallel genetic algorithm. In: Batyrshin, I., Sidorov, G. (eds.) MICAI 2011. LNCS (LNAI), vol. 7094, pp. 490–503. Springer, Heidelberg (2011). https://doi.org/10.1007/978-3-642-25324-9_42
2. Akiba, T., Sano, S., Yanase, T., Ohta, T., Koyama, M.: Optuna: a next-generation hyperparameter optimization framework. In: Proceedings of the 25th ACM SIGKDD International Conference on Knowledge Discovery & Data Mining, KDD 2019, pp. 2623–2631. Association for Computing Machinery, New York, NY, USA (2019)
3. Ames, B., Morgan, J., Konidaris, G.: IKFlow: generating diverse inverse kinematics solutions. IEEE Robot. Autom. Lett. **7**(3), 7177–7184 (2022)
4. Ardizzone, L., Kruse, J., Rother, C., Kűthe, U.: Analyzing inverse problems with invertible neural networks. In: International Conference on Learning Representations (2019)
5. Beeson, P., Ames, B.: TRAC-IK: an open-source library for improved solving of generic inverse kinematics. In: 2015 IEEE-RAS 15th International Conference on Humanoid Robots (Humanoids), pp. 928–935 (2015)
6. Bensadoun, R., Gur, S., Blau, N., Wolf, L.: Neural inverse kinematic. In: Chaudhuri, K., Jegelka, S., Song, L., Szepesvari, C., Niu, G., Sabato, S. (eds.) Proceedings of the 39th International Conference on Machine Learning. Proceedings of Machine Learning Research, vol. 162, pp. 1787–1797. PMLR, 17–23 July 2022
7. Coleman, D., Sucan, I.A., Chitta, S., Correll, N.: Reducing the barrier to entry of complex robotic software: a moveit! case study. J. Softw. Eng. Robot. **5**(1), 3–16 (2014)
8. Hendrycks, D., Gimpel, K.: Gaussian Error Linear Units (GELUs). arXiv e-prints arXiv:1606.08415, June 2016
9. Kerzel, M., et al.: Nicol: a neuro-inspired collaborative semi-humanoid robot that bridges social interaction and reliable manipulation. arXiv e-prints arXiv:2305.08528 (2023)
10. Kerzel, M., Spisak, J., Strahl, E., Wermter, S.: Neuro-genetic visuomotor architecture for robotic grasping. In: Farkaš, I., Masulli, P., Wermter, S. (eds.) ICANN 2020. LNCS, vol. 12397, pp. 533–545. Springer, Cham (2020). https://doi.org/10.1007/978-3-030-61616-8_43

11. Kerzel, M., et al.: NICO-neuro-inspired companion: a developmental humanoid robot platform for multimodal interaction. In: 2017 26th IEEE International Symposium on Robot and Human Interactive Communication (RO-MAN), pp. 113–120 (2017)

12. Kim, S., Perez, J.: Learning reachable manifold and inverse mapping for a redundant robot manipulator. In: 2021 IEEE International Conference on Robotics and Automation (ICRA), pp. 4731–4737 (2021)

13. Kraft, D.: A Software Package for Sequential Quadratic Programming. Deutsche Forschungs- und Versuchsanstalt für Luft- und Raumfahrt Köln: Forschungsbericht, Wiss. Berichtswesen d. DFVLR (1988)

14. Lembono, T.S., Pignat, E., Jankowski, J., Calinon, S.: Learning constrained distributions of robot configurations with generative adversarial network. IEEE Robot. Autom. Lett. **6**(2), 4233–4240 (2021)

15. Oreshkin, B.N., Bocquelet, F., Harvey, F.G., Raitt, B., Laflamme, D.: Protores: proto-residual network for pose authoring via learned inverse kinematics. In: International Conference on Learning Representations (2022)

16. Ren, H., Ben-Tzvi, P.: Learning inverse kinematics and dynamics of a robotic manipulator using generative adversarial networks. Robot. Autonom. Syst. **124**, 103386 (2020)

17. Smits, R.: KDL: kinematics and dynamics library. http://www.orocos.org/kdl

18. Starke, S., Hendrich, N., Zhang, J.: A memetic evolutionary algorithm for real-time articulated kinematic motion. In: 2017 IEEE Congress on Evolutionary Computation (CEC), pp. 2473–2479 (2017)

19. Volinski, A., Zaidel, Y., Shalumov, A., DeWolf, T., Supic, L., Ezra Tsur, E.: Data-driven artificial and spiking neural networks for inverse kinematics in neurorobotics. Patterns **3**(1), 100391 (2022)

20. Zhu, J.Y., Park, T., Isola, P., Efros, A.A.: Unpaired image-to-image translation using cycle-consistent adversarial networks. In: 2017 IEEE International Conference on Computer Vision (ICCV), pp. 2242–2251 (2017)

Robot at the Mirror: Learning to Imitate via Associating Self-supervised Models

Andrej Lúčny[(✉)], Kristína Malinovská, and Igor Farkaš

Faculty of Mathematics, Physics and Informatics, Comenius University Bratislava,
Bratislava, Slovakia
{lucny,malinovska,farkas}@fmph.uniba.sk
http://cogsci.fmph.uniba.sk/cnc/

Abstract. We introduce an approach to building a custom model from ready-made self-supervised models via their associating instead of training and fine-tuning. We demonstrate it with an example of a humanoid robot looking at the mirror and learning to detect the 3D pose of its own body from the image it perceives. To build our model, we first obtain features from the visual input and the postures of the robot's body via models prepared before the robot's operation. Then we map their corresponding latent spaces by a sample-efficient robot's self-exploration at the mirror. In this way, the robot builds the solicited 3D pose detector, which quality is immediately perfect on the acquired samples instead of obtaining the quality gradually. The mapping, which employs associating the pairs of feature vectors, is then implemented in the same way as the key–value mechanism of the famous transformer models. Finally, deploying our model for imitation to a simulated robot allows us to study, tune up and systematically evaluate its hyperparameters without the involvement of the human counterpart, advancing our previous research.

Keywords: association · imitation · deep learning · humanoid robot

1 Introduction

In nature we observe different forms of skills improvement. Sometimes, it is achieved through gradual learning, for which it is necessary to undergo many repeated attempts [6]. At other times we observe that the learning process suddenly occurred based on a single experience. Although we can be amazed by the current achievements of artificial intelligence, the acquisition of most skills is gradual and very lengthy, requiring each behavior pattern to be presented many times. Would it be possible to achieve a sudden improvement in a novel task in just one attempt, given a gradually and slowly prepared set of abilities? This question is especially urgent in mobile robotics, where we already have technical means for running deep learning models on board. However, on-board training or fine-tuning these models is a capacity problem.

In our previous work [13], we addressed this issue in an imitation game [3] between a human and a humanoid robot iCub [22]. (Please, do not confuse it

L. Iliadis et al. (Eds.): ICANN 2023, LNCS 14254, pp. 471–482, 2023.
https://doi.org/10.1007/978-3-031-44207-0_39

with the imitation game in the Turing test.) The goal was to teach a robot to imitate a human based on the human imitating the robot. Learning took place in two phases. In phase 1, the robot invited the human to imitate it. The robot created different hand positions, and the human imitated them with his body in front of the robot's camera. It allowed the robot to remember the associations between its body poses and the seen images. In phase 2, the robot imitated a human using the associations acquired in the first phase.

The associations acquired by the robot in phase 1 of the imitation game represent a list of representations of the image the robot sees and the poses the robot has manifested. Technically, ensuring that the robot correctly captures the moment a person takes its pose in the first phase was challenging. However, we simplified this so the person indicated it to the robot by whistling - since his hands are busy taking the right pose while interacting. The second phase of the imitation game relied on the fact that the robot's behavior has a stimulus–response nature. However, it was necessary to solve the problem of using the associations from the first phase because the person will never again be able to take the same pose the robot memorized. Therefore, we needed to design a mechanism to derive the robot's response to a new stimulus from the associations the robot had memorized and, above all, a suitable representation of the image and pose for this mechanism to work.

We use the attention mechanism [21], a generally known part of transformers, but in an unconventional way. Our model works with a set of key–value pairs that represent obtained associations. When we have a query at the input, we try to mix it from the available keys and create the output as an analog mixture of the corresponding values.

Associating the image with the pose from the raw data is technically possible, but it does not work. The image data space is too ample, sparse, and fluid to be mapped to another data space by a few associations. Its dimensions are of order hundreds of thousands and contain all possible image inputs, most of which the robot can never see. A slight change in the seen figure can lead to a dramatic shift in the point that represents its picture. Similarly, the pose space of the robot, although much smaller (maximum tens of degrees of freedom), contains many poses that are not reasonable to adopt. A small change in the hierarchically higher degrees of freedom results in a significant difference in the generated posture.

We use deep convolutional networks that process the data into feature vectors to overcome this. Each feature vector corresponds to a possible image seen or a reasonable pose assumed or, at most, some intermediate form between two such images or poses. Moreover, these spaces are continuous and preserve similarity: the feature vectors corresponding to the gradual change of the seen situation or the adopted posture represent a trajectory in the feature space. Thanks to these properties, we were able to implement the imitation game.[1]

The robot enters the game with two ready-made models: an image encoder and a pose decoder. Both can be obtained without the need for annotation.

---

[1] see the video at https://youtu.be/-3BVbU9BeRE.

As an image encoder, we used a pre-trained backbone of a medium-sized self-supervised vision transformer trained by the DINO method [4], which encodes the image into 384 features. Next, we obtained the pose decoder by training the variational autoencoder [10] from a dataset containing the robot's hand movements to randomly selected points around the robot, i.e., obtained during the so-called robot's babbling [15]. Then, in the first phase, the robot generated a pose from several selected posture feature vectors, waited for a signal from the human that it took the correct pose, encoded the image into the features, and saved both feature vectors into the association list. In the second phase, he encoded the image into features, calculated the corresponding pose feature vector from the associations, decoded it, and took the obtained pose. At the same time, the robot could lean towards some memorized posture or combine them appropriately (however, this ability depended on the so-called scaling factor of the association mechanism). An exciting feature of this solution was that the person could deceive the robot in the first phase. The robot learned a lousy reaction if the person did something else instead of the correct pose, for example, showed an object.[2]

The weakness of this approach was the human involvement, which limited the evaluation of the quality and impact of various system parameters. At the same time, the influence of two parameters was apparent. The first was the number of associations, and the second was the scaling factor of the association mechanism. Another undesirable feature was the need to notify the robot that the associating moment had arrived.

In this paper, we eliminate these limitations. We train the robot to learn the association between its pose and image in the mirror. It allows us to obtain a (3D) robot pose detector from ready-made self-supervised models without further training or fine-tuning, only based on associating. Then we evaluate it by imitating another robot with the same or similar visage.

Compared to the original solution, we must be able to arrange for the robot to eliminate redundant associations. In addition, our solution solicits both the encoder and decoder for poses. Then, in the first phase, the robot moves in front of the mirror by choosing a random pose feature vector, decoding it, and taking this pose. During the movement of the robot's hands into the new pose, the robot knows, thanks to proprioception, which pose it is currently passing through and can associate each one with the seen image, encoding both into feature vectors and remembering this pair if it is not redundant. The second phase proceeds almost the same way as in the original solution. We will replace the mirror with a view of another robot whose body we can manipulate. Then, by comparing the poses of the two robots, we can evaluate the detector's quality. Unlike within the original imitation game, we can fully automate and assess this process objectively. As a result, we can investigate the parameters' influence and evaluate the limits of the presented approach.

---

[2] see the video at https://youtu.be/_CBnCOnWRdY.

2   Related Work

Learning by imitation [2] is frequently addressed in cognitive robotics and human–robot interaction. Typically a robot is required to imitate the human companion, as in our previous research mentioned above.

Research on neural correlates of action understanding, namely the mirror neuron system theory suggests that the association between the visual and the motor modality, maintained by these special motor neurons, which also react to visual stimuli, may be the substrate for action understanding or at least mitigate the process of assessing the visual information [20]. In our past research, we built a multi-layer connectionist model of action understanding circuitry and mirror neurons, emphasizing the bidirectional activation flow between visual and motor areas in a simulated iCub robot [17] and extended the work to perspective-agnostic mirror neurons with results corresponding to biological data [16]. The gist of our modeling is to connect the high-level representations of the visual and motor aspects of motor actions in a hetero-associative manner. This allows the robot to understand and replicate the observed action using the motor primitives already in its motor repertoire.

The novel approaches to visual imitation learning usually utilize deep networks that can learn distributions and generate novel samples within, such as the Generative Adversarial Networks (GAN) [8] and Variational Autoencoders (VAE) [10]. Generative Adversarial Imitation Learning [5] extends the reinforcement learning (RL) paradigm to utilize a smaller expert data sample. Liu et al. utilize GANs and RL to translate the robot's observation of the demonstration into different contexts, such as different viewpoints, allowing the robot to repeat the observed action. Variational Autoencoders appear even more potent than GANs within this field. Sermanet et al. [19] implement imitation learning without any labels utilizing demonstrations in the videos from two different viewpoints yielding a viewpoint-invariant representation of the relationships between the end effectors and the environment with a metric learning loss driving the system to represent the viewpoints for the same action as similar embeddings in the deep model. Similarly, Bahl et al. [1] propose a system for imitating human actions from the videos recorded in the wild. They base it on reinforcement learning with agent-agnostic representations and conditional VAE employment.

On the path towards imitation via mirroring and building associations between high-level visual and motor modality representations, Zambelli and colleagues [25] proposed a multi-modal variational autoencoder to enable the iCub robot to match different modalities up to the point of being able to imitate an observed movement. Further in this line, Seker et al. [18] proposed the new deep modality blending networks (DMBN) with the essence of variational autoencoders, which endows the system to retrieve the missing information of the associated modal information, including different perspectives in the visual data. Garello and colleagues [7] use VAE to map the self-observation and third-person observed perspectives, hence building perspective agnostic representation of actions and using a similar paradigm as our previous MNS research inspired by imitation learning in infants. Namely, the parents tend to involuntarily imitate children right after they produce an action, which could also be a mechanism of the human MNS to emerge as a consequence of Hebbian learning as proposed by Heyes [9].

Šejnová and Štepánová [23] utilized the conditional VAE to enable a robot to incrementally learn simple actions from a limited number of demonstrations by a human. Unlike our approach, the labels are presented to the VAE when the robot demonstrates the task. The advantage is that the robot's performance can be assessed during learning. If the particular action receives more training examples, it could start with a minimum of examples and perform a kind of few-shot learning. Marcel and colleagues [14] use a VAE to model self-touch behavior in developing the body schema in early infancy using a simulated iCub robot with tactile skin. In their work, they iterate through the VAE projections using it as a control loop that will finally produce a movement sequence representing a trajectory from a neutral position to the point of contact of the agent's arm and its body, just from a single stimulation point.

Similarly to our current approach, Zahra and colleagues [24] proposed a two-stage model in which a robot first acquires motor primitives by motor babbling and subsequently learns via imitation. Interestingly, unlike other approaches based on deep learning, they use more biologically relevant spiking networks and self-organizing maps for forming high-level representations of movements similar to our above-mentioned models, which use recurrent self-organizing maps.

We studied the self-recognition of a robot in the mirror in [12]. At that time, we were working with a very simplified representation of the robot body, and it was a big question for us how a robot (or a human) could create a model of its seen body. In this paper, we partially address this question.

3   Our Approach

We aim to make the robot move in front of the mirror and learn to detect its pose from the image it sees. Then we demonstrate the learned ability by imitating the movements of its twin. The twin can be perfect or can vary in textures.

At the same time, we require that learning takes place immediately, based on short-term experience, employing only ready-made models for general image processing and robot poses. Similar to the imitation game mentioned above, we will distinguish two phases. In the first phase, the robot will perceive its image in the mirror, changing due to its babbling movements. In doing so, it gathers sufficient associations between the taken pose and the seen image, but it has to solve the problem with their redundancy. In the second phase, the robot will react to the other robot we can manipulate to take a predefined set of poses.

3.1   Ready-made Models

Our solution works with three models: image encoder, pose encoder, and pose decoder. The image encoder is the pre-trained backbone of a middle-sized visual transformer trained from a large set of non-annotated images with the DINO method, i.e., in the following self-supervised way. It transforms color images with a resolution of 224×224 into feature vectors of 384 real numbers. Its quality is impressive, demonstrated by several successful applications, including pose detection (of humans). Thus we are almost sure that the vector also contains information representing the robot's pose in the image. But, of course, they are in a very raw form: we use the backbone only, while the applications mentioned above add further processing layers. The model is relatively large, but its middle-sized version can fit into the 4GB GPU. Moreover, its inference only takes 0.05 s on an ordinary gaming notebook; thus, it is very suitable for building real-time applications.

We prepare the pose encoder and decoder by training a VAE from a dataset of the proper postures of the robot. We employ the iCub humanoid robot simulator, whose arm contains five significant degrees of freedom, three in the shoulder and two in the elbow joints. Together poses of the left and right arms are coded by ten angles. We collect the dataset using the robot's babbling. We randomly generate points in the robot's vicinity and use inverse kinematics to reach them if possible. Here, inverse kinematics replaces missing feedback that disallows the robot to feel one posture more and another less comfortable. In this way, we have collected 60,000 possible poses of both arms, with the same probability of the robot using the left arm, the right arm, and both arms symmetrically and independently. Then we train the VAE on the dataset. Since the pose space has a low dimension (ten degrees of freedom), we have used just ten input, six intermediate, two feature, six intermediate, and ten output neurons. Of course, the encoder part doubles, generating both the mean and the standard deviation logarithm as typical for VAEs. We have used ReLU and tanh activations since we converted joint angles from −180° to 180° into the range −1 to 1. Before training, we shuffled the dataset and split it into 50,000 training and 10,000 testing examples. The training required ten epochs with batch size 32 and took mere 92 s. Finally, we distilled the encoder and decoder parts of the trained model and saved them. Thus the encoder converts ten angles into two features, and the decoder the two features back to the ten angles.[3]

3.2   Association Mechanism

We employ an association mechanism known as attention [21]. It works with a set of l key–value pairs. When we have a query q as an input, we try to mix it from keys K and create the output as an analog mix from the corresponding values V, where

$$K = \begin{pmatrix} k_1 \\ k_2 \\ \vdots \\ k_l \end{pmatrix} \qquad V = \begin{pmatrix} v_1 \\ v_2 \\ \vdots \\ v_l \end{pmatrix} \tag{1}$$

All queries q and keys k_l are vectors of the dimension n, so K is an $l \times n$ matrix. Values v_l and outputs are vectors of the dimension m, so V is an $l \times m$ matrix.

---

[3] see the video at https://youtu.be/ZNkF5BTKOLU.

First, we find $c_i \in \langle 0, 1 \rangle$ that $\sum c_i k_i = pr_K(q)$, $\sum c_i = 1$, and $i = 1, 2, ..., l$, where $pr_K(q)$ is a vector similar to the projection of q into the subspace generated by the keys K. In doing so, we want c_i to express the similarity between the key k_i and the query q, so we can derive it from the dot product of $q^T k_i$, proportional to the angle that q and k_i make.

First, however, we have to get these similarities (positive for same, zero for perpendicular, and negative for opposite vectors) to $\langle 0, 1 \rangle$, which we can obtain by the function:

$$\text{softmax}(x_i) = \frac{\exp(x_i)}{\sum_k \exp(x_k)} \tag{2}$$

The coefficients with which we mix the keys k_i into something similar to the query q we, therefore, choose as:

$$c = \text{softmax}(\frac{qK^T}{d}), \tag{3}$$

where d is a constant that enables us to scale how much we mix from similar keys and how much from different ones. The smaller this constant is, the closer the coefficients are to the one-hot encoding. For $d = 1/n$, where n is the dimension of the keys, we always lean towards the dominance of one key, while the value $d = \sqrt{n}$ ensures that we constantly mix a little from the other keys. A proper d can be beneficial for the association mechanism to find the correct response, even for queries for which no similar key was memorized but can be expressed as a transition between two memorized keys. When we have the mixture coefficients c, which roughly correspond to the query, we can analogically mix the values of V to the output $o = cV$. So the complete response of the association mechanism A to a query q is calculated as:

$$A(q, K, V) = \text{softmax}\left(\frac{qK^T}{d}\right) V \tag{4}$$

The response of the attention mechanism to a query is the same as on its orthogonal projection to the subspace generated by keys:

$$A(q, K, V) = A(pr_K^{\text{ort}}(q), K, V) \tag{5}$$

since $qk_l = pr_K^{\text{ort}}(q)k_l$. This way, the mechanism generalizes when the query does not lie in the subspace generated by keys. Of course, the generalization is as good as the latent space is close to linear.

3.3   Technical Remarks

For implementation, we need a humanoid robot; we employ iCubSim, the simulator of the iCub robot [22]. We control it from Python via pyicubsim and OpenCV libraries. Further, we have used ONNX runtime for running the image encoder model. We do not need to train it; we have used a pre-trained backbone. We used Keras for training the VAE for postures, dissected its encoder and decoder parts, and converted them from h5 into the pb format for running under OpenCV. We have implemented the association mechanism in NumPy. Since the system operates in real-time, the integration employs a blackboard architecture [11] that helps us to combine slower and faster processes.

3.4 Method

We have a system with an image encoder F (perception), posture decoder G (action), and posture encoder H (proprioception). F transforms input images into feature vectors in the latent space L_F, H encodes posture features into $L_{G,H}$, and G decodes them back into the postures. The system has three parameters: the scaling factor d of the association mechanism, the mapping accuracy ε, and a termination condition (number of the collected pairs t). We can summarize the system operation into two phases in Algorithm 1.

Algorithm 1. Learning to imitate via association

F is image encoder, G is posture decoder, H is posture encoder
A is the association mechanism, K keys, V values
d is the scaling factor of A, ε is accuracy, t is the number of collected pairs

procedure PHASE 1(F,G,H,K,L,d,ε)   ▷ Learning mirror self-recognition
$\quad K = L = [\,]$ ▷ start with empty lists of keys and values
$\quad$**loop**
$\qquad i \leftarrow input()$ ▷ grab the image seen in the mirror
$\qquad k \leftarrow F(i)$ ▷ encode the image into a point in L_F
$\qquad p \leftarrow proprioception()$ ▷ get the current posture
$\qquad v \leftarrow H(p)$ ▷ encode the posture into a point in $L_{G,H}$
$\qquad w \leftarrow A(k, K, V, d)$ ▷ potential response w of A to k
$\qquad$**if** $\|v - w\| > \varepsilon$ **then**   ▷ if w differs from v too much
$\qquad\quad K \leftarrow K \cup \{k\}$ ▷ add k into keys K
$\qquad\quad V \leftarrow V \cup \{v\}$ ▷ add v into values V
$\qquad\quad$**if** $len(K) = t$ **then** exit   ▷ termination condition
$\qquad$**if** $undefined(o) \vee p \doteq o$ **then**   ▷ if the babbling movement is done
$\qquad\quad v \leftarrow random()$ ▷ generate a point in $L_{G,H}$
$\qquad\quad o \leftarrow G(v)$ ▷ decode it into angles of the new goal posture
$\qquad\quad output(o)$ ▷ set the goal posture, i.e., start a new babbling movement

procedure PHASE 2(F,G,H,K,L,d,ε)   ▷ Imitation
$\quad$**loop**
$\qquad i \leftarrow input()$ ▷ grab the seen image
$\qquad q \leftarrow F(i)$ ▷ encode the image into a point in L_F
$\qquad v \leftarrow A(q, K, V)$ ▷ response v of A to q
$\qquad o \leftarrow G(v)$ ▷ decode v to the posture o
$\qquad output(o)$ ▷ set the posture

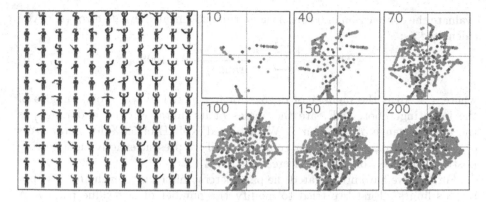

Fig. 1. *Left:* Visualization of the pose latent space with topographic organization. *Right:* Development of the key–value pairs over time. The red points represent the collected keys, and the green ones are redundant. (Color figure online)

In phase 1, we start babbling in front of the mirror and gradually collect keys K (image features) and values V (posture features) that provide us with mapping of L_F to $L_{G,H}$. We avoid redundant key–value pairs by checking the response of the association mechanism (Fig. 1). The babbling aims to reach a random but proper pose as we decode it from random features. In phase 2, we use the collected associations to imitate another robot (Fig. 2).[4]

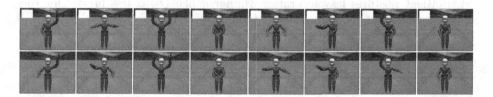

Fig. 2. An example of the learning imitation at the mirror via association. *Top:* The testing postures and their points in the latent space. *Bottom:* Imitated poses.

4   Results and Discussion

Both phases of our algorithm are fully automated so that we can assess its quality objectively (concerning the random nature of the babbling in phase 1). First, we prepare a batch of pose feature vectors corresponding to several good poses (Fig. 2) that we have not intentionally presented to the robot during phase 1. Then we manipulate another copy of the robot (i.e., we run phase 2), wait until the imitation finishes, and compare the postures of the two robots. Finally, we

---

[4] see the video at https://youtu.be/G6xWAKDMpsM.

evaluate the comparison in terms of the normalized mean absolute error (NMAE) calculated as:

$$\text{NMAE} = \frac{1}{s} \sum_{j=0}^{s-1} \frac{|\text{DoF}_j - \text{DoF}'_j|}{\text{range}_j} \cdot 100\% \tag{6}$$

where $s = 10$ is the number of degrees of freedom, DoF'_j are joints angles of the imitating robot, DoF_j are the angles of its imitated twin, and range_j is the angular range of the joint j. We achieved NMAE of 5.0% for parameters $d = \sqrt{384}$, $\varepsilon = 0.2$, $t = 100$. For comparison, if we present exactly eight testing postures to the robot, NMAE decreases to 1.14%.

Further, we have investigated the parameters' influence to evaluate this approach's limits. First, we tried to modify the number of key–value pairs t. A higher number enables us to map the latent spaces more precisely. However, the too-high value decreases the ability of the association mechanism to generalize the mapping. Many irrelevant items are within the $n = 384$ features the employed image encoder provides. Therefore t should be significantly lower than the dimension of keys. If they are equal, and the keys are diverse enough, the projection $pr_K(q)$ always equals the query q. As a result, there is not much generalization. For instance, if we change the viewpoint or the robot's color from red to blue, we could fail to recognize its posture. Therefore, the t providing the most stable behavior is about 200 (Fig. 3 left).

Second, we investigated the influence of the scaling factor of the association mechanism d. We fixed t and ε and tried to vary d. Lower d like $\frac{1}{n}$ (n is the dimension of keys) achieves a low error for the collected values but approximates the transient postures less accurately. Higher d like $\sqrt{n}$ is less precise for the collected values but generally more suitable (Fig. 3 right).

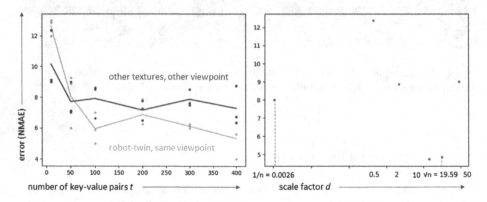

Fig. 3. The dependence of NMAE on the number of key-value pairs (left) and on the scaling factor of the association mechanism (right).

Finally, we believe the achieved error could be lower if we train a better VAE of poses. During its training, we followed the accuracy given by encoding and decoding the postures. However, it could be profitable also to consider the accuracy of decoding and encoding of the posture feature vectors.

5 Conclusion

In this paper, we investigated our approach to learning imitation by association. We presented an experiment in which a robot learns its posture model from its images seen in the mirror. We designed the procedure such that we could not only test our approach but also be able to objectively evaluate its quality and examine the impact of changing the parameters.

Our approach is technically interesting, mainly for mobile robots that can use deep learning models on board but lack the capacity for training and fine-tuning. In parallel, from the cognitive science viewpoint, we shed light on body modeling from seen images necessary for performing the imitation task. Namely, we point out that it can emerge quickly, stemming from the gradually developed general models dealing with perception and action separately.

The results of our experimentation provide us with several ideas for further development. We intend to prepare better output models with a more advanced association mechanism in the future.

We share the code at https://github.com/andylucny/learningImitation.

Acknowledgements. This work was supported by the EU-funded project TERAIS, no. 101079338, and partly by the national VEGA 1/0373/23 project.

References

1. Bahl, S., Gupta, A., Pathak, D.: Human-to-robot imitation in the wild. arXiv preprint arXiv:2207.09450 (2022)
2. Bandera, J.P., Rodriguez, J.A., Molina-Tanco, L., Bandera, A.: A survey of vision-based architectures for robot learning by imitation. Int. J. Humanoid Robot. **9**, 1250006 (2012). world Scientific Publishing Company https://doi.org/10.1142/S0219843612500065
3. Boucenna, S., Anzalone, S., Tilmont, E., Cohen, D., Chetouani, M.: Learning of social signatures through imitation game between a robot and a human partner. IEEE Trans. Auton. Mental Dev. **6**(3), 213–225 (2014). https://doi.org/10.1109/TAMD.2014.2319861
4. Caron, M., et al.: Emerging properties in self-supervised vision transformers. In: Proceedings of the International Conference on Computer Vision, ICCV (2021)
5. Dai, T., Liu, H., Anthony Bharath, A.: Episodic self-imitation learning with hindsight. Electronics **9**(10) (2020). https://doi.org/10.3390/electronics9101742
6. Dennett, D.C.: Kinds of Minds: Towards an Understanding of Consciousness. Weidenfeld & Nicolson, London (1996)
7. Garello, L., Rea, F., Noceti, N., Sciutti, A.: Towards third-person visual imitation learning using generative adversarial networks. In: IEEE International Conference on Development and Learning (ICDL), pp. 121–126 (2022)
8. Goodfellow, I.: Generative adversarial networks. Neural Inf. Process. Syst. (2016)

9. Heyes, C.: Where do mirror neurons come from? Neurosci. Biobehav. Rev. **34**(4), 575–83 (2010)
10. Kingma, D.P., Welling, M.: An introduction to variational autoencoders. Found. Trends Mach. Learn. **12**(4), 307–392 (2019)
11. Lúčny, A.: Building complex systems with agent-space architecture. Comput. Inf. **23**(1), 1–36 (2004)
12. Lúčny, A.: iCubSim at the mirror. In: Proceedings of EUCognition. Vienna (2016)
13. Lúčny, A.: Towards one-shot learning via attention. In: CEUR Workshop Proceedings, ITAT 2022, pp. 4–11. 3226 (2022)
14. Marcel, V., OâĂŹRegan, J.K., Hoffmann, M.: Learning to reach to own body from spontaneous self-touch using a generative model. In: IEEE International Conference on Development and Learning (ICDL), pp. 328–335 (2022)
15. Petrovich, M., Black, M.J., Varol, G.: Action-conditioned 3D human motion synthesis with transformer VAE. In: International Conference on Computer Vision, ICCV (2021)
16. Pospíchal, J., Farkaš, I., Pecháč, M., Malinovská, K.: Modeling self-organized emergence of perspective in/variant mirror neurons in a robotic system. In: Joint IEEE 9th International Conference on Development and Learning and Epigenetic Robotics (ICDL-EpiRob), pp. 278–283 (2019)
17. Rebrová K., Pecháč M., Farkaš I.: Towards a robotic model of the mirror neuron system. In: International Conference on Development and Learning and on Epigenetic Robotics, IEEE (2013)
18. Seker, M.Y., Ahmetoglu, A., Nagai, Y., Asada, M., Oztop, E., Ugur, E.: Imitation and mirror systems in robots through deep modality blending networks. Neural Netw. **146**, 22–35 (2022). https://doi.org/10.1016/j.neunet.2021.11.004
19. Sermanet, P., et al.: Time-contrastive networks: Self-supervised learning from video. In: IEEE International Conference on Robotics and Automation (ICRA), pp. 1134–1141 (2018)
20. Tessitore, G., Prevete, R., Catanzariti, E., Tamburrini, G.: From motor to sensory processing in mirror neuron computational modelling. Biol. Cybern. **103**(6), 471–485 (2010)
21. Vaswani, A., et al.: Attention is all you need. In: 31st International Conference on Neural Information Processing Systems, ACM (2017)
22. Vernon, D., Metta, G., Sandini, G.: The iCub cognitive architecture: Interactive development in a humanoid robot. In: IEEE 6th International Conference on Development and Learning, pp. 122–127 (2007)
23. Šejnová, G., Štěpánová, K.: Feedback-driven incremental imitation learning using sequential VAE. In: IEEE International Conference on Development and Learning (ICDL), pp. 238–243 (2022)
24. Zahra, O., Tolu, S., Zhou, P., Duan, A., Navarro-Alarcon, D.: A bio-inspired mechanism for learning robot motion from mirrored human demonstrations. Frontiers Neurorobot. **16** (2022). https://doi.org/10.3389/fnbot.2022.826410
25. Zambelli, M., Cully, A., Demiris, Y.: Multimodal representation models for prediction and control from partial information. Robot. Autonom. Syst. **123**, 103312 (2020)

Approximation of Binary-Valued Functions by Networks of Finite VC Dimension

Věra Kůrková[✉][iD]

Institute of Computer Science of the Czech Academy of Sciences,
Pod Vodárenskou věží 2, 18207 Prague, Czech Republic
vera@cs.cas.cz

Abstract. Distributions of errors in approximation of binary-valued functions by networks with sets of input-output functions of finite VC dimension is investigated. Conditions on concentration of approximation errors around their mean values are derived in terms of growth functions of sets of input-output functions. Limitations of approximation capabilities of networks of finite VC dimension are discussed.

Keywords: approximation by neural networks · bounds on approximation errors · VC dimension · growth function · high-dimensional probability · concentration inequalities · method of bounded differences

1 Introduction

Theoretical investigation of capabilities of feedforward networks have mostly been devoted to questions related to approximation of continuous functions on infinite domains (see, e.g., [1–3] and references therein). Instead, our approach is focused on approximation of functions on *finite domains*. Such domains model finite sets of data (formed e.g., by regular grids or scattered vectors in $\mathbb{R}^d$) that neural networks process in real applications.

The advantage of our approach is that real-valued functions on finite domains can be represented as *vectors in finite dimensional Euclidean spaces* of dimensions equal to the sizes of the functions' domains. Errors in their approximation by neural networks can then be studied in terms of Euclidean distances in $\mathbb{R}^m$, where m is the size of the domain. Typically, sets of data to be processes are large, so vectors modeling input-output functions are high-dimensional. Thus properties of high-dimensional geometry (see, e.g., [4–9]) can be exploited for study of approximation capabilities of feedforward networks.

In this paper, we explore distributions of errors in approximation of binary-valued functions on large finite domains by neural networks in terms of concepts from statistical learning theory. For this aim we employ the property of high-dimensional geometry called *concentration of measure*. It was discovered in statistical physics in study of distributions of velocities of large numbers

L. Iliadis et al. (Eds.): ICANN 2023, LNCS 14254, pp. 483–490, 2023.
https://doi.org/10.1007/978-3-031-44207-0_40

of molecules (see, e.g., [6]). Its first mathematical formulation appeared in the work of Lévy [10] who proved that values of a Lipschitz function on a high-dimensional sphere concentrate around their median. Mathematical theory of concentration of measure in a general setting of normed linear spaces together with related isoperimetric inequalities was elaborated by Milman and Shechtman [11]. A discrete version of this phenomena was independently discovered in high-dimensional probability by Chernoff [12] and Hoeffding [13] (see also the survey [14]).

We explore concentration of errors in approximation of binary-valued functions by neural networks using one of the tools from high-dimensional probability called McDiarmid Inequality [15]. It implies that functions on high-dimensional Hamming cubes $\{-1, 1\}^m$, which are sufficiently smooth, concentrate around their mean values. We apply this concentration theorem to neural networks of finite VC-dimension [16]. Combining concentration of measure and estimates of growth of sizes of sets of input-output functions, we derive conditions for concentration of approximation errors in terms of VC dimension.

The paper is organized as follows. Section 2 introduces basic concepts and notations on approximation of functions on finite domains. In Sect. 3, probabilistic estimates of approximation errors and conditions for their concentration in terms growth functions of sets of network input-output functions are proven. In Sect. 4, there are derived consequences of concentration of measure properties of hight-dimensional probability for limitations of capabilities of function approximation of neural networks of finite VC dimension. In Sect. 5, possible extensions of our results are discussed.

2 Preliminaries

We investigate approximation of binary-valued functions (classifiers) on finite domains $X \subset \mathbb{R}^d$ by feedforward multilayer networks with single threshold outputs.

For any $U \subset \mathbb{R}^d$ we denote by

$$\mathcal{S}(U) := \{f \mid f : U \to \{-1, 1\}\}$$

the *set of all binary-valued functions on U*, and by

$$\mathcal{F}(U) := \{f : U \to \mathbb{R}\}$$

the *set of all real-valued functions on U*. For any $X \subset U$ and any $\mathcal{H} \subset \mathcal{F}(U)$ we denote by

$$\mathcal{H}_X := \{g_{|X} : X \to \{-1, 1\} \mid g \in \mathcal{H}\}$$

the set of functions on X obtained by restricting functions from $\mathcal{H}$ to X.

Let $X := \{x_1, \ldots, x_m\} \subset \mathbb{R}^d$ be a domain of functions to be computed (modeling a set of data to be potentially processed by a class of neural networks). We identify $\mathcal{F}(X)$ with the finite dimensional Euclidean space $\mathbb{R}^{\operatorname{card} X} = \mathbb{R}^m$ and

$\mathcal{S}(X)$ with its subset $\{-1,1\}^{\text{card}X} = \{-1,1\}^m$ (in coding theory, it is called the Hamming cube). The advantage of the range $\{-1,1\}$ instead of $\{0,1\}$ is that all functions from X to $\{-1,1\}$ have l_2-norms equal to $\sqrt{m}$.

$\mathcal{F}(X)$ inherits from $\mathbb{R}^m$ the inner product $\langle f, h \rangle = \sum_{i=1}^m f(x_i)h(x_i)$ and the l_2-distance

$$\|f - h\|_2 = \sqrt{\sum_{i=1}^m (f(x_i) - h(x_i))^2}.$$

For $f \in \mathcal{S}(X)$ and $\mathcal{H} \subset \mathcal{S}(X)$, we denote by

$$\|f - \mathcal{H}_X\|_2 := \min_{h \in \mathcal{H}_X} \|f - h\|_2$$

the distance of f from the set $\mathcal{H}_X$, which represents the l_2-error in approximation of f by the set $\mathcal{H}_X$ (for X finite, the $\inf_{h \in \mathcal{H}} \|f - h\|_2$ is achieved and thus we write minimum instead of infimum).

We consider classes of *multilayer feedforward networks with fixed architectures and fixed types of computational units* and varying parameters. Their sets of input-output functions are parameterized families of functions. Here, we focus on feedforward networks with only one output unit in the last L-th layer. We assume that the output unit is a signum perceptron, which computes

$$\text{sgn}(\sum_{i=1}^k v_i y_i + b),$$

where y_i are outputs of units in the $(l-1)$-st layer, $v_i \in \mathbb{R}$ are weights, $b \in \mathbb{R}$ is a bias, and sgn denotes the signum function $\text{sgn} : \mathbb{R} \to \mathbb{R}$ defined as

$$\text{sgn}(t) = -1 \text{ for } t < 0 \text{ and } \text{sgn}(t) = 1 \text{ for } t \geq 0.$$

So we investigate networks computing sets of input-output functions which are subsets of $\mathcal{S}(X)$.

3   Probabilistic Estimates of Approximation Errors

An advantage of focusing on finite input domains is that sets of all input-output functions of networks with binary-valued outputs are finite. We show that their sizes play an important role in analysis of distributions of approximation errors.

Sizes of sets of functions induced on finite sets by various families of binary-valued functions have long been studied in statistical learning theory. Vapnik and Chervonenkis [16] defined the *growth function* $\Pi_{\mathcal{H}}(m) : \mathbb{N}_+ \to \mathbb{N}_+$ of any set $\mathcal{H} \subseteq \mathcal{S}(U)$ of binary-valued functions on any set $U \subset \mathbb{R}^d$ as

$$\Pi_{\mathcal{H}}(m) := \max_{X \subset U, \text{card}X = m} \text{card}(\mathcal{H}_{|X}).$$

So the growth function measures the maximal size that a given family of binary-valued functions $\mathcal{H}$ can induce on an m-point subset of U. Here we apply this measure to sets of input-output functions of multilayer feedforward networks with single signum perceptron outputs.

To prove a probabilistic bound on errors in approximation by neural networks in terms of growth functions, we employ one theorem of concentration measure type called the McDiarmid Bound [15]. This bound proves concentration of values of functions of independent random variables, which satisfy a discrete smoothness condition requiring that the function does not vary too much if one of its variables is changed. We call a function $\phi : B_1 \times \ldots \times B_m \to \mathbb{R}$ *coordinate-wise Lipschitz* with parameters $c_1, \ldots, c_m$ if for all $i = 1, \ldots, m$ and all vectors $b, b' \in B_1 \times \ldots \times B_m$ that differ only in the i-th coordinate,

$$|\phi(b) - \phi(b')| \leq c_i. \tag{1}$$

The following version of the McDiarmid Bound is from [17, p.70], where it was presented as one of the concentration bounds called *methods of bounded differences*.

Theorem 1. *[17, p.70] Let $\phi : B_1 \times \ldots \times B_m \to \mathbb{R}$ be a coordinate-wise Lipschitz function with the vector of parameters $c := (c_1, \ldots, c_m)$, and $Y_1, \ldots, Y_m$ be independent random variables with values in ranges $B_1, \ldots, B_m$, resp. Then for every $t > 0$,*

$$\mathrm{P}\Big[\, |\phi(Y_1, \ldots, Y_m) - E(\phi)| > t \Big] \leq e^{-2t^2/\|c\|_2^2}. \tag{2}$$

Note that Theorem 1 implies concentration of values of ϕ around its mean value $E(\phi)$ only for sufficiently small $\|c\|_2^2$.

We apply Theorem 1 to functions representing errors in approximation by feedforward networks. For a randomly chosen function f from $\mathcal{S}(X)$, let

$$Y_1 = f(x_1), \ldots, Y_m = f(x_m)$$

be random variables with values in $\{-1, 1\}$ induced by f. For any $h \in \mathcal{S}(X)$ we denote by

$$\phi_h(Y_1, \ldots, Y_m) := \sum_{i=1}^{m} (Y_i - h(x_i))^2$$

the function assigning to f the square $\|f - h\|_2^2$ of its l_2-distance from h.

Our main theorem gives an estimate of a distribution of approximation errors of uniformly randomly chosen functions from $\mathcal{S}(X)$ in terms of the growth function of an approximating set $\mathcal{H}_X$ (in particular, a set of input-output functions of a class of networks with binary-valued outputs).

Theorem 2. *Let $\mathcal{H} \subset \mathcal{S}(U)$, where $U \subset \mathbb{R}^d$, $m \in \mathbb{N}_+$, $X \subset U$ with $\mathrm{card}\, X = m$, $\mathcal{H}_X = \{h_{|X} \,|\, h \subset \mathcal{H}\}$, and $\lambda > 0$. Then for every $f \in \mathcal{S}(X)$ uniformly randomly chosen from $\mathcal{S}(X)$,*

(i) $\mathrm{P}\Big[\|f - \mathcal{H}_X\|_2^2 \leq 2m + m\lambda\Big] > 1 - e^{-\frac{m\lambda^2}{8}}$;

(ii) $\mathrm{P}\Big[2m - m\lambda \leq \|f - \mathcal{H}_X\|_2^2\Big] > 1 - \Pi_{\mathcal{H}}(m)\, e^{-\frac{m\lambda^2}{8}}$.

Proof. Let $f \in \mathcal{S}(X)$ be uniformly randomly chosen and $Y_1 = f(x_1), \ldots, Y_m = f(x_m)$ be independent random variables with values in $\{-1, 1\}$ induced by f. First, we verify that for every $h \in \mathcal{H}_X$, the function $\phi_h : \{-1, 1\}^m \to \mathbb{R}$ is coordinate-wise Lipschitz with "small" coefficients. Without loss of generality, we assume that the two vector variables differ in the first variable. Then we get $|\phi_h(1, b_2, \ldots, b_m) - \phi_h(-1, b_2, \ldots, b_m)| \leq 4$. So ϕ_h is coordinate-wise Lipschitz with all parameters $c_i = 4$. Hence $\|c\|_2^2 = \sum_{i=1}^m c_i^2 = 16m$.

By symmetry of the uniform distribution, for all $h \in \mathcal{S}(X)$ we have $E(\langle f, h \rangle) = 0$ and so $E(\phi_h(Y_1, \ldots, Y_m)) = 2m$. Setting $t := m\lambda$, we get

$$2t^2/\|c\|_2^2 = (2m^2\lambda^2)/(16m) = (m\lambda^2)/8.$$

Thus by Theorem 1 for all $h \in \mathcal{S}(X)$ and for f uniformly randomly chosen from $\mathcal{S}(X)$,

$$P\left[\left|\, \|f - h\|_2^2 - 2m \,\right| > m\lambda\right] \leq e^{-\frac{m\lambda^2}{8}}. \tag{3}$$

As for all $h \in \mathcal{H}_X$ $\|f - \mathcal{H}\|_2^2 \leq \|f - h\|_2^2$, the upper bound (i) follows from (3). The lower bound (ii) follows from

$$P\left[2m - m\lambda \leq \|f - \mathcal{H}_X\|_2^2\right] \geq P\left[(\forall h \in \mathcal{H}_X)\left(2m - m\lambda < \|f - h\|_2^2\right)\right] \geq$$

$$1 - \mathrm{card}\mathcal{H}_X \, e^{-\frac{m\lambda^2}{8}} \geq 1 - \Pi_{\mathcal{H}}(m)\, e^{-\frac{m\lambda^2}{8}}.$$

$\square$

As all functions in $\mathcal{S}(X)$ have norms $\sqrt{m}$, we can also consider bounds following from Theorem 2 for normalized functions. We denote

$$h^\circ := \frac{h}{\|h\|_2} \text{ and } \mathcal{H}_X^\circ := \{h^\circ \mid h \in \mathcal{H}_X\}.$$

By normalizing, we get from Theorem 2

$$P\left[\|f^\circ - \mathcal{H}_X^\circ\|_2^2 \leq 2 + \lambda\right] > 1 - e^{-\frac{m\lambda^2}{8}}$$

$$P\left[2 - \lambda \leq \|f^\circ - \mathcal{H}_X^\circ\|_2^2\right] > 1 - \Pi_{\mathcal{H}}(m)\, e^{-\frac{m\lambda^2}{8}}. \tag{4}$$

For example, setting $\lambda := m^{-1/4}$ the bound (4) implies the lower bound

$$P\left[2 - m^{-1/4} \leq \|f^\circ - \mathcal{H}_X^\circ\|_2^2\right] > 1 - \Pi_{\mathcal{H}}(m)\, e^{-\frac{m^{1/2}}{8}}$$

on the probability of an error in approximation of a uniformly randomly chosen f by a set of network input-output functions with the growth function $\Pi_{\mathcal{H}}(m)$.

4   Approximation by Networks with Finite VC Dimension

Theorem 2 and the bound (4) show that growth functions play a critical role in approximation capabilities of neural networks. In particular, networks with sets of input-output functions having polynomially increasing growth functions cannot well approximate most functions on large domains.

The following theorem by Vapnik and Chervonenkis [16, Theorem 1] states that a growth function $\Pi_{\mathcal{H}}(m)$ is either equal to 2^m or it is bounded by a polynomial.

Theorem 3. *[16, Theorem 1] For any set U and a subset $\mathcal{H}$ of $\mathcal{S}(U)$ either $\Pi_{\mathcal{H}}(m) = 2^m$ or $\Pi_{\mathcal{H}}(m) \leq m^r + 1$, where $r = \min\{s \mid \Pi_{\mathcal{H}}(s) < 2^s\}$.*

The growth function is related to the *VC-dimension* defined as

$$\dim_{VC} \mathcal{H} := \max\{m \in \mathbb{N}_+ \mid \Pi_{\mathcal{H}}(m) = 2^m\}.$$

The following bounds are known as the Shelah-Sauer Lemma [18,19], although they were proven earlier by Vapnik and Chervonenkis [16].

$$\Pi_{\mathcal{H}}(m) \leq \sum_{i=0}^{\dim_{VC}} \binom{m}{i} \tag{5}$$

and for $m \geq \dim_{VC}$,

$$\Pi_{\mathcal{H}}(m) \leq \left(\frac{em}{\dim_{VC}}\right)^{\dim_{VC}}. \tag{6}$$

Thus the growth function of a family of functions with finite VC-dimension is bounded from above by a polynomial of degree equal to the VC-dimension. Combining Theorem 2 with the equation (6) we obtain for $m \geq \dim_{VC}$ the following lower bound

$$\mathrm{P}\left[2m - m\lambda \leq \|f - \mathcal{H}_X\|_2^2\right] > 1 - \left(\frac{m}{\dim_{VC}}\right)^{\dim_{VC}} e^{\dim_{VC} - \frac{m\lambda^2}{2}} \tag{7}$$

on errors in approximation by networks with sets of inut-output functions $\mathcal{H}_X$ where $\mathrm{card}X = m$. By the bound (7) for a sufficiently large m (such that $\frac{m\lambda^2}{2}$ outweighs $\dim_{VC}(\mathcal{H})$), almost all binary-valued functions on a domain X of the size m have large errors in approximation by networks computing input-output functions from $\mathcal{H}$.

5   Discussion

We showed that growth functions of sets of input-output functions have an impact on almost deterministic behavior of approximation errors of uniformly randomly chosen binary-valued functions on large finite domains. Most of such functions have large errors in approximation by networks of finite VC dimension. So there is a trade-off between finite VC dimension and accuracy in approximation by feedforward networks.

Our probabilistic bounds assume that we have no prior knowledge about classification tasks or that all binary classifiers have the same importance. In such cases, the probability according to which random classifiers are chosen has to be uniform. In real applications, probabilities of tasks are not likely to be uniform. We investigated non uniform distributions of correlations of classifiers with network units in [20]. Influence of network depth and numbers of its parameters are subject of our paper [21]. Extension of probabilistic bounds for binary-valued functions to real-valued ones is a subject of our work in progress.

Acknowledgments. This work was partially supported by the Czech Science Foundation grant 22-02067S and the institutional support of the Institute of Computer Science RVO 67985807.

References

1. Kainen, P.C., Kůrková, V., Sanguineti, M.: Dependence of computational models on input dimension: tractability of approximation and optimization tasks. IEEE Trans. Inf. Theor. **58**, 1203–1214 (2012)
2. Telgarsky, M.: Benefits of depth in neural networks. Proc. Mach. Learn. Res. **49**, 1517–1539 (2016)
3. Yarotsky, D.: Error bounds for approximations with deep ReLU networks. Neural Netw. **94**, 103–114 (2017)
4. Gorban, A., Tyukin, I., Prokhorov, D., Sofeikov, K.: Approximation with random bases: pro et contra. Inf. Sci. **364–365**, 129–145 (2016)
5. Gorban, A., Tyukin, I.: Blessing of dimensionality: mathematical foundations of the statistical physics of data. Philos. Trans. Royal Soc. A **376**, 2017–2037 (2018)
6. Gorban, A.N., Makarov, V.A., Tyukin, I.Y.: The unreasonable effectiveness of small neural ensembles in high-dimensional brain. Phys. Life Rev. **29**, 55–88 (2019)
7. Kůrková, V., Sanguineti, M.: Model complexities of shallow networks representing highly varying functions. Neurocomputing **171**, 598–604 (2016)
8. Kůrková, V., Sanguineti, M.: Probabilistic lower bounds for approximation by shallow perceptron networks. Neural Netw. **91**, 34–41 (2017)
9. Kůrková, V.: Some insights from high-dimensional spheres. Phys. Life Rev. **29**, 98–100 (2019)
10. Lévy, P., Pellegrino, F.: Problémes concrets d'analyse fonctionnelle. Gauthier-Villars, Paris (1951)
11. Milman, V., Schechtman, G.: Asymptotic theory of finite dimensional normed spaces. Volume 1200 of Lecture Notes in Mathematics. Springer-Verlag (1986)
12. Chernoff, H.: A measure of asymptotic efficiency for tests of a hypothesis based on the sum of observations. Ann. Math. Stat. **23**, 493–507 (1952)
13. Hoeffding, W.: Probability inequalities for sums of bounded random variables. J. Am. Stat. Assoc. **58**, 13–30 (1963)
14. Vershynin, R.: High-Dimensional Probability. University of California, Irvine (2020)

15. McDiarmid, C.: On the method of bounded differences. In: Siemons, J. (ed.) Surveys in Combinatorics, pp. 148–188. Cambridge University Press, Cambridge (1989)
16. Vapnik, V.N., Chervonenkis, A.Y.: On the uniform convergence of relative frequencies of events to their probabilities. Dokl. Akad. Nauk SSSR **16**(2), 264–279 (1971)
17. Dubhashi, D., Panconesi, A.: Concentration of Measure for the Analysis of Randomized Algorithms. Cambridge University Press (2009)
18. Shelah, S.: A combinatorial problem; stability and order for models and theories in infinitary languages. Pac. J. Math. **41**, 247–261 (1972)
19. Sauer, N.: On the density of families of sets. J. Comb. Theor. **13**, 145–147 (1972)
20. Kůrková, V., Sanguineti, M.: Correlations of random classifiers on large data sets. Soft. Comput. **25**(19), 12641–12648 (2021). https://doi.org/10.1007/s00500-021-05938-4
21. Kůrková, V., Sanguineti, M.: Approximation of classifiers by deep perceptron networks. Neural Netw. **165**, 654–661 (2023)

Color-Dependent Prediction Stability of Popular CNN Image Classification Architectures

Laurent Mertens[1,2,3](✉), Elahe' Yargholi[4], Jan Van den Stock[5,6], Hans Op de Beeck[4], and Joost Vennekens[1,2,3]

[1] Department of Computer Science, KU Leuven, De Nayer Campus, J.-P. De Nayerlaan 5, 2860 Sint-Katelijne-Waver, Belgium
[2] Leuven.AI - KU Leuven Institute for AI, 3000 Leuven, Belgium
laurent.mertens@kuleuven.be
[3] Flanders Make@KU Leuven, Leuven, Belgium
[4] Department of Brain and Cognition, Faculty of Psychology and Educational Sciences, Leuven Brain Institute, KU Leuven, 3000 Leuven, Belgium
[5] Neuropsychiatry, Leuven Brain Institute, KU Leuven, 3000 Leuven, Belgium
[6] Geriatric Psychiatry, University Psychiatric Center KU Leuven, 3000 Leuven, Belgium

Abstract. The ImageNet-1k dataset has been a major contributor to the development of novel CNN-based image classification architectures over the past 10 years. This has led to the advent of a number of models, pre-trained on this dataset, that form a popular basis for creating custom image classifiers by means of transfer learning. A corollary of this process is that whatever weaknesses and biases the original model possesses, the derived model will also have. Some of these have already been extensively covered, but color sensitivity has so far been understudied. This paper explores the prediction stability of several popular CNN architectures when input images are subjected to hue or saturation shifts. We show that even small shifts in image hue can alter a model's initial prediction, with larger shifts introducing changes up to 60% and 40% of the time for AlexNet and VGG16 respectively. For all models considered, saturation changes have less impact. To illustrate the issue being inherited by models obtained through transfer learning, we confirm that EmoNet, a model derived from AlexNet, exhibits similar behavior. By further comparing a same architecture trained separately on ImageNet-1k, Places365 and Stylized ImageNet, we confirm that the issue is shared across datasets. Finally, we propose a new preprocessing data augmentation to alleviate this problem.

Keywords: Convolutional Neural Networks · Image Recognition · Reliable Machine Learning · Robust Machine Learning · Trustworthy AI

© The Author(s), under exclusive license to Springer Nature Switzerland AG 2023
L. Iliadis et al. (Eds.): ICANN 2023, LNCS 14254, pp. 491–503, 2023.
https://doi.org/10.1007/978-3-031-44207-0_41

1   Introduction

ImageNet[1] [2] is a large, publicly available, image dataset (14M+ images). Its images are organized according to the WordNet hierarchy, making it especially useful for image classification tasks, as target labels are readily available. In 2010, the ImageNet Large Scale Visual Recognition Challenge (ILSVRC) [12] introduced a particular subset of images from 1000 different categories known as the ImageNet-1k dataset, with an accompanying image classification challenge.

In 2012, a Convolutional Neural Network (CNN) now widely known as AlexNet [9] convincingly won this competition. This result led to quick and widespreak adoption of CNNs to solve image classification and recognition tasks; while AlexNet was the only CNN submitted in 2012, by the next year the majority of submissions were CNN-based. Other popular architectures that were either submitted to ILSVRC or trained on the ImageNet-1k dataset, and that will be evaluated in this paper, are VGG16 [13], ResNet18 and ResNet50 [5], and DenseNet161 [7].

Despite their popularity and successes, these architectures also have weaknesses, both ethical [1,14,16] and technical. The most famous in this latter category are arguably adversarial attacks [15]: tiny alterations to an original image, imperceptible to the human eye, that fool the network into misclassifying the image. Also visible alterations such as blurring, pixelation, addition of several types of noise, etc., severely impact model performance [6]. In summary, these networks tend to perform very well on the type of data they are trained on, but fail to generalize beyond that.

Within this context, this paper focuses on a type of alteration that seems understudied, namely color changes. Moreover, existing work, such as [3,11], focuses on comparison between the human vision system and CNNs. Both studies use models trained on ImageNet-1k—the former VGG-M and the latter AlexNet, VGG16 and VGG19—to investigate the color sensitivity and selectivity of unique CNN filters and layers. Their interest lies in decyphering how these CNNs encode color, and to what extent this overlaps with biological systems. The results obtained in [3] state that overall, the models they studied are more sensitive to changes in hue than in saturation, and that both affect model accuracy. Both results will be discussed and compared to our results below. Our focus lies solely on how color affects model robustness and performance. Although complete color invariance is not desireable, neither should a useful CNN model alter its predictions when small color shifts, that would not fool humans, are applied to images. An example of undesireable behavior is depicted in Fig. 1, which shows AlexNet misclassifying an originally correctly classified image when it is subjected to modest hue shifts. In this context, it is interesting to note that the original AlexNet paper [9] describes a data augmentation scheme that (last paragraph Sect. 5.1):

---

[1] https://www.image-net.org/.

[...] approximately captures an important property of natural images, namely, that object identity is invariant to changes in the intensity and color of the illumination.

For some reason, this specific augmentation disappeared from later implementations, e.g., the PyTorch implementation we use.

| Hue shift=0, | Hue shift=10, | Hue shift=20, | Hue shift=30, |
| label=French_horn | label=groom | label=groom | label=mortarboard |

Fig. 1. Example of AlexNet sensitivity to hue shifts, expressed in degrees.

We start by investigating the effect of applying hue and saturation shifts to ImageNet-1k images on ImageNet-1k trained models, both in terms of prediction robustness—i.e., does a prediction for an altered image differ from that of the original image, regardless of the correctness of that original prediction?—and accuracy. Next, we turn our attention to EmoNet [8], an image classification model obtained by taking AlexNet trained on ImageNet-1k, replacing its last layer with a 20 node linear layer and training only this new layer on a custom dataset of 137k images annotated with one of 20 emotion labels representing the emotion elicited by the images in an observer. The question we want to answer is to what extent this model obtained by means of transfer learning inherits its parent's properties. EmoNet forms an interesting case, because elicited emotions form a dimension that can also reasonably be assumed to be independent of moderate color changes; a few degrees of hue shift shall not make a puppy less cute. Following this, we look at some of the earlier mentioned CNNs, but trained from scratch on different large datasets. In particular, we consider Stylized ImageNet [4], a dataset derived from ImageNet-1k by means of style transfer, and Places365 [17], a dataset of millions of images annotated with one of 365 scene classes. By comparing the effect of color-related changes on a same architecture trained on different datasets, we determine if this effect is an inherent property of the architecture or a consequence of the training data. Stylized ImageNet is of particular interest, as its authors specifically constructed the dataset to obtain models that use more global ("style") rather than local ("texture") features.

Finally, we propose two image preprocessing steps, one related to hue, the other to saturation, to augment a model's robustness with regards to alterations in these dimensions. To demonstrate the effectiveness of these preprocessors, we focus on ImageNet-1k and show that one can simply continue training a pre-trained model using these additional preprocessors to achieve the desired effect; there is no need to train a model from scratch. All our code and models are available through our GitLab page [10].

The remainder of this paper is organized as follows: in Sect. 2 we explain the methodology used to test model robustness to hue and saturation changes, followed by a discussion of obtained results in Sect. 3. Section 4 deals with retraining pretrained models using additional preprocessing steps in order to increase model robustness to hue and saturation changes. The paper concludes with Sect. 5.

2   Exploring Color Robustness: Implementation

We perform experiments with a number of models that were trained by others on specific training sets. In our experiments, we test performance using a number of existing validation sets. Table 1 shows an overview of the model-training-validation combinations we consider. The ImageNet-1k train and validation sets consist of 1,281,167 and 50,000 images respectively. For Places365, the models were trained using 8,000,000 images, with the corresponding validation set containing 36,500 images. Our code is Python-based, using PyTorch[2] as deep learning framework and Pillow[3], often referred to as PIL, as image processing package. All ImageNet-1k models are standard PyTorch implementations. The SIN and Places365 models were obtained through their respective public Git repositories. EmoNet is officially released as a MatLab model, and was ported by one of the current authors to PyTorch[4].

Table 1. Overview of training and validation data per model. "$\langle ModelName \rangle$" is a placeholder for a valid architecture, "IN-1k" = ImageNet-1k, "SIN" = Stylized ImageNet, "train" = train data, "val" = validation data.

Model	Trained on	Validated on
AlexNet, VGG16, ResNet18/50, DenseNet161	IN-1k train	IN-1k val
$\langle ModelName \rangle$-SIN	SIN	IN-1k val
$\langle ModelName \rangle$-P365	Places365 train	Places365 val
EmoNet	IN-1k train + EmoNet	IN-1k val

2.1   Applying Hue Changes

For a given pre-trained model M and corresponding validation data V, we apply hue shifts with degrees $d \in [0, 10, 20, \ldots, 350]$ to obtain shifted data sets V_d. Note that $V = V_{d=0}$.

---

[2] https://pytorch.org/.
[3] https://pillow.readthedocs.io/en/stable/.
[4] This port is available at https://gitlab.com/EAVISE/lme/emonet.

To apply the hue shifts, we first load the images as PIL images, then transform them to tensors using PyTorch. These tensors, which encode RGB information, are then converted to HSV[5]. Following this, the H-dimension is shifted by the required amount of degrees, and the image converted back to RGB.

2.2 Applying Saturation Changes

To change the saturation level of an image, we use the `enhance(g)` method of the `PIL.ImageEnhance.Color` class, with $g \in [0, +\infty[$. Using color gain $g = 1$ returns the original image, $g = 0$ returns a black-and-white copy, values $0 < g < 1$ produce desaturated images and $g > 1$ saturates the image. Starting again from validation data V, we produce data sets V_g using the described approach with $g \in [0.00, 0.05, \ldots, 1.95, 2.00]$, where $V = V_{g=1}$. The upper limit value of 2 was chosen heuristically by visual inspection.

2.3 Assessing Model Robustness

For a given model M, we determine its reference predictions, defined as its predictions for $V = V_{d=0} = V_{g=1}$. We then let M process all other data sets $V_{d\neq0}$ and $V_{g\neq1}$, and check what percentage of predictions remain unchanged. For each data set, we also compute the accuracy and look at what percentage of originally correct and wrong predictions were left unchanged. In other words, this tells us whether the internal model representation of correctly classified images is more stable than that of wrongly classified images.

3 Exploring Color Robustness: Results

A graphical representation of the evolution of model performance with hue and saturation shifts for AlexNet-based models is depicted in Fig. 2. Due to space limitations, we do not include plots for the other models, but instead make those available on our GitLab page [10]. Just as the symmetricity of the hue shift plot can be explained by the hue shift being controlled by a 360-degree parameter, the non-symmetricity of the saturation shift plot follows from the g parameter being only lower bound, and non-symmetric around 1. Statistics for all models are shown in Table 2. Besides the familiar Top1 accuracy, this table also includes the following metrics:

- Equal predictions (*Equal*): for a given hue shift $d \neq 0$ or saturation shift $g \neq 1$, this represents the fraction of images for which the predicted label remains the same as the original prediction ($d = 0$, $g = 1$), regardless of the correctness of the original prediction.
- OverLap+ (*OL+*): the fraction of originally correctly classified images whose predicted label did not change.

---

[5] We use the code available at https://github.com/limacv/RGB_HSV_HSL for this.

- OverLap− (*OL*−): the fraction of originally wrongly classified images whose predicted label did not change.
- Original Position (*O.P.*): the position of the label predicted for the shifted image in the list $[l_0, l_1, \ldots, l_n]$ of labels ordered by their likelihood as predicted for the original image. That is, if O.P. = 0, the shift did not change the prediction, but if O.P. is, e.g., 2, this means that the label predicted for the shifted image was originally the third most likely label. The result tables show averages that were computed taking only non-zero values into account.

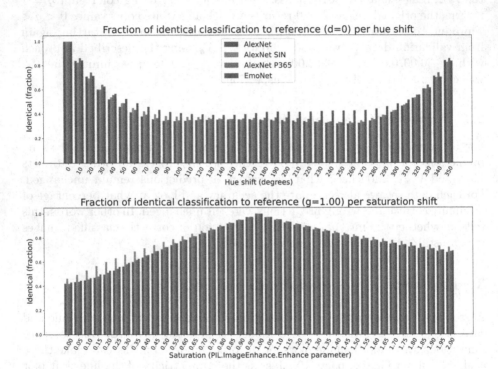

Fig. 2. Fraction of identically classified images compared to the reference prediction ($d = 0$, $g = 1$) for increasing hue and saturation shifts for AlexNet-based models.

For the Equal metric, we observe very similar results for the same architectures trained on different datasets. EmoNet does appear to perform slightly better than other AlexNet-based models wrt. larger hue shifts, but given that it only has 20 output nodes compared to 365 and 1000 for the other models, suggesting that larger perturbations are needed to switch output nodes, the overall similarities are remarkable. For saturation shifts, the differences are negligible. The slightly better AlexNet-SIN performance compared to AlexNet for saturation shifts is puzzling, given that both VGG16 and ResNet50 show the opposite behavior. Overall, the fact that SIN-trained models appear to be less robust wrt. both hue and saturation shifts than the ImageNet-1k models is intruiging, given that the aim of the SIN dataset is to create models that focus more on "global" than "local" features. Since hue and saturation shifts are global transformations, one would have expected the opposite. Our results confirm and expand on the findings of [3] that hue sensitivity is higher than saturation sensitivity[6], apparent from the much lower values for Equal d_{all} than for Equal g_{all}.

Turning to the OverLap metrics, it is noteworthy that images that are originally correctly classified consistently have a lesser probability of being misclassified after applying hue/saturation changes. This suggests that the internal model representations for these images are inherently more robust, although it is not clear at first sight why this is the case. The magnitude of the gaps between the OL+ and OL− metrics is striking. Even more so is the fact that, despite all models being less sensitive to saturation changes, the corresponding OL+/OL− gap lies considerably higher than for hue changes.

Finally, the O.P. results are in line with the previous results. As the number of output nodes diminishes, so does the O.P. Furthermore, for hue changes, the O.P. is higher than for saturation changes. For smaller perturbations ($|d| \leq 30$, $g \in {]}0.5, 1.5[_{\backslash \{1\}}$), the O.P. is markedly smaller than when considering d_{all} or g_{all}. As the size of the perturbation increases, so does the erraticness of the change in predicted label. This is specifically apparent in the very large gap in standard deviations between both regimes.

Concerning overall model performance, the top panel in Fig. 2 suggests that, for AlexNet and EmoNet, this more or less linearly decreases until it plateaus at around an 80° hue shift in either direction. Similar behavior can be observed for the other models, with the exception of ResNet50, for which the performance shows a slight bump around the 170°–180° region. In their paper, [3] report an average drop in performance of 31.6% over hue shifts, averaged over VGG16, VGG19 and AlexNet performance, with 42% for AlexNet alone. This matches our 41.5% for AlexNet[7]. In a non-reported experiment, we obtained 28.9% for VGG19, which combined with the 22.9% for VGG16 derivable from Table 2 amounts to a 30.9% average, closely matching their result. The slight differences can be explained by the useage of different pretrained models, namely CAFFE vs. PyTorch implementations. Turning to grayscale (corresponding to $g = 0$) vs. original images, they report average drops of 25% across all three networks, and 33% for AlexNet, compared to 25.5% and 40.2% for us respectively, 18.8% for VGG16. Although the average across networks matches, we can only speculate as to the larger implied individual differences indicated by the AlexNet mismatch.

---

[6] Note that [3] use "chroma" instead of "saturation", but given the similarity between both, our conclusion still stands.

[7] Divide "Top1 d_{all}" by "Top1 d_0, g_1" to compute this number.

Table 2. Pretrained model statistics wrt. hue and saturation shifts applied to input images. "Top1" = Top1 accuracy, "OL+/−" = overlap between predicted labels for $d_0 = 0$ vs. $d \neq 0$, and $g_1 = 1$ vs. $g \neq 1$, for originally correctly (+) and wrongly (−) predicted samples, "O.P." = Original Position of differing winning prediction for $d \neq 0$ or $g \neq 1$, d_{all} and g_{all} refer to all non-default (d_0, g_1) degree and color gain values, Equal $g \in]0.5, 1.5[\backslash\{1\}$ represents $d \in [-30, -20, -10, 10, 20, 30]$. Except for the "Top1 d_0, g_1" values, all normal case values represent averages and all superscript values represent standard deviations over the relevant parameter range.

	AlexNet	AlexNet SIN	AlexNet P365	EmoNet	VGG16	VGG16 SIN	ResNet18	ResNet18 P365	ResNet50	ResNet50 SIN	DenseNet161	DenseNet161 P365
Equal d_{all}	$.431^{.15}$	$.441^{.14}$	$.447^{.15}$	$.489^{.12}$	$.659^{.10}$	$.581^{.12}$	$.659^{.10}$	$.614^{.11}$	$.800^{.06}$	$.632^{.10}$	$.759^{.07}$	$.662^{.09}$
Equal $|d| \leq 30$	$.718^{.10}$	$.709^{.09}$	$.747^{.09}$	$.724^{.09}$	$.861^{.05}$	$.803^{.06}$	$.847^{.05}$	$.830^{.06}$	$.910^{.03}$	$.826^{.06}$	$.897^{.04}$	$.847^{.05}$
Equal g_{all}	$.746^{.15}$	$.786^{.13}$	$.756^{.15}$	$.758^{.15}$	$.883^{.08}$	$.857^{.09}$	$.874^{.09}$	$.842^{.10}$	$.950^{.03}$	$.885^{.08}$	$.946^{.05}$	$.863^{.09}$
Equal $g \in]0.5,1.5[\backslash\{1\}$	$.863^{.07}$	$.883^{.06}$	$.872^{.07}$	$.870^{.07}$	$.943^{.03}$	$.924^{.04}$	$.937^{.03}$	$.919^{.04}$	$.972^{.01}$	$.940^{.03}$	$.977^{.01}$	$.929^{.04}$
Top1 d_0,g_1	$.566$	$.400$	-	-	$.716$	$.522$	$.697$	-	$.803$	$.602$	$.771$	-
Top1 d_{all}	$.331^{.09}$	$.263^{.06}$	-	-	$.552^{.07}$	$.409^{.05}$	$.548^{.06}$	-	$.713^{.04}$	$.488^{.05}$	$.661^{.05}$	-
OL+ d_{all}	$.528^{.15}$	$.579^{.14}$	-	-	$.732^{.10}$	$.713^{.10}$	$.743^{.09}$	-	$.857^{.05}$	$.752^{.09}$	$.823^{.06}$	-
OL− d_{all}	$.305^{.14}$	$.349^{.14}$	-	-	$.475^{.12}$	$.437^{.13}$	$.465^{.12}$	-	$.568^{.09}$	$.451^{.12}$	$.541^{.10}$	-
Top1 g_{all}	$.505^{.06}$	$.382^{.02}$	-	-	$.688^{.04}$	$.511^{.02}$	$.668^{.04}$	-	$.798^{.01}$	$.591^{.02}$	$.762^{.02}$	-
OL+ g_{all}	$.855^{.14}$	$.846^{.14}$	-	-	$.917^{.15}$	$.874^{.14}$	$.915^{.15}$	-	$.938^{.15}$	$.897^{.15}$	$.934^{.15}$	-
OL− g_{all}	$.253^{.17}$	$.345^{.15}$	-	-	$.379^{.16}$	$.361^{.11}$	$.359^{.14}$	-	$.451^{.09}$	$.362^{.10}$	$.399^{.10}$	-
Top1 $|d| \leq 30$	$.501^{.04}$	$.367^{.02}$	-	-	$.681^{.02}$	$.500^{.01}$	$.662^{.02}$	-	$.782^{.01}$	$.580^{.01}$	$.747^{.02}$	-
OL+ $|d| \leq 30$	$.829^{.08}$	$.844^{.06}$	-	-	$.920^{.04}$	$.904^{.04}$	$.914^{.04}$	-	$.951^{.02}$	$.917^{.04}$	$.944^{.03}$	-
OL− $|d| \leq 30$	$.575^{.12}$	$.620^{.11}$	-	-	$.713^{.09}$	$.693^{.09}$	$.692^{.09}$	-	$.742^{.07}$	$.688^{.09}$	$.740^{.08}$	-
Top1 $g \in]0.5,1.5[\backslash\{1\}$	$.550^{.01}$	$.397^{.00}$	-	-	$.711^{.01}$	$.520^{.00}$	$.691^{.01}$	-	$.802^{.00}$	$.601^{.00}$	$.770^{.00}$	-
OL+ $g \in]0.5,1.5[\backslash\{1\}$	$.883^{.02}$	$.863^{.02}$	-	-	$.943^{.01}$	$.894^{.01}$	$.941^{.01}$	-	$.962^{.00}$	$.919^{.01}$	$.956^{.00}$	-
OL− $g \in]0.5,1.5[\backslash\{1\}$	$.197^{.04}$	$.310^{.04}$	-	-	$.337^{.04}$	$.344^{.03}$	$.319^{.03}$	-	$.444^{.02}$	$.346^{.02}$	$.381^{.01}$	-
O.P. d_{all}	58.5^{122}	40.6^{96}	29.5^{53}	3.7^{3}	28.0^{76}	26.5^{73}	25.3^{71}	13.0^{29}	31.6^{119}	24.5^{70}	19.1^{61}	9.9^{24}
O.P. $|d| \leq 30$	10.9^{37}	6.7^{23}	4.9^{13}	2.1^{2}	5.2^{18}	4.4^{16}	5.0^{18}	2.8^{6}	6.4^{45}	4.2^{14}	4.0^{15}	2.6^{6}
O.P. g_{all}	11.9^{40}	19.8^{55}	20.0^{44}	2.3^{2}	5.3^{20}	4.3^{17}	4.9^{18}	3.8^{10}	5.5^{23}	11.9^{36}	2.9^{10}	2.9^{8}
O.P. $g \in]0.5,1.5[\backslash\{1\}$	2.5^{5}	18.9^{52}	19.4^{42}	1.4^{1}	1.6^{2}	1.5^{2}	1.6^{2}	1.5^{1}	5.5^{22}	11.9^{36}	1.2^{1}	1.4^{1}

4 Increasing Color Robustness by Adding Extra Preprocessing Steps

4.1 Training of Models

For this experiment, we focused on the AlexNet, VGG16 and ResNet18 ImageNet-1k models. To increase their robustness to changes in hue and saturation, we apply random hue and saturation changes to input images during the training phase, on top of the standard ImageNet-1k preprocessing steps. The image processing is done as explained in Sects.2.1 and 2.2. The difference is that this time, the magnitude of the change is chosen randomly whenever an image is loaded. The number of degrees of the hue shift is sampled from a normal distribution $\mathcal{N}(\mu = 0, \sigma = 30)$, while the gain factor for the saturation shift is sampled from a normal distribution $\mathcal{N}(\mu = 1, \sigma = 0.5)$. The choice for these particular distributions is heuristic. For hue changes, $\sigma = 30$ was chosen as this range coincides with a steep descent in model performance and comprises hue changes that, as illustrated in Fig. 1, are not too extreme. For saturation changes, given the reduced model sensitivity, we opted to have 2σ span the entire covered spectrum.

The hue and saturation changes are applied right before normalizing the image. Model validation is performed on the original validation set.

As a starting point, we take the pretrained PyTorch implementations of the aforementioned models, available through the `torchvision` library. We then continue training these models using the ImageNet-1k train data, CrossEntropyLoss, dropout = 0.25, Adam optimizer with `weight decay` = 10^{-6}, batch size 64 for VGG16 and 256 for Alexnet and ResNet18, and the learning update rule:

$$lr_e = \frac{lr_0}{\sqrt{(e//2) + 1}}, \qquad (1)$$

with lr_e the learning rate at epoch e and the initial learning rate $lr_0 = 10^{-5}$. By virtue of the floor division ($//$), this means we update the learning rate once every 2 epochs. Training stops when either the best loss or the best weighted F1 score on the validation set lies 6 epochs behind the current epoch, with the model corresponding to this best epoch put forward as the final trained model.

Models were trained using hue ($+h$), and hue + saturation ($+hs$) preprocessing. Given the increased model sensitivity to hue changes, we opted not to train models using only saturation preprocessing. To check the effect of only retraining a CNN's classifier (class.; i.e., the final linear layers following the convolution layers) instead of the entire model, we also retrained the AlexNet classifier, consisting of the final 3 linear layers including the output layer, while keeping the convolution layers fixed.

4.2 Results

Metrics for our retrained models are depicted in Table 3. Plots depicting model performance are made available through out GitLab page [10]. Noteworthy is the fact that our retrained models retain the Top1 performance of the original models, but manifest clearly improved robustness to hue and saturation alterations. This means that separate sets of CNN filters achieve the same accuracy on the same dataset, but nonetheless show vastly different behavior when performing a specific transformation on the input images. Although the "AlexNet class." models already show a significant improvement in robustness compared to AlexNet, the fact that the full retrained models perform even better confirms the intuition that CNN filters are the crucial ingredient in obtaining robust models, rather than the linear classification layers. For all models, the additional preprocessing does not seem to alter the gap between OL+ and OL− for hue changes, i.e., they are both affected similarly, but additional saturation preprocessing has a clear positive effect for its corresponding gap. More striking is the large decrease in O.P., specifically for hue. For saturation, the effect is less pronounced[8], arguably in part because there is less room for improvement to begin with. Moreover, additional hue preprocessing tends to negatively influence O.P. for saturation changes, but using both hue and saturation preprocessing benefits the O.P. for both types of changes. All this suggests that these preprocessing steps contribute to creating more robust internal model representations.

5   Conclusion

This paper explores the prediction stability of the popular CNN architectures AlexNet, VGG16, ResNet18 and 50, and DenseNet161. We show that all models alter their predictions when input images have their hue shifted, with larger shifts increasing alteration frequency. Averaged over all hue shifts, relative model performance experiences a drop of 41.5%, 22.9%, 21.4%, 11.3% and 14.3% respectively for the aforementioned models, resulting in an average drop of 22.28% over all models; larger models show less sensitivity. The largest drops are observed within up to 30° shifts from reference, with performance stabilizing around the 80° mark. Moreover, models trained on ImageNet-1k, Stylized ImageNet and Places365 are compared, showing the training data has little to no effect on this issue. EmoNet, a model derived from AlexNet, is shown to inherit essentially the same behavior as its parent. Saturation shifts elicit similar but more restrained behavior, with an average performance drop of only 4.0% over all models. Importantly, for both hue and saturation alterations, the prediction for images originally correctly predicted tends to be more robust than for images originally wrongly predicted. We propose to include two additional preprocessing steps in the training process, namely random hue shifts and saturation changes, which, when used to retrain existing models, are shown to improve average prediction stability for hue shifts on ImageNet-1k with 19%, 13% and 12% for AlexNet, VGG16 and ResNet18 respectively. For saturation changes, 11%, 6% and 6% improvements are obtained, in the last two cases lifting stability up to 94% and 93%. Interestingly, these retrained models retain the original model's ImageNet-1k performance, leading to the question: How exactly can several sets

---

[8] We compare ⟨ModelName⟩ to ⟨ModelName⟩ +hs.

Table 3. Retrained model statistics wrt. hue and saturation shifts applied to input images. The original models are also included for easy comparison. "+h" = random hue shift added to train image preprocessing, "+hs" = random hue and saturation shift added to train image preprocessing, "class." means only the classifier was retrained instead of the entire model, "Top1" = Top1 accuracy, "OL+/−" = overlap between predicted labels for $d_0 = 0$ vs. $d \neq 0$, and $g_1 = 1$ vs. $g \neq 1$, for originally correctly (+) and wrongly (−) predicted samples, "O.P." = Original Position of differing winning prediction for $d \neq 0$ or $g \neq 1$, d_{all} and g_{all} refer to all non-default (d_0, g_1) degree and color gain values, $|d| \leq 30$ represents $d \in [-30, -20, -10, 10, 20, 30]$. Except for the "Top1 d_0, g_1" values, all normal case values represent averages and all superscript values represent standard deviations over the relevant parameter range.

	AlexNet	AlexNet class.+h	AlexNet class.+hs	Alexnet +h	AlexNet +hs	VGG16	VGG16 +h	VGG16 +hs	ResNet18	ResNet18 +h	ResNet18 +hs
Equal d_{all}	$.431^{15}$	$.528^{14}$	$.576^{14}$	$.587^{16}$	$.623^{17}$	$.659^{10}$	$.778^{11}$	$.793^{11}$	$.659^{10}$	$.769^{10}$	$.779^{10}$
Equal $|d| \leq 30$	$.718^{10}$	$.788^{07}$	$.817^{06}$	$.854^{05}$	$.877^{04}$	$.861^{05}$	$.938^{02}$	$.944^{02}$	$.847^{05}$	$.927^{03}$	$.932^{02}$
Equal g_{all}	$.746^{15}$	$.751^{15}$	$.820^{11}$	$.748^{15}$	$.857^{09}$	$.883^{08}$	$.880^{08}$	$.942^{04}$	$.874^{09}$	$.873^{08}$	$.931^{05}$
Equal $g \in |0.5, 1.5| \setminus \{1\}$	$.863^{07}$	$.865^{07}$	$.902^{05}$	$.861^{07}$	$.926^{04}$	$.943^{03}$	$.938^{03}$	$.972^{01}$	$.937^{03}$	$.934^{04}$	$.967^{02}$
Top1 $d_{0.9 1}$	$.566$	$.565$	$.564$	$.564$	$.565$	$.716$	$.714$	$.714$	$.697$	$.703$	$.702$
Top1 d_{all}	$.331^{09}$	$.400^{08}$	$.432^{07}$	$.428^{08}$	$.451^{08}$	$.552^{07}$	$.631^{06}$	$.644^{06}$	$.548^{06}$	$.623^{06}$	$.628^{06}$
OL+ d_{all}	$.528^{15}$	$.645^{14}$	$.701^{13}$	$.700^{16}$	$.739^{15}$	$.732^{10}$	$.847^{09}$	$.864^{09}$	$.743^{09}$	$.847^{09}$	$.856^{09}$
OL− d_{all}	$.305^{14}$	$.377^{14}$	$.414^{15}$	$.441^{17}$	$.473^{19}$	$.475^{12}$	$.605^{15}$	$.617^{16}$	$.465^{12}$	$.585^{14}$	$.599^{15}$
Top1 g_{all}	$.505^{06}$	$.508^{06}$	$.538^{03}$	$.506^{06}$	$.548^{02}$	$.688^{04}$	$.685^{03}$	$.709^{01}$	$.668^{04}$	$.674^{03}$	$.693^{01}$
OL+ g_{all}	$.855^{14}$	$.861^{14}$	$.884^{14}$	$.860^{14}$	$.887^{14}$	$.917^{15}$	$.919^{15}$	$.928^{15}$	$.915^{15}$	$.914^{15}$	$.927^{15}$
OL− g_{all}	$.253^{17}$	$.263^{18}$	$.352^{15}$	$.278^{18}$	$.356^{13}$	$.379^{16}$	$.413^{17}$	$.474^{10}$	$.359^{14}$	$.381^{15}$	$.453^{11}$
Top1 $|d| \leq 30$	$.501^{04}$	$.534^{02}$	$.545^{01}$	$.550^{01}$	$.556^{00}$	$.681^{02}$	$.709^{00}$	$.711^{00}$	$.662^{02}$	$.697^{00}$	$.697^{00}$
OL+ $|d| \leq 30$	$.829^{08}$	$.893^{04}$	$.916^{03}$	$.934^{03}$	$.949^{02}$	$.920^{04}$	$.974^{01}$	$.977^{01}$	$.914^{04}$	$.970^{01}$	$.972^{01}$
OL− $|d| \leq 30$	$.575^{12}$	$.652^{10}$	$.690^{09}$	$.750^{08}$	$.785^{07}$	$.713^{09}$	$.848^{05}$	$.862^{04}$	$.692^{09}$	$.828^{06}$	$.838^{05}$
Top1 $g \in |0.5, 1.5| \setminus \{1\}$	$.550^{01}$	$.550^{01}$	$.558^{01}$	$.548^{01}$	$.561^{00}$	$.711^{01}$	$.708^{01}$	$.713^{00}$	$.691^{01}$	$.696^{01}$	$.700^{00}$
OL+ $g \in |0.5, 1.5| \setminus \{1\}$	$.883^{02}$	$.888^{02}$	$.906^{01}$	$.891^{02}$	$.908^{01}$	$.943^{01}$	$.946^{01}$	$.950^{00}$	$.941^{01}$	$.941^{01}$	$.949^{00}$
OL− $g \in |0.5, 1.5| \setminus \{1\}$	$.197^{04}$	$.208^{04}$	$.312^{04}$	$.222^{04}$	$.329^{03}$	$.337^{04}$	$.371^{04}$	$.466^{02}$	$.319^{03}$	$.341^{03}$	$.440^{02}$
O.P. d_{all}	58.5^{122}	34.4^{84}	25.8^{68}	27.6^{72}	22.4^{61}	28.0^{76}	12.8^{41}	10.9^{36}	25.3^{71}	11.0^{36}	10.1^{34}
O.P. $|d| \leq 30$	10.9^{37}	4.3^{13}	3.1^{7}	2.4^{5}	1.9^{3}	5.2^{18}	1.7^{4}	1.5^{2}	5.0^{18}	1.6^{2}	1.6^{2}
O.P. g_{all}	11.9^{40}	38.6^{101}	10.6^{28}	36.0^{96}	9.6^{26}	5.3^{30}	5.0^{18}	4.7^{14}	4.9^{18}	9.0^{30}	2.2^{5}
O.P. $g \in |0.5, 1.5| \setminus \{1\}$	2.5^{5}	37.5^{97}	10.4^{27}	34.3^{91}	9.3^{25}	1.6^{2}	1.7^{2}	4.8^{14}	1.6^{2}	8.9^{30}	1.2^{1}

of convolution filters result in the same ImageNet-1k accuracy, yet show markedly different behavior when subjected to particular image transformations? We hope to address this question in future work.

References

1. Crawford, K., Paglen, T.: Excavating AI: the politics of images in machine learning training sets. https://excavating.ai/. Accessed 8 Mar 2023
2. Deng, J., Dong, W., Socher, R., Li, L.J., Li, K., Fei-Fei, L.: ImageNet: a large-scale hierarchical image database. In: 2009 IEEE Conference on Computer Vision and Pattern Recognition, pp. 248–255. IEEE (2009)
3. Flachot, A., Gegenfurtner, K.R.: Color for object recognition: hue and chroma sensitivity in the deep features of convolutional neural networks. Vision. Res. **182**, 89–100 (2021). https://doi.org/10.1016/j.visres.2020.09.010
4. Geirhos, R., Rubisch, P., Michaelis, C., Bethge, M., Wichmann, F.A., Brendel, W.: ImageNet-trained CNNs are biased towards texture; increasing shape bias improves accuracy and robustness. https://doi.org/10.48550/ARXIV.1811.12231 (2018)
5. He, K., Zhang, X., Ren, S., Sun, J.: Deep residual learning for image recognition. In: 2016 IEEE Conference on Computer Vision and Pattern Recognition (CVPR), pp. 770–778 (2016). https://doi.org/10.1109/CVPR.2016.90
6. Hendrycks, D., Dietterich, T.G.: Benchmarking neural network robustness to common corruptions and perturbations. CoRR abs/1903.12261 (2019), https://arxiv.org/abs/1903.12261
7. Huang, G., Liu, Z., Van Der Maaten, L., Weinberger, K.Q.: Densely connected convolutional networks. In: 2017 IEEE Conference on Computer Vision and Pattern Recognition (CVPR), pp. 2261–2269 (2017). https://doi.org/10.1109/CVPR.2017.243
8. Kragel, P.A., Reddan, M.C., LaBar, K.S., Wager, T.D.: Emotion schemas are embedded in the human visual system. Sci. Adv. **5**(7), eaaw4358 (2019). https://doi.org/10.1126/sciadv.aaw4358
9. Krizhevsky, A., Sutskever, I., Hinton, G.E.: ImageNet classification with deep convolutional neural networks. Commun. ACM **60**(6), 84–90 (2017). https://doi.org/10.1145/3065386
10. Mertens, L.: GitLab repository containing the code and additional material for this paper. https://gitlab.com/EAVISE/lme/nncolorstabilityanalysis-paper
11. Rafegas, I., Vanrell, M.: Color encoding in biologically-inspired convolutional neural networks. Vision Res. **151**, 7–17 (2018). https://doi.org/10.1016/j.visres.2018.03.010
12. Russakovsky, O., et al.: ImageNet large scale visual recognition challenge. Int. J. Comput. Vision **115**(3), 211–252 (2015). https://doi.org/10.1007/s11263-015-0816-y
13. Simonyan, K., Zisserman, A.: Very deep convolutional networks for large-scale image recognition. In: Bengio, Y., LeCun, Y. (eds.) 3rd International Conference on Learning Representations, ICLR 2015, San Diego, CA, USA, May 7–9, 2015, Conference Track Proceedings (2015)
14. Steed, R., Caliskan, A.: Image representations learned with unsupervised pre-training contain human-like biases. In: Proceedings of the 2021 ACM Conference on Fairness, Accountability, and Transparency, pp. 701–713. FAccT 2021, Association for Computing Machinery, New York, NY, USA (2021). https://doi.org/10.1145/3442188.3445932

15. Szegedy, C., et al.: Intriguing properties of neural networks. In: 2nd International Conference on Learning Representations, Conference date: 14–04-2014 Through 16–04-2014. ICLR (2014)
16. Yang, K., Qinami, K., Fei-Fei, L., Deng, J., Russakovsky, O.: Towards fairer datasets: filtering and balancing the distribution of the people subtree in the ImageNet hierarchy. In: Proceedings of the 2020 Conference on Fairness, Accountability, and Transparency, pp. 547–558. FAT* 2020, Association for Computing Machinery, New York, NY, USA (2020). https://doi.org/10.1145/3351095.3375709
17. Zhou, B., Lapedriza, A., Khosla, A., Oliva, A., Torralba, A.: Places: a 10 million image database for scene recognition. IEEE Trans. Pattern Anal. Mach. Intell. **40**, 1452–1464 (2017)

Improving Neural Network Verification Efficiency Through Perturbation Refinement

Minal Suresh Patil[(✉)] and Kary Främling

Umeå universitet, UNIVERSITETSTORGET 4, Umeå, Sweden
{minal.patil,kary.framling}@umu.se

Abstract. This paper presents a novel approach to efficient neural network verification through the use of adversarial attacks and symbolic interval propagation. The proposed method leverages low-cost adversarial attacks to quickly obtain a rough estimate of the first set of bounds, and then utilizes symbolic interval propagation to compute tighter bounds. We demonstrate the effectiveness of our proposed method on the popular MNIST dataset, which contains hand-written digit images. The results show that the proposed method achieves state-of-the-art verification accuracy with significantly reduced computational cost, making it a promising approach for practical neural network verification.

Keywords: Perturbation Refinement · Neural Network Verification · Adversarial Robustness

1 Introduction

Deep neural networks (DNNs) are widely used today. Their ability to generalise and thus work well even on previously unknown inputs is a key factor in their widespread use. Although this has many useful advantages, it could occasionally render DNNs unreliable. This dearth of dependability can actually come at a terrible price in applications that are either safety- or business-critical. Evidently, a trained network's instability is primarily caused by its inability to withstand input perturbations, or the fact that even minor changes to some inputs can significantly alter the network's output. In a lot of application domains, this is not ideal. Consider, for instance, a network that has been taught to alert aircraft to change their paths in response to approaching intruder aircraft. It is reasonable to anticipate that such a network will be capable of making sound decisions, meaning that the advice given in two situations that are strikingly similar should not diverge greatly. However, if that is not the case, then showing the network's lack of resilience through adversarial inputs can aid in both network improvement and determining when the network should hand over control to a more dependable entity.

When a network and an input are provided, an adversarial input is one that is very similar to the input but the outputs of the network for the two inputs are very distinct. Finding adversarial sources has been the subject of extensive research in the past [3,7,9,17]. Depending on whether they take into account the architecture of the network during the study or not, these approaches can be categorised as black-box or white-box techniques. Both of these groups have produced a wide range of techniques, from the creation of random attacks [14] and gradient-based approaches [1] to symbolic execution [18,22,26], fault localization [24], coverage-guided testing, SMT, and ILP solving [10,23].

Interval analysis is a method that's used to verify the safety and robustness of neural networks by estimating their output ranges for a given input. This is achieved by calculating both the upper and lower bounds of the output using interval arithmetic, as described in the literature [11]. To improve the accuracy of this approach, researchers have proposed a related technique known as symbolic interval analysis [22]. This involves approximating the output range of a neural network by computing the upper and lower bounds using symbolic mathematical expressions, which can result in tighter bounds and improved verification outcomes.

Robustness verification of neural networks is essential to ensure that they behave correctly and reliably in the presence of adversarial attacks or unexpected inputs. However, the verification process can be computationally expensive, especially for large and complex neural networks. Therefore, accelerating robustness verification of neural networks is crucial to make it feasible for practical applications. Numerous techniques have been proposed to utilize abstraction to achieve robustness [5,13]. Since ReLU activation function is commonly used in neural networks, it is more practical to investigate the problem of verifying robustness [15]. As ReLU networks have a piecewise-linear structure, the problem of verifying robustness can be transformed into a standard Mixed-Integer Linear Programming (MILP) problem, which can be tackled using branch-and-bound methods [6]. However, for large-scale ReLU networks, solving MILP problems for verifying robustness is still challenging. The difficulty of systematically searching the high dimensional and continuous input space makes it challenging to ensure that an adversarial example can be found, even if it exists. Therefore, machine learning models that appear robust to existing attacks may still have security weaknesses in practice. Off-the-shelf MILP solvers cannot make use of solutions gathered at a low cost via gradient-based adversarial attacks to quicken up its search. To tackle this issue, we propose *warm-starting* and *bounds tightening* techniques by integrate symbolic interval analysis to obtain tighter bounds for a gradient-based adversarial example which is formulated as MILP formulation. This can reduce the number of iterations required to converge to the optimal solution, and hence the computation time. The contribution is summed up as follow:

– An approach called *warm-starting* has been proposed to incorporate cheap solutions obtained from adversarial attacks, with the goal of reducing the search space that a MILP solver would otherwise have to explore. Additionally, a technique called *bound tightening* has been introduced to tighten the

bounds on the neurons, which can further improve the accuracy and efficiency of the MILP solver.
- A framework verifier for generating adversarial examples has demonstrated superior performance and has been validated on the MNIST dataset using three distinct neural network architectures and three different verification methods.

2 Related Work

Our work is connected to prior studies on attacking and defending deep neural networks, which encompass topics such as verification, testing, and creating adversarial examples. The existing research on neural verification can be categorized into two types based on constraint solving: methods based on Satisfiability Modulo Theories (SMT) problems [8,13] and methods based on Linear Programming (LP) [2,4]. These techniques are generally sound and complete i.e., no false negatives and no false positive respectively. But owing to the computational complexity, they have little capacity to scale. There are two methods, namely *approximation* and *abstraction*, that can be employed to achieve better scalability when verifying robustness. These techniques are known to be effective in achieving this objective [12,25]. Furthermore, there are numerous efforts aimed at either attacking deep neural networks (DNNs) or enhancing their resilience through the creation of adversarial examples. L-BFGS [19] was the earliest method developed for producing adversarial examples, while FGSM [9] utilizes gradient updates to create such examples. FGSM is capable of generating an adversarial example from an input with just one update, making it a relatively efficient technique. In our work, we employ FGSM attack to produce the rough set of bounds for the neurons before formulating into a LP problem.

3 Background

3.1 Robustness Against Adversarial Perturbations

The characteristics of a neural network can be inferred from the meaning and context of its specification. Typically, these characteristics are input-output (IO) properties that specify a particular relationship between the input and output of the network. One of the earliest IO properties that has been investigated is robustness, which requires the model's output to remain consistent even when minor modifications are made to the input value [7,16].

3.2 Gradient-Based Adversarial Attack

A small change made to the input to deceive the classifier's prediction is called an adversarial attack. If a neural network can withstand such attacks, it is probable that it can also handle other types of changes. However, this is not guaranteed, and therefore it is necessary to formally test the network's robustness against all potential alterations. In our work, the purpose of the finding adversarial examples is to reduce the search space by obtaining the perturbation bounds of the adversarial example before encoding it to a MILP solver. Numerous methods exist for creating adversarial attacks, which can be classified into two categories based on the attacker's objective: targeted attacks and untargeted attacks.

- *Targeted attack*: A targeted attack aims to cause the input sample to be misclassified to a specific target class, rather than just away from its original class.
- *Untargeted attack*: An untargeted attack does not have a specific desired output class, but rather aims to cause the input sample to be misclassified from its original class, regardless of what new output class it ends up being classified as.

Fast Gradient Sign Method. To create boundaries for the perturbations, we use the Fast Gradient Sign Method for the adversarial attack [9].

To produce a modified version of an original sample represented by x, we introduce a slight perturbation ϵ to each of its components through either addition or subtraction.

The technique involves analyzing the sign of the gradient of the loss function, which is denoted as $\nabla_x \mathcal{L}(x, y)$:

- If the gradient $\nabla_x \mathcal{L}(x, y)$ is positive, it indicates that an increase in x results in an increase in the loss function $\mathcal{L}$.
- Conversely, if the gradient $\nabla_x \mathcal{L}(x, y)$ is negative, it implies that an increase in x leads to a decrease in the loss function $\mathcal{L}$.

3.3   Symbolic Interval Analysis for Bound Tightening

Interval analysis is a method utilized in the verification of neural networks to study their behavior and ensure their safety and robustness. The process involves an estimation of the output range of a neural network for a given input through computing the upper and lower bounds of the output using interval arithmetic. In interval analysis, each neuron in the network is treated as a function that takes an input and gives an output. The input and output are both represented as intervals that express a range of possible values. Interval arithmetic operations are then used to propagate the input intervals through the network, resulting in the output intervals. The calculated output intervals are compared to the desired output range to determine whether the network is safe and robust. If the output intervals include the desired output range, then the network is considered safe; otherwise, it may be potentially unsafe, requiring further analysis. Interval analysis is a robust technique for verifying neural networks as it can handle non-linear activation functions and multiple layers. However, it may be computationally demanding and not scalable to larger networks.

The given Fig. 1(a), depicts a Naive Interval analysis of a three-layer Deep Neural Network (DNN) with weights assigned to edges, and bias vectors containing all elements as 0. Assuming the input intervals to the first layer to be [2, 4] and $[3,6]$, the output interval obtained after performing scalar operations over intervals layer-wise, is $[-5,7]$. However, here the output bound includes certain specific values that are infeasible in practical scenarios due to overestimation. For example, the value of -5 can only be achieved when neuron n_3 outputs 13 and neuron n_4 outputs 8. But to output 10 for n_3, the neurons n_1 and n_2 must output 4 and 5 simultaneously, and to output 8 for n_4, the neurons n_1 and n_2 should output 1 and 2 at the same time which also referred to as the *dependency problem*.

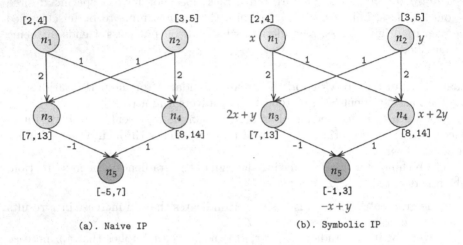

(a). Naive IP   (b). Symbolic IP

Fig. 1. Naive Interval Propagation vs. Symbolic Interval Propagation.

Symbolic interval analysis [22] or Symbolic Interval Propagation (SIP) is an approach utilized in the verification of neural networks to ensure their safety and robustness. This method involves approximating the output range of a neural network by calculating the upper and lower bounds of the output through the use of symbolic mathematical expressions. Symbolic interval analysis employs interval arithmetic to generate a group of mathematical expressions that represent the output range of the neural network. These expressions can be utilized to calculate the output range of the network for a given input and compare it to the desired output range to determine the safety and robustness of the network. Symbolic interval analysis is a powerful technique for verifying neural networks as it enables the analysis of intricate networks with non-linear activation functions and multiple layers. It is particularly effective for analyzing networks with piece-wise linear activation functions such as ReLU, as these networks can be challenging to evaluate using other verification methods. Figure 1(b), represents a symbolic approach to address the dependency problem. For neurons n_1 and n_2, let x and y represent the input variables. For neurons n_3 and n_4 can be symbolically represented as $2x + y$ and $x + 2y$ correspondingly and greater than zero since $x \in [1,3]$ and $y \in [2,4]$. Therefore, the symbolic interval for n_3 and n_4 is $[2x + y, 2x + y]$ and $[x + 2y, x + 2y]$ correspondingly and, similarly, the symbolic interval for n_5 is $[-x + y]$. Hence, for $x \in [1,3]$ and $y \in [2,4]$, the output interval is $[-1,3]$ which is computed as a tighter bound as compared to the naive approach of $[-5,7]$.

3.4 Mixed-Integer Linear Programming

Unstable Neurons. The non-linearity of activation functions $\mathcal{A}$ is a significant obstacle in the process of verification. Specifically, the ReLU activation function $\mathcal{A}\left(z_j^{(i)}\right) = \text{ReLU}\left(z_j^{(i)}\right) = \max\left(0, z_j^{(i)}\right)$ introduces complexities that must be addressed during verification. To tackle this issue, we define intermediate layer bounds $\mathbf{l}_j^{(i)} \leq z_j^{(i)} \leq \mathbf{u}_j^{(i)}$ that constrain the input of each ReLU neuron for a given input $x \in \mathcal{C}$. With these bounds, we can categorize the activation space of each ReLU neuron.

- Active and Inactive: When the bounds of an intermediate layer for a ReLU neuron satisfy the condition $\mathbf{l}_j^{(i)} \geq 0$ or $\mathbf{u}_j^{(i)} \leq 0$, it indicates that the ReLU neuron lies in either the linear active region where its output is equal to its input ($\hat{z}_j^{(i)} = z_j^{(i)}$) or the inactive region where its output is zero ($\hat{z}_j^{(i)} = 0$).
- Unstable: If $\mathbf{l}_j^{(i)} \leq 0 \leq \mathbf{u}_j^{(i)}$, we call this ReLU neuron as an unstable neuron, this circumstance frequently presents challenges to the process of certification.

We follow the MILP-based reformulation of ReLU networks [20], to encode the unstable neuron. We formulate a ReLU activation function as:

$$
\begin{aligned}
z_0 &= x \\
\hat{z}_{k+1} &= W_{k+1}z_k + b_{k+1}, \forall k = 0, 1, \ldots, K-1 \\
z_k &= \max\left(\hat{z}_k, 0\right), \quad \forall k = 1, \ldots, K \\
\hat{y}_x &= W_K z_K + b_K,
\end{aligned}
\tag{1}
$$

where the variable K denotes the number of layers. Each layer is determined by a weight matrix W_k and a bias vector b_k. The size of the weight matrix is $[N_{k+1} \times N_k]$, while the size of the bias vector is $[N_{k+1} \times 1]$. Here, N_k refers to the number of neurons in the kth layer. The specifications that define the encoding of the neuron are as follows:

$$
z_k = \max\left(\hat{z}_k, 0\right) \Rightarrow
\begin{cases}
z_k \leq \hat{z}_k - \hat{z}_k^{\min}\left(1 - \mathbf{b}_k\right) \\
z_k \geq \hat{z}_k \\
z_k \leq \hat{z}_k^{\max}\mathbf{b}_k \\
z_k \geq \mathbf{0} \\
\mathbf{b}_k \in \{0,1\}^{N_k}.
\end{cases}
\tag{2}
$$

where $\mathbf{b}_k$ is a binary variable.

4   The Perturbation Refinement Verification Framework

The methodology we have adopted involves the combination of gradient attack and symbolic interval analysis with the MILP-based method. The use of adversarial example from an attack aids in the provision of rough perturbation values, which we then utilize to establish the primary bounds. Following this, we leverage SIP to obtain more precise bounds for the hidden neurons. The application of tighter bounds results in decreased activation search space in the verification problem, thereby enhancing verification efficiency.

Algorithm 1: Perturbation Refinement

Input: DNN $\mathcal{N}$, input x, perturbation threshold ϵ
Output: Robust

1 $\widehat{\epsilon} := \text{FGSM\_attack}(x)$;   // Initial adversarial perturbation
2 $SymbolicBounds := SymbolicBoundpPropogation(x, \widehat{\epsilon})$
3 $MIPFormulation := MIPModel(\mathcal{N}, x, \widehat{\epsilon}, symbolic\_bounds)$
4 $\widehat{solver} := Constraint\&Objective(MIP\_formulation)$
5 $output := optimise(\widehat{solver})$
6 **if** *UNSAT* **then**
7 $\quad$ **return** Robust $\mathcal{N}$;   // returns a robust network
8 **end**
9 **else**
10 $\quad$ $x' := \text{get\_adversarial}(\widehat{solver})$;
    $\qquad\qquad\qquad\qquad\qquad\qquad\qquad$ // returns an adversarial example
11 $\quad$ **return** x';
12 **end**

Algorithm 1 displays an outline of our approach. Given an neural network $\mathcal{N}$, an input $x \in \mathbb{R}^n$ and a perturbation threshold ϵ. The FGSM attack is responsible for creating the initial boundaries for the adversarial example in line 1. In line 2, the SIP is utilized to establish tighter boundaries for the neurons than those from the original adversarial example. Between lines 3-6, an MILP problem is formulated that takes into account the input, $\mathcal{N}$, $\widehat{\epsilon}$, and the symbolic boundaries from line 2. The problem returns UNSAT if no adversarial example can be found, but it returns an adversarial example between lines 7-12.

FGSM Attack. In our method, we first compute a rough estimate ϵ using adversarial examples generated by the FGSM attack. This value is typically very close to the optimal robust radius, which helps to establish more precise input bounds. By having tighter input bounds, the number of binary variables is reduced, which in turn reduces the activation search space. Further, we constraint the adversarial attack that limits the magnitude of the perturbation that can be added to the input features of the neuron using the L-∞ norm. Mathematically, we can represent it as:

$$\|\delta\|_\infty = \max\left(|\delta_1|, |\delta_2|, \ldots, |\delta_n|\right) \tag{3}$$

where δ_i is the perturbation added to the $i-th$ neuron, and n is the total number of neurons. First, we define the L-∞ norm as the maximum absolute deviation between the original input and the perturbed input as shown in 3. Next we define the ϵ from the attack as the maximum allowable deviation between the original input and the perturbed input. Next, we set the bounds for each neuron in the network by taking into account both the L-∞ norm and ϵ. For example, if the L-∞ norm is 0.1 and ϵ is 0.05, the bounds for a neuron would be $[-0.05, 0.05]$, since any perturbation greater than 0.05 in either direction would violate both the L-∞ norm and ϵ. This ensures that the perturbed input stays within the allowable range.

By constraining the L-∞ norm of the perturbation added to the input of the neuron, the FGSM attack ensures that the resulting adversarial example remains within a certain "perceptual distance" of the original input, or that the output of the neuron remains close to its original output for small perturbations.

Epsilon-Robustness ϵ. Epsilon perturbation or epsilon-robustness is employed to represent the perturbation limits, ϵ, for a neuron x. Epsilon perturbation involves adding a small perturbation to the input of the neuron such that the output remains approximately the same. The procedure to encode perturbation bounds ϵ for a neuron x using ϵ perturbation:

- Determine the range of values that x can take. For example, if x is a pixel in an image, it might take values between 0 and 255.
- Choose a value for ϵ (this is obtained from the FGSM attack). This is the maximum amount of perturbation that is allowed for x.
- Scale epsilon to the same range as x. For example, if x takes values between 0 and 255 you can allow a maximum perturbation of 10%, you would scale epsilon to 25.5.
- Add or subtract the scaled epsilon value to x to create two new values: $x\_min = x - \epsilon$ and $x\_max = x + \epsilon$
- Use x_min and x_max as the new input values for the neuron x. This ensures that the output of the neuron will remain within a certain range, even if the input is perturbed.

By using ϵ perturbation to encode perturbation bounds for a neuron x, we can ensure that the neuron is robust to small perturbations in its input. This is useful in speeding up the verification process because since it provides low-cost solutions or information gathered via a gradient-based adversarial attack.

MILP Formulation. To formulate the bounded neurons bounded by ϵ into MILP solver[12], we follow the following steps:

1. The binary decision variables: We define binary decision variables for each neuron in the network, where the variable takes a value of 1 if the neuron is active and 0 otherwise.

---

[1] We use the Gurobi solver to tackle the MILP problem.
[2] https://www.gurobi.com/resources/chapter-1-why-mixed-integer-programming-mip/.

2. The objective function: The objective function can be defined to minimize the distance between the original input and the perturbed input subject to the constraints that we define in the following steps.

3. Define the constraints for the epsilon value: We can formulate the epsilon value constraint as a set of linear constraints that ensure that the perturbation of each neuron is within a specified bound. For each neuron, we can define two linear constraints to enforce the upper and lower bounds on the perturbation of the neuron obtained from the FGSM attack.

4. Solve the MILP: Once the MILP is formulated, we can solve it using an optimization solver to find the input that minimizes the distance between the original input and the perturbed input subject to the constraints that we have defined.

By formulating bounded neurons bounded by epsilon into MILP, we can find adversarial examples that are constrained by the epsilon value while preserving the behavior of the neural network.

5   Experimentation, Dataset and Evaluation

We compare our verification procedure's implementation with three existing verifiers, namely Venus [4], Neurify [21], and MIPVerify [20]. Venus Verifier is a software tool for verifying neural network models using a combination of abstract interpretation and SMT-based techniques. It is based on a novel approach that combines interval arithmetic and constraint propagation with SMT-based techniques such as CEGAR and IC3. Neurify is a software tool for verifying neural network models using abstract interpretation. It is based on the ReluVal algorithm, which is an abstract interpretation-based approach for analyzing ReLU neural networks. MIPVerify is a software tool for verifying neural network models using mixed-integer programming (MIP). It is a verification framework that is based on solving a sequence of MIP problems, where each problem checks if the output of the neural network model is within a certain range. In this work, we evaluate the effectiveness of our verification algorithm on the MNIST dataset, which contains handwritten digits ranging from 0 to 9. To ensure consistency, the images are preprocessed to have a size of 28×28 pixels and are normalized and centered. Each pixel of the image has a value between 0 and 255, with 0 representing black, 255 representing white, and intermediate values representing different shades of gray.

Table 1 displays the verification results on the first 100 instances using four different neural architectures and three different verifiers, with an epsilon value of 0.05. The metrics used to evaluate the verifiers are $V_{t(sec)}$ (total verification time), $\#Adv$ (number of adversarial examples computed), $\#SAT$ (number of instances verified as satisfied), and $\#UNK$ (number of instances for which verification was inconclusive). The experiments were conducted on a Linux workstation equipped with a Dual Xeon E5-2673 v3 (24 cores) and 64GB of memory. A time-limit was set to 120 min for each instance and an overall limit of 720 min. To minimize experimental errors resulting from parallel tasks, each verification task

Table 1. Verification on the MNIST dataset.

Method$(\mathcal{N}_1)\langle 784, 24, 24, 10\rangle \epsilon = 0.05$	$V_{t(sec)}$	#Adv	#SAT	#UNK
Ours	101.43	49	2	0
Venus	24.32	47	2	0
Neurify	398.42	47	2	0
MIPVerify	723.48	49	2	0
Method$(\mathcal{N}_2)\langle 784, 40, 20, 10\rangle \epsilon = 0.05$	$V_{t(sec)}$	#Adv	#SAT	#UNK
Ours	282.36	43	7	0
Venus	34.55	44	7	0
Neurify	timelimit	-	-	-
MIPVerify	1130.45	43	7	0
Method$(\mathcal{N}_3)\langle 784, 512, 512, 10\rangle \epsilon = 0.05$	$V_{t(sec)}$	#Adv	#SAT	#UNK
Ours	12335.32	41	7	0
Venus	2515.86	44	7	1
Neurify	memlimit	-	-	-
MIPVerify	34525.35	44	7	1
Method$(\mathcal{N}_4)\langle 784, 500, 10\rangle \epsilon = 0.05$	$V_{t(sec)}$	#Adv	#SAT	#UNK
Ours	513.43	2	46	0
Venus	18188.76	6	45	5
Neurify	timelimit	-	-	-
MIPVerify	18187.76	4	46	0

was run five times. The average of these results was then used as the experimental outcome. Our verifier performs better than the other verification methods on all four neural architectures. Additionally, we notice that Neurify reaches a time limit for the second and third architectures, denoted as $\mathcal{N}_2$ and $\mathcal{N}_3$, respectively, and a memory limit for the fourth architecture, denoted as $\mathcal{N}_4$. Venus, however, failed on $\mathcal{N}_4$ but outperformed on $\mathcal{N}_1$, $\mathcal{N}_2$, $\mathcal{N}_3$. On $\mathcal{N}_4$, Venus returns five #UNK case whereas our verifier returns zero #UNK thus ensuring completeness is achieved by always providing a solution to the MILP problem.

6 Conclusion

In conclusion, our paper has successfully demonstrated the potential of low-cost solutions derived from adversarial attacks to reduce the search space and streamline the verification process, while still maintaining high levels of accuracy. Future work in this area will involve comparing our approach with different adversarial attacks to further optimize the effectiveness of our method. By leveraging the insights gained from this study, we hope to contribute to the ongoing efforts to enhance the security and robustness of machine learning systems. In future work, we focus on robust optimization i.e., variability in the data or parameters of the problem, can lead to sub-optimal or even infeasible solutions. One way to address this is the objective function and constraints are reformulated to explicitly account for the worst-case scenarios of the uncertain data. Adversarial attacks can be seen as a way of generating such worst-case scenarios, and hence the adversarial solutions can be used as inputs to the robust optimization formulation. This can lead to more robust and reliable MILP solutions that perform well under various scenarios.

References

1. Alparslan, Y., Alparslan, K., Keim-Shenk, J., Khade, S., Greenstadt, R.: Adversarial attacks on convolutional neural networks in facial recognition domain. arXiv preprint arXiv:2001.11137 (2020)
2. Anderson, R., Huchette, J., Ma, W., Tjandraatmadja, C., Vielma, J.P.: Strong mixed-integer programming formulations for trained neural networks. Math. Program. **183**(1–2), 3–39 (2020)
3. Biggio, B., et al.: Evasion attacks against machine learning at test time. In: Blockeel, H., Kersting, K., Nijssen, S., Železný, F. (eds.) ECML PKDD 2013. LNCS (LNAI), vol. 8190, pp. 387–402. Springer, Heidelberg (2013). https://doi.org/10.1007/978-3-642-40994-3_25
4. Botoeva, E., Kouvaros, P., Kronqvist, J., Lomuscio, A., Misener, R.: Efficient verification of ReLU-based neural networks via dependency analysis. In: Proceedings of the AAAI Conference on Artificial Intelligence, vol. 34, pp. 3291–3299 (2020)
5. Bunel, R., Mudigonda, P., Turkaslan, I., Torr, P., Lu, J., Kohli, P.: Branch and bound for piecewise linear neural network verification. J. Mach. Learn. Res. **21**(2020) (2020)
6. Bunel, R.R., Turkaslan, I., Torr, P., Kohli, P., Mudigonda, P.K.: A unified view of piecewise linear neural network verification. Adv. Neural Inf. Process. Syst. **31** (2018)
7. Carlini, N., Wagner, D.: Towards evaluating the robustness of neural networks. In: 2017 IEEE Symposium on Security and Privacy (SP), pp. 39–57. IEEE (2017)
8. Ehlers, R.: Formal verification of piece-wise linear feed-forward neural networks. In: D'Souza, D., Narayan Kumar, K. (eds.) ATVA 2017. LNCS, vol. 10482, pp. 269–286. Springer, Cham (2017). https://doi.org/10.1007/978-3-319-68167-2_19
9. Goodfellow, I.J., Shlens, J., Szegedy, C.: Explaining and harnessing adversarial examples. arXiv preprint arXiv:1412.6572 (2014)
10. Gopinath, D., Pasareanu, C.S., Wang, K., Zhang, M., Khurshid, S.: Symbolic execution for attribution and attack synthesis in neural networks. In: 2019 IEEE/ACM 41st International Conference on Software Engineering: Companion Proceedings (ICSE-Companion), pp. 282–283. IEEE (2019)
11. Hernandez, C., Espf, J., Nakayama, K., Fernandez, M.: Interval arithmetic backpropagation. In: Proceedings of 1993 International Conference on Neural Networks (IJCNN-93-Nagoya, Japan), vol. 1, pp. 375–378. IEEE (1993)
12. Huang, X., Kwiatkowska, M., Wang, S., Wu, M.: Safety verification of deep neural networks. In: Majumdar, R., Kunčak, V. (eds.) CAV 2017. LNCS, vol. 10426, pp. 3–29. Springer, Cham (2017). https://doi.org/10.1007/978-3-319-63387-9_1

13. Katz, G., Barrett, C., Dill, D.L., Julian, K., Kochenderfer, M.J.: Reluplex: an efficient SMT solver for verifying deep neural networks. In: Majumdar, R., Kunčak, V. (eds.) CAV 2017. LNCS, vol. 10426, pp. 97–117. Springer, Cham (2017). https://doi.org/10.1007/978-3-319-63387-9_5

14. Kurakin, A., Goodfellow, I.J., Bengio, S.: Adversarial examples in the physical world. In: Artificial Intelligence Safety and Security, pp. 99–112. Chapman and Hall/CRC (2018)

15. Lin, W., et al.: Robustness verification of classification deep neural networks via linear programming. In: Proceedings of the IEEE/CVF Conference on Computer Vision and Pattern Recognition, pp. 11418–11427 (2019)

16. Madry, A., Makelov, A., Schmidt, L., Tsipras, D., Vladu, A.: Towards deep learning models resistant to adversarial attacks. arXiv preprint arXiv:1706.06083 (2017)

17. Papernot, N., McDaniel, P., Jha, S., Fredrikson, M., Celik, Z.B., Swami, A.: The limitations of deep learning in adversarial settings. In: 2016 IEEE European Symposium on Security and Privacy (EuroS&P), pp. 372–387. IEEE (2016)

18. Singh, G., Gehr, T., Püschel, M., Vechev, M.: An abstract domain for certifying neural networks. Proc. ACM Program. Lang. **3**(POPL), 1–30 (2019)

19. Szegedy, C., et al.: Intriguing properties of neural networks. corr abs/1312.6199, arXiv preprint arXiv:1312.6199 (2013)

20. Tjeng, V., Xiao, K., Tedrake, R.: Evaluating robustness of neural networks with mixed integer programming. arXiv preprint arXiv:1711.07356 (2017)

21. Wang, S., Pei, K., Whitehouse, J., Yang, J., Jana, S.: Efficient formal safety analysis of neural networks. In: Advances in neural information processing systems, vol. 31 (2018)

22. Wang, S., Pei, K., Whitehouse, J., Yang, J., Jana, S.: Formal security analysis of neural networks using symbolic intervals. In: 27th {USENIX} Security Symposium ({USENIX} Security 18), pp. 1599–1614 (2018)

23. Wang, S., Su, Z.: Metamorphic testing for object detection systems. arXiv preprint arXiv:1912.12162 (2019)

24. Wardat, M., Le, W., Rajan, H.: Deeplocalize: fault localization for deep neural networks. In: 2021 IEEE/ACM 43rd International Conference on Software Engineering (ICSE), pp. 251–262. IEEE (2021)

25. Weng, L., et al.: Towards fast computation of certified robustness for ReLU networks. In: International Conference on Machine Learning, pp. 5276–5285. PMLR (2018)

26. Yang, P., et al.: Enhancing robustness verification for deep neural networks via symbolic propagation. Formal Aspects Comput. **33**(3), 407–435 (2021)

Relative Intrinsic Dimensionality Is Intrinsic to Learning

Oliver J. Sutton[1]([✉])[iD], Qinghua Zhou[1][iD], Alexander N. Gorban[2][iD], and Ivan Y. Tyukin[1][iD]

[1] King's College London, London WC2R 2LS, UK
oliver.sutton@kcl.ac.uk
[2] University of Leicester, Leicester LE1 7RH, UK

Abstract. High dimensional data can have a surprising property: pairs of data points may be easily separated from each other, or even from arbitrary subsets, with high probability using just simple linear classifiers. However, this is more of a rule of thumb than a reliable property as high dimensionality alone is neither necessary nor sufficient for successful learning. Here, we introduce a new notion of the *intrinsic dimension* of a data distribution, which precisely captures the separability properties of the data. For this intrinsic dimension, the rule of thumb above becomes a law: high intrinsic dimension guarantees highly separable data. We extend this notion to that of the *relative* intrinsic dimension of two data distributions, which we show provides both upper and lower bounds on the probability of successfully learning and generalising in a binary classification problem.

Keywords: Intrinsic dimensionality · Classification problems · High dimensional data

1 Introduction

A *blessing of dimensionality* often ascribed to data sampled from genuinely high dimensional probability distributions is that pairs (and even arbitrary compact subsets) of points may be easily separated from one another with high probability [2,4–7,9,13]. Such a property is naturally highly appealing for Machine Learning and Artificial Intelligence, since it suggests that if sufficiently many attributes can be obtained for each data point, then classification is a significantly easier task.

However, although this provides a useful rule of thumb, it is far from a complete description of the behaviour which may be expected of high dimensional data, and a simple experiment shows that the precise relationship between data dimension and classification performance is more subtle (see also [8], Theorem 5 and Corollary 2). Suppose that data are sampled from two classes, each described by a uniform distribution in a unit ball in $\mathbb{R}^d$, and that the centres of these balls are at distance $\epsilon \geq 0$ from one another, as shown in Fig. 1. The classifier which offers the optimal (balanced) accuracy in this case is given by the hyperplane

L. Iliadis et al. (Eds.): ICANN 2023, LNCS 14254, pp. 516–529, 2023.
https://doi.org/10.1007/978-3-031-44207-0_43

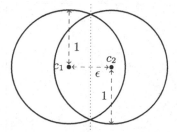

Fig. 1. Two unit balls separated by distance epsilon, and the optimal classifier (dotted) separating the two.

which is normal to the vector connecting the two centres and positioned half way between them. In Fig. 2 we plot the accuracy of this classifier as a function of the distance separating the two centres for data sampled from various different ambient dimensions d. The insight behind the blessing of dimensionality described above is immediately clear: when the data is sampled in high dimensions, for values of ϵ greater than some threshold value $\epsilon_0(d)$ depending on the ambient dimension d, the accuracy of this simple linear classifier is virtually 100%. Yet, what this simplified viewpoint misses is that, for $\epsilon < \epsilon_0(d)$ the probability of correctly classifying a given point sharply drops to close to 50%, demonstrating that raw dimensionality alone is no panacea for data classification[1]. On the other hand, data sampled even in 1 dimension may be accurately classified when the centre separation ϵ is sufficiently large: for $\epsilon \geq 2$ (when the two unit balls are disjoint), the two data sets are fully separable in any dimension.

What this simple thought experiment demonstrates is a fact which is not taken into account by previous work, such as [12]:

Determining whether data distributions are separable from each other must depend on a relative property of the two, and even genuine high dimensionality[2] alone is neither a necessary nor sufficient condition for data separability.

To lay the foundations of our approach, we propose the new concept of the *intrinsic dimension* of a data distribution, based directly on the separability properties of sampled data points.

Definition 1 (Intrinsic dimension). *We say that data sampled from a distribution $\mathcal{D}$ on $\mathbb{R}^d$ has* intrinsic dimension $n(\mathcal{D}) \in \mathbb{R}$ *with respect to a centre* $c \in \mathbb{R}^d$ *if*

$$P(x, y \sim \mathcal{D} : (x - y, y - c) \geq 0) = \frac{1}{2^{n(\mathcal{D})+1}}. \tag{1}$$

This definition is designed in such a way that the rule of thumb in the blessing of dimensionality described above becomes a *law of high intrinsic dimension*:

---

[1] Moreover, standard dimensionality reduction techniques, such as Principle Components Analysis, would not have any effect here since the data are uniformly sampled from d-dimensional balls.

[2] In the sense that dimensionality reduction techniques cannot be applied to find an equivalent lower dimensional representation of the data.

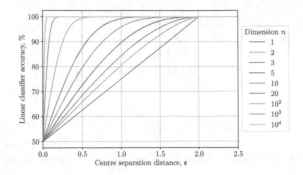

Fig. 2. Accuracy of the best linear classifier separating data uniformly sampled from two balls with unit radius and centres in $\mathbb{R}^n$ separated by distance ϵ for different dimensions n.

points sampled from a distribution with high intrinsic dimension are highly separable. The definition is calibrated so that the uniform distribution $\mathcal{U}(\mathbb{B}_d)$ on a d-dimensional unit ball $\mathbb{B}_d$ satisfies $n(\mathcal{U}(\mathbb{B}_d)) = d$ (see Theorem 1), although alternative normalisations are possible, and by symmetry $n(\mathcal{D}) \geq 0$ for all distributions $\mathcal{D}$. For $c = 0$, the expression $(x - y, y - c) \geq 0$ in the left-hand side of (1) is simply a statement that x and y are Fisher-separable [8].

Based on the same principle, we further introduce the concept of the *relative intrinsic dimension* of two data distributions, which directly describes the ease of separating data distributions.

Definition 2 (Relative intrinsic dimension). *We say that data sampled from a distribution $\mathcal{D}$ on $\mathbb{R}^d$ has* relative intrinsic dimension $n(\mathcal{D}, \mathcal{D}') \in \mathbb{R}$ *to data sampled from a distribution $\mathcal{D}'$ on $\mathbb{R}^d$, with respect to a centre $c \in \mathbb{R}^d$, if*

$$P(x \sim \mathcal{D}', y \sim \mathcal{D} : (x - y, y - c) \geq 0) = \frac{1}{2^{n(\mathcal{D}, \mathcal{D}')+1}}. \tag{2}$$

The relative intrinsic dimension is not symmetric, and satisfies $n(\mathcal{D}, \mathcal{D}') \geq -1$, with negative values indicating that $\mathcal{D}$ has lower intrinsic dimension than $\mathcal{D}'$, and data distributions with a low relative intrinsic dimension may be separated from distributions with a high relative intrinsic dimension.

To illustrate this, consider our previous experiment as an example and let $X = \mathcal{U}(B_1)$ and $Y = \mathcal{U}(B_2)$, where $B_1 = \mathbb{B}_d(1, c_1) \subset \mathbb{R}^d$ and $B_2 = \mathbb{B}_d(1, c_2) \subset \mathbb{R}^d$ are the unit balls centered at c_1 and c_2 respectively, and pick the centre $c = c_1$. When $\epsilon = \|c_1 - c_2\| \geq 2$ (the case when the data distributions are completely separable), we have $n(Y, X) = \infty$. This implies that points y sampled from Y can be separated from points sampled from points x sampled from X with certainty. The relative intrinsic dimension $n(X, Y)$ is an increasing function of the dimension of the ambient space in which the data is sampled with $n(X, Y) = 0$ in 1 dimension, implying that it becomes easier to separate points in X from points in Y as the dimension increases. These values of the relative intrinsic dimensions suggest that points from Y can easily be separated from points in

X by hyperplanes normal to $y - c_1$, while hyperplanes normal to $x - c_1$ do not separate X from Y.

Although the asymmetry may be slightly surprising at first, it is simply reflecting the asymmetric choice of centre $c = c_1$, which is located at the heart of the X distribution. The relative intrinsic dimensions described above would be reversed for $c = c_2$ and would be equal for $c = \frac{1}{2}(c_1 + c_2)$. A justification for this definition of relative intrinsic dimension is given by Theorem 2, where it is shown (in a slightly generalised setting) that these concepts of intrinsic dimension provide upper and lower bounds on classifier accuracy, indicating that it is indeed necessary and sufficient for learning.

There is a rich history of alternative charaterisations of the dimension of a data set, with each contribution typically aimed to solve a particular problem. For example, conventional Principle Components Analysis aims to detect the number of independent attributes which are actually required to represent the data, leading to compressed representations of the same data. However, as discussed above, the representational dimension of a data set does not necessarily give an indication of how easy it is to learn from. Several other notions of dimensionality are captured in the scikit-dimension library [3]. Perhaps the most similar notion of dimension to that which we propose here is the Fisher Separability Dimension [1], which is also based on the separability properties of data yet first requires a whitening step to normalise the data covariance to an identity matrix. This whitening step has both advantages and disadvantages: although it brings invariance to the choice and scaling of the basis, it disrupts the intrinsic geometry of the data. The Fisher Separability Dimension also does not address the important question of the *relative* dimension of data distributions and samples, which we argue is a concept fundamental to learning.

Our approach may appear reminiscent of Kernel Embeddings, through which nonlinear kernels are used to embed families of data distributions into a Hilbert space structure [11]. Although Kernel Embeddings and our work are motivated by very different classes problems, the common fundamental focus is on understanding the properties of a data distribution through the evaluation of (nonlinear) functionals of the distribution. Here we demonstrate how a single, targeted, property appears to encode important information about the separability properties of data.

An interesting question which arises from this work is how well the (relative) intrinsic dimension can be estimated from data samples directly. If it can be, then this could provide a new tool for selecting appropriate feature mappings for data and shine a new light on the training of neural networks. We briefly investigate this in Sect. 4, where we show that high order polynomial feature maps can actually be detrimental to the separability of data.

2 Separability of Uniformly Distributed Data

We investigate the separability properties of data sampled from a uniform distribution in the unit ball in various dimensions. This provides the basis for our definition of intrinsic dimension.

To simplify the presentation of our results, we introduce the following geometric quantities related to spheres in high dimensions. The volume of a ball with radius r in d dimensions is denoted by

$$V_d^{\text{ball}}(r) = \frac{\pi^{d/2} r^d}{\Gamma(\frac{d}{2}+1)},$$

and the surface area of the same ball is denoted by

$$S_d^{\text{ball}}(r) = \frac{d\pi^{d/2} r^{d-1}}{\Gamma(\frac{d}{2}+1)}.$$

Similarly, the volume of the spherical cap with height h of the same sphere (i.e. the set of points $\{x \in \mathbb{R}^d : \|x\| \leq r$ and $x_0 \geq r - h\}$) is given by $V_d^{\text{cap}}(r, h) = V_d^{\text{ball}}(r) W_d^{\text{cap}}(r, h)$, where

$$W_d^{\text{cap}}(r, h) = \begin{cases} 0 & \text{for } h \leq 0, \\ \frac{1}{2} I_{(2rh-h^2)/r^2}\left(\frac{d+1}{2}, \frac{1}{2}\right) & \text{for } 0 < h \leq r, \\ 1 - W_d^{\text{cap}}(r, 2r - h) & \text{for } r < h \leq 2r, \\ 1 & \text{for } 2r < h, \end{cases}$$

represents the fraction of the volume of the unit ball contained in the spherical cap. The function $I_x(a, b) = B(a, b)^{-1} \int_0^x t^{a-1}(1-t)^{b-1} dt$ denotes the regularised incomplete beta function, where $B(a, b) = B(1; a, b) = \frac{\Gamma(a)\Gamma(b)}{\Gamma(a+b)}$ is the standard beta function.

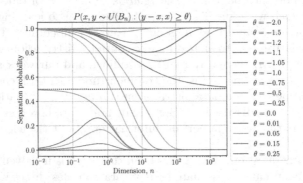

Fig. 3. The behaviour of $f_\theta(d)$, formally extended to non-integer values of d, for various values of θ. The function is only invertible for $-1 \leq \theta \leq 0$, and we note the asymptote of $\frac{1}{2}$ as $d \to 0$ when $\theta = 0$ and as $d \to \infty$ when $\theta = -1$

Theorem 1 (Separability of uniformly sampled points). *Let $\theta \in \mathbb{R}$, let d be a positive integer and suppose that $x, y \sim \mathcal{U}(\mathbb{B}_d(1, c))$, define*

$$R_\theta(t) = \max\left\{\frac{t^2}{4} - \theta, 0\right\}^{\frac{1}{2}}, \quad a_\theta(t) = \frac{1 - R_\theta^2(t)}{t} - \frac{t}{4}, \tag{3}$$

and

$$b_\theta(t) = 1 - a_\theta(t) - \frac{t}{2}, \tag{4}$$

and let

$$f_\theta(d) = \int_0^1 dt^{d-1} \big(W_d^{\mathrm{cap}}(1, b_\theta(t)) + R_\theta^d(t) W_d^{\mathrm{cap}}(R_\theta(t), R_\theta(t) + a_\theta(t)) \big) dt. \tag{5}$$

Then

$$P(x, y : (y - x, x - c) \geq \theta) = f_\theta(d), \tag{6}$$

and, in particular,

$$P(x, y : (y - x, x - c) \geq 0) = \frac{1}{2^{d+1}}. \tag{7}$$

Furthermore, f_θ may be simplified in the following cases as

$$f_\theta(d) = \begin{cases} 1 & \text{for } \theta \leq -2, \\ \frac{1}{2^{d+1}} & \text{for } \theta = 0, \\ \int_{2\theta^{1/2}}^1 dt^{d-1} \left(\frac{t^2}{4} - \theta \right)^{d/2} dt & \text{for } 0 < \theta < \frac{1}{4}, \\ 0 & \text{for } \frac{1}{4} \leq \theta. \end{cases} \tag{8}$$

and $f_\theta(d) \geq \frac{1}{2}$ for $\theta \leq -1$.

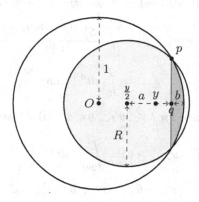

Fig. 4. The shaded area is the volume computed in the proof of Theorem 1. The two different shading colours indicate the two spherical caps used in the proof.

Proof. Without loss of generality, we suppose that $c = 0$, and consider points $x, y \sim \mathcal{U}(\mathbb{B}_d)$. Rearranging terms, we observe that

$$(y - x, x) = \frac{1}{4} \|y\|^2 - \left\| x - \frac{y}{2} \right\|^2,$$

and therefore, for fixed y, the set of x satisfying $(y-x, x-c) \geq \theta$ may be similarly described as those points x contained within the ball

$$\|x - \frac{y}{2}\|^2 \leq R(\|y\|) = \max\left\{\frac{1}{4}\|y\|^2 - \theta, 0\right\}.$$

Combining this with the condition that $x \sim \mathbb{B}_d(1,0)$, we find that x belongs to the intersection of the balls

$$\{x \in \mathbb{R}^d : \|x\| \leq 1\} \cap \left\{x \in \mathbb{R}^d : \|x - \frac{y}{2}\|^2 \leq R_\theta(\|y\|)\right\}. \tag{9}$$

This may be expressed as the union of two spherical caps, as depicted in Fig. 4. Comparing the triangles O, p, q and $\frac{y}{2}, p, q$ shows that the lengths a and b in the Figure are exactly those defined in (3) with $t = \|y\|$. Since y only appears through its norm, we deduce that

$$
\begin{aligned}
P(x : (y-x, x) \geq \theta \,|\, \|y\|) &= P(x : (y-x, x) \geq \theta \,|\, y) \\
&= \frac{V_d^{\text{cap}}(R_\theta(\|y\|), R_\theta(\|y\|) + a_\theta(\|y\|)) + V_d^{\text{cap}}(1, b_\theta(\|y\|))}{V_d^{\text{ball}}(1)},
\end{aligned}
$$

The result (6) follows by applying the law of total probability, which implies

$$P(x, y : (y-x, x) \geq \theta) = \int_0^1 P(x : (y-x, x) \geq \theta \,|\, \|y\| = t) p_{\|y\|}(t) dt,$$

where $p_{\|y\|}(t) = \frac{S_d^{\text{ball}}(t)}{V_d^{\text{ball}}(1)}$ is the density associated with $\|y\|$ for $y \sim \mathcal{U}(\mathbb{B}_d)$.

When $\theta \geq 0$, the ball centered at $\frac{y}{2}$ is entirely contained within $\mathbb{B}_d$, and so

$$
\begin{aligned}
P(x, y : (y-x, x) \geq \theta) &= \int_0^1 \frac{S_d^{\text{ball}}(t) V_d^{\text{ball}}(R_\theta(t))}{(V_d^{\text{ball}}(1))^2} dt \\
&= \int_0^1 dt^{d-1} \max\left\{\frac{t^2}{4} - \theta, 0\right\}^{d/2} dt.
\end{aligned}
$$

Since the integrand is zero for $t \leq 2\theta^{1/2}$, for $\theta \in (0, \frac{1}{4})$ we have

$$P(x, y : (y-x, x) \geq \theta) = \int_{2\theta^{1/2}}^1 dt^{d-1} \left(\frac{t^2}{4} - \theta\right)^{d/2} dt.$$

Moreover, $P(x, y : (y-x, x) \geq \theta) = 0$ for $\theta \geq \frac{1}{4}$, and in the simplest case of $\theta = 0$

$$P(x, y : (y-x, x) \geq 0) = \frac{d}{2^d} \int_0^1 t^{2d-1} dt = \frac{1}{2^{d+1}}.$$

On the other hand, for $\theta \leq -2$ we have $\sqrt{R_\theta(t)} \geq 1 + \frac{1}{2}t$ for all t, implying that the intersection (9) is the entirety of $\mathbb{B}_d$, and hence

$$P\left(x, y : (y-x, x) \geq \theta\right) = 1.$$

$\square$

The behaviour of $f_\theta(d)$ is illustrated in Fig. 3 for various values of the separation threshold θ. Heuristically, we observe the following limiting behaviour:

$$\lim_{d\to\infty} f_\theta(d) = \begin{cases} 1 & \text{for } \theta < -1, \\ \frac{1}{2} & \text{for } \theta = -1, \\ 0 & \text{for } \theta > -1, \end{cases}$$

which may be explained by the fact that when $\theta = -1$, the surfaces of the ball $\mathbb{B}_d$ and the ball centered at $\frac{y}{2}$ meet exactly at an equator of $\mathbb{B}_d$. The phenomenon of waist concentration (see [10], for example) implies that in high dimensions the volume of $\mathbb{B}_d$ is concentrated around its surface and around this equator, implying that this is the threshold value of θ at which the intersection of the two balls contains slightly more than half the volume of $\mathbb{B}_d$.

What these results suggest is that for any value of $\theta \in [-1, 0]$, the function $f_\theta(d)$ is an invertible function of d, and hence could be used as the basis of a definition of intrinsic dimension. In Definition 1 we use the behaviour at $\theta = 0$ to define our indicative notion of intrinsic dimension simply because it obviates the need to couple the scaling of the support of the distribution and the scaling of θ.

3   Few Shot Learning Is Dependent on Separability

We now consider the scenario of standard binary data classification, and show that the probability of successfully learning to classify data is intrinsically linked to the notion of relative intrinsic dimension. We focus on the case of learning from small data sets, as in this case the link is particularly clear to demonstrate.

Mathematically, we suppose that X and Y are (unknown) probability distributions on an d-dimensional vector space $\mathbb{R}^d$, and we have a sample $\{y_i\}_{i=1}^{k}$ of k training points sampled from Y and a sample $\{x_i\}_{i=1}^{m}$ of m training points sampled from X.

Since the problem setup is symmetric in the roles of X and Y, we only analyse the influence of training data sampled from Y. The role of the data sampled from X (alongside any possible prior knowledge of the data distributions) is incorporated through an arbitrary but fixed point $c \in \mathbb{R}^d$ in the data space.

We consider the following linear classifier to assign the label ℓ_X to data sampled from X and the label ℓ_Y to data sampled from Y:

$$F_\theta(z) = \begin{cases} \ell_Y & \text{if } L(z) \geq \theta, \\ \ell_X & \text{otherwise,} \end{cases} \tag{10}$$

where $L(z) = \frac{1}{k} \sum_{i=1}^{k} (z - y_i, y_i - c)$. In practice, the value of the threshold θ to be used in the classifier may be determined from the training data $\{y_i\}_{i=1}^{k}$ and $\{x_i\}_{i=1}^{m}$, although here we consider it to be a free parameter of the classifier.

Remark 1 (Comparison with similar classifiers). The classifier (10) may be equivalently be expressed in the form of the common Fisher discriminant with a slightly different threshold, viz.

$$F_\theta(z) = \begin{cases} \ell_Y & \text{if } (z - \mu, \mu - c) \geq \theta + \Theta, \\ \ell_X & \text{otherwise,} \end{cases}$$

where $\mu = \frac{1}{k} \sum_{i=1}^k y_i$ and $\Theta = \frac{1}{k} \sum_{i=1}^k \|y_i\|^2 - \|\mu\|^2$. Since the offset Θ to the threshold θ depends only on the same training data as θ, it is clear that the classifier we study is simply a Fisher discriminant. However, we choose to write the classifier in the form (10) because it simplifies some of the forthcoming analysis.

This classifier will successfully learn to classify the training data when both

$$P(F_\theta(y) = \ell_Y) = P(L(y) \geq \theta)$$

is large (where the probability is taken with respect to the evaluation point $y \sim Y$ and the training data $\{y_i \sim Y\}_{i=1}^k$), and

$$P(F_\theta(x) = \ell_X) = P(L(x) < \theta)$$

is also large (where the probability is taken with respect to the evaluation point $x \sim X$ and the training data $\{y_i \sim Y\}_{i=1}^k$). We now show that both of these probabilities can be bounded from above and below by the probability of being able to separate pairs of data points by margin θ. Corollary 1 to this theorem then shows how this simply reduces to upper and lower bounds dependent on the (relative) intrinsic dimension of Y and X when $\theta = 0$.

Theorem 2 (Pairwise separability and learning). *Let $\theta \in \mathbb{R}$ and define*

$$p_\theta(Y, X) = P(x \sim X, y \sim Y : (x - y, y - c) \geq \theta),$$

and let $p_\theta(Y) = p_\theta(Y, Y)$. Then, the probability (with respect to the training sample $\{y_i \sim Y\}_{i=1}^k$ and the evaluation point $y \sim Y$) of successfully learning the class Y is bounded by

$$p_\theta^k(Y) \leq P(F_\theta(y) = \ell_Y) \leq 1 - (1 - p_\theta(Y))^k, \tag{11}$$

and the probability (with respect to the training sample $\{y_i \sim Y\}_{i=1}^k$ and the evaluation point $x \sim X$) of successfully learning the class X is bounded by

$$(1 - p_\theta(Y, X))^k \leq P(F_\theta(x) = \ell_X) \leq 1 - p_\theta^k(Y, X). \tag{12}$$

Proof. Let E be the event that $F_\theta(y) = \ell_Y$ for $y \sim Y$. By definition, this occurs when y and $\{y_i\}_{i=1}^k$ are such that $\sum_{i=1}^k (y - y_i, y_i - c) \geq k\theta$. For each $1 \leq i \leq k$, let A_i denote the event that $(y - y_i, y_i - c) \geq \theta$. Then, $\bigwedge_{i=1}^k A_i \Rightarrow E$ and so $P(E) \geq P(\bigwedge_{i=1}^k A_i)$. We may further expand this using the law of total probability as

$$P\left(\bigwedge_{i=1}^k A_i\right) = \int_{\mathbb{R}^d} P\left(\bigwedge_{i=1}^k (y - y_i, y_i - c) \geq \theta \,\middle|\, y\right) p(y) dy. \tag{13}$$

Since the $\{y_i\}_{i=1}^k$ are independently sampled and identically distributed, it follows that the conditional probability satisfies

$$P\Big(\{y_i \sim Y\}_{i=1}^k : \bigwedge_{i=1}^k (y - y_i, y_i - c) \geq \theta \,|\, y\Big) = P(y' \sim Y : (y - y', y' - c) \geq \theta \,|\, y)^k.$$

Substituting this into (13) shows that $P(\bigwedge_{i=1}^k A_i) = \mathbb{E}_Y\big[(P(y' \sim Y : (y - y', y' - c) \geq \theta \,|\, y))^k\big]$, where the expectation is taken with respect to y. For a random variable X and a convex function g, Jensen's inequality asserts that $\mathbb{E}[g(X)] \geq g(\mathbb{E}[X])$. Applying this here (since the function $g(x) = x^k$ is convex for $k \geq 1$), we find that

$$P\Big(\bigwedge_{i=1}^k A_i\Big) \geq \big(\mathbb{E}_Y[P(y' : (y - y', y' - c) \geq \theta \,|\, y)]\big)^k$$

$$= \big(P(y, y' : (y - y', y' - c) \geq \theta)\big)^k.$$

Consequently, we deduce the lower bound of (11). The upper bound follows by arguing similarly and using the fact that $\bigwedge_{i=1}^k \text{not } A_i \Rightarrow \text{not } E$, from which it follows that $P(E) \leq 1 - P(\bigwedge_{i=1}^k \text{not } A_i)$. An analogous argument shows the result (12).   □

An immediate consequence of this theorem is that when $\theta = 0$, the probability of successfully learning can be bounded from both above and below using the (relative) intrinsic dimension of the data distributions.

Corollary 1 (Intrinsic dimension and learning). *The probability (with respect to the training sample $\{y_i \sim Y\}_{i=1}^k$ and the evaluation point $y \sim Y$) of successfully learning the class Y is bounded by*

$$\frac{1}{2^{k(n(Y)+1)}} \leq P(F_0(y) = \ell_Y) \leq 1 - \Big(1 - \frac{1}{2^{n(Y)+1}}\Big)^k, \tag{14}$$

and the probability (with respect to the training sample $\{y_i \sim Y\}_{i=1}^k$ and the evaluation point $x \sim X$) of successfully learning the class X is bounded by

$$1 - \Big(1 - \frac{1}{2^{n(Y,X)+1}}\Big)^k \leq P(F_0(x) = \ell_X) \leq \frac{1}{2^{k(n(Y,X)+1)}}$$

We note that the best lower bound which can be shown by (14) is $\frac{1}{2}$, due to the fact that the classifier with $\theta = 0$ will pass through the centre of the Y distribution. Despite this, Corollary 1 shows that the intrinsic dimension of Y is sufficient to know whether the probability of correctly learning the class Y is less than $\frac{1}{2}$. Arguing symmetricaly, a more refined analysis taking more account of the training set $\{x_i\}_{i=1}^m$ could instead show a version of the bound (14) which depends on the relative intrinsic dimension $n(X, Y)$.

These bounds are tuned to the case when the size k of the training set sampled from Y is small, and the upper and lower bounds separate from each other as

k grows, and alternative arguments would be required to get sharp bounds in the case of large k. However, even for large values of k, if the (relative) intrinsic dimension of the data distributions is sufficiently large or small, the bounds above will provide tight guarantees on the success of learning.

4 Learning with Polynomial Kernels

As an application of our proposed notion of intrinsic dimension, we use it to find the optimal polynomial kernel for a classification problem — i.e. the degree of the polynomial feature map in which two data sets become easiest to separate.

For fixed bias $b > 1$ and polynomial degree $k \geq 0$, let the polynomial kernel $\kappa : \mathbb{R}^d \times \mathbb{R}^d \to \mathbb{R}$ be given by

$$\kappa(x,y) = (b^2 + x \cdot y)^k. \tag{15}$$

There exists a polynomial feature map $\phi : \mathbb{R}^d \to \mathbb{R}^N$, where $N = \binom{d+k}{k}$, such that $\kappa(x,y) = (\phi(x), \phi(y))$ (see [12], for example, for details).

Consider

$$P(x, y, \sim \mathcal{U}(\mathbb{B}_d) : (\phi(x) - \phi(y), \phi(y) - c) \geq \theta),$$

where $c = \frac{1}{V_d^{\text{ball}}(1)} \int_{\mathbb{B}_d} \phi(z) dz$ is the empirical mean of the data in feature space. Then, expanding the inner product,

$$(\phi(x) - \phi(y), \phi(y) - c) = k(x,y) - k(y,y) + \int_{\mathbb{B}_d} \frac{k(y,z) - k(x,z)}{V_d^{\text{ball}}(1)} dz$$

$$= (b^2 + x \cdot y)^k - (b^2 + \|y\|^2)^k + \int_{\mathbb{B}_d} \frac{(b^2 + y \cdot z)^k - (b^2 + x \cdot z)^k}{V_d^{\text{ball}}(1)} dz.$$

Exploiting the spherical symmetry of $\mathcal{U}(\mathbb{B}_d)$, we have

$$\frac{1}{V_d^{\text{ball}}(1)} \int_{\mathbb{B}_d} (b^2 + x \cdot z)^k dz = \int_{-1}^1 \frac{V_{d-1}^{\text{ball}}((1-t^2)^{1/2})}{V_d^{\text{ball}}(1)} (b^2 + t\|x\|)^k dt = q(\|x\|),$$

for $b \geq 1$, where $q : [0,1] \to \mathbb{R}$ is given by $q(\|x\|) := b^{2k} {}_2F_1\left(\frac{1-k}{2}, -\frac{k}{2}; \frac{d}{2}+1; \frac{\|x\|^2}{b^4}\right)$, with ${}_2F_1$ denoting the hypergeometric function. Therefore $(\phi(x) - \phi(y), \phi(y) - c) \geq \theta$ if and only if

$$\cos(\beta(x,y)) \geq Q(\|x\|, \|y\|)$$

where $\beta(x,y) = \arccos(\frac{(x,y)}{\|x\|\|y\|})$ denotes the angle between x and y, and

$$Q(s,t) := (st)^{-1}\left(\left(\theta + (b^2 + t^2)^k + q(s) - q(t)\right)^{1/k} - b^2\right).$$

Geometric arguments show that for any $\alpha \in [-1, 1]$,

$$P(x, y \sim \mathcal{U}(\mathbb{B}_d) : \cos(\beta(x,y)) \geq \alpha \mid \|x\|, \|y\|) = T_d^{\text{cap}}(\alpha)$$

where $T_d^{\mathrm{cap}}(\alpha)$ denotes the proportion of the surface area of a unit sphere which falls within a spherical cap with opening angle $\arccos(\alpha)$, given for $d > 1$ by

$$T_d^{\mathrm{cap}}(\alpha) = \begin{cases} 0, & \alpha > 1, \\ \frac{1}{2} I_{(\sin(\arccos(\alpha)))^2}\left(\frac{d-1}{2}, \frac{1}{2}\right), & \alpha \in [0,1], \\ 1 - T_d^{\mathrm{cap}}(-\alpha), & \alpha \in (-1,0), \\ 1, & \alpha \leq -1, \end{cases}$$

where $I_x(a,b)$ is the regulalised incomplete beta function, and for $d = 1$ by

$$T_1^{\mathrm{cap}}(\alpha) = \left\{ 0 \text{ for } \alpha > 1; \quad \tfrac{1}{2} \text{ for } \alpha \in (-1,1]; \quad 1 \text{ for } \alpha \leq -1 \right.$$

Let E be the event that $x, y \sim \mathcal{U}(\mathbb{B}_d)$ are such that $\cos(\beta) \geq Q(\|x\|, \|y\|)$. Then, by the law of total probability,

$$P(E) = \int_0^1 \int_0^1 P(E \mid \|x\| = s, \|y\| = t)\hat{p}(s)\hat{p}(t)\,ds\,dt,$$

where $\hat{p}(t) = \frac{S_d^{\mathrm{ball}}(t)}{V_d^{\mathrm{ball}}(1)} = d t^{d-1}$ denotes the density associated with $\|z\|$ for $z \sim \mathcal{U}(\mathbb{B}_d)$.

The arguments above therefore prove the following theorem, from which Theorem 1 arises as a simplified special case when $k = 1$

Theorem 3 (Separability in polynomial feature space). *Let $k > 0$, let d be a fixed positive integer, and let ϕ denote the feature map associated with the polynomial kernel (15) with degree k in dimension d. Then, for $\theta \in \mathbb{R}$,*

$$P(x, y \sim \mathcal{U}(\mathbb{B}_d) : \langle \phi(x) - \phi(y), \phi(y) - c \rangle \geq \theta)$$

$$= d^2 \int_0^1 \int_0^1 T_d^{\mathrm{cap}}(Q(s,t))s^{d-1}t^{d-1}\,ds\,dt.$$

Figure 5 shows how the intrinsic dimension of the unit ball in various dimensions is affected by applying a polynomial feature mapping. Since the degree k polynomial feature map $\phi : \mathbb{R}^d \to \mathbb{R}^N$, where $N = \binom{d+k}{k}$, increases the apparent dimension of the space as k increases, the rule of thumb encapsulated by the blessing of dimensionality would lead us to expect that high order polynomial kernels should make the data more separable. However, this is not what we observe. Instead, the intrinsic dimension reveals that there is an 'optimal' polynomial degree, for which the data is most separable, and increasing the polynomial degree further beyond the point can actually have the detrimental effect of making the data less separable.

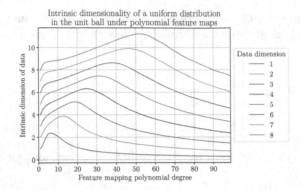

Fig. 5. The intrinsic dimension of the image of $\mathcal{U}(\mathbb{B}_d)$ under a polynomial feature map, for different polynomial degrees and data space dimensions d.

5 Conclusion

We have introduced a new notion of the intrinsic dimension of a data distribution, based on the pairwise separability properties of data points sampled from this distribution. Alongside this, we have also introduced a notion of the relative intrinsic dimension of a data distribution relative to another distribution. Theorem 2 shows how these notions of intrinsic dimension occupy a fundamental position in the theory of learning, as they directly provide upper and lower bounds on the probability of successfully learning in a generalisable fashion.

Many open questions remain, however, such as how to accurately determine the intrinsic dimension of a data distribution using just sampled data from that distribution, and how best to utilise these insights to improve neural network learning. This work also opens to door to generalising the concept beyond just simple linear functionals of the data distribution to notions of intrinsic dimensionality based around other more interesting models. The idea also generalises beyond examining individual points sampled from distributions, to studying the collective behaviour of groups, or 'granules' of sampled data.

Acknowledgements. The authors are grateful for financial support by the UKRI and EPSRC (UKRI Turing AI Fellowship ARaISE EP/V025295/1). I.Y.T. is also grateful for support from the UKRI Trustworthy Autonomous Systems Node in Verifiability EP/V026801/1.

References

1. Albergante, L., Bac, J., Zinovyev, A.: Estimating the effective dimension of large biological datasets using fisher separability analysis. In: 2019 International Joint Conference on Neural Networks (IJCNN) (2019)
2. Anderson, J., Belkin, M., Goyal, N., Rademacher, L., Voss, J.: The more, the merrier: the blessing of dimensionality for learning large Gaussian mixtures. In: Conference on Learning Theory, pp. 1135–1164. PMLR (2014)

3. Bac, J., Mirkes, E.M., Gorban, A.N., Tyukin, I., Zinovyev, A.: Scikit-Dimension: a python package for intrinsic dimension estimation. Entropy **23**(10), 1368 (2021). https://doi.org/10.3390/e23101368
4. Donoho, D., Tanner, J.: Observed universality of phase transitions in high-dimensional geometry, with implications for modern data analysis and signal processing. Philos. Trans. Royal Soc. A Math. Phys. Eng. Sci. **367**(1906), 4273–4293 (2009)
5. Gorban, A.N., Tyukin, I.Y.: Stochastic separation theorems. Neural Netw. **94**, 255–259 (2017)
6. Gorban, A.N., Tyukin, I.Y.: Blessing of dimensionality: mathematical foundations of the statistical physics of data. Philos. Trans. Royal Soc. A Math. Phys. Eng. Sci. **376**(2118), 20170237 (2018)
7. Gorban, A.N., Tyukin, I.Y., Romanenko, I.: The blessing of dimensionality: separation theorems in the thermodynamic limit. IFAC-PapersOnLine **49**(24), 64–69 (2016)
8. Gorban, A., Golubkov, A., Grechuk, B., Mirkes, E., Tyukin, I.: Correction of AI systems by linear discriminants: probabilistic foundations. Inf. Sci. **466**, 303–322 (2018). https://doi.org/10.1016/j.ins.2018.07.040
9. Kainen, P.C., Kůrková, V.: Quasiorthogonal dimension. In: Kosheleva, O., Shary, S.P., Xiang, G., Zapatrin, R. (eds.) Beyond Traditional Probabilistic Data Processing Techniques: Interval, Fuzzy etc. Methods and Their Applications. SCI, vol. 835, pp. 615–629. Springer, Cham (2020). https://doi.org/10.1007/978-3-030-31041-7_35
10. Ledoux, M.: The Concentration of Measure Phenomenon, vol. 89, American Mathematical Society (2001)
11. Smola, A., Gretton, A., Song, L., Schölkopf, B.: A hilbert space embedding for distributions. In: Hutter, M., Servedio, R.A., Takimoto, E. (eds.) Algorithmic Learning Theory, pp. 13–31. Springer, Berlin Heidelberg, Berlin, Heidelberg (2007)
12. Sutton, O.J., Gorban, A.N., Tyukin, I.Y.: Towards a mathematical understanding of learning from few examples with nonlinear feature maps. https://doi.org/10.48550/ARXIV.2211.03607https://arxiv.org/abs/2211.03607 (2022)
13. Tyukin, I.Y., Gorban, A.N., Grechuk, B., Green, S.: Kernel stochastic separation theorems and separability characterizations of kernel classifiers. In: 2019 International Joint Conference on Neural Networks (IJCNN), pp. 1–6 (2019). https://doi.org/10.1109/IJCNN.2019.8852278

The Boundaries of Verifiable Accuracy, Robustness, and Generalisation in Deep Learning

Alexander Bastounis[1] , Alexander N. Gorban[1,5] , Anders C. Hansen[2],
Desmond J. Higham[3] , Danil Prokhorov[4] , Oliver Sutton[5] ,
Ivan Y. Tyukin[5(✉)] , and Qinghua Zhou[5]

[1] University of Leicester, Leicester LE1 7RH, UK
[2] University of Cambridge, Cambridge CB3 0WA, UK
[3] University of Edinburgh, Edinburgh EH9 3FD, UK
[4] Toyota Tech Center, Ann Arbor, USA
[5] King's College London, London WC2R 2LS, UK
`ivan.tyukin@kcl.ac.uk`

Abstract. In this work, we assess the theoretical limitations of determining guaranteed stability and accuracy of neural networks in classification tasks. We consider classical distribution-agnostic framework and algorithms minimising empirical risks and potentially subjected to some weights regularisation. We show that there is a large family of tasks for which computing and verifying ideal stable and accurate neural networks in the above settings is extremely challenging, if at all possible, even when such ideal solutions exist within the given class of neural architectures.

Keywords: AI stability · AI verifiability · AI robustness · deep learning

Notation

$\mathbb{R}$ denotes the field of real numbers, $\mathbb{R}_{\geq 0} = \{x \in \mathbb{R} \mid x \geq 0\}$, and $\mathbb{R}^n$ denotes the n-dimensional real vector space, $\mathbb{N}$ denotes the set of natural numbers; $(x, y) = \sum_k x_k y_k$ is the inner product of x and y, and $\|x\| = \sqrt{(x, x)}$ is the standard Euclidean norm in $\mathbb{R}^n$; $\mathbb{B}_n$ denotes the unit ball in $\mathbb{R}^n$ centered at the origin $\mathbb{B}_n = \{x \in \mathbb{R}^n \mid \|x\| \leq 1\}$, $\mathbb{B}_n(r, y)$ is the ball in $\mathbb{R}^n$ centred at y with radius $r \geq 0$: $\mathbb{B}_n(r, y) = \{x \in \mathbb{R}^n \mid \|x - y\| \leq r\}$; $\mathrm{Cb}(\ell, y)$ is the cube in $\mathbb{R}^n$ centered at y with side-length $\ell \geq 0$: $\mathrm{Cb}(\ell, y) = \left\{x \in \mathbb{R}^n \mid \|x - y\|_\infty \leq \frac{\ell}{2}\right\}$; $\mathbb{S}_{n-1}(r, y)$ is the sphere in $\mathbb{R}^n$ centred at y with radius r: $\mathbb{S}_{n-1}(r, y) = \{x \in \mathbb{R}^n \mid \|x - y\| = r\}$; $\mathrm{sign}(\cdot) : \mathbb{R} \to \mathbb{R}_{\geq 0}$ denotes the function such that $\mathrm{sign}(s) = 1$ for all $s \in \mathbb{R}_{\geq 0}$ and $\mathrm{sign}(s) = 0$ otherwise; $\mathcal{K}_\theta$ is the class of real-valued functions defined on $\mathbb{R}$ which are continuous, strictly monotone on $[\theta, \infty)$, and constant on $(-\infty, \theta)$; $\mathbf{1}_n$ denotes the vector $(1, \ldots, 1) \in \mathbb{R}^n$.

L. Iliadis et al. (Eds.): ICANN 2023, LNCS 14254, pp. 530–541, 2023.
https://doi.org/10.1007/978-3-031-44207-0_44

1   Introduction

Data-driven AI systems and neural networks in particular have shown tremendous successes across a wide range of applications, including automotive, healthcare, gaming, marketing, and more recently natural language processing. Fuelled by high and growing rates of adoption of the new technology across sectors, robustness and stability are vital characterisations of AI performance.

The importance of AI stability and robustness is exemplified by the discovery of adversarial perturbations [12] – imperceptible changes of input data leading to misclassifications. These perturbations can be universal [8] (i.e. triggering misclassifications for many inputs), limited to a single attribute [11], or masquerading as legitimate inputs [2]. Sometimes, such AI instabilities can be typical [10,14]. Moreover, instabilities can also be induced by perturbations of the AI structure [13].

The issue of AI robustness is non-trivial and cannot be considered in isolation from other measures of AI performance: a model returning the same output regardless of the inputs is perfectly robust yet useless. A theoretical framework to approach the problem has recently been proposed in [1]. It has been shown in [1] that (i) there is an uncountably large family of distributions such that for an appropriately large data sample drawn from a distribution from this family there is an architecture so that any feed-forward neural network trained with that architecture has excellent performance on this sample, although (ii) every such network becomes inevitably unstable to one perturbation on some subset of the training and validation sets. Moreover, (iii) for the same distribution and the same data, there is a stable network possibly having a different architecture.

Here we show that the stability-accuracy issues have other unexplored dimensions and could be significantly more pronounced than previously thought. Our main result, Theorem 1 shows that there exist large families of well-behaved data distributions for which even networks achieving zero training and validation errors may be unstable to *almost any small* perturbation on nearly half of the training or validation data. Yet, for the same data samples and distributions, there exist stable networks *with the same architecture as the unstable network* which also minimise the loss function. Strikingly, there exist infinitely many pairs of networks, in which one network is stable and accurate and the other is also accurate but unfortunately unstable, whose weights and biases could be made arbitrarily close to each other. What is even more interesting, all this happens and persists when the values of weights and biases are made small.

This result reveals a fundamental issue at the heart of current data-driven approaches to learning driven by minimising empirical risk functions, even in the presence of weight regularisation, in distribution-agnostic settings. The issues is that such learning algorithms could be structurally incapable of distinguishing between stable and unstable solutions.

The rest of the paper is organised as follows. In Sect. 2 we introduce notation and problem setting. In Sect. 3 we state our main results along with discussion, interpretation, and comparison to the literature. Section 4 concludes the paper.

2   Preliminaries, Assumptions, and Problem Settings

Following [1], by $\mathcal{NN}_{\mathbf{N},L}$ we denote the class of neural networks with L layers and dimension $\mathbf{N} = \{N_L, N_{L-1}, N_{L-2}, \ldots, N_1, N_0 = n\}$, where n is the input dimension, and $N_L = 1$ is the dimension of the network's output. A neural network with dimension $(\mathbf{N}, L)$ is a map

$$\phi = G^L \sigma G^{L-1} \sigma \cdots \cdots \sigma G^1,$$

where $\sigma : \mathbb{R} \to \mathbb{R}$ is a coordinate-wise activation function, and $G^l : \mathbb{R}^{N_{l-1}} \to \mathbb{R}^{N_l}$ is an affine map defined by $G^l x = W^l x + b^l$, where $W^l \in \mathbb{R}^{N_l \times N_{l-1}}$, $b^l \in \mathbb{R}^{N_l}$ are the corresponding matrices of weights and biases. By $\Theta(\phi)$ we denote the vector of all weights and biases of the network ϕ.

In general, the activation functions σ do not have to be the same for all components and all layers, although here we will assume (unless stated otherwise) that this is indeed the case. In what follows we will consider feed-forward networks with activation functions in their hidden layers computing mappings from the following broad class:

$$\sigma = g_\theta, \ g_\theta \in \mathcal{K}_\theta, \ \theta \in \mathbb{R}. \tag{1}$$

Popular functions such as ReLU are contained in this class (that is the class of functions which are continuous, strictly monotone on $[\theta, \infty)$ and constant on $(-\infty, \theta)$). The condition of strict monotonicity of g_θ over $[\theta, \infty)$ can be reduced to strict monotonicity over some $[\theta, \theta_1]$, $\theta_1 > \theta$, with g_θ being merely monotone on $[\theta_1, \infty)$. This extension won't have any affect on the validity of the theoretical statements below, but will enable the inclusion of leaky ReLU activations (since then activation functions satisfying (1) can be constructed as a difference of a leaky ReLU function and its shifted/translated copy, and the results below therefore still follow) as well as "sigmoid"-like piecewise linear functions.

We will suppose that all data are drawn from some unknown probability distribution belonging to a family $\mathcal{F}$, and each element $\mathcal{D} \in \mathcal{F}$ of this family is supported on $[-1, 1]^n \times \{0, 1\}$. For any given $\mathcal{D} \in \mathcal{F}$, we will assume that the training and testing algorithms have access to samples (x^j, ℓ^j), $j = 1, \ldots, s + r$, $s, r \in \mathbb{N}$, independently drawn from $\mathcal{D}$, and which can be partitioned into training

$$\mathcal{T} = \{(x^1, \ell^1), \ldots, (x^r, \ell^r)\}$$

and validation/testing

$$\mathcal{V} = \{(x^{r+1}, \ell^{r+1}), \ldots, (x^{r+s}, \ell^{r+s})\}$$

(multi)-sets. Let $M = r + s = |\mathcal{T} \cup \mathcal{V}|$ be the size of the joint training and validation (multi)-set.

Further, we impose a condition that the data distribution is sufficiently regular and does not possess hidden instabilities and undesirable accumulation points which could otherwise trivialise our statements and results. In particular, for $\delta \in (0, 2\sqrt{n}]$ we will only consider those distributions $\mathcal{D}_\delta \in \mathcal{F}$ which satisfy:

If $(x, \ell_x), (y, \ell_y) \sim \mathcal{D}_\delta$ with $\ell_x \neq \ell_y$, then, with probability 1, $\|x - y\| \geq \delta$. (2)

Finally, we introduce the family of loss functions

$$\mathcal{CF}_{\text{loc}} = \{\mathcal{R} : \ \mathbb{R} \times \mathbb{R} \to \mathbb{R}_{\geq 0} \cup \{\infty\} \mid \mathcal{R}(v,w) = 0 \iff v = w\} \qquad (3)$$

which will be used to define the corresponding empirical loss functions for the model outputs $h : \mathbb{R}^n \to \{0,1\}$ on samples $\mathcal{S} \sim \mathcal{D}_\delta$ drawn from $\mathcal{D}_\delta$

$$\mathcal{L}(\mathcal{S}, h) = \sum_{(x^i, \ell^i) \in \mathcal{S}} \mathcal{R}(h(x^i), \ell^i). \qquad (4)$$

The subscript "loc" in (3) emphasises that the loss functions $\mathcal{R}$ are evaluated on single data points and in this sense are "local". It provides an explicit connection with the classical literature involving empirical risk minimisation, allowing us to exploit the conventional interpretation of the generalisation error as a deviation of the empirical risk from the expected value of the loss over the distribution generating the data.

3 Main Results

Having introduced all relevant notation, are now ready to state the main result of the contribution.

Theorem 1. (Inevitability, typicality and undetectability of instability) *Consider the class of networks with architecture*

$$\mathbf{N} = (N_L = 1, N_{L-1}, \ldots, N_1, N_0 = n), \quad L \geq 2, \ n \geq 2,$$

where $N_1 \geq 2n$ and $N_2, \ldots, N_{L-1} \geq 1$, and activation functions g_θ in layers $1, \ldots, L-1$ satisfying conditions (1), and the $\text{sign}(\cdot)$ activation function in layer L.

Let $\varepsilon \in (0, \sqrt{n} - 1)$ and fix $0 < \delta \leq \varepsilon/\sqrt{n}$. Then, there is an uncountably large family of distributions $\mathcal{D}_\delta \in \mathcal{F}$ satisfying (2) such that for any $\mathcal{D}_\delta \in \mathcal{F}$, any training and validation data $\mathcal{T}, \mathcal{V}$ drawn independently from $\mathcal{D}_\delta$, and every $\mathcal{R} \in \mathcal{CF}_{\text{loc}}$, with probability 1:

(i) *There exists a network which correctly classifies the training data $\mathcal{T}$ and generalises to the test data $\mathcal{V}$, satisfying*

$$f \in \argmin_{\varphi \in \mathcal{NN}_{\mathbf{N},L}} \mathcal{L}(\mathcal{T} \cup \mathcal{V}, \varphi)$$

with $\mathcal{L}(\mathcal{T} \cup \mathcal{V}, f) = 0$.
Yet, for any $q \in (0, 1/2)$, with probability greater than or equal to

$$1 - \exp(-2q^2 M)$$

there exists a multi-set $\mathcal{U} \subset \mathcal{T} \cup \mathcal{V}$ of cardinality at least $\lfloor (1/2 - q)M \rfloor$ on which f is unstable in the sense that for any $(x, \ell) \in \mathcal{U}$ and any $\alpha \in (0, \varepsilon/2)$, there exists a perturbation $\zeta \in \mathbb{R}^n$ with $\|\zeta\| \leq \alpha/\sqrt{n}$ and

$$|f(x) - f(x + \zeta)| = 1. \qquad (5)$$

Moreover, such destabilising perturbations are typical *in the sense that if vectors ζ are sampled from the equidistribution in $\mathbb{B}_n(\alpha/\sqrt{n}, 0)$, then for $(x, \ell) \in \mathcal{U}$, the probability that (5) is satisfied is at least*

$$1 - \frac{1}{2^n}.$$

Furthermore, there exist universal *destabilising perturbations, in the sense that a single perturbation ζ drawn from the equidistribution in $\mathbb{B}_n(\alpha/\sqrt{n}, 0)$ destabilises $m \leq |\mathcal{U}|$ points from the set $\mathcal{U}$ with probability at least*

$$1 - \frac{m}{2^n}.$$

(ii) *At the same time, for the same distribution $\mathcal{D}_\delta$ there is a robust network with the same architecture as f, satisfying*

$$\tilde{f} \in \underset{\varphi \in \mathcal{NN}_{\mathbf{N},L}}{\arg\min} \; \mathcal{L}(\mathcal{T} \cup \mathcal{V}, \varphi)$$

with $\mathcal{L}(\mathcal{T} \cup \mathcal{V}, \tilde{f}) = 0$, which is robust in the sense that for all $(x, \ell) \in \mathcal{T} \cup \mathcal{V}$

$$\tilde{f}(x) = \tilde{f}(x + \zeta)$$

for any $\zeta \in \mathbb{R}^n$ with $\|\zeta\| \leq \alpha/\sqrt{n}$, even when $|\mathcal{T} \cup \mathcal{V}| = \infty$.
Moreover, there exist pairs of unstable and robust networks, $f_\lambda, \tilde{f}_\lambda$ and $f_\Lambda, \tilde{f}_\Lambda$, satisfying the statements above such that the maximum absolute difference between their weights and biases is either arbitrarily small or arbitrarily large. That is, for any $\lambda > 0, \Lambda > 0$:

$$\|\Theta(f_\lambda) - \Theta(\tilde{f}_\lambda)\|_\infty < \lambda, \quad \|\Theta(f_\Lambda) - \Theta(\tilde{f}_\Lambda)\|_\infty > \Lambda.$$

(iii) *However, for the above robust solution $\tilde{f}$,*
   a) *there exists an uncountably large family of distributions $\tilde{\mathcal{D}}_\delta \in \mathcal{F}$ on which $\tilde{f}$ correctly classifies both the training and test data, yet fails in the same way as stated in (i).*
   b) *there exists an uncountably large family of distributions $\hat{\mathcal{D}}_\delta \in \mathcal{F}$ such that the map $\tilde{f}$ is robust on $\mathcal{T} \cup \mathcal{V}$ (with respect to perturbations ζ with $\|\zeta\| \leq \alpha/\sqrt{n}, \alpha \in (0, \varepsilon/2)$) with probability*

$$\left(1 - \frac{1}{2^{n+1}}\right)^{Mk}$$

but is unstable to arbitrarily small perturbations on future samples with probability $k/2^{n+1}$.

The proof of the theorem is provided in the Appendix.

3.1   Interpretation of Results

According to statement (i) of Theorem 1, not only are instabilities to be expected, but they can also be remarkably widespread: for sufficiently large data sets they may occur, with high probability, for nearly half of all data.

Statement (ii) of Theorem 1 confirms that a stable solution exists *within precisely the same class of network architectures*, although it is difficult to compute it by using only the loss functional $\mathcal{L}$ as a measure of quality. This shows that the architecture isn't necessarily the source of the instability. Moreover, a robust solution may be found in an arbitrarily small neighborhood of the specific non-robust one in the space of network weights and biases. As the construction in the proof shows, using networks with small Lipshitz constants can, counterintuitively, make the problem worse.

The robust solution, in turn, can also be unstable, as follows from statement (iii), part (a). This is reminiscent of a "no free lunch" principle for robust and accurate learning, although with a subtle distinction. In fact, as part b) of the statement states, there are solutions which may appear to be certifiably robust (and one can indeed certify the model on the training and validation sets), although there is no guarantee whatsoever that the certificate remains valid for future samples. To minimise the risks, one needs to certify the model on data sets which are exponentially large in n. This is particularly relevant for safety-critical settings, where the risk of failure must be calculated and bounded in advance.

Finally, we note that the instabilities considered in Theorem 1 become particularly pronounced for networks with sufficiently high input dimension n (see statement (iii) of the theorem). Moreover, statement (ii) shows that the fraction of perturbations around unstable points x in the sample which alter the network's response approaches 1 as n grows. These high-dimensional effects may still be observed in networks with arbitrarily low input dimensions if such networks realise appropriate auxiliary space-filling mappings in relevant layers. The technical point that the statement of Theorem 1 holds with probability one is due to the fact that the proof constructs data distributions which assign probability zero to certain sets, so there may exist training samples with probability zero for which the construction does not apply.

3.2   Discussion

Instabilities and Regularisation. The construction we used in the proof of Theorem 1 reveals that the instability discussed in statements (i) and (ii) of the theorem is inherent to the very definition of the binary classification problem and may not be addressed by regularisation approaches constraining norms of network's parameters and Lipschitz constants of non-threshold layers.

Indeed, consider just the first two layers of the network f constructed in the proof of the theorem, remove the sign$(\cdot)$ activation function, and introduce an arbitrarily small positive factor β (cf. (13)):

$$
\begin{aligned}
f_{\text{reg}}(x) = \sum_{i=1}^{n} & g_\theta(\theta) - g_\theta(\beta((x, e_i) - 1/\sqrt{n}) + \theta) \\
+ \sum_{i=1}^{n} & g_\theta(\theta) - g_\theta(\beta(-(x, e_i) - 1/\sqrt{n}) + \theta).
\end{aligned}
\tag{6}
$$

If the functions g_θ are Lipschitz then the Lipschitz constant of the function f_{reg} can be made arbitrarily small by setting β to some sufficiently small value. At the same time, the values of $\text{sign} f_{\text{reg}}(x)$ and $f(x)$ coincide. This implies that regardless of how well-behaved the function f_{reg} in (6) is, forced classification achieved either by the application of the sign function or, alternatively, through thresholding or softmax, brings instabilities.

In this respect, network regularisation by pruning, restricting norms of the network's weights, and forcing the network's Lipschitz constant to stay small do not always warrant robustness. Similarly, requesting that there is some non-zero margin separating the classes does not address or alleviate the problem either. The instability occurs due to the fact that the algorithm is required to produce a decision boundary, but is unaware that the data is placed directly on this boundary.

Adversarial Training. A potential way to overcome the instabilities formalised in statement (i) of Theorem 1 is to invoke a type of training capable of assessing that instabilities (5) do not occur. Adversarial training and data augmentation, whereby each data sample produces a set of points corresponding to perturbed data is an example of an approach which can potentially address the problem. The approach is not without its own challenges as one needs to ensure that all points in the sets $\mathbb{B}_n(\alpha/n, x)$, $\alpha \in (0, \varepsilon/2)$ are checked. The latter task can be computationally and numerically overwhelming for large n.

Dark Data. The final and perhaps the most interesting point in relation to the problem of verifiability is statement (iii), which can be related to challenge of the "dark data" – the data which exists but to which we don't have access [9] or, more generally, the missing data and the data which we don't have [6]. As the theorem states, high-dimensional distributions could be a very real source of such dark data, potentially leading to instabilities or non-verifiability.

4   Conclusion

Deep learning networks and models have convincingly shown ample capabilities in many practical tasks. When properly engineered, these models stunningly outperform shallower architectures (see e.g. [7,15] for examples and precise statements). Moreover, recent breakthroughs such as the emergence of Chat-GPT show exceptional power these models may bring. These models operate in high-dimensional spaces and process and execute decisions on genuinely high-dimensional data.

At the same time, and despite these remarkable achievements, the application of these highly expressive and capable models requires special care and understanding of their fundamental limitations.

Our work, by building on [1], reveals a new set of limitations which are particularly inherent to high-dimensional data. These limitations constitute the presence of nested uncountably large families of exceptions on which even moderately-sized networks may and likely will fail. The results also show that it may be computationally hard to verify both robustness and accuracy of models within classical distribution-agnostic learning frameworks based solely on the notions of risk and empirical risk minimisation. All these call for the need to rethink standard distribution-agnostic learning frameworks and introduce more appropriate models of reality into the mathematical setting of statistical learning.

The results, by showing fundamental difficulties with guaranteeing simultaneous stability, accuracy, and verifiability, highlight the importance of mathematical theory and methods for the continuous correction of AI models [3–5].

At present, the results do not include networks with classical sigmoidal activation functions. Detailed analysis of these types of networks will be the topic of our future work.

Acknowledgements. This work is supported by the UKRI, EPSRC [UKRI Turing AI Fellowship ARaISE EP/V025295/2 and UKRI Trustworthy Autonomous Systems Node in Verifiability EP/V026801/2 to I.Y.T., EP/V025295/2 to O.S., A.N.G., and Q.Z., EP/V046527/1 and EP/P020720/1 to D.J.H, EP/V046527/1 to A.B.].

Appendix

4.1   Proof of Theorem 1

Proof of Statement (i) of the Theorem. The proof consists of three parts. The first part introduces a family of distributions satisfying the separability requirement (2) and shows relevant statistical properties of samples drawn from these distributions. The second part presents the construction of a suitable neural network minimising the empirical loss function $\mathcal{L}$ for any loss function $\mathcal{R} \in \mathcal{CF}_{\mathrm{loc}}$ which successfully generalises beyond training (and test/validation) data. The final part shows that, with high probability, this network is unstable on nearly half of the data (for $s + r$ reasonably large).

Proof of statement (i), part 1. Consider the n-dimensional hyper cube $\mathrm{Cb}(2,0) = [-1,1]^n$. Within this cube, we may inscribe the unit ball $\mathbb{B}_n$ (the surface of which touches the surface of the outer cube at the centre of each face), and within this ball we may, in turn, inscribe the inner cube $\mathrm{Cb}(2/\sqrt{n},0)$ each vertex of which touches the surface of the ball and whose faces are parallel to the faces of the cube $\mathrm{Cb}(2,0)$. For any $\varepsilon \in (0, \sqrt{n}-1)$, the cube $\mathrm{Cb}(\frac{2}{\sqrt{n}}(1+\varepsilon),0)$ may be shown to satisfy $\mathrm{Cb}(2/\sqrt{n},0) \subset \mathrm{Cb}(\frac{2}{\sqrt{n}}(1+\varepsilon),0) \subset \mathrm{Cb}(2,0)$.

Let $V = \{v_i\}_{i=1}^{2^n}$ denote the set of vertices of $\mathrm{Cb}(2/\sqrt{n}, 0)$ with an arbitrary but fixed ordering, and note that each v_i may be expressed as $\frac{1}{\sqrt{n}}(q_1, \ldots, q_n)$ with each component $q_k \in \{-1, 1\}$. The choice of ε ensures that the set

$$\mathcal{J}_0 = \left\{ x \in \mathbb{S}_{n-1}(1, 0) \mid x \notin \mathrm{Cb}\left(\frac{2}{\sqrt{n}}(1+\varepsilon), 0 \right) \right\}.$$

is non-empty and that $\min_{x \in \mathcal{J}_0, \, y \in V} \|x - y\| > \frac{\varepsilon}{\sqrt{n}}$.

Consider a family of distributions $\mathcal{F}_1 \subset \mathcal{F}$ which are supported on $\mathbb{S}_{n-1}(1, 0) \times \{0, 1\}$, with the σ-algebra $\Sigma_{\mathbb{S}} \times \{0\} \cup \Sigma_{\mathbb{S}} \times \{1\}$, where $\Sigma_{\mathbb{S}}$ is the standard σ-algebra on the sphere $\mathbb{S}_{n-1}$ with the topology induced by the arclength metric.

We construct $\mathcal{F}_1$ as those distributions $\mathcal{D}_\delta \in \mathcal{F}$ such that

$$P_{\mathcal{D}_\delta}(x, \ell) = 0 \text{ for } x \in \mathrm{Cb}\left(\frac{2}{\sqrt{n}}(1+\varepsilon), 0 \right) \setminus V, \text{ and any } \ell, \tag{7}$$

with

$$P_{\mathcal{D}_\delta}(x, \ell) = \begin{cases} \frac{1}{2^{n+1}} & \text{for } x \in V, \, \ell = 1 \\ 0, & \text{for } x \in V, \, \ell = 0 \end{cases} \tag{8}$$

and

$$P_{\mathcal{D}_\delta}(\mathcal{J}_0, \ell) = \begin{cases} 0 & \text{for } \ell = 1, \\ \frac{1}{2} & \text{for } \ell = 0. \end{cases} \tag{9}$$

The existence of an uncountable family of distributions $\mathcal{D}_\delta$ satisfying (7)–(9) is ensured by the flexibility of (9) and the fact that $\mathcal{J}_0$ contains more than a single point (consider e.g. the family of all delta-functions supported on $\mathcal{J}_0$ and scaled by $1/2$). This construction moreover ensures that any $\mathcal{D}_\delta \in \mathcal{F}_1$ also satisfies the separation property (2) with $\delta \leq \frac{\varepsilon}{\sqrt{n}}$.

Let $\mathcal{M} = \mathcal{T} \cup \mathcal{V} = \{(x_k, \ell_k)\}_{k=1}^M$, denote the (multi-)set corresponding to the union of the training and validation sets independently sampled from $\mathcal{D}_\delta$, where $M = s + r = |\mathcal{M}|$. Let $z : \mathbb{R}^n \times \{0, 1\} \to \{0, 1\}$ be the trivial function mapping a sample (x, ℓ) from $\mathcal{D}_\delta$ into $\{0, 1\}$ by $z(x, \ell) = \ell$. This function defines new random variables $Z_k = z(x_k, \ell_k) \in [0, 1]$ for $k = 1, \ldots, M$, with expectation $E(Z_k) = \frac{1}{2}$.

The Hoeffding inequality ensures that

$$P\left(\frac{1}{2} - \frac{1}{M} \sum Z_k > q \right) \leq \exp\left(-2q^2 M \right),$$

and hence, with probability greater than or equal to

$$1 - \exp\left(-2q^2 M \right), \tag{10}$$

the number of data points (x, ℓ) with $\ell = 1$ in the sample $\mathcal{M}$ is at least

$$\left\lfloor \left(\frac{1}{2} - q \right) M \right\rfloor. \tag{11}$$

Proof of statement (i), part 2. Let $\{e_1, \ldots, e_n\}$ be the standard basis in $\mathbb{R}^n$. Consider the following set of $2n$ inequalities:

$$(x, e_i) \leq \frac{1}{\sqrt{n}}, \ (x, e_i) \geq -\frac{1}{\sqrt{n}}, \ \text{for } i = 1, \ldots, n. \tag{12}$$

Any function defined on $[-1/\sqrt{n}, 1/\sqrt{n}]^n$ (or which contains $[-1/\sqrt{n}, 1/\sqrt{n}]^n$ in the domain of its definition) and which returns 1 for x satisfying (12) and 0 otherwise, minimises the loss $\mathcal{L}$ on $\mathcal{T}$. It also generalises perfectly well on any $\mathcal{V}$. Hence a network implementing such a function shares the same properties.

Pick a function $g_\theta \in \mathcal{K}_\theta$ and consider

$$g_\theta((x, e_i) - 1/\sqrt{n} + \theta), \ g_\theta(-(x, e_i) + 1/\sqrt{n} + \theta), \ i = 1, \ldots, n.$$

It is clear that $g_\theta(\theta) - g_\theta((x, e_i) - 1/\sqrt{n} + \theta) = 0$ for $(x, e_i) \leq 1/\sqrt{n}$, and $g_\theta(\theta) - g_\theta((x, e_i) - 1/\sqrt{n} + \theta) < 0$ for $(x, e_i) > 1/\sqrt{n}$. Similarly $g_\theta(\theta) - g_\theta(-(x, e_i) - 1/\sqrt{n} + \theta) = 0$ for $(x, e_i) \geq -1/\sqrt{n}$, and $g_\theta(\theta) - g_\theta(-(x, e_i) - 1/\sqrt{n} + \theta) < 0$ for $(x, e_i) < -1/\sqrt{n}$. Hence, the function f given by

$$f(x) = \text{sign} \left(\sum_{i=1}^{n} g_\theta(\theta) - g_\theta((x, e_i) - 1/\sqrt{n} + \theta) \right. \\ \left. + \sum_{i=1}^{n} g_\theta(\theta) - g_\theta(-(x, e_i) - 1/\sqrt{n} + \theta) \right) \tag{13}$$

is exactly 1 only when all inequalities (12) hold true, and is zero otherwise. We may therefore conclude that

$$f \in \arg \min_{\varphi \in \mathcal{NN}_{\mathbf{N}, L}} \mathcal{L}(\mathcal{T} \cup \mathcal{V}, \varphi).$$

Observe now that (13) is a two-layer neural network with $2n$ neurons in the hidden layer and a threshold output. This core network can be extended to any larger size without changing the map f by propagating the argument of $\text{sign}(\cdot)$ in (13) to the next layers and appending the width as appropriate.

Proof of statement (i), part 3. Let us now show that the map (13) becomes unstable for an appropriately-sized set $\mathcal{M}$. Suppose that there are $\lfloor (1/2 - q)M \rfloor$ data points on which $f(x) = 1$, and by construction each is a vertex of $\text{Cb}(2/\sqrt{n}, 0)$. According to (10), (11), the probability of this event is not zero. Let x be one such point and let ζ be a perturbation sampled from an equidistribution in the ball $\mathbb{B}_n(\alpha/\sqrt{n}, 0)$ for some $\alpha \in (0, \varepsilon/2)$. Then, with probability $1 - \frac{1}{2^n}$, the perturbation ζ is such that $|f(x + \zeta) - f(x)| = 1$, since this is true for any ζ such that $x + \zeta \notin \mathcal{I} = \text{Cb}(2/\sqrt{n}, 0) \cap \mathbb{B}_n(\alpha/\sqrt{n}, x)$, and the set $\mathcal{I}$ is uniquely defined by the signs of exactly n linear inequalities which slice the ball into 2^n pieces of equal volume and so has probability $\frac{1}{2^n}$.

Finally, note that if there are at least m points $(u^1, \ell^1), \ldots, (u^m, \ell^m)$ in the set $\mathcal{U}$ then the probability that all $u^i + \zeta$, $i = 1, \ldots, m$ are outside of the corresponding intersections follows from the union bound, which completes the argument.

Proof of Statement (ii) of the Theorem. The argument used in the proof of statement (i), part 2, implies that there exists a network $\tilde{f} \in \mathcal{NN}_{N,L}$ such that $\tilde{f}(x)$ takes value 1 when the inequalities

$$(x, e_i) \leq \frac{1}{\sqrt{n}}\left(1 + \frac{\varepsilon}{2}\right), \ (x, e_i) \geq -\frac{1}{\sqrt{n}}\left(1 + \frac{\varepsilon}{2}\right), \text{ for } i = 1, \ldots, n. \qquad (14)$$

are satisfied, and zero otherwise. This network also minimises $\mathcal{L}$ and generalises beyond the training and validation data.

However, since for any $\alpha \in (0, \varepsilon/2)$ the function $\tilde{f}$ is constant within a ball of radius $\alpha/\sqrt{n}$ around any data point $x \in \mathcal{T} \cup \mathcal{V}$, we can conclude that $\tilde{f}$ is insusceptible to the instabilities affecting f.

To show that there exists a pair of unstable and stable networks, f and $\tilde{f}$ (the network $\tilde{f}$ is stable with respect to perturbations $\zeta : \|\zeta\| \leq \alpha/\sqrt{n}$), consider systems of inequalities (12), (14) with both sides multiplied by a positive constant $\kappa > 0$. Clearly, and regardless of the multiplication by κ, these systems of inequalities define the cubes $\mathrm{Cb}(2\sqrt{n}, 0)$ and $\mathrm{Cb}(2\sqrt{n}(1+\varepsilon/2), 0)$, respectively. Then

$$\begin{aligned}
f(x) = \mathrm{sign}&\left(\sum_{i=1}^{n} g_\theta(\theta) - g_\theta(\kappa((x, e_i) - 1/\sqrt{n}) + \theta) \right. \\
&\left. + \sum_{i=1}^{n} g_\theta(\theta) - g_\theta(\kappa(-(x, e_i) - 1/\sqrt{n}) + \theta) \right)
\end{aligned} \qquad (15)$$

encodes the unstable network, and

$$\begin{aligned}
\tilde{f}(x) = \mathrm{sign}&\left(\sum_{i=1}^{n} g_\theta(\theta) - g_\theta(\kappa((x, e_i) - (1 + \varepsilon/2)/\sqrt{n}) + \theta) \right. \\
&\left. + \sum_{i=1}^{n} g_\theta(\theta) - g_\theta(\kappa(-(x, e_i) - (1 + \varepsilon/2)/\sqrt{n}) + \theta) \right)
\end{aligned} \qquad (16)$$

encodes the stable one. These networks share the same weights but their biases differ in absolute value by $\kappa\varepsilon/(2\sqrt{n})$. Given that κ can be chosen arbitrarily small or arbitrarily large, the statement now follows.

Proof of Statement (iii) of the Theorem. Part a) of statement (iii) can be demonstrated following the same argument used to prove of statement (i) by replacing the cube $\mathrm{Cb}(2/\sqrt{n}, 0)$ with $\mathrm{Cb}(2/\sqrt{n}(1 + \varepsilon/2), 0)$.

Part b) follows by considering a slightly modified family of distributions $\mathcal{D}_\delta$ in which the set V is replaced with

$$V = \{v_i \mid i = 1, \ldots, 2^n - k\} \cup \hat{V},$$

where

$$\hat{V} = \{v_i(1 + \varepsilon/2) \mid i = 2^n - k + 1, \ldots, 2^n\}.$$

The probability that a single point from $\hat{V}$ is not present in $\mathcal{M}$ is $(1-1/2^{n+1})^M$. Since the samples are drawn independently, the probability that none of these points are present in $\mathcal{M}$ is $(1 - 1/2^{n+1})^{Mk}$. The probability, however, that a point from $\hat{V}$ is sampled is $k/2^{n+1}$.   □

References

1. Bastounis, A., Hansen, A.C., Vlačić, V.: The mathematics of adversarial attacks in AI-why deep learning is unstable despite the existence of stable neural networks. arXiv preprint arXiv:2109.06098 (2021)
2. Eykholt, K., et al.: Robust physical-world attacks on deep learning visual classification. In: Proceedings of the IEEE Conference on Computer Vision and Pattern Recognition, pp. 1625–1634 (2018)
3. Gorban, A.N., Grechuk, B., Mirkes, E.M., Stasenko, S.V., Tyukin, I.Y.: High-dimensional separability for one-and few-shot learning. Entropy 23(8), 1090 (2021)
4. Gorban, A.N., Tyukin, I.Y., Romanenko, I.: The blessing of dimensionality: separation theorems in the thermodynamic limit. IFAC-PapersOnLine 49(24), 64–69 (2016)
5. Gorban, A., Tyukin, I.Y.: Stochastic separation theorems. Neural Netw. 94, 255–259 (2017)
6. Hand, D.J.: Dark Data: Why What You Don't Know Matters. Princeton University Press (2020)
7. Kirdin, A., Sidorov, S., Zolotykh, N.: Rosenblatt's first theorem and frugality of deep learning. Entropy 24(11), 1635 (2022). https://doi.org/10.3390/e24111635
8. Moosavi-Dezfooli, S.M., Fawzi, A., Fawzi, O., Frossard, P.: Universal adversarial perturbations. In: Proceedings of the IEEE Conference on Computer Vision and Pattern Recognition, pp. 1765–1773 (2017)
9. Schembera, B., Durán, J.M.: Dark data as the new challenge for big data science and the introduction of the scientific data officer. Philos. Technol. 33, 93–115 (2020)
10. Shafahi, A., Huang, W., Studer, C., Feizi, S., Goldstein, T.: Are adversarial examples inevitable? In: International Conference on Learning Representations (ICLR) (2019)
11. Su, J., Vargas, D.V., Sakurai, K.: One pixel attack for fooling deep neural networks. IEEE Trans. Evol. Comput. 23(5), 828–841 (2019)
12. Szegedy, C., et al.: Intriguing properties of neural networks. arXiv preprint arXiv:1312.6199 (2013)
13. Tyukin, I.Y., Higham, D.J., Bastounis, A., Woldegeorgis, E., Gorban, A.N.: The feasibility and inevitability of stealth attacks. arXiv preprint arXiv:2106.13997 (2021)
14. Tyukin, I.Y., Higham, D.J., Gorban, A.N.: On adversarial examples and stealth attacks in artificial intelligence systems. In: 2020 International Joint Conference on Neural Networks (IJCNN), pp. 1–6. IEEE (2020)
15. Yarotsky, D.: Error bounds for approximations with deep ReLU networks. Neural Netw. 94, 103–114 (2017)

Componentwise Adversarial Attacks

Lucas Beerens and Desmond J. Higham[✉][iD]

School of Mathematics and The Maxwell Institute for Mathematical Sciences,
University of Edinburgh, Edinburgh EH8 9BT, UK
L.Beerens@sms.ed.ac.uk, d.j.higham@ed.ac.uk

Abstract. We motivate and test a new adversarial attack algorithm that measures input perturbation size in a relative componentwise manner. The algorithm can be implemented by solving a sequence of linearly-constrained linear least-squares problems, for which high quality software is available. In the image classification context, as a special case the algorithm may be applied to artificial neural networks that classify printed or handwritten text—we show that it is possible to generate hard-to-spot perturbations that cause misclassification by perturbing only the "ink" and hence leaving the background intact. Such examples are relevant to application areas in defence, business, law and finance.

Keywords: backward error · misclassification · stability

1 Motivation

It is well known that deep learning image classification tools can be vulnerable to *adversarial attacks*. In particular, a carefully chosen perturbation to an image that is imperceptible to the human eye may cause an unwanted change in the predicted class [7,15]. The fact that automated classification tools may be fooled in this way raises concerns around their deployment in high stakes application areas, including medical imaging, transport, defence and finance [11]. Over the past decade, there has been growing interest in the development of algorithms that construct attacks, and strategies that defend against them [1,6,10,12,13]. Amidst the background of this war of attrition, there has also been "bigger picture" theoretical research into the existence, computability and inevitability of adversarial perturbations [2,5,14,16,17].

In this work, we contribute to the algorithm development side of the adversarial attack literature. We focus on the manner in which perturbation size is measured. Figure 1 illustrates the benefits of our new algorithm. On the left, we show the image of a handwritten digit from the MNIST data set [9]. A trained neural network (accuracy 97%) correctly classified this image as a digit 8. In the middle of Fig. 1 we show a perturbed image produced by the widely used

LB was supported by the MAC-MIGS Centre for Doctoral Training under EPSRC grant EP/S023291/1. DJH was supported by EPSRC grants EP/P020720/1 and EP/V046527/1.

L. Iliadis et al. (Eds.): ICANN 2023, LNCS 14254, pp. 542–545, 2023.
https://doi.org/10.1007/978-3-031-44207-0_45

DeepFool algorithm [12]. This perturbed image is classified as a 2 by the network. On the right in Fig. 1 we show another perturbed image, produced by our new algorithm. This new image is also classified as a 2. The Deepfool algorithm looks for a perturbation of minimal Euclidean norm, treating all pixels equally. In this case, we can see that although the perturbed image is close to the original, there are tell-tale smudges to the white background. Our new algorithm seeks a perturbation that causes a minimal componentwise relative change; and in this context it will not make any change to zero-valued pixels. We argue that the perturbation produced is less noticeable to the human eye, being consistent with a streaky pen, rough paper, or irregular handwriting pressure.

Fig. 1. Showcasing the capabilities of our new algorithm, which seeks a perturbation that causes minimal componentwise relative change. Left: image from the MNIST data set [9], correctly classified as an 8 by a neural network. Middle: perturbed image produced by Deepfool [12], classified as a 2. Right: perturbed image produced by new componentwise algorithm, also classified as a 2. The componentwise algorithm does not change the background, where pixel values are zero. In the notation of Sect. 2, the relative Euclidean norm perturbation size, $\|\Delta x\|_2/\|x\|_2$, is 0.09 for Deepfool and 0.23 for the componentwise algorithm. This reflects the fact that Deepfool looks for the smallest Euclidean norm perturbation whereas the componentwise algorithm has a different objective.

2 Overview of Algorithm

We will focus on image classification, assuming that there are c possible classes. Regarding an image as a normalized vector in $x \in \mathbb{R}^n$, a classifier takes the form of a map $F : [0,1]^n \to \mathbb{R}^c$, where we assume that output class is determined by the largest component of $F(x)$.

Suppose $F(x) = y$ and we wish to perturb the image to $x + \Delta x$ with $F(x + \Delta x) = \widehat{y}$, where the desired output $\widehat{y}$ produces a different classification, so $\widehat{y}$ has a maximum component in a different position to the maximum component of y. In the *untargeted* case, $\widehat{y}$ may be any such vector. In the *targeted* case, we wish to specify which component of $\widehat{y}$ is maximum.

Because we seek a small perturbation, we will use the linearization $F(x + \Delta x) - F(x) \approx \mathcal{A}\Delta x$, where $\mathcal{A} \in \mathbb{R}^{c \times n}$ is the Jacobian of F at x, and F is assumed to be differentiable in a neighbourhood of x. Then, motivated by the connection to (norm-based) backward error developed in [4] and also by the concept of componentwise backward error introduced in [8], we consider the optimization problem

$$\min\{\epsilon : \mathcal{A}\Delta x = \widehat{y} - y, \quad |\Delta x|_i \le \epsilon f_i \quad \text{for} \quad 1 \le i \le n\}. \tag{1}$$

Here $f \ge 0 \in \mathbb{R}^n$ is a given tolerance vector, and we note that choosing $f_i = |x_i|$ forces zero pixels to remain unperturbed. Following the approach in [8] it is then useful to write $\Delta x = Dv$, where $D = \text{diag}(f)$ and $v \in \mathbb{R}^n$ so that our optimization becomes

$$\min\{\|v\|_\infty : \mathcal{A}Dv = \widehat{y} - y\}. \tag{2}$$

In practice, we found that the problem (2) encourages all components of v to achieve the maximum $\|v\|_\infty$, leading to adversarial perturbations that were quite noticeable. We found more success after replacing (2) by

$$\min\{\|Dv\|_2 : \mathcal{A}Dv = \widehat{y} - y\}. \tag{3}$$

Because $\Delta x = Dv$, in this formulation we retain the masking effect where zero values in the tolerance vector f force the corresponding pixels to remain unperturbed. We found that minimizing $\|Dv\|_2$ rather than $\|v\|_\infty$ produced perturbations that appeared less obvious, and this was the approach used for Fig. 1.

It can be shown that the underlying optimization task arising from this approach may be formulated as a linearly-constrained linear least-squares problem. To derive an effective algorithm, various additional practical steps were introduced; notably, (a) projecting to ensure that perturbations do not send pixels out of range, and (b) regarding each optimization problem as a means to generate a direction in which to take a small step within a more general iterative method.

In our presentation, we will show computational results on a range of data sets that illustrate the performance of the algorithm and compare results with state-of-the-art norm-based attack algorithms. We will also explain how a relevant componentwise condition number for the classification map gives a useful warning about vulnerability to this type of attack.

For full details we refer to [3].

References

1. Akhtar, N., Mian, A.: Threat of adversarial attacks on deep learning in computer vision: a survey. IEEE Access **6**, 14410–14430 (2018). https://doi.org/10.1109/ACCESS.2018.2807385
2. Bastounis, A., Hansen, A.C., Vlačić, V.: The mathematics of adversarial attacks in AI-Why deep learning is unstable despite the existence of stable neural networks. arXiv:2109.06098 [cs.LG] (2021)

3. Beerens, L., Higham, D.J.: Adversarial ink: Componentwise backward error attacks on deep learning. IMA J. Appl. Math. (2023). https://doi.org/10.1093/imamat/hxad017

4. Beuzeville, T., Boudier, P., Buttari, A., Gratton, S., Mary, T., Pralet, S.: Adversarial attacks via backward error analysis, December 2021. Working paper or preprint. https://ut3-toulouseinp.hal.science/hal-03296180. https://ut3-toulouseinp.hal.science/hal-03296180v3/file/Adversarial_BE.pdf. hal-03296180. Version 3

5. Fawzi, A., Fawzi, O., Frossard, P.: Analysis of classifiers' robustness to adversarial perturbations. Mach. Learn. **107**, 481–508 (2018)

6. Goodfellow, I.J., McDaniel, P.D., Papernot, N.: Making machine learning robust against adversarial inputs. Commun. ACM **61**(7), 56–66 (2018). https://doi.org/10.1145/3134599

7. Goodfellow, I.J., Shlens, J., Szegedy, C.: Explaining and harnessing adversarial examples. In: Bengio, Y., LeCun, Y. (eds.) 3rd International Conference on Learning Representations, San Diego, CA (2015). arxiv.org/abs/1412.6572

8. Higham, D.J., Higham, N.J.: Backward error and condition of structured linear systems. SIAM J. Matrix Anal. Appl. **13**(1), 162–175 (1992). https://doi.org/10.1137/0613014

9. LeCun, Y., Cortes, C.: MNIST handwritten digit database (2010). http://yann.lecun.com/exdb/mnist/

10. Madry, A., Makelov, A., Schmidt, L., Tsipras, D., Vladu, A.: Towards deep learning models resistant to adversarial attacks. In: 6th International Conference on Learning Representations, Vancouver, BC. OpenReview.net (2018). http://openreview.net/forum?id=rJzIBfZAb

11. Marcus, G.: Deep learning: A critical appraisal. arXiv:1801.00631 [cs.AI] (2018)

12. Moosavi-Dezfooli, S., Fawzi, A., Frossard, P.: DeepFool: a simple and accurate method to fool deep neural networks. In: 2016 IEEE Conference on Computer Vision and Pattern Recognition, NV, USA, pp. 2574–2582. IEEE Computer Society (2016). https://doi.org/10.1109/CVPR.2016.282

13. Papernot, N., McDaniel, P.D., Goodfellow, I.J., Jha, S., Celik, Z.B., Swami, A.: Practical black-box attacks against machine learning. In: Karri, R., Sinanoglu, O., Sadeghi, A., Yi, X. (eds.) Proceedings of the ACM Conference on Computer and Communications Security, Abu Dhabi, UAE, pp. 506–519. ACM (2017). https://doi.org/10.1145/3052973.3053009

14. Shafahi, A., Huang, W., Studer, C., Feizi, S., Goldstein, T.: Are adversarial examples inevitable? In: International Conference on Learning Representations, New Orleans, USA (2019)

15. Szegedy, C., et al.: Intriguing properties of neural networks. arXiv preprint arXiv:1312.6199 (2013)

16. Tyukin, I.Y., Higham, D.J., Gorban, A.N.: On adversarial examples and stealth attacks in artificial intelligence systems. In: 2020 International Joint Conference on Neural Networks, pp. 1–6. IEEE (2020)

17. Tyukin, I.Y., Higham, D.J., Bastounis, A., Woldegeorgis, E., Gorban, A.N.: The feasibility and inevitability of stealth attacks. arXiv:2106.13997 (2021)

Decorelated Weight Initialization
by Backpropagation

Alexander Kovalenko[✉][iD] and Pavel Kordík[iD]

Faculty of Information Technology, Czech Technical University in Prague, Prague,
Czech Republic
{alexander.kovalenko,pavel.kordik}@fit.cvut.cz

Abstract. A hybrid, trainable weight initialization method for neural
networks has been proposed to address potential training issues caused by
weight symmetry. By pre-optimizing randomly initialized weights, using
backpropagation, this method enhances parameter diversity. This efficient approach, applicable to any neural network architecture, decreases
symmetry and decorrelates weights, thus optimizing performance with
fewer trainable parameters.

1 Introduction

The stochastic nature of neural networks' weight initialization [4] imposes certain restrictions on model performance. Mainly, it can result in symmetrical
activation patterns that limit the network's representational capacity. This is
especially critical in resource-constrained models, where such patterns can significantly degrade performance.

Small, resource-constrained neural networks are indispensable in a wide range
of applications that require limited computational resources, real-time processing, or online retraining. Furthermore, a constrained number of parameters in
a neural network promotes learning of general rules rather than merely fitting
to a training dataset. Therefore, given the same performance, a smaller model
potentially has better generalization capability.

Weight initialization algorithms are typically non-deterministic and contain
an element of randomness, so symmetry in the distribution of weights is a matter
of chance. The similarity of the initial weights can also influence the network's
symmetry, which in turn affects the network's dynamics during training. This is
especially crucial in resource-constrained neural networks where weight redundancy is low. To address this issue, various methodologies have been developed.
For instance, orthogonal initialization has been reported to reduce overfitting
and improve system stability in recurrent neural networks [6,8]. Numerous initialization techniques have been developed [2,5], ranging from random weight
initialization and the widely-used Kaiming initialization [3], to unsupervised
pre-training with stacked autoencoders [1].

In this work, we present an efficient solution to decorrelate weights using
backpropagation. The approach is based on a trainable Gram matrix of the

L. Iliadis et al. (Eds.): ICANN 2023, LNCS 14254, pp. 546–550, 2023.
https://doi.org/10.1007/978-3-031-44207-0_46

model's layer weights. The Gram matrix [7], a specific type of covariance matrix that arises in the context of inner product spaces, has a determinant that provides a measure of the spread or volume of multivariate data. Leveraging the fully differentiable nature of neural networks, we employed data-independent weight decorrelation with backpropagation.

2   Our Contribution

In this work, we propose a hybrid approach to weight initialization that is both stochastic and trainable. This technique is suitable for neural networks of any architecture and activation function. The method is based on pre-optimizing stochastically initialized weights to enhance diversity among the network parameters. It is architecture-agnostic, data-independent, and computationally cheap. As a result, models with asymmetric initialization require far fewer trainable parameters to achieve optimal performance due to the decorrelated weights and lower symmetry.

3   Decorrelation by Backpropagation

Prior to the model training, an annealing process is employed. This process applies a data-independent loss function, backpropagated through the neural network, to decorrelate the weights. We define weight symmetry (inversely related to diversity, D) as the cosine distance between the rows of weight matrices in feed-forward layers and as the average cosine distance between individual kernels in convolutional layers. To enforce this symmetry, a straightforward approach that penalizes the Euclidean dot product of individual rows in feed-forward neural network weight matrices and the average Euclidean dot product of convolutional kernels is utilized:

$$1/D = \sum_i \sum_j (\mathbf{w_i} \cdot \mathbf{w_j})$$

$$L = 1/D + \alpha \bar{\mathcal{W}}(1 - \sigma(\mathcal{W})) \tag{1}$$

where D is diversity, $\mathbf{w_i}$ is the $i-th$ row of a weight matrix in feed forward layer, $\mathcal{W}$ layer weight tensor α is a regularization strength parameter. As seen from the equations above, the first term penalizes weight similarity (symmetry), therefore decorrelates the weight, while the second term is denoted to tackle abnormalities in the weight distribution, i.e. it penalizes weight mean and standard deviation that is largely distinct from the normally distributed ones. Even though the distribution penalization can be easily regularized by changing the α value, in the present work all the experiments were performed with $\alpha = 1$.

When reciprocal diversity and deviance from normally distributed weights are penalized, it becomes possible to effectively enforce asymmetric initial weights. This contributes to faster and more efficient neural network training, especially when the number of parameters is constrained and the dataset variance is high.

4 Decorrelation with Trainble Gram Matrix at Initialization

The main drawback of the above mentioned method is a pairwise comparison of the weights, therefore if the weight matrix is large. Therefore, here we describe another method to decorrelate the weights by maximizing the logarithm of the determinant of the Gram matrix. Since the determinant of a covariance matrix is related to the degree of correlation between the variables in the data, if the determinant is close to zero, some of the variables are highly correlated, which implies that the dataset has redundant information. This can be formalized as:

Let the linear layer weight matrix $\mathbf{W} = (a_{ij})_{1 \leq i \leq m, 1 \leq j \leq n}$ be of size $m \times n$, then if columns of $\mathbf{W}$ are linearly dependent, then there exist a vector $\boldsymbol{x} \in \mathbb{R}^n$ for some $n \in \mathbb{N}$ such that $\mathbf{W}\boldsymbol{x} = 0$. Then if $m > n$:

$$(\mathbf{W}^\top \mathbf{W})\boldsymbol{x} = \mathbf{W}^\top(\mathbf{W})\boldsymbol{x} = \mathbf{W}^\top \cdot 0 = 0 \tag{2}$$

alternatively if $m < n$:

$$(\mathbf{W}\mathbf{W}^\top)\boldsymbol{x} = \mathbf{W}(\mathbf{W}^\top)\boldsymbol{x} = \mathbf{W} \cdot 0 = 0 \tag{3}$$

Therefore, in this case, by penalizing the normalized logarithmic determinant of the Gram matrix ($\mathbf{G} = \mathbf{W}^\top \mathbf{W}$)) weight decorrelation can be achieved without pairwise weight comparison. Similarly to the previous case distribution abnormalities from $\mathcal{N}(0, 1)$ were penalized:

$$L = \log(\det(\mathbf{G}))/n + \alpha \bar{\mathcal{W}}(1 - \sigma(\mathcal{W})) \tag{4}$$

where $\mathbf{G}$ is Gram matrix, n – dimensionality of the Gram matrix, $\mathcal{W}$ layer weight tensor α is a regularization strength parameter.

Table 1. Results of the models on the CIFAR10 and CIFAR100 datasets

Model	MACs	Kaiming	Ours	Rel. Improvement, %
CIFAR10				
1	$0.204 \cdot 10^6$	57.85	**62.72**	8.4
2	$0.496 \cdot 10^6$	62.37	**66.87**	7.2
3	$1.37 \cdot 10^6$	65.16	**68.33**	4.9
CIFAR100				
1	$0.204 \cdot 10^6$	28.40	**31.76**	11.8
2	$0.496 \cdot 10^6$	31.24	**33.92**	11.7
3	$1.37 \cdot 10^6$	33.65	**35.52**	5.6

5   Accuracy on Benchmark Datasets

We conducted experiments on two standard image datasets: CIFAR10 and CIFAR100, using resource-constrained neural networks with 2 convolutional layers followed by 2 linear layers. To investigate the impact of convolutional layers on Multiply-And-Accumulate (MACs) operations[1], we varied the number of convolutional layers in the models. The fully connected hidden layers in all models consisted of 128 and 64 neurons. In total, we evaluated three different configurations with varying numbers of parameters: (1) 4 and 8 convolutional kernels of size 3×3 with default padding, stride $= 1$, and ReLU activation function (408 trainable parameters, $0.204 \cdot 10^6$ MACs); (2) 8 and 16 kernels with the same settings as above (1392 trainable parameters, $0.496 \cdot 10^6$ MACs); (3) 16 and 32 convolutional kernels with the same settings as above (5088 trainable parameters, $1.37 \cdot 10^6$ MACs)

To demonstrate the robustness of our proposed method, we applied batch normalization after each layer in the model. However, it is worth mentioning that the proposed method is applicable alongside batch normalization layers, and improves their performance.

The results are presented in Table 1. The decorrelated weight initialization approach led to a significant improvement of $> 11\%$ in validation accuracy, which diminishes as the model size increased. This phenomenon can be attributed to the ratio of efficient parameters: for overparametrized models, the number of efficient parameters responsible for correct reasoning is sufficient, even with symmetrical weight initialization. This is why pruning methods are effective. However, for resource-limited models, an excessive number of symmetrical weights decreases the number of effective parameters, leading to decreased performance.

References

1. Erhan, D., Courville, A., Bengio, Y., Vincent, P.: Why does unsupervised pre-training help deep learning? In: Proceedings of the Thirteenth International Conference on Artificial Intelligence and Statistics, pp. 201–208. JMLR Workshop and Conference Proceedings (2010)
2. Glorot, X., Bengio, Y.: Understanding the difficulty of training deep feedforward neural networks. In: Proceedings of the Thirteenth International Conference on Artificial Intelligence and Statistics, pp. 249–256. JMLR Workshop and Conference Proceedings (2010)
3. He, K., Zhang, X., Ren, S., Sun, J.: Deep residual learning for image recognition. In: Proceedings of the IEEE Conference on Computer Vision and Pattern Recognition, pp. 770–778 (2016)
4. Kumar, S.K.: On weight initialization in deep neural networks. arXiv preprint arXiv:1704.08863 (2017)
5. Narkhede, M.V., Bartakke, P.P., Sutaone, M.S.: A review on weight initialization strategies for neural networks. Artif. Intell. Rev. 55(1), 291–322 (2022)

---

[1] https://github.com/sovrasov/flops-counter.pytorch.

6. Rodríguez, P., Gonzalez, J., Cucurull, G., Gonfaus, J.M., Roca, X.: Regularizing CNNs with locally constrained decorrelations. arXiv preprint arXiv:1611.01967 (2016)
7. Sreeram, V., Agathoklis, P.: On the properties of gram matrix. IEEE Trans. Circ. Syst. I: Fundam. Theor. Appl. **41**(3), 234–237 (1994)
8. Vorontsov, E., Trabelsi, C., Kadoury, S., Pal, C.: On orthogonality and learning recurrent networks with long term dependencies. In: International Conference on Machine Learning, pp. 3570–3578. PMLR (2017)

Exploring Individuality in Human EEG Using Reservoir Computing

Hiromichi Suetani[1,2]($\boxtimes$) (iD) and Keiichi Kitajo[3,4] (iD)

[1] Faculty of Science and Technology, Oita University, Oita, Japan
[2] International Research Center for Neurointelligence (IRCN), The University of Tokyo, 7-3-1 Hongo, Bunkyo, Tokyo, Japan
suetani@oita-u.ac.jp
[3] National Institute for Physiological Sciences, National Institutes of Natural Sciences, Aichi, Japan
[4] The Graduate University for Advanced Studies (SOKENDAI), Aichi, Japan

Abstract. In the present study, we investigate the discernibility of individuality in brain dynamics at a macroscopic level, alongside fingerprints, facial features, and gait patterns, by employing a reservoir computer for time series prediction. Electroencephalograms (EEGs) are acquired from 100 participants during a resting state, and the reservoir computer is utilized to forecast these time series. The findings demonstrate that individuality manifests in the performance of time series prediction. Specifically, the predictive pattern, namely the prediction error as a function of the electrode's position, exhibits similarities within trials of the same participant while differing between participants. Furthermore, we illustrate that applying manifold learning to the predictive patterns facilitates the visualization of the similarity or dissimilarity among a substantial number of participants in a low-dimensional space. These results suggest the potential utilization of EEG signals for biometric authentication and other practical engineering applications.

Keywords: Individuality · Brain dynamics · Reservoir computing

1 Introduction

The brain consistently generates a diverse array of oscillations that occur across various spatiotemporal scales [1]. Similar to fingerprints, faces, or gait patterns, the inquiry into the extent to which these brain dynamics reflect individuality has long been a subject of interest [2]. In this present study, we employ a reservoir computing (RC) approach [3] to investigate the individuality of human brain dynamics at a macroscopic level, specifically in terms of predictability. When forecasting time series using a given model, the prediction error can be regarded as one of the indicators of the system's complexity or difficulty within a fixed class of dynamical models. For our specific time series forecasting model, we employ a reservoir computer and apply it to the resting-state electroencephalogram (EEG) data recorded from 100 participants, which has been employed in our previous studies [2]. We demonstrate that the predictive pattern reflects the individuality.

L. Iliadis et al. (Eds.): ICANN 2023, LNCS 14254, pp. 551–555, 2023.
https://doi.org/10.1007/978-3-031-44207-0_47

2   Materials and Methods

2.1   Experimental Paradigm and Data Acquisition

A total of 100 individuals actively participated in our experimental trials. All participants were provided their informed consent, which was duly approved by the ethics committee of RIKEN prior to the commencement of the experiment. Electroencephalogram (EEG) signals were recorded at a sampling rate of 1000 Hz Hz while the participants were in a state of rest, with their eyes closed, for a duration of 3 min. As part of the preprocessing stage preceding the main analysis, artifacts such as ocular movements and blink-related occurrences were eliminated through the implementation of an independent component analysis (ICA)-based procedure. Subsequently, 14 distinct segments, each spanning a duration of 5.5 s (equivalent to 5500 samples per segment), were extracted from the preprocessed EEG data of each individual for further analysis.

2.2   Eco State Networks

As a reserver computing approach, we introduce the subsequent echo state network [3] of N neurons defined as

$$\boldsymbol{x}_{t+1} = (1 - \tau)\boldsymbol{x}_t + \tau \tanh(gW^{\mathrm{rec}}\boldsymbol{x}_t + a_{\mathrm{in}}W^{\mathrm{in}}[u_t; b_{\mathrm{in}}]), \tag{1}$$

for simplicity. Here, $\boldsymbol{x}_t$ is the N-dimensional state variables of the reservoir and u_t is the EEG time series taken from an electrode, where t denotes discrete time (the unit time corresponds to the sampling time width of the recorded EEG) and $\tanh(\cdot)$ is applied to each component. The matrices W^{rec} amd W^{in} represent the connectivity within the reservoir and that from the input to the reservoir, respectively. The weight of each connection in W^{rec} is chosen firstly from a Gaussian distribution $\mathcal{N}(0, 1)$. Then, W^{rec} is divided by its spectral radius so that the resulting matrix is normalized. So, the parameter g controls the scaling of the inter-connectivity within the reservoir. The weight of each connection in W^{in} is chosen from a uniform distribution $\mathcal{U}(-0.5, 0.5)$. The parameters a_{in} and τ are the input scaling and the leaking rate, respectively. Then, linear superposition of the internal state $\boldsymbol{x}_t$ and a bias b_{out} is used as the output y_t of the reservoir as $y_t = W^{\mathrm{out}}[\boldsymbol{x}_t; b_{\mathrm{out}}]$, where the output matrix W^{out} can be determined in a linear way by minimizing a cost function such as ridge regression.

3   Results

We use one trial as the validation data, and the remaining 13 trials as the training data. Here, the purpose of the RC Eq. (2) is to predict the future ΔT seconds ahead. Figure 1(a) shows a demonstration of the RC's prediction of the EEG time series taken from an electrode (POz) for a single participant. The discrepancy between the output from the reservoir and the target EEG increases with an increase in the prediction time ΔT. Therefore, the normalized mean squared error (NRMSE) for the validation data was plotted as a function of the prediction time ΔT, which is shown in Fig. 1(b). Here, different colors indicate NRMSE for different positions of the electrode.

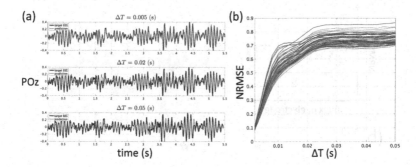

Fig. 1. (a) An example of EEG time series prediction via RC. The parameters are set to $g = 1.2, a_{in} = 1, \tau = 0.3, b_{in} = 0$, and $b_{out} = 1$, respectively. The regularization parameter for ridge regression is set to $\gamma = 0.001$. (b) The NRMSEs as functions of the prediction time ΔT for 63 EEG time series.

Of interest here is that the tendency of the prediction error depends on the position of electrode. Therefore, graphs depicting NRMSE as a function of the index of electrode (we call this function the predictability pattern) for eight different participants are shown in Fig. 2(a). In each of the panels in Fig. 2(a), the predictive pattern in the different colors indicate NRMSE on different trials. We found the following two interesting results. The first is that the predictive patterns for individual participants are similar across trials, which suggests that the system remains consistent for at least several minutes under the defined conditions of resting state with eye-closing. The second is that the shape of the predictive patterns differ from one another across participants. This means that spontaneous brain activity in the resting state differs from individual to individual, which is reflected in the predictive patterns.

To visualize the individuality of the predictive pattern in a low-dimensional space, we employ t-SNE [4] that is a state-of-the-art technique of manifold learning for dimensionality reduction. The result is shown in Fig. 2(b). Here, each point corresponds to a 63-dimensional prediction pattern for a single EEG segment, with different colors indicating different participants. It is evident that the participants' classes are adequately distinguished by the t-SNE embedding, where each participant is represented as a distinct cluster of points.

4   Summary and Discussion

We investigated individuality in EEG signals using RC and found that prediction patterns is useful for discerning individuals. Additionally, we demonstrated the feasibility of visualizing interrelationships among prediction pat-

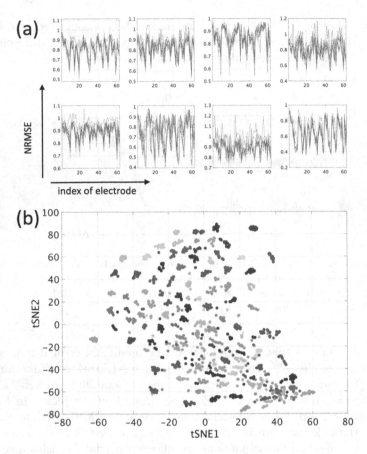

Fig. 2. (a) Predictability patterns of eight participants for resting state. (b) Embeddings of 1400 EEG segments (100 participants × 14 trials) with *t*-SNE. Each point corresponds to a 63-dimensional predictive pattern for a trial of a resting state and each color denotes each participant. The perplexity parameter for *t*-SNE is set to $k = 30$.

terns in a low-dimensional space using manifold learning. However, these findings depend on the chosen hyper-parameters. To address this, we are exploring a Bayesian optimization-based approach to mitigate variability. Comprehensive results, including further analyses, will be presented at the upcoming conference.

Acknowledgement. This work was supported by JSPS KAKENHI and MEXT KAKENHI Grant Numbers 19H04183 and 22KK0159, and 18H04948.

References

1. Buzsaki, G.: Rhythms of the Brain. Oxford University Press, New York (2006)
2. Suetani, H., Kitajo, K.: A manifold learning approach to mapping individuality of human brain oscillations through beta-divergence. Neurosci. Res. **156**, 188–196 (2020)
3. Jaeger, H.: The "echo state" apporach to analysing and training recurrent neural networks. GMD Report 148, German National Research Institute for Information Technology (2001)
4. Maaten, L., Hinton, G.: Visualizing data using t-SNE. J. Mach. Learn. Res. **9**, 2579–2605 (2008)

Learning Efficient Backprojections Across Cortical Hierarchies in Real Time

Kevin Max[1]([✉]), Laura Kriener[1], Garibaldi Pineda García[2], Thomas Nowotny[2], Walter Senn[1], and Mihai A. Petrovici[1]

[1] Department of Physiology, University of Bern, Bern, Switzerland
kevin.max@unibe.ch
[2] School of Engineering and Informatics, University of Sussex, Brighton, UK

Abstract. Models of sensory processing and learning in physical substrates (such as the cortex) need to efficiently assign credit to synapses in all areas. In deep learning, a well-established solution is error backpropagation; this however carries several biologically implausible requirements, such as weight transport from feed-forward to feedback paths. We present Phaseless Alignment Learning (PAL), a biologically plausible approach for learning efficient feedback weights in layered cortical hierarchies. Our dynamical system enables the simultaneous learning of all weights with always-on plasticity, and exclusively utilizes information locally available at the synapses. PAL is entirely phase-free, avoiding the need for forward and backward passes or phased learning, and enables efficient error propagation across multi-layer cortical hierarchies, while maintaining bio-physically plausible signal transport and learning.

Keywords: Credit assignment · Physical computing · Network plasticity

1 Summary

Neural activity is modulated through learning, i.e., long-term adaptation of synaptic weights. However, it remains unresolved how weights are adapted across the cortex to effectively solve a given task. A key question is how to assign credit to synapses that are situated deep within a hierarchical network. In deep learning, backpropagation (BP) is the current state-of-the-art for solving this issue, and may potentially serve as an inspiration for neuroscience. Application of BP to cortical processing is however non-trivial, due to several biologically implausible requirements it entails. For example, it requires information to be buffered for use at different stages of processing. Additionally, error propagation occurs through weights that must be mirrored at synapses in different layers, resulting in the weight transport problem. Furthermore, artificial neural networks (ANNs) operate in separate forward and backward phases, with inference and learning alternating strictly.

© The Author(s), under exclusive license to Springer Nature Switzerland AG 2023
L. Iliadis et al. (Eds.): ICANN 2023, LNCS 14254, pp. 556–559, 2023.
https://doi.org/10.1007/978-3-031-44207-0_48

We introduce Phaseless Alignment Learning (PAL) [4], a biologically plausible technique for learning effective top-down weights across layers in cortical hierarchies. We propose that cortical networks can learn useful backward weights by utilizing a ubiquitous resource of the brain: noise. Despite being usually treated as a disruptive factor, noise can be leveraged by the feedback pathway as an additional carrier of information for synaptic plasticity.

PAL describes a fully dynamic system that effectively addresses all of the aforementioned problems: it models the dynamics of biophysical substrates, and all computations are carried out using information **locally available** at the synapses; learning occurs in a **completely phase-less** manner; **plasticity is always-on** for all synapses, both forward and backward, at all times. Our approach is consistent with biological observations and facilitates efficient learning without the need for wake-sleep phases or other forms of phased plasticity found in many other models of cortical learning.

PAL can be applied to a broad range of models and represents an improvement over previously known biologically plausible methods of credit assignment. For instance, when compared to feedback alignment (FA), PAL can solve complex tasks with fewer neurons and more effectively learn useful latent representations. We illustrate this by conducting experiments on various classification tasks using a cortical dendrite microcircuit model [7], which leverages the complexity of neuronal morphology and is capable of prospective coding [2].

2 Theory

PAL utilises the noise found in physical neurons, as information is sent across the cortical hierarchy, see Fig. 1 (a). Neuronal dynamics are described in a rate-based coding scheme of a network with $\ell = 1 \dots N$ layers,

$$\tau \dot{u}_\ell = -u_\ell + W_{\ell,\ell-1} r_{\ell-1} + e_\ell + \xi_\ell , \tag{1}$$

with bottom-up input $W_{\ell,\ell-1} r_{\ell-1}$, and noise ξ_ℓ; the local error signal e_ℓ is used to update forward weights through $\dot{W}_{\ell,\ell-1} \propto e_\ell r_{\ell-1}^T$. Errors are passed down from higher layers through top-down synapses $B_{\ell,\ell+1}$ via $e_\ell = \varphi' \cdot B_{\ell,\ell+1} e_{\ell+1}$.

As suggested in [7], the different terms in Eq. (1) correspond to the different compartments of a pyramidal neuron, and the error is transported as the difference in firing rates of pairs of pyramidal and interneurons.

PAL learns from the noise ξ_ℓ accumulated on top of a stimulus signal as it passes through the network. Backprojections are learned using high-pass-filtered rates $\widehat{r}_{\ell+1}$ through the rule

$$\dot{B}_{\ell,\ell+1} \propto \xi_\ell \left(\widehat{r}_{\ell+1}\right)^T - \alpha B_{\ell,\ell+1} . \tag{2}$$

By exploiting the autocorrelation properties of neuronal noise, this learning rule dynamically achieves approximate alignment $B_{\ell,\ell+1} \parallel W_{\ell+1,\ell}^T$ for all layers **simultaneously**, and without interrupting the learning of forward weights (see Fig. 1 (b,c)). This allows networks which implement PAL to efficiently learn

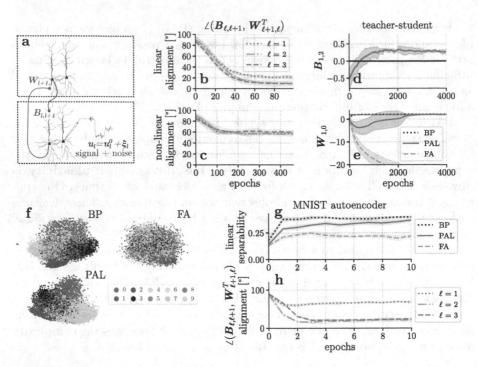

Fig. 1. PAL aligns weight updates with backpropagation in hierarchical cortical networks. (a) Cortical pyramidal cells as functional units of sensory processing and credit assignment. Bottom-up ($W_{\ell+1,\ell}$) and top-down ($B_{\ell,\ell+1}$) projections preferentially target different dendrites. Due to stochastic dynamics of individual neurons, noise is added to the signal. **(b)** We train the backward projections in a deep, dendritic microcircuit network of multi-compartment neurons with layer sizes [5-20-10-20-5] using our method PAL. All backward weights $B_{\ell,\ell+1}$ are learned simultaneously, while forward weights are fixed. Forward weights are initialised s.t. neurons are activated in their linear regime. **(c)** Same as **b**, but with weights initialised in non-linear regime. **(d)** In a simple teacher-student task with a neuron chain [1-1-1] of dendritic microcircuits, PAL is able to flip the sign of backwards weights, which is crucial for successful reproduction of the teaching signal. **(e)** PAL solves teacher-student task, where feedback alignment fails. The teaching signal (red dashed) requires positive forward weights, whereas all student networks are initialised with negative $W_{1,0}$. Note that PAL only learns the correct forward weights once the backwards weights have flipped sign (at epoch ~ 500). **(f-h)** PAL learns useful latent representations on the MNIST autoencoder task, whereas FA leads to poor feature separation. We train a network [784-200-2-200-784] using leaky-integrator neurons on the MNIST autoencoder task: **(f)** Shown are the activations after training in the two-neuron layer for all samples in the test set; colors encode the corresponding label. BP and PAL show improved feature separation compared to FA. **(g)** Linear separability of latent activation. **(h)** Alignment angle of top-down weights to all layers for networks trained with PAL. PAL is able adapt top-down weights while forward weights are learned at the same time. All curves show mean and standard deviation over 5 seeds.

all weights (feedforward and feedback) without phases, as opposed to many bio-inspired learning rules found in the literature (e.g., Difference Target Propagation and variants [1,3], AGREL [5,6], Equilibrium Propagation [8]).

3 Results

We have evaluated PAL on varius tasks: for an excerpt of results, see Fig. 1 (b-h). Additionally, we benchmark PAL using standard tests such as the MNIST digit classification task, where the dendritic microcircuit model (of network size: [784-100-10]) achieves a final test error 3.9 ± 0.2 % using PAL and 4.7 ± 0.1 % with microcircuits with FA. We emphasize that our results were achieved through simulation of a fully dynamic, recurrent system that is biologically plausible. Weight and voltage updates were applied at every time step, and populations of multi-compartment neurons were used as a bio-plausible error transport mechanism. Our findings demonstrate that PAL can efficiently learn all weights and outperforms FA on tasks involving classification and latent space separation.

We argue that PAL can be realized both in biological and, more generally, physical components. Specifically, it capitalizes on the inherent noise present in physical systems and leverages simple filtering techniques to distinguish between signal and noise where necessary. A realization of PAL (or a variant) in physical form, whether in the cortex or on neuromorphic systems, constitutes an elegant solution to the weight transport problem, while enabling efficient learning with purely local computations.

References

1. Ernoult, M., et al.: Towards scaling difference target propagation by learning backprop targets. arXiv preprint arXiv:2201.13415 (2022)
2. Haider, P., et al.: Latent equilibrium. Adv. Neural Inf. Process. Syst. **34**, 17839–17851 (2021)
3. Lee, D.-H., Zhang, S., Fischer, A., Bengio, Y.: Difference target propagation. In: Appice, A., Rodrigues, P.P., Santos Costa, V., Soares, C., Gama, J., Jorge, A. (eds.) ECML PKDD 2015. LNCS (LNAI), vol. 9284, pp. 498–515. Springer, Cham (2015). https://doi.org/10.1007/978-3-319-23528-8_31
4. Max, K., Kriener, L., García, G.P., Nowotny, T., Senn, W., Petrovici, M.A.: Learning efficient backprojections across cortical hierarchies in real time. arXiv preprint arXiv:2212.10249 (2022)
5. Pozzi, I., et al.: A biologically plausible learning rule for deep learning in the brain. arXiv preprint arXiv:1811.01768 (2018)
6. Roelfsema, P., Ooyen, A.: Attention-gated reinforcement learning of internal representations for classification. Neural Comput. **17**, 2176–2214 (2005)
7. Sacramento, J., et al.: Dendritic cortical microcircuits approximate the backpropagation algorithm. In: Advances in Neural Information Processing Systems. vol. 31 (2018)
8. Scellier, B., Bengio, Y.: Equilibrium propagation. Front. Comput. Neurosci. **11**, 24 (2017)

Neural Self-organization
for Muscle-Driven Robots

Elias Fischer[1]([✉]), Bulcsú Sándor[2], and Claudius Gros[1]

[1] Institute for Theoretical Physics, Goethe University Frankfurt a.M.,
Frankfurt am Main, Germany
`fischer@itp.uni-frankfurt.de`
[2] Department of Physics, Babes-Bolyai University, Cluj-Napoca, Romania

Abstract. We present self-organizing control principles for simulated robots actuated by synthetic muscles. Muscles correspond to linear motors exerting force only when contracting, but not when expanding, with joints being actuated by pairs of antagonistic muscles. Individually, muscles are connected to a controller composed of a single neuron with a dynamical threshold that generates target positions for the respective muscle. A stable limit cycle is generated when the embodied feedback loop is closed, giving rise to regular locomotive patterns. In the absence of direct couplings between neurons, we show that force-mediated intra- and inter-leg couplings between muscles suffice to generate stable gaits.

Keywords: self-organization · robots · muscles

1 Muscle-Driven Robots

A substantial effort is devoted to the development of robotic artificial muscles [9], with possible applications ranging from interactive soft robotics [7] to the recreation of human walking via compliant legs [2]. In comparison, only a somewhat limited number of studies have been devoted to the study of robotic control principles for synthetic muscles [1,4]. Here we examine control principles based on embodied self-organization that have been developed previously for robots driven by rotating actuators (motors) [3,6]. For pairs of antagonistic muscles that are controlled independently, viz without cross-control, we find spontaneous anti-synchronization due to the indirect coupling via the moving limb. Our studies are carried out using Webots, an open-source mobile robot simulation software developed by Cyberbotics Ltd [8].

The core processing unit of our controller is a single neuron with membrane potential $x(t)$ and a variable threshold $b(t)$. The neuron receives two types of inputs via constant synaptic weights, w_s and w_y, as illustrated in Fig. 1. The first, w_s transmits information about the current status $s = s(t)$ of the actuator, with the second, w_y, corresponding to an excitatory self-coupling:

$$\tau_x \dot{x} = -x + w_s s_{\text{rel}} + w_y y, \qquad s_{\text{rel}} = \frac{s - s_{\text{min}}}{s_{\text{max}} - s_{\text{min}}}, \tag{1}$$

$$\tau_b \dot{b} = y - y_b, \qquad y = \frac{1}{1 + e^{a(b-x)}} \tag{2}$$

where the neuronal activity $y \in [0, 1]$ is determined by a sigmoidal with gain a and threshold b. The time constants for the evolutions of membrane potential and threshold are respectively τ_x and τ_b. The position s of the actuator is bounded by physical constraints, such that $s \in [s_{\text{min}}, s_{\text{max}}]$. Using the relative position $s_{\text{rel}} \in [0, 1]$ as an input to the membrane potential, as done in (1), allows to directly compare the sizes of w_s and w_y. Entering (2) is the desired steady-state value y_b for the neural activity y. It is reached however only if activities would cease altogether.

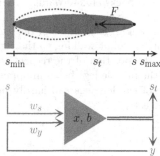

Fig. 1. Left: Six-legged robot driven by 24 muscles. Each leg is controlled by two pairs of antagonistic muscles, enabling movement both in up-down and forwards-backwards direction. Simulations were performed using the Webots open-source robot simulation software by Cyberbotics Ltd [8]. **Right:** Schematics of the single neuron controller. The neuron takes the current actuator position s and its own activation y as inputs, weighted respectively with synaptic weights w_s and w_y. The target position s_t determines via (3) the actuating force F [Link to the video]

The one-neuron controller acts by generating a target position $s_t \in [s_{\text{min}}, s_{\text{max}}]$ for the actuator, which in turn is translated to a force F via

$$F = -\gamma \dot{s} + K_s \frac{s_t - s}{s_{\text{max}} - s_{\text{min}}}, \qquad s_t = s_{\text{min}} + (s_{\text{max}} - s_{\text{min}})y \tag{3}$$

where K_s is the coefficient for proportional control and γ a phenomenological damping constant. The results presented are for critical damping. We assume with (3), that the target position s_t for the actuator is directly proportional to the neuronal activity $y = y(t)$. As a result, one has a sensori-motor feedback loop [3,6], with the actuator trying to reach a continuously updated target position. Biologically, muscles may exert force only when contracting, but not when expanding. This corresponds to the substitution $F \rightarrow F\left[1 - \theta(F)\right]$, where we use the Heaviside step function $\theta(x)$ to set the force to zero when $s_t > s$, viz when the length s would be increased.

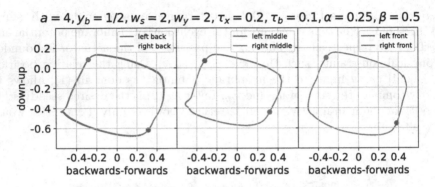

Fig. 2. The angle (in radians) of the legs of the robot shown in Fig. 1, viewed from the left side of the robot walking to the right after the initial synchronization phase. The dots show the position of the respective leg at the last time step, showcasing a tripod gait with the middle legs being in opposite phases to the front and back legs. The blue trajectory of the left legs can hardly be seen because the left/right trajectories align almost perfectly

Attractoring. The autonomous system, attained by setting $w_s = 0$ in (1), shows a super-critical Hopf transition at

$$w_y = \frac{4}{a} + \frac{\tau_x}{\tau_b}, \qquad (4)$$

which holds for $y_b = 1/2$. When w_y and/or a is large, the system oscillates spontaneously, acting as a central pattern generator (CPG). In this regime, the additional feedback $w_s s_{\mathrm{rel}}$ corresponds to a modulator. Here we concentrate on the case that the isolated neuron does not oscillate on its own, viz that w_y and/or a is too small for (4) to be fulfilled. Locomotion is generated consequently only when the feedback from the actuator is strong enough for an embodied limit cycle to emerge. We call this regime 'attractoring', which has been found to allow for increased behavioural flexibility [6]. Locomotion is embodied in the sense that the phase space of the resulting limit cycle contains the degrees of freedom of the body in addition to $x(t)$ and $b(t)$. We note in this context that it is important to use force signals for both real-world and simulated actuators, as the respective default PID controllers tend to be stiff.

Force Mediated Inter-muscle Coupling. The desired movement for a leg with two pairs of antagonstic muscles (up-down; left-right) is up-forwards-down-backwards. For this we expand (3) as

$$s_{t,1} = s_{\min} + (s_{\max} - s_{\min}) \cdot ((1 - \alpha)y_1 + \alpha y_2), \qquad \alpha \in [0,1] \qquad (5)$$

which corresponds to an embodied coupling via force superposition. The activity y_2 of a second neuron of the same leg influences the target position (and hence the force) generated by the first neuron, but not the first neuron directly. The order of coupling between the four muscles of a single leg is taken to be circular. The same principle is used for (indirect) inter-leg coupling,

$$s_{t,1} = s_{\min} + (s_{\max} - s_{\min}) \cdot ((1 - \alpha - \beta)y_1 + \alpha y_2 + \beta y_3), \qquad \alpha + \beta \le 1, \quad (6)$$

where y_3 is now the activity of a neuron from another leg. For the six-legged robot shown in Fig. 1, the contralateral pairs of legs are coupled via the up-down muscles for producing steps, while the inter-leg phase blocking is mediated solely via the upper muscles. We call this coupling principle 'force-mediated' coupling.

2   Results

For parameters in the attractoring regime, we present in Fig. 2 the time evolution of the positions of the six legs. One observes a stable tripod gait [Link to the video], which emerges without the direct coupling of the controlling neurons. A conceptually similar result has also been achieved by using pressure sensors and motors [5], albeit relying on CPGs for controlling the individual legs. Note that here oscillations would not be generated without feedback from the body and no forces are exerted when the muscles relax, so in this sense the locomotion is fully self-organized.

References

1. Geyer, H., Herr, H.: A muscle-reflex model that encodes principles of legged mechanics produces human walking dynamics and muscle activities. IEEE Trans. Neural Syst. Rehabil. Eng. **18**(3), 263–273 (2010)
2. Geyer, H., Seyfarth, A., Blickhan, R.: Compliant leg behaviour explains basic dynamics of walking and running. Proc. R. Soc. B: Biol. Sci. **273**(1603), 2861–2867 (2006)
3. Kubandt, F., Nowak, M., Koglin, T., Gros, C., Sándor, B.: Embodied robots driven by self-organized environmental feedback. Adapt. Behav. **27**(5), 1059712319855622 (2019)
4. Mohseni, O., Schmidt, P., Seyfarth, A., Sharbafi, M.A.: Unified GRF-based control for adjusting hopping frequency with various robot configurations. Adv. Robot. **36**(13), 641–653 (2022)
5. Owaki, D., Kano, T., Nagasawa, K., Tero, A., Ishiguro, A.: Simple robot suggests physical interlimb communication is essential for quadruped walking. J. R. Soc. Interface **10**(78), 20120669 (2013)

6. Sándor, B., Nowak, M., Koglin, T., Martin, L., Gros, C.: Kick control: using the attracting states arising within the sensorimotor loop of self-organized robots as motor primitives. Front. Neurorobot. **12** (2018)
7. Wang, J., Gao, D., Lee, P.S.: Recent progress in artificial muscles for interactive soft robotics. Adv. Mater. **33**(19), 2003088 (2021)
8. Webots: http://www.cyberbotics.com. open-source Mobile Robot Simulation Software
9. Zhang, J., et al.: Robotic artificial muscles: current progress and future perspectives. IEEE Trans. Robot. **35**(3), 761–781 (2019)

Novel Synthetic Data Tool
for Data-Driven Cardboard Box
Localization

Peter Kravár[1]([✉])(ID), Lukáš Gajdošech[2,3](ID), and Martin Madaras[2,3](ID)

[1] Faculty of Informatics, Masaryk University, Brno, Czech Republic
xkravar@fi.muni.cz
[2] Faculty of Mathematics, Physics and Informatics, Comenius University, Bratislava, Slovakia
{gajdosech,madaras}@fmph.uniba.sk
[3] Skeletex Research, Bratislava, Slovakia

Abstract. Application of neural networks in industrial settings, such as automated factories with bin-picking solutions requires costly production of large labeled datasets. This paper presents an automatic data generation tool with a procedural model of a cardboard box. We briefly demonstrate the capabilities of the system, and its various parameters and empirically prove the usefulness of the generated synthetic data by training a simple neural network. We make sample synthetic data generated by the tool publicly available.

Keywords: Synthetic Data · Neural Applications · Intelligent Robotics

1 Introduction

Automatic detection and localization of bins on a conveyor belt is an essential task in automated factories. This detection must be robust to guarantee the safe operation of robotic arms. It includes handling edge cases such as missing edges, occlusion, and variance in the materials and shapes of the bins. Moreover, in a specific scenario of package delivery factories, bins are made from a non-rigid cardboard material. These boxes are prone to various deformations, and their paper flaps are semi-randomly opened while being filled by workers and robots.

Analytical detection algorithms lack robustness and are hard to modify for new cases [5]. On the other hand, machine learning-based methods require data. Capturing real RGB-D samples in various scenarios in factories is costly. Therefore, the generation of synthetic data is recently a popular research topic [1,6], outlined by the boom of commercial solutions such as NVIDIA Omniverse[TM1].

---

[1] https://www.nvidia.com/en-us/omniverse/solutions/digital-twins/.

Supported by the TERAIS project in the framework of the program Horizon-Widera-2021 of the European Union under the Grant agreement number 101079338.

L. Iliadis et al. (Eds.): ICANN 2023, LNCS 14254, pp. 565–569, 2023.
https://doi.org/10.1007/978-3-031-44207-0_50

Following our previous work [3], in this short submission we propose a novel data-generation tool for the automated generation of training data containing cardboard boxes. We evaluate the results of a neural network trained upon this novel data against a baseline synthetic generator, which has no automatic parametrization and cannot produce boxes with paper flaps.

2   Generating Data

This project aimed to create a high-level system for generating synthetic datasets of 3D bin scans using Blender 3D compiled into a python module (bpy)[2]. We accomplished this by wrapping Blender's functionality into high-level classes representing respective parts of the 3D scanning pipeline. Our pipeline simulates the real scanning process of a structured light scanner. Render settings, scanner parameters and the behavior of random parameter generation are fully customizable by the user. The output of our system comes in the form of structured point cloud data. The camera transformation matrix and the volume box of the generated cardboard box are also exported and used as ground truth data.

2.1   Parametric Cardboard Box

Variety in synthetic data can be achieved by randomizing parameters of appropriate parametric model [2]. To generate virtual cardboard boxes, we have created a parametric model which approximates the most significant box features, see Fig. 2a for visual illustration. By changing the parameters, we are able to obtain a wide variety of virtual cardboard boxes. The box parameters are:

1. **Size** - box dimensions
2. **Flap Length** - flap dimensions
3. **Flap Width** - flap taper
4. **Open** - flap open angle
5. **Thickness** - cardboard thickness
6. **Bevel** - roundness of box edges

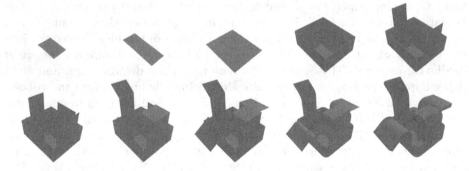

Fig. 1. Box creation process, operations are exaggerated for visual clarity.

---

[2] https://docs.blender.org/api/current/info_advanced_blender_as_bpy.html.

We have approximated a generic cardboard box as an object created using the corresponding sequence of steps as shown in Fig. 1. The steps include a series of extrusions, rounding corner edges, and adding thickness. The parametric model is implemented using Blender's Geometry Nodes system [4].

In real production, a box is assembled by folding a sheet of cardboard. The resulting object can therefore be closely approximated in 2D. Such 2D representation can serve as a UV map without visible seams, used for procedural shading of the parametric cardboard box, Fig. 2b shows the resulting rendered image.

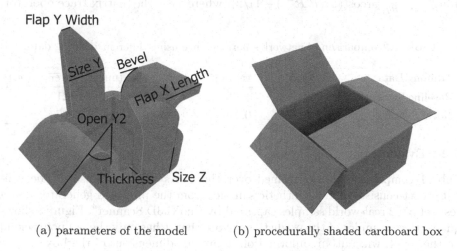

(a) parameters of the model   (b) procedurally shaded cardboard box

Fig. 2. Illustration of box parameters and the resulting rendered image.

2.2 Generation Parameters

The camera location was generated as a random unit vector in the positive XYZ part of a sphere scaled by uniformly distributed random distance in the $(1m, 1.7m)$ interval. The rotation of the scanner was then calculated such that the camera would point at world origin. Generation of boxes utilized random distributions for multiple parameters, ex. a single dimension was randomized as:

$$Size_X = 0.25 + min(max(-\sigma \times \gamma, \mathcal{N}(\mu, \sigma^2)), \sigma \times \gamma).$$

For our experiments, we set $\sigma = 0.1$ and $\gamma = 2.0$, each constant is in SI units.

3   Experiment

We have verified the added value of the proposed generator by training a neural network for 6D pose estimation of the cardboard boxes [3]. We have created two sets of synthetic training data, each consisting of 496 samples. The first set was

568   P. Kravár et al.

generated using a baseline generator, without the automated box parametrization, see Fig. 3a. The second set is generated using our novel tool. The data, together with loading scripts in Python is publicly available[3].

3.1 Metrics

Translation of the box origin is evaluated using Euclidean distance: $e_{\mathrm{TE}}(\hat{t}, t) = \| t - \hat{t} \|_2$. For rotation, we use model-independent angle distance between rotational axes calculated from corresponding rotation matrices as: $e_{\mathrm{RE}}(\hat{R}, R) = \min_{\hat{R}' \in \{\hat{R}_1, \hat{R}_2\}} \arccos((\mathrm{Tr}(\hat{R}'R^{-1}) - 1)/2)$, where Tr is the matrix trace operator.

Table 1. Comparison of network's performance using different training data.

Training Data	val $\overline{e_{\mathrm{TE}}}$ (mm)	val $\overline{e_{\mathrm{RE}}}$ (rad)	test $\overline{e_{\mathrm{TE}}}$ (mm)	test $\overline{e_{\mathrm{RE}}}$ (rad)
Baseline Synthetic	35.603	1.336	14.237	1.121
Novel Synthetic	4.326	0.240	12.161	0.787

3.2 Evaluation

Table 1 compares networks trained over the two synthetic datasets. The validation set consists of 100 synthetic samples from the proposed generator and a test set of 22 real-world samples captured by PhoXi 3D Scanner[4]. Figure 3 shows qualitative examples of the predictions. Note that it has only the 3D point cloud on the input, without any information about the dimensions of the boxes.

We conclude that the novel generator helped the network to generalize and learn to ignore paper flaps, showing promise in improving synthetic data tools for more successful training. Future work includes expanding this tool for additional possible variances, such as bins from semi-transparent plastic materials with a simulation of physical phenomena like light caustics in photo-realistic textures.

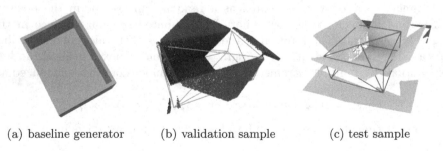

(a) baseline generator   (b) validation sample   (c) test sample

Fig. 3. Sample from the baseline generator and network predictions.

---

[3] http://www.st.fmph.uniba.sk/~gajdosech2/icann2023-dataset/.
[4] https://www.photoneo.com/phoxi-3d-scanner/.

References

1. Chen, K., et al.: Sim-to-real 6D object pose estimation via iterative self-training for robotic bin picking. In: European Conference on Computer Vision (ECCV), pp. 533–550 (2022)
2. Fedorova, S., et al.: Synthetic 3D data generation pipeline for geometric deep learning in architecture. In: The International Archives of the Photogrammetry Remote Sensing and Spatial Information Sciences (ISPRS Congress), pp. 337–344 (2021)
3. Gajdošech, L., Kocur, V., Stuchlík, M., Hudec, L., Madaras, M.: Towards deep learning-based 6D bin pose estimation in 3D scan. In: VISAPP, pp. 545–552 (2022)
4. van Gumster, J., Lampel, J.: Procedural modeling with blender's geometry nodes. In: SIGGRAPH Labs. N (2022). https://doi.org/10.1145/3532725.3538516
5. Katsoulas, D.: Localization of piled boxes by means of the hough transform. In: Michaelis, B., Krell, G. (eds.) DAGM 2003. LNCS, vol. 2781, pp. 44–51. Springer, Heidelberg (2003). https://doi.org/10.1007/978-3-540-45243-0_7
6. Periyasamy, A.S., Schwarz, M., Behnke, S.: SynPick: a dataset for dynamic bin picking scene understanding. In: IEEE CASE, pp. 488–493 (2021)

Reinforcement Learning with Memory Based Automatic Chunking for Complex Skill Acquisition

Shweta Singh[1]($\boxtimes$) (iD) and Sudaman Katti[2] (iD)

[1] IIIT, Hyderabad, India
shweta.singh@research.iiit.ac.in,shwetasingh@rde.gov.in
[2] Vishwakarma Institute of Technology, Pune, India
sudaman.katti19@vit.edu

Abstract. Transformers are rapidly gaining popularity in the field of reinforcement learning. This research work proposes a transformer model with enhanced stability and learning speed. Deliberate chunking is conscious in its nature, it is strategically intended to structure the material to memorize. Automatic chunking on the other hand, is unconscious, and continuous, this research work applies automatic chunking on transformers. Firstly, the memory buffer of the transformer is divided into chunks. A high level attention is then performed on summaries of these chunks to select the most relevant parts of memory during training. Thus, the transformer model learns to work on only the relevant parts of memory instead of performing self attention on the entire buffer. Gating connections which make use of gated recurrent units, layer normalization and positional encoding are also used for further improvement in performance. Training and testing for various visual navigation and robotic locomotion tasks is done.

Keywords: Transformers · Gated Recurrent Units · Convolutional Neural Networks

1 Introduction

Human learning and decision making works on recollection based on only relevant parts of memory. We can re-live specific past sequences of events in detail,without paying attention to everything in our memory. Reinforcement learning agents should work similarly in order to function effectively in complicated and long horizon tasks. The transformer mechanism used, should work on relevant subsections of memory instead of performing self-attention on the whole memory buffer. The architecture used in this research work does just that by modifying the transformer with a high level attention which learns the ability to select relevant chunks or sequences of events from memory during training. Layer normalization, gating and positional encoding are used to further improve the stability and performance of the transformer.

L. Iliadis et al. (Eds.): ICANN 2023, LNCS 14254, pp. 570–573, 2023.
https://doi.org/10.1007/978-3-031-44207-0_51

2   Methodology

The input observations are first pre-processed by an encoder which consists of 3 convolutional layers. Output of this CNN is then stored in memory and also fed to the transformer block. Memories are then split into various chunks and the output of the CNN acts as the query. Each chuck gets assigned a mean value using the PyTorch mean function which works around a specific dimension and attention is performed on these new summarised memories to find the top k chunks based on highest values. For the experiments in this paper, k was set to 3. These top k chunks are then detached to create a collection of relevant memories. Attention is again performed in the transformer, but this time, the new relevant memory is used (query remains the same). Layer normalisation and gating is then performed on the output of this attention. The final output of the transformer is then used to create a distribution over the action space such that based on the input to the CNN, there is always a specific action which will be taken. PPO (proximal policy optimisation) is used to perform consistent updates (based on the defined learning rate) and limit how far we can change the policy in each iteration through the use of KL-divergence which measures the difference between two data distributions. As a result, the model learns to select relevant parts of memory and take appropriate actions based on them during training (Fig. 1).

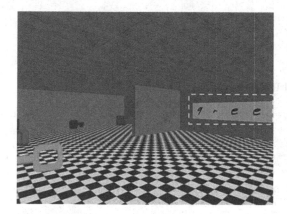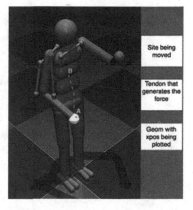

Fig. 1. The diagram to the left shows the visual navigation instructions task environment, the diagram to the right shows the robotic locomotion humanoid environment

The tasks implemented and their objectives are as follows-

1) Visual maze navigation task- Navigate a maze to find a goal
2) Collection task- Based on visual input, collect as many distinct objects as possible
3) Instructions task- Collect a specific colored object based on instructions displayed on a text box

4) Humanoid robotic locomotion task- Consists of a humanoid bot, the objective is to learn to balance and walk through manipulation of various body parts.

5) Quadruped robotic navigation task- Consists of a quadruped bot, the objective is to learn to move in a specified direction by manipulating its body parts

3   Results

Comparative study of regular transformer, transformer with relevant memory selection and transformer with relevant memory selection along with gating was done. Such comparison of algorithms in terms of entropy, rewards and value function loss was done for 3 visual navigation and 2 robotic locomotion tasks.

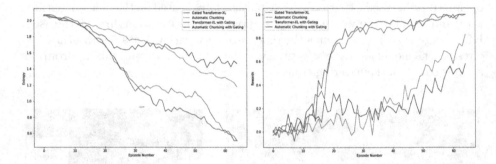

Fig. 2. Visual Instructions Task Results.

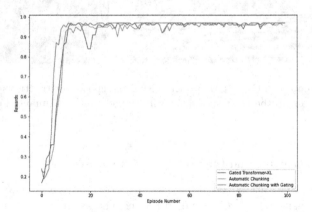

Fig. 3. Collection Task Rewards.

In Fig. 2, the red line corresponds to gated automatic chunking, green line corresponds to gated transformer-XL, orange line corresponds to automatic chunking and blue line corresponds to transformer-XL. The diagram to the right represents the mean reward across parallel workers per episode during training and the diagram to the left represents the entropy values during training. The X-axis represents episode number in all the above figures. Gated automatic chunking had the highest rewards and lowest entropy (randomness) during training. Decrease in entropy signifies successful training. Both gated algorithms showed superiority in terms of training time, randomness and rewards achieved. Gated Automatic chunking and automatic chunking showed better results as compared to gated transformer-xl and regular transformer-xl respectively. Similar reward values were found for the collection task as well as shown in Fig. 3. Higher rewards and consistent entropy values were found for other tasks as well. Similar to entropy, value function losses were found to decrease more and their stability was also higher.

4 Conclusion

Transformer with relevant memory showed better stability and was able to learn complex behavior more rapidly as compared to regular transformers. Gating, layer normalization and masking based on mean pooling led to consistent policy updates and higher overall rewards during training. The cognitive abilities of reinforcement learning agents can greatly benefit from chunking and relevant memory selection. This work is a deliberate effort to enable AI Agents with automatic chunking to learn complex skills in memory intensive environments using modified gated transformers.

References

1. Espeholt, L., et al.: IMPALA: scalable distributed deep-RL with importance weighted actor-learner architectures. In: International Conference on Machine Learning, pp. 1406–1415 (2018)
2. Jaderberg, M., et al.: Human level performance in 3D multiplayer games with population-based reinforcement learning. Science **364**(6443), 859–865 (2019)
3. Liu, P.J., et al.: Generating wikipedia by summarizing long sequences. In: The International Conference on Learning Representations (2018)
4. Yang, Z., Dai, Z., Yang, Y., Carbonell, J., Salakhutdinov, R., Le, Q.V.: XLNET: generalized autoregressive pretraining for language understanding. In: Advances in Neural Information Processing Systems (2019)
5. Sols, I., DuBrow, S., Davachi, L., Fuentemilla, L.: Event boundaries trigger rapid memory reinstatement of the prior events to promote their representation in long-term memory. Current Biol. **27**(22), 3499–3504 (2017)
6. Lampinen, A.K., Stephanie, C.Y.C., Banino, A., Hill, F.: Towards mental time travel: a hierarchical memory for reinforcement learning agents. In: Advances in Neural Information Processing Systems (2021)

Retinotopy Improves the Categorisation and Localisation of Visual Objects in CNNs

Jean-Nicolas Jérémie[1]([✉])[iD], Emmanuel Daucé[1,2][iD], and Laurent U Perrinet[1][iD]

[1] Aix-Marseille Université - CNRS, Marseille, France
{jean-nicolas.jeremie,emmanuel.dauce,laurent.perrinet}@univ-amu.fr
[2] Ecole centrale Méditerranée, Marseille, France

Abstract. Foveated vision is a trait shared by many animals, including humans, but its contribution to visual function compared to species lacking it is still under question. This study suggests that the retinotopic mapping which defines foveated vision may play a critical role in achieving efficient visual performance, notably for image categorisation and localisation. To test for this hypothesis, we transformed regular images by using a Log-polar mapping, and used this retinotopic images as the input of convolutional neural networks (CNNs). We then applied transfer learning on pre-trained networks on the ImageNet challenge dataset. Our results show that surprisingly, the network re-trained on images which were compressed by the retinotopic mapping performs as well as the re-trained network applied to regular images. Moreover, we observed that the retinotopic mapping improves the robustness and localisation of image classification, especially for isolated objects. This was specially acute on a custom version of the dataset which aimed to categorise images that contain or not an animal. In summary, these results suggest that such retinotopic mapping may be an important component of preattentive processes, a central cognitive characteristic of more advanced visual systems.

Keywords: Foveated vision · Convolutional Neural Networks · Transfer learning · Visual categorisation · Neuromorphic transformation

1 Introduction

The visual system in humans and many mammals is distinguished by a substantial resolution disparity between the central area of the visual field (fovea)

Authors received funding from the ANR project number ANR-20-CE23-0021 ("AgileNeuroBot") and from the french government under the France 2030 investment plan, as part of the Initiative d'Excellence d'Aix-Marseille Université - A*MIDEX grant number AMX-21-RID-025 "Polychronies".

L. Iliadis et al. (Eds.): ICANN 2023, LNCS 14254, pp. 574–584, 2023.
https://doi.org/10.1007/978-3-031-44207-0_52

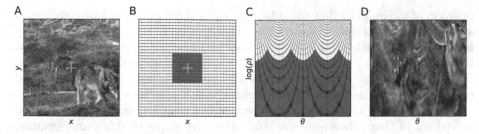

Fig. 1. We illustrate the process of transforming an example input image originally defined in Cartesian coordinates into retinotopic space using a Log-polar transformation. In (**A**), the input image is presented with the fixation point marked by a red cross. The regular grid representing the image is defined by vertical (red) and horizontal (blue) Cartesian coordinates (x, y), as shown in (**B**). As depicted in (**C**) to the image of the grid, by applying the Log-polar transformation, each pixel's coordinates with respect to the fixation point are converted based on its angle of azimuth θ (abscissa) and the logarithm of its eccentricity ρ (ordinates). This transformation results in an overrepresentation of the central area and a deformation of the visual space. When the transformation is applied to a natural image, as shown in (**D**), there is a noticeable compression of information in the periphery

and the peripheral regions, wherein the number of photoreceptors exponentially decreases with eccentricity [11]. Consequently, a natural question arises regarding the advantages conferred by these non-isotropic visual inputs in terms of information processing. Numerous hypotheses have been proposed regarding the role of this deformation of the visual field. One primary explanation is the coupling of foveal inputs with visual exploration : a retina with a fovea allows for efficient visual processing if the eye can actively move and focus its attention on specific points of interest. Studies have shown that this combination of saccades and foveal retina, coupled with an effective mechanism for detecting points of interest, significantly enhances visual acuity [3–5].

The most common approach to modeling foveal retinas involves reorganizing the pixels of an image into a Log-polar reference frame [9]. A Log-polar transformation organizes the visual field based on the angle and distance from the fixation point (eccentricity), with a resolution that exponentially decreases with the eccentricity. The primary role of a Log-polar transformation is to strongly compress the visual information, keeping high spatial frequencies at the center, but only low-spatial frequencies at the periphery. This conducts to process far less visual information when compared to the full resolution. Another important feature of the Log-polar transformation is the changing of the geometrical properties of the image, transforming rotations and zooms (homotheties) into translations [16].

We thus assess Log-polar visual processing on a well-known task, in the study of vision, that is the detection of an animal in a scene [6]. Applied to generic natural scenes, the task is such that the animal species is arbitrary. A further difficulty is due to the large variations in identity, shape, pose, size, and

576   J.-N. Jérémie et al.

position of the animals that could be present in the scene. Yet, biological visual
systems are able to efficiently perform such detection in images which are briefly
flashed [15]. Recently, deep learning algorithms have achieved an accuracy that
is currently superior to humans for some visual recognition tasks. However, the
tasks on which these artificial networks are typically trained and evaluated tend
to be highly specialised and do not generalise well, e.g. accuracy drops after image
rotation [8]. Here, we propose that a retinotopic mapping may be one essential
ingredient in that robustness and study the advantages of this transformation
in the context of image classification and localization.

2   Methods

2.1   Retinotopic Mapping

We implement retinotopic mapping, as found in some animal species such as
humans, so that visual information is concentrated at the center of gaze by
applying a transformation from the regular Cartesian pixel grid to a Log-polar
grid (see Fig. 1). This transformation is accomplished using Pytorch library's [10]
function : `grid_sample()`, it applies a grid to the pixels of the image in Cartesian coordinates. Therefore with a Log-polar grid, each pixel in Cartesian space
is assigned a new position in Log-polar space. We set the number of angles sampled (N_θ) and the number of eccentricity sampled (N_ρ) to 256 to get an output
image with a 256×256 resolution which was also used during the training process. All θ values are within a linear distribution in $[0; 2\pi]$, while ρ values are
within a logarithmic distribution in $\log 2([r_{\min}; r_{\max}])$. After analyzing various
$r_{\min}$ parameters (performed with a central fixation point), we set $r_{\min}$ to -5;
$r_{\max}$ fixes the radius and depend on the desired sub-sampling size. For instance,
setting $r_{\max}$ to 0 gives maximal ρ values range within a $\log 2$ distribution in
$[0.03; 1]$.

2.2   Transfer Learning

Transfer learning is a powerful technique that leverages knowledge gained from
solving one problem, such as ImageNet [13], and applies it to a different yet
related problem. Through our research, we successfully demonstrated the use
of transfer learning to retrain VGG networks [14], enabling their application to
various tasks. During the retraining process, we explored two network configurations: one with a retinotopic mapping at the input, and the other without.
We have shown in our previous study that an appropriate training process is
sufficient to produce performance with robustness comparable to physiological
data [8]. Also we have shown that it is possible to predict the likelihood of a
network trained on the animal task using the semantic link that connects the
outputs of a pre-trained network to a label library such as ImageNet [8]. Therefore, we expect similar results even though we did not examine the networks
re-trained on the animal task in this study. We extended the study by retraining

a Deep CNN RESNET101 on the categorization of 1000 ImageNet labels. This deeper network exhibited enhanced robustness, albeit at the cost of a higher computational load [7].

Each of these networks (i.e. VGG16 and ResNet101) is then re-trained with Log-polar inputs and compared with the baseline network on the Imagenet dataset. Two types of task will be exploited: (i) categorization of a tag of interest among the 1000 labels in ImageNet and (ii) categorization and localization of an animal. The study covers 4 networks: VGG16 CARTESIAN IMAGENET and VGG16 POLAR IMAGENET, RESNET101 CARTESIAN IMAGENET and RESNET101 POLAR IMAGENET (where only VGG16 CARTESIAN IMAGENET and RESNET101 CARTESIAN IMAGENET are not re-trained using transfer learning).

2.3 Data Sets

We have selected two datasets for our study. The first dataset is IMAGENET [13], which is widely used due to its extensive collection of images and associated labels. This dataset offers rich semantic links, enabling the construction of task-specific datasets, such as those focused on "animal" recognition. However, it is worth noting that IMAGENET exhibits certain biases, particularly with objects being centered in many images. This characteristic makes it suitable for applying a Log-polar transformation, where information is concentrated around the fixation point, which is considered the center of the image during training.

Despite its advantages, IMAGENET has limitations for localization tasks. For instance, it lacks multilabels, meaning there is only one label per image, and the proportion of bounding boxes relative to the image size is relatively small, which can limit the impact of certain analyses. To address these limitations, we also utilize the ANIMAL 10K [17] dataset. This dataset provides key points for each animal present in an image. By fitting Gaussians to these key points, we can generate heat maps centered around the label of interest, which, in this case, is 'animal', see Fig. 2. This approach enables us to improve localization and better analyze the distribution of animals in the images.

2.4 Likelihood Map Protocol

The CNNs described above are designed to categorise images by providing a likelihood value for each label. This likelihood is a probability that is, a scalar between 0 and 1) which predicts the probability that the label is present in the image. This allows to take a binary decision ("presence" or not) by choosing the label corresponding to the top likelihood, for instance. In our setting, we can also take different views from a large image and compute the likelihood for each of these, allowing to compare which view provides the best likelihood ("Bootstraping"). Views may consist for instance of cropping sub-images centred on different fixation points, with the fixation points aligned on a regular grid in visual space, see Fig. 3.

578   J.-N. Jérémie et al.

Original Image   Heatmap from keypoints full resolution   Reduce 8 x 8 heatmap from keypoints

Fig. 2. (A) The original image of the Animal 10k dataset. (B) A heat map constructed by fitting Gaussians to the key points of the Animal 10k data set (see Methods : Data sets). (C) The heat map constructed in (B) is normalized and reduced to an 8 × 8 resolution to be used as ground truth when evaluating the heat map. A threshold (0.2) is applied to reduce the heatmap field to the assumed contour of the animal

We used two parameters to define these maps: the first parameter is the resolution of the grid of fixation points. The second one is the size of the samples cropped at each of these positions define as the proportion of the input's Log-polar grid radius on the total input size (respectively Cartesian grid size, as the grid is a square for Cartesian samples see Fig. 3-A & C). The input grid values determine the size of the sample taken. For a sample size of ratio 1.0 representing the entire input image, the grid values will lie within [-1.0;1.0], for a sample size of ratio 0.33 representing 30% of the total size of the input, the grid values will lie within [-0.33;0.33]. In the next section, we'll refer to the ratio of sample size to input size.

This sample is then transformed or not by the retinotopic mapping before being used as input for the corresponding network see Fig. 3-B & D. Conveniently, a collection of samples for different fixation points can be process as a single batch, and we used here a range between 50 and 70 fixation points. This protocol define a likelihood map for any given network as the likelihood of categorising the presence of a label of interest (here "an animal") inferred at regularly spaced fixation points in the image.

3 Results

3.1 Average Accuracy

We observed that the network retrained on transformed images had a similar categorisation accuracy to that of the network retrained on regular images. This is surprising, given that the networks were pretrained on regular images and that images with a Log-polar transformation show a high compression of visual information around the fixation point and a degradation of textures in the periphery, see Fig. 4.

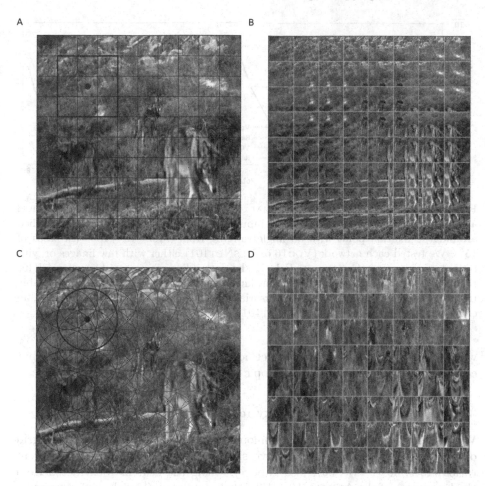

Fig. 3. Generating different views of a single image to compute likelihood maps. (**A**) For the networks using Cartesian inputs, we used a regular grid of 8 × 8 fixation points, which allow to crop samples, one particular view being highlighted. As shown in (**B**), this creates a batch of images which can be used to generate likelihood maps. (**C**)) Similarly, we used a similar grid for generating batches of Log-polar inputs, as shown in (**D**)). In (**B**) & (**D**) each samples correspond to 33% of the input (see text for more details)

In addition, we found that while the VGG16 network retrained and tested on regular images showed some degradations for different rotations, the categorisation results were much more invariant for the network including a retinotopic mapping (see Fig. 4). This phenomenon is a consequence of the translation invariance imposed by the structure of CNNs. Applied to the retinotopic mapping, this translation invariance in Log-polar space is transferred to a rotation and zoom invariance in the visual space [1]. The performance of RESNET101 with Cartesian or Log-polar mapping are similar. Surprisingly, while this net-

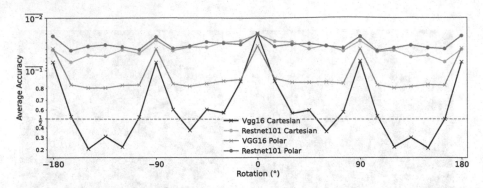

Fig. 4. Average accuracy over the Animal 10k [17] dataset, shown for both retrained and pre-trained networks with different input image rotations. The rotation is applied around the fixation point with an angle ranging from −180° to +180° (in steps of 15°). We tested each network (Vgg16 or ResNet101) either with raw images or with retinotopic mapping (Cartesian or Polar). The dotted line represents chance level. This shows that Vgg16 has a degraded performance compared to ResNet101, and notably that rotating images may have an adversarial effect on categorization performance, an effect which is less observed for ResNet101

work was not designed a priori for retinotopic images, we observe a slight, but consistent, advantage for the retinotopic mapping.

3.2   Likelihood Maps as a Proxy for Saliency

We tested the networks on the likelihood map protocol on a 8×8 fixed grid of fixation points varying the relative size of the input sample with different ratios (15%, 30%, 45%, 60%, see Table 1). Using the heat map extracted from the key points of the Animal 10k [17] data set as ground truth, "in" represents coordinates inside an animal (and respectively "out" coordinates outside an animal, see Table 1). For each point in the 8×8 grid, a likelihood value is obtained (probability of an animal's presence). Next, we calculate the average likelihood for all points located within the zone corresponding to the animal (likelihood "in") as well as the average likelihood for the zone that does not contain the animal (likelihood "out"). Next, we compare the values obtained in the "in" zone with those obtained in the "out" zone. A higher contrast indicates the network's better ability to identify regions of interest in an image. For the ResNet101, both performed well on the task even if the Cartesian tend to maintain a high accuracy outside the box. For the ResNet101 networks, the Cartesian version of the network seems to perform much less well than the Polar version in this exercise (see Table 1). If we consider a good categorization to be a high average probability on "in" coordinates (or a low probability on "out" coordinates), then in general, networks using Polar grids tend to be slightly more contrasted than networks using Cartesian grids, which is more manifest in the ResNNet101 case. From this perspective, we observe that image ratios ranging between 30%

and 45% appear to be best suited for highlighting the contrast between regions inside and outside the area of interest.

Table 1. Likelihood maps results for the VGG16 and RESNET101 networks and as computed on the IMAGENET challenge. Results are given as a fonction of the relative size of the samples with respect to the full image (Image Ratio). We highlight for each network the mapping which reaches maximal likelihood ratio for the "in" vs. "out" conditions.

	VGG16		RESNET101	
	Cartesian	Log-Polar	Cartesian	Log-Polar
Ratio	In/Out	In/Out	In/Out	In/Out
15%	**1.18**	1.14	1.06	**1.14**
30%	1.19	**1.24**	1.06	**1.20**
45%	1.10	**1.19**	1.01	**1.14**
60%	1.03	**1.07**	1.01	**1.06**

3.3 Accuracy After "Saccades" Protocol

In this part of the study, we focused on finding a label of interest by including a large number of fixation points per image. Thus, in addition to the central fixation point (1 point with a sample ratio of 100%), we applied a grid of 7×7 fixation points (49 points with a sample ratio of 33%) as well as a grid of 3×3 fixation points (9 points with a sample ratio of 60%). All 59 fixation points are processed in a single image batch. The use of one of these fixation points would correspond to the network response after a saccade to an area of high salience.

We applied this protocol to the 50,000 images in the validation set of the IMAGENET data set. If we only stop at the best position (Top 1), the performance of the networks is degraded compared to their accuracy without saccades, and the same is true for Top 5 (compared to the performance of Top 5 without saccades, not shown here). On the other hand, by adding a simple saccade selection strategy (Top Choice), we find that the accuracy of all networks exceeds their baseline level (Fig. 5).

4   Conclusion

A first and principal result of this study is proving the excellent capability of off-the-shelf Deep CNNs to deal with Log-polar inputs, that however represent a profound transformation of their visual inputs. The RESNET and VGG networks seem to effortlessly adapt to inputs where a large portion (the periphery) is heavily compressed, and the spatial arrangement significantly perturbed. The recognition rates achieved with Log-polar inputs are equivalent to those of the

Table 2. Accuracy after "saccades" results on the 1000 labels from IMAGENET. BASE represents the Top 1 accuracy of the network without saccades (state of the art accuracy), TOP 1 represents the accuracy using the post-saccade maximum likelihood as the predictor, TOP 5 represents the accuracy using the five post-saccade maximum likelihoods as the predictor. The TOP CHOICE represents the accuracy by taking the maximum post-saccade position if it is correct, otherwise we keep the pre-saccade prediction.

	VGG16		RESNET101	
	Cartesian	Polar	Cartesian	Polar
Base	**0.74**	0.55	**0.78**	0.74
Top 1	**0.69**	0.55	0.67	**0.69**
Top 5	**0.79**	0.70	0.830	**0.84**
Top choice	**0.74**	0.64	**0.85**	0.80

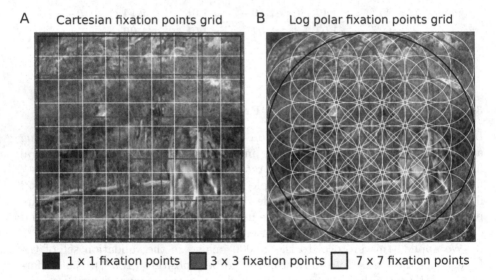

A   Cartesian fixation points grid   B   Log polar fixation points grid

■ 1 x 1 fixation points   ▨ 3 x 3 fixation points   ☐ 7 x 7 fixation points

Fig. 5. (A) Example of a superposition of Cartesian fixation points (respectively Log-polar in **(B)**) used to carry out the after "saccades" protocol. With a central fixation point (black), a 3 × 3 grid of nine fixation points, each corresponding to a 60% ratio of the input (blue) and a 7 × 7 grid of forty-nine fixation points, each taking a sample corresponding to a 33% ratio of the input (white).

original models. Additionally, the Log-polar transformation provides the added benefit of better invariance to zoom and rotation. However, this invariance comes at the expense of a reduced invariance to translation. For images that would not be centered on the region of interest, one would need to shift the fixation point to the area of interest, akin to eye saccades (Table 2).

The integration of a retinotopic mapping approach holds significant promise for enhancing the efficiency and accuracy of image processing tasks. Our results are consistent with physiological data on ultra-rapid image categorisation [6, 12]. The Log-polar compression employed in our approach allows for seamless extension to larger images without a significant increase in computational cost.

As a second result, the definition of saliency maps based on scanning the visual scene at a limited number of fixation points enables us to gain insights into Log-polar processing specificities: the Log-polar transformation provides a more focal view, thereby better separating the different elements of the image when focusing on its specific parts. In out case, it seems for instance to allow a more precise localisation of the category of interest, here an animal. It also gives us an insight into the features on which our networks actually rely. Such information can be compared with physiological data [2], used to design better CNNs, and ultimately allow physiological tests to be proposed to further explore the features needed to classify a label of interest. In particular, by focusing on the point of fixation with the highest probability in likelihood maps, we could envisage refining the training of the network our retinotopic mapping.

The accuracy performance of networks with a protocol that implements saccades in the process provides insight into the spatial modulation of network performance. It also allows us to extend the study of this type of network by implementing a strategy for choosing the optimal saccade.

Finally, the implementation of this robust categorisation, coupled with a refined localisation of a label of interest and the optimal selection of saccades, could allow us to extend this study to a more complex task. One such task is visual search (i.e., the simultaneous localisation and detection of a visual target), and the likelihood maps could provide the underlying pre-attentive mechanisms on which its effectiveness seems to depend.

References

1. Araujo, H., Dias, J.: An introduction to the log-polar mapping. In: Proceedings II Workshop on Cybernetic Vision, vol. 1, pp. 139–144 (1997). https://doi.org/10.1109/CYBVIS.1996.629454, http://ieeexplore.ieee.org/document/629454/
2. Crouzet, S.M.: What are the visual features underlying rapid object recognition? Front. Psychol. **2**, 326 (2011)
3. Dabane, G., Perrinet, L.U., Daucé, E.: What you see is what you transform: foveated spatial transformers as a bio-inspired attention mechanism. In: 2022 International Joint Conference on Neural Networks (IJCNN), pp. 1–8. IEEE (2022)
4. Daucé, E., Albiges, P., Perrinet, L.U.: A dual foveal-peripheral visual processing model implements efficient saccade selection. J. Vision **20**(8), 22–22 (2020). https://doi.org/10.1167/jov.20.8.22. 00003 Publisher: The Association for Research in Vision and Ophthalmology
5. Daucé, E., Perrinet, L.: Visual search as active inference. In: Verbelen, T., Lanillos, P., Buckley, C.L., De Boom, C. (eds.) Active Inference, pp. 165–178. Communications in Computer and Information Science, Springer International Publishing, Cham (2020). https://doi.org/10.1007/978-3-030-64919-7_17, 00001
6. Fabre-Thorpe, M.: The characteristics and limits of rapid visual categorization. Front. Psychol. **2**, 243 (2011)

7. He, K., Zhang, X., Ren, S., Sun, J.: Deep Residual Learning for Image Recognition (2015). https://doi.org/10.1109/CVPR.2016.90, 336 citations (INSPIRE 2023/7/20) 336 citations w/o self (INSPIRE 2023/7/20) arXiv:1512.03385 [cs.CV]
8. Jérémie, J.N., Perrinet, L.U.: Ultrafast image categorization in biology and neural models. Vision **7**(2), 29 (2023)
9. Maiello, G., Chessa, M., Bex, P.J., Solari, F.: Near-optimal combination of disparity across a log-polar scaled visual field. PLoS Comput. Biol. **16**(4), e1007699 (2020)
10. Paszke, A., et al.: PyTorch: an imperative style, high-performance deep learning library. In: Wallach, H., Larochelle, H., Beygelzimer, A., dAlché-Buc, F., Fox, E., Garnett, R. (eds.) Advances in Neural Information Processing Systems, vol. 32, pp. 8024–8035. Curran Associates, Inc. (2019)
11. Polyak, S.L.: The Retina. (1941)
12. Rousselet, G.A., Macé, M.J.M., Fabre-Thorpe, M.: Is it an animal? is it a human face? fast processing in upright and inverted natural scenes. J. Vision **3**, 440–455 (2003)
13. Russakovsky, O., et al.: ImageNet large scale visual recognition challenge. Int. J. Comput. Vision (IJCV) **115**, 211–252 (2015)
14. Simonyan, K., Zisserman, A.: Very deep convolutional networks for large-scale image recognition. arXiv:1409.1556 [cs] (2015)
15. Thorpe, S., Fize, D., Marlot, C.: Speed of processing in the human visual system. Nature **381**, 520–522 (1996)
16. Traver Roig, V.J., Bernardino, A.: A review of log-polar imaging for visual perception in robotics. Rob. Auton. Syst. **58**, 378–398 (2010)
17. Yu, H., Xu, Y., Zhang, J., Zhao, W., Guan, Z., Tao, D.: AP-10K: a benchmark for animal pose estimation in the wild. arXiv:2108.12617 (2021)

Safe Reinforcement Learning
in a Simulated Robotic Arm

Luka Kovač[1] and Igor Farkaš[2(✉)]

[1] Faculty of Computer and Information Science, University of Ljubljana, Ljubljana,
Slovenia
lk1114@student.uni-lj.si
[2] Department of Applied Informatics, Comenius University Bratislava, Bratislava,
Slovakia
igor.farkas@fmph.uniba.sk

Abstract. Reinforcement learning (RL) agents need to explore their
environments in order to learn optimal policies. In many environments
and tasks, safety is of critical importance. The widespread use of simulators offers a number of advantages, including safe exploration which
will be inevitable in cases when RL systems need to be trained directly
in the physical environment (e.g. in human-robot interaction). The popular Safety Gym library offers three mobile agent types that can learn
goal-directed tasks while considering various safety constraints. In this
paper, we extend the applicability of safe RL algorithms by creating
a customized environment with Panda robotic arm where Safety Gym
algorithms can be tested. We performed pilot experiments with the popular PPO algorithm comparing the baseline with the constrained version
and show that the constrained version is able to learn the equally good
policy while better complying with safety constraints and taking longer
training time as expected.

Keywords: safe exploration · reinforcement learning · robotic arm

1 Introduction

Reinforcement learning (RL) L agents need to explore their environments to
learn optimal behaviours. Sometimes an agent might perform a dangerous action,
therefore exploration is risky. Safe RL can be defined as the process of learning to maximize the reward and at the same time to ensure respecting safety
constraints during learning [2]. It is usually possible to train the agent in a simulated environment, and then after learning to transfer the learned policy to a
physical agent in the real world. However, because of difficulties in simulating
certain behaviours (e.g. human interaction, real-world scenarios in traffic, etc.)
agent's learning is transferred to the real world, where safety concerns are of
great importance.

To address these problems, OpenAI created Safety Gym, a suite of environments and tools for measuring progress toward RL agents that respect safety
constraints while learning [3], not only in testing. Safety Gym offers three different agent types (point, car, quadruped), different tasks (goal, button, push)

© The Author(s), under exclusive license to Springer Nature Switzerland AG 2023
L. Iliadis et al. (Eds.): ICANN 2023, LNCS 14254, pp. 585–589, 2023.
https://doi.org/10.1007/978-3-031-44207-0_53

and different safety constraints (hazards, vases, etc.). With those tools, one can create different layouts for trying out novel RL algorithms and having a common ground for benchmarking and evaluating them.

Our work integrates a new model of an agent (a robotic arm) into the Safety Gym environment. In a simulated environment, we are able to evaluate the agent's behaviour regarding the safety concerns. Research in this direction can produce significant contributions into human-robot interaction in the future.

An optimal policy in constrained RL is given by:

$$\pi^* = \arg \max_{\pi \in \Pi_C} J_r(\pi) \qquad \Pi_C = \{\pi : J_{c_i}(\pi) \leq d_i, \ i = 1, ..., k\} \qquad (1)$$

where $J_r(\pi)$ is a reward-based objective function and each J_{c_i} is a cost-based constraint function, involving thresholds d_i (a human-selected hyperparameters). These constraint functions form a feasible set (of allowable policies) Π_C that has been defined in the framework of constrained Markov Decision Processes [1]. In our case, $d_i = 1$, if the arm collides with the obstacle, otherwise it is 0. Hence, Lagrangian method uses a two-component loss function (reward-based and cost-based). In Eq. 1, the cost-based component is included within the space of acceptable policies Π_C. The optimization problem can also be expressed as

$$\max_\theta \min_{\lambda \geq 0} L(\phi, \theta) \doteq f(\theta) - \lambda g(\theta)$$

where the two terms of the loss function correspond to the reward and the cost, involving policy network parameters θ and Lagrangian hyperparameter λ [3].

2   Finding a Technical Solution

On one hand, it is positive that there exist various Python libraries and robotic simulators built on a variety of physics simulation engines. On the other hand, combining them or making extensions may often not be easy. Our primary motivation was to integrate safe RL algorithms with a robotic arm (not included in the Safety Gym library) that can be used in human-robot interaction. Finding a solution was not straightforward, though. The integration could be achieved in two ways: (1) Bringing a robotic arm model into Safety Gym framework, or (2) using a different or a customized environment with a robotic arm and integrate just the safety algorithms into it. This led us to the exploration of feasible options.

Safety Gym is built on the MuJoCo physics engine [5], so we first tried to import a Reacher model (a simplified robotic arm) from OpenAI Gym to Safety Gym. This should be compatible, since both are based on MuJoCo. But various technical problems (a lot of dependencies, the need to use older versions of Python and Tensorflow) discouraged us from pursuing this line of investigation.

Within the second option, we tried to connect Safety Gym with commonly used robotic simulator CoppeliaSim using PyRep library built on top of it – but this did not work due to incompatibility issues.

Finally, we used a PyBullet physics simulation engine that is built with python and is an open source project, so it is well documented and with a lot of examples already on the web. That helped a lot to set up the environment in the desirable way. Because there are already a lot of examples, we found the environment with a robotic arm that is implemented with PyBullet and is compatible with OpenAI Gym - panda-gym. Our source code with the installation guide and instructions of how to run the environment can be found here.[1] We also implemented two aditional arms to the environment – xarm and kuka – that can be used for training with safety algorithms.

3   Experiments

We used the Proximal Policy Optimization (PPO), a well-known efficient policy gradient method for RL [4] in our pilot experiments. We compared the basic PPO with its constrained version (cPPO) using the panda-gym robotics arm (with 7 DoF).

Regarding the action representation, we considered two options: (a) in PyBullet, the action representation is given by a vector $[dx, dy, dz]$ which means changes of the tip of the arm in 3D Cartesian space (we label it AR1). Those values are used to calculate the new position of the tip and via inverse kinematics to calculate how much the joints should change. (b) We also tested a "classical" actor output representation computed directly in the joint space as a 7-dim. vector of DoF angle changes in each step (AR2). These values are then directly added to move the arm (forward kinematics). We used dense reward hence simulating robotic vision enabling the robor to estimate

Fig. 1. Panda arm learned to reach the target (yellow cube) without colliding with an obstacle (red) in front of it. (Color figure online)

the distance between the tip and the target, which served as information for calculating the (inversely proportional) reward. Last but not least, we added an obstacle on the table in front of the target object (see Fig. 1).

In our four experiments (AR1/2, c/PPO) we used separate feedforward MLP policy networks with two hidden layers, each with 64 neurons, 1000 steps per epoch, maximum 200 epochs of training, and maximum number of steps per episode = 500. The experiments lead to two observations (see Table 1): (a) Regarding AR type, the agent learns faster (roughly with speedup factor of 2) and easier when using AR1 than AR2 (this is probably due to higher dimensionality of the state vector in the latter case). (b) Regarding the algorithm, cPPO yield lower average costs for both AR types. This makes Lagrangian PPO safer, with

Table 1. Average cost (with std) per one run of the classical PPO algorithm and its constrained version in case of Panda arm reaching for a target, using two action representation formats.

	PPO	cPPO
3D	17.6 ± 1.3	11.9 ± 3.6
7DoF	23.8 ± 5.0	17.0 ± 1.9

---

[1] https://github.com/lukakovac99/robotic-arm-safeRL.

a tradeoff for length of training. Performance of both algorithms in case of AR1 is illustrated in Fig. 2.

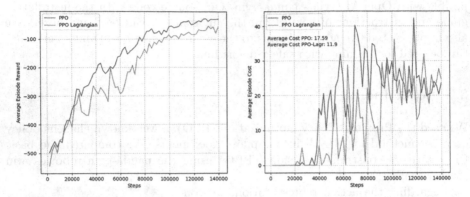

Fig. 2. Comparison of PPO and cPPO using panda arm in terms of reward (left) and cost (right). Constrained PPO is slower in learning and reaching the reward. On the other hand, it is keeping the cost at lower values hence making the arm behavior safer.

4   Conclusion

We presented pilot results with a robotic arm (panda gym) environment that is compatible with OpenAI Safety Gym, and verified the correct functionality on a selected algorithm (PPO). Constrained (Lagrangian) PPO algorithm was observed to have a longer learning time, but eventually learned the policies at the same level of efficiency while being all the way safer.

The available code provides opportunities for experimenting with the robotic arm in various setups, trying also other algorithms available in Safety Gym (TRPO, cTRPO and CPO), adding a proper obstacle representation, obstacle generation methods, or developing different safe tasks for the agent to perform.

Acknowledgment. L.K. was supported by Erasmus mobility stipend, and I.F. by the Horizon Europe project TERAIS, no. 101079338 and by the national project APVV-21-0105.

References

1. Altman, E.: Constrained Markov Decision Processes. Routledge, New York (1999)
2. García, J., Fernández, F.: A comprehensive survey on safe reinforcement learning. J. Mach. Learn. Res. **16**(1), 1437–1480 (2015)
3. Ray, A., Achiam, J., Amodei, D.: Benchmarking safe exploration in deep reinforcement learning. arXiv preprint arXiv:1910. 01708 7(1.), 01708 (2019)

4. Schulman, J., Wolski, F., Dhariwal, P.: Proximal policy optimization algorithms. arXiv preprintv arXiv (2017)
5. Todorov, E., Erez, T., Tassa, Y.: MuJoCo: a physics engine for model-based control. In: IEEE International Conference on Intelligent Robots and Systems (2012)

Author Index